LIFE ON THE LINE

FAYE WATTLETON

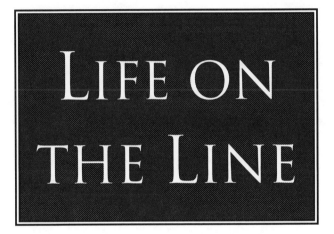

LIFE ON
THE LINE

BALLANTINE BOOKS

NEW YORK

To Mama and Felicia,
my past and my future.

CONTENTS

FOREWORD

The day before Independence Day 1989 was the end of the Supreme Court's spring term. Sunny, humid, and as unbearably hot as Washington, D.C., gets, it was a day to breed impatience and trigger tempers. The glare from the gleaming white steps of America's grandest courthouse made it especially hard for me to read the Court's decision in *Webster v. Reproductive Health Services*. The flurry of activity and chatter among the media and other interested parties added to my difficulty in focusing on the words of the justices. Nonetheless, over the shoulder of NBC's veteran Supreme Court correspondent, Carl Stern, I had to glean the essentials of the majority opinion—hurriedly, before I had to step in front of the television cameras.

I felt as though I was reading the obituary of a close relative or loved one who had suffered a prolonged illness. I may have anticipated the death; still, words cannot begin to describe the sense of loss and dejection I felt at that moment. We'd hoped against hope in regard to the *Webster* case. In the papers before us, the Court had decided how far states could go in restricting the provision of abortion. Given persuasive lobbying by the now conservatively inclined balance of the Court, and given the unpredictability of its center, the decision could have been the vehicle to overturn *Roe v. Wade*, which recognized a woman's constitutional right to abortion.

Jet-lagged from a long journey from Egypt, I'd arrived in New York on July 1, the day before the decision was to be handed down (according to "reliable sources"). July 2 found me standing on the steps of the court-house amid throngs of lawyers, activists, and the media. Of course, we should have known better: By time-honored tradition, the date of release of the Court's decisions is one of the most closely guarded mysteries of that imperial body. With the arrival of 10:00 A.M., the hour that the Court delivers its opinions, all eyes were fixed on the doors to the side of the majestic steps leading to the Court's main lobby. We searched for signs of the lawyers designated to receive the opinion. Surely, they would soon venture forth, hands filled with thick sheaves of white paper and, more than likely, heads buried in their contents. When they emerged empty-handed, we knew that the decision would be released the following day—the last day of the Court's session. There was much conjecture about the reason for the waiting game. Some theorized that the delay was strategic; that the Court was about to issue a highly controversial decision and did not want to be around for the uproar it would produce among the media and the public.

On July 3, crowds—larger than those of the day before—gathered on the plaza below the temple of justice. Pro- and anti-choice demonstrators faced off in heated exchanges. Others marched back and forth with signs and banners. One abortion opponent shouted "Babykiller!" over and over through a bullhorn. His chant was met by "Not the church, not the state, women will decide their fate!" from an equally energetic band of reproductive rights defenders. The Capitol police, out in force, seemed impassive in the midst of this hurly-burly.

Dozens of television cameras, including all three national television networks and CNN, were primed for live broadcasts. By arrangement, I was to be interviewed by Jim Miklaszewski of NBC. The short exchange would be impromptu. There would be no chance to study my notes while I was being painted with television makeup. There would be very little time to hear from my staff, "Be sure to make this point."

After skimming through the nine-page summary of the decision, I searched the crowd for Eve Paul, Planned Parenthood's vice president for legal affairs, and Roger Evans, our litigation project director, praying to get that last-minute briefing from them before going in front of the cameras. My gaze found many heads buried in those incendiary papers; it didn't find theirs. They knew that improvising from a quickly scanned decision before a television audience of millions was not the way I preferred to do things. I wanted desperately to discuss matters with them now, in order to avoid making embarrassing mistakes. After I finished, I was scheduled to take part in another impromptu press conference—a "stakeout," in newsspeak. To bring a semblance of order to the chaos, the print and broadcast media had arranged their mikes and cameras in a large circle in the center of the Court's plaza. There, each side of the case could make statements regarding the Court's decision, then field questions from reporters. *Where are they?* I raged inside myself, feeling exposed and abandoned. They'd hear from me about this, I vowed.

As the media circus coalesced, I synthesized as best I could what I'd read of the Court's opinion and played over in my mind some of its more crucial points. As far as I could tell, it meant big trouble for us, but as I forced myself to focus on the issues, my initial gut reaction made me realize that I had to be careful not to overstate the damage done this day. No, *Roe* had not been overturned. But its major tenets as we knew them—including limitations on states' regulation of abortion—had suffered serious blows. It appeared to me that women were now more vulnerable to further assault by state legislatures.

After many years of watching television commentary—both my own and that of others—I knew that *how* I responded was as important as what I said and could give an impression that reached far beyond the moment. I had to be careful not to launch panic. Women confused by messages they received about the ruling could conclude erroneously that abortion was now illegal.

I worried about the heat itself, and the fact that my sheer physical misery would magnify my distress. Would the oppressive tension I felt make my mind go blank when the hot lights for the camera were turned on?

Stay calm, I told myself.

This setback could cause some to give in, assent to it, and just hope that no further limitations would be allowed. But such an acceptance would be harder on women than the sixteen years of battles that had preceded it. Damaged though *Roe* might now be, it was still intact, although I didn't need the instruction of my disappearing staff to tell me that its future was far from certain. It was essential that I project confidence and a conviction that, while the decision was a blow, the battle to preserve reproductive rights would continue.

The tumult on the plaza seemed nothing but a dull roar in the wake of my anxiety. My stomach churned and my hands were damp. I was having serious trouble concentrating and organizing my thoughts. One or two cogent remarks from the attorneys would have calmed me. Finally I spotted, in the futile distance, Roger Evans. Too late; I'd have to go it alone. I'm not sure if it was the weather or anxiety that turned the temperature from hot to sizzling. My forehead was moist. Under my jacket, my blouse was soaked. Perspiration rolled down my rib cage as I stepped before the television cameras. Dr. Jack Willke, president of the National Right to Life Committee, lurked in the background.

But suddenly, almost magically, the anxiety slipped away. Miklaszewski asked me well-informed and provocative questions. He was precise in setting parameters for the answers. But if he knew what he wanted, I also knew what needed to be said about the ruling. When he asked me what the pro-choice movement planned to do in the wake of the *Webster* decision, I answered:

> Our anticipation is that we will fight on to make certain that all women in this country continue to have access to safe abortion. We are not daunted by this Supreme Court decision. We think it is an outrage that the Supreme Court does not see fit to protect women's rights through the Bill of Rights, but leaves it up to the vagaries of the state legislatures to decide what women will do with their reproductive decisions. We will fight on in every state to assure that every woman has access to a safe and legal abortion. This does not mean that this battle is over. It only means that we will fight on because women must be protected in this country.[1]

Even as I spoke, I thought about the ways that the debate over women's bodies would become more political than ever; the prospects for future conflict depressed me. There had been so much strife already. The Court had shielded women from those who would fully recriminalize abortion, but now it was allowing a wider opening. It didn't take a wild leap of imagination to see how this gap could be used to erode the protections guaranteed by *Roe*—protections we'd fought so hard to preserve.

While Miklaszewski was interviewing me, Doug Gould, my vice president of communications, and Bebe Bahnsen, who worked with the Washington media on our behalf, were hastily correcting and adjusting the statement we had prepared for the decision. Doug handed me the statement as soon as the interview was over. I moved toward the ring of reporters, cameras, and microphones.

Randall Terry, the leader of Operation Rescue and one of the more confrontational voices for the opposition, was giving impromptu remarks to various reporters around the plaza. As I walked past, he turned toward me. Blond and bespectacled, Terry would have appeared to be the all-American clean-cut man, were it not for his maniacal manner.

"Faye, you made a mistake in your statement," he called out. "*Roe* was decided seven to two, not six to three. God loves you and is ready to forgive you, if you give your heart to him."

The cameras captured Terry's remark and his aggressive posture. I felt embarrassed, and momentarily furious with myself for making the error—minding facts was my obsession. And of all the people to catch that mistake, I thought. I kept walking.

As the smoldering sun beat down on the crowd, I waited while Ellie Smeal, former president of NOW, finished her comments on the new developments. When she began to thread her way out of the compressed body of reporters and observers, I squeezed up to the mikes to read Planned Parenthood's official statement. It decried the Court's *Webster* decision and called for massive political organizing to counter the opening that antiabortion forces would now use for pressuring state legislatures to chip away at a woman's right to control her fertility.

I'd just taken my first question from the press and was about to answer when, out of the corner of my eye, I noticed a dark-suited figure moving toward me. Stepping up to the microphone into which I was speaking, he began, "I'm Doctor—"

I then recognized who this bully was. It was Jack Willke.

Not letting him go any further, I broke in: "Excuse me, I'm answering a question."

He looked stunned as he stepped back. "Pardon me. Go ahead. Go ahead."

I had answered several more questions when I felt a hand shoving my right arm. I looked over my shoulder at Dr. Willke. It was as though something had come over him that he could not control. He was again moving in to the microphone.

"I'm Dr. Jack Willke. I'm president of National Right to Life."

For a moment, I was stunned. What did he think he was doing? An impulse to hit him came over me—an impulse that, while arguably justified, was not the answer. Cameras of all the networks were rolling. An image of Willke and me engaged in physical combat flashed through my mind as "Picture of the Week." That was the last thing I needed. Nevertheless, the tension I'd felt only moments earlier turned to trembling rage.

"Excuse me, I'm not through," I said as I shook his hand away.

The reporters, observing the conflict, spoke up in my defense. "Let her speak!" they yelled. "We're not finished asking her questions!" Willke retreated behind me. "We're tired of hearing from men, anyway," one lone female voice added amid the clicking shutters and the whirring television cameras. This comment brought forth some cheers.

I am not the first woman in my family to hold my ground in the face of opposition. As I watch my daughter near adulthood, I'm certain that I won't be the last. My great-grandmother, Mariah Williams, born to a slave, had faced down a white straw boss who had tried to take her son away to work the fields. She stood on her porch, ax in hand, to protect what she believed in. Here, on the steps of the Supreme Court, Jack Willke had assumed the same role for me as that white straw boss. In that moment of confrontation, the spirit of Mariah burned in my blood: "I understand why you want to stand up to the indignity. I felt the same. But the eyes of the entire nation are on you, Alyce Faye. Don't give an inch. Keep your dignity."

LIFE ON THE LINE

CHAPTER I

INDOMITABLE SPIRIT

I have never believed in the impossible. My mother is a preacher who is the daughter of a preacher. The roots of my character can be found in the values of a family of doers, a family of independent thinkers with strong wills and convictions. In keeping with this heritage, I have never been able to accept the notion that there are some things I cannot do, some things I cannot change. I have always told myself that it is all just a matter of figuring out *how*. But time and again, life has taught me just how difficult change can be; I have had to learn and relearn that it takes more than will and intellect to make things happen.

I suppose that my first conscious encounter with the impossible came when I was five or so, one sunny Sunday afternoon in early summer. As was family ritual, we'd returned from church to feast on my mother's Sunday dinner of fried chicken, collard greens, sweet potatoes, and cornbread muffins, and my father's pride—delicious hot peach cobbler.

My father was a hardworking man, but luckily for all concerned, he'd found that his never-fail cobbler had nothing to do with hard work. He loved Mama, and he loved showing her up in the kitchen.

"I can bake better than your mother any day," Daddy would boast, and in truth, the smell of baking peaches filling our home at 1241 Walton Avenue is a memory that remains with me to this day.

But this was a special Sunday. Grandpa Deanie, my mother's father, had come up to St. Louis from Mississippi to visit. Our home was overflowing with family and friends from church—Mama's sisters, my aunts Alice, Evie, and Ola, and her cousins Stella and Jerome—all wanting to catch up on the doings of relatives still living down south.

As for me, I was less interested in family gossip than in simply seeing Grandpa Deanie again. He was a gentle man, tall and handsome, with straight black hair, smooth bronze skin, dark, deep-set eyes, Caucasian features, and perfect white teeth, all of which lent his face a kind of matinee idol elegance. I loved it when he picked me up and gave me warm hugs and bathed me in his broad radiant smile. And for days beforehand, I'd enjoyed the sheer excitement in the air and the bustle of preparation.

There were no sisters or brothers for me to play with, and I lived among ever-busy adults who often ignored my chatter and left me to create my own entertainment. But a kitchen full of grown-ups talking and laughing was a kitchen full of opportunities for getting attention, and at an early age, I could be quite talented at demanding it. I had to be: Given their daily tasks of survival, it was the only way I could find a place for myself.

At last, probably needing some peace from my jabbering, Mama ordered, "Go outside and play, girl." I took heartily to that suggestion. I loved climbing the trees in the backyard, especially the large shady maple with the variegated trunk that towered over the small lawn of my family's redbrick two-story house. My favorite playmate, Miss Sue, lived next door. Although she was several years older than I, I was tall for my age and precocious, and those two things made up for the difference in our years.

Miss Sue was always ready for the adventures that I conjured up for the two of us, so when I called for her over the wire fence that separated our yards—"Come on, Miss Sue, let's climb trees!"—she promptly appeared.

We heard the lively, laughing voices of the adults in my house as we scaled the maple higher, then higher still toward the branches that offered unobstructed views of yards identical to ours, separated by white wooden picket fences, and many boasting brick barbecue pits at the back.

As Miss Sue and I took turns swinging from limb to limb over the lawn, I watched a blackbird take to the air to escape our commotion. I remember thinking, If that bird can fly, why can't I? There was no one to tell me that it was impossible.

"Look at me, Miss Sue. . . . Tweet, tweet, I'm a bird." With this pronouncement, I flapped my arms and pushed off from the safety of the sturdy limb, out into the stillness of the warm, late-afternoon air.

I woke two hours later, dizzy, and suffering from a pounding headache. Mama and Grandpa Deanie stood over my bed, their hands clasped in prayer. "Lord, take care of this child," my mother intoned. "You know we can't keep her still. We pray that she has no serious injuries. Watch over Alyce Faye, Lord."

"She's in the Lord's hands," I heard my grandfather say, touching one of my hands softly. I slipped into and out of a spinning and throbbing consciousness.

Mama and Grandpa Deanie, both preachers of a fundamentalist faith, believed in the power of divine healing—calling on the power of God through prayer, and spurning medical intervention. Certain that their faith in prayer was all that was necessary, they had not taken me to a hospital, but instead let me sleep (something I now know to be the worst possible response to what might have been a serious head injury). I did survive the fall, with nothing more than a minor scrape under my right eye, and the next morning I was up and on the move. So I couldn't fly? Who cared. That was yesterday. The new day brought hope that some other possible delight was around the corner. My indomitable spirit shielded me from the adult censure that I evoked by my steady intrusion into adult thoughts and ways. The only child of George and Ozie Garrett Wattleton, born on July 8, 1943, a steamy St. Louis summer day, I'm sure I was not what my parents expected.

Like many other southern black Americans, my parents, before they met, had joined the second wave of migrants crossing the Mason-Dixon line in hopes of finding new opportunities in the industrial cities of the North.

I know little of the history of my father's family in Alabama, but my mother's rich heritage, rooted in the flatlands and piney woods of northern Mississippi, profoundly shaped our family's life. Mama is the oldest daughter of second cousins—Eugene and Ola Branson Garrett. They were, respectively, the grandson and granddaughter of Lydia and Lucy, sisters and slaves on a plantation owned by one "Colonel John Williams." Originally from Warren County, North Carolina, the Colonel had brought Lydia and Lucy with him to Mississippi as chattel when he moved, sometime in the 1840s, to a rural stop on the road known as Farmhaven. It is not known whether the sisters and their seven siblings were bought as a lot or if their parents were sold or separated from them by death, but when the Colonel later returned to North Carolina, he granted all but one of them their freedom to stay in Mississippi. The eighth-born, a sister, chose to return east with him.

At Farmhaven, deep in Mississippi cotton country, Lydia gave birth to Mariah Williams, my grandfather's mother. Mariah always claimed she was born in the "year of surrender." That would have been 1863, the year that Mississippi surrendered to the Yankees after the fall of Vicksburg. As a child, I remembered my great-grandmother as a tiny black-skinned woman with broad African features. Mariah possessed a name common among the Yoruba tribe of Nigeria. Although she was not born a slave, she grew up during the difficult days of the post-Reconstruction South when the difference between freedom and slavery was remarkably small. According to family lore, a white man, Tom Garrett, a traveling salesman from Garrett, Arkansas, settled in Madison County and there sired children by both white and black women. One of the latter women was Mariah, who in 1884 gave birth to Eugene, the man I would come to know as Grandpa Deanie.

My mother remembers Mariah as being "a woman of great conviction and a lot of gumption. Nobody ran or walked over her." She raised her young son alone, and, if his regal bearing as an adult was any evidence, raised him with pride and dignity. Mariah grew fruit—peaches, plums, and figs—and vegetables, canned them, and made a modest profit selling them to white folks in Canton, the county seat. Eventually, she saved enough money to buy several acres of red-dirt farmland, which her son's children would inherit.

Family legend has it that a straw boss came up to Mariah's house and spotted Eugene sitting on the porch.

"Boy, where's your mama?"

The young man nodded toward the screen door, where Mariah, having heard the man's voice, now stood.

"I want to hire your boy to work my field," the straw boss told her.

Mariah stepped out onto her porch. The screen door slammed behind her. "He ain't for hire," she said, shielding her eyes against the glare of the summer sun with a hand to her brow.

He glanced at Deanie, who now stood behind his mother. And she—never one to waste words—picked up the ax that leaned against the side of her house. Lifting it into the air, she shouted, "I'll split his head open with this ax handle before I let you work my boy." She would have preferred to see him dead rather than see him a slave, whether or not his indenture was cloaked in the euphemism of the straw boss's "hire."

The stunned overseer made a quick retreat, no doubt thinking she was crazy and just might make good on her word and either way he wouldn't gain a worker. Surely it took courage and determination for Auntie 'Riah (as we called her, after the African vernacular of respect for an elder) to stand her ground. Mississippi lynchings had been provoked by less. I like to think that the ties between this brave woman and her progeny, though separated by time, are bound by blood.

Grandpa Deanie grew tall—over six feet tall, lanky, and handsome. Some say that he was given favor by whites because he was so often mistaken for one of them. As I remember him, he was a soft-spoken man of relatively few words.

Although my grandfather was not an educated man, he was an eloquent speaker. At eighteen, Grandpa Deanie answered his "calling" to the ministry in the Church of God. He believed God wanted him to commit his life to ministering to the rural churches scattered along the gravel roads and amid the cotton fields and pine groves of northern Mississippi.

A fundamentalist offshoot of the American Holiness movement, the Church of God was founded by D. S. Warner in the 1880s. It quickly gained a following among white families of the Midwest, and then by the 1890s took root among southern black families. It drew its founding tenets from the Methodist faith, the traditionalist approach of the young American Holiness movement, and the Pentecostal ideology that emphasized the transformation of the person through acceptance of the divine power of the Holy Spirit. The doctrine of the church that would establish its general offices in Anderson, Indiana, was derived from the Bible, both the Old Testament and the New, and "not from the councils of man."

The Church of God is grounded in the belief that the reward for those free of sin and living a Christian life is to be accepted into heaven. According to the Book of Revelation, on the final Judgment Day, the Lord will examine the lives of all who have inhabited the earth. Those who do not repudiate their sins and live a life free of sin will be condemned to the eternal fires of hell. Because one can never know when the moment of final judgment will arrive, one's life must always be lived in a state of readiness.

In keeping with the principles of the Church of God and the prescription, "In all things acknowledge Him and He will direct thy ways" (Proverbs 3:6),[1] Grandpa Deanie applied his staunch religious beliefs to all endeavors: The Bible provided the moral guideposts for every aspect of his life. For years, he traveled on the Sunday circuit as a preacher. Having started and served several churches nestled in the red-clay farmlands, he preached one Sunday a month to each of the small congregations. But he didn't confine himself to one undertaking. Grandpa Deanie opened a small general store, and soon took up work as a blacksmith, carpenter, bricklayer, and builder, and at a dusty turn in the road sixteen miles outside Canton, he set up a sawmill and sold cut lumber from his mother's land.

The handsome young minister, considered to be a catch by the marriage-minded women in his vicinity, married his second cousin Ola Branson, the granddaughter of his grandmother Lydia's sister Lucy. His various enterprises were necessary to support his new wife, and the five sons and four daughters that would eventually be born to them: Ernest, William Eugene, Coleman, Thomas, Ozie, Robert, Alice, Evie, and Ola. Mama remembers, "My daddy trained bird dogs and went hunting for food. And he sold hides and skins," while my grandmother, Mama Ola, as she was known, had babies, worked the garden, raised chickens, and sold eggs, milk, butter, and fruit. From the proceeds of her ventures, Mama Ola would buy the things that she could not make or grow—socks, shoes, underwear, and caps. She made clothes from used fifty-pound-size cotton flour sacks, which could be bleached and dyed. The children helped their parents by chopping wood, picking cotton, shelling peas, and doing other such work. The older boys helped with logging, and with slaughtering chickens, cows, and pigs for meat.

It was a hardscrabble life. Although much of the produce from the garden was canned and put up for the winter, my mother remembers that the supplies often ran low by early spring; meals became smaller and relied more heavily on hunted food. But when hard times fell, they landed not on my mother's family alone, and Grandpa Deanie then took particularly to heart the Matthew 19:19 scripture, "Love thy neighbor as thyself." My aunt Alice still recalls the steady flow of neighbors to and from their house: "As their minister, he married our neighbors and when they died, he buried them. If they didn't have money to afford a casket for a dead baby, he'd build one. . . . If we had cornmeal and there was somebody that didn't have a meal, he would give them some of what we had. We took care of the community and the community never forgot that. They loved our daddy."

The quiet life of Farmhaven, Mississippi, belied the upheaval taking place in the world around it. There had been waves of immigrants and a world war. And the long struggle for women's rights was finding a place on the national stage. In 1911 Jane Edna Hunger founded the Working Girls Home Association, later known as the Phillis Wheatley Association, to campaign for equal rights for black women in the workplace. In 1913 Margaret Sanger, then a young nurse from New York City, went to France to study birth control methods. In 1915 Mama was born. In 1916 Sanger opened her first birth control clinic, in New York. In 1917 American women won the right to vote. Meanwhile, the southern states were busy enacting a string of new Jim Crow laws that would reverse the liberality of the Reconstruction era. My mother's family lived in a state whose governor was considered the most vicious segregationist of them all—James K. Vardaman, who had won his place through speeches against "the threat of Negro domination."

Then came the Roaring Twenties and the depressed Thirties. Neither had much economic influence upon the lives of my mother's family, whose existence had never depended upon the whims of Wall Street or industry. Life had always been a struggle for them and for most everyone around them. But if the economic plight of the nation at large didn't affect them directly, the brutal racial climate did. In the mid-Thirties, Grandpa Deanie had noticed that the county provided local white children with a yellow bus to transport them to their school. Black children had no other choice but to walk to their school.

My grandfather decided to do something about this injustice. Out of sheet metal, he fashioned a bus-like shell, outfitted it with seats and doors, and loaded the contraption onto a truck chassis to complete his "school bus" for the black children of Farmhaven. His twenty-one-year-old son, Robert, the youngest of the Garrett boys, was to be the bus driver.

On a chilly November afternoon in 1938, Uncle Robert was nearing the end of his route. Only one child remained on the bus. When he was about three quarters of the way across a bridge outside Farmhaven, Uncle Robert spotted the yellow school bus barreling toward him. The country-road bridge was only wide enough to carry one bus at a time. But it soon became clear that the bus carrying the white children wasn't going to stop to wait for the young driver to clear the span.

"I had two options: keep moving forward or steer the bus into the water," Uncle Robert remembers. "I decided to keep going."

The two buses sideswiped each other. Although the damage was minor, knowing the law concerning accidents, he stopped the bus on the other side of the bridge. Shaken but unhurt, he remained in his seat. Then the lone little girl on his bus screamed, "That man! He's got a gun!" She began to cry.

Uncle Robert didn't move. "You don't expect someone to shoot you. . . . But that man walked right up to the bus and, without a word, lifted a twelve-gauge shotgun and opened fire point-blank at me. He shot only once. As I saw the gun come up to my face, I threw up my left hand. Some of the number-six bird shot pellets blew my thumb away. One pellet hit me in the chin, and another destroyed the tissue in my left eye. I remember landing in the dirt road outside the bus. The other driver went back to his bus, inspected the damage to it, climbed in, and then drove away."

A white farmer saw what happened, and he was soon joined by a friend of Grandpa Deanie's who happened to drive up in his shiny one-seater Chevrolet. Uncertain of the seriousness of my uncle's condition, the two men tried to stem the bleeding of his various wounds before they picked him up from the road and placed him in the car.

After a quick stop at the Garrett family store to tell Mama Ola what had happened, the men sped the injured youth to Dr. Bowman, the only black doctor in nearby Canton. Dr. Bowman concluded that Uncle Robert needed emergency surgery, but his surgical practice was limited to the Afro-American Hospital in Yazoo City, some sixteen miles away—too far for Uncle Robert to be transported safely. Dr. Bowman was not allowed to practice at Canton's all-white King's Daughters Hospital, even under such circumstances. But he knew a white doctor who might treat my uncle's wounds.

It turned out that the white doctor also knew Grandpa Deanie. He arranged for his friend's son to be admitted to King's Daughters Hospital, where he could practice, but could not treat blacks. The doctor operated there on the wounded young man, anyway. His eye was too badly damaged to save, but the doctor was able to rebuild its socket sufficiently to install a prosthetic eye. Despite the lengthy surgery, "To this day twenty-four shotgun pellets remain inside my body," Uncle Robert claims.

The Garrett home erupted in anger upon hearing the news of the shooting. The older boys wanted to exact revenge upon the man who had shot their younger brother. They knew who he was and were ready to hunt him down. Uncle Ernest "raged like a bull" about killing the man, but Grandpa Deanie intervened. Uncle Robert remembers their father telling his angry sons, "Getting revenge isn't going to solve anything. You'll get over it and we'll go on with our lives. 'Vengeance is mine, saith the Lord.' " There would be no swaying his religious beliefs, even under trying circumstances. And there would be no questioning his resolve. But besides placing great faith in a higher power, my grandfather was a wise, practical man. He understood how the Jim Crow South worked. There were no laws to protect his sons if they resorted to violence. Most certainly, there would have been more bloodshed. At the very least, their house could have been burned to the ground.

Fortunately (if any good fortune can occur under such circumstances), the shooting outraged many townspeople. "There were no practicing black lawyers, no NAACP in Canton," Uncle Robert recalls. But a white lawyer came to Grandpa Deanie and asked if he could represent the family in the case against the assailant. With the attorney's help, the assault was brought to the local courts.

On the day that the case was tried, the entire family went to the little courthouse off of the oak-draped town square in Canton. The judge asked Uncle Robert if he could identify the man who shot him. The tall, hazel-eyed young man pointed to his scrawny attacker. The facts were recited and the evidence was presented, but the man was found not guilty. Such was southern justice.

"I had no feelings about what the court did," Uncle Robert recalls. "My daddy was more concerned about protecting his family and living in the community, and we all abided by his decisions. But I did carry a Smith and Wesson revolver every day that I drove that bus. And true to Daddy's belief in the Lord exacting revenge, the man died a horrible death from TB some three years later, when I was away at Tuskegee Institute."

CHAPTER 2

THE ROOTS OF CONVICTION

My mother was the eldest daughter and the apple of her father's eye, but that did not exempt Ozie Garrett from backbreaking work. With Mama Ola bearing children every other year, the burden of domestic duty fell heavily on Ozie's shoulders. "Mama showed me how to bake cakes and fry chicken when I was but a small child, because she wasn't able to do anything herself. She was so sick she couldn't take care of the children, either—little Ola used to call me Mama when I was only thirteen."

As I reflect upon my grandmother's life, I also think about Margaret Sanger's spearheading efforts in the early days of the birth control movement. When, in 1921, she founded the American Birth Control League (which would later evolve into Planned Parenthood Federation of America), Sanger had women like my grandmother in mind: women whose health was weakened by the strain of bearing each new child, women whose families suffered the economic consequences of one more mouth to feed. For Sanger's mother, there had been eighteen pregnancies before her body buckled under the burden. For my grandmother, there had been at least nine. And they were but two victims of the same oppression and ignorance.

Margaret Sanger understood my grandmother's reality, and with her keen ingenuity she set about to make sure that "Negro" women were not left out of her movement. In 1939, with people like Mary McLeod Bethune and W.E.B. Du Bois on an advisory panel, she formed the Negro Project, an alliance between the black leadership, workers' unions, and civil rights and healthcare organizations. Many have criticized the project, calling it racist, a eugenic plan of white supremacy. Within the birth control movement there was racism, just as there was and is in so many other aspects of American life. And she did court eugenicists—a movement more popular than her cause—so birth control could quickly find a place in mainstream society. However, in seeking the support of such black leaders as Du Bois and Bethune, she proved that her motive was to have birth control gain legitimacy among Negroes in its own right. To say that Sanger's intent was anything but that is to discredit her work and her movement.

But Sanger's initiative was too late for Mama Ola. By the time it got under way in the early 1930s she'd borne the last of her children. A heavy part of the burden of their care had fallen on my mother, who, besides doing household chores, was expected to work with her mother, brothers, and sisters in the family-owned cotton fields. From the first light of dawn until sundown, my mother and her siblings would drag long muslin sacks with tar-coated underbellies down rows of plants whose bolls, bursting with the foamy white cotton, would be reduced to barren brown stalks by late fall. Their backs were bent by the fifty- to hundred-pound bags of cotton, which they then emptied into a wagon at the edge of the field, until the full container was hitched to two horses for the journey to the cotton gin. If there was a new baby in the family, it was brought to the field and placed on a blanket pallet at the end of the rows. As the cool temperatures of autumn drew near, the children were sometimes joined in the fields by day workers Grandpa Deanie had hired to collect the last of the cotton before the rains came. Grandpa Deanie was himself often too busy with his various businesses to join in the work.

My mother's first forays into the cotton field had come of her own volition. "When I was three," she says, "I wanted to follow Daddy, Mama, and my brothers into the fields, so Mama made a cotton bag out of a fifty-pound flour sack and hung it over my shoulder." But by the time she had reached her teens, the weighty muslin sack to which she'd graduated represented a heavy burden for a girl already weary from oppressive "women's work." One hot Mississippi day changed all that.

It was midday. The sun was high and my then sixteen-year-old mother stood between the tall rows, her hands stinging from the pricks of the spike-tipped cotton bolls. Her back ached. She straightened her body and let the weight of the sack, now filled with cotton, fall from her shoulders. She took one long look at the white clapboard house that sheltered her family. She glanced up at the sun, then back at the house, which seemed to beckon her. Right then and there, she decided she was never going to pick another handful of cotton. She dropped her burden and marched down the shallow gullies of the field toward the house. To this day she can't explain it: "I just went to the house and sat down."

Her parents were shocked to find their daughter home when they came in for the noontime break. "What's the matter with you?" they demanded. Usually a child returning early from the fields meant illness or injury, but my mother responded, "I've made up my mind. . . . I'm not going to pick any more cotton."

They were speechless. Such defiance simply didn't happen in the rural South. Respect, deference, and obedience to adults were unquestioned values. All her life, my mother had honored her parents—especially her father, with whom she had a special bond. But she had reached her limit.

"You can whip me every day, but I'm not going back. I know that Jesus has saved you, so I know you won't kill me. I'll take my whippings, but I won't go to the field again." In those days, corporal punishment was freely administered for fear of "sparing the rod and spoiling the child." Because she was both willing to accept their punishment and unwilling to give them the desired results of that punishment and because she'd never been one to compromise, her parents had no choice but to accept her decision. Mama did not go back to the cotton fields.

Grandpa Deanie and Mama Ola were probably not altogether surprised by my mother's defiance. Even within a family their neighbors thought "different"—"The Garretts act just like white folk. They don't cry much at funerals"—Mama had always been considered one apart. With her smooth skin darker than all her siblings', her long black hair, and her regal manner, she was the exception. "She was the one who carried her purse under her arm while we held her school books," Aunt Alice laughs. She was also the one who traveled with her parents on the Sunday circuits. But this act of rebellion put them in a real quandary. They could not countenance a revolt, not while the rest of the children continued to work in the fields every day. Besides, by this time, Grandpa Deanie was a much-revered community leader. If a beating would not bring their daughter to her senses, they had to find another way out of their dilemma.

At a church meeting, Sister O'Neill, the portly, pleasant-faced matriarch of an Ohio family, had an idea. "Why don't you let Ozie come live with us and our daughters?"

Her offer must have appealed to my grandparents, partly because it promised a consistency with the Church of God way of life, but just as importantly because it held the opportunity for their daughter to get a high school diploma "up north." Though Grandpa Deanie had not been formally educated, he always wanted his children to get the best schooling he could provide. To his mind, the education in the integrated schools of the North was infinitely better than the all-black high school in Canton. And so my mother was sent north.

Mama had never envisioned leaving her family, and she soon found herself desperately homesick. Although the O'Neills had opened their home and hearts to the teenager, they were not her kin, and Columbus, Ohio, was a jarring change from Farmhaven, Mississippi. She begged her parents to let her come home again, although she would not agree to go back to the cotton fields, but they rejected her tearful pleas. She had no choice but to settle into her new life. Soon she began to turn toward the familiar—the church—to relieve the emptiness she felt inside.

As the months passed, Mama found herself listening more closely to the sermons and heeding the minister's calls to search the Bible to find God's purpose for her life. I'm sure that the church also answered her yearning to retain a strong emotional connection to her father, who still traveled the country roads to preach to sparse congregations.

Mama remembers she experienced the first intimations of a spiritual transformation as an adolescent in Columbus. "One Sunday, I attended services and heard the minister preach. Around this time, one of my teachers had complimented me on my looks and figure. She said I should be a model and I even thought about it," Mama recalls. "But my minister was an electrifying preacher. His words penetrated my heart. I got saved and immediately gave my life to God. All thoughts of being a model vanished. I felt truly blessed to be chosen to serve God."

At seventeen my mother was passing from gawky adolescence into graceful adulthood. With hips taking the shape and fullness of her African heritage, luxurious hair, dark bronze skin, and a lovely smile that could light her entire face, she was said to have been quite a beauty. Her sisters remember her as being as stern and determined as she was engaging and funny.

A few months later, she received another message from God through her Bible study—her calling to the ministry. Despite the many obstacles that lay in the path of a woman in this work, my mother never doubted the mission she had been called to fulfill. "Go into all the world and proclaim the good news to the whole creation," Jesus had commanded his disciples upon his resurrection.[1] Although it would be some years before my mother would heed this command, her passion to follow in her beloved father's footsteps began to take precedence in her life.

Two years after they had sent her away, Grandpa Deanie and Mama Ola let my mother return to Farmhaven. There she began her apprenticeship in her father's churches. From the beginning, her elegance and her oratorical skills, perhaps learned from her father, commanded notice, as did, of course, her gender. On returning home, she further honed her budding speaking talents at 4-H forums, eventually winning an oratorical competition that led her to the national competitions in Washington, D.C.

But the adage that one can never go home again proved true for my mother. She soon found herself shuttling back and forth between Mississippi and the homes of the O'Neills and other friends in Ohio. In

Columbus, her pastor allowed her to continue her speaking, which she did to growing acclaim. On a trip to St. Louis for an extended visit with cousins who were also members of the Church of God, she predictably became deeply involved with church activities there. It was also in St. Louis that the beautiful Mississippi girl would meet a very light-brown-skinned and light-brown-eyed young man up from Alabama.

My father, who would become an emotional and practical support for my mother's ministry, was a proud man. George Edward Wattleton was born and raised in an all-black town outside Anniston, Alabama. Hobson City, he often bragged, had its own "colored mayor, colored sheriff, and colored chief of police." Daddy had come to St. Louis because it was a branch of the black migratory circuit that led job-seekers to such other industrial cities as Chicago, Detroit, Indianapolis, and Cleveland. Daddy cut a dapper figure with his fastidious dress and his fondness for sweet-smelling colognes that he generously slapped on his face with big, hardworking hands. And he was never without a hat perched jauntily on top of his bald head that shone "like new money." Even when he was engaged in the daily ritual of washing his beloved car, the hat, whether a brown wool fedora or a breezy Panama straw, was his ever-present signature.

My parents were introduced to one another by mutual friends, and after six months of chaperoned flirtation in which my mother was plied with countless barbecued ribs and chicken dinners, my father asked my mother to marry him. Although she thought Daddy was "a nice young man," Ozie Garrett was not one to make rash decisions. Because Daddy was not a member of the Church of God, she would be choosing to "yoke" herself to an unbeliever. Her faith was being tested against the strength of her heart.

My mother fashioned a reply that would buy herself more time and maybe even get her off the hook. "I'll have to go home to Mississippi to think about it. I have to talk it over with my daddy."

Afraid that Grandpa Deanie would not give his blessings, and that she would not have the courage to cross him, Daddy, no slouch either at getting what he wanted, offered, "I'll pay your way home if you marry me first."

My mother accepted. The two were in their mid-twenties when they married, in March 1939. When my mother returned to Farmhaven, not long after her marriage, Grandpa Deanie greeted the news with typical pragmatism: "Your husband must love you or he's a fool to let you leave him to come here by yourself."

As it turned out, it was Daddy's Methodist family that found the marriage unacceptable. Daddy's commitment to my mother was so strong that he chose their rejection over forsaking her. While he would demonstrate little interest in becoming involved in Mama's growing religious devotion,

Daddy did profess his beliefs in the Church of God's teachings and claimed to be "saved." In time he would become essential to her next calling—her evangelical career.

Because my father had only a seventh-grade education, the North offered him few opportunities. He took janitorial jobs and my parents lived on my father's twenty-two-dollar weekly pay. Hard though their early years may have been, they were also good ones. They weren't a particularly sentimental or demonstrative pair, but their love and accommodation for one another was understood.

From the beginning, Mama didn't rail against those who claimed "God didn't call women to preach." Neither did she ever let the biases against women in the ministry weaken her resolve. That even after marrying she held to what she believed was God's will for her made her position all the more unorthodox. The Bible holds: "Wives be subject to husbands as you are in the Lord."[2] Subservience to men, be it to her Church of God brethren or her husband, never seemed to enter Mama's mind, and she continued her ministry in St. Louis without concession to Bible instructions on submission to masculine authority.

As the Depression waned, the dark clouds of another world war loomed. Although President Roosevelt had tried to keep the country out of any conflict by proclaiming American neutrality, the Japanese had other plans. Soon after I was born, on July 8, 1943, my father's infantry unit was shipped to England and France to fight Hitler. Daddy eventually landed KP duty after suffering severely frostbitten feet, which pained him the rest of his life. Meanwhile, like many women of that time—and especially African American women—my mother worked in a bullet factory to help make ends meet and to serve the war effort while he was away.

After Mama Ola died in 1942, my mother's two teenaged sisters, Evie and Ola, came north to live with us. A little later their sister Alice, after whom I was named, and her husband David, arrived. "Never rent," my mother always said. They had saved enough to make the down payment on the house on Walton Avenue, and it was there that we all—four sisters, two husbands, and one child—settled together. The house stood at the beginning of a block of nearly identical redbrick two-family structures with neatly manicured postage-stamp front yards. Each house was adorned with two little front porches and a large picture window between them, one porch leading to the first floor and the other to the steps to the second level.

When my family first moved to the neighborhood, it was mostly white, Jewish, and working class, but as more black families moved in, the whites fled to the quiet suburbs of Wellston and University City. As it evolved into a mostly black enclave, the neighborhood thrived in a way that hardly seems to exist today. People sat on their front porches late into the night, talking with each other over their hedges. During the summer months, the fragrance of pork ribs roasting on open pits drifted through the backyard air. Jovial male boasting over the wire fences about who could make the best "St. Louis barbecue" or discussions about who the St. Louis Browns would next defeat gave the neighborhood an atmosphere of warm comity. I feel sad that my child will never know what it is to grow up in such a tight-knit community of strivers.

I had the run of the house and, for that matter, the immediate neighborhood. All day long, I ran up and down the staircase between my mother's and aunts' flats while they cleaned house, did laundry, or worked at their sewing machines. And when I tired of that, I'd climb on my red tricycle and tour the world. Around the corner, there was a cabstand, a Chinese restaurant, a drugstore, Reed's ice cream parlor, and Dr. Evans's office. I could most often be found at one of those locations, chatting up a storm with the cabdrivers (whom my mother considered unsavory) or some newfound friend. "Lord, you and that tricycle," she would sigh as she brought me back to the safety of our home one more time.

Saturday nights were festive at our house, as family, neighborhood friends, and sometimes visiting relatives gathered for fried chicken, macaroni and cheese, collard greens, cornbread, and Kool-Aid. There was always lots of laughing, piano playing, and talk of politics and church activities. Above all, there was storytelling, mining experiences past and present, and the humor in them. I did my best to keep up with the adult conversations and to get a word in edgewise when I could.

When I was still quite small, my mother took me to a clinic to get my wrist sutured after a nasty fall from my speeding tricycle onto a broken milk bottle. The doctor asked my mother for permission to conduct a few tests. Not certain what the doctor had in mind, she reluctantly agreed.

After a time, the doctor returned me to my mother, shaking his head. "This young lady is remarkable. . . . She doesn't stop talking. She should be put into school immediately. She could be a genius."

Mama bristled at the very idea. "There's a fine line between genius and insanity," she would tell me in later years. "I didn't want a genius. I wanted a normal child with a normal future."

Despite her worries, I was soon sitting on the small low chairs of Mrs. Howard's Nursery School. There, my energy was channeled in healthy engagement with other Negro children my age, and into my fascination with the new things I learned. I was not quite three at the time.

After my father returned from the war, he took up the same work he'd left behind. To support the household, he and Uncle David, Aunt Alice's husband, worked from sunup until well after I was asleep, each holding two and three jobs at a time. Daddy worked as a janitor or a hauler, or labored in factories. My uncle did much the same.

Mama and Aunt Alice went into business as dressmakers. The two, who had learned to sew as teenagers in the 4-H Club, could make suits that looked "store bought," and they did equally professional-looking alterations. Soon trade poured in, especially from the church members who wanted new garments made for holidays and special occasions. At those times, Aunt Alice would sew all night to finish the frocks, nodding off from time to time.

Mama and Aunt Alice set up shop in the first-floor parlor, whose wide-sashed window between the two porches looked out over the street. From the sidewalk, a passerby could see their heads bent over their machines, just above the advertisement for their services, their faces illuminated by the small lights that guided their stitching, or by the sun when it streamed in. The radio entertained the southern sisters as they toiled over the tedium of zippers, buttons, and hems. The radio antics of "Pepper Young's Family" and "Stella Dallas" accompanied the sound of the whirring motors of the busy Singer sewing machines.

During the day, the parlor was often filled with women of every shape and size trying on the creations that my mother and aunt had crafted for them. Around Christmas and especially Easter, our home was a madhouse of pins, patterns, fabrics, and scissors. During my stopovers in the work-room, I'd watch the women socializing, laughing, gossiping, totally at ease with one another in a way I'd later learn was common to women the world over. They would spell out the words if they didn't want me to know what they were talking about. Sometimes they used pig Latin. In time, I usually figured out what they were talking about. There were no approving men in the workroom, just women who knew how they wanted to look, women whose sense of themselves was made powerful by this knowledge. I'd see pride and self-confidence reflected in their faces when they looked in the long mirror propped against the wall. Their presence had a tremendous influence on my awareness of the power of appearance, on my image of who I would eventually become and how I would present myself. Occasionally, I got an outfit, too. I always loved pretty clothes, so I didn't mind holding still while Mama or Aunt Alice pinned up a hem so it would fall just right against my ever-lengthening legs.

This is not to say, though, that I was a paragon of patience. True to my mother's belief that we are all "born in sin and shaped in iniquity," I had my moments. When I was but three years old, I visited my fierce will upon my mother in a way that neither she nor Aunt Alice has ever forgotten. At family gatherings we still laugh at the memory of it.

Even before I could pronounce it correctly, I loved milk and pestered my mother many times a day for a glassful. At night, a warm glass of it could be counted on to quiet my restless body.

On this day, Mama and Aunt Alice were engrossed in their sewing when I interrupted them with, "Mama, I want muck." I repeated the demand several times. She gave no evidence that she had heard me. Eventually, without a word, my mother rose from her sewing table and started for the kitchen to get my drink. But I wasn't convinced of the purpose of her mission.

I followed her up the hallway, past my small bedroom and toward the kitchen at the back of our flat. "I want muck," I repeated several times as I trailed my silent mother.

Before we had left the sewing room, however, I had picked up a straight pin and clutched it between my fingers as I continued to insist. Finally, impatient with the uncertainty of whether my desire would be satisfied, I ran up behind her, took aim, and plunged the pin squarely into her backside. My always dignified mother let out a yelp, grabbed her pricked behind, and whirled to face me.

"Girl, why did you stick me with that pin?" she demanded.

"I want muck." I'm told I said it without blinking or flinching.

I'm not sure why my mother didn't punish me. Perhaps she was simply too amazed. Perhaps she considered that she hadn't responded to one of my many requests with her typical immediacy. But I am sure it became clear to her that day, if not earlier, that even when it looked as though I was about to get what I wanted, I still would persist and persist, until I had it in hand.

If, upstairs and downstairs, our house was all hustle and bustle during the week, Sundays were quite another matter. The Bible stressed modesty, but it also instructed that Christians accept that the body is a vessel of the Holy Spirit. Thus it was incumbent upon those who were saved to keep that place where the spirit of God dwells clean and well groomed. No makeup was allowed, except for a little loose powder "to take the shine off my nose," as my mother would say. Without a sense of inconsistency, however, hair was straightened with a hot comb, then styled in the latest upswept fashions of the Forties, and held in place with a decorative comb. For church, our four ladies always wore hats and gloves, and rayon dresses or suits cut on the bias or sewn in gores to cling softly to their bodies. A dab or two from the cobalt blue bottle of Evening in Paris perfume finished the toilette.

Dressed in our best, we'd head for the Church of God on Garfield Avenue. We'd attend church again that evening and on Wednesday evenings. On special occasions, there were afternoon services and dinners afterward in the church fellowship hall. Occasionally, on Sunday evening (and these were my favorite moments at the Church of God) we'd go to a slide show, where visiting missionaries reported on their compassionate work in faraway places.

"Modesty in all things" was a basic credo of my family's faith, and the church we attended gratified it by eschewing all elaborate ornamentation. It was a simple square building with white asbestos shingle siding and two heavy wooden front doors painted a golden orange. Inside were rows of connecting wooden seats with armrests. Simple, stained-glass windowpanes filtered the sunlight that fell upon the piano, the raised pulpit, and the singing and praying faithful. Behind the minister, over the baptismal pool, was a large painting of a white Jesus, portrayed as a shepherd tending his flock of sheep. A wooden cross adorned the front of the rostrum. There were no lighted candles or burning incense.

Prior to the Sunday service, my father would drop me off at Sunday school, where I would be taught that Jesus loved me and all the little children of the world. I remember the round-cheeked Sister Epps, her felt hat perched just so and its net veil grazing her forehead, standing in the main sanctuary before we went to our classrooms. She'd welcome us in her high-pitched "Good morning, boys and girls" voice. And when we were settled in our seats, she'd announce, "This morning we are going to talk about Jesus. We are going to learn about the little boy Jesus and his mother, Mary—" By then we were rapt with attention as the tale unfolded. Then we'd sing the hymn:

> *Jesus loves me, this I know,*
> *for the Bible tells me so.*
> *Little ones to Him belong.*
> *They are weak, but He is strong.*

I'd find myself absorbed by the stories of David and Goliath, of Daniel in the lions' den, the parables of the values of faith—and by a belief that one could overcome any obstacle.

In church, small child though I was, I was expected to remain quiet and attentive for more than two hours. There were moments of entertainment, however. I enjoyed inspecting the ushers and their movements around the room. The women, each dressed in a white uniform, white stockings and shoes, and each adorned with a fancy white lace handkerchief worn as a flowery corsage out of the left breast pocket to which their brass name tags were affixed, stood with one hand folded across the back of the waist. The other was free to point the churchgoer to an empty seat or to pass the offering plate. Daddy or Mama would always have given me a nickel, tied up in the corner of my white cotton handkerchief, and I'd unwrap it and drop it into the shallow silver bowl with a green felt bottom. Among the other church members, my fascination was always drawn to the women and the way they were dressed. They, like my mother and aunts, were clothed in latest-fashion suits and dresses, and their hats were bedecked with veils, feathers, and flowers. It always seemed to me that they sat with one shoulder cocked higher than the other—with a lot of attitude.

The burgundy-robed choir, directed by Lee Cochran, sang syncopated hymns that were surely more lively than their original Church of God authors—white folks back in Indiana—had intended them to be. But that didn't mean dancing in the aisles like the "holy rollers." Never. The singing was spirited, but rarely did anyone stray from their seats. The prayers were fervently led by the minister and accompanied by a staccato of vocal "Amens," raised hands, and private prayers, but there was none of the unintelligible "speaking in tongues" that the Pentecostals were said to do. The collection plates were passed once, not numerous times in the way of the Baptists, unless there was a guest preacher. In that case, a "love offering" would be collected after the sermon.

The preacher went on forever, it seemed to me, but not on one point as is often characteristic of African American churches. No, in the Church of God, multiple Bible verses were read to make many points. I liked to sit on the center aisle with my friend, Janice, who was the preacher's daughter. There, we wouldn't miss the ushers or the occasional "saint," so overcome with the spirit of worship that he or she would step out into the aisle and walk up and down.

If the Jesus we learned about in Sunday school class was kind, protective, and all-loving, the Jesus I encountered in the morning worship service was harsh, judgmental, and capable of exacting severe punishment upon sinners. I heard of the Second Coming of the Lord, of Judgment Day, and the fiery pit for those who did not live a holy life. I learned the "thou shalt nots" of the Ten Commandments, and the certainty of eternal hell for those who did not repent their sins made those rules seem worth obeying. By this score, I came to understand that the "pleasures of the world" weren't to be had in this life, that we should all prepare for the hereafter, which would only be paradise if we'd been faithful to God.

After we got home from church, before "Sunday dinner," which was served in the early afternoon, Aunt Alice would read the funny papers to me. Doing the voices and acting out the scenes, she would laugh harder than I would at the antics of Li'l Abner and Daisy Mae, Dagwood and Blondie, or Pogo.

After Miss Sue, Aunt Alice was my best playmate and closest confidante. Where my mother was reserved, serene, Aunt Alice was quick with a laugh and always seemed brimming with emotion and humor. And also unlike my mother, she showed her affection freely and easily. I loved the warmth of her bosom and the tightness of her hugs. I loved it when she rained kisses all over my face.

When I was four, my mother received her third "calling." She was to give up domesticity and fulfill a ministry of evangelism. Now, instead of attending one church and occasionally preaching, she would serve wherever and whenever she was invited. She believed her calling to be ordained, just as the disciples had been ordained when Jesus ordered them to leave off their secular lives to join his mission. Her reputation as a commanding presence in the pulpit was growing locally and spreading far beyond St. Louis. She was getting invitations from all over the country asking her to speak at revivals, which are akin to spiritual retreats. Each night over a week or ten days, worship services were held and a visiting minister sermonizes. Mama took these requests as affirmation of God's purpose for her.

Facing the dilemma of what to do with me during her revival tours, given that Evie and Ola were off at college, Mama accepted a church member's offer to look after me for a while. The woman was known for "training children," and her reputation was enhanced by the children in her charge who sang at church gatherings. My mother recalls that the performances were "most impressive," and contributed to her confidence in the woman's care. Perhaps because of her own positive experience with the O'Neill family in Columbus, Mama truly believed that all church members followed the Bible's teachings of kindness, charity, and discipline.

Instead of letting me stay with my aunt Alice when she was away, Mama packed a small bag of my possessions and handed me over to Gladys Brown, who lived in Evanston, Illinois. I was frightened by the sudden change in my life, baffled about the reason why I was being sent away.

Miss Brown was a stout, dark-skinned woman with wide hips and knees that knocked so severely she seemed to rock as she walked. Her thin graying hair and missing teeth gave her the look of a witch. I feared her the instant I first laid eyes on her, but there was nothing I could do. In my parents' eyes, she was saved and therefore trustworthy. After my parents drove away, there was no one to rescue me from the torture I was about to endure.

My musical training began immediately. Every evening, we children gathered around her at the upright piano and we sang at the top of our lungs, "I come to the garden alone, while the dew is still on the roses. . . . The voice of God is calling." I was alone, but it was no garden.

Miss Brown worked as a domestic in one of the beautiful homes along the Evanston shoreline of Lake Michigan. Every afternoon, she donned a white dress and went to her job—after locking me in a small cold room for safekeeping. I would remain there until she came home in the early evening. The three or four other children in her care at the time were old enough to take care of themselves, but too young to assume responsibility for me.

During her absence, the other children would get into mischief, mainly breaking into forbidden cupboards, eating forbidden food. When Miss Brown returned and discovered the loss, the children told her they'd let me out and I'd committed the thievery. The minute I heard the padlock slip off the latch and the door opening, I'd begin to tremble. Seeing her face contorted with anger, I'd protest, "I didn't do it! I didn't do it!" But my denials didn't matter as she led me to the bathroom to strip and beat me with a large leather strap. Sometimes the other children would hold me down when I tried to resist or flee. Sometimes a bar of soap would be shoved into my mouth and my head held under cold rushing water from the bathtub faucet. Then, sobbing from the stinging welts on my arms, legs, back, and buttocks, I'd be sent back to the same cold, locked room, where I'd climb back up on the high bed, crawl between the sheets, and fall into a troubled sleep. I'd waken with the sunrise, fearful of the regimes of "training" and brutality that the gathering day invariably held.

Like so many children who find themselves in such circumstances, I was certain that I had provoked the abuse. In vain attempts to deter Miss Brown's wrath, I'd try to be *perfect*, try to sing with all my might without making a mistake. But every day I knew that I had failed when I heard her shrill voice shouting, "Who ate the Cracker Jacks?" And the "saint of God" who was supposed to teach me to sing gospel songs and recite Bible verses would usher me to my torture.

Eventually the abuse escalated to a level where it could no longer be concealed: a sore on my leg would not heal. To "treat it," Miss Brown had boiled an Epsom salts brew in a galvanized metal foot tub and tossed towels into it to make a "hot pack." She sat me down and told me to hold still while she laid the steaming cloths on my tender skin. As one of the older boys held me immobile, I screamed and screamed as the scalding fabric wrought its damage. After an eternity, she lifted the towel from my withering skin and sent me to my cold bed. The next morning, my skin lay on the sheets and my leg was an open wound. Terrified and in great pain, I started to cry again. When she let me out, she wrapped the raw, seeping wound on my leg with a bandage smeared with ointment.

The sore, which was now a serious burn, was noticed at the prekindergarten that I attended several mornings each week. A large, kindfaced white man in a business suit, who said he was a policeman, asked me about it and about other scars on my legs and arms. At the same time, one of the members of the church, fearing that I was being mistreated, called my mother and said, "There's a sore on her leg that won't heal." Alarmed, Mama quickly came for me.

My mother says that I used to sing a lot before I went to Evanston. I did not sing anymore. But time does heal wounds. Though the scars on my legs never altogether vanished, neither did my resilient spirit. In my familiar surroundings, I was soon back to my old tricks, playing and chatting like a magpie.

When I returned to St. Louis, my mother enrolled me in a kindergarten at the Washington School, a bulky brick structure a few blocks from our home. Two weeks later, she received a call from the kindergarten teacher. "Mrs. Wattleton, this child never stops talking and won't stay in her seat. She follows me around all day, telling me, 'I will help you with the babies.' "

I was only four and a half and they'd decided to put me in the first grade. After one term, I was sent home with a note attached to my collar. I was being promoted to the second grade. This, Mama was not prepared to hear. She would not have her worst fears realized and see me pushed to the brink of insanity. Off to school she marched, and demanded to know why I was being sent to second grade. "I don't want her moved too fast," she told the teacher.

The teacher shrugged. "She's doing the work. We might as well let her."

Her eyes flashing in angry concern, my mother grabbed my hand and we headed home. I was confused and frightened. I didn't know whether I was going to be subjected to one of my mother's stern tongue-lashings or the spanking she always threatened to give me but never did. But soon she looked down at me and sighed. "Girl," she said, "I just don't know what we're going to do with you."

CHAPTER 3

MISSISSIPPI SUMMERS

It was the custom of many African Americans recently settled in the North to go down south to visit relatives for a few weeks each summer, trading the oppressive heat of city brick and concrete for the humidity of Georgia, North and South Carolina, Alabama, and Mississippi. For my family this usually meant an August pilgrimage to the church's Mississippi state camp meeting, in Farmhaven, at the site of Grandpa Deanie's church. There we met up with my mother's relations, including Ernest, W.E., Coleman, and their growing families. Of the brothers, only Uncle Robert had moved north.

Church of God camp meetings were held all over the country. The largest, which was held at the church's headquarters in Anderson, Indiana, convened during the summer months and consisted of a gathering of church members for a week or so of daily morning, afternoon, and evening worship. Originally, these spiritual retreats entailed camping out under tents, trees, and stars, but at the camp meetings I recall, tabernacles and rustic dormitories had been built to shelter the faithful. During the days, crafts programs, sing-alongs, and other organized activities occupied the children, but we were also allowed to roam the grounds freely, making up our own games, swinging on the swings, and climbing on the jungle gyms on the playground. From time to time, I'd search my mother out to get a nickel for a soda pop or a "snowball." In the evenings, everyone was expected to shower and change into cool cotton dress, and appear for evening services together.

If parents couldn't make the journey during the early summer, children were often "sent down south" by themselves to get away from the perceived dangers of long days of school-less idling. The summer that I was six, I made the long trip by myself. My parents were to come down in July for the Mississippi state camp meeting. When Mama woke me that hot, sunny morning, I was itching with excitement and pride. My first solo journey signaled that I was at last a "big girl" in her eyes. My anticipation of the wonderful things that waited for me—seeing my family; fishing; eating watermelon fresh from the garden—was briefly dampened by my mother's steady stream of instructions: "You be good." "Don't fall and break anything." "Stay in your seat on the train . . . no running around." "And for goodness' sake, don't talk too much." But as we walked through the grand marble-walled station with its vaulted ceiling and broad promenade to the waiting trains hissing steam, my heart was pounding wildly.

Mama asked the conductor to make sure that I switched over to the Illinois Central's "City of New Orleans," which stopped in Carbondale, then she handed him my sturdy cardboard suitcase. A Jim Crow law still in effect in the late Forties prohibited black people from eating in the dining cars, so the lunch she had packed for me—a shoe box filled with fried chicken, hard-boiled eggs, potato salad, and pound cake—would have to sustain me. As I stretched to reach from the step stool to the high step of the train, Mama reminded me, "Behave yourself, do you hear?"

One last hug, then the silver metal door quickly snapped shut behind me. The kindly conductor helped me to find a seat. There, my excitement soon gave way to anxious concern about the unknown. I waved to my mother through the train's window. Her smile was reassuring. As the train started to move, I settled down with my Barbara Stanwyck coloring books and my Bible stories book, and surveyed the vicinity for people to talk to. The trainmaster passed by from time to time to check on me. But Mama had instructed me not to run up and down the aisles, and even in her absence, I did not care to test the consequences of disobeying her. My caretaker always found me sitting quietly.

At Carbondale, the conductor lifted me down from the high steps of the train and walked me to the second train. I rode another nine hours before the engine pulled into the small brick station of Canton, Mississippi. My feet had no sooner touched the step stool on the platform than I rushed into the waiting arms of my aunt Lou Doris, the wife of my mother's brother Coleman. Her pastel cotton skirt and simple white cotton sleeveless blouse, with the Peter Pan collar so popular in the Fifties, contrasted with her smooth café au lait complexion, dark eyes, long wavy black hair, and sparkling smile. To me she was one of the most beautiful women in the world. When the embraces passed, I stood very tall and straight. "Girl, you sure have grown," Aunt Lou marveled. "Look at those long legs! How's your mama and daddy?" I felt proud that I was being recognized as a "big girl."

As we walked past the station to her car, I caught a glimpse of words—black letters on white signs hanging over two water fountains. I could read "Colored" and "White."

Before leaving town, we stopped to say a quick hello to my mother's eldest brother, Ernest, and his wife, Sadie. Their white shingled home, built in what could generously be called a patchwork style—rooms had been added on and there were unfinished interiors—reflected my uncle's start-stop ways.

"Honey, Ernest never finishes anything. He'd rather go fishing," Aunt Sadie lamented. And yet, there was certainly an air of southern grace and an elegance about the Victorian settee and the globed *Gone With the Wind*-style lamp.

There was a warmth about the place. Uncle Ernest and Aunt Sadie held to Grandpa Deanie's often quoted credo, "This house is a friend to every man." In those years, their home was always open to any traveling relative. Some years later, in the Freedom Summer of 1964 and at no small peril to their own family, they would offer their home as a safe house for college students from the North who came to register black voters.

Aunt Sadie persuaded Aunt Lou that we must stay long enough for supper: crispy fried perch that Uncle Ernest had caught that day. We didn't tarry long, though. It would soon be night. As we headed out of town, we passed the square, shaded by magnificent Spanish moss–draped oaks and the broad oily leaves of large magnolia trees. This was the same square where blacks stepped aside to let whites pass or were pushed aside if they hadn't stepped quickly enough. The same square where my uncle Robert had been brought for a doctor's care; the square that bore the weight of the courthouse that saw his assailant freed. We passed sprawling clapboard churches, and large, gracious houses as we headed out to Highway 16. What I didn't understand at that young age was that these guileless struc-tures stood as a memorial to the pain of my ancestors. We traveled the road deeper into "the country," where I'd soon be playing with my cousins, Junior, Odessa, and Coleman Wesley.

About five miles out of town, we stopped at Aunt Lou's house. She and Uncle Coleman lived with their sons, Roland and Coleman, Jr., in a small bungalow attached to a country store, the one that Grandpa Deanie had built and that they now ran together. Surrounded by a white cross-tie fence, the little house overlooked one of my mother's favorite fishing holes, a still-water pond well stocked with perch and bass.

Uncle Coleman was a man of few words. Family lore held, "You ask Coleman a question, you'll get the answer next week."

Faithful to family tradition, Uncle Coleman and Aunt Lou earned their living through several enterprises. She ran the small grocery store, where he lent a hand when he wasn't working as an industrial arts teacher or helping to run the family sawmill up the hill behind the house. Grandpa Deanie's mill was now in the hands of his three surviving sons, Coleman, Ernest, and William Eugene (W.E.). Uncle Thomas had died of brain cancer. I fondly remember the aroma of freshly cut wood and the clouds of dust that settled on their dark curly hair. Mushrooms thrived in the damp sawdust that carpeted the floor.

Farmhaven, our final stop, eleven miles up the road and the original site of Mariah's homestead, was where the rest of Mama's large clan lived. Their neat white clapboard houses were scattered amid the gently rolling hills of cotton that spread as far as the eye could see. The homes, each seeming to vie with one another for whitewashed cleanliness, were surrounded by glorious gardens of zinnias and gladioli, and rows of lacy petunias. In the vegetable garden out back, watermelon, lima beans, okra, tomatoes, and a few stalks of corn guaranteed vegetables not just during the summer months but, once canned, all winter as well.

I usually stayed with Uncle W.E. and Aunt Zenobia because the oldest of their eight children were around my age. My uncle and aunt were highly regarded by their neighbors—after all, Uncle W.E. was Grandpa Deanie's son, and Aunt Zenobia was a teacher. Education in Farmhaven had often meant a one-room schoolhouse where children of all grade levels sat together with books cast off from the white schools. In the 1960s, Uncle W.E. and Aunt Zenobia would run the first Head Start program in that rural area. And when the Freedom Rides and the Voting Rights Act would help to open the doors to political strength for African Americans, Aunt Zenobia eventually became an administrative judge for the Farmhaven area of the county.

By late summer, my cousins, including Odessa, the oldest daughter, and Coleman Wesley, who was my age and my favorite, picked cotton in the family's fields all day long. At first, figuring that their company was worth the toil, I went to the fields with them several times, but I quickly gave up. I didn't like being stuck by the sharp points of the dried cotton bolls. I hated the clammy early morning dew as it soaked through my shoes, dress, and skin. With the long muslin sack slung over my back growing heavier as the reward for my labor, the sun beating down on my shoulders, and buzzing horseflies circling my head, I decided cotton picking wasn't for me. Like Mama before me, I couldn't believe that I'd been put on earth to do work like that.

As a guest I wasn't obliged to do such labor, but that meant spending my days lonely and bored, reading comic books, filling in coloring books, and trundling from house to house in search of company. But everyone was usually in the fields, except for my elderly grand-aunts. Grandpa Deanie's sister, Aunt Annie, lived across the road from Uncle W.E., and cared for Mariah, who had taken to her bed years earlier for reasons no one really understood. I was always grateful when Uncle Ernest drove out from Canton to take me fishing with him.

When my cousins came home, they were tired and their knees were crusted with the red Mississippi soil. Every once in a while, I'd help Odessa. She, like my mother and many other eldest daughters in large rural families whose mothers were still engaged in childbearing, shouldered a heavy burden of cooking, cleaning, washing, and ironing for her large family, besides working in the field. Odessa was rail thin and by the end of the day her hands were swollen from the heavy work. I felt guilt and empathy, so I'd help with the dishes once in a while—but such emotions did not extend to cotton picking. Happiness on these summer evenings was hearing Uncle W.E. break open a watermelon on the front porch, then eating the sweet jagged chunks, the juice running down our faces and arms.

On later visits, when I was in my early teens, I would join my cousins in a newfound defiance. We all knew that we were forbidden all "worldly" amusement that did not glorify God, and especially from anything inviting the temptations of the flesh, like dancing, smoking, drinking, and, of course, sex. Nevertheless, we'd gather around a small radio on the back porch or in Odessa's bedroom and secretly listen to music broadcast from Randy's Record Shop, in Gallatin, Tennessee, or to programs from Del Rio, Texas. We'd hear the blues of B. B. King, Muddy Waters, Bo Diddley, Lonesome Sundown, and Howlin' Wolf. We'd fall asleep to the rhythms of the Mississippi Delta and to the tiny light of the illuminated dial, which cast a glow over our secret transgressions.

On Saturdays, we'd pile ourselves into Uncle W.E.'s car for a trip to Canton. This being the early 1950s, segregation was still enshrined in law and deeply embedded in the texture of the antebellum town. Unless blacks were domestics, they were not to be seen on the shady streets of Canton's white sections. But commerce has a way of being color-blind, so we were free to shop for groceries and supplies, and patronize Mr. Montgomery's general store and the gas pumps on the road into town.

Our business finished, we generally headed for the black section of town, where, as in my neighborhood in St. Louis in pre-integration days, the elite, professionals, and poor people mingled in easy harmony. The center of black commerce—"the holler"—was the place to promenade, to flirt, to see and be seen. From Saturday midday until well after midnight, it was packed with people dressed in fresh casual attire. The smells of barbecued ribs and fried perch and catfish mingled with the familiar fragrance of dime-store perfume. Juke joints blared Mississippi Delta blues, and we'd slip into their smoky darkness to listen to Fats Domino and Ike and Tina Turner, and to watch couples jitterbug. Years later, when I traveled through the teeming marketplaces of African villages, it all felt strangely familiar.

Sunday mornings jolted me back to the hustle of getting dressed in our finest, against an acceptable (by even Mama's lights) but no less blood-stirring musical backdrop of the Swan Silvertones, The Five Blind Boys, The Soul Stirrers, and Sister Rosetta Tharpe. After a hearty breakfast of fried chicken, rice, and biscuits lathered in butter to sop up the heavy dark Brer Rabbit syrup, we'd climb into a car or pickup for the short drive down the dusty road to Grandpa Deanie's church. My extended kin made up nearly half the congregation.

In contrast to the stylish sophistication of the folks who had gone north, the simple tastes of my southern kinfolk tended toward cotton dresses—with brooches to make sure the neck opening remained modestly closed—bare legs and wedge-heeled sandals. The men wore short-sleeved cotton shirts and slacks and sometimes Panama hats just like Daddy's. They were country people, practical in their ways as in their dress. And there was style in this simplicity. The natural glow on the sun-kissed complexions seemed more beautiful than the matte-powdered faces of the St. Louis women.

Going to church taxed my patience even more in Mississippi than in St. Louis. The God of my southern family was a highly decorous deity who was less tolerant of the amens, clapping, and lively music that characterized the services I went to up north. The sermons were dry, didactic, and inter-minable. I spent miserable hours on the hard, straight-backed benches in that sultry sanctuary. Handheld cardboard fans, each advertising the local funeral home, moved the heavy air and the scent of sweat and cheap per-fume from person to person. The open windows admitted a pungent piney breeze from time to time, or the chirping buzz of crickets, a dissonant accompaniment to our stolid renditions of "When We All Get to Heaven" and "Onward Christian Soldiers."

I could hardly wait to get to the Sunday dinners sometimes held in the fellowship hall lined with wooden picnic tables and benches. There each family unpacked wicker baskets laden with fried chicken, baked ham, potato salad, greens, and yellow cake with chocolate or white coconut icings. This bounty was then laid out for everyone to share on long wooden tables that spanned the open room. But most often we'd stop off and visit with my great-aunts Bessie, Mandy, and Lucille. In the best southern tradition, we'd be offered food and refreshment wherever we stopped.

Down south, on Sunday evenings there was no church worship, so kids congregated on Uncle W.E. and Aunt Zenobia's porch. My popular cousins attracted friends from miles away. We sat late into the night, laughing and talking. We'd chase fireflies, collecting them in jars, then pulling them apart to explore more fully the wonder of their neon glow. If the dissection was made at just the right moment, the light of their abdomens would continue for minutes longer. Without the city lights to soften the blackness of the skies overhead, the stars shone as sharp as diamonds against the black velvet of a jeweler's display tray and often seemed close enough to touch. An occasional truck or car passing on Highway 16 would remind us that there was a world beyond our porch.

If we were feeling brave, we sometimes sneaked off to a juke joint in the woods and bought Royal Crown colas and some salted peanuts and poured them into the fizzing drink. Taking in the mournful strains of gut bucket blues, we'd watch couples slow-drag to the music. I was always afraid we'd get caught, but my cousins never seemed to care.

The Sunday revelry always ended too soon, as my cousins had to be ready to rise at the crack of dawn, when the cotton leaves were still heavy with dew. The morning would return my cousins to the fields, and me to my lonely boredom.

Much though I loved the country and my family there, after a few weeks I longed for the congestion of city life, and by the end of my visit I was ready to go.

CHAPTER 4

ON THE ROAD AGAIN

By 1949, Mama's evangelism was full-time. She, like hundreds of itinerant preachers, was taking her crusades to small-town America, calling on sinners to repent their wrongful deeds and find salvation in the word of God and so save themselves from the eternal hellfire and damnation that otherwise awaited them.

Mama's reputation as a dynamic and hard-hitting preacher had led to invitations to speak not just to black congregations, but to white ones as well. Soon, requests from all over—Alabama, Louisiana, Mississippi, and the Midwest—filled her calendar. My parents bought a used, two-toned brown, four-door DeSoto as snappy as my father's carefully creased trousers, and we took to the road.

Although we'd still call St. Louis home and would often return in the summer for visits with our relatives, my parents and I would spend very little time there ever again. Like a vaudeville troupe we were in constant motion, making stops in such exotic locales as Plaquemine, Louisiana; West Middlesex, Pennsylvania; and Albion, Nebraska, logging thousands of miles in the name of my mother's relentless crusade to win souls for Christ. I can still see Daddy at the steering wheel, his left elbow resting on the open window, his right hand guiding the heavy sedan. His shirts were often drenched by the time we reached our destination. Still, his hat left his head only occasionally, when he lifted it to swab his round, bald head with the large white cotton handkerchief he always carried, while Mama dabbed at her brow with the lace-trimmed linen ones that rarely left her hand. By September, Daddy's left arm was sun-baked several shades darker than the one that steered.

In the summers, I usually traveled with my parents. My constant chatter proved taxing for both of them, especially my father. He was not a man of great patience—certainly not after long hours in the car with little relief but the sultry breeze blowing in through the open car windows. At such times my mother came up with countless clever little games to keep the peace.

When the summers inevitably drew to a close, my mother was determined that I complete each school year in one location. So each September from second grade to my junior year in high school, she and my father left me in the care of church friends or relatives, mostly in Louisiana and Mississippi. They chose to see Miss Brown as the exception to the rule. I was always anxious with the arrangements, worried about fitting into both a new home and a new school. Knowing that I would be saying good-bye in nine months' time made making friends difficult, and making best friends all but impossible. And though I never again endured physical brutality, those impermanent "homes" were governed by strict rules enforced mostly without the love and tolerance of my family. I was left to my own devices, to adapt to every circumstance. It was a lonely, guarded existence. Memories of Aunt Alice's laughter and hugs and Reed's ice cream cones left me yearning for St. Louis. Sometimes I would go "home" for the Christmas holidays, and sometimes my mother would stop and visit me during the school year. When she'd leave again, I would cry so hard it seemed my heart would break.

But if I often felt helpless, if I often longed to return to the redbrick house on Walton Avenue—the home made busy and beautiful by the industrious verve of my extended family, where playmates could join me in my backyard play—I did not feel resentful. Had I been, I don't know what difference it would have made. I figured it was God's will. There were times when it was hard to tell where God stopped and Mama began. But this I did know; Mama would not tolerate reports of bad behavior, whether it was my not keeping my personal possessions neat, not doing my schoolwork, or sassing my caretakers. On one occasion, when my parents came to pick me up, a teacher with whom I'd been left in Franklin, Louisiana, reported to my mother that I had given her mother some back talk. The grim-faced adults scrutinized me as though they were trying to find visual proof of the Devil dwelling within me. Mama did not give me the benefit of offering an explanation, although I doubt that I could have come up with one, as my brain was so paralyzed by fear. My mother then unleashed what I dreaded most—a lengthy tongue-lashing that began "The Devil is working on you, girl." And as if to seal the guilt for my misdeeds within my soul, she ended in an emotional crescendo of tearful prayers.

* * *

My father loved his cars and took great pride in them. They were his thrones of power within our family. Over the years, their numbers would include Dodges, DeSotos, and Packards, always purchased used, always kept meticulously clean and waxed to a blinding sheen. Still, beauty was no shield against mechanical failures; inevitably, they happened. And inevitably they meant bickering between Mama and Daddy, especially when the unplanned mechanic's bills stressed their precarious budget. Every once in a while, the heat from the sun-drenched asphalt became so intense that a tire would blow out. But aging engines and the scorching summer sun weren't the only culprits in car breakdowns. Our road woes were often caused by Daddy himself. He seemed, indeed, driven to test the limits of the gas tank and my mother's patience. It was she who, spotting a gas station on the road up ahead, would urge, "George, you'd better stop. The needle is on empty."

Watching the station disappear in the rearview mirror, sitting straighter, then fixing his light brown eyes on the road ahead, he'd reply, "I'm driving, O.B. I know what I'm doing. I'll tell you when the tank is empty." She would flash her eyes in impatience and let out a heavy breath.

If we made it to the next gas station before the engine died, my mother and I would have to endure his chortling for hours—even days. And of course such successes only gave him more ammunition for the next "I know what I'm doing."

Too often, though, we'd find ourselves sitting in the car on the side of the road, waiting for help to arrive or watching Daddy walk off into the distance in search of a few gallons of gasoline to get the engine primed so that we could roll slowly into the next station. I remember those times well. Sometimes I was afraid. Sometimes, sitting there in the sweltering heat, the plastic covers protecting the seats growing intolerably hot, I was simply bored by my surroundings.

Another offense that was guaranteed to set off verbal fireworks was Daddy's refusal to ask for directions. Not even if it was obvious that we were lost. Not even if we were covering the same stretch twice. Only after we had wandered a bit and he could not deny that we were lost would he pull to the side of the road and pore over a map with my mother or stop at a filling station and ask for directions. "The Devil is working on George." Thus did my mother always chalk up Daddy's irascible behavior. And somehow, we always managed to arrive on time at our destination.

When I think about my father, I find that these little quirks in his character served a purpose for him and were testaments to his need to maintain control over a life that was ever changing. He was always supportive of my mother's work; without him, Mama would never have been able to travel as widely and as often as she did. But Daddy was not passive in any regard, and always stood his ground when confronted by my mother's forcefulness.

Sometimes I would tremble when he yelled at her for pressing him too hard on his inclination to speed. It was a power struggle between them in which there could be no winner. Nevertheless, the tussle lasted as long as their marriage. In so many ways they were perfectly matched.

Traveling was neither pleasant nor easy for black people in those years. We never stayed in hotels, because "colored" were not allowed. We had to plan to drive from well before daybreak until late into the night, when we'd arrive at the home of some church members. After long hours on the road, my mother would take up monitoring my father's drooping eyelids. "George, wake up," she would shout in alarm.

And as usual, he would resist. "O.B., I'm not 'sleep."

But if fatigue really began to overtake him, we would sometimes pull over to the side of the road and he would sleep for a few minutes. Perhaps this wasn't the safest thing to do, but there were no alternatives. Other times, Mama, a competent driver, would take over the wheel.

We packed our meals, because my parents weren't about to receive food from the back windows of restaurants that would not allow us to enter their front door. And when my father stopped at filling stations, he always asked if they had a bathroom for "colored." If the attendant said they did, Daddy instructed him to fill the tank. If they didn't, we would drive on until we found a station that did. When we couldn't find one, my mother and I would relieve ourselves on the side of the road, squatting discreetly between two open car doors; Daddy would walk off into the bushes.

Once, en route to a revival meeting in Louisiana, we crossed the bridge from New Orleans and stopped at a gas station in Algiers.

"Do you have a bathroom for colored?" Daddy asked.

"Sure," answered the attendant, pointing to the back of the station. Feeling the urge strongly, I ran behind the station, where I found no sign of an outhouse or any room with a door, nothing but a hole in the ground. It said "nigger" to me. Nothing more, nothing less. My eyes stung at that insult. But my heart was pounding, because I knew what was about to happen when I reported this to Daddy.

I ran back to my father and told him that there was nothing behind the service station but an open pit. His vexation flaring, Daddy whirled around to face the attendant.

"You told me there was a bathroom for colored," said my father, accusingly, his gaze hardening into a glare.

"What else do you expect?" the attendant drawled.

"George, let's go," Mama demanded.

"Stop pumping the gas," Daddy shouted, his caramel eyes flashing, anger rising in his voice, paying no mind to Mama. He paid for the small amount that had already flowed into our tank while my mother looked on in disgust. But he wasn't willing to let his protest end with an economic boycott.

As we began to drive away, my father yelled back through his open window, "You know we're not dogs!"

Wielding his meager economic power, my father rejected the degrading treatment by the white man. He headed the car back to the open road, raging at the indignity. At such moments, my mother, like her father, would calm the scene. Soon we pulled over to the roadside as we had done so many times. There, the marshy grasses would serve our need.

I was upset and angry that I'd been sent to urinate in an open pit, and proud that my father had rejected such treatment. But I was still too young to appreciate the danger he had put us in. This was the Deep South.

When my mother's engagement took the form of a tent revival, Daddy would join the men of the host church in pitching a large, rented tent. He'd help the men set up the chairs and erect the platform that would serve as the pulpit and as a stage for the choir. Great care was given to the installation of the sound and lighting systems. Preparations completed, Daddy sometimes drove around the local neighborhoods with a loudspeaker perched atop our car. His amplified voice was accompanied by a backdrop of religious music announcing that night's services. Though the revivals weren't on the scale of the Billy Graham extravaganzas, which were gaining popularity around this time, they did create quite a stir; something like the circus coming to the small towns. The curious often came to see what all the commotion was about.

Sometimes, Daddy would stay for the duration of the meeting, taking up whatever short-term employment he could find—construction work, most often. Other times, he'd drop us off and return to his job, if not back in St. Louis, then wherever my parents had taken up temporary residence. As the revival drew to a close, he would make the long drive back to pick us up.

Mama usually entered the church or revival tent after the start of services, in the midst of singing, praying, and shouting. She'd climb the steps to the platform in front of us with the authority of a woman on an important mission. Her presence was commanding, dignity and prepossession manifest in her regal carriage: shoulders square, back ramrod straight, head held high. In one hand she carried her black leather Bible with the onionskin pages; in the other, her purse and a stole to protect her shoulders against the night chill.

Dressed in a simple skirt and a white blouse of cool cotton or luminous silk, she was beautiful to me. Faithful to her strict beliefs, she did not adorn herself in any way. But with her flawless skin, and black hair flecked prematurely with gray and pulled into a neat bun at the nape of her neck, she hardly needed ornamentation.

I often heard people tell Mama, "Sister Wattleton, you're so beautiful." While she never said so, it was clear that Mama understood that the power of her message and her ability to draw people to her was enhanced by her physical beauty. Morning and night, she cleansed and treated her flawless skin with rubbing alcohol and Noxzema face cream. She worked hard to keep both message and medium in fine form.

My father and I would already be seated in the church, both of us enduring the preliminary hymns, prayers, offerings, and testimonies until it was time for Mama to take charge of the pulpit. I brimmed with pride at the sight of her. Following a lavish introduction, she would step up to the rostrum and, with a minimum of smiling acknowledgments, launch her sermon.

Invariably, she began, "Turn with me in your Bibles. . . ." The authority of her voice and the flash of her eyes having secured the attention of her audience, she would read several passages of scripture with perfect diction. She developed her theme slowly, methodically, using the Bible lessons skillfully to buttress her message of salvation from sin of every kind.

Mama's sermons often focused on the sins of the flesh, especially fornication and adultery, words whose meanings I did not fully understand. She exhorted women to dress modestly. Later she would caution, "No pants." Mama didn't jump around the stage, didn't yell or scream. Using her small, expressive hands freely to make her points, she stood with her feet fixed on the floor behind the rostrum. Her gaze took constant measure of the attentiveness of her audience. Occasionally, she'd stop the forward momentum of her words to stress a point. My mother's powerful physical presence—her beauty and self-assurance—and her commanding oratory, which combined well-honed English with her scholarly presentation of the texts and the inherited eloquence of her father, held audiences, sometimes over two hundred strong, transfixed.

Though Mama and the other evangelists often crafted harrowing images of eternal damnation, their sermons were founded in the conviction that people could change, be called to a life of goodness. This message offered hope and inspiration to many who flocked to hear them—hope of blissful escape in the next world from the hardships they knew so well in this one.

When the sermon concluded, forty-five minutes to an hour later, the crush of repentant sinners at the altar in front of the stage would affirm my mother as a compelling messenger of God. Gratitude for her heartfelt message was reflected in the collection plate. As Mama's reputation grew and with it the traveling my parents needed to do, my father found holding a regular job more and more difficult, and the collections provided a major source of our family's income.

Never able to muster Mama's public piety, I often felt uncomfortable with the demonstrations through which church members showed their devotion. Eventually, I would come to believe that one's relationship with God is a private matter; but there were times when the strength of my mother's oratory propelled me into the remorseful crush at the altar to "get saved." I'd feel tremendous guilt, although I was never certain what my sins were—maybe telling a fib, sassing my mother, sneaking into the balcony of a movie house, going to the juke joint with my cousins. But one thing was certain: I was terrified if somewhat skeptical of the hellfires that awaited me if I didn't get saved. Yet, even though I got saved over and over again, getting saved never seemed to stick.

For all our pride in her, Daddy and I found it hard to live up to the standard of Mama's holy aura. We didn't have a calling yet; we were supposed to present a united front of propriety consistent with her teachings. He was her husband and I was her daughter and everything we did, she believed, reflected on her. Daddy's lack of religiosity was a source of great consternation for my mother, and he often had to defend himself against her reproachful lectures.

"George, you were asleep while I was preaching," she would complain. "If the preacher's husband can't stay awake, what will people think?"

"No, O.B., I wasn't," he would reply time and again. "I heard everything you said."

As for me, I was aware that much was expected of "Sister Wattleton's daughter." It was assumed that I would be restrained in manner, as proper girls should be, and plain in appearance, with a Bible tucked under my arm and its scriptures floating easily from my tongue. It was supposed that I would be actively involved in the rituals of religious worship—playing the piano, singing, ushering, testifying, or praying.

I wasn't supposed to like boys and was warned to steer clear of the sexual dangers that lurked behind "boy craziness," but there wasn't much danger of this. As I grew into adolescence, the boys of the church seemed to prefer the lighter-skinned girls with straight, wavy hair; shapely legs; and beautiful singing voices. I may have been the preacher's daughter, but my relative closeness to the seat of righteousness gave me no status with the roving hormones of the Church of God boys. I cannot ever remember having a "boyfriend" within the church. Furthermore, I was tall—taller than most of the adolescents my age. The people I loved the most, my family, were tall and stately, and my mother always followed her certain command, "Stand up straight. Don't sit on your back," with a reassurance that "Models are tall."

Though I may not have given my mother cause for concern about being "boy crazy," I showed scant evidence of other aspects of devotedness. When we were together, she did her best to mold me in her vision. In our home, daily Bible or meditation reading and prayer—usually before I went off to school—was all but ritual. And for eight years, I was forced to take piano lessons wherever I went, so that I could play for the church. The only thing I got out of the piano lessons were thick knuckles. And when I sat in the church or in the hot humid air of the revival tent, I struggled mightily to maintain a semblance of propriety as nagging mosquitoes stabbed at my bare legs. I dared not squirm in my seat, whisper with my friends, or chew gum lest I solicit a reprimanding glare from the pulpit.

Once, while we were at a Mississippi camp meeting where I knew my mother wasn't scheduled to preach, I saw her headed for the tabernacle, dressed in her preaching uniform. I asked in surprise, "Mama, you're going to preach today?"

"The preacher who was supposed to preach couldn't make it and they asked me to take his place," she replied.

Never reluctant to give my opinion and never believing that I would be kept from doing so, I complained, "I sure do get tired of your mouth."

And in a moment of sympathy, my mother laughed at my frankness. I had, after all, received a daily dose of her ministry at the eight revivals and camp meetings we'd already attended that summer. She continued on her way.

CHAPTER 5

PREACHER'S DAUGHTER

When I think back on my mother's single-minded devotion to her ministry, I understand why God came before everything else. How else could she have overlooked the toll that her calling would take on her husband? How else could she have reconciled the separation from her only child that it would demand? I am sure that it was the very fervor of her commitment that my mother drew upon for the courage necessary to confront the obstacles posed by her gender and race.

Mama had been invited to one of her first tent revivals by the black congregation in the tiny northern Louisiana town of Oak Grove. In an unusual exception to tradition, whites of the denomination would also be in attendance. There had been much debate about integrating the black and the white congregations in the Church of God in the late 1800s, but in 1910 the church settled on voluntary segregation. In doing so, they were following the logic expressed by C. W. Naylor in his assertion that race made no difference in salvation, but that "there are social differences which we cannot ignore without serious consequences. Both white and colored are better off as a result of social separation that would be mixed together [*sic*] in these relations."[1] As this was 1950 in a domain where Jim Crow was still a vigorous social regulator, the fellowship of blacks and whites under the same tent constituted an unusual, if not disturbing, occasion.

But Mama's courage was not diminished. She remembers, "We would go to the tent for services—black and white together—and across the way I could see white people gathering in back of a house, sitting out in the yard under a large umbrella. I thought they were just eating and visiting together out there every evening."

After a few nights, Mama concluded that they were listening to her sermons, which were being projected by a loudspeaker. She also thought that they would eventually join everyone else under the big tent. But night after night, they came to the same backyard and watched from the same cloak of darkness. From early in her ministry, Mama believed her faith would provide her with all that she needed to confront this or any situation.

One night Mama decided to address her silent witnesses. Pointing toward the dark void beyond the tent, she said into the microphone, in a voice that challenged without fear or reticence, "If you can't come under the tent to worship with us because of the color of our skin, I know one thing we can do together, we can all roast in hell for your not doing it."

Apparently my father leapt up and, as my mother describes it, fled the tent as though someone were shooting at him. Coming from Alabama, he knew that retribution was more likely to be taken out on him than on his brazen wife. Later that night, safe behind the closed door of their host's guest room, my father demanded, "O.B., have you gone crazy? Don't you know that somebody could have shot you!"

"I never even thought about it," Mama answered calmly.

Later, my parents learned that there *had* been talk of tarring and feathering my mother. "I guessed it was the Ku Klux Klan. But I wasn't scared," my mother says. "I was just preaching freedom. And I certainly wasn't going to bend to their threats." But Mama's determination to carry on was not shared by the sympathetic whites who'd worshiped in the tent. They didn't return, for fear of putting her life, and perhaps their standing in the community, in jeopardy.

Later still, Mama learned that the mayor of Oak Grove admitted to being part of the backyard crowd, and that he'd intervened on her behalf. "Our town needs to hear that lady's message," he told those threatening to run her out of town.

While my mother never considered leaving the ministry in the wake of such danger, she knew that she had to rely on more than the Lord to protect her husband, her daughter, and herself. My mother recalls a sign posted at the entrance of another Louisiana town: NIGGER, READ AND RUN. "Since we had bad tires on the car, I prayed that we didn't get a flat before we got through there."

For all my parents' attentiveness to signs of "sinful transgression" when I was in their care, they continued to yield responsibility for my emotional and physical well-being to church members. They assumed that as long as they were Church of God folk, my moral upbringing would be fine.

Shortly after we took to the nomadic life, my mother was preaching at a revival in northern Louisiana. It was cotton-picking season and she allowed me to go to the cotton fields with my new acquaintances at the church. It was a chance to enjoy the company of my playmates during the day and earn a little cash. We would be in the care of one of the older church members. In the half-light of dawn, we climbed onto the large hauling truck that made the rounds in the black quarter to collect field workers. But I didn't like picking cotton in Louisiana any more than I did in Mississippi.

Just before midday, the white straw boss singled me out. "I've got to go into town to buy supplies. Would you like to ride in with me, little girl?"

I wasn't aware of any danger, but my chaperone, Sister Key, was. I saw a look of worry in her gentle eyes as she straightened from her position over the lush green cotton stalks. She said nothing. I'm certain she was afraid she would anger the sun-beaten white man.

We climbed into his pickup and were soon on our way down the dusty road, toward town. I saw Sister Key standing over the bent backs of the hunched laborers, watching us leave. It didn't take me long to understand why she was so tense.

Just as we turned onto the paved road, the man slowed the truck and pulled it over to the side. He switched off the engine and turned to me, smiling. I wasn't sure what that meant, but intuition told me something was wrong. Just then, he reached his hand past the gearshift in the floor— the only obstacle between us—and before I knew it, his large red hand was pressing hard against the part of my dress that covered my pubis. My frightened reflex was a violent shove of his hand from my body. It seemed to startle him. His face grew redder.

I said nothing; I didn't know what to say. At seven, all I knew was that I felt embarrassed and frightened. I started to cry.

The man whirled the truck around and headed back toward the field. When I spotted my friends, I leapt out of the now slow-moving vehicle to run to them. I never revealed what happened. They never asked.

In the summer of 1953, Mama was asked to preach at a revival for a white congregation in Nebraska. Daddy was not going to join us, so, for the first time in my short life, I would be in the midst of only white people. The only other colored face that I would see for the two weeks of the revival would be my mother's.

Mama and I took the train to Albion, a small farming community in the middle of the corn and alfalfa fields of central Nebraska. We would be staying in the home of the host pastor, and Mama, anxious to make a good impression, reminded me during the train ride that we must not reinforce the negative racial stereotypes of blacks as unclean, unkempt, or speaking in dialect; and I must be a polite and helpful guest.

"Help with the dishes and don't leave your washcloth on the sink," she instructed. "And I brought the hot comb to take care of that nappy hair of yours."

At ten, I was an old hand at adapting. Still, I had no idea what to expect in Albion, no comparable experience to draw on. I wasn't afraid, because I was with my mother, but I was anxious. First sight of our Alabama-born hosts, the McCulloughs, did much to calm my anxieties. Sister McCullough was a big, tall woman with laughing, vivid blue eyes. Her husband, rosy-cheeked and ever smiling, exuded enthusiasm. "Sister Wattleton, I can't tell you how happy we are to have you," he blurted out as he energetically pumped Mama's hand.

The McCullough sons, David, Ron, and Dale, were fresh-scrubbed, all-American teens. As they rounded out the reception line of smiles, I suspected that, like me, they had gotten some parental priming for our arrival. Here, far from the South, the hand of fellowship within the Church of God was being extended freely and kindly across racial lines. Nevertheless, I vaguely sensed that our hosts' effusiveness flowed in part from their own anxieties.

They took our bags and led us to the second-floor guest room. As I sat down cautiously on the double bed and looked out the window at the bright sunlight reflecting off the white steepled church outside, I wondered about what lay ahead.

My worries were soon forgotten in play with the McCullough boys and other neighborhood children and in riding borrowed bicycles on the wide, mostly empty, tree-shaded streets of the small town. Sometimes we played jacks or fiddlesticks on the concrete porch, or frequented the neighborhood confectionery. Mama, as was her custom, stayed in the guest room throughout the day, praying, reading the Bible, and preparing her sermons.

Every day at noon, lunchtime was announced by a siren blaring from the town's water tower and we children ran back to the parsonage for what were, to me, marvelous delicacies—banana and mayonnaise sandwiches on white bread, cottage cheese, potato chips, and raw vegetables. After the meals, faithful to my mother's instruction, I helped clean up. Then I returned to my outdoor adventures, which soon included sailing down the street at high speed without holding on to the handlebars.

While we were in Albion, I was introduced to the trials of conforming to a standard of beauty that did not value my African features. A day of vigorous play under the hot summer sun in that pre–chemical straightener era meant sweaty, kinky hair. Mama's thick, heavy, straight hair was unaffected by the heat, but she'd packed all the necessary equipment to tame my own soft but rambunctious mass of corkscrew curls. Late each afternoon, the preparation of my exterior for nightly services became a ritual. The companion odors of burning hair and roasting alfalfa, the latter wafting from the processing plant on the edge of town, filled the still afternoon air.

These secular ministrations began with bathing, dousing my emerging underarm pubescence with liquid Avon deodorant, rubbing Vaseline on my legs, "so that these white people won't see the ash on your legs," and pulling out a small can of liquid fuel to heat the straightening comb. I would sit on the floor between my mother's legs, facing out, my arms wrapped around her knees to anchor me while she tugged at my resistant hair.

"Hold still!" Mama would command as I tried to dodge the searing sweep of the comb.

"Hold your ear down," she'd order to avoid inflicting third-degree burns on me with the heated metal. Not only would a burn hurt me; more important, it might reveal our efforts to transform our looks into a semblance of white folks'.

Keeping my hair straightened was all but impossible since the spiral strands would reappear as soon as I began to perspire.

During the nightly services, members of the Church of God from Columbus, a small town nearby, used to come to hear "the colored lady preacher." They talked of needing a pastor for their church, and before we headed east, they asked my mother if she would consider the post.

Without hesitation, she accepted. Again, the invitation was for her a demonstration of "God's calling." It simply would not have done to question the details or the wisdom of it. My father would acquiesce. I was not asked. I was thrilled by the prospect of my parents' settling in one place for a little while and my being able to stay with them. Maybe I'd even be able to get a bicycle, I thought.

We drove into the town of ten thousand inhabitants in the middle of the night. Like Albion, its streets were wide, and the silhouettes of the broad-trunked trees and houses set behind large lawns gave a sense of elegance and tranquillity. But when we pulled up in front of the four-room house attached to the back of the stucco-and-brick church, my heart sank. It sank even deeper when we opened the door and beheld a living room and two bedrooms slightly larger than the double beds and the dressers that filled them. In my room was a dressing table made from wooden crates and a sheet of wood that rested on top. It was draped in pink cotton. At the back of the apartment was a kitchen, a minuscule closet with a commode and a sink, and a shower in the basement. Or, if we preferred, we could use a galvanized metal washtub for baths. The members of the church had stocked the small refrigerator with cold milk. A package of Oreo cookies sat on a cabinet. There was no television, and the only other amenities were a piano, which became the site of my torture as I practiced endless scales on its keys, and a small Bakelite radio that my mother kept tuned to the homilies of commentator Paul Harvey at lunchtime and soap operas after I returned from school. But, such as it was, this was my first stable home since we'd pulled up stakes in St. Louis, and far better than any place I'd been since.

Everything seemed so charming, so orderly and predictable, in that quiet little town. But when my father went in search of construction and janitorial jobs, he was turned down repeatedly. Only then did a church member reveal to him one of the town's unwritten rules: No blacks were to be hired in Columbus.

Since my mother's resigning her position was out of the question, Daddy had no choice but to commute some eighty miles to Omaha to find work. For two years, he'd leave early Monday mornings and come home late Friday nights, and Mama and I would stay behind in a town where we knew black people were unwelcome.

I never heard Daddy complain. I have since wondered whether this situation provided him with an easy escape from Mama's ministry. Though devoted to Mama, he was still a proud man. I can imagine that the spring in his manner when it was time for him to depart came from the satisfaction of being able to hold on to his identity.

Members of my mother's congregation tried to downplay the significance of our color. One member, when asked her opinion about having a black pastor, disingenuously replied, "Oh, is she black? We really hadn't noticed." I still remember the first time Mama and I went to shop for groceries. We were walking down the tree-lined street when suddenly we found ourselves in the midst of a sea of white faces pointing, snickering, whispering, and staring at us. In every direction, people had stopped in their steps to gawk. Some were surely seeing black people for the first time. I was not a stranger to this mutual sense of otherness, but I was overwhelmed by the strength and lopsidedness of the feeling. I remembered my father telling us how members of his segregated army unit had their coats lifted so that their "tails" could be examined; this was not so different. We tried to go about our shopping as though this arm's-length assault weren't happening. Finishing our grocery shopping, we walked on to the dry goods store. The curious eyes tracked us. People stepped to the side and peered out the windows to watch us as we passed.

My mother was incensed by the callous rudeness of the stares. As for me, while I had seen signs that had read "Colored" and "White" in the South, this experience was altogether different. At ten years old, I felt humiliated and isolated. Nothing could have prepared me for this experience, and I cried all the way back to our small apartment. Once there, I ran into my room, closed the door, fell on the bed, buried my face in my pillow, and wept uncontrollably, distraught by the idea that we would be living in this town indefinitely. All I wanted to do was to go back to St. Louis, back to the security of the familiar—to be back in the house on Walton Street, playing with Miss Sue or reading the funny papers with Aunt Alice; back to smell the grass of Forest Park; to see the monkey show at the zoo; to drink a cool, bitter lemonade while sitting through a boring aria at Forest Park Opera, where Evie and Ola took me to escape the sweltering night heat and humidity of our brick house on Walton. But they were gone, too—Evie was married and supporting her husband while he attended Meharry Medical School in Nashville, Tennessee, and Ola was married and living in Indiana.

But it didn't matter what I felt. To rebel against my mother's calling would have been to rebel against God. I remembered the Sunday school song that Sister Epps had taught us, "Jesus loves me, this I know, for the Bible tells me so," and to its refrain, repeating over and over in my mind, I curled up and drifted into a sorrow-induced slumber.

I did enjoy going to school. The schools in Columbus were better than any I'd attended before—cleaner, with better books, and with teachers who gave me more attention than any I'd ever known. I even made a few friends—all girls. I was rarely invited to parties, however, or other social events by my classmates. In seventh grade I tried out for a spot on the cheer-leading team, figuring that it would unquestionably establish status with my peers. I was not chosen. Somehow, I knew all along that I wouldn't be. I'd practiced the chants over and over, but when it had come time to audition before the entire junior high, I was struck by stage fright. I managed to go through the motions, but not with the same exuberant abandon I'd mustered in the church basement. Maybe I wasn't good enough to be a cheer-leader, but I'll always believe that it was more than that.

During our second year in Columbus, when I was in the seventh grade, I had a crush on a blond, blue-eyed boy named Steven. He'd been quite friendly to me, but then someone informed me that, while he liked me, he didn't want to go steady. I was hurt and frustrated by this rejection. Just like any other eleven-year-old, I was searching for acceptance and approval, and I was out of luck. In the adolescent social world of Columbus, Nebraska, I was neither openly rejected nor embraced; neither hated nor loved, recognized nor ignored.

I turned inward for comfort, and used fond memories of my reigning status at 1241 Walton to buoy my confidence. And I found a sense of importance and worldliness in talking with my classmates about a city they had only read about—big, faraway St. Louis. I substituted hard work and academic achievement for social companionship.

Mama and Daddy bought me a set of the *Encyclopædia Britannica*, and I'd leaf through the burgundy, leather-bound volumes every day. Once, by accident, I happened upon a sequence of diagrams showing the stages of a fetus developing within the uterus. About to enter pubescence, I was trans-fixed by the images. I'd hardly begun to examine the diagrams when my mother entered the room, and I slammed the book shut. For days after, I searched for those pictures, but I never found them again.

Racial seclusion affected my mother, too, but differently. Mama was accustomed to preaching before audiences that responded with encouraging "Amens" or an occasional "Sister Wattleton, preach the Gospel!" In Columbus, she had to learn to stand before a roomful of silently attentive people—people who listened to her sermons with nary an amen, save as a ritual response. And in Columbus, realizing the distraction caused by the contrast between the dark color of the back of her hand and the paleness of her palm, she kept the back of her hand turned toward the audience, mitigating the issue of her color. Whatever sacrifices needed to be made to lead a Christ-like life, Mama was more than willing to make.

In the emotional turbulence of my preadolescence, I cried a lot of tears in Nebraska. And yet the whole of life wasn't contained in that midwestern town. The world beyond its borders seemed to be changing. Americans were dying in the Korean conflict. Senator Joe McCarthy was conducting his communist witch-hunts, ruining careers and lives. A polio epidemic raged uncontrollably, crippling and killing thousands. But still, the 1950s were different from the anguished 1930s and the wartime 1940s. There was growth, a sense of change, of hope. There was more talk about greater rights for women. And a few years later, in 1957, a movement that would shake America began with Rosa Parks, a bus seat, a young minister named Martin Luther King, Jr., and a boycott.

I recall one afternoon in Columbus, when I arrived home from school and found my mother listening to the radio. The Supreme Court had just announced its ruling in *Brown v. Board of Education*. Mama told me that segregation in public schools had been outlawed. Only eleven years old at the time, I had no knowledge of how or why the Court had decided to mandate school integration. It was my mother's exuberance and pride that impressed me. And I was old enough to understand that the Court had confirmed to society what my parents had often told me to help me through my time in Columbus: I might be the only black child in school, but I mustn't in any way feel unworthy of sitting in a classroom with white children. I had a right to be there.

CHAPTER 6

BUDDED, BLOSSOMED, AND BLOOMED

Throughout our two-year pause in Columbus, Nebraska, Mama had continued to accept revival commitments. Eventually, though, the twin burdens of ministering to her flock and stumping the revival circuit for souls grew to be more than even she could bear. And her ministry was one of repentance and conversion, more trailblazing than pastoral. She resigned from her position as minister in the spring of 1955.

The final, crushing blow to her Nebraska ministry had come when the Cuddefords, the couple who had been instrumental in persuading her to accept the pastorate, accused her and my father of dishonesty.

Daddy had worked out a signal with Mama to let us know that he had arrived safely in Omaha, where he returned every Sunday to prepare for the beginning of his workweek. He would place a person-to-person call to our home in Columbus and ask for himself. Whoever answered the telephone would then tell the operator, "George Wattleton is not here." I often heard Daddy's voice as he thanked the operator, which assured me that he had made his journey safe and sound.

Proud of his scheme, Daddy bragged to a group of men in the church about it. Shortly afterward, the Cuddefords—the church's head couple—asked to meet with my parents. When they entered our tiny apartment, I stayed in my bedroom, for I could sense trouble. I didn't hear much of what they were saying, but I did make out, "You're stealing from the telephone company. You're a cheat." And then I heard something that I had never heard before or since—Mama sobbing in her bedroom as though her heart would break.

In spite of their pain, the relief I felt when Mama told me that we were leaving Columbus was tremendous. I had made friends—mostly among church families, where my status as the preacher's daughter counted for something—and I had adapted to being the only colored child in town. But I craved the sense of belonging that adaptation never affords. I'd be leaving Columbus, Nebraska, feeling that it was a place that I had passed through and survived, a social vacuum in which my parents and good grades had been my only emotional anchors. Even if I didn't know where I would next be left, when fall came round, that uncertainty seemed safer, more familiar, than life in Columbus had ever been. Wherever we might next stop, I was certain we would never again be isolated from others of our race.

The strains of traveling had worn on Mama, her strength of faith notwithstanding. So Mama and Daddy used their small savings to make a down payment on a thirty-foot Silverstream with two bedrooms, a bathroom, a comfortable living room, dining area, and kitchen. The trailer would be our home wherever we stopped.

We pulled out of the Nebraska town and headed for the old homestead in St. Louis, where I would stay with my aunts while my parents headed for Texas. Mama was promised support there while she rested and regained her strength. My days in St. Louis were spent in the familiar, loving surroundings of my family, the church, and the city I'd been longing for.

I often imagine how different things would have been for me had my childhood not been divided between the road tours and the shuttling back and forth between Church of God families. But the truth is that, despite her frequent absences, my mother had a clear—and for the time, unconventional—vision of the woman she wanted me to become and the opportunities she wanted me to have. She was committed to making that vision a reality, and to doing so while still meeting the demands of her ministry. Her own example utterly bypassed the feminine stereotyping of that era, whether it confined women to the house in the Ozzie and Harriet model or stuffed them into the racial pigeonhole that assigned black women, especially, to labor as household servants. And in a conviction fostered by her father's belief in the value of education, Mama was determined that I receive the best possible education.

So it was that, after a nostalgic summer divided between St. Louis and Mississippi, I was sentenced again to spend the school year in the deep bayou country that embraced Franklin, Louisiana, with the same maiden schoolteacher and her mother who had complained of my sassing when I'd stayed with them years earlier. All too well, I remembered the boot camp regimen of their household—if my bed was not perfectly made and all my dresser drawers were not neatly closed, I had to walk the two or three miles to school, reflecting all the while on the error of my ways; how weekends were filled with cleaning, washboard laundering, and picking pecans from their trees.

"But I don't want to go back there!" I pleaded in the face of my mother's insistence. I didn't want to be torn away from my parents again, abandoned. I had grown more used to living with my mother than I'd realized. This time, being separated was harder than ever.

Although my mother had not always been affectionate or attentive to my needs, her love was far superior to any I'd encountered with my caretakers; it buoyed my ability to cope with the life that her dedication required of me. Quite simply, I adored her. A sip of water from her glass always tasted better than a sip from my own. None of this mattered this time, just as it hadn't mattered at other times.

Not long after I arrived, a fierce tropical storm hit the Louisiana coast. For two days, the furious winds shook every inch of that old house. As we huddled together in the old lady's candlelit bedroom, I thought we would be blown away and I'd never see my parents again. When it had passed, all I wanted to do was to go to them, wherever they were. When I learned that my mother would be speaking in the area and that we would be going to hear her, my heart leapt with hope.

By the time we entered the simple redbrick church in the small town of Ferriday, Louisiana, the worship service had already begun. Mama was on the platform—ankles crossed, head back, regal. She saw me come in, and smiled. I'd have to wait until the service was over before I could hug her.

After the benediction, I headed to the front of the church to greet Mama. My father grinned broadly and came toward us, but Mama was quickly surrounded by people wanting to "shake Sister Wattleton's hand." As I watched the electricity of her smile, which rivaled that of the most supreme diva, pride welled up in my chest. When she was finished, Mama hugged me close, and I began to plead to go with her. Soothingly, she rejected my pleas. "No," she said gently. "You're in school." Smoothing my hair with the palm of her hand, she continued, "I have revivals to do. We'll come for you when school is out."

I began to weep. I wanted and needed her, but she believed God needed her more.

My father was less patient with my tears. He looked at me and said, simply and firmly, "You can't come. You have to go back to school."

"Now, don't cry," Mama instructed. "Be a big girl."

I wondered if it pained her to see me in tears. Years later, she told me that it did.

I kept thinking about my mother and how much I wanted to be with her all the way back to the lonely house at the end of a lonely seashell road in the Cajun country of Louisiana. There I would remain for six more long months.

The following year, when I was thirteen, Mama was asked to serve several churches in the familiar landscape of rural Mississippi. She'd learned that Tougaloo College Preparatory School, outside Jackson, was the best high school for blacks in the state, so she and Daddy settled their mobile home within walking distance of the school. It was my mother's hope that I would be able to stay at Tougaloo for all four years of high school. If the Lord "called" her again, I could take advantage of the school's boarding facilities.

For the first time since we'd left St. Louis, I looked forward with excitement and anticipation to a new school. I would be able to sing in the school choir, play sports, have a social group, and maybe even find a sense of belonging. But far better than those things, shortly after arriving at Tougaloo, for the first time I found a best friend.

Nell Braxton was the daughter of the Tougaloo football and track coach. Like me, Nell was long-legged. Her silky bronze skin, pouty lips, large liquid eyes, and small chiseled nose gave her face a sensuous magnetism that attracted a lot of attention as we walked across the shady lawns of Tougaloo's campus. I coveted her long, lusciously abundant hair, which she wore in two thick braids across the crown of her head. She coveted my hair, which I wore loosely curled.

Our backgrounds differed, but we also had a great deal in common. She, too, had spent much of her childhood moving to different cities because of her father's coaching career. She longed to be in one place long enough to have a "best friend." Although the restrictions governing Nell's household were more flexible than mine, I found her parents stiff and formal. Her parents, children of well-to-do devout Episcopalians, allowed Nell to engage in activities my mother banned—going to dances, listening to popular music, experimenting with makeup so long as she kept it simple, and wearing jewelry—yet they didn't allow her to wear her hair down or associate with kids they disapproved of. Set apart from our peers, we found comfort in each other's company.

Nell and I spent hours in her parents' living room listening to Lloyd Price, Little Richard, and James Brown records, and talking about the boys we liked or the chemistry class we hated. She taught me basic bebop steps, so I knew what to do when I stayed late after sports events to attend forbidden sock hops. I didn't have a terrific sense of rhythm, but I loved the dances even though I was afraid someone would see me and tell my parents.

Faithful to the church's doctrine forbidding adornment, I had not worn lipstick or jewelry; but one afternoon, Nell and I returned from our noontime bebop practice with our lips painted to a cherry glow, and took our places in Mrs. Jones's English class. Walking between the rows of desks, she suddenly stopped at ours and took one long, hard look.

With her eyes fixed on us, hands on her high hips, and sarcasm sharpening every word, she said, "Young ladies are like flowers. In the ninth grade, they're buds. In the tenth grade, they begin to blossom. In the eleventh grade, they continue to blossom, and in the twelfth grade, they bloom. I see that over the course of a lunch hour, two members of this class have budded, blossomed, and bloomed."

Years later, Nell and I would laugh hysterically over that scene, but on that day, in the silence that fell over the room, no one dared so much as a snicker. My best friend and I wanted to slide beneath our seats. But the humiliation didn't last long. Despite the risks of my mother's rebuke, I was soon painting my lips bright red on my way to school every day. I'd rub them almost raw to remove all lipstick traces before I returned home to the Silverstream in the afternoon.

Quoting Romans 7:19–21, "For I do not do the good I want, but the evil I do not want is what I do. Now if I do what I do not want, it is no longer I that do it, but sin that dwell within me. So I find it to be a law that when I want to do what is good, evil lies close at hand,"[1] my mother would have warned that I was undergoing the traditional battle between God and the Devil. While I wouldn't have agreed, I couldn't deny that some sort of battle was taking shape in me. For the first time in my life I'd found myself belonging, although not fully so, with my peers. In the excitement of their company the pressures to conform were eased by the fact that my best friend and I shared similar restrictions.

My changing body offered its own contradiction with my mother's faith. I couldn't have been much more than eleven—the same age I'd been when I'd come across the illustrations in the *Encyclopædia Britannica*—when I began to notice a certain sensation in my pelvis that I didn't understand and couldn't stop. I knew that it was something that I dare not discuss with my mother. With most families in the Church of God, much of life, certainly on matters of sex, remained undiscussed.

I'd had one conversation of a sexual nature with my mother in my whole life. I must have been nine or so at the time. We'd been sitting in the DeSoto, parked at an angle on the town square in Philadelphia, Mississippi. I remember that it was hot. Flipping through the pages of *Life* magazine, I happened upon a picture of a beautiful white woman in a white evening gown. I read the advertisement, then asked my mother, "What's a Modess?"

My father's snicker hinted that I was treading on forbidden territory, while my mother turned to face me. A harsh look came over her face.

"Don't you ever ask me anything like that again," she said. There was an edge to her voice that I couldn't remember having heard before. "And don't you ever ask me anything like that in front of anybody. They might think you're fast." She did not answer my question.

Although she eventually prepared me with supplies for menstruation, my mother and I never discussed its purpose in a woman's life. Looking back, I wonder if she herself knew enough of the facts to convey them. But her rejection of even my timid attempt to satisfy my curiosity settled any ideas I might have had about approaching her on such subjects. It wasn't until the day they separated the boys and girls at school that I was educated even remotely about human sexuality. The girls were shown *Personally Yours*, a film about menstruation produced by one of the sanitary napkin companies. It acknowledged that menstruation did not occur if one was pregnant, but made no reference to how pregnancy did occur or anything related to it.

As it turned out, my dream of staying in one school for four years was just that—a dream. At the end of a thrilling year of basketball games, sock hops, singing with the choir, and my first best friend, Tougaloo Prep, with too few students and too little money, closed. "Au revoir, but not good-bye," we sang through tears at the end of graduation ceremonies.

My mother was invited to work with some churches in Texas, so I had to say good-bye to my classmates and teachers at the tiny school. Nell and I hugged each other and sobbed. We promised to write every day, but, of course, we couldn't keep the promise. Twenty-five years passed before we became best friends again.

"We'll find a place where George can get a job and we won't move until you finish school," Mama promised again. They bought a new and bigger mobile home, and we settled in Port Lavaca, outside Houston, where my father had found work in the Alcoa aluminum plant.

As the pressures for social acceptance escalated, so did my battles between conformity with my peers and obedience to the strictures of my upbringing. In Port Lavaca, I didn't have the security of a best friend with similar restrictions. There would be no dating for me—not until I was "sweet sixteen," Mama decreed. No prom. Not that it would have been possible to conform, anyway. Port Lavaca's Calhoun High School had been integrated after the *Brown v. Board of Education* decision, but the majority of the student body had remained white. It was a far less friendly place than even the school in Columbus, Nebraska, had been.

I joined the drama club and played the bell lyre in the band. Our school was small and those colored students participating in school activities were few. I was an outsider again. When we traveled on band trips, the four colored students clung together, not so much because we wanted to but because we were ignored by the white students. But we were more comfort to one another than we knew. Once, on a trip to Austin for a band competition, I was the only black student selected, and I went without them. I tried to strike up conversations with several band members, but my attempts inevitably failed. I was left to myself while clusters of the white kids laughed, talked, and enjoyed the sunny University of Texas campus and the camaraderie of equals.

Sometimes I'd sneak to the movies after school with the new friends I was making and sit in the balcony of the film house. *Carmen Jones,* starring the beautiful Dorothy Dandridge and the young and handsome Harry Belafonte, was my favorite.

When Mama went out on the revival circuit, I was allowed to stay behind, in the care of Daddy and church members Mama hired to stay with me. I finished my junior and senior high school requirements in one year, and at sixteen I was eager to find my way to college.

Ever since I can remember, my childhood fantasy was to be a missionary nurse. Perhaps it came from my mother's encouragement. The occasional slide show at church, given by missionaries to Africa, had captured my sense of adventure and fostered the dream. I'd grown up thinking that I too would go to "Kenya Colony," which was all I knew of Africa.

Mama's enthusiasm was founded not so much on my devoting my life to caring for sick people as on my committing myself to a life of service. It was not sufficient to be a nurse; the profession had to be a channel through which I would serve God's design for me. But now, after all the years, all the miles, churches, and sermons, the religious element of missionary work had lost its appeal. The dreams of service in exotic places had evolved into dreams of a white uniform and cap, and of helping people.

Commitment was the cornerstone of my mother's life. Over the years, I'd not only been witness to her commitment to her work, I had also seen her ingenuity and independence, traits that run at least as deep as to link her—as much in spirit as in blood—with her grandmother Mariah.

In the late 1950s most women who wanted careers, especially black women, prepared for teaching, social work, or nursing—professions that assured employment. Not only would nursing truly suit my dreams, it would provide security for my future.

In my last year at Calhoun High, the guidance counselor strongly urged me to pursue a college degree in nursing, rather than go to a three-year nursing school. The degree would provide a strong foundation if I chose to change professions, she advised me, and there was talk of phasing out the training of nurses in nonacademic hospital settings. I was excited by the counselor's idea.

When I mentioned it to my parents, my father scoffed. "O.B., why should we waste our money to send her to college? We'll never get anything out of it; she'll never amount to anything."

Harsh though it sounds, my father's attitude about higher education was common among fathers of his generation: An investment in a college education for a woman was an investment of dubious returns. But the irony was that while he had spent most of his marriage devoted to the work of a woman, he seemed to have little faith in my potential. Perhaps he worried that college would expose me to a more corrupt world. Then again, maybe he feared encouraging the development of another independent woman. Daddy wanted me to get a diploma at a nursing school, thereby learning a trade without risking the expense and the moral dangers of college. My mother's younger sister, Ola, also weighed in on the side of nursing school. She thought I should go to the one at St. John's hospital, affiliated with the church school in Anderson, Indiana. She and her husband, Isom, a minister and teacher, had met there, and I suspect that she hoped I too would find a good Church of God husband there.

But my strong-willed mother thought differently. Although I'm sure she was disappointed that I no longer talked of becoming a missionary, she saw ministering to the sick as a worthy ideal. Mama had not gone to college herself, yet she held education in the same high regard that her father did when he sent her up north for high school. She agreed with my guidance counselor that I ought to pursue the college degree. I was exhilarated.

Although my parents couldn't afford a college education, Mama expressed her faith that something would happen to make it work out.

CHAPTER 7

BREAKING IN THE BLUES

The summer following my graduation from high school, my mother became pastor of a large congregation on the east side of Cleveland, Ohio. Around that time she heard from Josephine Johnson, a friend from her high school days in Columbus, Ohio, that the state university had an excellent nursing school and, better still, that it provided free room and board for nursing students. I was relieved when I learned that the tuition was less than $100 per quarter—an amount Mama told me that they could manage. In addition, the prospect of my being in Columbus, where she'd found God and her ministry, eased any concerns she may have had. And I would be close to her friend, who could make sure I didn't take on sinful ways or stop attending church.

The day before registration, I took a Greyhound to Columbus, where I stayed with Josephine and her daughter, Barbara. The next morning, with encouraging words, they left me at the grassy, open expanse known as the Oval. In the center of the sprawling campus, surrounded by the imposing buildings ringing the Oval, I felt terribly small.

I found my way to the old stone and brick administration building and, with butterflies in my stomach, climbed the creaky wooden steps that led to the second-floor registrar's offices. I filled out my application to get into the courses required of a pre-nursing student. After waiting in line for what seemed an eternity, I finally reached the counter.

"As an out-of-state student, your tuition will be three hundred and fifty dollars this quarter," said the clerk. I couldn't believe my ears. Where would we get that kind of money?

My eyes searched the woman's impassive face for a solution to my financial woes. "But the catalog said it was less than one hundred dollars," I pleaded, feeling my stomach twisting into a tight knot.

"You're not a resident of Ohio," she replied flatly.

I thought quickly. "But we live in Cleveland, my parents live in Cleveland. . . ."

Sighing deeply, the woman pushed my application toward me and pointed an accusatory finger at a section of the form. "It says right here on your application that you've lived at your Cleveland address for less than a year. Your parents must live in the state of Ohio for one year before you are a legal resident and eligible for residents' fees."

She offered no alternatives, no mention of scholarships, student aid, or loans, and I didn't know enough to inquire about them. I was only seventeen years old, and I was devastated.

I stumbled away from the registration desk, trying to find my way out of the blurring room. My thoughts and feelings wavered between shock and resignation: How could my dream be snatched away so quickly? . . . It doesn't matter. . . . This is the end. . . . I'll have to go to a hospital nursing school. . . . Maybe someday I'll be able to put myself through college. . . .

There was no way I could imagine my parents finding the thousand dollars necessary for my first year's tuition, plus the costs of room and board.

In a daze, I wandered around, searching for a telephone. How would I tell my parents about this problem? How would they respond? Would they just say, "Come home"?

In going to college, I knew I was entering an institution that many within the church viewed with skepticism. Some deemed it a corrupting influence and cause for people to question their faith.

As I prepared to call home, I thought about my father's reservations about the value of a college education for me. I knew I would find no advocate in him. And yet, having dared set foot onto Ohio State's campus, I was more certain than ever that I wanted to attend. I hoped that this financial setback would not force Mama to abandon her commitment to my college education.

I took a deep breath and made the call. "Mama, the tuition is three hundred and fifty dollars a quarter," I wept into the phone receiver, my self-control giving way instantly to the weight of my disappointment. "We're not legal residents yet, so they say I have to pay out-of-state tuition fees."

"Well . . ." Mama paused. And then, her voice calm and measured, she spoke the words I feared most. "You'll have to come home. We can't afford it."

Daddy picked me up at the Cleveland Greyhound station that afternoon.

"Well, you came back home," he said simply and with finality. But still the expression in his eyes seemed sympathetic—the soft soul beneath the bluster.

When I walked into the parsonage, Mama greeted me with her usual message of hope, "We'll pray on it."

I couldn't be comforted. I headed to my unfamiliar bedroom. I didn't know how to pray for the miracle I needed, but again and again over the next few days, I heard my mother praying to God to "work something out." She appeared serene. "If the Lord wants you to go to Ohio State, He'll work it out," she reminded me from time to time.

By the end of the week, through a "miracle" that has never been revealed to me, Mama came up with the funds. "The Lord provides if you have faith in Him."

I felt I was emerging from a nightmare. Everything was going to be manageable. I'd be registering late—but I'd be registering.

On a fall morning in 1960, God having answered my mother's prayers, I paid the fees and entered Ohio State University. It was too late to get a dormitory assignment, but for ten dollars a week I found a tiny room to share on the second floor of a rooming house. As the landlady led me upstairs, she recited a litany of household rules. She would not tolerate loud music or loud talking; there was to be no noise of any kind after 10 P.M. Male guests above the first floor were out of the question. Mama's spirit, it seemed, had followed me to Ohio State to keep me on "the right path." And this woman wasn't even a Church of God woman.

I was not prepared for the shabbiness of the room I was to inhabit. Most of the floor space was taken up by two metal-framed twin beds with mattresses that sagged so deeply, I'd only be able to find a comfortable sleeping position on the very edge. I would have to share a four-drawer dresser and a metal cabinet. My prospective roommate, another freshman, also from Cleveland, sat Buddha-style on her bed. "Hello, I'm Devonne," she said, smiling coolly. Her large eyes, shaded by heavy lids lined with dark brown pencil, examined me closely as she twisted her single large braid over her shoulder. Her brown skin was flawless, and in the face of her sophistication and aloof manner, I felt quite plain.

Rooming settled, and knowing that I would have to work to help cover my expenses, I scoured the classified ads in the campus newspaper. "Marketing firm near campus needs statistical clerk," one ad read. Good at math, I called for an interview at the company's office, conveniently located near the Student Union. The morning of my appointment, I entered a large desk-lined room, where students sat hunched over their work, entering inventory numbers into adding machines from long sheets of paper. I was hired to work twelve to sixteen hours a week for a little more than twenty dollars a week after withholdings. It just barely covered my incidental financial needs, but I was happy to have any money at all.

The rooming house offered my first experience of living among people who were not of the church. But I'd lived in so many different settings—why not another? And I didn't spend a whole lot of time there, returning only at bedtime.

On Saturday nights, my new acquaintances at the rooming house would often go to fraternity and sorority parties and dances. In the beginning, they'd stop by and ask me to join them. I'd politely decline, explaining my reservations on religious grounds, and they eventually left me alone. I think they understood. My roommate, whose cool manner, I quickly learned, was simply a front for shyness, didn't go out much either. Despite the questions growing within me, I was still trying to remain faithful to church teachings. And I dared not distract myself from my studies and work. Often, on Saturday nights, I'd be the only student in the large house on 11th Avenue, and I would watch television with the landlady on her black-and-white set.

It wasn't long into my first quarter before I realized that, despite my strong academic performance in high school, I was ill-prepared to meet the rigorous requirements that my first Ohio State courses demanded, and there were no tutors, no special remedial programs to help me catch up. As far as I could tell, at Ohio State—a vast, impersonal place with forty thousand students—no one cared whether I succeeded or failed. But I was at Ohio State through my mother's steadfast faith and wily resourcefulness, and I was determined to make it. Toward that end, I spent many hours at the library and in study lounges at the Student Union.

Every Sunday morning and every Wednesday night, for the first part of my freshman year, I regularly attended services at the Hilltop Church of God. The Church of God has no central doctrinal authority to assure uniform consistency from one congregation to another, so Hilltop's minister saw to it that adherence to the Bible and to "what God requires of us" was rigid and narrow, and his strictures were even more demanding than my mother's. Mama believed that modesty in dress was appropriate; this minister preached that even a wedding ring was pagan and sinful. Mama associated with people of other faiths; this minister insisted that we "had to keep separate from nonbelievers."

Perhaps because my exposure to Mama's devotion had been disrupted so often by our separations, perhaps because I'd left home when I had just turned seventeen and my value system was not yet firmly in place, perhaps because this minister's interpretations were so very extreme, I soon found myself questioning this church, and its obsession with personal mores as evidence of the state of one's heart and soul. This didn't seem to fit with what I was seeing around me. Some of my rooming-house mates danced, some smoked, some drank; all wore makeup; and in the style of the Sixties, their skirts were, to my eyes, incredibly short. I hadn't noticed any of them reading the Bible or attending church. According to my mother's teachings, all this meant they were living in sin, and if they didn't repent, they were certain to burn in Hell's eternal fires. But they didn't seem evil or dangerous to me. And the dire predictions of Judgment Day didn't seem relevant to the world into which I was beginning to move.

Nevertheless, I felt loyalty to a God who'd answered my mother's prayers, just as I still felt the strong influence of her expectations. And I was certain she'd find out if I did not regularly appear at church. So I continued to make my long trip across town.

By the spring quarter, however, I found myself moving more confidently into the world beyond the church's influence. I'd become quite friendly with one of my housemates—a young woman named Vicki, who lived on the third floor and who wore her hair in a high beehive style and painted the rims of her almond-shaped eyes with black eyeliner. The hems of her skirts were above her knees. I was convinced that Vicki, with her high-fashion style, glamour, and emphatic New Jersey accent, possessed more style than anyone I'd ever met. Trying desperately to remain faithful to the legacy of the Garrett women's pious sense of beauty, I wore only the faintest trace of makeup. But Vicki and I found common ground: We both came from families that were struggling so that we could attend college, and we were both struggling with the academic challenges posed by our courses. But most important of all, we shared the experience of being two of only several hundred colored students in that vast student body.

Not that our Ellisonian sense of invisibility wasn't beginning to change around this time: In my freshman year, Marlene Owens, daughter of the heroic track star Jesse Owens, was homecoming queen. Perhaps she had been selected for a number of reasons: the changing times, her father's fame, her own beauty. No matter the cause, we all felt pride in her recognition.

In the winter, Vicki joined a sorority and hoped that I, too, would join it. I was reluctant. I knew very little about sororities, but I remembered Mama's warnings about "secret societies" and I didn't want more pressure on my already wavering attempts to remain faithful to my upbringing.

But Vicki was persistent. "You'll like the girls in Alpha Kappa Alpha, they're heavy," she said, meaning they were bright and studious. "AKAs are also interested in community service."

Vulnerable to the lobbying of the East Coast sophisticate and to my longing for a sense of community, I decided to pledge Alpha Kappa Alpha. I gained a circle of friends and a special African American sanctuary within the predominantly white world of Ohio State. I would later miss many sorority-sponsored social events because of my academic load and my heavy schedule of work in the hospital, but AKA remained an integral part of my college experience and gave me a stabilizing sense of belonging. And such sorority volunteer programs as our organized visits to nursing homes on Sunday afternoons and our tutoring kids in inner-city schools offered me my first glimpse of civic-mindedness independent of a religious framework. Many of the friendships I made there still endure.

In the middle of the spring quarter, the list of those admitted to the School of Nursing was to be posted. I was hopeful because I'd been able to maintain the C+/B− average necessary for acceptance, and there was the new emphasis on integration and equal opportunity. But there were times when I'd been plagued by doubts. If I didn't get in, my father would be proven right—the money spent would have indeed been "not worth it," and my mother's insistence that I get a college degree would be deemed a misplaced confidence. The money my parents could not afford would be wasted. And my dream of getting a college degree would end.

My hands were quivering by the time my eyes found my name in the Ws. I kept repeating to myself: "I made it! I made it!" I'd been admitted to the Ohio State University School of Nursing. I called Mama to tell her the news.

"You mean you *got in?*" she asked, her voice lilting not in challenge but in search of confirmation. "Oh, Faye, oh, Faye, you're going to be a nurse," she said proudly.

I would have to immerse myself in the demands of nursing school for the next thirty-six months, with no break—not even summers—until graduation. But I knew I could do it.

As I faced a challenging summer of anatomy, physiology, and microbiology, I was haunted by my inadequate academic background, especially in science. There was simply so much to remember and so little time for priming the pump of my memory. I quit my part-time job to gain more study time.

In a hot laboratory, we were introduced to our first cadaver. By day, the pungent odor of the fluid that preserved the body for our scholarship made it hard for us to breathe, let alone concentrate. I'd sit at my desk, into the small hours of the night, alternately nodding off and studying the insides of a cat, preserved in formaldehyde. With the help of my new roommate, Jan Ruffin, an Alpha Kappa Alpha pledge and a beginning nursing student, I had snuck the animal out of the anatomy lab. Daily, if not hourly, I'd lecture myself: "You can do it. Just keep trying!" Sometimes I'd think about my white classmates—many of them seemed to be breezing through the material. I knew if I'd had a better high school education, my task now would be easier. I just studied harder and kept telling myself that I would prevail.

During that term, we were also introduced to clinical nursing. In the nursing school's classrooms, set up like hospital rooms, we were taught how to tightly fold and tuck hospital bedsheet corners like a boot camp draftee; how to bathe bedridden patients, provide skin care and back rubs; how to take temperatures and empty bedpans. We learned to give injections to oranges and to one another and we pored over the beginner's textbook of diseases, a tome that would become our constant companion.

Late in the summer, I met and began to date a fellow student, Fred Woodson. I'd met him in a department store where we were earning extra money as temporary workers tallying inventory. When he asked me out for pizza, I was smitten. Fred was four years older than I, had graduated, and was applying to dental school. Although he wasn't a "church boy," he was friendly and shy, hardly the stereotype of the dangerous sinner I'd been taught to avoid. His great-grandfather had been a founder of the Wilberforce Seminary in Ohio; his mother's family were major landowners in Macon, Georgia; his father was head of the math department at Central State College. By my lights, he was a true southern aristocrat. Although initially his parents disapproved of me, probably because I didn't come from "the right family," he became my steady boyfriend for the rest of my college years.

Once in a while our socioeconomic differences would give rise to conflict. I had very little money, and so I made my own clothes. I'll never forget the time that I appeared in the lobby of my dorm for a date in a new red-and-white gingham cotton dress with ruffled sleeves, feeling pretty. That is, until I saw Fred's face fall as he stood before me.

"What's *that* you've got on?" he said. Seeing the shock on my face did not stop him. "Where did you get that from? Wait a minute, you can't go out with me looking like a Beverly Hillbilly."

I was shattered. Homemade clothes just could not measure up to the expectations of a young man reared with the professionally made finery that his parents could afford. Over time, though, and with a little more maturity on my part, I grew into my own sense of prepossession and style, and Fred left off his commentary.

The rewards for hard work came at the end of summer, when our entry into the School of Nursing was confirmed and Jan and I and over a hundred other students moved into the dorm for student nurses. Studying together during the brutal summer, Jan and I had become quite close and we decided to be roommates. Also from Cleveland, Jan was tall, full-figured, and as reserved as I was talkative. Her sandy hair and light brown eyes gave her an aura of mystery, accentuated by the clouds of cigarette smoke that surrounded her. Like so many other college students in Columbus at the time, she loved to listen to Nancy Wilson recordings, and would sing along with her own lovely voice. Both Jan and I were greatly helped by the free room and board—but as soon as our nursing experience permitted, both of us would have to find work to help meet our other expenses.

When classes began we were issued our student uniforms—sturdy sky-blue cotton shirtwaist dresses. They would be washed, starched, and ironed hundreds of times in the hospital laundry over the next three years. We'd wear them to class and for hospital duty. In the clinical area, we'd fasten a stiff white pinafore to the dress, and add a stiffly starched, simply styled white cap, bobby-pinned to the back of the head. Of course, we always had to wear white stockings and white shoes.

I'd spent most of my freshman year waking at the reasonable hour of 8 A.M., but at 6 A.M. on the day of my first shift at University Hospital, I was startled awake by banging on the door, bright lights, and a loud chorus of "Wake up, you sleepy sophomores, it's breaking in the blues day!"

Forty-five minutes later, in a great wave of over a hundred female figures dressed in blue and white, we entered the modern brick-and-glass building where our clinical rotations were to begin. We broke up into preassigned groups and made our way to designated spots in the hospital for our first assignments in hands-on care. I was nervous and apprehensive as I walked down the shiny halls, past the rooms of still-sleeping patients in the eerie quiet. I was about to find myself exposed to the human aspect of nursing in a way that no amount of laboratory practice could ever have prepared me for.

At the nurses' station, we were greeted by our clinical instructor, Miss Daubenmire, a pretty blond woman. She would guide our awkward attempts to provide simple care and comfort to patients. The summer had been rife with war stories about how tyrannical these instructors could be, but Miss Daubenmire greeted us with a smile that morning, and my fears vanished. She told us that our first task would be to give simple hygiene care to a patient.

I was assigned to Mr. Yancy. Having reviewed his chart the night before, I consulted it briefly for any recent developments before entering his room. He had advanced cirrhosis of the liver, and while he was fully coherent, he was also terminally ill. My job would be to make him as comfortable as possible, to provide him with a clean bed, a bath, a back rub, and clean sheets. On that first day, every one of these basic nursing tasks seemed formidable, but my patient eased my worries with a weak smile and a pleasant "Hello."

Given the early hour, he couldn't have been overjoyed to see me, but he showed no displeasure as I set about my assigned tasks. I took his temperature and blood pressure, and counted his pulse and his respirations. I then pulled the steel washbasin out of the bedside cabinet, clanging it with nervous clumsiness.

I filled it with warm water, testing it with the sensitive skin of my elbow, as we'd been taught. Mr. Yancy took the cloth into his bony yellow hands and washed his face, but that effort alone sapped all his strength. Now I would put my bed-bath skills to their first test. "Why couldn't I have been assigned to a patient who could get out of bed?" I asked myself anxiously. Cleaning his body while intravenous fluids flowed through a tube and needle into his arm unnerved me. What if air got into his veins and caused an embolism that killed him? But, over the summer, it had been drilled into us that nervousness was never to interfere with giving a patient care in a calm and confident manner, so I tried hard to steady my hands so that Mr. Yancy would not sense my lack of confidence.

From time to time Mr. Yancy's pleasant smile reassured me that he was grateful for the care and that he appreciated my efforts. Occasionally Miss Daubenmire would come into the room and inquire, "Is everything all right?"

I'd just finished his bath when the breakfast tray arrived. The task of rolling up the head of his bed and arranging his meal as attractively as I could came as a great relief from the stressful effort of the bathing. I then left Mr. Yancy to eat his soft food in peace and went to my patient's chart to record his condition and the care I'd just given him.

While the patients were having their breakfasts, my clinical instructor checked on my progress and reassured me that I was doing well. I still faced intimidating challenges, though: I had to help Mr. Yancy dress in clean bed clothing, change his sheets while he still lay in his bed, and give him a back rub to relax him before he had to endure the various tests that had been ordered to monitor his disease. I was praying that I would get everything done by the time I left the ward at noon to head for my afternoon classes. Mr. Yancy's wife arrived while I was giving him his back rub. I found her presence calming as I struggled awkwardly through my tasks. But I was proud: I'd managed to get through the morning's work with the IV needle intact and Mr. Yancy alive in his bed.

I repeated the same routine, growing in confidence, for more than a week. In that time Mr. Yancy seemed to grow weaker, although he wasn't in pain. One morning I arrived on the unit and found that my assignment had changed. Mr. Yancy had died quietly over the weekend. I was distressed by the news. I'd grown fond of the gentle, pleasant man. And yet I'd been able to hold on to a measure of detachment that my many years of transitional associations had forced me to develop.

To some, "detachment" may connote coldness, even callousness. And I cannot claim that cold characters never find their way into the medical community. But it can be the key to survival in a profession serving the suffering and dying. Such detachment does not mean indifference, or a lack of empathy or compassion. It simply means that without detachment, the emotional costs of caring for the injured, sick, and dying could become overwhelming, and burnout inevitable.

During my sophomore year, the clinical experience of rotating among wards of patients being treated for medical conditions and wards of patients being prepared for or recovering from surgical procedures, honed my basic nursing skills and sorely tested my endurance. Like interns and residents, we were coping with the strain of long hours and a total lack of regard for the physical limits of the human mind and body. There was never a time when we were not under scrutiny. Staff nurses who were not our instructors watched us carefully, and our clinical professors stopped us in the halls and grilled us about various diseases, nursing care plans, and the latest developments of our assigned patients. We'd have to recite, on demand, the actions, reactions, and contraindications of the drugs we administered, and the meaning of the results of our lab tests.

After returning from the hospital at noon, I would often try to take a quick nap before heading to classes from 1 to 5 P.M. My nights were devoted to the study of patient charts and textbooks. But there would be no buckling: not to fatigue, not to stress, and certainly not to the distractions outside my professional training—whether the church, sorority events, or my boyfriend, whose departure for dental school in Tennessee had necessitated the long-distance romance that suited my full life.

Wednesday-night church services had already gone by the wayside, and regular Sunday attendance was getting harder. In the spring of my sophomore year, I began looking for a church nearer the campus. The prospect of attending worship outside my denomination was a hurdle. As I visited Methodist, Episcopal, and nondenominational churches that catered to college students, I felt guilty about my lack of faithfulness and was certain God would punish me.

But other issues had begun to influence my evolution away from the Church of God. Over the years, many people have assumed that I must have rebelled against the restrictions of my childhood. The truth is that the nursing profession, based on the total acceptance of another human being without regard for lifestyle or religious affiliation, was about to take me further from my religious upbringing than any act of defiance ever could. In the Church of God, one was judged by one's personal conduct; after all, it determined where one would spend eternity. Not so paradoxically, however, I would remain close to the fundamental values of that upbringing: service and care. Nursing was about caring for people—about providing kindness, patience, and above all, compassion to others, regardless of their personal conduct.

My care could not be predicated upon any such sense of judgment. Moral and religious values had no place in the way I gave a bed-bath, and washed, creamed, and massaged callused feet. Without judgment, I would gently restrain an alcoholic whose body was racked by delirium tremens. Without thinking that the devil was at work, I could stand before a patient whose internal agony was being purged on me in a wave of violent expletives and quietly ask if I could do anything to make her more comfortable.

It was ironic that my movement outside the teachings of the Church of God would travel on the tracks of the very profession that my mother had dreamed of my entering. The truth was that my sense of satisfaction in my work did have its spiritual aspect. If I was not devoting myself to God, I was devoting myself to the care of others. If I was setting aside differences, judgment, or prejudice to provide impartial care and compassion, I was also coming to understand how small our differences are in comparison to the sameness that bonds us.

CHAPTER 8

JUDGMENT DAY

After a year devoted to learning the basics of nursing, it was time for specialty rotations. My first placement was in pediatrics at Children's Hospital in Columbus. From there I would move to quarter rotations in communicable diseases, medicine, surgery, public health, obstetrics, and psychiatry.

After my pediatrics rotation, the chronically understaffed Children's Hospital—or Kiddies, as we called it—welcomed Jan and me back on a part-time basis, to shore up its overwhelmed personnel. Not only would I be earning desperately needed money for personal expenses to ease the strain on my parents, I'd be continuing work I had enjoyed. As an only child, I had never spent much time with young children before. I liked being with them, and found them much easier than working with adults.

Every Friday after classes, Jan and I headed for Kiddies to work for a few hours. On Saturdays and Sundays we worked the entire 3 to 11 P.M shift if the hospital needed us—and they usually did.

Often, we would be assigned to a ward with an abundance of critically sick children and too few nurses to care for them. As I tossed my white pinafore over my head and anchored it to the waist of my blue cotton dress and attached the stiff white cap to the back of my head with bobby pins, I hoped I wouldn't have to miss my supper break or work much later than 11:30 and miss the last bus back to campus. Most of all, I hoped I wouldn't be assigned to a desperately ill child. Injury and suffering in the young is hard to watch, and I found that when a child's pain was great and the hope for recovery slight, my still-developing objectivity all but deserted me.

In addition, at Kiddies I didn't have the reliable support of my nursing professors.

My worst fears were realized the evening the supervisor announced my assignment. She glanced down briefly at the chart that listed the number of children and the number of nurses on the wards: "There are two kids up on Three-West who need constant care," she said, looking up from the chart.

"Constant care." To me the words meant, "You can't leave these kids for a minute or they could die." Although I had never experienced the death of a patient during my shift, I never stopped dreading the possibility.

No doubt reading the anxiety on my face, the supervisor continued, "They're both comatose with severe head injuries." Comas meant tracheotomies, feeding tubes, IVs, catheters, drugs. Unconsciousness meant reduced circulation and bedsores. To reassure me, she added, "I think you're up to it."

As I headed toward their room, I stopped by the nurses' station to check the girls' charts. Their conditions had moved to the long-term vegetative state that is sometimes the result of brain damage that doesn't kill, but doesn't necessarily heal either. They'd had several surgeries to remove blood clots on their brains. The attention I'd be giving them verged on intensive care, although I had no specialized training in this area.

When I walked into their room, I felt as though I had entered a vault containing two helpless children. The girls lay quietly in fetal position, their eyelids half opened. My only comfort was the window overlooking the nurses' station—nearby help if I needed it. The fizz of oxygen being pumped into the young girls' lungs through the holes in their windpipes created a strangely soothing curtain of sound that shut out the bustle of the hospital. The on-and-off clicking of the motor attached to the rubber mattresses on which the girls lay punctuated the steady hiss of oxygen.

Norma Jean, five years old, was blond with wispy hair. Karen had luxuriant dark brown hair. Both girls had tubes connected to their bladders, tubes connected to their arms, tubes traveling from their noses to their stomachs. The hospital was fighting a valiant battle to keep these little girls alive, to feed them, to drain their waste, to keep them oxygenated, to not give them more fluids than their kidneys could handle, and to clear their lungs so they could breathe, with the hope that they would somehow recover. Every two hours, the girls were to be fed, given medication to control their seizures, have their fluid intake and urine output checked, be turned in their beds to prevent bedsores, and have their vital signs and level of consciousness checked by opening their eyelids, pointing a small flashlight at their pupils, and watching the response of the black spots in the middle of their irises. After each test I put ointment in their eyes to prevent the corneas from drying out and becoming ulcerated. Every few minutes, the gurgling sounds from their tracheotomies warned me to suction them before mucus blocked off their breath. Working around their tubes, I bathed the children and changed their beds at least once during my shift. If there was time, I was to put their arms and legs through a series of motion exercises to prevent their muscles from shortening and freezing their joints. There never was enough time to do everything well, and that distressed me.

I had to keep careful track of time. If the antiseizure medication was given late, the children could be vulnerable to seizures; if I lost a sense of how long I'd been involved in one child's care, the other's trachea could become blocked. I would do this for eight hours at a time—my stomach in knots every minute.

Norma Jean, fair-skinned, with a cherubic face, had been in a coma for weeks. Her mother never came to visit her, but her father, a short, wiry man from Appalachia with sad eyes, came every Sunday. He told me Norma Jean's injury had been caused by "falling down one step and hitting her head."

I'd watch him as he sat beside her, mournfulness etched on his weathered face. He'd hold her hand, stroke her golden hair, and bend over to kiss her forehead. Sometimes he'd try to hug her. But mostly he just sat there, watching her intently, as if willing her back to reality.

Over the weeks that I cared for Norma Jean, I couldn't help but wonder: How could a simple fall from one step do so much damage? Why didn't Norma Jean's mother come to visit her? What did she know about the circumstances of her daughter's injury? But in that era of the "traditional family," violence against children at the hands of their parents simply wasn't the first thing we considered in the emergency room. The battered child syndrome was not well recognized, and so we accepted their parents' word for what happened. I had no proof that the cause of Norma Jean's injuries was not as it was described, but over the years my suspicions grew.

Karen had been hit by a car. Her mother, often joined by her father, kept a constant vigil at her bedside. They spoke to her of their love, of her toys, of her little siblings waiting for her back home. They sometimes spoke of their concern that their daughter might not recover, but mostly they dwelt fiercely on the fact that she was alive. They clung, as to a life raft, to the thought that where there was life, there was hope. By the time I was assigned to another ward, their child was attempting to speak and we were able to prop her up in a chair for short periods.

These families represented two extremes of a host of problems and emotions that I was to witness at Kiddies. There were parents overwhelmed by the grief of watching their terminally ill child move toward his or her final moment, parents so consumed by the demands of attending to their ailing child that their other children were not receiving the love and care they needed, and parents who didn't know how they were going to manage financially. And always, I perceived an element of self-blame in them—a sense that somehow they had not protected their child well enough, that somehow they could have prevented the catastrophe from occurring. Mothers of babies with severe birth defects often stood over their children with faces that spoke their guilt.

But there were also moments of profound joy and satisfaction: watching children who went home restored, children whose recovery from serious injury or surgery seemed nothing short of miraculous, children undaunted by their handicaps. Picking up and hugging a small child or stopping at another's bedside for a few moments of play would lift my spirits and ease the ache in my back and feet from the long hours of work in ways that were hard to convey.

I was never able to hold Norma Jean or Karen, for fear of accidentally disconnecting one of their many tubes, but I hoped that my talking to them while I worked reached beyond the mechanical procedures I performed so incessantly. When I was eventually given a new assignment, I felt satisfied that I'd helped to keep their airways open, their bodies properly hydrated, their skin healthy, and their seizures under control with medication. Yet I had grown attached to them and whenever I was in the hospital, I would stop to look at their motionless bodies through the window. Over the weeks, I watched their physical bodies continue to grow while their cognitive development remained locked by their injuries.

In a pediatric hospital, caring for children who are the victims of disease, abuse, neglect, accidents, and debilitating abnormalities is the norm. I'd often find myself wondering to Jan if there were any healthy, happy children in the world. Certainly I saw demonstrations of tremendous strength and love, but the simple existence of so much suffering of children in one place was oppressive. The very randomness of tragedy scared me into a growing sense that it was better not to bring a child into the world than to force it to suffer some of what I saw.

The stresses of learning my chosen profession were not confined to the walls of Children's Hospital. On my rotation on a medical unit during my junior year, I was assigned to care for a quadriplegic patient, a young man in his early twenties who had broken his neck in a diving accident. One evening, confident that I'd accomplished the tasks of his physical care satisfactorily, I prepared to go back to the dorm to study.

As I walked down the corridor toward the elevator, my instructor, Miss Plummer, a tall, rail-thin woman with gray hair, a beak nose, and squinty eyes, came running after me. "Where do you think you are going, young lady?" she demanded, her features contorted by outrage.

"Back to Neil Hall," I answered quietly.

"And leave your patient in *that* condition?" Miss Plummer snapped. She grabbed the back of my collar and commanded, "Come with me."

Miss Plummer was the only nursing professor in my college experience who was consistently unpleasant toward me, consistently finding fault with my work. My being constitutionally incapable of paying obsequious deference to her surely didn't help matters. I was offended by her grabbing me, but knew the consequences of challenging her.

With her white hat flapping, Miss Plummer marched me back up the corridor and into the startled young man's room. "Look at him!" she spat, pointing at him and then at the area near his bed. "The sheets on his bed are loose and messy. There's all sorts of rubbish on his bed table. His hands are not resting comfortably on a pillow. And you're leaving the hospital?!" Disdain colored her every word.

By now, I was at once terrified and deeply humiliated. Though the housekeeping aspect of nursing may not have been my primary concern, I was not a messy person, and I didn't see anything that I had done in this instance to warrant such a fierce reprimand. I made a few adjustments to the room in order to satisfy Miss Plummer, clearing away all extra paper and packages of various instruments and supplies. We then stepped back into the hall, where she continued her tirade. I stood silently, with my eyes downcast, as the pain welled up within me.

As I walked back to the dorm, angry tears—the ones I'd refused to give Miss Plummer the satisfaction of seeing—came to my eyes and streamed down my cheeks. Even where I'd struggled academically, no one had suggested that I might not make the grade. Nor had I experienced any real doubt that I couldn't overcome the challenges; there had been no cause for it. I was furious at the injustice of the irate professor's rebuke, furious that I'd been unable to defend myself from her abuse. Her harsh criticism did not make me want to learn or to perform better. It was strange to me that, as a teacher, she didn't seem to understand the basic rule of human motivation—affirmation—even in the face of imperfection. Miss Plummer would never offer me encouragement—she would only stand stubbornly in my way as I strove to reach my ultimate goal of getting a college education.

The weight of nursing responsibilities, both grand and tedious, coupled with the burden of extra work at Kiddies, suddenly seemed more than I could bear. For a few hours, I thought about quitting nursing. By morning's light, though, my resolve had returned. I would not let her win the battle by crushing my aspirations. I resolved again that Miss Plummer was just a fact of life until my rotation changed.

No sooner had I recovered from the trauma of Miss Plummer's supervision than I careened into a mistake during my surgical rotation that could have ended my career. One night, another student nurse and I were distributing medications on a surgical ward. Like Kiddies, the nursing staff at University Hospital was in short supply during the evening shift. Student nurses were assigned to fill the gaps. Kathy was working on one side of the unit and I on the other. A woman on my side turned on the light, signaling that she needed attention. When I entered her room, she moaned, "Can I have something for the pain? I'm hurting pretty bad. . . ."

"I'll check, and be right back," I promised her.

An order on the patient's chart permitted an intramuscular injection of one hundred milligrams of Demerol and fifty of Seconal every four hours, and when I found no indication that any medication had been administered within the last four hours, I prepared the mixture and gave the woman her shot. I made a note on my assignment sheet to record my action in the chart as soon as I'd finished passing out medications to the other patients.

An hour or so later, the woman switched on her signal light again. I must have been tending another of my charges, because my classmate answered her call. The woman was again complaining of pain from her incision, and Kathy, seeing no notation of the previous injection, gave the agonized woman another dose of the prescribed painkillers. A few minutes later, as we were on our way to the nurses' station, Kathy said, "I gave Mrs. Klein in Ten-oh-three-B medication for pain."

I stopped dead in my tracks. "You did what?"

"I gave her medication for pain," Kathy repeated. "She put on her call light and you were busy, so I answered it. She was complaining of a lot of pain and I checked her chart and she hadn't been given anything for more than five hours, so I gave her an injection of a hundred milligrams of Demerol and fifty milligrams of Seconal."

"But I gave her the same injection an hour ago. I hadn't had time to stop and put it in on her chart."

Kathy's blue eyes grew wide as she began to comprehend the error we had just made. Without a word, we put our trays down on the metal counter and ran to the woman's bedside.

She'd fallen into a deep sleep and did not respond to our urgent calling of her name. Her face was pale, and her skin felt damp when I gently shook her arm and called, "Mrs. Klein, Mrs. Klein." She did not move. Kathy reached for her other wrist and began to count her heartbeats.

"Her pulse is over a hundred," she whispered anxiously.

Her respirations dropped to three to four per minute. My throat, now dry as sand, allowed "Oh, my God, Kathy, what if we killed her?"

Kathy's face turned red as a beet and her wide blue eyes seemed flooded by rivers. She stared at me speechless.

The lump in my throat seemed to grow larger by the second. The nurse in charge was tied up in another patient's room, changing a surgical dressing, so we immediately paged the resident doctor. When we told him what had happened, his urgent "I'll be right up" slightly reassured us.

A few minutes later, the young, bespectacled doctor strode up to the nurses' station. "Where is the patient?" he asked coolly. Our fears were not eased by his now casual demeanor.

"Ten-oh-three-B!" we blurted in unison.

He headed down the corridor toward the patient's room and we had to keep ourselves from stepping on his heels as we followed him. At her bedside, the resident loudly called out the woman's name. She still didn't respond. He then pulled back the sheet and blanket that covered her and called her name again, this time rubbing the index and middle finger of his left hand vigorously over her chest. She stirred. In a moment, an unintelligible sound escaped her throat. Instantly, he turned and said, "She'll live" and casually walked out the door, leaving us anxiously watching our patient as if the strength of our presence could bring her back to consciousness.

As the doctor predicted, the woman did not die. She did, however, have a long night's sleep. The incident was written up by the nurse in charge, then reviewed by her supervisors and ours.

When we appeared before our starchy professor the next day, we had no idea what the consequences would be, except that, if worse came to worst, we would be dismissed. My error in not promptly recording the injection was duly noted. But Miss Diller, who seemed to like Kathy about as much as Miss Plummer liked me, showed my classmate no mercy for failing to consult me before giving any medication to a patient at my end of the unit.

For me, this was the final straw. I decided that I did not want to be a clinical nurse. I didn't especially enjoy dressing wounds, dispensing medication, changing bedpans and linen, straightening bedside tables; and at nineteen, I certainly did not feel comfortable with the risks inherent in caring for critically ill patients. Although the operating room nurses told me, "You have a knack for this," I hated the tension of handing doctors instruments and sponges during surgery. With the harrowing incident of what seemed to be nearly killing a patient, the dangers were brought home to me in a whole new way. None of my previous struggles to overcome my academic obstacles, financial trials, and exhaustion, could possibly compare. Still, I couldn't quit. I'd managed to escape the humiliation of expulsion, and I'd have to find the strength to make my way through disillusionment.

Whenever things became almost more than I could bear, I'd call Mama. She'd tell me she'd pray for me, or she'd say, "God won't put more on you than you're able to bear," or "All things are possible with God, if you trust Him."

One afternoon in August of 1963, during the first rotation of my senior year, I was assigned to a medical unit on the afternoon shift. I entered one patient's room, with a tray of medication in my hand, and was stopped by the image and voice on a small television screen of Martin Luther King, Jr., standing on the steps of the Lincoln Memorial. I knew that the civil rights march on Washington was being held that day, but going to Washington and being part of it was a thought that never occurred to me. Political activism was far removed from my life at the time. I had little concept of social change. Surely, I'd known racial injustice, but I had sheets to change, injections to give, bedpans to empty, and a profession to learn.

And yet, the power of Dr. King's words, "I have a dream . . ." held me awestruck and immobile with rapture, as they did the patient in the room and the rest of America. When the speech was over and the emotional cheering of the hundreds of thousands in Washington began to subside, I was jolted out of my trance by the demands of the day. I had to return to dispensing medications and hurry on to the next patient in an effort to make up for lost time.

Nearing the end of my senior year, I was still uncertain about my future in nursing. But the first day of my obstetrics rotation, I knew I had found my place. That certainty was due in part to the influence of my nursing professor Ethelrine Shaw, one of only two African American professors in the school. Dr. Shaw was said to be firm and exacting, and her crisp, business-like "Good morning, Miss Wattleton" when I met her seemed to fit her reputation. But in the interview, I learned that her formal manner belied a great deal of warm encouragement, which she shared generously.

Unlike many of my professors, Dr. Shaw placed more emphasis on the postpartum care of a given patient than on the recitation of physiology and treatment methodology. Perhaps it was the soft fullness of her quiet smile, or the kindness in her large eyes, but no matter the cause, the hallway drills so intimidating from others were, with her, genuine learning experiences that motivated me to work hard to meet her expectations.

During the weeks that would prove pivotal in my chosen career, I came to understand the full picture of human reproduction. From the beginning, my experience of caring for women through delivery, watching babies being born, and caring for babies during their first days of life obliterated my memories of the dread that I'd felt when I had to face the care of a suffering patient. By the time I'd donned my surgical cap and mask and entered the delivery room to observe the birth of a baby for the first time, my heart seemed to accomplish one beat on every other try. Although we weren't there to assist, we helped the moaning patient to position her legs wide open in the stirrups of the delivery table. Then we stepped back to let the professionals do their work.

The anesthesia nurse placed the plastic mask over the woman's face, and in a few moments her suffering was over. We watched the doctor cleanse the birth area. Although the patient was not fully conscious, the heavy sedation did not stop her from pushing down as though she were having a bowel movement. Her body strained, once, twice, and a crown of black curly hair appeared in the distended vaginal opening. All at once, the mask I wore seemed suffocating. At the sight of the baby's head emerging from the woman's body, I squirmed with empathic discomfort.

I know I was supposed to feel a sense of awe—and in time, when I'd grown more accustomed to the physical drama of birth, I would. But all I was conscious of at this particular birth was the tremendous agony that the mother must have felt when the baby's body wrenched open what seemed to be her entire lower body. When the baby suddenly slid out into the obstetrician's skilled hands and let out its cry, I was less struck by wonder than by the need to get out of the room and catch a breath of fresh air before I passed out.

When I grew more used to childbirth, though, the satisfactions of obstetrical nursing surpassed even the joys of watching a young child's return to health. Assisting women in delivering life uplifted me in ways that I couldn't explain. I enjoyed feeding the babies in the nursery, holding them, being witness to the early bonding between mother and child.

When we visited an evening clinic at the local Planned Parenthood affiliate—my first encounter with the organization I would one day lead—the kind concern of the counselors, as they spoke to the women, adult and married, about various birth control methods (the Pill had been on the market for only a few years) was a continuation of the atmosphere of the obstetrics ward that I so enjoyed.

By the end of the quarter, I was certain that obstetrics was the area to which I wanted to devote my life. Perhaps the allure was as simple as being drawn to the beginning of life, rather than to the end and all the struggles in between. At birth, all was new—a clean slate. Teaching mothers to care for their babies so they stayed healthy and unharmed was an irresistible opportunity.

During that same senior year that I saw so much joy, my surgery rotation taught me about the sadness that can also accompany pregnancy. The beautiful young wife of a resident physician at the University Medical Center was admitted for treatment of a severe kidney ailment. She was in her seventh month of pregnancy, and the team of doctors who attended her had concluded that carrying her pregnancy to term was likely to cause kidney failure and possibly death for her, and held uncertain consequences for the fetus. For these reasons, they believed that her pregnancy should be terminated.

In Ohio at that time—except in instances where it would save a woman's life—abortion was illegal and punishable by a prison term unless a woman was able to persuade a committee of doctors to agree to the procedure. Given the resident's wife's life-threatening condition and her connections at the hospital, it probably wasn't hard to get the review committee at the institution to approve the termination of her pregnancy. Because the woman's pregnancy was in its second trimester, a dilation and curettage, or

D & C, as the standard practice is commonly known, was not possible. In this procedure the opening to the uterus is expanded and a sharp, spoon-shaped instrument is inserted to scrape its contents. Later, technological advances brought about by the legalization of abortion would allow for the dilation and evacuation procedure at this late stage. But doctors in 1963 had no choice but to perform a hysterotomy, a major surgical procedure that involved opening the uterus through the abdomen, with all the attendant risks, to remove the fetus.

Given the tremendous debates that would arise around the legalization of abortion, and about late-term abortion, it seems strange to recall the practicality with which this case was handled. Because of the rareness of the young woman's circumstances, her case was the subject of any number of conversations that year, not only among nursing students but among doctors on their rounds. I don't recall hearing one mention of ethical conflict over the abortion or of sentiment toward the fetus. The woman's health was of foremost concern. Her life could not be jeopardized for the sake of her pregnancy.

Neither do I recall any reference being made to the case of another woman, whose access to abortion had not been so easy. The story of Sherri Chasen Finkbine, the celebrity host of the local *Romper Room* children's television show in Phoenix, Arizona, had been splashed in the headlines all over the nation the previous summer. Early in her fifth pregnancy, Sherri Finkbine had taken a tranquilizer that her husband had brought back from Europe. To her horror, she later learned that it had been thalidomide, a medication that had just been traced as the cause of grotesque fetal deformities. Faced with the strong possibility that her fetus was severely deformed, Finkbine sought an abortion.

As in Ohio, Arizona permitted abortion only to save the life of the woman. And as in Ohio, the statute often was circumvented by the well-connected. Once she had the assurance of her doctor that the procedure was arranged, Finkbine, as required, sent a letter to an abortion review committee, made up of two to four doctors who were not her physicians at the hospital where the abortion would be done. She affirmed in the letter that continuing the pregnancy would cause her to have a complete mental breakdown. Suicide was probably implied.

The abortion was duly approved and scheduled, when Finkbine, worried that other pregnant women might unknowingly take the drug, told her story to a newspaper reporter under conditions of anonymity. The next day, July 23, 1962, *The Arizona Republic* carried a front-page headline that read, "Drug Causing Deformities in Infants May Cost Woman Her Baby Here." As the story was printed and broadcast across the country, the Catholic bishop and the fundamentalist clergy in Phoenix publicly condemned the scheduled abortion.

Sherri Finkbine's identity was revealed during the well-publicized court proceedings in which the hospital sought permission to perform the abortion. Concerned about bad publicity, the hospital canceled the operation. Sherri then found herself unable to get a legal abortion anywhere in the United States. She and her husband considered going to Japan, but their requests for visas were denied by the Japanese embassy. Desperate, the couple flew to Sweden, where a doctor performed the procedure after subjecting her to grueling interviews.

When she came home, she was ordered to give up her television show. "You are unfit to handle children," she was told by a vice president at the Phoenix affiliate of NBC.

In my work at Kiddies, I'd often cared for children whose bodies had been deformed, not by thalidomide but by other causes, such as German measles, which caused deafness, heart abnormalities, and blindness, and by severe physical malformations caused by vitamin deficiencies during their mothers' pregnancies. I'd cared for children born with fluid on the brain or with no brain, or with mouths and lips so incompletely formed as to leave gaping holes, making the feeding of formula a horrendous task. I remember the expressions on the parents' faces when they left their children's bedsides—the looks of powerlessness and devastation. I was saddened in ways that I will never forget and prayed that I would never be forced to confront such a fate if I became a mother.

In those years, fathers weren't allowed in the delivery room and were therefore not witness to either the wonder of birth or the many complications that can accompany it. I remember one young father's face when the doctor took him into a conference room to explain the significance of his child's deformity. His baby was anencephalic, born with very little brain, and therefore consigned to certain death. Shortly after the father emerged from this sad meeting, his wife was wheeled into the hallway, and he rushed to her side. As he bent over to embrace her, their grief revealed itself in mingled tears and helplessness. Their only choice was whether to withhold food or liquid to hasten their child's death. The baby died within a few days of its birth, and they were spared having to make the wrenching decision.

Today, severe deformities that are incompatible with life outside the womb can be diagnosed in utero by sonogram, and couples can decide whether they wish to continue the pregnancy. For most couples, this is a devastating experience. And it's being made more difficult as politicians debate whether to make terminating a pregnancy safely at this late stage a federal crime.

At Kiddies, I'd seen the suffering of children, and now I was witnessing the suffering of parents. I couldn't help but think that it would be more compassionate to end a pregnancy at the point of discovery, even late in the term, than to make a woman continue a pregnancy and endure the long hours of labor and the agony of birth, knowing that her baby could not live.

I was not alone in my observations. Sherri Finkbine's case, along with the stories of thousands of deformed infants born during the German measles epidemic of 1964 and 1965 to women unable to get hospital abortions, brought the misery caused by the antiabortion laws to light. Slowly, a consensus started to build among health professionals, religious leaders, feminists, and much of the American public that the existing situation was intolerable.

This intolerance of needless suffering took root in an America that was willing to see old limits shattered so that new perceptions, morals, and values might emerge. The equal rights movement was gathering strength, its proponents determined to see an egalitarian society where women would not be denied their rights and privileges. Blacks were challenging traditional societal attitudes, mores, and laws that perpetuated inequality. Every social and cultural issue was being examined, dissected, and filtered during America's battle to shed its moral schizophrenia. One nation existed on paper, in its treasured documents, while another existed in reality. The reproductive rights movement, which was begun by a group of revolutionary young women in the early years of this century and which had lain dormant for decades, was again emerging front and center in the nation's consciousness.

CHAPTER 9

A GRADUATE WITH A MISSION

On June 14, 1964, Ohio Stadium was a sea of nine thousand black robes. After four years of grueling work, I'd earned the privilege of wearing one of them. I knew that my family was up in the stands—Mama, festive in a dress of soft voile, and a large hat covered with bright organdy flowers; Daddy, dapper in his brown suit and matching hat, tilted just right. All the extended St. Louis family were there, too—my aunts Alice, Evie, and Ola. They were proud.

And I was proud. I'd made it, and that was no small achievement. I had a clear sense of what I wanted to do within my profession.

Ethelrine Shaw had helped me decide. I'd approached her after my obstetrics rotation to discuss my interest in studying for a Master's in maternal and child health. Given the struggles that my family and I had gone through in order to afford nursing school, this ambition might have seemed unreasonable. They certainly could not support graduate studies. But from my earliest years, I'd learned that obstacles were not impossibilities, they were simply meant to be overcome.

"I know that if I want to specialize, I'll have to get a higher degree," I said to Dr. Shaw, my unspoken thought being that such a degree was required if I wanted to escape bedside nursing. At that point, I was sure that was exactly what I wanted to do.

"Absolutely," she approved. "But if you do, be sure to get into a program that offers midwifery training. It's the wave of the future."

I didn't fully understand what she meant and I didn't have the nerve to ask for clarification. But inspired by her encouragement and the terse authority of her suggestion, I didn't ask any questions.

The graduation procession had started at nine o'clock and was over by eleven. We were back at Neil Hall by noon. I didn't know how I'd get myself to graduate school, but I hardly cared in that exhilarating moment when I received my Ohio State diploma in its crimson leather cover. "Bachelor of Science in Nursing," it read. I savored my victory. "Girl, you made it," Mama kept repeating, a broad smile filling her face.

Daddy was pleased, too, although more restrainedly so. I'd graduated. I was going to amount to something after all. I knew that my struggle for his respect was far from over—that I would have to prove myself to him time and time again—but it didn't matter, not that day.

After everything was packed into my parents' car, we headed a small caravan to the small Ohio town where Mama now pastored. That evening, the cooking, laughing, and happy talk were reminiscent of the old days in the big house on Walton Avenue. I think the happiness had less to do with the particular occasion than with the sheer pleasure of our all being together once again.

A week later, Jan and I headed for a long weekend trip to visit her sister, Joi, in New York before we returned to Columbus and the state-sponsored examination to qualify for a license to practice nursing. I had never been there before; but St. Louis was hardly rural. As it turned out, we took only a few excursions—saw the Statue of Liberty, went to a Broadway play, and shopped. Too uncertain to venture out alone, we mostly watched television in Joi's tiny apartment while she was at work.

Soon I was back in Ohio, trying to figure out where I would apply. I briefly considered joining the Peace Corps, but the two-year stint as a volunteer would have taken me too far off track from my plans for graduate school.

After sitting for the state board, I buckled down in search of work. On the meager salary I was likely to earn as a graduate nurse, it would take forever to save what I needed for more than a year of graduate school, even if I was lucky enough to get a fellowship. But with a college degree, I could look for a better-paying teaching or administrative position. Since I now planned to focus on maternal health and midwifery, I decided to apply for positions in obstetrics.

My alma mater summarily rejected my application for an entry-level position—I had been neither a straight-A student nor an inductee into the nursing honorary society. I didn't take this setback to heart. I was quite sure not meeting their standards had more to do with my having had to work to support my education than with a lack of ability. Studying sometimes had to come second to paying for the opportunity to study. If my B− average was another obstacle to overcome, so be it.

During my senior-year rotation in public health, I'd enjoyed living in Dayton, where I'd been assigned to the Dayton Public Health Service, so I decided to apply for a teaching position at the Miami Valley Hospital School of Nursing there. The response came within days. There was an opening to teach students in the labor and delivery department, and I was invited for an interview.

The day of my appointment found me a bundle of nerves, but the reassuring smile of the nursing school director restored my confidence. I recall little of that meeting, but I do recall my fervent hope that the director would give the inexperience of my youth the benefit of any doubt. I was temporarily staying with my parents, who were now in Washington Court House, about thirty-five miles from Dayton. I impatiently awaited the results of my state boards and the outcome of my job interview.

It was strange and a little uncomfortable to be living with Mama and Daddy again. Although I'd visited them during every break, the times we had together over the last four years had been relatively short. I'd spent most of my time sleeping off the exhaustion of my rigorous schedule. These breaks had been few and far between—two weeks off at the end of the summer and a week off during the quarter breaks, and I began to see how much my time away from the rigors of their lives had changed me. While I didn't smoke, drink, or use drugs, by my mother's meter I was still not saved. I didn't read the Bible daily or attend church each time the doors opened. My dresses were too short and I wore lipstick and jewelry.

Life in the tiny farming town and in the small church community my mother led was a far cry from my life in Columbus. The sole excitement of a Washington Court House summer was going to the Old Timers Day Sale on the town square, where all the merchants sold their wares at discount prices and where games, raffles, and food stands added to the small-town revelry. Although I tried to avert Mama's wrath, I didn't fall comfortably into lockstep with their church schedule of Sunday-morning, Sunday-night, and Wednesday-night services. Sometimes I'd drive out to the edge of town in my green Nash Rambler and have a foot-long hot dog and an A&W root beer at the drive-in or a banana split at the Dairy Queen. Mama and Daddy made the usual rounds of camp meetings, and when they were home Mama was immersed in the duties of ministering to her flock.

I'd been home for almost a month when the call from Dayton came. The director of the nursing program said, "Assuming you pass your state board exams, you have the job as an instructor in labor and delivery nursing at a starting salary of five thousand dollars per year. My assistant director thinks I'm making a mistake. You're so young. You've just graduated. You have little nursing experience. You have no teaching experience at all. But I told her, 'This one's different. I think she can do it,' and I'm sure you will."

Her words sent my spirits soaring. "Thank you," I answered, breathless with excitement. "I'll make sure you aren't disappointed."

My new job was to start at the beginning of the fall term, in August. I called my friends, dispersed by this time in different parts of the country, and bragged about my salary. "Can you believe it . . . five thousand dollars!" In 1964, this sum was unheard of for a graduate nurse fresh out of college. I counted the days until I would be free of my parents' straight-laced home.

When August finally rolled around, I moved into a small rooming house in Dayton. I expected it to be my home for two years, the time I figured it would take me to save for graduate school—with the extra help of a government grant.

At a few minutes before seven o'clock on the first morning of my new job, I walked into the instructors' ground-floor office of the squat brick building of Miami Valley Hospital's maternity and gynecology wards. There I was greeted courteously, but without much enthusiasm, by my two fellow instructors. The head of the department, much more welcoming, gave me an energetic handshake along with her cheery hello. She was a kind, pleasant woman in her fifties who liked to regale us with tales of growing up in another part of Ohio.

During the summer, I had turned twenty-one—only a few years older than the students I'd be teaching. There was no orientation, so I didn't have the foggiest idea how to proceed. But I was hired to teach them to provide sound nursing care to patients in labor, to deliver their babies and help them recover from labor. I would do my best. Having no other guidance, I proceeded to instruct as I had been instructed—with high expectations, and little tolerance for students who weren't prepared. To my students the women who passed so quickly through their care were a blur of procedures and of coping with the stress. I didn't yet have the perspective to help my students comprehend the practical, human applications of the skills and knowledge they were acquiring.

The students wasted no time in letting me know my deficiencies: Their first evaluation of my work was that I was excellent in conveying the theory of nursing practice, but that I should ease up a bit on my expectations. The students were complaining that I was impossible to please. I'd been so focused on their knowing the material and becoming the best nurses possible that I'd forgotten how inspiring the warmth and wisdom of Dr. Shaw had been. After a few more months' experience and a little more confidence in my ability, I realized that my students were right. Performance and understanding were two very different things.

On Fridays, I drove to my parents' house as soon as my shift was over, at three-thirty. If I walked in the door after five, Daddy would greet me with a terse "Where have you been?" I was expected to stay until Sunday afternoon after service. The tension that had not flared over the summer flared now, as I reconnected with a world outside their realm.

As the months passed, I began spending some weekends in Dayton, and my parents demanded to know why. I never had an answer that would comfort them. I wanted to shout, "I'm not a bad person. I don't commit crimes. I'm not dishonest. I'm dedicating my life to service. I just can't live my life as a carbon copy of yours. I'm trying to find my own way." Re-entering the sanctuary of the holy community every Friday, only to return to the secular world on the Monday that followed it, was becoming almost impossible for me.

Could two such different worlds be reconciled? I couldn't convey my thoughts and feelings to my parents without risking my mother's rebuke and her unhappiness at my being "lost." I didn't believe myself to be a sinner. I was committed to the work of caring for others—and a lifetime commitment to that work was what I now had firmly in mind. In its emphasis on service, nursing was compatible with the dictates of the Church of God. In other ways—most especially the aspect of nursing that necessarily forswore moral judgment of a patient—it was not.

But more than my work was drawing me away from my mother's faith. Not long after settling in Dayton, I'd met James Annie. She was another recent college graduate, a social worker who moved into the rooming house shortly after me. Comparing notes on our living arrangement, we agreed it was uncomfortably confining even though we planned to remain in Dayton only two years—she would be marrying her fiancé, then in the Air Force in Germany, and I would be heading to graduate school. We found a house to share.

As I'd moved through one rotation after another in college, I'd gained the skills necessary to become a nurse, dealt with life and death, and always worked to make ends meet. But beyond going to the monthly sorority meetings, I'd found little time for a social life. Distance having cooled my romance with Fred, I felt comforted knowing he was still in my life and that I'd probably marry him someday. By senior year, though, I felt more comfortable with an increasingly active social life. By the time James Annie and I and a third housemate, Barbara, were living together, with the pressures of study and work behind me, I was drawn to testing my social wings.

We led the busy lives typical of so many young women—shopping, giving parties, dating, and going to nightclubs. Our telephone rang constantly. Suddenly, I seemed to be the focus of a great deal of male attention. My dates urged me to enter beauty contests or to pursue a career in modeling. I was so flattered by their attention that I broke off my four-year relationship with Fred, to explore new relationships. These included my posture toward myself. Never had so much been made of my looks, and with my feet not yet firmly planted in maturity, I found myself wanting to accentuate them. I began seriously studying the use and application of makeup. When I was a child, Daddy had called me "clumsy," and it had stuck with me, so I took a charm school course to learn how to walk and sit with grace. It didn't take me long to realize that I had to exercise self-restraint if I was to save enough money to continue on the path I'd planned for myself.

Midway through our second year in Dayton, James Annie got married. She and her new husband, Sam, were moving to California. On the way out of town, she stopped by the hospital to say good-bye to me and to collect the birth control prescription she'd asked me to get for her. On the highway just outside Kansas City, a car pulled out in front of their tiny Volkswagen bug and hit them. James Annie was critically injured, and died the following day.

When I called home distraught, Mama, after expressing regret, responded in accusatory tones that I'd failed to lead my roommate to God because I hadn't upheld the standards of His church. She believed that James Annie, never having repented her sins, was eternally lost.

Even as my mother spoke her piece, I disbelieved it. That didn't mean I wasn't deeply hurt by her judgment. When I think about it now, I realize how absurdly funny James Annie—so full of life and humor—would have found this exchange. But I said nothing, beaten down by the loss of James Annie and Mama's reproach.

About a year into my whirlwind social life, I met a man whom I started to date on a regular basis. Although it was the mid-Sixties and the birth control pill was gaining popularity, freeing more and more women from the risks of unwanted pregnancy, Fifties values still held sway, and the stigma of sex outside marriage was still strong. As I contemplated intimacy, all the teaching I'd been given on fornication, which had meant so little to me as a child, assumed a powerful relevance. And the attitudes of my friends were not a whole lot more liberal. We didn't discuss sexuality—not intercourse; not pregnancy; and certainly not abortion—unless there were complications or reports of an arrest of a doctor performing illegal abortions.

Our aspirations lay not only in the security of our careers, but in cherished dreams of marriage and child-rearing. We were expected to be virgins until marriage; to acknowledge that we were not, even to our closest friend, was to risk rejection and being branded as "loose." Then as now, the same standards did not apply to men—they were expected to sow their wild oats. But with whom? That was unclear. Unless you were preparing for marriage, contraception was not discussed. After all, why would virgins need birth control?

So, all alone, like so many other single women with boyfriends, I worried about pregnancy. Though I was surrounded by obstetricians and gynecologists every day and human sexuality was the substance of my work, I was still too embarrassed to discuss contraception with anyone. Instead, I took my chances with foam and condoms. And every month, my worry mixed with guilt, I waited for the cramps that announced the onset of my period or the quiet that would confirm my fear. I was fortunate—the cramps always arrived. Others were not so lucky.

It was at Miami Valley Hospital that I first became aware of the lengths to which some of the unlucky women went. They were placed in a back room in the labor section of the obstetrics ward, isolated from women with full-term pregnancies. They were usually admitted to the unit complaining of hemorrhaging. If their uteruses seemed small on examination and if their descriptions of the onset of their bleeding and pain were vague or evasive, it was assumed that the pregnancy had been ended with help. Unless there was concrete evidence of an illegal abortion—a high fever or an object caught in their vagina—the women rarely admitted to having had abortions. They knew they could be investigated by the police, who would press them for the name of the abortionist.

As a nursing instructor, I did not personally attend these women, but the nurses and doctors who did discussed their cases in a way that accented the stigma. Members of the medical establishment have the same values as the rest of society. Even for them, sexuality outside of marriage and the termination of pregnancy at one's own hand are isolated at the extreme end of the spectrum of secrecy. The discussions of staff about their patients' suspect conditions were conducted in lowered tones. The women being cared for had participated in a criminal act and it was spoken of as such.

Any fertile, sexually active female, single or married, stood some chance of finding herself trapped in a web of concealment and shame. Though I was a caregiver, as a woman I was not exempt from such a predicament.

CHAPTER 10

HARLEM: AN AWAKENING

By early 1966, after more than a year spent teaching labor and delivery nursing at Miami Valley Hospital, I had to move on. Initially, I'd found the work challenging and rewarding. It hadn't taken long, though, before the repetitiveness of teaching the same material month in and month out with little time for building a personal rapport with my students began to wear on me.

More significantly, this period, devoted exclusively to the healthcare of women, confirmed my interest in obstetrics. I felt as comfortable with women as they experienced one of the most fundamental yet awesome aspects of their bodies as I had felt years earlier in Mama's sewing room.

As Dr. Shaw had prophesied, midwifery was taking hold as a specialty in nursing. There were articles in professional journals about its practice and potential. There were reports in newspapers about its growing acceptance. There were those who believed it would become so widely practiced across the country that most healthy pregnancies and deliveries would be handled by these specially trained nurses, freeing doctors to focus their skills on problem pregnancies and complications. At the same time there was also an undercurrent of concern that they would be perceived as competition by doctors.

I heeded Dr. Shaw's advice, and applied to two universities for graduate school—Catholic University, in Washington, D.C., and Columbia University, in New York City. Both offered midwifery training. And both invited me to enter their programs with the promise of a U.S. Public Health Service Training Grant, a now dismantled governmental financial package that paid my tuition and a small stipend.

Columbia's program appealed to me more. It offered a Master's of science degree in maternal and infant care with certification in midwifery, and I'd be able to finish the program in a little over a year. I accepted, packed my belongings, and said good-bye to my colleagues at Miami Valley Hospital.

The August morning that I was to leave found Mama, Daddy, and me in the driveway, with Mama praying for our safety on the road and my protection in New York. Daddy was going to drive me to the city, and Mama smiled proudly as we climbed into my car, which I had arranged to be sold when Daddy returned. My father seemed quite pleased with my decision to attend graduate school, and the long trip from Ohio to New York was filled with pleasant conversation.

Though neither of my parents had ever visited New York, I think their pride was accompanied by considerable relief that I was leaving behind my singles life to return to the more cloistered and regimented world of study and hard work. As for me, I was a lot less anxious than I thought I'd be. I was in New York to study, and Columbia's medical center would be the center of my existence. Its scale was not nearly so vast as the city in which it was situated.

Maxwell Hall was a tall, darkly aged building overlooking the Hudson River and the George Washington Bridge. But when I opened the door to the two-room apartment to which I had been assigned, my spirits sank. It was clean, but the view was of the shadowed driveway and courtyard. These tiny, dreary quarters would be home for a year.

On the first day of classes, I was surprised to discover that there were only two people in the program besides me—Ruth, a young woman from Cleveland whose kind brown eyes and gentle manner gave her something of a saintly aura, and Linda, an outgoing nurse from Rochester. I liked both women instantly, and over the course of the year, Linda and I would become quite close, sharing as many adventures of the city as our meager budgets allowed.

The three of us were excited by the prospect of learning midwifery while getting a master's degree. The nursing professor assigned to oversee our program—a tall, portly woman named Carol—was just as enthusiastic about this profession as we were. Her jaunty movements and staccato speech gave a sense of perpetual motion. In her Long Island accent, she'd rave about the superior care that midwives could provide to women experiencing normal pregnancies. And as if her enthusiasm wasn't striking enough, we were in awe of Carol's interactions in the prenatal clinic, her patience and the time she took to teach the women she would select to demonstrate to us how it should be done. I was amazed that it didn't seem to matter to her that in the real world of a busy hospital, a nurse would never be allowed to spend an hour with a woman explaining the steps of labor and practicing breathing exercises. And yet the effect this care had on the women was clear—when we saw them at subsequent visits they seemed less frightened by the prospects of childbirth, asked more questions, and when they returned to the postpartum clinic, they were much happier than women who had not received the midwife's intense care.

Shortly after the semester began, I was tremendously excited to learn that my clinical work would primarily take place at Harlem Hospital, now part of the Columbia Presbyterian Medical Center. For the first time in my career, I would work in a setting that mainly served black people.

The old Women's Hospital building—a wing of Harlem Hospital—was dingy. The postpartum wards were large and open, with metal beds lining the walls. In the summer, we sweltered in the smaller non-air-conditioned labor and delivery rooms, especially when it came time to don a face mask, a cap, a long cotton gown over the scrub dress, and rubber gloves for delivery.

I had cynically expected Harlem Hospital to be overcrowded and poorly equipped, with an overworked and callous staff. Nothing could have been further from the truth. The commitment of the midwifery instructors brought back fond memories of Dr. Shaw. There was Pat, thin and boyish, with a crackling southern accent. Jean, her colleague, was chatty and friendly, with an easy smile. Pat and Jean worked long hours running the midwifery service and working alongside Linda and me to ensure that we learned the compassionate care (and total dedication they practiced as the hallmark of midwifery. The pregnant heroin addict and the pregnant child in her early teens required and deserved as much nonjudgmental empathy, diligent attention, and time as was needed to guide them safely through childbirth.

Being back in the clinical area as a student was jarring at first, and my initial disorientation was compounded by the nonmidwife staff nurses with whom we worked. Although we were registered nurses, to them we were, simply, "students"—a student in midwifery and a student of basic nursing, they seemed to believe, were one and the same—and we were routinely questioned about our abilities to perform the most basic tasks without supervision. Once, when I was assigned for a brief time at Physicians and Surgeons Hospital, a nurse in charge of the labor room stopped me on my way toward a patient's room. I was carrying a tray of supplies for setting up and starting the intravenous fluids that would sustain her through labor.

"Where are you going with that?" she asked, her tone full of challenge. "You have to wait for your instructor."

Though taken aback, I stood my ground. "But I'm an R.N. I have taught nursing. I don't need an instructor to supervise a procedure that I've been performing and teaching for years now."

"I don't care. You're a student and you'll have to wait," she replied curtly.

I paged Carol, and after some negotiation with the reproving nurse, I started the intravenous fluids—alone.

The conventional image of a midwife is of a woman with modest training who is not a nurse and delivers babies in the home. The truth is that nurse-midwives practice in hospital settings. As a student of midwifery at Columbia I would learn how to manage all aspects of prenatal, delivery, and postpartum care under standing doctor's orders, without requiring a doctor's presence so long as the progress of the pregnancy and delivery were within normal limits. I would be trained to recognize the outer limits of normalcy and, when it was appropriate, consult with the doctor and assist him or her in managing any complications.

I learned about complications—about what can go wrong and how quickly it can go wrong—in the case of a woman named Delores Harris, who was carrying her eighth child. Mrs. Harris was a sweet-faced woman, soft-spoken and shy, with the browned skin of her Caribbean heritage. She was obese from the remnant weight gains of her previous pregnancies and appeared at each prenatal visit in neat cotton pastel dresses that were several sizes too large, the better to accommodate her distending abdomen. As the months grew cooler, she stretched a sweater over her expanding girth. This pregnancy was categorized as high-risk for complications, because seven others had preceded it, but Mrs. Harris exhibited no evidence of complications during her prenatal visits to the clinic. Thus, under the surveillance of my instructors, I was assigned to manage her pregnancy as it progressed along a normal course through delivery.

Although the business of having babies was nothing new for Mrs. Harris, she faithfully kept her clinic appointments. She seemed to enjoy the chats we had about the progress of her pregnancy, her diet, and her aches and pains, while I performed her physical exams, checked her urine and blood pressure, the fetal heartbeat, and the size of her womb to determine its consistency with the length of her pregnancy. I enjoyed them, too. There was nothing of the transient connection between a nurse and a patient as I'd witnessed and experienced it before. As her midwife, I saw her as *my* patient, not *a* patient. And I wasn't *a* nurse, but *her* midwife.

I was in the prenatal clinic seeing patients one early evening when Mrs. Harris came to the hospital for delivery. I was bent over the swollen abdomen of an expectant mother, listening through the stethoscope to the rapid heartbeats of her fetus, when the door to the small examining room was opened slightly and Jean poked her head into the curtained cubicle to say quietly, "You have a patient in labor."

Taking the metal instrument from my head and ears, I excused myself, and stepped into the corridor to ask, "Who is it?"

"Mrs. Harris. When you finish up with this patient, get up to labor and delivery as soon as possible. You know that she's a grand multip. She'll probably go fast."

I wound up my examination and rushed to the labor ward, changing into a baggy blue cotton scrub gown, slipping a cap over my head, pulling the string tight and tying it at the nape of my neck as I went.

Mrs. Harris was already wearing the not very modest light blue gown, secured at the neck, open down the back, that was designed to facilitate the frequent pelvic examinations and monitoring of the fetal heartbeat that charted the progress of delivery.

Upon seeing me, she smiled wearily, just as a contraction peaked. I gently passed my hand over her abdomen, above the umbilicus and just below her breastbone, to assess the strength of the muscles of her womb pushing the fetus into the birth canal. Although she was in active labor, the response of these muscles did not seem especially strong to me.

I knew that after seven labors and deliveries, expansions, and contractions, Mrs. Harris's uterus was well-worn and might be a little tired. The muscles that had probably functioned with vigor during the birth of her first child were less resilient. Perhaps they would not work as efficiently, especially after delivery, as we would need them to.

After almost three hours, the mouth of the uterus was completely open. If this were Mrs. Harris's first delivery, we would have waited until we could see the baby's head pushing against the outside of the birth canal before determining that birth was imminent. But the tissues in her lower pelvis and birth canal were pliable and yielding after repeated stretching. There was no more time for vaginal examinations. One last check of fetal heartbeats at a time when the fetus was under the most stress and we had to get our moaning patient into the delivery room, so that we could control the delivery if things started to happen quickly. I hurried out into the hallway and found a gurney. After pushing it alongside the bed and locking its wheels, I helped Mrs. Harris shift the heavy load of her pregnant body onto the narrow span. Pat joined me and we wheeled her into one of the delivery rooms, actually no bigger than the labor room and just as dingy. Then we helped her move again over to the birthing table. Mrs. Harris's legs were guided into the cold metal stirrups mounted on each side of the lower end of the table. As the nurse who was to assist us applied restraints to her wrists, Pat and I headed to the sinks outside the delivery room to scrub our hands and arms as close to sterility as we could get them.

Mrs. Harris's position, with her legs splayed high and wide, was absurd and unnatural, even torturous, for any woman, let alone one in severe pain. But this was for our convenience as I prepared to guide the baby out of her body. While Pat and I put on our sterile gowns and rubber gloves, I rolled through my mind the steps for guiding the release of a baby from its inner sanctum, just as I did before each delivery that I attended.

By now, my patient was straining down as though she was having a bowel movement—a reflex action often triggered by the pressure of the baby's head on the rectum. If we couldn't get her to stop pushing until she could be prepared, there was the probability that her pushes would force the baby through the birth canal too quickly, causing injury to both of them.

Scrubbed and clothed in our sterile attire, we stepped up to the delivery table. The nurse who would be assisting us quietly and firmly urged through her mask as she stood at Mrs. Harris's side and held her hand, now immobilized by the leather strap, "Breathe deeply, breathe deeply."

Luckily Mrs. Harris's second stage of labor had not progressed as quickly as we'd feared it might. With everything set, we needed her to push again. "Push!" we prodded in chorus. "Push!" But our interventions—her elevated legs, the nitrous oxide gas passing into her lungs and being absorbed into her bloodstream—made it hard for her to comply.

There I stood before Mrs. Harris in full sterile gear, with Pat peering over my left shoulder—waiting for the first glimpse of a head. The exhaustion of the woman sprawled before us was now hidden from us by the folds of starched, sterilized cotton sheets. Our attention strictly focused on the safe passage of the baby from the only area of her body that was still exposed, now illuminated by the powerful delivery room lamp overhead. I touched her abdomen through the sterilized sheets. Her contractions were not powerful. The nurse assisting us continued to comfort and encourage her.

"Puuuush!" we urged again quietly. There was no exclamation needed in prompting her pushes, for we knew that one good one could result in the baby's landing in our hands with force. We wanted to keep everything in control.

Mrs. Harris groaned and twisted her pelvis, shuddering and moaning as each contraction exhorted her body to expel the baby. She tightly gripped the silver metal handlebars at each side of the table. In another few moments we saw the first patch of black hair—the baby's head moving toward us. We needed one more push. Even as the fear gnawed at me that something would go wrong, excitement welled up in me just as it did each time I delivered a baby.

"I . . . I . . . I need to rest . . . need to catch my breath," Mrs. Harris stammered when the nurse-anesthetist momentarily took from her face the mask that administered the mild anesthetic.

"Now we're almost there, just one more push," I answered in encouragement. "Don't stop . . . we're almost there."

Suddenly, Mrs. Harris let out one long deep grunt and more of the baby's head began to emerge through the opening of her vagina. The firm head, now pressing on the wall of her rectum, stimulated Mrs. Harris's urge to bear down. She needed no further coaching. I watched the head turn sideways, and with the outside of my gloves now slick with amniotic fluid, I cupped it and guided the upper shoulder and then the lower one as they passed under Mrs. Harris's pubic bones. She grunted once more and the round, slippery body of her child slid into my hands.

I placed the infant onto the sheets covering most of its mother's body. The mask was removed from Mrs. Harris's face and she smiled weakly and attempted to lift her head. After applying two metal clamps to the umbilical cord to stanch the blood flow, I cut the cord of life that had nurtured the fetus for almost a year. As I gently stroked the length of the baby's back, she started to cry lustily. It was then that Mrs. Harris finally caught a glimpse of her new baby girl and smiled.

So far, so good, I thought.

We stood quiet, awaiting signs that the organ that had attached the baby to the wall of the womb, and had efficiently conveyed nutrients and oxygen and removed waste in the baby's blood had, its duties done, separated from its host. We watched for a trickle of blood and more of the umbilical cord to appear at the distended opening to the birth canal.

Minutes later, the section of the umbilical cord still attached to the mother began to slip out of the birth canal, the sign that the afterbirth was about to be expelled. I tugged once, gently, on the clamp still attached to it and soon the deep-purple disk of tissue filled my hands. Again, so far, so good. Maybe we were getting out of this one okay, I thought, and began to relax a bit.

I asked for the administration of Pitocin, a drug that would help her uterus to contract tighter to close off the blood vessels from which the placenta had been fed. A rush of blood gushed from Mrs. Harris's vagina. This, too, was normal, a result of the womb's clamping down on the uterine vessels after the placenta is detached, squeezing the blood out of them. I dabbed the area to be sure that there were no tears to her vagina that would need a stitch or two to repair. But instead of dwindling to a trickle of fluid, the blood kept coming. The flow began to increase, and increase significantly. Sensing danger, my alert midwifery instructor ordered me to place one hand on Mrs. Harris's abdomen and one hand behind the neck of her cervix, high into her vagina. She hoped that the pressure from squeezing the two walls of tissue together would mechanically close the vessels and quell the bleeding until the Pitocin could do its work. But because Mrs. Harris's tissues were so expanded and undefined, it was hard to distinguish what was what between my gloved hands. With blood now flowing in what seemed to be a river, I tried in vain to execute my instructor's directions. Panic rose inside me as I tried to visualize where the cervix, now thin and flabby, could be. It wasn't the cervix familiar to me through my prenatal examinations. It wasn't the cervix of labor. It wasn't even the cervix of a woman who had just given birth to her first child. I could feel nothing. I reached and squeezed and reached again and squeezed. The blood kept flowing.

My God, she's going to bleed to death if we don't do something, I thought, and yet I didn't want to accept that I couldn't manage the situation. My hands began to tremble.

"There, I think I have it," I assured my instructor. But I didn't have it. The blood kept coming. The large arteries that had served her fetus so perfectly were now pumping what seemed to be gallons of blood into my hands and the stainless-steel basin that I propped with my abdomen against her elevated pelvis. Pat asked our assistant nurse to open the intravenous line so that more fluid could replace Mrs. Harris's dissipating life force. Though it seemed like hours, it was only minutes—vital minutes—that had passed.

"Do you have it?" Pat asked calmly but urgently this time.

"I'm not sure," I acknowledged, knowing that nothing had changed.

"Step aside, let me get in there," Pat, the seasoned nurse-midwife, ordered firmly. Within moments, her experienced, skillful maneuvers and the drugs administered earlier combined to cause the lazy uterus to contract, shuting down the blood flow from Mrs. Harris's uterine arteries. Finally, the crimson flood stopped. I breathed a deep sigh of nervous relief, hoping that it would not start up again.

Fortunately, obstetrical emergencies were infrequent. By the end of my training, I had delivered the twenty babies required at that time for midwifery certification and I had cared for many more women in the prenatal clinic and on the postpartum wards. But the memory of Mrs. Harris would always stand out. For many reasons, she'd been a special patient to me, but the lesson that childbearing can be a dangerous endeavor transcended even our warm rapport.

Training at Harlem was not just about prenatal care, deliveries, and healthy babies with happy mothers. It was also about the other side of childbearing—unwanted pregnancy.

I remember walking into a ward one afternoon, while a group of doctors were discussing the prognosis of a pretty teenager. Her condition was terminal, the doctors said. I looked over at her, lying so quiet against the white sheets in a room separated from the large ward of mothers recovering from delivery. It struck me that she was only a few years younger than I. She looked as healthy as any normal teenager, her eyes bright and her skin clear, showing no obvious signs of pain or distress. Though the tubes in her body gave witness to the fact that she was dying, it was hard to believe.

Unable to afford the services of an abortionist, the girl and her mother had concocted a solution of Lysol and bleach and injected it into her uterus. The potent mix of chemicals had been absorbed by her blood-stream, badly damaging her kidneys. Her other vital organs were shutting down and there was nothing that could be done. She was so pretty, so young, and had it not been for one fatal mistake, the world could have been hers.

The year that I was there approximately 6,500 women entered Harlem Hospital suffering from the complications of incomplete abortion.[1]

When we'd sit in the nurses' lounge during breaks, the nurses who were more experienced than I would tell their war stories. It was then that I began to comprehend the sheer force of women's need to end pregnancies they were not prepared to handle, and the tremendous dangers they were willing to face to do so. We were all aware that the dangers fell most heavily on poor women, because women who were well-connected could afford to go to doctors who knew what they were doing. I was also aware that what I heard and saw was only the smallest fraction of the pain that women in Ohio and New York and all over the country were suffering. The girl in the prime of her adolescence was only one of between eight and ten thousand women who died each year in the United States from abortions that had gone awry.[2]

One nurse remembered, "There was this one woman . . . she told me that she was picked up on a street corner and put in a car blindfolded so she would never know where she had gone. The blindfold stayed on throughout the procedure. Afterwards, she was dropped off, still bleeding, on the same street corner where the whole ordeal had begun. She wound up here with a temperature of a hundred and five degrees, but she made it. We had to call the police, but she wouldn't say anything to them."

Commonly, the illegal abortionist, using a crude instrument or surgical dilator, would open a woman's cervix until contractions and bleeding started, and then send her to the hospital to be "cleaned up."

"We couldn't break the law and risk losing our licenses, so we refused to perform D and Cs unless blood and fetal tissues had already been passed and the suspect 'miscarriage' was already under way when the patient was admitted," one doctor recalled. "This meant that the woman hemorrhaged, and went through a lot of humiliation and pain before she could receive medical treatment, but what could we do?"

At Harlem Hospital, I learned from my colleagues that women came to the hospital with knitting needles, sticks, pieces of coat hanger inserted in their cervixes, often beyond their reach. There, the tools jabbed into their bodies and tore the tissue in their uterus, vagina, and sometimes even their intestines. Or sometimes they'd have bought unsterile witch hazel sticks over the counter at the pharmacy, which they'd insert into their cervix; there they would gather moisture, expand, and dilate the cervix until contractions started. Sometimes rubber catheters made to empty the bladder were pushed into the uterus and left for several days, until it and the inflammation it caused provoked violent contractions and bleeding.

Whenever unsterile objects were used, whether catheters, witch hazel sticks, or coat hangers, infection was virtually inevitable. Those women who didn't get medical attention quickly enough risked infections that would make future pregnancies impossible, or worse, the infection might spread into the Fallopian tubes and out into the abdomen. In these instances, death from infection could occur quickly, despite massive doses of antibiotics.

If corrosive solutions, like those the teenager had used, were injected into the uterus in the hope of irritating the cervix into dilation, the chemicals could often burn holes through the tissues, causing hemorrhages and only occasionally inducing abortions. Some of these solutions were made with tablets of potassium manganate, a caustic chemical used to purify water. If the woman did not dissolve the tablets in water to make a diluted douche, but inserted one directly into her vagina, she would arrive at the hospital hemorrhaging from holes the size of dimes burned into her vaginal walls. When these ulcers bled, a woman would often think she had initiated an abortion, although she was actually still pregnant.

Any injury to a woman's internal organs served as a convenient point of entry into the bloodstream for bacteria. The virulent tetanus (or lockjaw) bacteria was the most deadly. Blood poisoning (septicemia) would attack every vital organ. Eventually the kidneys would swell and shut down, or gangrene, the result of circulatory cessation, would develop.

Even in the face of such devastation, the cases were discussed, not as the outrages that they were, but in hushed tones in casual moments in the nurses' lounge or in more formal reviews of recovering patients' charts. But the odors of the fatal infections caused by illegal abortion and the hopelessnesss of saving them are unforgettable for anyone who cared for those desperate and doomed women.

Three years after my training at Harlem Hospital, the antiabortion laws that had loomed over the lives of women for a century would be reexamined. In 1970, New York would be one of the first states to put an abortion reform law in place, guaranteeing women access to the choice of ending unwanted pregnancy legally and safely. But that was too late for the teenager that I remember and the countless other women who met her fate.

The strange thing was that little emphasis was given to preventing unwanted pregnancy in the structured aspects of our training. Family-planning services were offered in the hospital's outpatient clinics. There, we observed doctors fitting diaphragms and nurses instructing women on the still-revolutionary technology of oral contraception. Given the reality of the lives of poor women who possessed only one safe option in facing an unwanted pregnancy—to carry it to term—in my mind, voluntary prevention should have been given top priority.

Although much of my time was spent within the confines of the hospital, the reality of life in America's largest and most dynamic black communities couldn't help but awaken my political consciousness. Harlem meant jazz clubs and Adam Clayton Powell, Sr.'s Abyssinian Baptist Church, and the ghosts of Langston Hughes and Marcus Garvey. Sometimes, Jan, my college roommate who was studying for her master's in psychiatric nursing at Rutgers University, would come into the city and we'd slip out for a night at Minton's Playhouse. I remember seeing pianist Horace Silver and the late trumpeter Lee Morgan. We'd spend hours talking about James Baldwin's *Another Country* and Claude Brown's *Manchild in the Promised Land*.

But Harlem was more than the richness of a cultural heritage. It was the Sixties, and the entire nation was being swept into the turbulence of radical self-appraisal. The Vietnam War protests churned the conscience of the country. The inner cities, electrified by the dream of Martin Luther King, Jr., and the assassination of Malcolm X, smoldered with a sense of pride, militancy, and rebellion. For the first time, I found myself working with predominantly black colleagues caught up in the momentum of the times. At the top rungs of the social and professional ladder, the privileged class of doctors, dentists, nurses, and social workers engaged in vigorous debates over the subtle and explicit effects of racism in America. Some saw redoubtable virtue in the nonviolent approach of the civil rights movement. Others brought the issues into our immediate realm, contesting that the "white power structure" that had recently taken over Harlem Hospital and made it part of the Columbia University Medical Center was oppressive and paternalistic, damaging the comity of the traditionally black hospital. All the while, the sounds of Motown spilled onto the streets from loudspeakers on street corners on 125th. Black Power slogans were graffitied on subway trains, walls, and abandoned buildings.

And yet, if there was pride and angry defiance, there was also despair. Nothing in my experience—certainly not in the shelter of the church, but not even my time at University Hospital, Kiddies, or Miami Valley Hospital—prepared me for all I would see. I witnessed that despair in more ways than one in Harlem that year. Not only were there the women who bore unwanted pregnancies and some who took desperate measures to end them, but heroin addiction and all of its consequences continued to ravage the community. Men, their heads nodding and their bodies limply folded over at the waist, stood along the sidewalks where I caught the shuttle uptown to my apartment.

Mercifully, the pregnancy rate among true heroin addicts isn't high. Disenfranchised from healthcare, when they do conceive, they often carry their pregnancies to term without prenatal care and arrive at the hospital in active labor. In those days they'd show us the most reliable vein into which the intravenous fluids should be connected. The babies born to these women would scream shrilly and endlessly as the effects of the absence of the drugs supplied by their mothers' blood left their nervous systems irritable. They were given mild sedatives to reduce the possibility of convulsions brought on by too-rapid withdrawal from their mothers' drugs, and to ease them into a gradual withdrawal. The nursery attendants would stop up rubber nipples with cotton to prevent the intake of air, and place the nipples in the tiny mouths to pacify the infants' tumult. Sugar water also helped.

But more fundamentally, what chance did these children have? Mother Hale had not yet opened her home to such babies. A lucky few might be adopted into loving, caring homes, where they stood a fighting chance to live the lives that their biological mothers could not provide. But most would begin a long journey into the foster care system and toward a greater likelihood that their lives would also be locked in poverty and despair.

Heroin addiction was so far outside the realm of my life experience that I was fascinated by it. I did my master's thesis on photoelectrophoresis, then a common test that could be used to screen for drug use during the pre-natal period, so the mother's newborn might be treated immediately after birth to ease the effects of narcotic withdrawal. In those years, worries about the possible violation of civil liberties were not as keenly considered as they are today. The treatment couldn't solve the problems that spawned the mother's troubled life, but perhaps it could lessen the suffering of its youngest victims.

Then there was the violence. One evening, I was standing on the front steps of the hospital, waiting for the shuttle to take me home, when I saw a fight break out across the street. One of the combatants suddenly pulled a long knife and stabbed the other in the abdomen. The man fell to the pavement, clutching his wound. His companions picked him up and ran past me through the door of the emergency room. I'd never witnessed such raw violence in such proximity. All night long I wondered if the wounded man had died. The next morning, I asked the emergency room staff about his condition, and they told me that his liver had been lacerated, but he would live.

I realized, amid all of this, that there was no separating the conditions that had brought the country to the brink of racial and class cataclysm—no teasing apart poverty, violence, drug addiction, racial pride, and militant protest from the forces arrayed to maintain the established order. I did not wear my hair natural, nor did I don a dashiki, but seeing the conditions in which people were existing brought home the meaning of social injustice. I began to appreciate as I had never done before how fortunate I had been, how, by the randomness of my birth, I had not been forced to survive as my patients had. No, life had not been easy since we left Walton Avenue, but compared to the world that I was working in, I had much to be grateful for.

This consciousness that others did not have the same opportunities humbled and angered me and catalyzed my innate sense of outrage over injustice. I was getting an education that would put me in a position to do something about the suffering that poverty and lack of choices imposed. It would be my obligation to use everything I learned to fight injustice and lack of power and its consequences the best way I could.

As I neared completion of the requirements for my degree, I found myself with several choices for my next career move. Ruth Anne Yauger, who had been my public health professor when I was on my senior-year rotation in Dayton, called and asked me to return there as her deputy in charge of the Visiting Nurses Association and maternal and child health programs at the Dayton Health Department. As I was considering her offer, Dr. Donald Schwartz, chairman of Obstetrics and Gynecology at Harlem Hospital, asked me to consider joining him in starting a new midwifery service in the Ob-Gyn Department of the Albany Medical College, in Albany, New York, where he would soon assume the department's chairmanship. I was over-whelmed by both offers, exhilarated by the notion that unknowingly I had made a favorable impression on a former professor and that a highly respected specialist considered me capable of taking on such a responsibility so soon after completing my graduate training.

I was caught up in my work at Harlem Hospital, caring for women whose lives were defined by their daily struggle for survival. At the same time I longed for nursing of a different kind. I wasn't unfamiliar with all of the aspects of the Visiting Nurses Association that would be the focus of my position in Dayton. I'd made several home visits to mothers whose infants I'd delivered at Harlem Hospital. Sometimes I'd been uncomfortable as I walked down dimly lit tenement hallways, oppressive with the odors of poverty, climbed the stairs, and knocked on a door that opened to an apartment furnished with the barest essentials. But when the door had opened, and I saw the woman I'd come to know over the course of her pregnancy, my uneasiness would leave me. My focus was again on her and her baby.

These women were always glad to see me—"my midwife," they'd say, as they invited me into their homes. Questions like "Does the baby have any diaper rash?" "How do you sterilize the baby's formula? Could you demonstrate it for me?" and "What is the color of your vaginal drainage?" seemed trivial in comparison with their life struggles. On one occasion, I found that the mother's public assistance check had not arrived. She was diluting formula that she had been given at the hospital with water to make it last.

I knew I could never care for the many needs of the women in Harlem by serving them one by one. But if I were an administrator in public health, I could dedicate myself to changing the system that served them. Some might have thought returning to Dayton was a retrenchment. Perhaps it was. But when I thought about my two years at Miami Valley Hospital, I realized that Dayton, with its universities and high-technology defense industries, was far from an intellectual backwater. Like New York, this midwestern city had poverty in the midst of progress. Perhaps this poverty wasn't on the same scale as Harlem, but it represented a need all the same. And more to the point, given the size of the city, and my position as number-two person in the department, I felt I might be able to have some real influence on the situation.

I discussed it with Mama, but I don't think that her "Girl, why don't you come back to Dayton" had so much to do with my professional well-being as with her need to see me safe from the dangers of New York. The truth was that I was still quite young. At twenty-four I instinctively responded to my need for the security of the familiar, even as I set about testing myself and my evolving framework of values. I also needed to answer a call I couldn't yet name. I would almost call it providence—that first step in a direction that would lead to all the other steps on my way to the Planned Parenthood Federation of America. I accepted the Dayton offer and left New York right after my final exams.

CHAPTER 11

PRENATAL CARE AND
PARENTAL CONSENT

When I hear teenage pregnancy characterized as a relatively new phenomenon and evidence of a national moral decline, I can't help but think back on the young women I attended in Dayton thirty years ago. I believe that the continued high rate of teen pregnancy and unintended pregnancy among adult women reveals not a moral decline, but our society's continuing failure to address sexuality early enough and honestly enough as a natural aspect of human development.

Teenagers were having sex and getting pregnant in 1967, and had been for a long time before that. The stigma of teenage pregnancy has always been powerful (though less so today), but contrary to popular illusion, it has never been powerful enough to quash sexual urges and deter the early initiation of sexual intercourse. I've learned that my parents' approach to the subject was fairly typical, which meant that most adolescents received little information about their sexuality beyond a discussion of its most practical aspects—if they got that much. Girls learned how to deal with the hygienic demands of menstruation, and boys were told, "If you get that girl pregnant, you're going to marry her." But threats of a shotgun marriage didn't tame raging hormones thirty years ago any more than they would today. Without the free teen clinics that came into being in the late Sixties, teenagers had primarily their wiles to guide them away from pregnancy— and wiles, when applied to sexuality, are only haphazardly effective.

The youngest child I cared for, I'll call her Toya, was only thirteen years old and had been brought to the clinic by her exasperated mother. Toya had been impregnated by a neighborhood boy. Abortion was still illegal, and even if she and her mother had wanted to do so, having her pregnancy ended by illegal means raised the specter of serious danger to the youngster. Her mother brought her to our neighborhood prenatal clinic.

"Hello, I'm Miss Wattleton. I'm the midwife and I'm going to take care of you," I offered in my most cheerful and reassuring nurse voice. Toya stole a quick glance at me, then returned her blank gaze to the floor. The image of that youngster sitting stiffly on the edge of the examining table, lost in the overlarge paper examining gown, is as troubling to me today as it was the moment I first saw her. Pimples marked the oily skin at her temples. Her hair was brushed into a then-fashionable straightened flip. Her mother, perhaps in her late thirties, stood next to the table with her arms crossed, shifting from one leg to the other.

My assistant had prepared her for the pelvic examination. A public health nurse would be following up. I needed only to determine whether Toya's immature pelvis would provide adequate space for a normal delivery or whether she should be referred immediately to the hospital clinic. Even adult women find this proceeding less than pleasant. Without a doubt, it is the hardest thing about the initial prenatal visit for sexually inexperienced girls. Barely out of virginity, their vaginal muscles are naturally tight and their fear makes relaxation during the examination virtually impossible.

I asked her a few questions necessary to gauge her pregnancy: "When was the first day of your last period?" "Have you had morning sickness?" "Are you taking vitamins?"

Her mother answered the questions as the silent child's eyes remained fixed on the tiles of the floor. Then, as if unable to stop herself, the mother blurted out, "I don't know how this happened."

I'd heard those words before as mothers wrestled with anger, despair, guilt, and worry over their teenagers' pregnancies.

"I don't know what we're going to do," this mother grieved.

And I had my own feelings to wrestle with. The vision of a pregnant girl in her early teens summons powerful emotions in most people, including the professionals who care for her. Many of these emotions are founded in compassion; some are founded in judgment. As I looked at this child, questions came to my mind, challenging my ability to be objective: What was she doing having sex? Was she exploited by an older man? What on earth will she do with a baby? She'll probably have another before she's grown.

I'd seen the devastating effects of abortion at Harlem Hospital; but here was the problem when desperate measures to end the pregnancy had not been taken. This pregnancy would cause irrevocable damage to the young girl's future—and in all likelihood, to her child's future. The judgmental side of me ruled: If this wasn't a case for ending pregnancy, I didn't know what was. The compassionate side prevailed: It's not for me to judge; I have to take care of her.

When confronted by such complex circumstances and such troubling emotions, caregivers often flee to procedures. Still inexperienced in handling such cases, I was no exception.

"Now, I'm going to examine you with this one finger," I told Toya, holding up the index finger of my right hand. "That doesn't look big, right?" She watched me, her expression a blend of skepticism and terror.

"My finger has lots of jelly on it. That's so it will go in without hurting you. I will tell you everything I do before I do it. Once you get used to one finger, I'll put two fingers in so I can get a good idea of how your pregnancy will go."

In truth, even before I started, I felt defeated in my attempt to effectively explain the uncomfortable procedure to a child who should have been more concerned about her friends approving of her hairdo than of a stranger examining the most private part of her body. Even with her mother standing there, making it all so real, the girl seemed isolated from what was happening to her.

The instant I touched Toya's genital area, she straightened her knees and pushed her bottom away from me, using the leverage of her feet in the fixed metal frames. I told her calmly that I would examine her very slowly and would stop each time she asked me to.

We repeated this drill several times, and all the while Toya's mother sighed and sighed, impatient with her daughter's inability to cooperate. Twenty stressful minutes later, I had obtained a Pap smear and a less than satisfactory evaluation of the measurements of her pelvis. I judged that if she had an average-size baby, she should be able to deliver without a cesarean section. But to be on the safe side, I would send her to the hospital clinic for an evaluation by a doctor.

Following the exam, I tried to talk to Toya about her pregnancy. It was of no use. She was far too upset by the ordeal to answer my questions beyond a simple, nearly inaudible "yes" or "no." I felt certain that she wouldn't remember a thing I said. I'd have to settle for making more progress with her during subsequent visits, when she wasn't so frightened and the air wasn't so full of her and her mother's unhappy tension. I decided to defer prenatal instruction, but gave her mother vitamins for her.

Because she was so young, Toya was transferred to Miami Valley Hospital's clinic for care during her eighth month of pregnancy. After she delivered her baby, I visited her at home and felt stunned, once again, watching a child trying to adjust to the presence of a newborn. Toya smiled weakly from the sofa where she sat holding her infant son. The public health nurses would work with the family for many months to make sure that she and her baby received the necessary health care, and that arrangements were made for other services. The agency's social worker would help her apply for public assistance, for which she was now eligible, so she could get back into school. They would be working against very long odds.

There were others who came to the clinic like Toya—not so young, but not much older, either. With each encounter I gained a deeper understanding of the tragedies that pregnancies and parenthood meant for those who were so young. If only one girl lost her childhood because she'd gotten pregnant, lost the chance to paint her lips and dance in the living room as Nell and I had done, she was one too many. The societal consequences of teenage pregnancy challenged me, and the individual encounters informed and troubled me.

Pregnant teenagers wouldn't be the sole focus of my work at Dayton, but their vulnerability and often their poverty made their circumstances particularly poignant. Without exception, they lacked the physical, emotional, and economic resources of adult women, and in those days, few voices advocated prevention of their pregnancies.

In 1967, I didn't know that my inclination toward maternal healthcare, which had drawn me into the problems of teenagers and poor women, would someday lead me to fight for the reproductive rights of all women. I was drawn to Dayton because of the possibility of influencing the services of an agency. I didn't see it as a bold decision—it was just the next step for me after Harlem, as logical to me as my grandfather's building a bus when he saw children walking to school one by one.

Overseeing the child health program was also part of my job. And I believed that the well-being of children was best secured by caring for their mothers.

Arriving that first day at the multipillared entrance to the Dayton Municipal Building, which housed the visiting nurses' offices, I was too excited to take the elevator. I bounded up the wide marble stairs to the fourth floor and up to the windowed barrier. Behind the glass were the same two gray-haired nurses who had struck fear in my heart when I was a student, by way of that brusque, no-nonsense manner seasoned nurses used toward novices. This time, their broad smiles were reassuring.

"We've been waiting for you," said Dorothy. "I'll tell Ruth Anne that you're here."

"By the way, how many babies have you delivered?" her companion inquired.

I felt proud to say, "Twenty." I kept telling myself that what I lacked in experience would certainly be compensated by the uniqueness of my training. And I had been promised that I could quickly put to use, in the city's health department, what I had learned in New York. All the same, I was glad that Ruth Anne appeared before I had to answer any more questions.

As a professor, Ruth Anne Yauger had been aloof and didactic, but I'd always sensed a kind spirit behind her stark demeanor. I saw a sadness in her eyes when she smiled that I believed revealed her grief over the sudden death of her husband a few years earlier. Ruth Anne was a chain-smoker, and her slender, diamond-adorned fingers betrayed a slight tremor as she lifted a cigarette to her lips.

Speaking with a soft stutter that her students had learned to recognize as a sign of nervousness, she greeted me warmly, now as a colleague. "C'mon in. We're delighted that you're back. I want to hear all about New York."

The institutional-green walls of her office were decorated simply, with documents of her profession—a doctorate and other degrees, and an array of honorary nursing society certificates—together validating the brilliance of this reticent woman.

From a long, friendly conversation centered on my graduate school experiences, we turned to my new responsibilities. They would entail supervising the nurses who visited mothers and babies in their homes after delivery, and overseeing such special programs as well-child clinics, birth preparation classes, and pregnant teenager education. I was also to make certain that all the nurses on staff were kept informed of the latest developments in maternal and child health.

Working with nurses providing care to people in their homes rather than in the hospital, where there is a greater measure of control over a patient's return to health, was a perspective different from the one I had just left. Another adjustment was that my administrative role, with one exception, would remove me from direct patient care. Still, returning to the familiar environment of my undergraduate training made getting reacquainted with the agency's operations an easy task.

Unlike New York, with its extensive public hospital and clinic systems, Dayton's privately owned hospitals retained private physicians and residents to care for the poor in their clinics. The hospitals were required to submit reports to the health department on all women who delivered without prenatal care: They and their babies were considered high risks for complications because of inadequate medical supervision. Similar reports were filed on "preemies," babies weighing less than five pounds. We were mandated to follow up on these cases by making home visits. After comparing the previous two years' reports and the total number of births, I calculated that an astonishing 30 percent of these women had received no prenatal care. Many of them had delivered low-birth-weight babies, thus compounding the problem. I learned that Dayton's infant mortality rate was among the highest in Ohio. There was little doubt in my mind that inadequate or nonexistent prenatal care contributed to these fatalities.

After monitoring the hospital and follow-up reports for several months, I concluded that we had to find a way to reach women before the birth of their babies. In New York, I'd visited the Maternal and Infant Care Project, which had been successful in reaching such women through prenatal clinics set up in their own neighborhoods. The program, administered by nurse-midwife Dorothea Lang, was closely allied with the public hospitals, and nurse-midwives provided the bulk of the care. I thought a similar program could work in Dayton, even though it could be tricky to arrange with private hospitals. I went to Ruth Anne and laid out my reasons for setting up clinics in two of Dayton's inner-city neighborhoods.

"If you can get the doctors to cooperate, we'll try to find the money," she said. "But you'll need the support of the county health commissioner."

I knew many of the obstetricians and gynecologists at the three hospitals from my teaching days at Miami Valley Hospital, and I felt certain that the recent Medicaid legislation would make these very conservative, mostly Republican doctors skeptical of any proposal that smacked of socialized medicine. But as it turned out, the imprimatur of my position in city government helped me. The heads of the Ob-Gyn services at each of the three major hospitals allowed me to make my proposal at their staff conferences. If they had reservations, they didn't air them to me.

The first presentation was at Good Samaritan Hospital. The best way to garner support for the idea was to be sure my audience understood the exact nature and scale of the problem. I knew that doctors responded to numbers and statistics. Like my mother, whom I'd watched prepare the text for her sermons, day in and day out—"Study to show thyself approved of God,"[1] she'd quote—I knew that nothing could substitute for thorough preparation: not emotion, but hard evidence. I'm no firebrand crusader, though indignation over injustices has always provoked passion within me. But even if I had been inclined to preach, I knew my audience. These were not social activists.

"I have prepared a few transparencies that I think illustrate the problems of women delivering without having received prenatal care," I began in my best attempt to be coolly official and not reveal the knot of anxiety in my stomach.

Many of these doctors had delivered poor women who had come to the labor room without prior care. They all understood the particular tensions of caring for women at a crucial moment when so little was known about the pregnancy. Every doctor had a story to tell, but none had a perspective on the way that story fit into the big picture. But Dayton's unacceptable death rate for babies under the age of one mandated that the medical community do something new and different. And to transform my idea into reality as a citywide effort, I needed the cooperation of all the hospitals.

I outlined the creation of a prenatal clinic program patterned after the

New York Maternal and Infant Care Project. Some of the doctors were concerned that my proposal offered an opening for nurses to encroach upon the practice of medicine. But the majority decided, "What can it hurt? We don't see these women before delivery anyway."

Months later, after settling on a protocol that set limits on my practice, the three hospitals agreed to participate in the program. Assisted by a public health nurse, I would attend to the women's prenatal care, examining and counseling them and treating their minor problems. Patients with complications would be referred to the hospital of their choice, where doctors would take over.

I wouldn't be granted hospital privileges to deliver babies—the doctors weren't ready to go that far—so in the ninth month, the women would be transferred to the hospital prenatal clinics. Their deliveries and early postpartum care would be handled by staff doctors. I would then visit each of the women in their homes after they and their newborns were discharged. Public health nurses would keep track of them to make sure they returned to the hospital for the postpartum examination.

The cumbersome process taught me an early career lesson: Change happens not so much by leaps and bounds, but by persistence and increments, while never losing sight of the larger goals. The prenatal clinics were a first step. I resolved that I would eventually gain approval for hospital deliveries before my mission was fully achieved, but at least, for now, I had managed to open the door to reaching women early in their pregnancies.

Another key to making the program work was situating the clinics in places easily accessible to women, especially those who were neither on welfare nor sufficiently well-off to pay for private care—the women who often get lost in the cracks of the healthcare system. The city owned facilities where it offered health and social services to the community. Given a portable examination table and a table to conduct the necessary blood and urine analyses, we could quickly convert an ordinary room in such a facility into a prenatal clinic. We located one site in primarily black West Dayton and another in primarily Appalachian East Dayton. As a result of radio public service announcements, leaflets distributed to churches and community groups, and word-of-mouth promotion by the visiting nurses, requests for appointments were soon crossing the agency's switchboard. We were in business. One small step had been taken toward turning a hidebound system into one that reached out to women where they lived.

Until the mid-Sixties in Dayton, and in many other parts of the country, adolescent girls who became pregnant were expelled from school. If their impregnators were of school age (although research would eventually show that the majority were adults) they would also be expelled—but only if they acknowledged their responsibility for the pregnancy. Shortly before my arrival at the health department, this practice was "reformed." Pregnant schoolgirls were no longer expelled, but they were removed from their regular classrooms and sent to the Daytime Center for Girls, which was sponsored by the Board of Education and located at the central YWCA. There, each semester, between twenty and thirty girls would receive the academic support they needed to keep pace with their classmates. Though the basis for this arrangement was never expressed in policy as such, sequestering those girls from their classmates was clearly designed to "protect the virtue" of other teenagers.

At the Daytime Center for Girls, one of the earliest facilities of its kind in the country, the students received prenatal, delivery, and postpartum care and "parenting" classes, which were taught by public health nurses involved in the maternal and child health programs. A nursery for newborns offered care for infants until the sixth week, or until the girls finished the semester and were able to return to their regular schools.

However good our intentions were, the program couldn't undo the effect of years of personal neglect, which was the inevitable result of society's neglect. It couldn't mend the damage done by low self-esteem, inadequate education, and limited resources. It couldn't prevent the babies from being raised in the very circumstances that had shaped their mothers' lives. Nor did the center have the means to offer child care on a long-term basis. Unless there was an unemployed adult (most often the teenager's grandmother) at home willing to care for the baby, who would quickly become an active toddler, the odds were in favor of the teenager giving up her battle to stay in school.

And there was one thing about teen pregnancy that we hadn't been prepared for: Contrary to the conventional and cynical assumption that a teenager's first pregnancy would "teach her a lesson," especially if she was forced to carry the pregnancy to term, second pregnancies were—and are—common. That shouldn't have surprised us, since the factors that made the youngster vulnerable in the first place could only be addressed remedially during the few months she spent with us.

Nevertheless, the first girl who returned to the center pregnant for the second time took us by surprise. Linda was, at seventeen, in the older range of the girls we served. Most were fourteen to sixteen. Her fashionably styled hair and trendy clothes conveyed a sophistication that most of the other girls had not acquired. But her outstanding academic performance was discussed in weekly program review conferences, which included a public health nurse and the social workers and teachers who worked full-time in the program. Linda had returned seventeen months after her first delivery, four months pregnant. Her teachers were aghast, as though they had been betrayed.

"Definitely college material," "A real standout," "If anyone could make it, this girl can," they had concluded during her first pregnancy.

This time around, the odds were stacked more heavily against Linda's future. For teenagers, coping with one child was a struggle; managing a second baby usually tipped the scales into dependency. College was now a remote possibility; it was unlikely that Linda could overcome the burden of parenting alone, without public assistance. The probability of her being trapped in a cycle of lost opportunities, struggle, and poverty left us with a sense of futility.

At that moment, I realized that our attitudes were as much at fault as society's. The entire philosophy of the center reflected the values of adults toward teenage sexuality. ("We might encourage sexual intercourse if we discuss contraception.") Our work, so accepting and supportive of these girls who'd been segregated from their peers, was rooted in remediation, not prevention. I don't ever remember our saying, "How can we help these girls to keep from getting pregnant again?" or "Shouldn't we try to work with the schools to encourage discussion on prevention?" Discussion of birth control was part of the sixth-week exam that followed delivery, but it didn't include the values and pressures that underlay our charges' sexual decisions. We left these girls as we found them. Like so many parents, we behaved as though hard experience had endowed the teenagers with the common sense to have "learned their lesson."

After three years of supervising the nurses who rotated through the program, I reached the conclusion that we were working on a few pieces of a very complex puzzle of sexuality and its manifestation in pregnancy. We needed to stop theorizing about the most effective punishment for sexuality and start thinking pragmatically about how to avoid its tragic consequences. But this was still the 1960s, and even as professionals, we didn't talk frankly about sexuality.

A year after my return to Dayton, Konrad Reisner, a member of the board of Planned Parenthood of Miami Valley, called me and asked if I would be interested in joining their board. My only contact with Planned Parenthood up to this point had been the several evenings of observation I'd spent at a Planned Parenthood clinic when I was in college. However, the little I knew about its work for the prevention of unwanted pregnancies appealed to me in light of the problems that I was seeing in my work at the health department. The regularity of repeat pregnancies was growing more and more troubling for the staff at the Daytime Center. Planned Parenthood's very name suggested that the problems we were facing could be avoided. Perhaps it would offer a way to reach youngsters before they were excused from their regular classrooms or walked into the prenatal clinic.

Konrad continued, "Virginia Kettering and some of her friends just put together the donations to get us started, so we're pretty new."

I knew who Virginia Kettering was. The daughter-in-law of the co-inventor of the switch starter for automobile engines, she was renowned in Dayton for her generosity and commitment to local causes. As for Konrad Reisner, I knew that he was head of the local Family Service Association, which offered counseling for adoptions and troubled families. The supervisor of the Daytime Center was a social worker with his agency.

Konrad gave me a brief sketch of the affiliate's history, explaining how, in the 1930s, community opposition had forced it to close down. The new plan was to open Planned Parenthood birth control clinics around Dayton to complement the one in operation at Miami Valley Hospital. They hoped to use a mobile unit and expand to the surrounding counties. They were about to receive a federal antipoverty grant with which they would be able to start an educational outreach program.

I accepted Konrad's offer with little further thought.

After a few board meetings, I discovered that Planned Parenthood required that teenagers—that is, teenage girls—obtain their parents' written consent, or a referral from a social service, health agency, or minister, before they could receive contraceptives. I couldn't believe it. Didn't it make sense for an organization whose explicit purpose was to prevent unwanted pregnancy to make birth control easily accessible for every sexually active person?

The Daytime Center didn't offer contraceptive services—Planned Parenthood did. The revelation that Planned Parenthood stood on pretty much the same ground as everyone else disillusioned me. I knew that the teenagers with whom I worked weren't checking in with their parents to get permission to have sex or get pregnant. This stipulation requiring parental approval, or an "appropriate substitute," failed to respect that fact. It also failed to acknowledge that while it was relatively easy for a teenager to give in to sexual drives and pressures, it was a lot harder for her to make and keep an appointment at a family planning clinic. There, she would have to acknowledge her sexual activity to strangers and admit an intent to continue having sex in the face of the prevailing social taboo. It took maturity and a sense of self-worth for a girl to take responsibility for the consequences of her actions.

In good conscience, how could the Dayton affiliate of Planned Parenthood place one more obstacle in her path, when all around us kids were getting pregnant? No one at the board meetings spoke about how girls would rather not be mothers if they could avoid it, how society's double standard encouraged young men to explore and experiment with their sexuality in adolescence while keeping young women bound to the ideal of virginity until marriage, how withholding knowledge and the means to prevent pregnancy was simply a means of controlling their behavior.

In what was to be an experience of resistance to an idea that to me seemed so logical, so self-evident, the board rejected my suggestion to reconsider its policy on teens and contraceptives. "Someone should give their consent," one board member argued. "If a girl can't go to her parents, a minister or a social worker gives her another avenue." The lack of connection to the circumstances of teenagers' lives reflected in their well-meaning conclusions troubled me. "Minister?" I asked. "Social worker? How do they find these people if they don't already know them?"

Instead of discouraging me, the rejection made me even more determined to see the situation changed. Every month, I attended the board's meeting with that special purpose in mind. When the business part of the meeting finished, I would repeat, "I would like to discuss our policy on serving teenagers." I gave as vivid a presentation as I could about the girls that I was seeing in the prenatal clinic and that the public health nurses taught at the Daytime Center, without compromising anyone's privacy or inviting judgment about a particular case. I felt as though I was arguing on behalf of all young women who needed to see restrictive attitudes and practices change.

"But we don't want to appear to be encouraging teenagers to have sex," one member worried.

"If my husband ever learns that one of our daughters is being seen in a Planned Parenthood clinic without his permission, you'll have hell to pay," one well-to-do board member threatened.

I didn't give up. Frankly, I didn't care whether I annoyed or angered them. I persisted with uncompromising stubbornness and utter exasperation at my colleagues who refused to acknowledge both human nature and the devastating consequences of teen pregnancy. I believed that what I had seen could not be refuted. My willfulness, evidenced in my early years, to my mother's painful dismay, would harbinger my tenacity in future battles.

"These kids *are* having sex whether we want them to or not," I'd say over and over. "And if they're already having sex, how can our clinics possibly be considered to be encouraging them? Shouldn't we at least try to help them avoid pregnancy?"

Most board members advocated counseling. I didn't disagree. I just couldn't accept that in 1969, almost a decade after the sexual mores of the country had been transformed by the arrival of the birth control pill, this group was still holding fast to the idea that a sexually active teenager had a "problem" and needed counseling and permission *more* than she needed the means to prevent pregnancy. If we kept doing what most board members wanted, we would just end up seeing more girls at the Daytime Center.

In the end, I'm not sure whether the board consented to my proposals because they were persuaded by my arguments or because they simply grew tired of discussing the subject. But by the time of my appointment to the position of executive director of Planned Parenthood of Miami Valley in September 1970, teenagers in Dayton, Ohio, could receive contraception upon request without their parents' consent. And by that time, teenagers had another option: *legal abortion*—not in Ohio, but in New York.

Shortly after I'd returned to Dayton, my parents had moved back to Texas, where my mother served a small congregation outside Houston. From that base she continued to travel the revival circuit. In the early part of 1970, she called me and asked me to come to Houston immediately. "George is in the V.A. Hospital," she told me.

I heard urgency in the somberness of Mama's voice. My throat tightened and my heart pounded. She rarely showed evidence that the problems she faced couldn't be worked out and she had never made such a request of me, so I knew that my father's condition must be serious.

When Daddy had applied for a health card for clearance to work as a cook in a restaurant that specialized in barbecued ribs and chicken, the required X ray revealed a spot on his lungs. Despite the technician's recommendation that he get it checked out by a doctor, Daddy hadn't taken the matter seriously. "George was not about to go see a doctor without being sick," Mama remembers now. "He was scared of doctors. He was scared of sick folks. And he was scared of dying."

He went to work and forgot all about the warning. One evening in the restaurant kitchen, the meat caught fire in the brick pit and my father inhaled clouds of heavy smoke. By the fourth day, he told Mama his chest was hurting so badly that he wanted to go to the V.A. Hospital.

No beds were available there, so Daddy had to return home. "I'm going back there," Daddy told Mama the next day, after a particularly brutal night of pain. "They're going to take care of me . . . I'm so sick." It was then that Mama called me.

A week later, Mama and I met with the surgeon at the Houston Medical Center. Describing the exploratory surgery that was scheduled for the next day, his tone was not reassuring. "If it's simply scar tissue or a benign growth, we'll take it out and look around to be sure everything is clear."

"And if it's not?" I asked.

"If we find a malignancy and it has not spread, we'll take out the lung. He can manage just fine with one lung. If it is cancer, and it has spread to the surrounding tissue, we'll try to remove the majority of the tumor and give him radiation to slow its growth," he replied, in the clinical tones that were so familiar to me as a nurse and so frightening to me as a daughter.

Mama and I went back to Daddy, where he lay in the large open ward of beds. His shiny forehead knitted with a mix of curiosity and fear as he searched our faces for some indication of the situation.

"What did the doctor say?"

"They're going to see what's up and then we'll know," I replied in the most comforting tones I could summon. My mother stood beside the bed close to Daddy and stroked the sheets, as if such closeness might provide him some solace and the power of divine healing that she so strongly believed in. "George, you know that the same God that made you is the God that can heal you," she said with an air of reassurance.

And for the first time that I could recall, my father gave verbal witness to his belief in the power of God to heal him. "Yes, I know."

"Let's say a word of prayer," Mama said as I'd heard her say so many times before. "I don't have any oil to anoint you, George, but the Lord will hear our prayers anyway." Touching the top of his hand lightly with one hand and his forehead with the other, she turned her face heavenward and began softly, "Our Heavenly Father, we come to you on George's behalf . . ."

By the time she finished her prayer, even though only Daddy and I could hear what she was saying, the force of her prayer had hushed the ward. We kissed Daddy good night. He seemed so vulnerable between the white sheets, his eyes wide and unblinking. We promised we'd be there in the morning before he went into surgery.

The next morning, we arrived at the hospital around six-thirty. Then, Daddy lay quiet in a soft white surgical gown, but smiled when Mama and I pulled a couple of metal chairs close to his bed and sat silent, watching him in the dim, early-morning ward. All three of us were lost in the quiet of our thoughts and prayers. Soon, he was placed on the large-wheeled gurney, and as the sheet was being pulled over his body, he looked at Mama and said plaintively, "O.B., pray for me."

"George, God is able," she reminded him.

We waited for five hours. Mama reminisced about the years they'd spent together; how Daddy had driven her from place to place; and also about how cantankerous he could be whenever she challenged his authority about the car, the roadways, or his driving habits. Their life together was an idiosyncratic one, and their capacity to find accommodation with one another would fit few other models. Surely, without Daddy's unstinting service to her ministry, my mother's message would have been greatly limited.

Just after noon, the tiny waiting area filled as several members of the church joined us. Not long after, the surgeon appeared and we stood. I tried to read his face for a hint of what we were about to hear.

Taking off his mask, he sighed and spoke slowly. "We didn't remove the lung."

No one spoke. No one moved. I felt the oxygen being sucked out of the room. My stomach began to churn and my hands trembled. "How long does he have?" I asked, fighting back tears.

"Six to nine months," the doctor answered quietly. "I'm sorry. The cancer has progressed too far. We took out most of the tumor, but it has spread outside the lung and involved other tissue. We don't recommend radiation. He should do well for several months. You'll want to believe that the cancer is cured, but in time, he'll begin to fail, and there won't be much we'll be able to do."

After the young surgeon left, we all sat in silent disbelief. Finally, one of the women spoke. "Sister Wattleton, let's pray."

Daddy was only fifty-eight years old, and he was going to die. How could this be? He'd always been strong and vital. He rarely got so much as a cold. It was Mama who always seemed to have physical aches and complaints, about which he was solicitous. But his most dire complaint before this was an aching back after a hard day's work.

Daddy's recovery went as smoothly and quickly as the doctor had promised. He was released from the hospital after a week or so. I returned to Ohio and stayed in frequent contact by telephone.

Daddy was soon strong again, and though we never discussed the seriousness of his situation, I think he suspected the worst. He seemed quietly resolved to do the things that gave him pleasure. As for Mama, she was praying for his divine healing. My parents' thirty-one-year marriage, which had sometimes borne the stress of verbal conflicts and power struggles, softened into a mutually loving and supportive one. They went fishing together and took drives around the countryside. As a long-standing devotee of good nutrition, Mama put Daddy on a regimen of the best fruits and vegetables she could grow or find, not forgetting to include his favorite foods: collard greens, cornbread, and, of course, hot peach cobbler. During our telephone conversations, she would proudly report on the good care she was giving him.

By the middle of the summer, although Daddy was growing weaker, he seemed strong enough for a journey that was especially important to him— to the Garrett family in Mississippi. Mama drove Daddy to Canton, where after stopping over in New Orleans, he'd be looked after by Aunt Sadie and Aunt Lou. But his particular desire was to visit Uncle Ernest and Uncle Coleman, their husbands. They were like brothers to him, and he was especially fond of Uncle Ernest.

However briefly, Daddy was recapturing something of those happier times of reunion as he now revisited his "brothers" and their wives. Afterward, he planned to go to Louisiana to visit friends, and there Mama would meet him and take him back to their home in Houston. But Daddy had been in Mississippi for only a few days, when Aunt Sadie called to tell Mama that they thought he'd suffered a stroke. Could she come for him immediately? When my mother arrived, she found Daddy able to speak coherently, but he'd lost dexterity on his right side. He could no longer button his shirt or feed himself. He spent his time resting quietly on the sofa.

When they got back to Houston, Mama took Daddy back to the Veterans Hospital. When she called me with this news, I feared the worst, and quickly arranged to go to Texas.

The first sight of my father told me that his condition was far more serious than the "stroke" he may or may not have had. He'd lost a lot of weight. His left eye bulged slightly from its socket and fluid eased out of the corners. X rays confirmed that the cancer had spread to his brain. The "stroke" had been the cancer now destroying the nerve centers vital to his life.

I greeted Daddy with a kiss on his still-shiny bald head.

"How are you?"

His eyes revealed the answer before he spoke. "I'm afraid that I'm not going to be able to walk."

The lump in my throat gave way to the churning in my stomach. Something terrible, something I could not control, was about to happen. My eyes burned from the salty tears that I didn't want him to see. *My father is going to die,* I thought. For the first time, reality sank in. I did not know an existence without my daddy, and soon he would be gone. The world as I knew it would be changed forever.

Even then, no one talked to Daddy about dying. We didn't pretend that it wasn't happening, but neither did we overtly acknowledge that death was imminent. Mama and I were at Daddy's bedside every day, but we abandoned him to his thoughts and fears, for the sake of taking each day and each new development as it came. We hoped for the best. Mama believed that the miracle of healing was possible.

Daddy denied having any pain. He didn't lose much more weight, but his strength was ebbing rapidly. Fortified by the prayers of the members of the church, Mama held on to her uncompromising faith for his healing, while I tried to cope with the harsh reality of his approaching demise.

One evening, I sat next to my father. My mother had gone home to rest after a long vigil at his bedside. The women of the church also came to relieve her when I couldn't. I held one of Daddy's bulky hands, so rough from the years of toil, and put a cool cloth over his eyes. He thanked me, squeezed my hand in an emotional way that I had never felt before, and asked me to come closer.

"I want to tell you something," he began softly. "I know I'm going to die." He paused, as though expecting confirmation. In my silence, I obliged him. Then he took the cloth from his face and opened his eyes wide in the way that I knew to mean no nonsense. His light brown irises appeared to pick up flecks of fire in their flash. It was the first hint, since he'd taken ill, of his former vigor and his well-known irascibility. "When I die, I want you to be sure that I am buried next to Daddy Garrett." My mother's father (Grandpa Deanie) had himself died from lung cancer in 1951. "My people will pressure your mother to take me back to Alabama. I don't want to be buried in Alabama. I want to be next to Daddy Garrett. Promise me that you won't let them take me back to Alabama?" The tone of his voice carried the rising inflection of a question. But this was no question. It was a command.

"Daddy, I promise." My voice shook.

In that moment, my father had affirmed me in a way that he had never done before. He had openly acknowledged his respect and trust in me by putting me in charge of assuring that his wishes for his final resting place were honored. Furthermore, he had passed to me the mantle that he had carried for more than thirty years—the mantle of protecting Mama, who was so outwardly independent, but whom he considered too vulnerable to stand up to his family. At that moment Daddy had made me an ally above all others. It was a level of respect that I would never have predicted.

"Okay," he said, squeezing out a smile.

After a second surgery, Daddy's condition improved somewhat, so I went home to Ohio and back to work at the health department. Two weeks later, on September 3, 1970, he passed away.

Mama remembers the night before his death. She'd been sitting at his bedside and he looked up at her and said, "O.B., you go home. You're tired." To the end, Daddy was tending to her needs above his own.

The next morning, the telephone rang in my parents' apartment. The simple and chilling words cut straight to my mother's heart. "Mrs. Wattleton, this is the V.A. Hospital calling. We wish to inform you that at five forty-five this morning, George Edward Wattleton passed away." I didn't have to hear the words to know their cool, Teletype formality.

I returned to my mother's side, to help in the preparations for my father's funeral in Houston, and for his body to be carried to Mississippi for a second service. As I had promised him, Daddy would be buried beside Grandpa Deanie in the Garrett cemetery just up the hill from the Farmhaven church, beneath the tall swaying pines under which I had scampered as a child. When Mama called to discuss the arrangements with me, she pleaded, "Out of respect for your father, please bring a dress that covers your knees. "

Daddy's family wanted to bury him in Alabama, but they offered no resistance when I told them of Daddy's request to be laid to rest next to my mother's father.

The sunny September morning of the Houston services offered me my first glimpse of my father after his death. Because he had not endured a prolonged illness, he looked much as he always had, slightly thinner but peaceful, and dapper, in his favorite brown suit. I saw his body, but my father was gone forever. I could not control my sobs.

Demonstrating their respect and fondness, mourners overflowed the large, white, steepled church. More than two hundred people had come from congregations in Texas and Louisiana to pay tribute to him and to lament his passing. All was in keeping with what I wanted for my father—until the minister, chosen because he was a family friend, began to preach the memorial sermon. Rather than honoring my father's life and the role that he'd played in my mother's ministry, he began, "Now, preaching at a funeral is preaching to the living, not to the dead. I want to preach to you about where you will spend eternity. We don't know whether George will make it to heaven, but you, the living, have a chance to make things right."

I couldn't believe my ears. Over the course of my twenty-seven years, I'd heard a lot about divine retribution for leading a sinful life, but I'd never heard anything like this. My sorrow gave way to shock. This was the man whom Daddy had struggled in his last days to visit in Louisiana? *This* man, who now questioned his worthiness for heaven? *This* man, who dared to assume that my father, never a self-righteously pious man, had not found peace despite all of his work and service? My shock turned to fury.

Though I'd never felt as close to my father as I did to my mother, I'd come to accept his impatience as being just "his way." I had never doubted that he loved me. The level and consistency of his devotion to my mother's cause was something I would not fully appreciate until many years later. I would slowly come to admire his steadfastness in holding on to his own identity in the face of those who expected Ozie Wattleton's husband to be a public embodiment of her ministry.

"If he doesn't stop this, I'm going to get up and walk out," I whispered loudly to my mother. She commanded me to silence with a sweeping flow of her hand, just as her glare had stilled me when I was a child whispering to a friend in the pews during a revival meeting. I could see from her expression that she too was displeased; but still, she would not countenance a reproach of the mortal man who dared to pass judgment on my dead father's eternity.

Whenever I think back upon that moment, I find myself indignant all over again. Perhaps it was a stepping-stone in shaping my determination to fight for understanding rather than for the kind of harsh and dogmatic judgment that was pronounced, without a qualm, over Daddy's coffin.

After the service, we flew my father's body to Mississippi. While Mama and I watched through the large window of the departure lounge as his casket moved along the conveyor belt into the belly of the airplane, my father's passing struck me again. Images of him flowed like movie reels: the whistles; the hat; the chamois lovingly dragged over the shiny automobile metal; the impatience with my announcements of, "Daddy, I need to go to the bathroom." I saw again his struggle to maintain a measure of self-possession by challenging systematic racism, and his expressions of love that came in his offerings of food. I remembered the time he gave me my first "real" watch that he'd bought in an Omaha pawnshop and that stopped running a week later; the affection in his eyes when he watched my mother mount the pulpit; his genuine pride when he told me, "Girl, you got your master's degree"; and finally, "Promise me . . ." Later, I would often wonder what he would have thought of my work. I think that seeing his daughter on television, trading sound bite for sound bite with Pat Buchanan on *Crossfire*, would have made him laugh out loud and brag to the gas station attendants. He would have doted on his granddaughter, Felicia.

We were met by all of my uncles and aunts in Canton, where my father lay in the "holler," at People's Funeral Home, in 1970, the town's only mortuary for blacks. The Mississippi funeral would be a family affair, an homage on the passing of an important member of my mother's clan. Daddy was deeply loved by his adopted family and they openly displayed it in their grief.

Mama and I rode in the car behind the hearse that led the procession to Farmhaven. We headed out past the magnolias and Jimmy Montgomery's store, toward Highway 16, on which my parents and I had traveled so many times together. We passed Aunt Lou and Uncle Coleman's store, and the pond on whose banks I'd once stood screaming, "Daddy's drowning! Daddy's drowning!" as Daddy, an expert swimmer, dove into its cool, calm waters while Mama sat on the bank, fishing pole in hand. When we turned off the highway and moved on past the Garrett homestead to the church, the caravan of cars behind us was blurred by clouds of red dust and by tears.

Once again, hundreds of people converged on the small church that Grandpa Deanie had built. My mother's brothers, his pallbearers, fondly recalled the times they'd spent with him and his verve for life. But the contrast between the life that had embraced him and the life that had rejected him couldn't have been more striking. The Wattleton women from my father's estranged family wore black. The Garrett women wore white.

Soon it was time to take Daddy to where he wanted to be, under the pine trees next to Grandpa Deanie. Crickets chirped in the late-summer grass as Daddy was lowered into the red earth.

I have never heard a melodious whistle or caught the scent of Double-mint gum on a cigarette smoker's breath without thinking of Daddy.

CHAPTER 12

MAMA'S LOSS,
PLANNED PARENTHOOD'S GAIN

Twenty-four years after the fact, I learned that 1970 had been a year of twofold loss for my mother. "It was a year that I will never forget. I lost my husband and I lost my daughter," she remembered. "George died and you went to work for Planned Parenthood."

We were in my mother's gray 1989 Buick, a present from her congregation in Atlanta, Georgia, where she now lived and pastored; and I was driving. It was Christmastime and, after years of coaxing from the South, my daughter Felicia and I had traded the special pleasures of a New York Christmas—finding the perfect Christmas tree among the many that were lined up along the piers of lower Manhattan, decorating it on Christmas Eve, sipping hot mulled cider while listening to Andrae Crouch and the Winans singing carols—for a larger family gathering at Aunt Ola and Uncle Isom's house in Laurel, Mississippi.

I thought back to 1970. Yes, Daddy's death had made it a year of great loss for me, too. But it had also been a year of milestones: I left my job at the Dayton Health Department to become executive director of Planned Parenthood of Miami Valley, Ohio, and that year I met Franklin Gordon, the man who would become my husband. It was also the year that New York became the first state to decriminalize abortion, the first major breakthrough for the reform of reproductive rights throughout the country.

We were rounding the perimeter of Birmingham, Alabama, and Mama had been talking about how much she missed Daddy. Her revelation, stark and lacking any preamble, took me by surprise. Indeed, she had chastised me over the years: about the length of my skirts and the regularity of my church attendance. When I accepted the job at Planned Parenthood, I didn't need to be told that I had chosen to further a cause that contradicted the tenets of my mother's faith. I had occasionally heard her pronounce in her sermons, "God commands us to be fruitful and multiply. The word of God is as true today as it was the day it was written." I'd even been told that Mama had publicly requested prayers for my salvation after I'd taken the job at Planned Parenthood Federation of America. Still, she'd always seemed to take pride in the advances of my career. It had not occurred to me that her pride had its roots in such a profound sense of loss.

I might have become aware of that paradox had we, at any point, discussed my work in depth. But we never had. Yet I was certain that she had gathered information about the organization to familiarize herself with its work. To this day, I cannot imagine challenging my mother's religious beliefs. Had she lectured me about the sin of my work, I would have listened, and, as Mama had done before me, gone on to do what I believed was right. I knew that she believed children to be the gifts of God, and that no measures should ever be taken to interfere with their creation. Her future in eternity rested on her faithfulness to all of her beliefs. There was no room for compromise in the teachings of the scripture, no place for contemporary adjustment. Yet Mama never attacked me for my work or my beliefs.

For my part, I never expected to persuade her to accept that unwanted pregnancy was a potentially tragic situation, demanding safe intervention. This conviction challenged point-blank her faith that God takes care of all problems. Not only would an attempt to "convert" my mother have invited her rebuke; it would have meant being hypocritical to my own values, which included respecting the personal beliefs of others and their right to hold them without harassment.

As we left the Birmingham area and drove down the broad stretch of road that cut through the iron-rich mountains of Alabama, very near my father's birthplace, Mama went on, "I was proud of your accomplishments, but I believe in what the Bible teaches. 'Thou shalt not kill.'"

I heard her words, but I had a hard time reconciling them with the world that I now knew, a world from which her faith had sheltered her.

"But, Mama, I have never told anyone to kill. My work has been devoted to preventing unwanted pregnancies, and to giving women the right to choose how to control their fertility and trusting them to make the decision for themselves."

"Yes, but God said He would supply our every need. He knows the number of hairs on our heads and watches over the sparrows."

"But people *aren't* taken care of," I asserted. I knew what her reply would be.

"That's because they haven't found God."

For Mama, all of life was unalterably directed toward the realm of God, and her mission was to persuade everyone who listened to her to join her in seeking a place in that realm. For me, life had its spiritual aspects, but it was also an earthly endeavor consisting of day-to-day struggles. My commitment was, and is, to making sure that all people have the freedom and the power to make choices that will help them survive this life, one that is not without its own rewards. There was no middle ground between our two perspectives.

When I'd been offered the executive position at Planned Parenthood of Miami Valley, I was already deeply familiar with the tragedies women endured. I grieved for thirteen-year-old children, whose bodies were barely mature enough to sustain their pregnancies; for seventeen-year-olds who died from illegal abortions; for women like Sherri Finkbine, who had been made to withstand humiliating odysseys in order to prevent the birth of their fatally damaged fetuses; and for young children stranded in a vegetative state by physical abuse. My professional experiences, rather than my religious upbringing, informed my decision to take the job offered to me.

Throughout the discussion between the two of us, Felicia had sat silent in the backseat with our dog, Benji, curled on her lap. Felicia was no stranger to her grandmother's judging ways. Indeed, as a child accustomed to having her views respected, she'd occasionally been offended by my mother's outspoken and uncompromising discipline, whether over a television program she wanted to watch or over her desire to wear her hair in a certain way.

I kept on driving, in the spirit of my father—except that he would have argued at length with Mama. I didn't. A heavy silence surrounded us in the car for many miles.

Unbeknownst to me, the wheels had been put in motion for my transition from the health department to Planned Parenthood. Around the time Daddy's cancer was diagnosed, I was asked to join several other board members on the search committee to find a replacement for the only executive director that Planned Parenthood of Miami Valley had known in its brief five-year history. We had interviewed several candidates, and for one reason or another, none quite met our expectations. By early summer we were meeting again over a lunch at the King Cole, Dayton's only French restaurant, when Konrad Reisner leaned over and whispered in his heavy Teutonic accent, "Why don't you apply for the job?"

He told me that he and the other members of the committee had agreed that they wanted me to be the next executive director. Though kind and pleasant in demeanor, Konrad had been a leader in the German resistance movement before World War II, and he was not one to make idle suggestions. I was stunned.

I laughed nervously. "You mean me?"

"Yes, you. We think that you'd do an excellent job."

He didn't elaborate, and I was too timid to ask what made them think so. Being on the search committee, I'd felt fully capable of making judgments about candidates' qualifications, but I hadn't considered that my own might be sufficient for the job. I was surprised that, again, someone seemed certain that I could do more than I felt sure I could do.

I didn't say yes, but I didn't say no. I asked Konrad to let me think about his suggestion. I drove home that evening, trying to figure out what reasons I might give to justify declining the offer. I'd just turned twenty-seven, so one part of me thought: I know, I'll tell them that I'm too young, and that I've never had the responsibility of running a whole organization. But then I answered that excuse with: What's so magical about age? How do I know I can't do this job if I don't try? And the job offered the allure of professional advancement and financial reward. I woke up in the middle of the night, frightened by thoughts of responsibilities that I had not experienced before, ones I would have to shoulder alone, without the security of a superior to assume the ultimate responsibility.

With dawn's light, I felt safer. And as soon as I got to my office at the Municipal Building, I called Konrad and told him I would resign from the committee and submit my application for consideration. My two-degree and two-job résumé was pretty thin, but after a brief informal interview (because I was on their board, they were already familiar with my positions on Planned Parenthood's issues), I was offered the job.

In the same September that my father died, I embarked upon a venture that would take me far from the back roads of the South and the Midwest that he, my mother, and I had traveled together, and into worlds that I could not possibly have imagined.

On joining the board of Planned Parenthood, I had little sense of the organization, beyond the services it provided at its Columbus and Dayton clinics. I didn't know, and wouldn't know, until I became president of the Planned Parenthood Federation of America, that the organization had begun with one woman's fervent wish to empower women by freeing them from the limitations of uncontrolled childbearing.

Margaret Sanger was born in Corning, New York, in 1883. As a young woman, she served as a nurse in New York City, where she became appalled at the toll exacted on women's lives and bodies by self-induced abortion. But this was an era when many considered her ideas too crude, if not altogether heretical, to discuss in polite society. However, the late nineteenth century was the time when the campaign for women's rights, led by such crusaders as Elizabeth Cady Stanton and Susan B. Anthony, had risen up against the Victorian cult of motherhood and the expected submission of women to the whims and desires of men. Perhaps realizing that the ideas they expressed were radical enough in themselves, these women did not speak to the legitimacy of a woman's own sexual needs.[1] Neither did they challenge the idea that motherhood was the proper vocation of a woman. Instead, they advocated "voluntary motherhood," which included the unpopular views that men should curb their sexual urges and, more important, that a woman should be able to reject her husband's sexual advances. These early activists argued that if a woman could choose when to have children she would be a better mother, with better children. In this way, the voluntary motherhood movement laid the foundations for the public discussion of birth control.

But the forces of oppression were not to move aside easily. Anthony Comstock, who was born in New England in 1844 and moved to New York City as a young man, launched a crusade to pass laws that would wipe out "vice and obscenity," which he perceived to be overtaking the city and the country at large. His vehicle to repress any advances made by the voluntary motherhood movement was the Society for the Suppression of Vice, which he founded in 1869. By 1873 Comstock had accumulated an impressive collection of pornographic material, which by his standards included any information about contraception and abortifacients, and he carted it to Washington to exhibit to members of the United States Congress. There the collection's detailed exposition received far more attention than it would have gotten otherwise. (One hundred years later, Senator Orrin Hatch and some of his colleagues orchestrated a similar demonstration, exhibiting films and sex education materials, and demanding that I answer for our violation of public morality.)

Comstock's presentation had its desired effect when the shocked senators and representatives passed a federal statute prohibiting the mailing of "every obscene, lewd, or lascivious, and every filthy book, pamphlet, picture, paper, letter, writing, print, or other publication . . . designed, adapted, or intended for preventing conception or producing abortion, or for any indecent or immoral use."[2] Many states extended the prohibitions to include the discussion, publication, or advertising of any information discussing contraception or abortion, and Connecticut outlawed contraception altogether. The federal laws and their state counterparts became known as the Comstock Laws, and they would continue to wield some influence until as late as 1983, when the last of the laws was struck down.

During the early years of the twentieth century, even as Comstock battled on, Margaret Sanger had taken her nursing practice to the tenements of New York City. It was clear to her that white wealthy women had long had the knowledge and the means to circumvent the Comstock Laws that made safe and effective contraception state and federal crimes; poor women did not. By the thousands, they suffered the debilitating and often fatal consequences of uncontrolled childbirth.

Sanger recognized that a woman's powerlessness could never be overcome without challenging the prevailing notion that her primary role in society, and even her duty, was to bear children. She and her colleagues, the unstoppable revolutionary Emma Goldman among them, set about making the birth control issue explicit in public and political forums. Like their predecessors, they didn't minimize the value of motherhood, but rather sought to provide women with the means to control their own fertility.

Sanger's passionate defense of women's reproductive rights must surely have been prompted by her mother's death after eighteen pregnancies. Later, she also recounted the case of a young woman who had begged her for information on contraception. Legally hamstrung, Sanger had been unable to answer her pleas, then learned that soon after her visit, the young woman had died from an illegal, self-induced abortion. Sanger claimed that the young woman's tragedy had played a pivotal role in shaping her vision of reform.

In 1914, when she was brought up on felony charges for her "obscene" views on women's sexuality and her revolutionary activities, she fled to Europe, leaving her husband and small children behind. In the more progressive circles abroad, Sanger honed her vision and her knowledge of contraceptive methods. She returned home to stand trial. However, after much visibility and public support had been generated, the charges were dismissed and Sanger returned to her work with zeal.

In 1916 Sanger opened her first birth control clinic in the impoverished Brownsville section of Brooklyn. There, in the guise of "consultations," for which she charged ten cents, she offered contraceptives: diaphragms, condoms, suppositories, and the Mizpah Pessary, a device that blocked the opening to the womb, which was Sanger's recommended form of birth control. The demand for these services was, as Sanger had known it would be, overwhelming.

Ten days after the clinic's opening a police raid forced Sanger and her sister, Ethel Byrne, to close it down. Both women and a co-worker were arrested. Their subsequent trials and convictions for establishing the clinic and for giving out illegal information on contraception provoked a maelstrom of publicity. Cannily sensing that the publicity could be turned to their cause, Ethel staged a hunger strike in jail and was force-fed by prison authorities. Even Governor Charles S. Whitman entered the fray, offering to pardon all three miscreants if Margaret Sanger promised to stop all her birth control work. At first she refused the stipulation, but when she saw

how weak her sister had become, she conceded to it. Her promise to the
governor was one she would not be able to keep.

Despite the attention her work was receiving, Sanger later described the
time between 1917 and 1921 as her "leaden years." She was constantly
short of money for her cause, and her new magazine, *The Birth Control
Review*, lost its mailing privileges. Rather than letting it die, she and her
collaborators resorted to selling it on Times Square street corners. And the
publicity surrounding her jailing had strengthened her opposition as much
as it had rallied her supporters. Hotels that allowed her to speak in their
conference rooms were boycotted. The mayor of Boston threatened to
revoke the license of any establishment that allowed her to speak there. In
response, she appeared at one gathering with a wide strip of white tape covering her mouth.

Even as Sanger's movement proceeded, women were working in concert
to emancipate other aspects of their lives. In the upper and middle classes,
they were determined to deconstruct the cloistering vestiges of Victori-
anism and to redefine women's social, political, and economic power. And
women were achieving higher levels of formal education, and forging
careers in professions that had formerly been reserved for men. But as far as
Sanger was concerned, nothing was so fundamental to the establishment of
women's equality as the freedom from sexual repression.

The first American birth control organization, the National Birth Control
League, had been created in 1915 by Mary Ware Dennett in New York
City. Although started by a liberal group, the organization did not want to
be identified with Sanger and others with "radical" tactics. The NBCL dissolved only four years later, in 1919, when World War I turned public
attention to other causes. Following the demise of the NBCL, Mary Ware
Dennett organized the Voluntary Parenthood League, whose primary aim
was to repeal the federal statutes on birth control.

Sanger would not join a group with so narrow a focus, nor one she had
no hope of controlling. Her vision was of groups that would conduct federal and local legislative work and would also open clinics across the country
and conduct research. Financed by Mrs. George Rublee, Mrs. Paul Cravath,
Mrs. Dwight Morrow, and other prominent New York women, Sanger
worked in 1920 and 1921 to organize the American Birth Control League.
More support was consolidated from the well-to-do, many of whom were
ardent libertarians, after police raided a meeting at Town Hall in which
many of "their own" were taking part.[3] Eventually the medical profession
would also endorse the league.

In 1921, Sanger organized the first American Birth Control Conference,
which was held in New York City. Her movement quickly spread to other
parts of the country as she traveled tirelessly to promote the creation of

birth control clinics. By 1930, there were fifty-five centers in twenty-three cities in twelve states, from Bangor, Maine, to El Paso, Texas.

In 1938, the courts removed a major barrier to the advancement of the birth control movement. Judge Augustus Hand of the Second Circuit Court of Appeals in New York handed down a reinterpretation of the Comstock Laws, allowing the public transport of "things which might intelligently be employed by conscientious and competent physicians for the purpose of saving life or promoting the well-being of their patients."[4]

For Sanger, such triumph was bittersweet. Her movement had taken hold, but she could no longer determine its direction. She had always been a radical, even a zealot, who had proposed an idea and worked singlemindedly to promote it. But the people she'd convinced to join her movement did not always share her priorities or her commitment. That reality was underlined in 1942, five years after her official retirement due to poor health. The leadership of the organization was now mostly in the hands of men, who changed the name from the Birth Control Federation of America to the Planned Parenthood Federation of America.

Sanger's purpose had always been to give women the ability to control their lives by controlling their fertility. She believed the euphemistic emphasis on "parenthood" rather than on the sexual and reproductive life of women was enough to undermine the social and political significance of her mission. The change of name alienated Sanger from the organization and the movement she'd devoted her life to building. In 1966 (the same year I began my graduate studies in midwifery), Margaret Sanger died, having lived to see the birth of another of the twentieth century's most important movements—the women's equal rights movement.

I hadn't previously discussed the possibility of my leaving the health department with Ruth Anne Yauger because (perhaps presumptuously) I didn't want to be talked out of it. The search committee had honored my desire for secrecy. Now I had to tell her. I wasn't looking forward to the task.

"I wanted to meet with you to tell you that I am planning to resign. I've accepted a position at Planned Parenthood to be their executive director."

"Oh, my," Ruth Anne answered, her eyes widening in surprise. "Is there anything we can do to keep you?"

Perhaps it was unfair of me, but I felt her words were simply rhetorical, a reflex response to the unanticipated news rather than a genuine effort to make me stay. But I was so relieved that the meeting wasn't going to be unpleasant that I hardly minded. My strength restored, I went on without qualms. "No. I've already accepted the position."

Ruth Anne smiled enigmatically and said, "We'll miss you," her words mingling with smoke from her cigarette. "Well, it will be a great opportunity for you, though," she added, smiling more enthusiastically. I began to suspect that she was more relieved than disappointed.

I walked back to my office feeling strangely ambivalent: sad that more hadn't been made over my decision, unsettled that she placed such emphasis on the great opportunity for me, and yet relieved that there hadn't been a scene. I felt keen satisfaction in having created and implemented the neighborhood prenatal program, the health component of the teenage pregnancy program, and the maternal and child health services within the department. Nevertheless, I knew Ruth Anne had been frustrated by the single-mindedness of my focus on the maternal and child health programs. She'd hired me to be her deputy, and had needed and tried to get me involved in helping her carry out the broader administrative demands of the agency's work. Although I had longed for the opportunity to implement the kind of changes that only an administrator could, I focused my efforts on the area where I'd had the bulk of my training—women's and children's health. I was neither mature enough nor professionally responsible enough to see the broader picture and devote a reasonable amount of attention to things that didn't interest me. Had I been, I might have made more of a contribution and I certainly would have been better prepared for what was to come.

Planned Parenthood of Miami Valley was located in East Dayton, a part of town where immigrants from the Appalachian Mountains of Kentucky and West Virginia had settled in hope of finding work at the General Motors or National Cash Register plants. The small, slightly ramshackle offices that the fledgling organization called its headquarters occupied the second floor of a two-story building and consisted of a cramped reception area, two offices, and two open cubicles that passed as offices. It would have been impossible to offer medical services at that location. They were carried out in mobile units.

Because the reception area opened onto the large area where most of the workers sat, everyone was able to watch as Pat, the assistant director who'd been temporarily in charge, greeted me.

"Here, let me show you to your office, then I'll introduce you to the staff," Pat offered. My office was a small room lined with imitation wood paneling, carpeted with a dark brown shag rug, and furnished with a Formica-topped metal desk, a black vinyl swivel chair, and two dark, tweed-upholstered side chairs. An air conditioner filled the lower part of the front window; above it, a double thickness of dirty panes further rationed the light. The long fluorescent ceiling lights cast their cold blue glow over my grim new home. I put my things down on the desk and followed Pat around the cramped space to meet my staff, who were polite but distant.

What transpired next was even more unnerving. Pat and I returned to my office to begin my orientation with the agency's operations. With a disquieting mixture of sympathy and thinly veiled delight at my discomfort, Pat told me that on my first day on the job, I was to prepare the next year's budget and write the federal grant requests. While I'd done some budget work before, I had no experience with anything on this scale. To make matters worse, the budget was due to the board in weeks, not months.

Then I understood. This was my first trial by fire, my introduction to intraorganizational power politics at Planned Parenthood. Pat was in control, and I had no choice but to depend on her to help me get the job done. This was not a good start. Yet I feared that if I appeared to panic, the message would get back to the board that I wasn't competent to hold the position.

If my master's degree and professional training as a nurse-midwife mattered at all to my new colleagues, they weren't letting on. No allowances were made for my age or my lack of administrative experience. My assistant director provided the program background for the budgets, but she had not carried full responsibilities, so there were limits to her knowledge about the overall operations. But young and inexperienced though I was, I also was old beyond my years at coping with unexpected situations: All those temporary homes I'd had to survive as a child had taught me how to size up situations and adapt to their realities, until I could either change them or get away from them.

It took only a few days to figure out that, for now, all loyalty here was to Pat. Her office was a beehive of activity, staff questions, reports, and chatting. Mine was a quiet, solitary place where I struggled with the budgets and a mountain of grant applications. Sometimes I'd stop by Pat's office to join in the conviviality; the conversations continued as though I were invisible.

While this was the first time I'd encountered such a cool reception, it wouldn't be the last. I sometimes found myself in my office in tears, frustrated by the discoveries of withheld information that could have helped me, terrorized by late-breaking crises that could easily have been contained much earlier. I was also learning another important lesson: Being the director didn't automatically earn respect from this group, or, for that matter, regard. I often longed for the camaraderie and the supportive professional atmosphere created by my former colleagues, but there was no turning back. Just as I had learned to live successfully with virtual strangers, and just as I had held my own, even excelled, in a different school every year, there was no doubt in my mind that I would succeed here.

I had to familiarize myself with our outreach programs. The Planned Parenthood clinics were set up much like the health department's neighborhood prenatal program. The mobile units that provided the medical services consisted of vans outfitted with all the equipment, supplies, and staff necessary to operate a birth control clinic at any location. They traveled to churches and community centers throughout six counties. A doctor—

usually a resident from one of the local, non-Catholic hospitals who was moonlighting to earn extra money—would perform the examinations and prescribe the appropriate methods of birth control. In later years, when attracting doctors interested in family-planning work became more difficult, we hired specially trained nurse-practitioners.

The mobile units had a set circuit, visiting the same location at the same time every month. Appointments were made by telephoning the main office; or women simply walked into the clinic. With our poster advertisements, the regular touring schedule, and word of mouth, people in the neighborhoods and towns where our vans stopped came to know when and where to expect us.

Difficult though I had found coping with the administrative rigors of running an agency, by the end of the first year things became more manageable. The tiny affiliate struggled through the difficulties new organizations face. Nevertheless our patient load and our budget were growing. The work consumed me—not the management aspects of the operation that I was rapidly mastering, but the cause Planned Parenthood served: empowering women to control their sexual and reproductive lives. I was also learning that we were pushing against society's deepest conflicts and taboos over sexuality and women. My position would force me to repeatedly test my commitment to the thornier aspects of the movement.

Throughout that demanding and lonely first year at Planned Parenthood, I sought solace in the life I'd made for myself outside work. When I'd first returned to Dayton, I hadn't rejoined the social whirl of my earliest days there. The Dayton scene seemed less exciting after the bright lights of New York City. Parties and nightclubs were not nearly so satisfying as spending time with old friends. I settled into a quietly domestic life of sewing, candlemaking, and learning to work with ceramics. On Saturday mornings my friend Lucille, one of the nursing supervisors at the health department, would come by. Lucille was a jovial, wonderful woman whose gold-capped teeth glistened against her dark skin. Together we'd spend the day prowling through fabric and crafts stores. By dusk, we'd return home laden with goods and dreams of the things we would make "to save money." Some of those things actually got made.

And of course there was Franklin. Shortly before moving to Planned Parenthood, I'd been invited to a community action conference sponsored by the Junior League, an organization I had resigned from a year or so earlier when the Dayton chapter decided not to endorse the Equal Rights Amendment. Not unlike countless other conferences bred of Great Society ideals, this one consisted of a series of panels and discussions—on this occasion, an exploration of ways to increase the collaboration between volunteer organizations and government agencies.

I was walking into an afternoon session when, behind me, a baritone voice inquired, "Hey, girl, have you ever played basketball?" References to my height were not unfamiliar—not since I was fifteen and had grown into my full height of almost six feet—and my back stiffened. I turned to address the offender with the cool glare and stony silence with which I met such rude questions from complete strangers. But when I found myself face-to-face with a tall, handsome man whose smile turned into a chuckle, then to a laugh at my indignation, I grinned sheepishly.

"My name is Franklin Gordon," he said, introducing himself, his voice bearing the trace of an East Coast accent and the cadence of the jazz musician that he was. As his heavy-lidded eyes surveyed me, I had to look away.

I suppose I must have mumbled something in reply, said my name or something, but to be honest, I was too dazzled by Franklin's charm and physical presence to remember much of what I said.

We spoke several times during the conference, and I learned that he ran a human relations program for the city of Grand Rapids, Michigan. One night during the cocktail hour, I watched Franklin as he played a few jazz tunes at the piano. I was taken by his sophisticated air; he seemed so different from the men I'd occasionally dated in Dayton. Ten years older than I, he came from a place where people of intellect, like the doctors back in Harlem, debated the issues of equality and rights.

After the conference, Franklin returned to his home in Michigan and I went on with my work in Dayton. I was startled and elated when I picked up the phone at work several days later and heard his voice at the other end of the line. Before long we were speaking regularly with one another, and through our long telephone conversations my attraction to Franklin grew. I learned that he'd graduated from Morehouse College in Atlanta, where he'd been active in the early days of the Student Non-Violent Coordinating Committee (SNCC). And since graduation, he'd worked within government agencies investigating race discrimination cases. I may not have been Black Panther material, but Franklin's intellectual militancy resonated with me. We had lively discussions about the political philosophies of Elijah Muhammad, Malcolm X, and Louis Farrakhan, about *Black Rage* and *Soul on Ice*. Before long, I was in love with Franklin. Six months after we'd met at that first convention, he and I met again. By this time we knew our feelings were mutual, and Franklin decided to move to Dayton.

Franklin didn't send me flowers, but he wrote me poems, and the notion of such a tenderness located somewhere within this large man tugged at me. I thought about what kind of a life I wanted to build. I was not looking for him to take care of me, but I felt we could have a life of sharing. We each had our causes: His lay in race relations, mine in the well-being of women. But there were other things, too: the pleasures we found in tooling around the back roads of Ohio in my shiny red Porsche, realizing our mutual love for antiques and for bargains at auctions and flea markets, and spending quiet evenings watching television. And though Motown was more to my taste, I gained some appreciation for the sophisticated jazz idiom that Franklin played and listened to.

I'd not been in any particular hurry to get married. My life was filled with the demands of career and community involvement; but with my twenty-ninth birthday coming, I realized I wasn't getting any younger. Franklin and I decided to get married. There was no dramatic moment to the decision, no moonlight, roses, or champagne. It just seemed like the right thing to do.

When I'd called my mother to tell her our plans, there was silence at the other end of the line. But I wasn't surprised. I'd known she wouldn't approve of my marrying outside the faith. "You'll be sorry," she said. "I know he comes from good people. Seventh-Day Adventists are clean living." But I knew the rest—he wasn't saved, and that meant that my distance from the Church of God, which in Mama's mind had already been established by the nature of my work and my lifestyle, would only grow. But just as religious differences had not stopped my mother's marriage to my father, so they would not stop mine to Franklin. We were deeply in love, and for me, that was sufficient.

At the end of August 1972, Franklin and I were married. We didn't have much money—we wanted to save for a down payment on a house, and Franklin was planning to go back to graduate school to get his master's in social work—so we slipped off to the justice of the peace. The gray official called his wife into his office to witness our vows.

As we walked out of the justice's small office, we laughed as we asked one another, "Do you think it's legal?" Afterward, we celebrated with a quiet dinner in a romantic Cincinnati restaurant that overlooked the Ohio River.

CHAPTER 13

THE NEW YORK REFORM:
A NEW DAY FOR WOMEN

"**I** just found this package of birth control pills in my daughter's dresser drawer and it's got Planned Parenthood's name on it," a woman's voice shrieked over the telephone.

I'd heard about such calls. The staff fielded them, and until this moment, when everyone else was out at the clinics, I'd been spared. I'd hardly had a moment to think of a response when the irate woman raged on. "What are you people doing? Did you give these pills to my daughter? I demand an explanation!"

I resorted to clinical protocol. "First," I replied calmly, "I cannot tell you whether your daughter is a patient of Planned Parenthood or not. In order to protect our patients' privacy, we never reveal their names."

"But I *demand* to know."

"I cannot say if she came to Planned Parenthood, but if she did, perhaps your daughter is trying to prevent an unwanted pregnancy," I said, trying to direct the woman's attention to the most important issue, as I saw it.

"But you're only encouraging her to have sex," she screamed into the receiver. If it was possible, she seemed even more furious than when we'd begun our conversation.

Maybe explaining would work. "When kids come to us—and I'm not saying your daughter came to us—they're usually already having sex, and doing so for a long time."

This woman was not about to be swayed from her rage by such generalizations. With flashing indignation, she countered, "I'm going to get a lawyer on you people. As a parent, I have a right to know. I'll charge you with assault and battery."

I hoped that it would calm her if I told her that I didn't think teenagers' having sex was a good idea either. I added, "But if your daughter is having sex, wouldn't it be even worse if she got pregnant?"

"Maybe it would teach her a lesson," she said as she slammed down the phone.

I understood all too well the difficulty of letting go of the notion of "teaching a girl a lesson." It had been the conventional thinking at the Daytime Center for Girls. But how could forcing a teenage girl to live through pregnancy, childbirth, and the lifelong responsibility of parenting, be judged an appropriate "lesson"? It was a punishment inflicted on two persons, not one. And the sentence was for life.

The essence of that phone conversation—the mother's anger, and my attempts at conciliation—played itself out over and over again at Planned Parenthood of Miami Valley. Sometimes, as in this case, it was birth control pills; sometimes it was an appointment slip for clinic services, or Planned Parenthood's logo on a pamphlet that they'd found in their daughter's room, that had provoked the parent's—most often, the father's—angry call. Daughters were the focus of concerns. I never heard a mother or father complain of finding condoms or Planned Parenthood literature in their son's room.

I always tried to remain calm while parents railed on about a conspiracy between Planned Parenthood and sexually errant children to undermine their authority. Sometimes after a few back-and-forth oral tussles, their anger would abate. Then I'd try to help them see that while their daughters might not be conforming to their moral standards, they were at least attempting to avoid becoming pregnant or contracting a sexually trans- mitted disease.

These conversations, whether they ended in a slammed-down phone or in tentative dialogue, were inevitably draining. And each conversation left me more convinced than before that teenagers not only needed a safe place to turn as they began to contend with their sexual maturation, but they also needed protection under the law.

In these years, as I was building on my understanding and confirming my personal values about the importance of our work in the day-to-day con- flicts over reproductive control, others were addressing the big picture of the laws that limited the decisions that women could make. The first step toward actual legal reform of abortion laws had been taken in 1962, the year Sherri Finkbine encountered so many obstacles to ending her troubled pregnancy. It was the passion of women—haunted by the continuing hor- rors of illegal abortion, the tragedies of babies born damaged by the

German measles epidemic and Finkbine's nightmare; liberated and empowered by the introduction of the birth control pill; and galvanized by agitation for the recognition of the equality of women set forth in the Equal Rights Amendment—that really set the wheels of reform in motion.

Although the Pill had empowered women to enjoy their sexuality with almost no fear of pregnancy, they still did not have full control over what happened if they found themselves pregnant when they didn't want to be.

In 1962 the American Law Institute (ALI) approved a Model Penal Code to permit abortion in cases of rape and incest, to preserve the physical or mental health of the woman, or to prevent the birth of a child afflicted by grave physical or mental deformity.

As much of an advance as this may have seemed, however, the revised ALI Code still did not leave the decision to end a pregnancy solely to a woman and her physician without government intervention. It required that all abortions be certified in writing by two physicians. That the panel of doctors was smaller than had been required before did not mean a woman could avoid the humiliation of appearing before arbiters who had the final say over a decision regarding her own body. It has always been clear that medical practitioners are, by tradition, a conservative lot when they stand to risk economic loss in the form of civil or criminal penalties. Only the most courageous and idealistic doctors were willing to consider the needs of these women above all else.

Nevertheless, with this measure of freedom in their hands, women began to articulate Margaret Sanger's message: that a woman's power, her equality, was inextricably connected to her ability to control her own life. With the energy and turmoil of the political and social revolutions of the Sixties as a backdrop, the campaign for reform was galvanized. By 1967, women's groups, students, individual activists, and health professionals were vigorously fighting for the reform or repeal of state abortion laws. Such groups as the Association for the Study of Abortion and the National Association for the Repeal of Abortion Laws (NARAL) were established. The National Organization for Women (NOW) added an abortion-rights plank to its platform and organized rallies outside state legislatures and courts. Women marched on the American Medical Association's national convention, demanding that the doctors sign a petition for abortion-law repeal. And in New York City, a feminist group called Redstockings held a "speak-out" where, for the first time, women spoke openly of their experiences with the horrors of illegal abortion.

The campaign gained momentum as large medical professional and human rights organizations came on board. For reasons as varied as their constituencies, the American Medical Association (which had been instrumental in criminalizing abortion in the first place), the American College of

Obstetricians and Gynecologists, the American Public Health Association, and the American Civil Liberties Union joined in the fight to decriminalize abortion. And in 1968 and 1969 the American Public Health Association and the American Medical Women's Association stepped in.

Given the force of its founder's convictions, Planned Parenthood was also a participant in the movement toward reform, although not aggressively so. In 1969, it released the following statement, culled from Margaret Sanger's memoirs, in which she had written:

> The optimum method of birth control is the consistent employment of effective contraception but in practice this goal is sometimes not achieved. It is, therefore, desirable that provisions respecting abortion not be contained in State Criminal Codes. Planned Parenthood believes that since abortion is a medical procedure, it should be governed by the same rules as apply to other medical procedures in general when performed by properly qualified physicians with reasonable medical safeguards.[1]

Perhaps the most profoundly humane statements made on the subject at this time came from the religious denominations. A number of them were involved in the Clergy Consultation Service, a network that helped women to obtain abortions, either illegally but safely from doctors in the United States who were willing to risk arrest, or in safe clinics abroad.

From 1965 on, such organizations as the Religious Action Center of Reform Judaism, the American Baptist Convention, the United Presbyterian Church, and the General Conference of the United Methodist Church all issued statements advocating abortion reform and affirming the principles of freedom, equality, and human dignity. In this astonishing period of activism, even traditionally conservative American institutions were moved by the drive for social justice.

With such pressures, a radical change in laws and institutions was inevitable. Clarity began to emerge in the struggle for reproductive rights in the years between 1967 and 1970, when twelve states reformed their abortion laws. In 1967, Colorado became the first, following the suggestions of the ALI's Model Penal Code.

Later in 1967, Ronald Reagan, then the governor of California, signed a law that was similar except for its exclusion of fetal deformity as a justifiable reason for abortion. Nearly all other "reform" states fashioned their laws more or less on the ALI model, although some "reforms," notably Georgia's, contained so many conditions that it made actually obtaining a legal abortion almost impossible.

Even in New York, a state where there had been long-standing support for legal abortion, reform was a fragile, setback-ridden process. Liberalization also gained momentum in 1967, when Al Blumenthal, a Democratic assemblyman from Manhattan, introduced a bill in the state legislature based on the ALI Model. The bill was defeated both in 1967 and 1968 because, as Blumenthal remarked, "apparently the political rule of the day [was] to abort abortion."[2]

Assemblywoman Constance Cook, a Republican from Ithaca, had supported the bill on what she called the "half-a-loaf theory"—it was better than nothing. To her, its defeat indicated much more than the opposition of organizations like the New York State Catholic Church Committee. The ALI-type reform simply hadn't fired the political ardor of zealous reformers, the frontliners of a revolution. "Women were not going to ask a man or anyone else whether they could have an abortion," she said.

Later in 1968, Cook got a phone call from a woman on Long Island who'd been actively lobbying for the reform bill, and the two arranged to meet with several other advocates for change. Cook summarized the session for me: "The women began, 'Well, we don't like the bill.' And I said I didn't like the bill at all. They said, 'Well, what we'd really like is outright repeal of the law.' I said, 'That's great. I would, too.' At the time, the idea seemed far-fetched. I didn't think it could be done, and I told them so. . . . But they asked, 'What would we have to do to get it passed?' I told them they'd need a real grassroots campaign all over the state. And that's what happened."

By January 1969, Cook and Franz Leichter, a Manhattan assemblyman, introduced a repeal bill at the same time that the Assembly was considering Al Blumenthal's expanded "half-a-loaf" bill.

After a fierce lobbying campaign on both sides of the issue, the Cook and Leichter repeal bill was passed. On April 11, 1970, Governor Nelson Rockefeller signed into law New York's revision of the sections of its penal code dealing with "homicide and abortion." New York became the only state to make abortion legal without restrictions. This reform—the most liberal abortion reform in the country—became effective two months before I took up my position at Planned Parenthood in Dayton.

Just as Sanger's movement that began in New York had sparked the creation of birth control clinics all over the country and fostered a revolution, so too the stunning new developments in New York generated intense interest in communities nationwide, including Dayton. I soon found myself called upon by groups who wanted to know how the changes had been accomplished and what they meant for women.

Armed with the facts as they were reported in the press and discussed at meetings with other Ohio Planned Parenthood executive directors who were beginning to help women travel to New York for legal abortions, and inspired by memories of suffering women whose futures would have been safeguarded by such reform, I began to publicly address an issue that had been shrouded in taboo and silence for longer than I had lived. Legal abortion was strange new terrain, still mysterious within the veil of shame where it existed. Nonetheless, the subject now stimulated intense interest.

On one noteworthy occasion, I was asked to be the keynote speaker and address the changes taking place in reproductive rights since the New York reform at a Founders' Day luncheon of an African American sorority. I felt comfortable in the elegant hotel dining room filled with fancy suits and flower arrangements. That one of the first formal speeches of my career would be received by an African American audience made me especially pleased. Several hundred women were gathered here—women who, for their lack of visibility in the activist ranks, were often characterized as being "out of touch" with the pro-choice movement, and thus allowing its detractors to classify the struggle as the folly of white, middle-class women.

Over the years I've spoken to hundreds of groups on a host of issues related to reproductive rights. While there have always been a few people of color in attendance, the audiences have been, by and large, middle-class whites. Speaking to a mostly African American audience is always what it was at that brunch in Dayton—a different experience for me. Out of shared tradition there is an understanding, a bond, between the audience and me. We know who is first endangered by sexual and reproductive oppression and the first to bear the most tragic consequences: poor women and teenagers. And that means a disproportionate number of African American women.

The audience sat in rapt attention as I talked about the revolution in sexual and reproductive rights, technology, and services. This forum would have been improbable even a year earlier. In this dignified setting, I expected the middle-class, primarily professional women to be restrained in their concern about such issues. But that day, they engaged me in dialogue during the question-and-answer session that was as frank as any I have ever participated in on college campuses.

They wanted to know the details. "Is the pill safe?" "What services does Planned Parenthood offer?" "How did the abortion law in New York get passed?" "What's going on here in Ohio?" "How can women from Dayton get abortions in New York?" Their interest was proof that the issue was important to them; and it was important to me to understand that.

Women's interest in controlling their fertility was not exclusive to white, liberal activists, nor to lower-income women. It was, and is, universal, crossing ethnic, racial, religious, educational, economic, and geographic boundaries. The realm of abortion was shifting from the back alley to the safety of the medical establishment, or at least to the periphery of it.

Reports by the renowned abortion researcher Christopher Tietze helped to shape Americans' understanding of the prevalence of illegal abortion.

Tietze, as a senior consultant to the Population Council, estimated that in the 1960s, one million women had had illegal abortions, with a death rate of 1,000 per 100,000 abortions.[3] No one would ever know how many women had been forced to carry unwanted pregnancies to term, although abused and neglected children who managed to get the attention of outside agencies offered some indication. Nothing—not statistics, not real-life scenarios, and certainly not our own imaginations—could have prepared healthcare providers for the numbers of women who would seek to end their unwanted pregnancies when illegal abortion *in one state* suddenly became history.

As powerful a role as the New York reform played in bringing about the collapse of the old order and saving the lives of women, it also created its own horrors. Because women flocked to the state from all over the country, abortion became a booming business for the enterprising—the scrupulous and the unscrupulous alike. Clinics and hospitals were swamped; overnight, new clinics sprang up. Some doctors set up shop in their offices.

Because it was virtually impossible for women from other states to find their way through this confusing maze, a host of intermediaries sprang up. They advertised in newspapers, magazines, the Yellow Pages, and on public transportation and billboards throughout the nation. "Your abortion is an operation. You'll require all the rest, comfort and compassion you can get," stated one. "Low cost, safe, legal ABORTION in New York/Scheduled immediately," read another. Another referral agency even hung a banner from a low-flying airplane that circled Miami Beach during Christmastime. "Abortion Information," it read, and displayed a New York telephone number.[4]

For a booking fee, sometimes more than a hundred dollars, these so-called referral services were supposed to make the arrangements for a woman's transportation to and from New York, her hotel room, and the abortion itself. Some were reputable and provided the services they promised, but many more were boiler-room operations that gave the caller nothing more than the number of the clinic with which the agency was "affiliated."

In theory, competition leads to lower prices. But theories didn't even come close to predicting what actually happened in New York. Given the tremendous demand, profiteering was inevitable. Park East, a clinic with an excellent reputation, had prices to match: $575 for an early abortion done on an outpatient basis. If the procedure was conducted in a private hospital, the obstetrician's and the anesthetist's fees could add another $300 to $400 to that figure. Then, of course, there was the referral agent's "cut."

By comparison, nonprofit clinics like those at Planned Parenthood of New York or Women's Services charged $200 to $300 for early abortions;

less if a woman couldn't afford it. Flower Fifth Avenue Hospital charged $450 for second-trimester saline abortions; while at Kings County Hospital, one of New York's larger public hospitals, the cost was $270, but only New York City residents were eligible. When all was said and done, a New York abortion could add up to around $640. And that didn't include the costs of travel, shelter, or meals.

Women who managed to pull together the resources for the abortion and related expenses still may not have anticipated all the costs. Sometimes it seemed that everyone who could take advantage of the woman's situation did so. Cabdrivers were paid to steer women to particular clinics.[5]

Undoubtedly the overwhelming majority of the 173,900 procedures performed in the first year after repeal were done in a safe and humane manner. However, in what had virtually overnight become a $150 million business, the potential for abuse was enormous—particularly since the changes had outpaced the state's ability to regulate and monitor the new facilities. A woman who called a "referral agency" had no way of knowing whether she was being directed to a safe, well-run clinic, or if she was being led to an unsafe "abortion mill" that was in business for profit, as had been true of illegal practitioners during the Prohibition era. With few exceptions, women who could not afford the quoted price were left to their own devices to make do.

The testimony of "Kathy D." at a hearing held by Manhattan borough president Percy Sutton is poignant witness to the desperate circumstances that some women found themselves in. Though not every woman was subjected to such a brutal experience, that any woman had to endure it at all—and in a legalized system, no less—showed the hardest and most inhumane edge of reform.

I, Kathy D., am 18 years old and live in a suburb of Boston. In late July when I discovered that I was pregnant, I called a referral service in New York City. They told me to contact Dr. Frank S. at his office on Park Avenue.

I called the doctor and his secretary told me the cost would be $300. It took me two weeks to get the money together, then I made the appointment, and my husband, brother and I came to New York. We had $343 and our return tickets to Boston.

The doctor said, yes, his fee was $300 but the hospital cost $275. We left his office and I was crying so much I couldn't see the buildings. We sold our bus tickets back. We called everyone we knew but we couldn't raise any more money. That night we stayed in Central Park. Early in the morning we saw some blood banks on 40th Street. We got $10 each for a pint of blood. Farther along the block was another blood bank. I was too dizzy to give more but Richie and Ken each got $20 more.

We spent another night in Central Park, very hungry, since we'd only had one hot dog each all day. The next day I kept throwing up and crying. We tried to beg but were too ashamed. That night we slept in Tompkins Square. The next morning we still needed $25 more. We called the doctor but he refused to lower his price. At that, my husband was so desperate he walked along St. Mark's Place trying to solicit a homosexual. Instead, he met a woman from Women's Liberation who lent us $25. Later we found out I could have had the abortion for much less, but neither the doctor nor the referral agency ever suggested I could get a cheaper one elsewhere.[6]

I can imagine the terror that I would have felt had I been in her place. Fortunately, Kathy D. had her husband and her brother to support her. Many women had no one.

Exactly what drove this couple to take such desperate measures was not revealed, but the willingness to face degradation and danger in order to end an unwanted pregnancy was not erased by a governor's pen. Just as they'd been hallmarks of the back alley, degradation and danger were, ironically, the hallmarks of lawful abortion, given that few options existed outside New York.

By February 1971, the media and women's and consumer groups had uncovered enough abuses in what Planned Parenthood of New York City called the "Abortion Racket" to prompt the Attorney General to hold hearings. Women complained not only about outrageous prices and inadequate care but also about graft.

In May of 1971, one "referral agency," Abortion Information Agency, Inc., was found guilty of brokering professional services, fee-splitting, and practicing medicine without a license. In an opinion later upheld by the appeals court, Judge Sidney H. Asch wrote: "The law which sought to emancipate women from servitude as unwilling breeders did not intend to deliver them as helpless victims of commercial operators for the exploitation of their misery."[7]

It took almost a year for lawmaking to catch up with the mercenaries, but on June 28, 1971, the governor signed a bill banning commercial "referral agencies." The new law restricted referral services to the medical profession and to nonprofit groups like Planned Parenthood and the Clergy Consultation Service.

But this wasn't the only problem besetting women who flocked to the state by the hundreds of thousands. Four months after the repeal, the *New York Times* reported that, according to city hospital statistics, as many women as ever were being admitted for complications of botched abortions. And there were horror stories associated with even hospital abortions, typically involving delays, misinformation, profiteering, and outright intimidation: A seventeen-year-old girl, seeking a $160, simple first-trimester abortion at a municipal hospital when she was nine-weeks pregnant, was told to come back in six weeks for an examination. The more complicated abortion she would then require would cost $325, paid in advance. When a low-income mother of three came to the hospital for her abortion, she was told: "We stick a needle in your belly to kill the baby." Still another woman was subjected to great suffering when she was asked "upon admission to a voluntary hospital, to sign a fetal death certificate as 'maternal parent of the deceased.' "[8]

The women who had the most traumatic experiences were those who had had second-trimester abortions (performed by injecting normal saline into the uterus to cause contractions and expulsion of the fetus and the surrounding tissue). They told about the emotional toll of lying in a hospital bed, sometimes without attendants, at the moment the fetus was expelled.

Eventually, the system got so out of hand—particularly in New York City, with its dense concentration of doctors and medical facilities—that the city instituted regulations to rein in the incompetent and unethical. Abortions could be performed only in hospitals, or in hospital-affiliated clinics, or in independent clinics that had blood banks, fully equipped operating rooms, laboratory and X-ray facilities, and a staff of obstetricians, anesthetists, and registered nurses. The unsafe, fly-by-night abortion providers could not meet such standards of safety and soon became a horror of the past.

Most of the more established Planned Parenthood affiliates in Ohio took an active role in making arrangements for getting women to New York. But the Dayton affiliate was largely funded by government grants. By federal law those monies could not be used to fund abortion-related activities, and our private funding primarily supported our administrative operations. When women called us, or were diagnosed with unwanted pregnancies in our clinics, we provided them with a list of three or four safe and reasonably priced clinics whose names we'd gotten from the local Clergy Consultation Service.

If we heard from these women again, it was after they returned from New York. Sometimes, they came to us for an examination, generally six weeks after the procedure, to make sure their bodies had healed properly and to get birth control. Most were satisfied with their experience. A few told us of the assembly-line atmosphere in the abortion clinics. Some had been discharged to return home while still medicated, nauseated, and sometimes bleeding. Airline attendants became the unsung heroines of the time, supporting women when they became sick on airplanes. We sometimes saw women with complications like continuous bleeding or infection because few doctors in Dayton were willing to get involved with "cleaning up" the complications of an abortion.

Nevertheless, in the three years preceding the *Roe v. Wade* decision, reform in New York, flawed though its practice often was, saved the health and lives of thousands of women. The New York model, requiring only that a woman give her consent to a licensed physician to perform an abortion up to twenty-four weeks of pregnancy or to save her life, became the lodestar for nationwide reproductive liberation.

Before long, the forces that had opposed the liberalization of the law geared up to repeal the reform. Even Richard Nixon got involved. In a letter dated May 6, 1972, to Cardinal Terence Cooke, head of the Catholic Archdiocese of New York, the president wrote, "I would personally like to associate myself with the convictions you deeply feel and eloquently express."[9] New York governor Nelson Rockefeller, who was then also Nixon's campaign manager for the state, and who had repeatedly said he would veto any repeal of the abortion law, was furious. Aides to the president later said that the letter was not supposed to have been released. But more likely, it was Nixon's bid to get Catholic support for his reelection campaign.

Certain to get the govenor's veto, the repeal of the abortion law passed the Assembly 79–68 and the Senate 30–27 on May 12. On May 13, Nelson Rockefeller made good on his promise to reverse the legislative action, saying, "I do not believe it right for one group to impose its vision of morality on an entire society."[10] But a governor's veto was a slim reed on which to hang a woman's right to choose abortion.

Meanwhile, in Congress Bella Abzug, the indefatigable representative from New York City, was trying to harness the pressure for reform in the states to get a pro-choice plank on the 1972 Democratic party platform. She was unable to persuade George McGovern to endorse her plan. But a little opposition has never stopped Bella; in fact, it usually has the opposite effect. She turned to her colleagues at the National Women's Political Caucus, and they caused a stir about the need for reform at the Democratic Convention.

Knowing the issue was making its way through the Supreme Court in the *Roe v. Wade* case, but also wanting to take advantage of the attention received by abortion rights activists at the convention, in 1972 Bella introduced legislation in the House, based on the constitutional right to privacy set forth in the First, Third, Fourth, Fifth, Ninth, and Fourteenth Amendments, that would establish a federal statute reforming state laws and prohibiting state interference in a woman's decision to terminate an unwanted pregnancy. (Senator Robert Packwood, R-OR, had introduced a similar bill in 1971.) But Bella's bill was still in committee when the Supreme Court decision in *Roe v. Wade* made it unnecessary.

CHAPTER 14

ROE V. WADE:
COMPLETING THE REVOLUTION

"High Court Rules Abortions Legal the First 3 Months"

—*New York Times* banner headline,
January 23, 1973, beneath another banner headline,
"Lyndon Johnson, 36th President, Is Dead"

On January 22, 1973, a little more than two years after I'd become the executive director of the Dayton affiliate of Planned Parenthood, Franklin and I turned on the evening news and there, amid somber reflections on the death of Lyndon B. Johnson, architect of the Great Society, came a bulletin announcing the Supreme Court's decision in *Roe v. Wade* and *Doe v. Bolton*. It was the end of illegal abortion as we knew it.

Looking back from the perspective of this thoroughly plugged-in age of CNN, E-mail, faxes, and the Internet, I find it hard to fathom how I could have been so startled by that news. When I spoke with other Planned Parenthood directors around the state the next morning, I found that we all shared the same sense of utter disbelief at the Court's sweeping decision. The national offices had communicated no strategy for addressing the implications of such a landmark decision.

In part, I attribute our surprise to the fact that the New York reform had taken a good deal of pressure off the need for nationwide reform. We knew that, although a woman might still suffer the indignity of exploitation and the discomfort of less-than-perfect medical care, she could, if she was able to get to New York—where the clinics were now more effectively regulated—obtain a safe abortion. Nevertheless, New York was a long way from California, Mississippi, and Idaho. In those places, and in the country at large, there were still more women facing unsafe abortions than not. Rather than asking ourselves "what if," we'd adjusted our vision to what seemed to be the realm of possibility. This does not justify our ill-preparedness for the *Roe* decision. As the head of a reproductive health-care agency, I should have been asking myself "what if" and planning contingencies.

I remember sitting in my second-floor office several days later, watching the cars flash by on the street below. The high court's decision seemed so distant, so far removed from my day-to-day concerns of running the affiliate. We were in the midst of negotiating for an office building to house the affiliate's rapidly expanding programs and its first stationary clinic. We needed space for surgical rooms in which to provide the male and female sterilization services we'd just added. And I had been devoting my attention to community outreach and education programs, while adding counseling services to our clinics. To Franklin's consternation, I'd often work late into the night trying to figure out how to make our budget work. Now that we were reaching nearly eight thousand women a year, there never seemed to be enough money to do everything that was asked of us.

I'd simply been working my way through the administrative weeds when suddenly the ground beneath them shifted. I would soon find myself snapped to attention.

The legal basis for the *Roe v. Wade* case dated back to 1859, when a law was enacted in Texas prohibiting abortion except when, as determined by a doctor, it would save the life of a woman.

The trail of the eventual nullification of this Texas law began in 1961 when Estelle Griswold, the executive director of the Planned Parenthood League of Connecticut, was accused of providing contraceptives to young couples. Her action was an open challenge to Connecticut's Comstock Laws, which since 1873 had prohibited the distribution and the use, even by married couples, of contraceptives. Mrs. Griswold and Dr. C. Lee Buxton, the medical director of the clinic, were convicted for their violation of the law. After the Connecticut Supreme Court of Errors affirmed their conviction, they took their case to the United States Supreme Court. They argued that the law violated their rights to privacy and free speech. However, it wasn't until some ninety years after Comstock, in 1965, that the Supreme Court finally ruled that a ban on the use of contraception was unconstitutional.

Eight years later, Justice Harry Blackmun, writing for the seven-to-two majority in *Roe*, concluded that the right of privacy set forth in *Griswold* was broad enough to include a woman's right to have an abortion, "whether it be founded in the Fourteenth Amendment's concept of personal liberty and restrictions upon state action, as we feel it is, or, as the District Court determined, in the Ninth Amendment's reservation of rights to the people."[1]

Blackmun may not have had to write the opinion at all if it weren't for "Jane Roe," an unmarried and pregnant Dallas woman, who wished to terminate her pregnancy. In 1970, her request was denied and she agreed to accept the offer of two young Texas lawyers—Sarah Weddington and Linda Coffee—to argue the case for her abortion before the Dallas Division of the United States District Court. In May of that year, the two lawyers, driven by the conviction, as Sarah later said, that "women [could] not make any decisions about their lives that [were] of true significance, about employment, family, anything else, unless they [could] decide under what circumstances to have children,"[2] argued that the Texas law violated a woman's right to privacy under the First, Fourth, Fifth, Eighth, Ninth, and Fourteenth Amendments to the Constitution.

On June 17, the court ruled in their favor. However, the court did not officially enforce its decision, citing the federal policy of noninterference with state criminal prosecutions. This left the Dallas District Attorney, Henry Wade, free to prosecute anyone caught performing an abortion. While seeking an abortion was no longer illegal, performing one was.

The district court's failure to grant an injunction, combined with Wade's defiance of the ruling, provided Jane Roe's lawyers with a strategic opportunity. Short-circuiting the regular appeals process, they went straight to the Supreme Court, seeking a court order to prevent any prosecutions on the basis that a state law had been declared unconstitutional, but local authorities were refusing to abide by it. On May 4, 1971, the Court announced that it would hear the case, along with a Georgia case, *Doe v. Bolton*.

Doe v. Bolton contested Georgia's reformed abortion law, which was based on the ALI model, and which permitted abortion in cases of danger to the life or health of the woman, grave fetal deformity, or incest. The case comprised twenty-four plaintiffs, including "Mary Doe," a twenty-two-year-old Georgia citizen who was pregnant, impoverished, and who already had three children, two of whom were in foster care; two nonprofit organizations that advocated abortion reform; and an assortment of doctors, nurses, clergymen, and social workers. Margie Pitts Hames, a Georgia lawyer, had brought the case to the United States District Court for the Northern District of Georgia, seeking both a declaratory judgment that the abortion statutes were entirely unconstitutional and an injunction against the enforcement. When the District Court did not comply, she, like Weddington and Coffee, took the case to the Supreme Court.

In its decision on these cases, the Supreme Court responded to the state of Texas's argument that life begins at conception with:

We need not resolve the difficult question of when life begins. When those trained in the respective disciplines of medicine, philosophy, and theology are unable to arrive at any consensus, the judiciary, at this point in the development of man's knowledge, is not in a position to speculate as to the answer.[3]

A woman's right to abortion was not unconditional, however. In an attempt to balance the woman's right to privacy with the state's authority to regulate and protect health and potential life, the Court further defined its position based on the three trimesters of pregnancy. During the first trimester, when abortion is safest, a woman, in consultation with her doctor, has the right to choose abortion free from any state regulation or interference. In the second trimester, the state's interest in preserving the health of the woman becomes "compelling," and the state may regulate abortion, but only to ensure the "preservation and protection of maternal health."[4] (Permissible regulations might include setting qualifications for the person performing the abortion, or the facility in which the abortion was to be performed.) The state's interest in protecting potential life may become "compelling" at the point of viability, when the fetus can survive outside the uterus, roughly at the beginning of the third trimester. After viability, the government can limit or ban abortions, but never when the woman's life or health are threatened. Thus, the Court ensured that even when the state has the most power to regulate abortion, concern for the fetus can never take precedence over the life and health of the woman. At one stroke, the Court's decision had rendered unconstitutional and thus unenforceable all restrictive state laws then on the books.

Although on the surface the opinion was remarkable, those within Planned Parenthood who had been involved with the reform movement, as well as those of us who could take no credit for it, were suspicious that the few restrictions that the Court gave the states power to enact would be used against women to frustrate their will and prevent them from exercising their right. And even where state power didn't get in the way, a woman's decision to have an abortion in the first trimester was contingent on a consultation with her physician, which meant a physician could still be an obstacle to a safe, legal abortion.

Ironically, a hundred years earlier, when women had far fewer legal rights, they had more power over this particular aspect of their fertility. Until the late nineteenth century, abortion legislation and practice in the United States followed British common law: Abortion before "quickening," usually during the fourth or fifth month of pregnancy, was not a crime; in fact, pregnancy was not considered proven until the woman felt the fetus move. While abortion after quickening was criminal, it was never considered murder, and judges consistently ruled that the woman involved was not punishable. So pregnant women were regularly treated for "menstrual blockage," or they sought a cure for "cold."

Most of the laws against abortion in the United States were enacted during the Comstock crusades between 1860 and 1880. But Comstock wasn't the only one who'd fought against a woman's right to have an abortion. The American Medical Association had launched a concerted campaign to prevent "irregular" or uncertified doctors, many of whom were women, from performing abortions on the ground that the procedure was simply too dangerous for untrained hands. (The campaign probably had less to do with public safety than with a desire to shut out the competition.)[5]

Behind the AMA's proclaimed reasons and ulterior motives lay the same contempt for women that fueled Comstock's rage, the same fear of what would happen if women had the power to control their own reproductive lives. Nothing made it clearer than the *1871 Report of the AMA Committee on Criminal Abortion:*

> Admitting . . . the fashionable view that young females are restrained from sinning owing to the fact that they dread detection and exposure, what will be the effect when they are informed that . . . exposure is no longer a . . . consequence—that the timely interference of an abortionist will . . . do away with all such unnecessary scruples. . . . [I]f they are restrained from sinning . . . by fear of exposure, they also avoid the horrid crime of foeticide, which . . . must necessarily follow.[6]

Those words were written in 1871. In 1992, Pat Robertson, head of the Christian Broadcasting Network and erstwhile presidential candidate, in a letter paid for by the Christian Coalition of Chesapeake, Virginia, and sent to households around the country, declared: "The feminist agenda is not about rights for women. It is about a socialist, anti-family political movement that encourages women to leave their husbands, kill their children, practice witchcraft, destroy capitalism and become lesbians."[7]

At the end of the nineteenth century, the combined forces of Comstock's zeal and the ostensible determination of the private medical establishment to preserve women's safety convinced the American public that abortion had to be stopped. So pervasive was that conviction that even as Margaret Sanger's campaign for birth control made strides, abortion remained virtually unmentionable. Banished to the back alleys, the constitutional right to end an unwanted pregnancy did not exist until Jane Roe and her lawyers brought the issue to the Supreme Court.

Many have argued, as they did after the New York repeal, that the same legal recognition of abortion granted by *Roe v. Wade* would eventually have been achieved had the process of reform at the state level simply continued. They concluded that by preempting the give-and-take of legislative debate, the Supreme Court (and in particular Justice Blackmun, who wrote the decision) practically invited the backlash that rose up against it.

There is no evidence to justify that argument. Between 1970 and 1973, only one state, Florida, had reformed its abortion laws and adopted an ALI-type bill in response to a ruling of the state Supreme Court—hardly a testament to the state legislative process or the cumulative momentum for reform. More ominously, in some states, efforts to repeal the so-called "ALI reforms" that had progressed so steadily between 1967 and 1970 were under way. Opponents to reform were popping up like toadstools after a rain around my uncles' sawmill in Mississippi.

No sooner had the *Roe* decision been handed down than our phones began to ring off their hooks with women asking whether they could get an abortion at Planned Parenthood. We responded: "We have no plans to open an abortion clinic at this time. You can call your doctor or the Clergy Consultation Service." The truth was that, while I'd thought about how our new facilities could easily accommodate surgical services, I'd not so much as raised the question of what we'd do if abortion became legal with my staff and board.

Some might conclude that I was uncomfortable with the subject. But I wasn't, even though according to my mother's faith abortion is among the most serious of sins. The suffering of women who had been forced to endure unwanted pregnancies and the dangers for those who had sought to end them—the women I'd met and heard about over the years, and the hundreds of thousands of women whose stories I'd never known—had long before taught me a pragmatism that transcended my personal, religious, and ethical beliefs. But in Dayton, in 1973, I wasn't connecting my convictions with my work at the affiliate or women's newly recognized right. Had we been more actively involved in helping women get to New York, or had the national organization issued a rallying call encouraging us to integrate pregnancy termination into our programs, I'm sure that my unconscionable fogginess would have cleared and I would not have blundered so badly.

I was soon made to feel embarrassed for my lack of awareness. In the spring after *Roe v. Wade* was handed down, I got a call from Anita Wilson, a woman I knew, mainly through her work with the Dayton Clergy Consultation Service. "We're thinking about opening a first-trimester abortion clinic," she told me. "But first we want to know what Planned Parenthood plans to do. We'd like to come in to discuss it with you."

I asked Cheri Liskany, the supervisor of our clinics, to join Anita and her colleague Laurie Heindel in my second-floor office. Anita got right to the point. "We don't think Dayton needs two abortion clinics. If Planned Parenthood plans to establish a clinic, we'll probably abandon our thoughts of opening one. What do you plan to do?"

Not wanting to reveal that we hadn't even discussed the possibility, I bluffed my way around her question. "Well, of course we will be discussing it further, but at this point we don't know what we're going to do."

"How could you not know what you plan to do?" Anita asked, coming at me with incredulity.

She was right, of course. How could we not know? The Supreme Court, in making abortion legal, had just given the go-ahead not only to making abortion safe, but to bringing it into the mainstream of medical care. To the best of my knowledge, these two women were not trained health professionals. They and other activists like them had been helping women by lobbying and bringing lawsuits. Although I'd been in the trenches, and had witnessed the destruction of women's health, they understood what I had not—that though women now had the constitutional right to choose to end a pregnancy safely, it was a hollow promise if they had no way to safely take action on that choice.

After more discussion about whether their clinic could be sufficiently profitable if we became a competitor, I told them that I'd discuss the matter with my board. We ended the meeting amicably.

Cheri and I returned to my office after the women left.

"Ms. Wattleton, I think it would be a good idea if we started a clinic," said the large-framed nurse with big brown eyes.

I was startled. It was the first time we'd spoken about the possibility in other than theoretical terms. But obviously she'd given it some deeper thought; after all, the burden of implementing an abortion service would fall most heavily on her shoulders.

"Why do you say that?" I asked, trying not to sound surprised.

"Well, I think that it would be good for us to offer the service to our patients. That way we wouldn't have to keep referring them somewhere else. We should take care of them ourselves."

Unlike the women who'd just left, two activists soon to become clinic operators, we were two nurses trained to care for patients. Cheri saw abortion as an extension of the birth control services we already provided, a way of serving women more completely. I did, too. Contraceptives failed, and people weren't always perfect, especially when caught up in moments of passion. Women got pregnant who would do anything not to be.

"With our new surgery rooms, recovery room, laboratory, and some additional equipment, it wouldn't take much to operate a clinic once a week," Cheri assured me.

"Do you think the clinic staff would support it?" I asked.

"We haven't talked about it, but not all of them would have to be involved. We could schedule the ones who volunteered. I'm sure that enough would want to do it to cover the clinic. We'd only need one doctor, a nurse, and a couple of assistants. Our surgical rooms meet the state's requirements."

She was right. In July of 1973 we'd moved our offices to a low, three-story postwar structure with pink-and-blue art-deco panels under expansive windows. With our name and our newly designed logo in place over the entrance, we were establishing ourselves as a visible presence and a stable agency in the community. We had space for a stationary clinic and vasectomy services, and we now had adequate facilities to extend our services to include abortion.

Before approaching the board, I spoke with Dr. Alan Baker, the medical director of the affiliate, to find out what he thought about our offering abortion services, and whether he would be willing to recruit doctors to perform the terminations. He said he would think about it and discuss the matter with his wife.

In the meantime, since they hadn't gotten a definitive answer from us, in August, Anita Wilson and Laurie Heindel opened the Dayton Women's Health Center. They performed abortions up to the tenth week of pregnancy for a fee of $175.

Shortly before the board meeting, Dr. Baker called me back to say, "Faye, I'm sorry. I can't be involved. My wife does not want me to be known as an 'abortionist.' If you go ahead with the service, I may have to resign."

I was stunned and frustrated that he used his wife's objection as his reason for opposing our proposed abortion services. Dr. Baker had a lot of influence in the medical community. The prospect of his affiliation being severed over this issue was not a pleasant thought. I felt certain that the board would not agree to establish abortion services if it would result in his resignation. Nevertheless, if I didn't press ahead, we'd be bowing to the pressures of shame still cast upon a woman's newly recognized right.

Planned Parenthood of Miami Valley, like most Planned Parenthood affiliates, had been formed by a group of people committed to serving the poor in their community and had been blessed with the means and the connections to launch a new organization to carry out this mission. The board was not made up of social activists, but rather of individuals from Dayton's power structure: businessmen and -women, lawyers, educators, and women who considered themselves "professional volunteers." Their reasons for serving on the board varied widely, but for the most part, providing birth control services for the poor was their primary concern.

Conservative though their views sometimes were, the board had supported every proposal I'd brought before it: from providing support to train nurses to be nurse-practitioners to expanding our educational programs into a center for the training of family-planning professionals from developing countries. The new building was a major commitment. However, I don't mean to suggest that we had a rubber stamp board. My proposals were thoroughly studied and discussed. Still, I calculated that I could persuade them to support the development of an abortion clinic.

My instincts told me that the subject would be controversial and to approach it carefully, practically, and with restraint. At the meeting, I described the needs of our patients based on the inquiries that we were receiving. Then I outlined the steps for setting up a clinic. Finally, I broached the difficulty in getting physician coverage. I concluded: "If we don't offer the service, others will, and some of our patients may not continue coming to us."

I quickly discovered that in the minds of the board members, abortion was not seen as a logical extension of our services; it was something very different. Trying to persuade the board that we ought to provide services to end unwanted pregnancies was altogether different from persuading it to provide teenagers with pills without their parents' knowledge or to offer vasectomies. They listened to my proposal, but made no decision one way or the other. After the meeting, Fred Smith, the board president and chairman of the Huffy Corporation, said he thought that the board would be open to discussing the matter, but he could make no predictions about the outcome.

I decided to call Frankie Stein to ask for her help in persuading the board to approve the proposal. Frankie headed the small unit at the national office assigned to work with affiliates who were considering whether to offer abortion services. I knew that there was a loan fund for affiliates that needed financial assistance in opening abortion clinics. It was established with a $400,000 grant from the Scaife Family Foundation and a $600,000 line of credit from Citibank. Frankie enthusiastically agreed to come to Dayton to meet with the board.

Instead of giving us a step-by-step recipe for opening an abortion clinic, Frankie gave a brief overview of what other affiliates were doing. Then she moved into a series of probing questions.

"If there was no statistical evidence to support the need to provide abortion services, would you provide them?" she asked.

"Would you provide these services because they would offer continuity with the rest of the care you provide your patients?" (This was a variation on the theme Cheri had sounded.)

"Would you provide services because Planned Parenthood is recognized for its excellent services, and abortion is in the range of your other medical services and should be offered to the community according to the same standards?"

"Would you provide abortion services because it is your responsibility to do the right thing?" she asked.

I had no qualms about answering yes to each of Frankie's challenges. They all touched upon my instincts to provide the best and most comprehensive services to our patients. But as I looked around the room, I saw only solemn faces. The board was used to hearing facts. They were not prepared, however, to probe their own beliefs about abortion. No one challenged the young woman. No one stood up to say, "I'm against abortion," or "Abortion is murder." Neither did anyone embrace it and say, "Abortion is a service, now legal, that women need, and we should provide it."

Frankie's provocative questions seemed to stimulate thought more than inquiry. Although she did most of the talking that day, she never got to "Now that you've decided to offer abortion services, this is how you set them up . . ." For she knew, wisely, that until the why of it was settled, it wouldn't matter how well we implemented the service, because there would be prolonged internal dissension.

Years later, Frankie would remember that "it took a committed executive director, at least one committed board member, and at least one committed doctor to get abortion services started." As far as I could see that day, we had met only one of the three necessary criteria.

At subsequent board meetings, discussion circled warily around Frankie's four questions. At the heart of the board's reticence, I suspect, there lurked that sadly persistent sense that, whether it was legal or not, abortion simply was not "respectable."

As New York had done for the rest of the country in the few years before *Roe*, the opening of Anita and Laurie's Dayton abortion clinic relieved us of immediate pressure. We could still have our book fairs and our recipe-tasting and wine-sipping events, but the board's inaction conveyed the message that providing abortion services was something that "people like us" did not do. At the very least, we shouldn't be one of the first in line to offer such services.

But the board's unwillingness wasn't the only catch. Dr. Baker had told us that not only would he not recruit and supervise doctors, he wouldn't oversee the development of operation protocols for abortion procedures. I was certain that pushing him to the point of resignation would cause strife on the board and have repercussions, especially in the medical community. Although violence didn't yet play a large role in our discussions, as reports of the actions of the forming backlash to *Roe v. Wade* began to circulate, we were becoming aware of the disturbing opposition to abortion's legalization. The pro-criminalists were not about to let the Court have the final word. Fred Smith kept pointing out that we now occupied our own freestanding building. "What is there to prevent someone from planting a few sticks of dynamite?" he asked.

If my work at the Dayton Health Department had shown me what it was like to realize a dream, I now understood that simply having a vision didn't mean being allowed to implement it. But if my affiliate would not provide abortion services—at least not yet—women could go to the new Dayton Women's Health Center, south of town.

As it turned out, most Planned Parenthood affiliates were no more eager than mine to embrace abortion services. Moral questions aside, our reliance upon government grants that prohibited abortion-related activities chilled nascent enthusiasm. Some of the larger affiliates didn't feel so constrained. The Houston affiliate, for example, started its service the day after the decision came down. Affiliates in California, Texas, New York, Minnesota, and even nearby Cincinnati also reacted swiftly. And Planned Parenthood of New York City, experienced in performing abortion since the New York reform that preceded *Roe v. Wade*, became the clinic upon which other affiliates modeled their programs.

In the nation at large, the existence of clinics established primarily to provide abortion helped perpetuate the notion that the procedure was still not "legitimate." Even though some Planned Parenthood affiliates provided abortion services, the federation's lack of unity on this crucial issue perpetuated the negative perception. If Planned Parenthood's national leadership had taken a more aggressive stand and urged all affiliates to provide abortion services, the "respectability" of the organization might have established it as an integral part of reproductive healthcare before the opposition to legality consolidated and took hold. We had the structure and the facilities; we had the credibility of history; we had the tradition of excellent services firmly established in communities throughout the country. The effect could have been profound. Instead, in the face of the most important breakthrough for women's liberation of the twentieth century, the nation's principal family-planning provider largely equivocated into the ambiguity of "Not now." And I sat squarely in its midst.

In fact, the national leaders were actually congratulating themselves that Sanger's vision was now a reality, at least in the United States. I first realized this at a meeting of executive directors of the thirty-five largest Planned Parenthood affiliates, in Montecito, California. The chairmen of the board and the executive committee came to speak with us about our concerns about the state of the organization. The Pill had made contraception almost perfect; the federal family-planning program was providing it and other contraception to low-income women and teenagers; abortions were now legal. What was there left to do? They concluded that we now needed to mount a strong international initiative aimed at helping developing countries to limit their populations.

There I sat, feeling that my affiliate and most of the others were not doing all we could to make the promise of the Court's decision a reality for women in the United States, while the national office was setting its sights on the women of Africa and India. I needed help making Planned Parenthood's mission a reality in my city, not a vision for some far-off land. Something wasn't right about this picture.

The freedoms provided by the birth control movement had brought the sexual revolution to its peak, and some people were holding Planned Parenthood responsible. Despite our abdicating our right to provide abortion services after *Roe v. Wade*, my affiliate became the lightning rod for Dayton's budding backlash.

In mid-1976, I learned that our work was being condemned as immoral, evil, and destructive from the pulpit of the Sacred Heart Roman Catholic Church, two blocks up the street from the affiliate. Father Roger Griese was the parish priest of the church. In his sermons, it was reported that he repeatedly characterized our programs as encouraging sexual promiscuity and moral degeneration. Anti–Planned Parenthood literature was distributed at Sunday masses, and donations were solicited to support the church's antiabortion activities. And Father Griese did not confine his one-man campaign to the walls of Sacred Heart; he promised to show up at county commission meetings, and to oppose Planned Parenthood's funding.

At the time, I was unaware that Father Griese's activities were part of a pattern forming in Catholic parishes throughout the country, part of the Pastoral Plan of the American Conference of Catholic Bishops. But I soon heard similar tales from executive directors around the country. Ann Mitchell at the Cincinnati affiliate was under especially heavy fire from the archdiocese there.

In the spirit of informing Father Griese about Planned Parenthood's programs, I invited the fervently outspoken man to visit our offices. I hoped that if he learned more about what we did, he would, at the very least, stop condemning our work. Perhaps he would even support us on some points.

Cheri and I listened, dismayed, as Father Griese made it forcefully clear that as far as he was concerned, there was no redeeming value in Planned Parenthood's philosophy, let alone its programs, even if we never provided abortions. He warned that unless we announced our commitment to teach that marriage was the only acceptable circumstance for having sexual intercourse, he would continue to publicly denounce us. Father Griese, who had been married before he decided to enter the priesthood, went on at great length about the sacredness of marriage and the family. As if in evidence of his current celibacy, he raised his large beefy palms and declared that since the loss of his wife, "these hands [would] never touch female flesh again." He also wanted us to know that in addition to speaking out against us at every opportunity, he would do all he could to see that our funding from the county government was cut off.

I looked at him in utter amazement. His words reminded me of my mother's many sermons on the dangers of "the flesh." But even more, they elicited memories of her warnings about "the Church of Rome." According to Mama, it was "a political institution, not a religious denomination." Preparing for the Second Coming of Christ (which could happen at any moment) didn't include getting involved in politics. The aim of the Catholic Church, she insisted, was to conquer and politically dominate the world. As such, it was a force to be feared as much as communism.

By the time I encountered Father Griese, I had long since rejected Mama's characterizations as exaggeration, if not religious bigotry. But at that moment, sitting across from him, anger welling up inside me, I found it hard to dismiss her views. As his polemic continued, I struggled to remain calm. When our meeting drew to a close, I thanked him for coming and escorted him to the door. I realized that I had just been given a glimpse into the heart of this issue, and it wasn't just about abortion. Father Griese didn't rail about the evils of "killing innocent life." His focus had been on sex outside of marriage and the dangers of touching a woman's body. I concluded that the problem was really about his own repugnance toward women being sexual. Abortion was just the flashpoint. The real worries ran deeper. If women's bodies were released from the intrusions of governmental and religious edicts, society (and the Father Grieses of the world) would be forced to acknowledge the power of a woman freed from reproductive constraints.

As fanatical as his actions may have seemed to me in 1976, Father Griese's enunciations were entirely consistent with the Catholic Church's reaffirmation of its views on sex, contraception, abortion, and women. In 1968, Pope Paul VI had issued *Humanae Vitae [Of Human Life]*, condemning all artificial birth control, sterilization, and abortion. Far from being the anticipated official confirmation of the liberating trend in the Church that had begun with Vatican Council II, it was a giant step backward into a rigid past.

More than being a rejection of the sexual and reproductive revolution of the Sixties, this was seen by many Catholics and non-Catholics alike as a harsh rejection of the challenge the women's movement posed to the traditionally subordinate role of women in the Church and in society. Unwilling to trust the moral strength of its teachings to compel its followers to lead lives faithful to its doctrines, the Church decided that a more powerful incentive was needed. Compulsory pregnancy and childbirth would not only continue to restrict women, but also punish them for transgression.

The Catholic campaign against family planning and birth control had begun in the United States even before *Humanae Vitae*. In 1965, after *Griswold*, the National Conference of Catholic Bishops had created a family life division to run a campaign against contraception. Ten years later, in 1975, the conference issued the Pastoral Plan for Pro-Life Activities "to shape our laws, to protect the life of all persons including the unborn." Formally moving the Church into U.S. politics, the Pastoral Plan consisted of three parts: an education and public information campaign; a "pastoral" effort toward women who had been personally involved in abortion decisions; and a "public policy effort directed toward the legislative, judicial and administrative areas so as to ensure effective legal protection for the right to life."[8] It was the blueprint for the grassroots activities in parishes across the country—including, of course, Dayton. Mobilized to achieve the plan's antiabortion objectives, Catholic activists eventually organized under the banner of the National Right to Life Committee.

By the time Father Griese's campaign was in full gear, a similar backlash was growing in East Dayton, among Appalachian immigrants. They had brought Protestant fundamentalism with them from the mountains of Kentucky and the hollers of West Virginia. I was very familiar with this clear and rigid brand of religion in which all issues were boiled down to right and wrong, good and evil, righteousness and sin.

But at that point East Dayton was not a political force in the community, and the vociferous evangelical ministers in small neighborhood and store-front churches were generally ignored by the political elite—at least until 1976. Then, in a drive led by a fundamentalist Protestant minister, Reverend Estrich, candidates running from East Dayton gained control of the school board on the platform of "Save Our Children." The stunned liberal establishment was wholly displaced.

The new school board demanded that "Planned Parenthood be banned from the schools." Our sex education programs, they charged, were teaching kids to have sex, so that we could then distribute birth control pills to them. The truth was that we did not actually operate any programs in the schools. We simply served as a resource to teachers and made presentations to students when invited.

This new phenomenon, which would later be called the Religious Right, had scored a major upset, and the shock resonated throughout the community. East Dayton's fundamentalist Protestant influence could no longer be denied. Soon, its disciples began attending county commission meetings, calling for a return to "traditional values," which meant no more county funds for Planned Parenthood.

From its beginnings in 1965, Planned Parenthood of Miami Valley had enjoyed broad community support and the backing of the Montgomery County Health Commissioner, Dr. Robert Vogel. In fact, fearing controversy, he had recommended that all federal family-planning funds flow to Planned Parenthood. He later persuaded the county commissioners to allocate funds, not for medical services but for educational programs.

Before long, the voices of the anti-choice activists from different sides of town joined together to form a powerful ideological alliance for a common social agenda. Planned Parenthood became a popular target for denunciation in their pulpits and public forums. Even though we still did not provide abortions, our affiliate's events, and sometimes the clinic itself, began to be picketed by antiabortion activists.

Father Griese, joined by his East Dayton compatriots, showed up at the county commission meeting where we were present to ask for the renewal of our small county grant. The bombastic priest stood at the lectern in the hearing room and accused the county of encouraging teenage promiscuity and promoting immorality if they continued to give us any money whatsoever.

Dr. Vogel, who was also Catholic, stood up after Father Griese's tirade and spoke strongly in favor of continuing to fund Planned Parenthood. His arguments before the commission, and ours, carried the day. Our grant was safe—for this round. Relieved, Konrad Reisner and his wife, Else, who had accompanied me to the hearing, and I pulled our papers together and headed toward the door. Somehow, we ended up in the same elevator as Father Griese. As the elevator reached the first floor, Konrad, ever the gentleman, said, "We'll walk you down to your office, Faye."

"Oh, you don't need to do that," Father Griese called. "We're not going to hurt her."

"At least our opponent has a slight sense of humor," Konrad muttered as we walked out of the building.

CHAPTER 15

WORKING MOTHER

Franklin, being ten years older than I, was anxious to start a family soon after we were married. I had not been so eager. In fact, when he first mentioned the idea, I thought it was just this side of insanity. I was struggling to meet every new demand of my job with Planned Parenthood: coping with my own inner drive to meet women's needs, managing the Dayton affiliate's growth and raising the visibility of our programs in the community, and allocating what had grown to be a budget of one million dollars.

We had just bought our first home, an eight-room English Tudor–style house. As much as we loved this new home—its stained-glass windows, warm wood paneling, and big fireplace—we were struggling to pay for it and the few repairs that it really needed. Franklin was commuting to Ohio State, where he was working toward his master's degree in social work, and could contribute to our budget only his stipend and the money he made playing the piano on weekends at private clubs. Two evenings a week, I worked at a prenatal clinic at a neighborhood health center to help make ends meet. I simply could not risk the possibility of a pregnancy jeopardizing my gainful employment and our financial stability. And I wasn't sure I was ready to give up our way of life as a childless couple, not after just a year. We could come and go as we pleased, our only concern being whether or not our pets were fed.

We had a choice. We waited another year.

But by the end of 1974, at the age of thirty-one, I, too, was aware that time was passing, and felt ready to expand our twosome. Franklin had begun to work in his field in the spring, and I told him that I thought the time had come. I'm not sure who I was trying to convince, him or me. Prospects of the unknown did not thrill me. True, I'd helped many women adjust to motherhood, but the chief lesson I had derived was that each experience was unique. What would it mean to me? How would it be unlike anything I'd ever seen? And what effect would it have on our marriage, which still seemed so new? The answers to these questions I did not know.

"Are you sure you want to do this?" I asked Franklin one evening when we were doing the supper dishes.

"Yeah, I'm ready," he answered with a sly smile.

Once we'd made the decision, there was no going back.

By late January 1975, I suspected that I was pregnant and made an appointment to see Dr. Baker, who was also my gynecologist. Franklin took me to the appointment and waited outside in the car. When I returned, half an hour later, I had only just closed the car door before exulting, "My test was positive. I'm due in October."

Franklin responded with a quiet "I need to get used to the idea." I had been hoping for joy and celebration, and his response, so low-key for something we both had wanted, was a letdown. Maybe his earlier enthusiasm had given way to the sort of uncertainty that I had felt before. Whatever the reason, our ride home wasn't spent in excited planning for the baby, but in the usual, safer conversation about work and our recent acquisitions for our home.

The beginning of my pregnancy was, in every respect, a normal one— including the misery of the so-called *morning* sickness, only I suffered with profound nausea from the moment I woke in the morning to the moment I lay down to sleep at night. Dr. Baker wanted me to take the drug Bendectin to ease the discomfort. I refused. Not wanting anything to harm my fetus, I took nothing stronger than multivitamins. (Bendectin has since been implicated in causing birth defects.) The wretched feeling stopped three months to the day from the start of my pregnancy.

Then, at about the fourteenth week, I started spotting dark blood. It wasn't a lot—but it was more than enough to frighten me about the possibility of a blighted fertilized egg, or damage to the fetus from an interruption in blood supply. Fearing miscarriage, I called Dr. Baker and he asked me to come to his office. As I carefully maneuvered myself off the examining table, I felt fragile, fearful.

"Now listen," he said. "I want you to take it easy and I don't want you dieting." He recommended that I take supplemental hormones and reassured me that, with some bed rest, I should be fine. "The hormones will make the placenta that is lying in the lower part of your uterus stick to the sides a little better. . . . You're just a little old to be doing this," he added with a chuckle.

When I looked at him in feigned indignation, he replied, "You're a nurse-midwife. You know that age increases the chance of a low-lying placenta."

Yes, I did know, but this was *my* pregnancy. *I* was having a baby.

Dr. Baker's casual manner didn't comfort me, but I accepted the direction. We agreed that if the bleeding got any worse, we would discuss whether the pregnancy should continue. Franklin and I decided that if the bleeding did not stop, we would terminate the pregnancy rather than risk having a severely damaged child who might suffer as I'd seen such children suffer. Fortunately, it was a choice we didn't need to make.

That night, I called Mama and asked her to pray for us. I took a few days off and stayed in bed. The bleeding stopped.

As the pregnancy progressed, my bonds with the life developing inside me grew stronger. In the middle of the night, I'd be awakened by movements—kicks and punches. By the eighth month the two of us would embark upon an unspoken dialogue while Franklin slept beside us. With each stretch that pressed hard against my bladder as if to make sure that I was awake, I would search in vain for a position of comfort until quiet settled in again.

As a seasoned hand at labor and delivery, I could have forgone Lamaze classes, but in body and mind I was not a nurse-midwife; I was a pregnant woman. I dragged my reluctant husband to the classes so that someone else could teach us to do what I had taught so many couples to do. It wasn't that Franklin was hostile to the idea of Lamaze class; men of his generation simply were not conditioned to do such things. In the mid-Seventies the shift toward family-centered maternity care, in which the father was involved in most aspects of pregnancy and birth, was relatively new.

Franklin was shown how to use pillows to support me in different positions and instructed on how to detect a contraction so that he could help me to breathe deeply, relaxing the abdominal muscles around the uterus. And he was warned about the difficulties of the final stage, when the baby started to move out of the uterus through the short passage to independent life. The look on Franklin's face as he struggled with the pillows made me want to laugh with sympathy—this kind of nurturing was so clearly not for him. And neither was I exactly obsessed with Lamaze. I didn't practice the breathing every day, as was suggested. And as for relaxing one's body when it was racked with pain—well, it just didn't seem very practical to me, even though I taught it as the ideal way to control the "discomfort of labor." But I did look forward to having Franklin with me in the labor and delivery room.

If Franklin and I didn't savor every moment of Lamaze class, there were other things that we did together in happy anticipation of our baby. We painted our spare bedroom yellow and I made curtains and ruffled skirts for the bassinet. I was committed to rocking the baby as much as I could, and so we found the perfect Victorian rocker, upholstered in soft burgundy velvet, at a flea market. Its low seat and high back would give endless comfort during the many hours each night that the baby and I would spend together.

When I announced to my staff that I was pregnant, they were more expressive than Franklin had been. "Oh, Miss Wattleton, that's wonderful. We'll give you a big baby shower," Cheri promised. But several members of the board were perplexed. Since there had been no fanfare when Franklin and I got married, they'd assumed I was single and about to become an unwed mother—this was not suitable for a Planned Parenthood executive director. Two of them called Fred Smith and asked him how they were to handle this problem. Fred, laughing, assured them, "Miss Wattleton is not a Miss, she is a Mrs., and her husband's name is Franklin Gordon."

It was an amusing moment. But the contretemps also showed me that in the minds of the two who spoke up—and probably in the minds of many who hadn't spoken—my lifestyle and conduct were tied to the image of the organization. If I did anything socially questionable, it would not simply be my individual reputation at stake, but the group's credibility. And so it would be for the duration of my Planned Parenthood life. Attention to my rectitude would become even more important in later years.

I had looked forward to breaking the happy news to my colleagues from the other affiliates at the Great Lakes Region Planned Parenthood conference in the spring. However, before I'd had a chance to say anything, I was invited to lunch by executive directors Ann McFarren and Carol Wall, of the Gary, Indiana, and Akron, Ohio, affiliates. I assumed that this was just one of the friendly get-togethers we tried to arrange whenever we converged for these professional meetings.

Ann, like me, was a nurse. She had preceded me at Planned Parenthood by several years. I admired her grit as she struggled to expand an affiliate in economically depressed Gary, Indiana, an area with so few resources. I admired Carol for much the same reason, for Akron offered similar challenges. She and I had gotten to know each other well as members of Planned Parenthood Affiliates of Ohio, a group that met once a month in Columbus to share experiences and ideas and to lobby the state legislature for family planning funding.

Ann and Carol had both been more involved in abortion reform than I had been. But they never wielded that fact against me—not when they had described the troubles they were encountering as they helped women get to New York prior to *Roe v. Wade*; not later, when Ann opened her affiliate's first abortion clinic to picketing and bomb threats; and not now.

Once we were seated in a dim corner of the Chicago hotel restaurant,

Ann went straight to the point. "We want you to become a candidate for the next chairmanship of NEDC."

The National Executive Directors' Council (NEDC) was composed of the executive directors of the affiliates. The chairperson represented their interests on the national board. If my life had depended upon it, I couldn't have been more surprised.

"We've been thinking about the mess the federation is in," Carol continued. "The best way to get the national office on the ball is to have a chair of NEDC who can make them understand the affiliates' views. We think that person is you."

"You know that the affiliates aren't getting what we need," said Ann, citing the lack of support in the face of growing opposition by pro-criminalist forces. "If there are to be changes," she continued, "we believe you'd be the one to convince the national office to make them."

Stunned, I asked, "Why me?" It didn't occur to me that this was the fourth time in my young career that I had been so approached.

"Because we think that you won't back down and that you'll be able to get the national board to move in the right direction. The candidate being put forward now would be a disaster," Ann concluded, with Carol nodding in agreement.

By this time, many executive directors were beginning to experience the effects of the gathering backlash. Picketing and vandalism were being reported from every part of the country. The National Right to Life Committee had consolidated the pro-criminalist forces (those who do not stop at condemning abortion but are dedicated to making it, once again, a criminal act) into a unified movement. Invectives by local Catholic and fundamentalist churches on Planned Parenthood clinics were becoming more and more bold and inventive. The affiliates were calling for "Eight-ten" (the national headquarters are at 810 Seventh Avenue in New York City) to provide stronger leadership to counter the growing opposition.

"We also think it's time to break up the old boys' network in Planned Parenthood," Ann continued, her infectious laugh seeming to launch the idea beyond dispute.

"The men want to run everything," Carol added.

This being the spring of 1975, I was just starting to feel feathery movements in my lower abdomen. Thinking that I had a foolproof escape, I announced, "I think I should tell you, before we get too much farther into this conversation, that I'm pregnant and scheduled to deliver during the time of the annual meeting in Seattle."

After hearty congratulations and hugs, Ann got back to the business at hand. "Well . . ." she paused, "we'll just have to get you elected without your being there. Or maybe you could come to the meeting with your obstetrician?"

We all laughed.

Other concerns besides my delivery date flashed through my mind. Even if I accepted their challenge and by some long shot won the position, over the next two years I would have to travel to board meetings and other Planned Parenthood forums in different parts of the country, even as I tried to run my affiliate. Time had passed, and Pat, the assistant director who had been so resistant to me, had left. I now had a supportive staff, but the job still was not easy. It just didn't seem like the right time to plan to be away from the office. And the responsibility of motherhood lay ahead. I was planning to nurse my baby, so if I took on a national position that involved a lot of traveling, the baby would have to come with me.

"I don't think I should do it. Maybe the next time around."

They were not to be put off. "No, now is the time. We need you now," Carol pressed on.

I countered: "There is no way I can get elected if I am not in Seattle to speak for myself."

"We think you can," they insisted, offering to run the campaign, make the speeches, and track the inclinations of potential voters. "Think about it. Don't say a final no," they pleaded.

I returned to Dayton two days later without having given them an answer. Certain that he would object, I approached Franklin gently. "What do you think about my running for the chairmanship of NEDC?"

After I explained to him what it was about, without hesitation he encouraged me to go for it.

"But it would mean traveling all over with the baby."

"That's okay with me," he answered quite simply.

I could do no worse in the job than the other leading candidate, I figured. If I lost, I'd still have my day job, and if I had enough support to get elected in absentia, maybe the force of that goodwill would carry over to my role as the executive directors' representative. Perhaps I really could help the national board understand the problems affiliates were facing, and help convince its members that we had to become more proactive.

I reported the proposal to Cheri and the officers of my board. They were as supportive as Franklin. They seemed proud, certain that, whether I won or not, the image of the affiliate would be enhanced by the invitation.

The next week I called Ann and told her that they could submit my name for nomination.

"Great!" Ann replied, and, with a burst of laughter, resurrected the idea of my bringing my doctor with me.

At my next prenatal visit, I jokingly mentioned to Dr. Baker that my colleagues would like to see me in Seattle on my expected delivery date. He laughed and said, "Not a chance."

The summer months were not too uncomfortable for me—I wasn't that large; besides, having been born in the middle of a hot St. Louis summer myself, I love the heat. The anticipation of the baby minimized my discomfort. When October rolled around, I still went to the office every day, figuring that nothing about my body and my enlarging uterus altered my capacity to think and do my work.

In early October we held our annual book fair. Several years earlier, we'd realized that we needed to do more to gain the support of the general Dayton community and, especially, to raise more money. We decided to follow the successful lead of Planned Parenthood of Iowa, and established a used-book sale. The first sale took place in a church hall; now in 1975, the event had grown so large that the sale filled the coliseum at the county fairgrounds. We sold thousands of recycled books over the course of a week. And as the fairs were always held in the fall, they became festivals of apple cider and pumpkins, as well. By then, we were making close to $100,000, but more important, we'd attract dozens of volunteers who were committed to helping Planned Parenthood services reach people in the community.

I had come to look forward to the event, but this year, the opposition saw the book fair as one more way to attack our work. They had petitioned against our being granted permission to use county property to hold the fair. Unsuccessful in that effort, about fifty of them showed up at the fairgrounds with placards declaring that Planned Parenthood was engaged in killing babies—even though we still did not offer abortion services.

The conflict, of course, made the event even more attractive to the local media, who came to witness the classic confrontation of good and evil. I was asked to speak to the reporters about the book fair and about Planned Parenthood, and to express my opinion on the noisy picketers who were attempting to leaflet every car that entered the parking lot and to shout at the hundreds of people who chose to cross their picket line to buy books. Altogether, it was quite a moment—the antiabortion disruption condemning Planned Parenthood for being against family and children, and me standing before television cameras, doing nothing to camouflage the size of my nine-month-distended abdomen, discussing why Planned Parenthood was so important to women, children, and families.

In mid-October, while my partisans were campaigning for me in Seattle, I stayed behind in Dayton to await the baby's arrival. At precisely seven o'clock on the morning of October 19, the day before my due date, I was awakened by contractions. I lay quietly for about an hour after the first tightening of the powerful muscles of my womb, and then shook Franklin's shoulder. "Wake up, wake up. I'm in labor."

"How do you know you're in labor?" he asked.

"Because I'm having contractions."

"How far apart?"

"They aren't exactly regular—anywhere between ten and fifteen minutes apart—but I think that this is the real thing."

"Do you want to go to the hospital?"

"No," I told him. "I want to go to the office."

After delivery I planned to be away from the agency full-time for three months (although, as I had agreed, I would come in at intervals and for board meetings). I had assumed I would have the baby later than my due date, instead of precisely on the day her birth was predicted, so I hadn't quite tied up every loose end. This being October, the budget had to be in fairly final shape before I went off to give birth.

I put on the maternity dress I had worn most often during my pregnancy, a muu-muu that had stylishly concealed my abdomen. I'd gained forty-three pounds, but my swollen belly offered the only outward evidence of my pregnancy. Franklin teased me about my resemblance to *Sesame Street*'s Big Bird.

When we entered the office that Sunday morning, the janitorial workers looked up from their vacuuming, startled by my appearance. "Miss Wattleton, what are you doing here?" exclaimed one woman.

When I told her that I'd gone into labor and wanted to get some work tied up before the baby arrived, her jaw went slack. She looked at me as though I were crazy, and then her demeanor turned sympathetic. "Well, hurry and get it done. I don't want to deliver a baby here," she said, laughing.

Before settling in the reception area with the Sunday paper, Franklin again inquired, "Are you sure you want to do this?"

I reassured him, "There are a lot of women all over the world who go into the fields in labor. I won't take long."

I was familiar enough with what I was doing to know how much time I had. If the contractions had been closer or if the amniotic sac surrounding the baby had broken, I would have asked that we head for the hospital immediately. As it was, I calculated that I still had some hours to go. I thought that if I busied myself, I would not be wholly consumed by my growing discomfort.

An hour or so later, with my contractions coming at precise ten-minute intervals, we headed back home. I called Dr. Baker and, as I had expected, he instructed me to remain there until my contractions were close to five minutes apart. By early evening, they were of such regularity and strength that I was now feeling real pain in my lower back and abdomen. I called Dr. Baker again. "Maybe you should head down to Kettering," he advised. "I'll meet you there."

I was scheduled to deliver at the Seventh-Day Adventist Kettering Hospital. When we arrived, I was admitted and placed into a private labor room. As the night wore into a weary, painful, early morning, Franklin coached me through my contractions. His support—mostly his insistence that I "Relax. Relax," and then, after the contraction passed, "You're not relaxing"—was not exactly true to the Lamaze form, and his observations sometimes annoyed me. Who *ever* dreamed up relaxing when you're in such excruciating pain? I asked myself. But Franklin was doing his best, and I knew more than he did about labor. The truth was that I was simply a woman having a baby and needed all the support that I had ever taught others to give.

By three o'clock that morning, with the opening of my womb complete, Dr. Baker decided it was time for me to move to the delivery room. The pain was becoming unbearable. The birth canal was only a few inches long, but it seemed a brutal eternity before Felicia's head passed through it.

"Can't you give me something to dull the pain?" I pleaded.

"No, I expect the baby to be born in the next two hours, and we don't want the medication to suppress the baby's breathing just when it needs to expand its lungs."

I knew he was right. Barbiturates should not be used if birth is anticipated within the two hours. I remembered times when it had been hard to get a baby to breathe because its mother had been overly medicated, but I wasn't a nurse at this moment.

"But I'm in so much pain," I moaned.

"We'll give you something after delivery," he promised.

"But I feel as though I'm suffocating from the pain."

"It won't be much longer," he assured me. "Try to relax."

Shortly thereafter, I crawled onto the gurney to be wheeled into the delivery room. There I suffered the same fate to which I had subjected so many women—being strapped in stirrups, my legs apart in the air while my every wish was to simply bend over, squat, and push the baby out. With no painkillers except the local anesthetic for the episiotomy, the pain was the most intense that I'd ever experienced. The coldness of the air and of the hard, unyielding table accentuated the intensity of my misery and the impossibility of what I was being asked to do.

I felt little joy in any of this, and wondered about all those women who claim that once they're in the delivery room they're so happy that they feel little pain. I no longer believed, as I was taught in midwifery school, that the pressure of the baby's hard skull against the soft tissues of the birth canal has a numbing effect.

The commands commenced: "Push! Push!" With my feet and legs floating to the ceiling, this seemed a gravitational impossibility, if not downright ludicrous. During the last few pushes the doctor slipped large metal spoons around Felicia's head and gently guided it as he cut a small incision at the back of my birth canal to make the opening wider. The local injection didn't work very well. I felt it all.

Before her head was all the way out, Franklin announced, "It's a girl."

"How can you tell?" I challenged, momentarily diverted from the business at hand and the enveloping contraction.

"I can just tell," he said.

Within a few seconds, his certainty was confirmed.

At 4:06 on October 20, 1975, Felicia Megan Gordon arrived into the world.

"Is she okay?" I asked anxiously.

I could almost hear Franklin grinning through the surgical mask.

"Yes, yes. She's fine," Dr. Baker assured me just as she began to cry lustily. He laid her on my abdomen, cut her cord, and rubbed her back. She was briefly taken away to be wrapped in warm receiving blankets, and for that moment, I grew anxious. "Are you sure there isn't something wrong after all?" I asked.

"Her Apgar is nine," the nurse announced. I knew that a score of nine out of ten on this assessment of a baby's color, breathing, and heart rate was nearly perfect. Her fingertips were just not as rosy as they would be a few minutes later, when her peripheral circulation was getting established.

Felicia was placed next to me. During the last few weeks of my pregnancy her night jabs and kicks had grown fierce. And in the loneliness of the early-morning darkness, my attachment to her grew. I'd even taken to talking to her. I tried to imagine what our baby would look like. Would she have Franklin's large, sultry eyes or my longer-than-life arms and legs? Maybe she (I mostly thought in terms of "she") would be blessed, as I had been, with adolescent-acne-free olive skin, or the chestnut brown of her father's skin, or a blend of both. I prayed that she would inherit her father's musical talents and my facility to empathize with others' misfortunes. In the back of my mind, I felt certain that I would get my just rewards and give birth to a child that would be as much of a challenge to me as I had been to Mama and Daddy.

Now, as she lay beside me, I could look at her. She was perfect in every way. Masses of black hair swirled all over her perfectly round head and away from her forehead in a distinctive cowlick over her right eye. Although I had just given birth to this beautiful creature, I somehow could not believe that she was mine. She felt strangely alien to me. I had expected to feel immediate identity, but I didn't, yet I couldn't stop gazing at her.

I wish I could put my legs down, I thought as Dr. Baker did his repair work while keeping up a steady stream of pleasant chatter with Franklin.

Ours was a wanted child—wanted very much by both her father and her mother. Nevertheless, the transition from the freedom of being part of a childless couple to the responsibility of caring for a new life was not automatic. I would have to get used to being a mother. The nurse gently helped me put my baby to my breast, and she suckled vigorously.

During the many hours of labor I had not given any consideration to what was happening in Seattle, where another event was taking place that would change the course of my life forever. When the nurse finally took Felicia from me and placed her in the warm incubator to take her to the nursery, my thoughts turned to NEDC. I knew that hours after I'd arrived at the hospital, the election would have taken place for the chairmanship. What had happened?

It was three hours earlier in Seattle, not yet a respectable hour for calling Konrad Reisner, our delegate to the national conference, to learn of my fate. The suspense was overwhelming. By eight o'clock I could wait no longer.

Before I asked any questions, I told his wife, Else, our good news. She then passed the receiver to Konrad.

"I had a baby girl."

Through his "Great!" amid laughter, I asked, "Did I win?"

"Yes, you did. How's the baby?" he asked, returning the conversation to the more immediate event.

I then placed a call to my mother, and afterward found myself overwhelmed by the need to see my baby.

I slid out of bed and slipped on my long cotton housecoat and slippers and eased my way down the hall to the large windows that overlooked the neatly lined bassinets of the nursery. I spotted our daughter immediately. She stood out among the dozen or so babies in the nursery. Lying on her stomach with her head to one side, she was sleeping peacefully. Though she did not move and I could not touch her, I stood there watching her for a long while, until a faintness came over me and I slowly made my way back to my bed.

An hour later, at 9:00 A.M., Felicia's pediatrician walked into my room, looking somber. I immediately sensed that something was wrong. I had not seen Felicia up close since I nursed her on the delivery table, but there had been no reason to believe that she was not healthy.

The boyish doctor, notorious for his ubiquitous smile and crewneck sweaters, sat down cheerlessly. "We have the results of the analysis on the cord blood. Your baby has a severe ABO incompatibility."

Our baby had inherited her father's blood type, A, which was the opposite of my O type. During pregnancy, with the exchange of blood cells over the placenta, my blood had built up antibodies to her blood and those antibodies had passed into her bloodstream. Now that she was independent of my body, the residual antibodies were destroying her blood, and quickly.

All of the blood in her body had to be exchanged for blood that had none of the lethal cell-destroying antibodies. Her body could then make new blood free of the dangerous substances.

"We'll have to do a complete blood exchange and hope for the best. Sometimes it takes several exchanges before things settle down. Of course, there are risks."

I understood the severity of the situation and was terrified. Blood transfusions, especially in newborns, can be dangerous. One transfusion is often not enough, and with each exchange the risk increases of brain damage or even death. But the breakdown in her red blood cells was raging. There was no real choice—they had to do an immediate exchange transfusion. Dr. Bloom asked me to sign a consent form. I tried to call Franklin, but he wasn't home; I consented to going forward with the procedure. There was no guarantee that one transfusion would work, but it was certain that without it Felicia could not live.

When I finally reached Franklin and told him what was happening, the news shook him as well. He asked if the baby was going to be okay. Pretending confidence, I reassured him that they had detected the problem early and, while there was some risk, it was unlikely that complications would arise. I called Mama back and asked her to pray for Felicia's recovery. "God is able," she said, and told me that she and Ola were on their way.

Although Felicia's blood cells continued to break down very rapidly for a short time after the transfusion, the process soon simply stopped, and her condition stabilized. A second transfusion was not necessary.

Felicia and I had to remain in the hospital for another five days, to be certain that she wasn't going to have further problems. I was perfectly happy to stay put as Felicia slept quiet and safe under a lamp designed to minimize the effects of the rapid destruction of her blood cells. I'm not so sure that the hospital was as delighted about our extended stay, however. For five days the quiet haven of the maternity ward was cast into a tumult. The telephone rang constantly in my room as colleagues in Seattle called to congratulate me and to give me blow-by-blow accounts of my election and its aftermath; family members called the front desk to check on us; my executive assistant, Earl Estes, came in once a day to work with me on office matters; and bouquets of flowers were marched into my room until it began to resemble a funeral parlor.

Five days after her birth, Felicia and I were discharged, and a couple of days later my mother and Ola arrived. Mama cooked me a big pot of rich vegetable stew—"I've put seven vegetables into this soup," she proudly announced. "Even chopped up the beet leaves."

Ola bathed Felicia, and both women doted on her. And Franklin was just plain giddy. "The three Fs," he called us, glad that he'd insisted that our daughter be named "Felicia," rather than "Taylor," which I'd preferred.

Konrad came and, picking her up from her bassinet draped in yellow and white organdy, promised to attend her high school graduation. He was sixty-five at the time. He fulfilled his promise.

Four days later I visited my office to prepare for a finance committee meeting to approve the budget that would go before the board in November.

Mama and Ola left after a week's stay, and Franklin and I were on our own. Franklin helped a lot with the cleaning and cooking and proved to be a real pro at changing Felicia's diapers. If I'd ever had any worries about the arrival of a new member in our family, they quickly disappeared in the shared care and devotion to our beautiful new child.

For the first few weeks Felicia would do little more than sleep, and I began to worry about it. I phoned my mother one day in distress: "You know, she sleeps so much, I wonder if she'll ever wake up."

My mother, with her southern-style wisdom, replied, "She'll wake up one day. Don't worry, she'll wake up."

And she did. Felicia was a healthy child in every way. Her temperament was gentle, she rarely cried, and from two months on she gurgled and laughed with little provocation.

Those first three months were a time of discovery, exhaustion, and joy. We bought a "Snugli," and carried Felicia on our chests. Saturday mornings, Franklin would put her in the pouch and, with a cup of coffee in hand, take her with him to visit with his friends in the neighborhood. He and I debated the virtues of subliminal jazz conditioning—he thought that if it was played softly in her nursery at all times, she would definitely grow up to be highly intelligent. I thought Felicia would be intelligent because of her genes, and she fretted when the music was on. Franklin fretted if I turned it off. "If you leave it on," he'd say, "she'll get used to it."

The most wonderful times of all for me were the nights when I would quietly leave our bed and go into Felicia's nursery, pick up the gently sleeping child, rock and sing softly to her, or simply look at her. I couldn't take my eyes from her perfectly shaped head and her slender, tapered fingers. She'd stir occasionally and look up at me with her drowsy eyes as if to confirm my sanity. Breastfeeding offered me some of the most intimate moments that I would ever have with her. As the days, weeks, and months wore on, my initial sense of wonder about her grew into a preoccupation that continues to this day.

Felicia and I took our first plane trip together to New York in December, when she was six weeks old, to attend my first national board executive committee meeting. Felicia's need to eat did not always coincide with the meeting breaks, so I occasionally found myself speaking at the microphone of Planned Parenthood meetings while breastfeeding her. What else was I to do? For discretion's sake, I'd slip a cloth diaper over my shoulder and her head. Most people couldn't see what I was doing. But when some board members were told, they were taken aback, shocked, and after-the-fact embarrassed. I felt that that was their problem. My concern was to feed my child *and* to carry out my responsibilities.

When the three months' maternity leave wound to a close, the post-partum depression that so many mothers feel shortly after delivery descended upon me without mercy, triggered not by the usual hormone-driven letdown, but by profound anxiety over hiring someone else to care for our baby. The mere thought of leaving her for hours at a time brought me to tears. But I had to return to work.

Memories of my own childhood were all too vivid—the feelings of abandonment and loneliness, the pain of a stranger's hand raised against me. Might my child be harmed in any way, and I not know it until the harm was already done? Mama assured me, "I wouldn't worry about it unless you notice a change in her sunny personality."

I was determined that Felicia be cared for in the familiarity of our home. It was something we could rearrange our priorities to do, and I was grateful for that flexibility.

Few referral agencies in Dayton placed child care workers, so I was left to advertise in the local newspaper and to inquire about candidates among friends and colleagues. When one neatly groomed woman came for an interview, she seemed nervous, unable to look at me directly, yet she'd been recommended by a friend as being quite loving, and was herself the mother of a grown son. She picked Felicia up and swayed her in her arms, while going on about Felicia's beauty. Franklin had left the decision up to me, and, although he'd expressed some reservations about this particular woman, I was desperate. I hired her.

On the first of February, I left her in the care of our new housekeeper and returned to work full-time. Because I was still breastfeeding, I'd come home at lunchtime to feed Felicia; with a supplemental bottle in the afternoon, she was able to get through the rest of the day. As for the long hours that I used to spend at the office, they stopped. I would have to be home, not only to relieve the child care worker, but also to feed my baby. Sometimes I'd bring work home, although caring for a totally dependent child made concentration on professional matters all but impossible. Given the pressures of running the affiliate, chairing NEDC, and balancing my family responsibilities, I lived in a state of permanent exhaustion. Franklin was patient, though not thrilled with the treadmill my life seemed to be turning into.

Nonetheless, things seemed to run smoothly—at least for several months. And then one day my secretary buzzed me. "Ms. Wattleton, your housekeeper is on the line and she says there is an emergency." My heart sank with that horrible fear every parent knows—that something has happened to their child in their absence. The housekeeper told me that there had been a "small fire" in the kitchen.

"There's soot everywhere," she said, "but I'm cleaning things up."

While there was no damage, there was a lot of smoke, she reported. I dropped the telephone, pulled on my coat, flew down the stairs and out of the building to hail a taxi to take me home. I didn't call Franklin, because I didn't want to take the time and I knew that he'd be upset with me for having hired this woman in the first place. For some time prior to the fire, he'd been monitoring the lowering volume of gin in our liquor cabinet. Neither of us drank gin. This would be the final straw.

The woman said she'd forgotten that she'd left the skillet on when she'd gone to take care of Felicia. I dismissed her on the spot. I hadn't the foggiest idea where I would find a replacement, but she had to go.

CHAPTER 16

FAMILY VALUES:
HOLDING IT ALL TOGETHER

"It's about time that an organization that primarily serves women be headed by a woman," Joan Draper argued.

"But is a woman capable of doing the job? . . . After all, it's a very big one," B. T. Hollings wondered aloud as he shook his head in doubt.

The presidency of the Planned Parenthood Federation had been vacant for almost four months, and the debate in the search committee over who the next president should be had become as heated as the steamy August streets outside our New York suite.

I slid back in my chair, captivated by the sparring between Joan, a young white woman from a conservative part of Utah, and B.T., a middle-aged African American obstetrician from Houston, Texas.

As I listened to the back-and-forth, I recalled being told, "We've got to break up the old boys' network," when I was approached about running for the chair of the NEDC.

Even so, until that moment, I hadn't given much thought to the predominance of men in top leadership positions at Planned Parenthood. I hadn't even found it ironic that since Margaret Sanger stepped down in 1942, an organization *founded by a woman, primarily for women*, had not been *led* by a woman. By not advocating for change, I'd been a passive colluder in the kind of thinking my female colleague was inveighing against.

"Look," Joan continued. "Women could do no worse than the men in messing up this organization. It would simply be an outrage—an act of hypocrisy—if we put a man in as the head of an organization primarily focused on women's health."

And I agreed with her: It wouldn't have been appropriate to offer the presidency of this particular organization to a man when women had finally been granted full control of their reproductive lives. The image of a movement is vested in the persona of its leaders. Joan's argument echoed the calls of women demanding the ability to shape their destiny—so why not shape the destiny of a multimillion-dollar international organization?

In the spring of 1977, Jack Hood Vaughn, a former director of the Peace Corps and a former ambassador to Colombia, had resigned as president of Planned Parenthood Federation of America. His tenure had been short and tumultuous. At the June board meeting, the chairwoman, Tenny Marshall, had caught up with me and asked, "Will you serve as the executive directors' representative to search for Jack's replacement?"

Currently, she also served as PPFA's unpaid president until a new executive could be found. Tenny was a Main Line Philadelphia matron, reserved, elegant, and gentle in manner. But her engaging smile and large, soft brown eyes belied a formidable strength, so I supposed her question, as she stared hard at me, unblinking, to be more a directive than a request. And yet it had distinct appeal.

As a member of the national board, I'd done my best to educate the federation leadership about the real-life concerns of the affiliates and of the dangers inherent in the rising opposition to Planned Parenthood's mission. It seemed to have fallen on deaf ears. The executive directors kept telling me, "We need strong leadership." But less and less was coming from a national office that was paralyzed by the death of its longtime, revered leader, Dr. Alan Guttmacher, and the short tenures of its last two presidents. It seemed incapable of providing the affiliates with a clear sense of mission.

During my two years on the PPFA board I'd learned how difficult it was to get things done. At board meetings, often with Felicia in my arms, I argued for "more aggressive political involvement," since the 1976 presidential elections were fast approaching. "We need to do more to put forth our issues," I pleaded. Congressman Henry Hyde (R-IL) was attacking poor women with his amendment that would cut off Medicaid funds for abortion, and Senator Jesse Helms (R-SC) was pushing for a constitutional amendment to reverse *Roe*.

Since the board seemed incapable of coming up with a political plan of action that the entire federation could use to repel the growing political backlash, the NEDC steering committee decided to produce one.

David Andrews, the executive director of Planned Parenthood of San Antonio, Texas, and Ann McFarren placed the plan before the steering committee directors, who represented different regions of the country. We were exhilarated. It included concrete measures—such as media, voter guides, and registration and get-out-the-vote campaigns—that would build our influence in shaping the political debate, if not the political terrain. The only problem was that some of our ideas were illegal for a nonprofit organization.

When Harriet Pilpel, Planned Parenthood's general counsel, heard my presentation, she went ballistic. "You simply cannot do some of these things. They're illegal. We could lose our tax exemption," she protested.

We were chastened. We hadn't even considered getting a legal opinion in the matter. Nevertheless, our rejected plan stimulated debate over what we *could* do legally. It was a step forward.

Since my two-year term as chairman of the NEDC was coming to an end, Tenny's offer was my last chance to have a significant impact on the organization's future.

When our search for a new president got under way, the eleven-member committee represented many facets of the organization—the new, more politically engaged generation as well as the traditional leadership; the affiliates as well as the national organization. Indeed, we were a disparate group in many ways. But from the beginning, we were united in our desire to find a strong leader who could rebuild this national organization into a forceful national movement. Julian Allen, an African American lawyer from Gary, Indiana, who had been both a law partner and a close adviser to Gary's former mayor Richard Hatcher, chaired the committee.

We spent many days that summer holed up together in New York City hotel suites and conference rooms, developing a job description, interviewing candidates, and debating the future of Planned Parenthood. By summer's end, our short list of half a dozen candidates left us uninspired. The lengthy search and the prospect of facing the national convention in October without a new candidate was wearing upon us.

Some felt strongly that we needed a seasoned manager from within Planned Parenthood. "We've had enough of these outside people who don't know anything about the organization," Andy Greensfelder, a lawyer from St. Louis and chair of the national board's executive committee, argued. Joan Draper held to her conviction that we needed a woman. The doctors on the committee insisted on a stronger presence from physicians in the organization. Phyllis Vineyard, a proper New Englander, lectured us about not "losing sight of overpopulation and our international work." And Martha Diener, Tenny's Pennsylvania neighbor, warned that if we didn't hire Al Moran, there would be a great split in the organization, and whoever got the position would have "hell to pay."

Al Moran was the executive director of Planned Parenthood of New York City. A sometimes blustery, silver-haired Irishman in his early fifties, with a pair of piercing blue eyes and a voice that could flatten his opposition, he'd made an impressive track record in the social welfare community even before coming to Planned Parenthood in 1966. Al had also been a leader in the New York abortion reform movement. Under his management, the New York City affiliate became the first to offer abortion services. An uncompromising and articulate advocate for reproductive rights, some said Al was "the conscience of the Planned Parenthood movement." Three years earlier, he'd applied for the presidency of the federation, and he'd been a front-runner to replace Jack Vaughn. I was an admirer of Al's work, and had encouraged him to put his hat in the ring again.

In early September, back in my office in Dayton, I began to get phone calls from executive directors around the country urging me to become a candidate myself. Although I'd been expecting a letdown when my term as NEDC chair ended, I wasn't eager to consider their suggestions. All the meetings and travel and correspondence had been exciting, but a strain. I was looking forward to spending more time with Franklin and Felicia. My job was secure, my board was happy with me, and I was happy with them. The accommodation, pride, and encouragement they'd shown for my national work had won over my wholehearted loyalty. Why would I want to leave all of that?

Dayton was also the kind of place in which I liked to live. Franklin, Felicia, and I had a home we loved, in a quiet, integrated neighborhood in the middle of the city. I enjoyed my volunteer commitments outside the affiliate, including a term on the board of the local Urban League. I'd found a church that I liked a lot. It was a Church of God, but one where the minister preached more about love and compassion than about judgment. Franklin and I had had Felicia baptized there and were thinking of enrolling her in the Christian school on the church property. In the meantime, I trusted the woman I'd found to care for her after the departure of the first woman. We'd enrolled Felicia in a three-days-a-week program at the Downtown Child Development Center, because as an only child, we felt she needed the companionship of other children, and because we didn't share my mother's fears that we'd be releasing the demon of her genius. The center had accepted her even though she wasn't yet potty trained. I asked them not to make an issue of it, and they didn't. But she'd only been at the school two days when she declared, "Mommy, I want training pants." I bought them for her, and that was her potty training. I was happy with our life and hardly wished to disrupt it.

Besides, having observed PPFA's inability to effectively address our political opponents and the national board's resistance to change, I couldn't imagine the stress of trying to fix those long-standing problems. Running a million-dollar local agency was one thing. Running an international organization with a budget of tens of millions of dollars and almost two hundred local affiliates, all of which made different demands, plus having a seventy-five-member board to keep happy—was something altogether different. I didn't even tell Franklin about the calls I was receiving.

By the time the annual convention met in New York in October of 1977, we were six months into the search for the new president and still had not reached a consensus. Those of us on the search committee found ourselves subjected to a steady barrage of lobbying, both for and against the front-runner, Al Moran.

On the first day of the meeting, David Andrews was elected to replace me as chair of NEDC. An energetic former Peace Corps volunteer, David was four years younger than I. We'd collaborated on resolutions and tactics to challenge the reluctant national board to resist the political head winds. We'd also agitated for an end to Jack Vaughn's tenure. His international interest reflected the board's view that the domestic situation was under control. We knew this was far from true. However, our agitation didn't determine his departure nearly so much as his highly controversial attempt to bring a semi-autonomous division of the national organization under his direct control. In response, the head of the division had negotiated a separation that resulted in the creation of the Alan Guttmacher Institute, a special affliate located in Washington, D.C., for research, education, and policy analysis.

That night, exhausted from all the meetings, I retired early to my hotel room. I was almost asleep when I heard a knock on the door. I asked who it was, and a crisp, no-nonsense voice answered, "Faye, it's Ruth Green." Ruth was the executive director of the Tucson affiliate. We'd served together on the NEDC steering committee and had grown very fond of each other.

When she entered the room, the expression on her face told me she had come on a serious matter. Sitting at the foot of my bed, she said, "You have to do it. You simply have to do it."

I didn't have to ask her what she meant. More than once that day, I'd been urged to become a candidate. Ruth went on, "I've been sent here by a group of executive directors, and we want you to go for it."

She didn't name her backers and I didn't counter with my lack of qualifications. Instead, I said, "Ruth, I really appreciate your confidence in me, but you know I've been on the search committee and it would really be awkward for me to become a candidate now."

"We know that's a problem. That's why we want you to resign from the committee at this meeting—then it won't be too late to become a candidate. The organization needs a new image," she continued. "We need someone who understands Planned Parenthood from the inside. And you're one of us, an executive director."

"Felicia's only two years old," I told her. "I don't see how I can do such a big job, with all of the traveling and long hours."

Ruth didn't break stride. "We gave you a lot of help with her when you were chair of NEDC. You'll get plenty of help again."

This woman will make any promise, I thought, smiling to myself. Having my colleagues hold my baby while I conducted a steering committee meeting or stood to speak before the national board was one thing, but I couldn't quite see anyone signing up to baby-sit when I needed to catch an early-morning plane and the housekeeper was sick.

"Al Moran is emerging as the only candidate," Ruth continued. "We think you're the only one who would be more attractive." And then she cut her argument down to its most basic element: "Planned Parenthood needs a woman as its head."

While Al had his partisans and detractors, so did I. When rumors circulated that I was being pressed to apply, Sherri Tepper, the executive director of Rocky Mountain Planned Parenthood, who had never warmed to me, had cornered David Andrews and told him, "It's ridiculous to think about Faye being president. Even with all my credentials, I couldn't be president of Planned Parenthood, and if I couldn't be president, how on earth could someone like Faye be president?" Maybe Sherri had a point, I'd thought wryly.

Ruth stood to leave. At the door, she turned to face me. "Faye, you simply have to go for it. We need you."

That statement, so simple and clear, called out above those objections I had marshaled. Ruth had appealed to the impulse to do service I'd inherited from my mother. I lay in my hotel bed that night thinking about what it might mean for me, a woman and an African American, to head Planned Parenthood and about what needed to be done. The movement, founded in 1916 by a woman who'd been willing to go to jail to provide women with birth control, seemed locked in caution and complacency. Just as women's sexual and reproductive lives had become political pawns when Comstock took his battles to Congress a little over a century earlier, the revisionist agenda was creating the same kind of nightmare. Restraining orders on Congressman Henry Hyde's amendment to cut off funds for abortions for poor women had been lifted with the backing of President Carter. The Planned Parenthood of Minnesota headquarters had been fire-bombed and severely damaged that past February. The televangelists were growing increasingly political, and sex education, contraception to minors, and abortion—which they felt destroyed "traditional values"—were at the top of their hit lists. Even contraception for adults—whose acceptability had been broadly taken for granted since the availability of the birth control pill in 1960 and the subsequent availability of services to poor women (effected by the 1969 passage of Title X of the Public Health Service Act)—was becoming the focus of increasing attack. If ever there was a time that Planned Parenthood needed to return to its original purpose and activist roots, that time was now. We had no choice but to change fast and radically.

Sleep did not come. Ruth had put me on the spot and she knew it. I certainly couldn't do any worse than my predecessor—and I do know the organization, I told myself. But what if I failed—and on a national scale? *And what about Felicia and Franklin?*

I decided I couldn't risk it, but that I'd talk it all over with Franklin before telling Ruth no. In the meantime, I'd be careful not to acknowledge any interest in the position or my backers would doggedly pressure me, and my detractors would go all out to rally opposition to me. The meeting was charged enough; we needed no more fireworks.

When the convention came to a close, I promised Ruth that I would make a decision before the next search committee meeting—after I had discussed the matter with my husband.

Much to my surprise, the idea didn't displease Franklin at all. In fact, he'd immediately responded, "Yeah, yeah, you'd be terrific, and it would also give me a chance to get back to the East Coast."

"But what about your job?" I asked, taken aback by this unexpected show of enthusiasm. I hadn't forgotten the price Daddy had paid when Mama accepted "the call" to go to Nebraska before he'd known there would be no livelihood for him there, let alone a meaningful one.

But my father always figured he could manage somehow, and so did Franklin. "I can always get a job," he said. "People always need social workers."

"But we'll have to sell this home that we both love."

"I know, but it's not the last Tudor on earth. There are lots of them around New York. You'll see."

It seemed that it was he who had to convince me, rather than the other way around. I guess I'd been hoping that Franklin would object so strenuously that the decision would be made for me. Instead, I found myself with the full weight of our future on my shoulders. There were no easy outs.

When I informed the search committee that I was resigning so I could be considered for the position, Julian Allen grumbled, "You know you've really waited too long, don't you?"

"I know—but the committee will have to decide whether I'm a strong enough candidate to overcome the problems posed by my late entry," I answered somewhat cavalierly, hoping they'd save me where Franklin hadn't.

I called Fred Smith, now president of the board in Dayton, to tell him my decision. "Are you sure you want to do this to your family?" he asked.

Given Franklin's hearty encouragement, it hadn't occurred to me I was "doing" anything to anyone.

When I told Franklin of Fred's concerns, he chuckled and said, "I think everything will be fine."

Franklin and I had pursued our separate careers quite successfully over the five years of our marriage. Whenever there had been a shift in our work that meant taking on additional responsibilities, we'd always figured out a way to make it work. I assumed—and I think Franklin did—that we would cope with this move just as we'd coped with all the other changes. But I've often wondered if Fred would have asked Franklin the same question if the situation had been reversed. As it would turn out, Fred's question was more prescient than I could have imagined.

My interview with the search committee in New York was relatively informal and relaxed—after all, my would-be interrogators already knew where I stood. Still, I returned to Dayton with no sense of whether they'd take my candidacy seriously. "If I don't get the nod, it won't be the end of the world," I told myself, not yet having embraced the idea wholeheartedly. I turned my attention to the work of the affiliate.

Franklin grew more excited about the possibility with each passing day. But when I telephoned Mama to tell her of my decision to apply, she responded, "I hope you don't take the job," her voice flat.

Just as my mother's sense of mission had compelled her, something within me now seemed to be pulling me toward the position. Trying to offer Mama some comfort, I assured her, "Don't worry. They won't name a black person. And they haven't had a woman running the organization since Margaret Sanger."

"Who is Margaret Sanger?" she asked.

"The founder, Mama, the founder."

On January 15, 1978, Andy Greensfelder called. "Are you sitting down?" he asked.

"Yes, I am," I answered.

"The search committee has unanimously decided to recommend that you be appointed the next president of Planned Parenthood Federation of America. And the executive committee has just approved the recommendation. The recommendation will be sent to the board for consideration at its meeting two weeks from now in Kansas City."

My mind raced in the moment of silence that followed Andy's enthusiastic announcement. The only question that I could think to ask was, "Did the committee have a difficult time making the decision?"

"Oh, it didn't take them long at all. In fact, I was sort of annoyed. Here we had gone to all the trouble to prepare a lengthy report, and we'd even rehearsed our strategy for confronting any opposition. But a couple of members were more concerned with catching their planes to the Super Bowl in New Orleans," he said, laughing.

His cheerful exasperation broke the ice. I laughed, and thanked him for the good news.

"Well, congratulations and good luck. I know you'll do a good job."

I told him I wished I could be so confident. The full board had yet to vote, and anything could happen. I kept him on the line just chatting for a little while longer, as if needing the sound of his voice to confirm the reality. The momentum of events was now out of my control.

Andy later told me more about the search committee's final meeting. It hadn't taken them long to clarify that the members favored either me or Al, and the other candidates were set aside.

"The discussion went around the table," Andy said, "and it soon became apparent that more of us were leaning toward you. You being young, a woman, black—we had a sense of hey, this is a little bit exciting. We had all the logical reasons to choose you, too, of course—your record in Dayton and so on—but I think in a way we made an emotional decision and then lined up the logical reasons to support it. And there were enough of us on the committee who just felt really good about going with you."

That I was the only person the search committee recommended to the board didn't mean my candidacy would go uncontested. Al's supporters offered his name as an alternative to mine. The two weeks of frantic lobbying were torture. I flew to St. Louis to discuss the terms of my potential employment with Tenny and Andy. Tenny, who I believed was unenthusiastic about my advancement, thought it would be "a nice gesture" if I accepted a lower salary than Jack Vaughn had been paid.

"Absolutely not!" I answered indignantly. "The work and responsibilities will be the same if not greater, and you want me to take a lesser salary than someone who did not last?"

They backed down, and agreed to give me the salary and benefits Jack had received—if the board approved my nomination.

Finally, on January 27, the full national board gathered in Kansas City, Missouri, in the middle of a blizzard that buried the area in more than two feet of snow. But the marooned board was able to get down to business.

Snowbound by the same storm in my house in Dayton, I hung on the periodic phone calls from David Andrews and Ann McFarren, who, once again, were "managing my campaign."

"Things are tense," they told me. "Al's supporters are working hard . . . Your supporters are counting votes, lobbying, and recounting votes."

"There shouldn't be a problem," David optimistically assured me. "But you never know what can happen at a Planned Parenthood board meeting!" he added with a laugh.

Early on the second day, David called to tell me that a board member had banged on the door of his hotel room at the wee hour of two or three o'clock, saying there was a rumor that there would be a motion to reject the search committee's recommendation and keep Tenny Marshall on as president. Another rumor had it that some were discussing bringing a lawsuit to block my appointment; because I had been on the search committee, they would charge "conflict of interest" if I won the vote. No one was sleeping.

By the time Tenny's phone call came that afternoon, telling me that the board had selected me by a vote of 54 to 6, none of it seemed real. I was too numb even to feel surprise. "Okay," I said quietly.

"You don't seem too excited—are you having second thoughts?" said Tenny, startled. I assured her that nothing could be farther from the truth, I just needed some time to think about what all this meant. Was she still looking for a way to get me to call the whole thing off? I wondered.

I put my hand over the receiver and whispered to Franklin, "I got the job." His face lit up with a broad smile.

In a sort of anticipatory nostalgia, even as my conversation with Tenny continued, I thought about all the people we'd be saying good-bye to— close friends with whom we had Thanksgiving and Christmas dinners, at one home one year and another the next, friends with whom we'd play bid whist on Saturday nights and listen to the latest soul music. I would miss my closest friend, Sarah, with whom I went shopping and traded recipes.

I loved our home. I liked the large yard, where I worked the flower beds in the spring and planted bulbs in the fall, and where Felicia stumbled through her first steps, the grassy carpet easing her falls. I liked thinking of Franklin out in our garage, polishing his beloved old green Jaguar sedan to the same high gloss that my father used to enjoy creating.

And then there was the hugeness of the unknown. From where I'd sat, it was easy to say, "If I had that job I would . . ." Now that I had it, I had some idea what I would be facing in New York, but no idea what would happen if I failed. Though I'd never have confessed it to anyone, part of me thought I'd be lucky to last five years. After that we could return to Dayton, and make a new home in safe familiarity.

But for now, there was no turning back.

"We hope you can get into Kansas City to make a statement," Tenny said.

"That may be nearly impossible," I said with a laugh, reminding her that the Dayton airport was still closed. I promised to get a flight out as soon as I could.

After I hung up, I dialed my mother's number. "Mama, I got the job," I said, trying not to sound too happy.

There was a long silence. "Well, I hope that you'll do well," she replied evenly, without emotion. This was followed by another long pause; then, each word spoken with hesitation: "When do you start?"

The next morning, the airport opened just in time for me to catch the flight that would get me to Kansas City about an hour before the board meeting was scheduled to adjourn. I put on the yellow "Ultrasuede" coatdress that I'd laid out the night before. Franklin drove me to the airport and kissed me good-bye, saying, "Good luck. Things are really about to change in a big way."

He was happy. I was scared.

I'd worked on my acceptance speech the night before, but the hour in the quiet sanctuary of the airplane, away from Franklin's high spirits and Felicia's needs, gave me the chance to rewrite and refine it. I desperately wanted my first act as president to set the tone for my leadership. But being a novice at writing and delivering speeches, I felt anxious and kept revising and re-revising. Then I thought about how Mama would take command of the moment. I felt my back straighten and my spirits rally. I would be among friends. And as for my detractors—well, they wouldn't like what I said, no matter what it was.

When I arrived, I was greeted with handshakes and hugs. Martha Diener, who considered herself a "professional volunteer," embraced me with her pearl- and gold-jeweled arms. Usually dignified, today her delight was childlike. "I'm so proud of you," she said in her cigarette-raspy voice that could compel the boardroom to dignified silence. "I know you'll do great things." During her second embrace, though, she whispered in my ear: "Just remember, this organization eats its young."

Feeling heady, buoyant, I stepped up to the podium to give the speech that I hoped would be a call to action. First I thanked my colleagues and acknowledged my excitement. And then I said:

> I am proud to be a part of this organization today. You have demon-strated unparalleled courage. You have made a statement to the world that race, sex and age did not cloud your vision as you sought and selected a competent leader. The effect will be to herald a new day in our federation and for the Planned Parenthood movement. You, too, should be proud.

It was then time to lay out my hopes for the years ahead:

> There is much work to be done, but I feel confident that as a team, we will meet the challenges that face us. We will meet them aggressively and successfully. The issues are complex—not always clearly defined and always interrelated.

I wanted the board to understand where I believed our priorities should lie. I listed them, and issued my call to action:

- Access to safe abortion.
- The development of new, safe, acceptable contraceptives.
- Effective means for reaching teenagers.

• Effective sex education programs.
• Effective delivery systems for rural populations.

Then I continued:

Unfortunately, the battle lines have been drawn for us. The enemies of reproductive freedom are tireless; we must be just as zealous lest we lose the battle, permitting the repressive dogma of a vocal minority to erode the right that we consider basic: the right of a woman to manage her own fertility. We must not shrink from controversy.

I am moved by two profound commitments: to Planned Parenthood becoming the foremost leader in the reproductive rights movement; and to the excellence of our service delivery system: our affiliates.

I challenge you to examine carefully your involvement in our organization. If your energies are not directed toward either or both of these goals, perhaps a moment of reflection and reevaluation is necessary.

There will be difficult times ahead. Within our family there will continue to be diverging opinions on how we should go about our vital work. We must not be troubled, for healthy debate will strengthen us.

There may be times when you feel that I am pushing too hard or moving too fast. I pray for your tolerance in the knowledge that we must run to catch up and then keep ahead of our opposition. I, too, will be patient in the recognition that not all of us will be at the same place at the same time. The climate is ripe for the development of exciting policies and programs. We must not look back, but look forward to the bright promise of our future. I know that we will meet the challenge.[1]

It was January 30, 1978. I was thirty-four years old, trained as a nurse-midwife, and the new president of Planned Parenthood Federation of America—its youngest president ever, the first woman to head it since its founder, Margaret Sanger, and the first African American president. I was proud and honored on each of these counts, but I felt that my being an African American was a vital aspect of my leadership; that it provided insights and experiences that I am certain would have been missing had I not been black.

Throughout my career, I'd been moved along by the circumstances of opportunity and by the confidence of others when I myself had little. Perhaps if I had not succeeded each time I'd taken on a new challenge—whether it was teaching at Miami Valley Hospital, working at the Dayton Health Department, directing Planned Parenthood of Miami Valley, or heading the council of my executive director colleagues—I might have been more resistant to the calls to serve. But, like my mother, the model before me, I had succeeded—in large measure because of the encouragement, support, and assistance of mentors and friends each step of the way: from Ruth Anne Yauger at the health department to Konrad Reisner and Cheri Liskany at the Dayton affiliate, to Ann McFarren and Carol Wall in other affiliates, and, in days to come, David Andrews and Fred Smith in the national organization.

As the president of Planned Parenthood, I would have to take things one day at a time, but I had a vision and I was determined to achieve it.

CHAPTER 17

REPRODUCTIVE RIGHTS
UNDER SIEGE

In 1978, when I was selected to become its president, the Planned Parenthood Federation of America was a network of 189 affiliates in forty-three states and the District of Columbia. PPFA served over a million people a year, fielding a staff of three thousand paid employees and twenty thousand volunteers, and deploying an operating budget of over $100 million. We were one of the largest healthcare organizations in the country. By virtue of our widespread clinic network, we were much better known for our contraceptive services than for our abortion advocacy. Indeed, though some affiliates had fought in the reform movement, we were by no means boldly in the forefront. But in the minds of some, as Father Griese had made so clear back in Dayton, we were guilty by association. The form that our persecution would take was becoming harrowingly clear.

On the night of February 23, 1977, the administrative offices of Planned Parenthood in St. Paul, Minnesota, were burned with damages totaling $250,000. Bullets were subsequently fired into the building, and a bomb that failed to explode was found in front of the clinic's windows. Kidnap threats had been made against board members' children, and one child had been removed from school because of death threats.[1]

In Omaha, Nebraska, on August 18, 1977, at least four bottles of gasoline were thrown through a clinic window and ignited, causing $35,000 worth of damage. Within hours, the local newspaper received letters, one of which had words clipped from a magazine and glued onto a piece of paper. It read, "You'd bomb a concentration camp—why not abortion centers?"

The return-address area was marked, by the same means, "For Life." Nevertheless, although several of the letters were signed, and clinic personnel discovered that someone had bought gasoline from a nearby convenience store that evening and paid for it by check, police came up with no suspects.[2] Such apparent apathy on the part of local law-enforcement agencies, from constables to courts, would prove to be commonplace.

Cincinnati, Ohio, Jack Willke's hometown, offered yet another case of the escalation to violence. Family planning in general, as well as abortion in particular, had come under relentless attack from the pulpit of then Archbishop Joseph Bernardin. One Planned Parenthood clinic, which provided only contraceptive services, was picketed daily by protesters who took down the license plate numbers of cars belonging to the staff and clients and used them to obtain home addresses and phone numbers for further harassment.

In November 1977, a man entered another Cincinnati Planned Parenthood clinic, which also did not perform abortions, and set fire to a crib in the reception area. At a third Planned Parenthood clinic—which did provide abortion services—a firebomb hit a window air conditioner but did not explode.

In February of 1978 a chemical bomb and packets of anti-choice literature were thrown through a plate-glass window of an abortion clinic not affiliated with Planned Parenthood. The bomb's key ingredient was an acid reportedly on the government's list of chemical-warfare agents. The clinic had to be closed for nine days, and all rugs and upholstered furniture replaced.[3]

The protesters' rigid adherence to one set of beliefs and their condemnation of all others was hardly new to me. It was, after all, the bedrock of fundamentalist beliefs. But I had been raised to the words of Romans 12:19-21: "Vengeance is mine. I will repay, saith the Lord. Therefore if thine enemy hunger, feed him; if he thirst, give him drink. . . . Do not overcome evil by evil, but overcome evil with good."[4] The use of violence to extort conformity to a moral or religious tenet was terrifying. It was as though our clinics were at war, and the violence was increasing.

Three weeks before, when I was appointed president of Planned Parenthood, on January 6, 1978, in coordinated actions all over the country—including Omaha, Nebraska; New York City; Minneapolis, Minnesota; Anchorage, Alaska; and Fairfax, Virginia—demonstrators forced their way into clinics and disrupted services by distributing literature, singing anti-choice songs, sitting-in, or chaining themselves to the doors of the procedure rooms. In some cases, the trespassing was called legal by law-enforcement officials, some judges, and certainly the demonstrators themselves, who all justified it in terms of a person's "right" to trespass to "save the life of another."[5]

In Cleveland, Ohio, during the night of February 15, 1978, a clinic was broken into. All of the furniture was slashed, telephone and electrical lines were cut, and an iodine-like substance was thrown on walls, floors, and ceilings. Police were called, but declined a request for investigation. Three days later, someone posing as a deliveryman entered the clinic and threw a substance believed to have been gasoline into the eyes of a technician. She remained sightless for several hours. He then set a fire that destroyed the entire clinic. Twenty patients were in the building at the time; at least one had to flee wearing only a laboratory coat. The arsonist was never caught.[6]

If law enforcement was benign at best, then the press perhaps unwittingly compounded the atmosphere of tolerance with its failure to see the implications of the far-flung but related acts of violence. For the most part, the local media did not cover the picketing that was steadily becoming more ugly and more disruptive. And in some cases, newspaper editorial positions actually rationalized the tactics of the disrupters, allowing that arguably, their actions were an acceptable response to procedures that some viewed as a crime.

Some may assert that reporting the activities of protesters only encourages them, that if they are not given the spotlight of attention, they will lose interest. I would counter that, by not reporting such assaults until they become so violent that they cannot be ignored, the perpetrators are empowered by tacit acquiescence. In other words, the absence of strong condemnation of harassing and threatening tactics invariably leads to the mistaken interpretation that the violence is tolerable.

But as dangerous as the arsonists may have been, for the moment they did not constitute the greatest threat to reproductive rights.

Less than a week after I had been named president of Planned Parenthood, there was a press conference at the federation's New York offices. No more than half a dozen newspaper and magazine reporters showed up, along with a couple of television crews (perhaps more curious than expectant). But the room was crowded with members of my new staff, who were interested in hearing what I had to say.

Roe had been under steady attack not only by anti-choice extremists, but also by congressmen and senators who, beneath the vaulted ceilings and crystal chandeliers of the Capitol, were hard at work undermining the Supreme Court decision with a number of recently passed and impending amendments and resolutions.

I began my first statement to the press by announcing my plans to challenge the most ominous threat—the Court's lifting of the injunction against the amendment proposed by Henry Hyde to prohibit the use of Medicaid funds for abortion. In effect, the amendment cut off federal funding for poor women to exercise their legal right to abortion.

If even one woman was denied access to abortion, that was more than enough reason to fight the Hyde Amendment. But apart from the fact that it was the first blow to *Roe*, the amendment involved much more than abortion, and that made it a defining issue for us. I hadn't forgotten Father Griese making clear to me that the real issue was the whole of a woman's body and all of the rights and powers it might encompass. This early focus on distinct *aspects* of the newly recognized right to abortion convinced me that it was merely the first step in a larger agenda. I felt that if we didn't secure the right to abortion for the most vulnerable women with the immediate reversal of Hyde, the ability of *all* women to exercise their reproductive decisions, including abortion, would be put in jeopardy.

I knew that challenging a threat like the Hyde Amendment in my opening speech also meant challenging Planned Parenthood's long-standing restraint on the subject of abortion. But as the new president of an organization whose founding principles had included advocacy for the rights of poor women, I couldn't ignore it. There was simply too much at stake for all women and for the work of Planned Parenthood *not* to do so, and forthrightly.

More in keeping with the organization's traditional role, as I had done in my maiden speech to the board, I also announced initiatives in contraception, the prevention of teen pregnancy, and reproductive biology.

In the question-and-answer session that followed my statement, few reporters responded to the substance of what I'd said. Instead, several asked me to confirm that I was the first woman president since Margaret Sanger—they expressed disbelief. And there were a number of questions about how it felt to be the first black person to head Planned Parenthood. Not only was I the first black to lead the organization, but the whole of it was primarily white, and especially so at the executive director and board levels.

I've been asked this question many times since, and I can never figure out how to answer it. I've never known how it feels to be anything else. But, as I've said before, I believed that my ethnic identity gave me firsthand experience with those who suffered the most from the oppression of illegal birth control and abortion.

Along with the press conference, there had been a press release that covered many of the points of my public statement. It began:

FAYE WATTLETON, 34, NAMED PRESIDENT OF NATIONAL PLANNED PARENTHOOD OF NEW YORK, February 2—The new president designate of the nation's principal family planning organization called today for a three-pronged national drive to restore the provision of abortions under Medicaid, to spur development of a new generation of contraceptive methods, and to formulate a national strategy for reducing the incidence of adolescent pregnancy.

The press release also quoted part of my speech regarding the growing wave of violence and the principle that would frame my discussions and debates for years to come. I was determined not to engage in the polemic of the right and wrong of any aspect of reproductive rights, including abortion. And if Planned Parenthood had made the values of self-determination the bedrock of our work, we had to believe that "freedom of speech" meant freedom of speech for everyone. Though our opponents might say obnoxious things, as long as their views did not rise to the harassment of others, they had a right to them, I said.

> [The organization would] seek not to silence these people, but to create and protect a world in which all people have the opportunity, as they do, to express their opinions and pursue practices consistent with their own beliefs, free of coercion or manipulation by those whose opinions are different from theirs.

I was pleased with the press release and the way it expressed my vision—until I came to its last paragraph:

> A health professional with a degree in nursing from Columbia University, Ms. Wattleton currently serves as the Executive Director of Planned Parenthood of the Miami Valley (Dayton, Ohio) and is former Chair of the National Executive Directors Council. Before joining Planned Parenthood, she was with the Public Health Nursing Service of Dayton, Ohio. Married with one child, Ms. Wattleton resides in Dayton, and will be moving to New York in mid-April.[7]

When I read these words now, I remember the disappointment I'd felt because they overlooked the aspects of my work that I was most proud of: There was no acknowledgment that I was coming to the national office after building a small five-year-old affiliate into one of the largest in the country. And my membership on the national board and the nature of my involvement there passed unremarked. There was no welcoming quotation (from the chairperson of the board)—a standard feature of press releases written to mark the accession of an executive. I felt as though I was being presented as the lowest common denominator. I was too proud to challenge the modest portrayal.

I believed that my mandate was to provide the strong leadership that had been lacking over recent years. I knew I had the support of the colleagues who had helped me to earn this post. But what about the people who didn't know me—those upon whom we depended for so much of our financial support? How could I inspire their trust? How could I lead if the evidence of my competence to do so was so limited?

* * *

Since we hadn't sold our house in Dayton, and Franklin had not yet resigned from his job with the Montgomery County Mental Health and Mental Retardation Board, I planned to commute back and forth to New York for several months, beginning in April, when I'd take on full responsibilities of the PPFA presidency.

At first, Franklin resisted the idea of Felicia being left solely in his care. "Why don't you take her with you?" he asked, remembering the days when she'd traveled with me to Planned Parenthood national board meetings. I explained that this time I wasn't going to be away for just a few days of meetings. And Felicia, once a world-class sleeper, had now transformed into a cheerful and very active toddler. I'd be living in a hotel and it would mean consigning our daughter to one small room and the care of a stranger. It wouldn't have been fair to her and would have terrified me. I was still deeply concerned about leaving her with anyone. "I'd never forgive myself if . . ." remained a kind of mantra, and I could not forget my terror over the baby-sitter's words, "It was just a small fire . . ." Eventually, I was able to persuade Franklin that, for now, it was better for Felicia to stay in Dayton, in his and our new housekeeper's care.

Saying good-bye to the staff at the affiliate was more difficult than I would ever have imagined on that first morning seven years earlier. The staff still consisted of fifty or so people; but now instead of a large cadre of outreach workers, our numbers also included a professional counseling staff, a professional community education staff, and a growing fund-raising and public relations department. Together, we'd brought about tremendous changes at Planned Parenthood of Miami Valley. We still served the same six-county area, but the number of people our clinics reached had grown from about three thousand to almost ten thousand. The budget had tripled. There had been difficult times, too, but we'd weathered them.

The staff's work and loyalty had brought recognition to the affiliate locally, nationally, and internationally. We could never have done so much without their dedicatation.

I couldn't thank the board enough. The members had supported and encouraged almost everything that I had tried to do. But even as I prepared to take on bigger tasks, I was nagged by the thought that had I not been distracted by my national work, if I had had a little more time, I would have found a way to gain the board's support for the provision of abortion services.

I felt as though I was saying good-bye to a very close-knit family when I said good-bye to the board—and especially to Konrad, who had found me, and Fred, the seasoned corporate executive, who had joined Konrad in mentoring my development as executive director. Fred would take a new lease on his mentorship when he became the next chairman of the national board. He used to say to me, "Faye, you're like a thoroughbred racehorse. All I need to do is keep you on the track and let you run." Both men, much older and wiser than I, were close personal friends; in many ways, father figures.

On April 17, I arrived at my new office on the seventh floor of 810 Seventh Avenue in New York City.

If the press had found more novelty in my age, my gender, and my race than in my plans, such was not the case throughout the organization. I soon learned that giving abortion such a prominent place in my vision for Planned Parenthood was, in the minds of many of my colleagues, a major blunder, if not outright heresy. It hadn't occurred to me that anyone within Planned Parenthood *wouldn't* be outraged by the possibility of poor women not having the same access to their recently recognized rights as affluent women did.

I was quickly made to understand that despite being an organization whose founding passion was the liberation of all women from sexual and reproductive bondage, Planned Parenthood was not—and had never been—an organization made up of individuals who agreed on every point of principle—even founding principles.

After my public statements had been circulated to the affiliates, Tenny Marshall, who had returned to her position as chairman of the board, received a number of expressions of distress about my "agenda to drag the organization unnecessarily into the abortion controversy." Some were even afraid that I was about to make PPFA an "abortion organization" instead of one whose primary work was preventing unwanted pregnancy. And to my astonishment, there was a charge that I had a "radical political agenda" that would "destroy Planned Parenthood as we know it."

I spent the first month of my presidency traveling the regional meeting circuit of affiliates scattered around the country. In the desert setting of El Paso, Texas, the site of one of Margaret Sanger's first organizations, three women from the Waco affiliate asked to meet with me privately.

When I joined the women—all in their early thirties, well-coiffed, well-turned-out, and jeweled (Texas style)—in a quiet corner of a hotel dining room, I was taken aback by their reason for wanting to meet with me: "Abortion may be okay in New York, but abortion doesn't play well in our town."

"You're pushing too hard on abortion and your public statements have hurt our affiliate."

"You're going to throw the baby out with the bathwater."

"You will not be welcome in Waco if you keep on pushing the abortion issue." These words took me back to Mama's account of having been threatened with being run out of town for her provocative statements on racial intolerance.

Clearly, my appointment had left these women feeling vulnerable to the anger of their community. Instead of confronting our opposition, they confronted me, who they feared would provoke controversy. And their worries about their community support in the face of that anger were deep and genuine. They clearly could not see how much more profoundly their work would be compromised if we weren't outspoken in our challenge of the Medicaid restrictions. Nothing I could say at that point would convince them.

"I appreciate your letting me know your concerns," I said—as I would say at the end of dozens of similar meetings over the next fourteen years. "I believe that these attacks threaten more than abortion, and I can't see backing down. We must defend all women."

I had no supporters among these three women, but the battle wasn't about approval. It was about the right thing to do, and this unpleasant challenge, so early in my tenure, did not shake my conviction.

The wariness on the part of my colleagues was hardly limited to west Texas towns. The resistance that I'd encountered when I tried to get abortion services started in Dayton had offered me my first glimpse of ambivalence even among those who are firmly committed to reproductive rights, and who have demonstrated their commitment through their work. This ambivalence, which our opposition exploited over and over, was prevalent throughout the reproductive rights movement.

When I gave speeches at Planned Parenthood events early in my tenure, I was often asked why I didn't talk more about the "good things" Planned Parenthood did; or I might hear, "We would just like to have a speech on contraception or teenage pregnancy or world population control." Sometimes I was asked to avoid the subject of abortion and politics altogether. When affiliates requested restrictions on my speech—"We don't want Faye to talk about abortion"—I would decline the invitation. I refused to promise not to discuss every aspect of reproductive choice.

I thought that most in the organization believed in unfettered reproductive rights, and I was fairly certain that those who requested my silence on "abortion and politics" were not motivated by concern over the Father Grieses of the world. The desire for silence seemed to be motivated by the hope that if we weren't so visible, we wouldn't attract controversy. Yet all around us was the evidence that we were the focus of the enemies of women's reproductive rights whether we assumed a high profile or not. I didn't believe that we would alienate our supporters by standing up for our principles. I believed that we would gain more support if we did not veer from these principles.

Underlying the ambivalence that some affiliates were expressing was a judgmental core—the feeling that ending a pregnancy is undesirable. The implication of judgment rankled me. I was taught, "Judge not, that ye be judged." On matters so private, so intimate, who are any of us to judge another's way?

Whenever we gave way to the thinking that the decision to have an abortion was one of "last resort," we were making an implied judgment that "no one would do it unless there was absolutely no other way." And where did that leave women who made the decision to end a pregnancy when there was another way? Abortion is often a woman's first choice. Even as we supported the right to choose abortion, by revealing such attitudes, we implied that abortion was immoral and shameful. For many women it is a morally correct decision to make, and that shouldn't be repudiated by implication or direct assaults.

I was certain this lack of uncompromising conviction weakened us. And I believed that the opponents of women's rights would continue to attack our ambivalent spots in the hope of wearing us down.

I didn't go so far as Margaret Sanger had and put tape over my mouth in protest of the attempted censorship, but I wasn't going to keep silent either. I believed that talking openly about abortion, even just saying the word, was crucial to erasing the stigma placed on the practice and on the women who choose it. In time, the requests to restrict my words stopped and invitations to speak came from every part of the country. Eventually, I would give an average of fifty speeches each year. But I was under no illusion that there was no ambivalence among my listeners.

Some of my soon-to-be inherited charges at the national offices also thought that my appointment was a blatant mistake; that the likelihood of my succeeding on the national level was virtually nil. Tenny Marshall was said to have announced my appointment to the staff: "The board has selected a thirty-four-year-old nurse from Dayton, Ohio, to be president of PPFA." One senior member asked, "How long is her contract and what is the buyout clause?" I wouldn't let such resistance as his set the tone for my tenure, so I asked Tenny to make certain that he wasn't at PPFA by the time I arrived. Now, openly supportive, she obliged.

Quibbles aside, I felt strong support, goodwill, and a spirit of hope for my success from many throughout Planned Parenthood. And with respect to the public at large, I was the subject of more press attention than I or anyone else expected. The *New York Times* announced my arrival with: "Planned Parenthood's New Head Takes a Fighting Stand." Its article explored the more controversial aspects of my opening statement, and the political significance of an African American woman taking such a prominent role in a movement sometimes criticized for being eugenic. When the reporter asked me if I thought that my being black would help "diffuse criticism" from other blacks who felt that birth control and abortion were forms of "black genocide," I answered: "We should not be concerned with increasing our numbers, but with the quality of life. What's really important is that black women have equal access to determine when they will have children."[8]

I was featured on the cover of *Working Woman*. And *Essence, Ms.,* and *People* magazine did feature articles. The coverage I received, like the questions asked at the press conference, focused mainly on the firsts I represented. But some, like the *New York Daily News*, wrote articles dissecting my opening statement against the backdrop of Planned Parenthood's conservative image. *Essence,* for example, noted that, since abortion had only just recently been added to the roster of Planned Parenthood services, it was "too early to tell" whether I could lead the organization to a position of major influence in the areas of our reproductive rights."[9]

This sense of healthy skepticism, of "we'll wait to see," was not intimidating. But it did serve notice that I would be under the media's scrutiny until I made good on my promises. But from the beginning, I did not fear the press, which would eventually become our best channel to reach millions in the name of women's reproductive rights.

Working Woman wrote, "[S]he's a mother and she works. She's all of the things she represents."[10] While I wanted it known that my life had dimensions beyond PPFA, I was reluctant to discuss Franklin. I did not believe that he should be obliged to play a part in my professional purpose. But Felicia was part of me in a whole different way. I wanted people to know that motherhood was central in my life; that it was possible to be a good mother and still be committed to an ideal and to *this* career.

One or two articles noted my looks and manner, as *Essence* did when it wrote, "With her fresh laugh and bright friendly eyes, Faye Wattleton looks like a college student. You keep expecting for her to show some hard edge . . . She's slim and graceful, impeccably dressed."[11]

I was my mother's daughter. Having learned from her how valuable one's appearance could be to having one's message heard, I did my best to follow her lead. One look at some of the photographs from the first months, though, showed that I could use some help with my hair and makeup if I was to live up to my mother's standards (and that my appearance would need to be adapted to a national stage monitored by all those ever-ready cameras). This time I sought advice from my African American staff. "Honey, I know just what you need . . ." concluded Sandy Grymes, one of our regional directors. Soon I was in the care of a person who would become a close friend, hairstylist Bruce Clark, who also arranged for a makeup artist to advise me, and upon whom I would rely for the fourteen years that I found myself the focus of press attention.

From my viewpoint, all this press attention was unexpected, but at times comforting in light of some of the objections that were being raised about my statements. Those concerns aside, the board was thrilled to see so much focus on the organization, even if some of its members would have preferred gentler words.

That spring, when the round of regional meetings was over, I turned my attention to getting the internal house in order, which also included our international division, established in 1971. It had become the largest State Department–financed, U.S.–based family-planning assistance program, supporting projects in twenty-five developing countries.

The affiliates were clamoring for programs that would support and assist them locally, which meant that I would need to attract top-level people with leadership experience to help me guide the organization through the inevitable turbulence. That would take time. In the meantime, I needed all the help I could get from my affiliate colleagues.

One of the first people I reached out to was Al Moran. I respected his leadership and his many achievements; but most of all, like many in Planned Parenthood, I admired his uncompromising stand on reproductive rights and his fearlessness in challenging anyone who did not uphold his high standards or who in any way attacked them. I knew he must have felt betrayed by my encouraging him to apply for the presidency, and then becoming a candidate myself. But given that we existed in the same city, I hoped we could put aside any harsh feelings and join together to move the organization forward. His icy response dashed any hope I might have had about letting bygones be bygones. "You can depend on my presence," he said flatly. That was the sum of that conversation. However, in time, he and I would be able to forge a congenial working relationship. But for now, I would have to make do without his support.

By June, David Andrews, a rising star in the federation, had accepted my invitation to join me as executive vice president. David was a brown-haired, brown-eyed Texan of medium height and stocky build, whose accent suggested southern intelligentsia. He had served in the Peace Corps in Ecuador, and upon his return to America with his beautiful Ecuadoran wife, he joined an antipoverty agency in San Antonio. From there he was recruited to become the executive director of the city's Planned Parenthood affiliate. David's ready laugh relieved the tensions of many trying situations. He was often the gentle counter to my forthrightness, but on principle we stood shoulder to shoulder.

Mary Beth Moore, who had been a devoted member of my staff in Dayton, also responded to my urging to come aboard as my special assistant handling board matters.

I was determined that we stay focused on our mission to serve and empower women through the availability of birth control education and medical services. A strong defense of abortion rights didn't mean that our mission to care for women's health could be diluted or overshadowed. In fact, it was our service aspect that would continue to reinforce the credibility of our voice in all our public and political debates.

I also knew that if we stood up to the gathering forces of the opposition, we would be subject to public scrutiny in ways we'd never been subject to before. The standards of every aspect of our work had to be above reproach. I would soon learn that attaining reproachlessness wasn't as easy as I might have assumed. I hadn't been at Planned Parenthood two weeks when I realized that the damage someone could do—inadvertently or otherwise—would play a role in my middle-of-the-night terrors.

My first real-life nightmare was *Abortion Eve,* a comic book published by Nanny Goat Productions, in Laguna, California. Six months prior to my arrival it had been reviewed in the October 1977 issue of *Getting It Together,* a bimonthly Planned Parenthood publication directed at young people. *Abortion Eve* recounted the sagas of four different "Eves" as they went about making different decisions about their unwanted pregnancies. However, the review failed to mention that the back cover of the comic book depicted Mary, the mother of Christ, in a satirical and irreverent cartoon. When our review was picked up by the anti-choice press, Planned Parenthood was accused of having endorsed the whole book.

By summer, the protest letters and condemnation from Catholic leaders were at full cry. Demonstrators formed protest lines outside our front door on busy Seventh Avenue. More than three hundred people turned out for one two-and-a-half-hour demonstration. The commotion eventually required police barricades. Several of the picketers' placards claimed that Planned Parenthood had defiled "the person of Our Lady" by promoting *Abortion Eve.* One speaker described us as the "maggots on the rotting flesh of a declining civilization."

On May 1, 1978, barely two weeks after I assumed my responsibilities as president, and while I was shuttling to regional meetings, we released the following apology:

> We take this opportunity to publicly repudiate *Abortion Eve* and to call on all groups involved in the reproductive health issues to confine their public messages within the bounds of decency and respect both for truth and for the religious and other sensitivities of their audience.[12]

The protests continued.

Meanwhile, another embarrassment was brewing. Our largest affiliate, Rocky Mountain Planned Parenthood, in Denver, headed by Sherri Tepper (who had opposed my candidacy), had produced many outstanding educational materials. The affiliate even had its own publishing subsidiary. However, it had also created a series of cartoons ridiculing the pope, army generals, Phyllis Schlafly, members of Congress (for various sexual peccadilloes and hypocrisies), and Secretary of Health, Education and Welfare Joseph Califano. Although the cartoons had been produced as in-house humor, they circulated among the executive directors of the largest affiliates. The executive director in Chicago filed the cartoons. When he was away from his office and a college newspaper requested a political cartoon on abortion, one of his staff members, who recalled seeing cartoons he thought were humorous, went to the executive director's files, pulled them, and sent copies off to be published in the school newspaper.

While some of the cartoons were quite clever, what one can create and circulate as a private individual is very different from what one can do under the banner of an organization whose stock-in-trade is the public's goodwill. The press excoriated us. Members of Congress condemned Planned Parenthood as an organization engaged in irresponsible demagoguery, and charged that we were thus untrustworthy to receive federal funding. There were calls for an investigation to determine whether or not the government's Title X funds had been used to create the cartoons. Once again I had to send off apologies, not only to affiliates, who were starting to catch heat as well, but also to the subjects of the cartoons.

Abortion Eve and the cartoons were lumped together by Planned Parenthood's opponents, and the combined crisis escalated so quickly that for several weeks—when I could least afford the distraction, given the management restructuring under way—I did virtually nothing but focus on containment. My ability to respond to the Denver situation was made more difficult by the preexisting tensions between Sherri and me. When I tried to reach Sherri to arrange a meeting to discuss the matter, she would not take my calls. When David and Jeannie Rosoff from the Alan Guttmacher Institute contacted her, she said, "It's just a tempest in a teapot." When they pressed further, suggesting that her acts had imperiled the future of Title X funding for Planned Parenthood, she dismissed even the possibility of considering it.

Tenny Marshall called the board president of the Denver affiliate and asked to meet with the board of directors to impress upon them the seriousness of our situation and to persuade them to publicly acknowledge their mistakes.

Tenny, David, and I flew out to Denver. In a face-to-face confrontation that evening, Sherri sat in stony silence, furious at the rebuke our presence signified. I would have been furious, too. With more experience I probably would not have escalated the incident to such a visible level. But I also knew that in spite of the need to maintain harmony in the organization, it was also important to make tangibly clear that such productions would not be countenanced.

Our next step was to create a memorandum titled "What We Say and How We Say It." In the communiqué, I said that Planned Parenthood must continue to abide by its reputation for respect and sensitivity toward the personal views of all people. I recognized that most attacks on us would come from antiabortion extremists, determined to use any opening they could find in our materials to reduce our public support, and to convince the government that it should no longer fund our programs. To guard against those dangers, we had to emphasize issues rather than people. Unlike antiabortion organizations, we received public funds for the provision of our services. That, I stated, made us "much more visible, and in a sense more vulnerable, than organizations that do not have the same direct link with the government." While we could mention the increasing political activities of the Roman Catholic Church, we could not dishonor any religious, ethnic, or social group, or personally insult or libel any specific individual. Although our opponents might resort to the rhetoric of slander, shock, and ridicule, such tactics employed by us could not be tolerated. We were expected to be civil and rational.

I also took the opportunity to lay out the importance of our not letting our opponents claim for their own, words that represent basic American values—*family*, *morality*, and *life*. These values, I argued, were central to our mission. I was setting the tone for my internal leadership.

Things settled down eventually, and we didn't lose our Title X funding. And I learned some essential lessons in the process. The most significant was one that I'd begun to understand in Dayton: The focus of the opposition's attacks would not be confined to the issues of reproductive rights, which included abortion. Increasingly, the very existence of Planned Parenthood would be the issue.

CHAPTER 18

REFUSING TO SURRENDER
THE POOR

W hen I first started my job at the national offices, after spending a few weeks in a grungy, midtown Manhattan hotel, I was lucky enough to rent a small apartment in the nurses' residence at Columbia, where I had lived during my graduate school days. But after three months of commuting back and forth to Dayton, I found myself experiencing those old childhood pangs of anxiety when I didn't know where my next home would be. I longed for the time when Franklin, Felicia, and I would all be together again, and worried about finding a house we liked and could afford. The demands of reorganization and damage control at Planned Parenthood offered little time for the task of house hunting, but Franklin was still wrapping up his work in Dayton and we didn't have the money for him to repeatedly fly out to help me. Having no time in my fourteen-hour workdays to look at houses, I decided to stay in New York for a few weekends to find the right place for us.

Tenny had suggested that I look for an apartment in the city, but I was accustomed to freestanding houses, to trees and shady lawns. I was beginning to realize that there would be little that was predictable or secure about so much of my life, and that I needed the peace and sense of security that such things offered. I didn't want Felicia to grow up without a swing in her backyard, grass under her feet, and quiet streets where she could learn to ride her bicycle. Franklin agreed. After much inquiry, advice from my staff, and trips to several New York suburbs, I found what I thought we would like: a Tudor-style home in New Rochelle, a racially and economically integrated community on Long Island Sound about thirty minutes north of the city. As we'd now sold the house in Dayton for less than half the asking price of this one, it fell in a range we could afford—especially if we could bring the price down a little bit.

The next weekend, Franklin and Felicia flew out from Dayton and we piled into a rented car for the trip to New Rochelle. When we drove up the driveway of our new home, I felt I was entering a lacy wonderland. English garden flowers lined the long sloping lawn just as the white crab apple blossoms were giving way to the leaves that would cool the yard from the summer sun. Birdsong and the fragrance of early summer completed the picture of the traditional home that, from the time of my vagabond childhood, I'd always dreamed of. As I walked into the entry foyer, I instantly felt at home amid the leaded glass windows, sunken living room, fireplace, and large bedrooms and bathrooms. All was larger and more gracious than the house in Dayton had been. Franklin's "Wow!" confirmed that I'd found the perfect place for us. We made the down payment a few days later, then returned to Dayton to pack and say good-bye to our friends and neighbors and head east, hopeful and expectant.

Felicia was not quite three at the time, so securing her care was my next priority. A Montessori school five minutes away from our house would serve as a perfect setting to nurture Felicia's boundless curiosity and energy—but first things first. I had to find reliable child care. When Mona walked up to our door, fortune once again smiled on us. Sent by a referral agency, Mona was a short round woman with soft sad eyes. She'd recently come to the United States to join her husband, who had fled South Africa under death threats for his political activities in the then-outlawed African National Congress. She wore the knitted cap that so commonly covered the heads of black women in her homeland. She'd worked as a registered nurse in Soweto, but had no standing in her profession in the United States, until she took additional training.

I could not have wished for a more gracious or gentle person to care for our daughter. In the years she was with us, Mona taught Felicia many things about her country, and reinforced the values of politeness, of sharing, and of loving. One of Felicia's special pleasures was to hear Mona say, "Sweetheart, if you eat your salad you can watch the soap operas." As for Mona, I suspect that, given the distance that lay between her and her own daughters and son, who were still in South Africa, Felicia gratified her need to love a child.

As he had presumed, Franklin quickly found a job running a program for the Police Athletic League in Brooklyn, and our lives soon settled into a habit of rising early so Franklin could drive me to the station to catch the train that would get me to the office before nine. He would then continue on to Brooklyn. In the evenings, around seven, we'd reverse the routine.

Some nights, when I was forced to work late, I'd arrive home weary and too late to see Felicia before she fell asleep. That's when I'd remember Tenny's advice, and acknowledge to myself that we'd paid a high price for the luxury of grass and trees.

But I took to heart a caution from Fred Smith—"You've got to take care of yourself, because no one else is going to do it"—and kept my weekends inviolate. With the rare exception of a board meeting overlapping into a Saturday, I accepted no commitments over those two days. Franklin, Felicia, and I would do the usual things a working couple must see to on the weekends—the cleaner's, the grocery store, car repair. We looked forward to dinner at a nearby Chinese restaurant, or to a movie. Occasionally we would see a Broadway show, but mostly we preferred to recuperate at home from the week's rigors. When Sunday night came around, I'd cook enough food for the week ahead, and wrap up the dinner-size portions in foil and put them in the freezer. It was a ritual that satisfied my need to take care of my family, even when I couldn't be with them.

As little time as I spent there, I felt I had a home again. I felt anchored as I immersed myself ever deeper in the task of running PPFA.

Almost from the moment the Supreme Court ruled in *Roe v. Wade*—five years before I'd first come to the national offices—attempts had been made to overturn the Court's decision. Jesse Helms, the Republican senator from South Carolina, sponsored a constitutional amendment to establish the fetus as a person from the moment of conception. But amending the Constitution is a cumbersome and difficult process, so those who were opposed to legal abortion soon shifted to the more achievable goal of imposing other restrictions on abortion rights. Congressman Henry Hyde was in the vanguard of this opposition to *Roe*.

When the *Roe* decision declared abortion to be a legal medical procedure, since the Medicaid program was the nation's healthcare financing program for the poor, it meant that Medicaid would automatically fund legal abortions for poor women. Because the distribution of Medicaid funding was legislated at both state and federal levels, Hyde and his cohorts decided to take aim at *Roe* through federal legislation.

On June 24, 1976, Congressman Hyde introduced an amendment to the Labor–Department of Health, Education, and Welfare (L-DHEW) bill stating, "None of the funds appropriated under this act shall be used for abortions or to promote or encourage abortions."[1] This meant that Medicaid funds, appropriated to give poor women the same access to medical care as affluent women, could not be used to pay for abortion. No exceptions, even to save the life of a woman, were allowed in Hyde's original plan.

This was an election year, and members of Congress were beginning to feel the pressure from anti-choice activists. Hyde's proposal added to that pressure, since a vote against it could be construed as a vote for taxpayer-supported "murder," as abortion was considered to be by the amendment's supporters. Roll call votes piled still more pressure on those legislators who were opposed to the implications of Medicaid restrictions.

The foes of abortion knew that they had the sentiments of the American public working largely in their favor. Most Americans are in favor of a woman's right to have an abortion, but there is an aversion to the poor and welfare. Public dependency undermines our values of self-sufficiency by appearing to indulge irresponsibility, especially when such behavior involves sexual conduct. Even those who are pro-choice are tempted to buy into the notion that publicly funded abortion relieves poor women of the consequences of their "promiscuity," and should therefore be restricted.

There are many arguments for helping poor women gain access to abortion services, the first of which is that it is legal. It is also not fair to discriminate against them. Put in harsh economic terms, raising children in poverty is a lot more costly than abortion. But those who use this reasoning risk charges of "Nazism" or "genocide" against the poor.

In the Senate, Robert Packwood (R-OR) offered an amendment to strike the Hyde Amendment, calling it unconstitutional. After considerable debate, the Senate deleted the amendment from its version of the bill.

Jesse Helms represented the opposition to poor women when he asserted that "whatever the Supreme Court has said about a woman's right to privacy with respect to abortions does not translate . . . into an affirmative duty on the part of the federal government to use public funds to finance the termination of human life."[2] After extended and heated debate, maneuvers to avoid a roll call vote failed.

But after a joint House-Senate conference committee had ironed out all the differences on the entire appropriations bill *except* for the Hyde amendment, debate over it resumed in the House.

Congressman Parren Mitchell (D-MD), who had worked as a probation officer, conveyed a visceral understanding of the consequences of driving poor women to dangerous situations:

Have the Members seen the results of a coat-hanger abortion? Have the Members seen the illness that women suffer when they get caught up in these abortion rackets? Have the Members seen the result of an abortion performed by a rusty penknife? Have you seen what that does to a woman physically and psychologically? I have.

All we would do today under the Hyde amendment is to leave those ugly, brutal options open to one class of people: those at the very bottom. . . . We cannot live with that on our conscience.[3]

But in a speech that managed to affront all women, Congressman Hyde pulled out all the stops:

> Abortion is an inhuman solution to a very human problem. The only virtue to abortion is that it is a final solution. Believe me, it is a final solution, especially to the unborn child.
>
> Mr. Speaker, let the poor women of America make a list of those things that society denies them and which are enjoyed by rich women. Decent housing, decent education, decent food, decent income, and then say to them, "Now, those will take second place. But we will encourage you to kill your unborn young children. Besides, there are too many of you anyway."
>
> If rich women want to enjoy their high-priced vices, that is their responsibility. They can get the finest heroin in the world that is not available on the street. They can get a face-lift. They can fly to Las Vegas and gamble. That is fine, but not at the taxpayers' expense.
>
> Mr. Speaker, let us not make the innocently inconvenient scapegoats for our futility in finding human solutions to these human problems. When the mother, who should be the natural protector of her unborn child, becomes its adversary, then the legislature has a duty to intervene.
>
> Birth is no big deal. It is just a change of address.[4]

Pat Schroeder, Democratic Congresswoman from Colorado, responded to that outrage:

> Nowhere in the public record is there a rebuke of such characterization of women by men who will never deliver a baby or spend a single moment of their lives wondering whether they're pregnant, being pregnant and not wanting to be. Yet they have the temerity to judge that birth is no big deal and to compare abortion with such "high-priced vices" as heroin addiction and gambling in Las Vegas. The contempt for women that was embodied in the denigrating failure of the Congress of the United States to acknowledge that women are more valuable than fetuses, should even today outrage any woman who cares one whit about her worth.[5]

On August 23, 1976, the Senate again voted down Hyde's amendment by a tally of 53–35. But barely a month later, the members of the conference committee announced agreement on a modified amendment, which provided that Medicaid-funded abortion would be allowed *only* "where the life of the mother would be endangered if the fetus were carried to term." It was ratified by both houses.

What happened in between the two votes? Nothing . . . except they all realized that both the new fiscal year and the coming elections were pressing harder. The appropriations bill contained funding for nearly all federal labor, health, and social programs. No one wanted to risk disrupting government services over the single issue of abortion for poor women. The legislators decided that as they hit the campaign trail, it would look much worse for them if they didn't pass the appropriations bill than if they voted for a measure that "everybody knew" was unconstitutional and that sacrificed the rights of poor women.

Although he supported the Hyde amendment, President Ford vetoed the bill, claiming that he didn't like the level of appropriations in it. Congress overrode his veto, and on September 30, 1976, the Hyde amendment became law. It would take effect in the fall of 1977. Unless the Supreme Court struck the amendment down, antiabortion activists had scored their first major victory in their campaign to recriminalize abortion for all women. The *Roe v. Wade* decision was not yet four years old.

The same day Congress overrode Ford's veto—September 30, 1976—Cora McRae, a New York Medicaid recipient in the first trimester of a pregnancy she wished to terminate, filed a class-action suit with the District Court of the Eastern District of New York against the Secretary of the Department of Health, Education and Welfare on behalf of all women "who [were or would be] prevented from obtaining medical termination of their pregnancies by the Hyde amendment."[6] Planned Parenthood joined in the challenge along with a number of others.

The case was assigned to Judge John F. Dooling, Jr., of the Federal District Court for the Eastern District of New York. On October 22, Judge Dooling enjoined DHEW from putting the amendment into effect. He ordered DHEW to continue making federal reimbursements for abortion services nationwide, while the case was under consideration.

So far so good. But then, the following summer—on June 20, 1977—the Supreme Court decided three cases, *Beal v. Doe, Maher v. Roe,* and *Poelker v. Doe,* all of which involved limitations imposed by state and local authorities on the ability of poor women to exercise their right to obtain abortions, limitations based on the denial of Medicaid funding for the procedure when it was "nontherapeutic" or "elective." In all three cases, the Court upheld the limitations as constitutional.

The *Poelker* decision was handed down along with *Maher.* As in *Roe v. Wade,* the majority was 6–3. The decision was written by Justice Lewis Powell:

> *Roe* did not declare an unqualified "constitutional right to an abortion," as the District Court seems to think. Rather, the right protects

the woman from unduly burdensome interference with her freedom to decide whether to terminate her pregnancy. It implies no limitation on the authority of a state to make a value judgment favoring childbirth over abortion, and to implement that judgment by allocation of public funds. . . . An indigent woman who desires an abortion suffers no disadvantage as a consequence of Connecticut's decision to fund childbirth; she continues as before to be dependent on private sources for the service she desires. The indigency that may make it difficult—and in some cases, perhaps, impossible—for some women to have abortions is neither created nor in any way affected by the Connecticut regulation.[7]

Justices William Brennan, Thurgood Marshall, and Harry Blackmun dissented. Brennan saw the dangers implicit in the decision, and he wrote:

I had not thought the nature of the fundamental right established in *Roe* open to question, let alone susceptible of the interpretation advanced by the Court. The fact that the Connecticut scheme may not operate as an absolute bar preventing all indigent women from having abortions is not critical. What is critical is that the state has inhibited their fundamental right to make that choice free from state interference.[8]

Another decision came on August 4, 1977. Judge Dooling, who had first placed the restraining order to block the implementation of the Hyde Amendment pending his decision, lifted it. Apparently, government attorneys had convinced him that the attending physician's good-faith certification of "life endangerment" would be sufficient for Medicaid reimbursement to continue. Still, Judge Dooling would not make a final decision for two more years. For now, we could only hope.

Once the flurry of coverage over the novelty of my appointment died down, I assumed that I would mostly be left alone. But by the end of 1978, I found myself being drawn more visibly into public debate. Requests for network television appearances were increasing. By this time I was relatively comfortable with speaking before large groups of people, but I still wasn't confident when it came to expressing my views on television. I turned to Dorothy Sarnoff, the well-known television coach, for help. After two sessions, she said, "Either you have it or you don't. I've seen them all—and you have it." So I was on my own, learning to live with my faithful pre-interview jitters and to rely on my innate ability to think quickly on my feet.

My first national media test came in the late Seventies, on *The Phil Donahue Show*, when it was still in Chicago. I was invited to appear with

Congressman Henry Hyde. The idea of going head-to-head with one of the most prominent nemeses of the pro-choice movement had me tense and nervous. The prospect of doing so on national television left me almost frozen with anxiety. And then there was the issue of my being outraged over the ugly intent of his amendment and the reprehensible language he had used to promote it. I wasn't sure I'd be able to stay calm, rational, and in control of my thoughts with him seated next to me.

Once we were on the air, the partisan applause, especially the applause against me, unnerved me even more. My hands shook and my throat dried out. I tried my best to hide my terror with a plastered-on smile that was supposed to exude confidence. But Hyde's self-righteous pomposity and lack of regard for poor women—and all women—infuriated me. And the false familiarity of his conversation during commercial breaks—"A trip to Hawaii would be great right now"—sickened me. When Hyde said before the millions of people tuned to the program that I was encouraging women to "kill their unborn," I found myself drawing upon skills that I'd learned in nursing school—how to remain composed and resolute while under tremendous pressure. This was just the first of many times that I'd have to draw upon them, as I and the organization I represented became lightning rods for debate in the increasingly rough-and-tumble political environment of sexual and reproductive politics.

At the beginning of the program the audience response had been fairly evenly divided on the issue. But by the end of it the mood had shifted. One woman stood up and said to Hyde, "I'm against abortion, but I'm also against someone like you telling me what to do."

I hadn't been in New York long before I began hearing one name bandied about—David Garth. People talked about him in tones of reverential awe. He was a "political guru" they said, a strategist who won election after election and furthered progressive causes. He had co-chaired, along with Eleanor Roosevelt, the committee to elect presidential hopeful Adlai Stevenson, and had guided the campaigns of New York governor Hugh Carey, New York City mayor Ed Koch, Pennsylvania senators John Heinz and Arlen Specter, West Virginia governor Jay Rockefeller, and Los Angeles mayor Tom Bradley. He had helped elect former New York mayor John V. Lindsay, and he would later help Rudolph Giuliani become mayor of New York City. Al Moran, at Planned Parenthood of New York City, had sought David Garth's advice for his affiliate's successful public education campaigns on abortion.

Realizing the nature of our opposition and its growing strength in Congress, I had made an appointment early in the fall of 1978 to meet with Garth and his colleague, Judy Press Brenner, to see if they would be willing to study and analyze Planned Parenthood's political situation and advise us on how best to proceed. At the meeting, we all concluded that there was far too much to lose if Planned Parenthood maintained its long-standing avoidance of political issues.

I received David Garth's report late in January, with the winter board meeting hard upon us. To avoid repeating a past mistake, I forwarded a copy to our general counsel, Harriet Pilpel, and to the head of our legal division, Eve Paul, for a preliminary vetting even as I sent it to the board members for their perusal before the meeting.

Within hours, Eve called and announced that she had to meet with me "immediately." Hearing urgency in her voice, I agreed to see her right away. I then phoned David Andrews and asked him to join us.

Eve had joined Planned Parenthood shortly before I had; she oversaw the legal matters and the litigation that we were being drawn into with greater frequency. Prior to Planned Parenthood, she had worked with Harriet in private practice on many of the First Amendment and reproductive rights cases in which Harriet had played such a prominent role.

Eve was characteristically willing to see all sides of any issue, but that afternoon, she marched into my office indignant, eyes flashing. She waved the report in her hand, her bearing and authority making her presence fill the room. Her agitation tightened the tension in my office even before she spoke. "This document is illegal!" she exclaimed.

David and I looked at her, incredulous. "Illegal? What on earth do you mean?" he challenged.

"It's illegal," she repeated in a higher key, as though she believed that might help us understand English better. "We are a (501)(c)(3) organization and we cannot get involved in political activity."

Yes, I explained, I knew. We had encountered the same arguments from Harriet Pilpel when NEDC had made its proposal to the national board in 1976. But this wasn't our proposal. It was the report of an outside consultant.

"What we do with it, and how, is our business."

But Eve was adamant. "As a nonprofit organization, we simply cannot legally accept the report's recommendations. David Garth is saying that we should get involved in the elections. We can't do that. Even reading the report could be construed as illegal." And in finality she said, "Harriet insists that all copies of the report be collected before the board meeting."

"But it's not *our* report," I repeated, now getting impatient. "Certainly there's no harm in hearing what Garth has to say, even if we reject his advice."

"That's not the point," said Eve, holding firm. "We paid for it, didn't we?"

By the time the board meeting arrived, Eve and Harriet had prepared a memo disclaiming any involvement in the report's preparation or recommendations. A copy was slipped under the door of each board member's hotel room.

I had not thought to say anything more alarming to the board officers beyond "The report is creating some controversy among our lawyers, but I think we have everything under control." Before he even stepped to the podium in the New York Sheraton ballroom that cold day in February 1979, neither Garth nor I was prepared for the donnybrook that would befall us.

The opening shot came from Al Moran. This was the first political initiative of my presidency. Al had promised in a subtly threatening way that I could expect to hear from him, but I had not anticipated his message arriving with such flair and on an initiative that I would have predicted he would, if not support, at least not oppose. David Garth's ads for his affiliate were considered among the most effective in the federation.

When an envelope was handed to Fred Smith, who was battling valiantly to maintain order as he introduced David to the crowd, I caught sight of the words "By Hand." The room was racked with tense anticipation. At that moment, I couldn't imagine what was inside the envelope. As Fred pulled out its contents and I spotted the Planned Parenthood of New York City letterhead, my pulse quickened.

Al Moran had had this letter hand-delivered, to be read at the meeting.

"Is it supportive?" I whispered to Fred.

After scanning the letter, he passed it over to me. Al's letter decried the idea of the organization becoming involved in politics, invoking the traditions of Planned Parenthood as a social conscience, unsullied by the unpleasant business of partisanship. The letter urged the board to reject David Garth's conclusions and recommendations.

With the large crystal chandeliers tinkling in the background, Garth pulled no punches: If Planned Parenthood intended to see that reproductive rights were preserved, we had no choice but to enter politics.

He began by acknowledging that our goals—providing contraceptive services, curbing the rate of teen pregnancy, preserving unrestricted access to abortion, and improving contraceptive technology—were appropriate for a service-oriented organization founded on a commitment to reproductive freedom. He continued:

> Unfortunately, if the federation continues to follow its past course of action, it is highly unlikely that these goals will be achieved. . . .
>
> Public policy can also be influenced by a quicker, more direct process—the electoral process—in which organizations can help elect or defeat candidates on the basis of specific issues. This process is more powerful than the legislative process. But this process is closed to you because of your nonprofit tax status; so that what is recognized as

political clout—the ability to get the right people into office to make the right decisions on public policy—is an influence you don't have.

And though we didn't need to be reminded, Garth then went on to tell us about our opposition:

The right-to-life movement is already strong—and growing stronger. It is organized and effective. It is maximizing the perception of its strength through a carefully orchestrated public relations, political, and lobbying effort. . . .

And right-to-lifers are unabashed in saying that they are *just getting started* . . . In essence, they are seeking to become an institutionalized political force . . . *PPFA is not.* . .[9]

Without sugarcoating his opinion, Garth told us that we'd gotten into our present dilemma because we'd relied so heavily on court decisions, rather than developing a coherent vision that would allow us to challenge the opposition on our own terms: "The Supreme Court decision did more than just legalize abortion," he said. "It neutralized you, it robbed you of your rallying cry, your most provocative issue, your activist identity." Meanwhile, he pointed out, the same kind of energy that had driven the abortion reform movement was mobilizing our opposition to reverse reform.

Garth now laid out our options. We could take no political action and content ourselves with doing our service work, and lobbying legislatures and litigating in the courts to preserve reform "without the benefits of strategic action and purposeful political action." Given the changing political climate, this meant that:

Achieving PPFA's stated goals would remain an unrealistic dream. Instead, there would probably be more firebombings of Planned Parenthood clinics, more harassment, more network news documentaries portraying the strength of the opposition, and more erosion of family planning rights . . . It is possible to see an America where, once again, PPFA is a fringe group instead of the more mainstream and respected leader it is today—or where it ceases to exist at all.[10]

The second path we could consider was one of self-protection, where we held on to our moderate image while our opponents strengthened their longtime political viability by moving beyond abortion to fight other aspects of reproductive freedom, including "unrestricted teenage contraception and sex education in the schools."

Garth then presented us with our final option. "If you are serious about achieving your goals and fulfilling your leadership potential," he said, "in fact if you want to survive . . . [you have to be] able to 'play power politics' and that means being able to influence elections. . . . That is why the right-to-life organization is winning."[11]

He proposed that we increase our lobbying ability and credibility; bring ourselves directly into the electoral process through the establishment of an appropriate structure; and develop our grassroots support into a political force.

If ever I had witnessed the phenomenon of "kill the messenger," it was at the moment that Garth concluded his presentation. Planned Parenthood people are usually polite to guest speakers, even those with whom they strongly disagree, but at that moment the room exploded with angry objections. David Garth's advice never had a chance.

People were outraged at the mere suggestion that Planned Parenthood enter into electoral politics, with one member going so far as to say, "We must avoid using the word 'politicking.'" They were even angrier at Garth's daring to suggest that we had no choice but to follow his advice if we were to remain true to Planned Parenthood's founding principles.

In spite of the open hostility, not everyone on the board was opposed. "What I'm hearing you say," one board member commented, "is that we're going to go out of business unless we [engage in] this type of political action, and several things will happen if we do . . . we'll increase membership, increase contributions, achieve our goals, build upon everything we believe in." Several also shared Garth's view—and mine—that time was of the essence; that whatever we did, delaying a course of action would only weaken our position. The elections were little more than a year away. Political revolution was being shaped, and the area of reproductive rights was already one of its most hotly contested territories.

The maverick philanthropist Stewart Mott, who had been a longtime major contributor to Planned Parenthood, stood up and condemned the report. Although he agreed with Garth's fundamental proposal, he felt that it was not appropriate for Planned Parenthood. Perhaps he just couldn't tolerate not being the bold originator, so he made an audacious move of his own. He called for any interested parties to meet him in the corner of the ballroom to discuss forming a political action committee. When the lawyers, Eve and Harriett, sprung to their feet, insisting that no such conversations could take place in an official Planned Parenthood meeting, Mott, with a marigold blossom beaming in his lapel and holding the Garth report aloft like a tour guide's flag, headed into the corridor with a handful of interested board members in tow. They were now private citizens, having severed their ties to Planned Parenthood by leaving the room to attend to the birth of their own organization, which would eventually join with others to become Voters For Choice.

Fred gaveled the confused gathering into recess.

After Garth's report was rejected, I left the meeting limp from the battle and very much aware that I'd been given one more lesson in how difficult it would be to move Planned Parenthood from the inside out. If there had been ambivalence within the organization over my taking an aggressive public stand on the abortion issue, it was clear to me that Planned Parenthood would pay greater deference to its members' qualms about offending political party sensibilities than to our central role of defending women's reproductive rights.

Once the commotion settled down, the board decided to create a task force to study what should be done given the external opposition we were now facing. Its report came in late 1979 and recommended that rather than move into politics, as Garth suggested, we should direct our efforts to the areas of public relations and litigation strategies. The contrast between the two proposals was stark and painful to me. Public relations and litigation were vital, but stopgap; political engagement stood the chance of transforming the political landscape to secure women's rights.

The Monday after the Garth debacle, my vice presidents arranged a gathering of all the staff to express their support for what I had attempted to do. I was overwhelmed and grateful. In the years to come, I would find these people a source of comfort and a refuge from battles both internal and external.

If any good came of the David Garth venture—and I'd soon learn to look for progress in even the smallest increments—it was in the implementation of the task force recommendations that we hire a public relations firm to guide the development of a positive image for Planned Parenthood. We retained the firm Manning, Salvage and Lee. One of their first actions was to commission a national poll for us on abortion. The findings indicated that most Americans considered abortion "killing." Not "murder," but "necessary killing," and that most felt it was wrong, but accepted that there were circumstances where it was necessary. By a broad majority, those Americans polled believed that it was not the business of the government to get involved, but when forced to come down on one side about the morality of the issue, the majority opposed abortion.

Our mission was not to force the issue of right or wrong in the public's mind, the public relations analyst advised us, but to keep putting women and the complexities of their lives forward, to keep asking "What if?" and to keep illuminating the complications that no government is fit to address in its laws. In so doing, the pollsters concluded, we could keep the public in the middle because of their moral ambivalence.

Time would show that, two years before Ronald Reagan's inauguration, the Planned Parenthood national board had rejected the advice that I believed could have altered the course of the reproductive rights movement for the remainder of the century. Had we vigorously committed ourselves to transforming the political landscape, the Senate might not have lost some of its strongest pro-choice stalwarts, and Ronald Reagan's political coattails might not have swept so many anti-choice legislators into *both* the House and the Senate in the 1980 elections.

Instead, while the antiabortion movement was organizing to get a president elected, we decided to tie one hand behind our backs—a two-fisted defense of the high ground on which we stood was deemed too unseemly.

At the Metropolitan Executive Director's Council several months later, the executive directors of the thirty-five largest Planned Parenthood affiliates concluded that my leadership was wholly unacceptable, even dangerous, to the integrity of the organization. They requested that a delegation from their group meet with me and Fred Smith, who was now the board chairman, to discuss their angst.

We gathered in another dimly lit hotel lounge to discuss the council's concerns. The affiliate executive director in Baltimore, one of the people who had opposed my appointment, was the spokesman for the delegation. He expressed dismay that I was pushing the organization in a direction that would lead to its demise through the loss of community support and funding. He went on to claim that the group was considering calling for a vote of "no confidence."

Angered by the executives' presumptive statement, Fred asked whether they had discussed their concerns with me before bringing me to the chairman of the board to lodge their complaints. When they admitted they hadn't, Fred challenged them on their lack of proper professional procedure and dismissed their complaints. "Folks, this is no way to run a railroad," he told them, a bit of advice I've never forgotten and for which I am eternally grateful.

Although dissension seemed to float just beneath the surface, no one ever again risked a face-to-face confrontation.

CHAPTER 19

HOW MANY DAUGHTERS
MUST DIE?

P̲oor women weren't the only ones vulnerable to the assault of the opposition. Even as Hyde proposed his amendment in Congress, many states were responding to the *Roe* decision by moving to restrict the rights of teenagers. In the guise of "protecting" teenagers from their own youthful lack of judgment, and securing the "authority" of parents, a host of laws were being introduced in state legislatures that required parents' consent before their minor children could receive abortion services. But no one who was aware of the tragedies that befell women of all ages before *Roe*, when they were forced to face hospital review boards or turn to illegal means, should have been surprised that the same result would come of demanding that teenage girls disclose their illicit acts to their parents or face a court of law. Nothing brought this fact home more vividly than a story I heard in October 1991, nearly twenty years after the first of these laws had taken effect.

It was a soggy Portland, Oregon, afternoon. I was to speak at a rally opposing a referendum to make parental consent prior to a minor's abortion state law. The proposal was to be put to the voters a week or so later. The cold and steady drizzle didn't discourage the hundreds of exuberant activists who filled the downtown park in the City of Roses. When I arrived with my now necessary phalanx of security guards, the Indigo Girls were in full swing. Their guitars, harmony, and songs of protest against women's inequality were warming the spirits of the damp crowd.

The off-duty detectives spirited me from the van into a tent behind the stage. As the dry shelter and a cup of hot apple cider were warming my body and easing my pre-speech anxieties, Karen Bell approached me and introduced herself. Her warm brown eyes, soft but firm voice, and friendly midwestern manner made me feel as though we'd met before. Karen and her husband, Bill, were receiving support from Ellie Smeal's Fund for the Feminist Majority to travel the country campaigning in Congress and in state legislatures against attempts to pass parental consent laws.

As we sat together, I asked Karen about the experience that had made them so determined to fight against parental consent laws. The story she began to tell me was finished onstage before an audience of hundreds, hushed by the power of the Bells' reality.

Becky Bell had been the first victim of Indiana's laws requiring parental consent for abortion. Her parents, Karen and Bill Bell, told the heartbreaking story of their daughter's death at seventeen from an infection caused by an illegal abortion. Becky had lost her life because she couldn't face disappointing her parents, and she'd felt it useless to appear before an anti-abortion judge to request permission for a legal abortion.

Near the end of their speech, Karen Bell told of leaving yet another notebook at Becky's grave bearing the title "Notes for Becky."

"There have been eight notebooks filled," Karen told us. "Friends, girls who heard about her, Billy [Becky's older brother] and Bill and I write in them. So many have written, 'Becky, we've done what you did and we'll never tell either, but we lived.' "[1]

By the time Karen and Bill finished, there were few dry eyes in the crowd. As a mother I ached for the Bells then and I ache for them now, for I cannot imagine the horror of life without my child. I was awed by the courage it took for this mother and father to travel the country, reminding those who wanted to ignore the real-life consequences of the laws they heartlessly passed; awed by the conviction that helped them to face the kind of pain that only the loss of a child can bring, so that others might not have to experience it.

Not only did I feel tremendous compassion for Karen, Bill, and Billy Bell; I also found myself filled with fury that their child had been killed as the result of politicians engaging in the most pernicious form of lawmaking. How was it possible that fifteen years after abortion was legalized, a young girl could suffer such a fate? How could it be that in the race to do anything possible to repeal all women's rights, teenage girls were also being endangered? And how was it acceptable to uphold parents' rights at the expense of their children's?

And I thought of my own daughter, who was then sixteen. If we, like the Bells, had lived in Indiana, and if Felicia had gotten pregnant, she would have needed my permission to put an end to her condition. If she hadn't turned to me, she'd have had to put her fate in the hands of a judge who knew nothing about her life. And if she decided not to do either of those things, I might have been, as Karen is and as Bill is, a regular visitor to my daughter's grave.

As a mother, I can hardly deny my longing to protect my daughter. Even now that she's grown into adulthood I long to have her in my arms again, to have control over every aspect of her life. I know this yearning is hardly unique to me. But I also know that over the years my ability to regulate her day-to-day decisions has grown less effective as she has become more independent. Perhaps the need to pretend otherwise is part of the reason that most Americans, pro-choice and anti-choice alike, are ambivalent about or in favor of parental consent laws—just as the Bells were, before discovering the real reason for Becky's death.

The Indiana parental consent law was not a novelty. In fact, parental consent laws tend to get passed with relatively little objection, for sexual activity among teenagers challenges our values about its propriety. And pro-choice politicians quickly discovered that parental consent laws are a convenient device for gaining the support and the votes of those opposed to abortion—without offending their pro-choice constituents. In 1991 parental consent and notification laws were in effect in seventeen states; in 1996 they are in effect in twenty-seven states.

The first parental laws surfaced in Missouri and Massachusetts within a year of the *Roe* decision. Interestingly, neither law was advanced by a group specializing in teenage problems. The Missouri law was a bold attempt to test the limits that the courts would allow. Besides placing other restrictions on abortion, it required an unmarried woman under the age of eighteen who sought to end her pregnancy to submit the written consent of a parent or a person acting as a parent, unless the abortion was "certified by a licensed physician as necessary in order to preserve the life of the mother."[2] Abortion providers were subject to criminal penalties if they overlooked this regulation.

Three days after the statute became effective, two Missouri physicians and Planned Parenthood of Central Missouri brought suit in the United States District Court for the Eastern District of Missouri, challenging its constitutionality. Representing the plaintiffs was Frank Susman, a St. Louis lawyer who had fought to strike down Missouri's restrictive abortion law that had been in effect before *Roe v. Wade.* On January 31, 1975, the court ruled, two to one, that, with one exception unrelated to the parental consent issue, the law was constitutional.[3] The decision was immediately appealed to the Supreme Court, where the case was heard on March 23, 1976, with Susman again presenting the case for the plaintiffs, and State

Attorney General John C. Danforth (who sixteen years later would shepherd Clarence Thomas through the Senate to the Supreme Court) defending Missouri.

Susman argued that no other criminal statute in Missouri made parental consent necessary for the medical treatment of minors. In fact, as Susman pointed out, in keeping with a trend begun in the 1960s to allow minors more authority over their healthcare, minors in Missouri could *by statute* be treated for "VD, drugs, and pregnancy, excluding abortion . . . without the knowledge or without the consent of the parents. In other words, they [could] perhaps be sterilized, receive contraception, bear children, and do all the other pregnancy-related acts without the consent of the parents, with the sole exception of abortion."[4] Susman drew derisory attention to the fundamental flaws of a statute that might force a seventeen-year-old youngster who had been "emancipated" by marriage but was single again (as the result of the death of her spouse, or divorce) to obtain her parents' consent to terminate a pregnancy.

Susman then moved on to more practical aspects of the statute. He questioned whether the institution of the family could truly be better preserved by requiring a child to give birth to a child she didn't want than by allowing her to end a pregnancy that her parents wanted her to continue. While, under the statute, parents could force a child to give birth by withholding their consent, there were no legal responsibilities or financial obligations that would require them to help raise their grandchild.

And then there was the simple fact that the "morbidity and mortality rates for minors . . . being pregnant are much greater than they are for adults, . . . [as are] the emotional distress and psychological burden [of] unwanted pregnancy." With regard to Missouri's contention that consent should be required because teenagers are too immature to think for themselves, Susman noted: "Doctors face the same question [of psychological maturity] when treating an adult. The mere fact that the adult is over twenty-one does not really mean, automatically, that she is capable of giving an informed consent."[5]

All of these arguments were fine, but they seemed safely abstract, given the law's potential to cause suffering and to create dangerous situations for women. What about the girl whose youth was interrupted and whose hopes for the future were limited by childbirth? What about the life of the unwanted child? What about the girls who—like Becky Bell—took desperate measures to end their pregnancies without their parents' knowledge? The issue cried out for compassion and the deepest understanding of the impact that the laws would have upon the living, breathing reality of a teenager herself.

While Susman told me that "the minors [provision] did not have special importance" to him, and that he "would probably give up the minor's consent provision before the spousal consent provision,"[6] I saw parental consent provisions as part of the whole unacceptable effort to restrict abortion. The fear of pregnancy has long been regarded as the primary mechanism for regulating a teenage woman's sexual activity. The idea of freeing a teenager from this fear—whether by granting her access to contraceptives or to abortion—poses a threat to those who would oppose it. It forces society to face a troubling issue: deep ambivalence about the sexuality of our children.

The Court ruled that the Missouri law and its many restrictions were unconstitutional. Even so, the split decision didn't bode well for teenage girls. The decision was 6–3 on all of the law's provisions except one: the parental consent requirement for minors, where the vote was 5–4.

That the issue of parental consent hung in the balance was illuminated by Justice Harry Blackmun's opinion for the majority. He suggested that a parental consent law that did not "give a third party an absolute, and possibly arbitrary, veto over the decision of the physician and his patient to terminate the patient's pregnancy" and that provided "sufficient justification for the restriction" might meet constitutional requirements.[7]

Justice Potter Stewart was joined by Justice Lewis Powell in concurring on this point and in clarifying their stand on the issue:

> There can be little doubt that the State furthers a constitutionally permissible end by encouraging an unmarried pregnant minor to seek the help and advice of her parents in making the very important decision whether or not to bear a child. That is a grave decision and a girl of tender years, under emotional stress, may be ill-equipped to make it without mature advice and emotional support.[8]

Encouragement was hardly the purpose of parental consent laws: they were designed to compel, and euphemisms can never veil that fact. By referring to *unmarried* minors, the justices only confounded the issue further. Were they deciding the case on the basis of a teenager's tender years, or was it really her unmarried state that they wanted to safeguard against? Perhaps their decision was based on a vestige of some earlier time, when in marriage a young woman passed from the ownership of her parents to the ownership of her husband and the decisions about her well-being were likewise transferred.

Stewart and Powell then followed Blackmun's lead when they proposed the actual mechanism for avoiding that "absolute and possibly arbitrary veto" of parents. In their blueprint for the laws that are now on the books of thirty-eight states (Indiana, where Becky Bell died, among them), they suggested that parental consent might pass constitutional muster if the states provided for "judicial resolution of any disagreement between the parent and the minor."⁹

The justices had been drawn into the fictional ideal that a teenager could find "mature advice and emotional support" only from her parents or a judge. They ignored the fact that most parents don't talk to their children about their sexual development: How, then, would those same parents easily approach the murkier end of the sexual spectrum?

The justices also implied that health and social service professionals in "abortion clinics" were "unlikely" to offer "adequate" counsel, reflecting their skepticism about the medical profession and their suspicion that physicians, nurses, and counselors might have ulterior motives. This smacked of the familiar pro-criminalist rhetoric that abortion clinics are governed by a craven indifference to anything but making money. I can only say that the willingness to face persecution—taunts, picket lines, stink bombs, harassing telephone calls, arson, bombings, kidnappings, death threats, and even murder—requires tremendous conviction and a degree of selflessness not usually prompted by greed.

Justice John Paul Stevens, who usually voted with the liberal wing of the court and had voted with the majority in *Roe*, dissented on the decision and sent an even more disturbing signal about future decisions regarding minors:

> In my opinion . . . the parental-consent requirement is consistent with the holding in *Roe*. The State's interest in the welfare of its young citizens justifies a variety of protective measures.[10]

Reflecting some understanding about the reality of putting teenage girls in jeopardy, but then dismissing the fear of it as probably exaggerated or invalid, Justice Stevens nevertheless argued that a political forum still should be allowed to make the rules. Ironically, in later rulings, he grew more sensitive to the ways that limits on minors adversely affect their lives, until he eventually opposed parental consent laws.

Far from protecting teenagers from harm, parental consent requirements put them in harm's way. With Court sanction, young girls—as adult women once did—now risked dying for the sake of keeping a secret. If the law's true motive was to keep minors from the harm caused by incompetent or wrongly motivated healthcare providers, it would require that parents be notified and give their consent on *all* care for reproductive health, including prenatal care. But as Frank Susman pointed out, there were no such restrictive laws in Missouri—or anywhere else—when it came to treatment for venereal disease or for prenatal care.

* * *

On the same day that teenage girls in Missouri narrowly won the right to make their own reproductive decisions in *Danforth*, the Supreme Court stripped Massachusetts teenagers of such autonomy when it refused to find unconstitutional an act that protected "unborn children" and maternal health within constitutional limits.

This act had originally been passed into law in 1974 by the Massachusetts legislature, over the governor's veto. The same year it passed, the law was challenged in a suit brought by William Baird, the longtime crusader for reproductive rights, along with others, in the name of "Mary Moe," an unmarried minor "residing at home with her parents, and desirous of obtaining an abortion without informing them."

A year later, Massachusetts declared the 1974 law, particularly its parental consent statute, unconstitutional. The Massachusetts attorney general, Francis X. Bellotti, appealed this decision before the Supreme Court, and the case became known as *Bellotti I*.[11]

Instead of deciding whether the 1974 "act" was unconstitutional in its entirety, the justices chose to rule only on the law's controversial parental consent statute, and to reinterpret it as "preferring," rather than mandating, parental consultation and consent. Once they reconfigured this part of the Massachusetts legislation so a minor would have the opportunity to turn to the courts without first consulting her parents, the judges no longer had to find the law unconstitutional.[12] (It would be another five years before the Court, with only Justice Byron White dissenting, declared that this insistence upon parental approval was unconstitutional.)

Again deeply divided on the rationale for reaching this conclusion, the justices handed down three separate concurring opinions that together spelled out, even more explicitly than *Danforth*, what sort of parental consent law would *not* violate the Constitution. Justice Powell wrote for the majority:

> . . . Many parents hold strong views on the subject of abortion, and young pregnant minors, especially those living at home, are particularly vulnerable to their parents' efforts to obstruct both an abortion and their access to court. . . .
>
> We conclude, therefore, that under state resolution such as that undertaken by Massachusetts, every minor must have the opportunity—if she so desires—to go directly to a court without first consulting or notifying her parents. If she satisfies the court that she is mature and well enough informed to make intelligently the abortion decision on her own, the court must authorize her to act without parental consultation or consent. If she fails to satisfy the court that she is competent to make this decision independently, she must be permitted to show that an abortion nevertheless would be in her best interests. If the court is persuaded that it is, the court must authorize

the abortion. If, however, the court is not persuaded by the minor that she is mature or that the abortion would be in her best interests, it may decline to sanction the operation. . . .[13]

Thus with *Bellotti I*, the "judicial bypass" was born. If reproductive rights advocates were uncomfortable with teenage girls' being forced to seek their parents' approval to obtain an abortion, then these teenagers would be offered another alternative: seeking permission from the lower courts. But the judicial bypass process offered its own unnecessary humiliations that echoed those endured by all women in the pre-*Roe* era who had to get the approval of a medical panel in order to end a pregnancy. If a girl did not persuade a judge of her maturity, he could still permit the abortion if he found it to be in her best interests. However, the judge could also deny her request for an abortion and force her to continue her pregnancy to term. Paradoxically, the same judge who pronounced a girl too immature to have an abortion would be concluding that she was mature enough to be a mother without her parents' consent.

Perhaps the Supreme Court justices placed such faith in the wisdom of the lower-court judges that they regarded the judicial review process as offering a reasonable way of protecting teenagers from harm at the hands of abusive parents. But what safety, kindness, and respect could a teenager expect to find in a system that forced her to appear before a judge with a lawyer at her side on such a private matter? How could she not feel like a delinquent? And what "encouragement" would a judge provide that a doctor, nurse, social worker, counselor, or minister could not?

Furthermore, the Court's decision was made in the name of the well-being of teenage girls, but there were no companion provisions to "protect" boys. There was not, nor would there be, discussion, let alone legislation, that touched upon the idea that teenage boys or adult men who impregnated women might face either their parents or a judge.

After the Supreme Court decision was handed down, the Massachusetts Supreme Court responded to a request from the Planned Parenthood League of Massachusetts, and issued some guidelines for judges. Accordingly a judge can ask a pregnant teenager about her life, her work and educational experience, about what she knows of the abortion risks and of the alternatives, whether she is living independently of her parents or is about to, what her plans are for the future, and the extent to which she has consulted with others.

Still, many argued that the Court had structured a reasonable compromise between the rights of minors and the rights of parents by allowing young women a way out through the courts. Some contended—and some still contend, even when apprised of the clandestine and nightmarish experiences of many girls and the death of at least one girl—that if minor medical procedures like ear piercing required parental permission (although in fact there is no law in any state mandating parental permission for ear piercing), surely it was reasonable that the more serious abortion procedure should have parental or judicial oversight. Such reasoning fails to recognize the proliferation of parental consent laws and that pregnancy is a quantum difference from abortion.

This decision, coming down just as the Hyde amendment was about to begin its legislative and judicial journey, was the first chip in the *Roe v. Wade* armor.

After the *Bellotti* decision was handed down, pro-choice supporters in Massachusetts became invested in making the bypass system work—"until we can get the law changed," they would say. Jamie Sabino, a private lawyer, who also headed the state's judicial bypass referral panel of two hundred or so lawyers willing to represent teens, described the court process:

> In most cases a hearing is held four or five days after the teen contacts the attorney. But first the teen has had to go to a clinic; the clinic has her call the Planned Parenthood Counseling Referral line, an 800 number; the referral counselor gives the teen the protocol, tells her the choices, and, if she chooses to go to court, gets a lawyer for her. Then the minor has to contact the lawyer, which can take two or three days, and then have the hearing, and then often wait several days after the hearing to have the abortion. And keep in mind, some of these teens can only make one phone call a day, because they have to call from school, because they can't call from home.[14]

Delays of a week or two weeks may seem insignificant, but they're not. Because of ignorance, fear, or shame, a teenage girl is often slow to realize or admit to herself that she is pregnant. By the time she does, she's often well into her first trimester and any further delay jeopardizes her safety, as we saw in Becky Bell's case. Abortions performed at eleven or twelve weeks of pregnancy are three times more dangerous for women than abortions performed at or before eight weeks. The nine percent of all abortions performed in the second trimester accounted for 53 percent of all abortion deaths between 1981 and 1985.[15]

This sad fact is compounded by the irony that the bypass system rendered parental consent laws little more than grueling charades. In a study conducted for the *American Journal of Public Health* in 1988,[16] it was found that only the smallest fraction of teenagers in Massachusetts were judged to be too immature to be denied a bypass of their parents' approval—nine of four hundred seventy-seven cases. And in eight of these nine cases, the judge granted the petition anyway as being in the minor's best interest. Of the eleven thousand petitions in Massachusetts over the next ten years there were only fourteen denials, eleven of which were overturned on appeal, and the remaining young women found other legitimate means of obtaining their abortions.

After all the secrecy, humiliation, trauma, and delay, most girls found themselves allowed to keep the knowledge of their pregnancy from their parents, but at the cost of having their pregnancies further advanced, and thus their abortions made much riskier and more expensive. By seeing to it that they are "tried" in family or juvenile court when they are seeking a medical procedure that is not a crime, the Massachusetts law succeeds to some degree in recriminalizing abortion for teenagers.

The political barricades should have been stormed when the Massachusetts law was first handed down in 1974, and protest made against the abridgment of minor women's rights. But the backlash to *Roe* hadn't yet consolidated itself enough to assume the dangerous momentum that forced us to take note of its full power and the intent of our opponents. I was still head of the Dayton affiliate, and few of us there saw *Baird v. Bellotti* as a national phenomenon.

Later, however, when I was at the federation headquarters—and more and more states were taking up this weapon against teenagers, I remembered Mama's counsel that "a good offense is the best defense." I decided to raise the idea of an offensive posture at a board meeting. I felt we needed to put the recriminalists back on the defense by fighting to pass state laws that explicitly protected minors' rights to confidentiality in all reproductive healthcare.

I knew I'd be touching another sensitive nerve—Planned Parenthood board members reacted much like other Americans on the issue of teen sexuality. Some still expressed concern about the defensibility of charges that our contraceptive services encouraged promiscuity. Campaigning in state legislatures for minors' rights to control their fertility, releasing them from government regulation, would be a difficult step for many to take. All the same, after approaching the board I went to affiliate groups, trying to rally support for at least considering the idea. Again, I found that what was a self-evident course of action to me was wholly unrealistic to them. Fearing loss of funding and our base of support, they worried what might happen if our opponents made headway in their efforts to cast us as condoning teenage immorality and undermining parental authority.

Although I was unable to persuade the board and affiliates to take a proactive stand against parental consent laws, their consciousness had been raised on the issue. It was a beginning. Accepting that limited progress would have to suffice for the moment, I still found it difficult to step back and take the longer view, to keep pressing forward while stuck in a position that frustrated my ideals.

It's tempting to think that parental consent laws are exceptions in effect in twenty-seven states, and that a teenager can still obtain an abortion in the other states. But to do so is to ignore the realities of all those teenagers who, for whatever reason, are unable to withstand the difficulty and shame of obtaining parental consent or judicial bypass and are also unable to avoid these restrictions by traveling to another state. It also ignores the impact of these pregnancies on the young women who are forced to carry them to term.

There are those who romanticize the plight of pregnant teenagers—especially poor teenagers—saying that they get pregnant deliberately so that "they'll have something to love." Evidence does not support this myth for the vast majority of youngsters: Of the over one million teenage pregnancies in the United States each year, 84 percent of them are unintended.[17] Apart from the philosophical argument, the hard evidence is overwhelmingly against teenage parenting:

- Thirty percent of teenage mothers do not complete high school.
- Often because they don't have adequate educations, teenage parents can't get decent jobs; and the likelihood that no father will be present accounts for the fact that their family income will be about half the amount earned by the average family.
- Even if they do marry, teenage parents are far more likely to become divorced than are teenagers who delay childbearing.
- Thirty-two percent of babies born to mothers seventeen and younger have health problems.
- Children of teenage mothers consistently score lower than children of older mothers on measures of cognitive development. Rather than declining over time, the educational deficits of children born to adolescent parents appear to accumulate.[18]

The courts, legislatures, and society cling to the fantasy of parental involvement, but successful parental involvement doesn't begin during a child's adolescence. Parents must guide the development of sexuality from the earliest years of their children's lives if they are to have a meaningful influence during puberty. Sexuality is a complex area of human development, and there are no simple or perfect answers to its many facets. It is not susceptible to government regulation without placing women's, minors', and adults' lives on the line.

CHAPTER 20

STANDING FIRMLY
ON MIDDLE GROUND

On January 22, 1979, the sixth anniversary of *Roe v. Wade*, Eleanor Smeal, the president of the National Organization for Women (NOW), issued invitations to forty advocacy groups on both sides of the abortion debate to attend a mid-February meeting in Washington, D.C. The intent of the meeting was "to begin a dialogue and to make an initial attempt to seek areas of consensus on fertility-related issues, excluding abortion itself."

From the outset, I did not like the premise of the meeting. I could not see how any sort of consensus with opponents to reproductive rights would not mean compromising on a woman's fundamental rights. Further, I couldn't imagine what difference the consensus of any group—whether sitting around a conference room table or in seats of Congress, or standing in pulpits around the country—should make in the way a woman conducted her personal life. Who had appointed any of us the moral arbiters of a woman's right to practice the freedom that *Roe* had finally allowed her?

After my executive staff and I consulted with the staff of the Alan Guttmacher Institute on how to handle the invitation, I phoned Ellie.

Then only casually acquainted with her, I began by telling Ellie how much we appreciated NOW's good intentions. But then I expressed my concern that they might not fully appreciate the risks. "There's no reason to believe anything good will come of this," I told her. "In fact, given the nature of the pro-criminalists, it could be used against us. If you insist upon going ahead with this meeting, we won't agree to any statement that condemns abortion as a woman's right."

Ellie didn't scold me for intransigence, but in her reply she, too, was firm: "If we don't try to talk, we'll never get anywhere. At least we have to try."

"You don't know what these people can do," I warned.

Though Ellie may have considered our position as the kind of extremism that precludes "compromise," at least she could be sure that none of the pro-choice groups would bring in a bloody metal instrument or rubber catheter to make our point. That could not be said for the other side. However, she and her colleagues felt that the good that might come from such a meeting was worth the gamble.

Ellie and I ended our exchange pleasantly, but unspoken between us were the subtle tensions that had long existed between the pro-choice organizations and the leaders of the Equal Rights Amendment movement, who had resisted embracing the abortion issue as a part of the drive to pass the ERA. It is said that ERA leaders feared that the contentiousness of the debate would splinter the fragile alliances necessary to move the ratification to victory.

I believe this was a strategic error, especially after the emergence of the backlash after *Roe*. Had the movement integrated abortion rights and fought against the threats to these rights, a key aspect of women's lives, into its campaign, many more women would have felt impelled to fight for the amendment. As it was, the ERA officially died in 1982.

But, in 1979, with the fate of the ERA still down the road, I was troubled by the possibility of our showing any weakness in our position, so I had no choice but to attend the confab. Cory Richards, director of the Alan Guttmacher Institute's Washington office, also attended.

As I flew down to Washington, I again reflected on David Garth's warning of just two weeks earlier: "The right-to-life movement is already strong—and growing stronger. It is organized and effective." I braced myself for the worst.

It was a sunny day, cold and brittle, when representatives from eight antiabortion organizations and twenty pro-choice groups gathered in a drafty conference room of the Hotel Washington. We were seated at tables arranged in a large square, which made greetings tense, difficult, and easily avoidable. The leaders of the represented organizations were assured seats at the table. Others sat in chairs lining the wall. The room was full, but not packed. Oddly, although the leaders of the pro-criminalist movement were (and are) virtually all male, on that day the only two men in the room were Cory and former television talk show host Morton Downey, Jr.

Not everyone who had been invited showed up. Nellie Gray of the March for Life rejected the invitation ("I do not negotiate with babykillers," she is reported to have said), as did Carolyn Gerster, who was president of the National Right to Life Committee, the largest anti-choice organization.

The Wanderer, a right-wing Catholic newspaper, warned that proponents of abortion might somehow try to sucker pro-criminalists into easing up on their "drive to put abortion where it belongs—in the realm of serious crime."[1]

In her opening remarks, Ellie expressed the reasons for NOW's gathering us together in this disparate assemblage. "There has never been an attempt for the pro-choice and antiabortion leaders to meet and talk about our differences," she began. Then, to her credit, she acknowledged that some of us had expressed our suspicions that any expectation of agreement was hopelessly naive. Still, she said, she was hopeful. "Even if we cannot reach a consensus, at least an attempt will have been made."

After we'd introduced ourselves around the table, the talks began easily enough. But it didn't take long before our worst suspicions were confirmed.

Ellie asked if we could all agree that family planning should be universally available.

"No, we can't agree to that," replied Mildred Jefferson, the most prominent pro-criminalist leader in attendance.

Jefferson was an African American doctor, former president of the National Right to Life Committee (1975–1978), and then head of the Right to Life Crusade. This Boston doctor, an active leader in the pro-criminalist movement since 1970, sat to the left of Ellie Smeal. I sat at the table to the left of the titular head table, where Ellie and Jefferson were assigned.

Throughout the day, Mildred Jefferson would be treated like a special guest, speaking to most points, commenting more frequently than anyone else, and making provocative statements about "killing the unborn."

The opening gambit from the pro-criminalist side was: "Teenagers should not have access to contraception. And not only are we opposed to teenagers having access to contraception, we are opposed to any woman receiving contraceptives that are abortifacients." (They considered such methods as the pill and the intrauterine device as fitting this category.) By this interpretation, any method that interfered after the union of the sperm and egg was an abortifacient.

We haggled over this point until both sides despaired of a resolution. We then turned to the idea of education, and were making a little progress when we became aware of the hour. It was nearing midday and we all knew that NOW had announced a press conference for three o'clock. By early afternoon, the pressure to come up with some sort of joint statement grew intense. The room started to feel cramped and airless with all the tension as we struggled to do the impossible—fashion an acceptably optimistic statement about what we had accomplished. Minutes before the deadline, we settled on calling our discussions "wide-ranging and amicable throughout" (although by this time I felt no sense of amicability and doubted that anyone else in the room did either). We cited the need for "reproductive education at every stage in the human life cycle by parents, schools, religious groups, and other community organizations," and expressed the hope that future discussions would be arranged, although I don't believe that anyone in the room had a modicum of desire to sit at the same table ever again. I know that I certainly didn't.

A few minutes before three, we moved to an adjoining room filled with reporters from newspapers all over the country. The cameras of all the TV networks were primed. Ellie, who was to make the prepared statement, moved to the podium; Mildred Jefferson was given the seat to the right of the podium, but the chair to the left of it was empty. I was uncertain where to sit and hesitated briefly to see how the arrangements would take shape. However, Cory Richards spotted the empty chair at Ellie's side and gave me a gentle push toward it. "Sit there," he ordered sharply.

Just then, two young women, part of a group calling itself People Expressing a Concern for Everyone (PEACE) that had staged demonstrations at abortion clinics, moved toward the front of the room. Morton Downey, Jr., had sat with them during the day. Now he stood at the back of the room, close to the door, and watched, a grim smile on his lips.

I had a sinking feeling that we were about to be treated to something extremely unpleasant. My stomach began to tumble, because I didn't know what it would be, and whether it could be managed in a way that would not embarrass us. My pulse began to race. One of the young women cradled in her arm an object wrapped in a blue receiving blanket. She made sobbing sounds as she moved toward us. The other one, trailing behind her, read solemnly aloud from the Bible. By now every eye in the room had turned from Ellie to them.

They climbed the three steps up to the platform where the organizational representatives were seated. Ellie stopped speaking and turned toward them in stunned silence. They kept walking toward the podium.

"We have listened all day to your discussions about the annihilation of 'our sisters,'" said the one with the bundle. "We are no longer going to sit quietly while you discuss the murder of 'our sisters' just like the one that we are carrying." And then, in full view of the television cameras, they opened the blanket, revealing a dark brown, fully formed fetus that appeared to be of five to six months' gestation. There were audible gasps, and the room broke into horrified upheaval. The cameras moved in to catch a shot of the exposed, lifeless fetus as the young women were rushed off the platform. They closed the blanket as they were rebuked and hustled from the stage.

Clearly shaken, her face flushed, Ellie turned to me and asked, "What do I do now?"

I'd seen how easy it was for raw emotions to seem like hysteria when flashed on television, and this was the last emotion we needed the public to see. Once again, my training as a nurse-midwife steeled my instinct to remain calm among quickly shifting situations.

"First you must get out of view of the cameras. Let me get to the podium," I answered firmly, although I felt sympathy for her. She'd been abruptly shaken from the realm of abstract discussion by the force of the brutally tangible. Grasping the lectern to calm myself, I tried to collect my thoughts as the two women and their mentor headed out the door at the back of the room.

I wasn't shaken by the sight of a dead fetus. It was completely intact. I suspected it was the result of a spontaneous abortion. Having spent part of my career in the labor and delivery rooms, where women delivering still-born fetuses were not uncommon, it wasn't the first that I'd seen. But what goes on in a delivery room and what gets shown on network television are entirely different matters. Adrenaline was now raging through my veins. I was outraged that these people would stoop so low to make their point. In spite of Planned Parenthood's collective misgivings, a small part of me had wanted to believe what our opponents all claimed—that they truly respected life. But for those who would parade a dead fetus before the national media for dramatic effect, to shock and horrify, there was no place for pretense.

I was furious that they had betrayed the goodwill of those less cynical than I, people who'd gathered with the sincere hope of creating a dialogue. I was angry that NOW had not heeded our warnings, and had gone ahead with this event without appreciating the risks. And I was frustrated that, rather than being able to express my anger, I had to don the mask of being calm, measured, and rational—as I had been taught all my life to be. I confined myself to denouncing the action as being "totally outside the spirit of the meeting."

I was, of course, no stranger to zealotry—religious zealotry in particular. Tent revivals had been a way of life in the summer months of my childhood. People took their vacations from work then, and the weather suited outside gatherings. And when we weren't assembled beneath the canvas of the revival tents, radios broadcast the exhortations of preachers in the living room of my home and those where I was left to stay. Lacking altars, the radio preachers commanded their listeners to put their hands on the radio while they prayed for them to be freed from the burdens of illness and hard luck. Lacking collection plates, they promised their followers instant healing and good luck if they were sent a "love offering" and a "prayer cloth" (handkerchief), which they vowed to return, anointed with holy oils.

But whether projected from the pulpit of the revival tent or from the radio in the living room, the fundamentalist oratories had always had a consistent theme: the sins of the flesh—lying, smoking, dancing, drinking, gambling, and especially sex (fornication and adultery)—were at the root of America's moral decay and would bring us all to the pit of eternal hellfire. Responsibility for sexual regulation has historically been placed squarely at the feet of women. From Eve's transgression in the Garden of Eden through the sins ascribed to Bathsheba, Delilah, and Salome, women have been the ones to bear the reproach and recrimination.

My mother had only a microphone to amplify her messages to dozens of people at a time. But the radio evangelists reached thousands across the country with their calls for repentance. By the late Seventies, the television evangelists had extended their grasp to millions from the pulpits of glitzy cavernous structures with names like Cathedral of Tomorrow and the Crystal Cathedral. Their show business productions of singing, praying, and testifying, and their leading men bearing names like Bakker, Falwell, Humboldt, Robertson, and Swaggart would revolutionize evangelism—and politics as we knew it. Unlike those preachers who sweated it out under the tents, and the gimmicks of the invisible radio sermonizers of the Fifties of my childhood, the modern-day crusaders were blow-dried, well-tailored, and manicured media celebrities. Their wives were occasionally stars in their own rights, but usually relegated to the traditional role of singer—the most famous of whom was Tammy Faye Bakker. The serious business of controlling the message was firmly in the hands of men.

The social upheavals of the Sixties and the political eruptions of the Seventies, teenage pregnancy, and later the scourge of the AIDS epidemic, gave saliency to the theme of the wicked bringing about the moral disintegration of our society. Yet, even though the audience of the faithful grew ever larger, and the television productions grew ever more lavish, and the contributions that maintained this sophisticated communications machinery were more than keeping pace with that demand, the doctrines of hope, of life in the hereafter for the believer, the fear of eternal damnation for the transgressor, and the certainty of the disintegration of our society remained the same.

These messages launched on the airwaves were as familiar to me as my skin. I knew the passions they evoked—I will never forget how frightened I became during the sermons of my childhood as I imagined the end of the world coming at any moment, and the terror of the vision of a pit of fire and devils with pitchforks while I burned for all eternity. Nor could I forget the weeping "sinners" at my mother's altars. I could not have failed to understand and respect the power that fervent beliefs had in shaping and controlling the thoughts and behavior of those who "believed." I recognized the strength of a faith that clung to a promise of an eternity for which this life was merely preparation and the obligation to be unerringly faithful to the commandments of God, for which heaven is the reward. While many watched the newfangled evangelists with bemused distaste, I could not dismiss the potential of this fundamentalist religious revival.

Some of my mother's convictions weren't all that different from those of the new evangelists, especially with regard to lifestyle. But Mama's mission was the transformation of the human heart—the conversion of those who heard her message from a life of sin to one free of transgressions according to the teachings of the Bible.

The religious broadcast empire that had once been the realm of radio preachers now encompassed five TV cable networks and dozens of radio stations, as well as real estate holdings that served lavish tastes. By the end of the Seventies, it was estimated that almost 130 million Americans watched televangelists every Sunday morning.[2] There was no question in my mind that, given the compounding power of modern technology, the influence would be formidable.

The evangelism of the late Seventies was gaining momentum beyond the southern roots of fundamentalist Protestantism, and the undertones were beginning to sound quite different from those that I'd known as a child. Calling the faithful to repentance wasn't enough; controlling the hearts and minds of the faithful wasn't enough either. Not only did the new religious leaders have their eyes set upon what Jerry Falwell called "the return of this country to moral sanity,"[3] but through the wonder of television, they had millions of followers—many of whom, they knew, would do at least one thing that they asked: send money to support their ministries. This gave these leaders tremendous power to implement their vision.

By the early Eighties, in a development that was probably inevitable, given the danger of the corrupting influence of power, the televangelists set their sights on an even more powerful mechanism than persuasion to enforce religious dogma. Under the banner of restoring "Judeo-Christian ethics" to America, their messages began to take on increasingly political tones. They declared it the obligation of Christians to elect to public office God-fearing men (women went unsolicited for such elevation), men who were committed to ending legal abortion, stopping the busing mandated for racial integration, and returning prayer to public schools.

"Not voting is a sin against Almighty God," Pat Robertson proclaimed.[4] Though my parents had always voted, I'd never heard them, or anyone else in the Church of God, suggest that their religious views should be enacted into law, or that God had ordained voting. Such declarations unsettled me. This was religion that, trading heavily on its emotional impact to affect government, was going dangerously awry. The merest notion of enacting the fundamentalist tradition into law—all that fear of hellfire, all that passion for repentance, and, especially, all that malevolent moral judgment—was a deeply frightening development.

Richard Viguerie, a political organizer who was said to have made a fortune by setting up direct mail fund-raising enterprises that catered to right-wing organizations, calculated that the conservatively estimated 15 million Americans who regularly watched Falwell's *Old Time Gospel Hour* could become the base of a new political majority.

In one of the earliest and most successful attempts to define this group, Ed McAteer, the field director of the Conservative Caucus, set up a meeting between Howard Phillips, one of the funders of the Conservative Caucus, Falwell, and himself to discuss how to bring disparate fundamentalist religious groups together in common purpose without drawing the scrutiny of the Internal Revenue Service.[5]

Not only did they come up with a number of initiatives to capture a force of committed activists, they also came up with a rallying cry that would galvanize the country—"The Moral Majority." By implication, anyone who disagreed with their agenda was immoral. The Moral Majority would soon become the best-known and most powerful right-wing religious movement in America.

But Moral Majority, Inc., which became Jerry Falwell's base of operation, did not represent the whole of the religious right. In order to create a more united front, McAteer founded the Religious Roundtable as a so-called nonpartisan, interdenominational branch of the Conservative Caucus to encompass every faction of the religious right. Under the umbrella of the Religious Roundtable, McAteer managed to bring right-wing political leaders like Viguerie, and theoreticians like Paul Weyrich and Terry Dolan, into the same circle with prominent evangelical leaders, for seminars and strategy and training sessions. Together, these men formed the political leadership of what became known as the New Right.

Given that not all the groups courted by the New Right—the National Conservative Political Action Committee, the Eagle Forum, and Young Americans for Freedom among them—agreed with every aspect of the New Right agenda, there had to be a common bond that would hold them together. They found this in their commitment to ending legal abortion and busing, and in reintroducing prayer in public schools—"the social agenda," as it came to be known.

Meanwhile, the Catholic Church's involvement in political activities was also gaining momentum. That trend had begun in 1965, when the National Conference of Catholic Bishops had created the Family Life division to campaign against contraception to counter the Supreme Court decision in *Griswold* legalizing contraception. Although I'd witnessed this unlikely alliance between fundamentalist Protestants and Catholics in Dayton, I'd never have imagined that such an alliance could endure at the national level. However, there were those who believed that the New Right would succeed in coupling its vision with the Catholic hierarchy's well-developed political apparatus. This could bring about a profound political shift in the country. They were not wrong.

Jerry Falwell vigorously embraced his role as spokesman for the Moral Majority. He believed that America's Founding Fathers intended separation of religion and state, but not God and state, and he revealed his commitment to politics in comments like the following:

> When you're dealing with moral issues you're talking about something that touches the majority of the people of this nation . . . as part of the electorate, we have not only a right but a responsibility to speak out. We . . . the moral majority . . . still believe that the commandments are valid for today.[6]

I knew there was no hope for compromise on any issue from those who believed their mission to be divinely ordered by God, because the future of their soul in eternity hinged on it. I began to fear that if national policy ever became governed by such convictions, one of our most fundamental freedoms—religious liberty—could be so weakened as to become meaningless.

The New Right's emotionally charged rhetoric on abortion was the most inflammatory aspect of their so-called social agenda. In the days preceding the 1980 elections, when leaders of the Moral Majority stoked the zeal of their supporters, Pastor David Rhodenizer said, "I believe abortion is first-degree murder. Any candidate who would stand for abortion is a part of that first-degree murder and he will be held accountable to God."[7] A year later, Falwell vowed that the Eighties would be "the decade in which abortion on demand will be brought to an end." He had prepared his followers for that closure by claiming his "position on abortion [came] from the word of God."[8]

In a matter of months that seemed more like a year, as we faced the 1980 elections, I often thought about David Garth's predictions—particularly his point that the real goal of the pro-criminalist movement was to restore women to the conditions of enforced motherhood. And I thought about how one of our hands was tied behind our backs—the hand that could have challenged the Moral Majority's political ascendancy—even as we faced an opposition that held the denial of the rights of women as its galvanizing mission and aimed to make enforcement of that denial the government's mission.

How could I convey to my colleagues at Planned Parenthood my understanding of these dangers I knew so well? How could I get them to see that there was a whole other world of people out there—people trying to get to heaven by not only changing their lives, but by "saving" the souls of others, and—their dedication having been exploited for political purposes—by "saving" our secular nation from destruction through the imposition of their religious values in law? How could I persuade them that tending to our image wouldn't even begin to effectively challenge a movement fueled by faith in the divine?

Change is hard to create. No one at Planned Parenthood was going to take my word on faith—they needed evidence. That evidence would come through attacks on the most vulnerable women—the young, the poor, and the sick—those who were to lose their ability to exercise their reproductive rights.

In a book published in 1980, Pat Robertson declared that "we have together with the Protestants and the ethnic Catholics enough votes to run the country, and when the people say, 'We've had enough,' we're going to take over."[9] To make its way to the White House and Congress, the New Right had only to identify its party affiliation.

The fundamentalist Protestants and Catholics had traditionally voted Democratic, but for many of them this time, cleaving to the Democratic Party was out of the question if for no other reason than its pro-choice platform. If, however, they converted to the Republican Party, the so-called New Right would have to challenge the party's historically moderate base on social issues by solidifying its power in the right wing. For its part, the Republican Party wanted those new voters and candidates to help topple the incumbent Democratic president and reclaim the White House with a candidate who only a few years earlier had been deemed too conservative to head the party's national ticket.

The task force that had been formed in reaction to the Garth Report had called for the implementation of a grassroots lobbying program, and although I anticipated resistance and obstacles, political realities demanded that we move forward to build as vigorous a structure as was legally feasible for a nonprofit organization. I knew that even if we could not influence who got elected, effective lobbying required transforming our role from "educating" Congress to advocating for specific action. We needed our own operation in Washington to do that. The Alan Guttmacher Institute (AGI) had represented Planned Parenthood in Washington for years, but their primary mission was research and policy analysis. The lobbying it could do was limited because of its need to preserve its credibility and reputation for objectivity.

Determined to see us build our own lobbying operation to defend our issues, I set about enlisting the support of the officers of the board and affiliate representatives. Most of the people I spoke with understood why we should make such a move, but they were wary of conflict with AGI.

I phoned Jeannie Rosoff, who was now the president of the AGI, and tried to reassure her fears: "I have no desire to hurt AGI in any way—we need you to remain the credible research organization that you already are. But we also need a direct lobbying operation to take the hard positions that could tarnish the objectives of AGI. I'd really appreciate your cooperation."

We agreed to meet and discuss this the next time Fred Smith was in town. The tension was palpable in the room the day we met. Jeannie was no less worried now than when I'd first broached the subject. Her French accent still strong after more than thirty years in America, she sputtered, "This is simply another assault on AGI. If you want to build a strong lobbying organization you should go out and work with local affiliates to build a network of constituents to lobby their members of Congress in the states. A Washington lobbying operation, per se, is of no value without an active grassroots organization."

She was right, of course, but I believed that developing local activists was not enough. We also needed a visible presence on the Hill to represent our interests there to the collective legislative body. Besides, even an active grassroots organization would need Washington-based coordination in order to channel the views of local citizens on congressional actions.

Fred and I spent more than an hour in trying to rally Jeannie's support. We failed to convince her, and she set out to mobilize opposition to the proposal before we could present it to the board.

Among the people most successful in our own effort to stem the internal opposition was Win Forrest, our vice president for development. He'd been hired by my predecessor, and had quickly become an invaluable participant in our organizational deliberations. Tall and rail-thin, Win was a Texan who had spent most of his career in fund-raising for colleges and universities. His reserved professional demeanor hid a brilliantly channeled competitive streak.

Win had a keen sense of how organizations work, and his patience perhaps sometimes exceeded even his considerable management skills in delivering the results he sought. At meetings, he would often sit over long dinners or over drinks or coffee late into the night, listening patiently to the concerns of board members and affiliate directors. And just as patiently, he'd explain why a certain course of action was the right one. He'd even managed to get some people to forget their reservations about me, as he advocated on my behalf.

And then there was Joan Dunlop, vice president for public affairs, who would have direct responsibility for setting up the office. Tall, elegant, and British, Joan made speech after speech advocating for the proposal. Though affiliates were dazzled by her accent, most remained troubled about our getting too deeply involved in politics.

As I entered the board meeting, where I would propose the lobbying operation, I had the heart-sinking feeling that, despite all our campaigning, the outcome was a toss-up.

The discussion over the issue was acrimonious. The accusations that I was trying to build a political empire were painful to me, for such charges were not about the issue; they were about me. I told myself again that I'd have to build a layer of toughness around my emotions so that the challenges to my proposals would not weaken my leadership. But I'm human, and the words hurt. Still, part of me knew that the resistance had less to do with me than with the proposal itself, just as part of me understood that a large, mature organization didn't change its ways quickly or easily. It didn't dampen my raging frustration, nor still my swirling emotions.

Given our growing opposition, I didn't feel that we had the luxury of time for the organization to grow more accustomed to me or mull over the idea of change. I was determined to salvage as much as possible of David Garth's argument, and whatever I could salvage, I would count as progress.

After a full airing of all sides of the issue, the board voted by a narrow margin to approve the proposal for the establishment of a lobbying office in Washington. The office was opened in 1981.

Whenever I emerged from difficult battles, especially those inside Planned Parenthood, I longed to get home to my family to recharge my emotional batteries. Though my executive staff would always comfort me immediately, there was nothing like seeing Felicia to set my world straight. I used to go straight to her bedroom the moment I got home. If I was lucky, she'd still be awake to tell me of the day's happenings. But this night I found her in a gloomy mood.

"What's the matter, my bubbling brown sugar?" I asked as I wrapped her in my arms.

"Patrick said he didn't like black people because they're ugly. Patrick said he didn't like me," she replied, her voice sulky and heavy with sadness. Her distress tapped my childhood memories of Nebraska, and the isolation and humiliation that I'd felt when my skin color set me apart from an entire town. It called up those relentless clandestine operations to turn my hair straight so I wouldn't look too black. I could imagine that she felt as I had that day in Columbus, Nebraska, when I ran to my room awash in tears because I was different.

"Well, honey, God made you and He made you beautiful," I answered. "The next time Patrick says anything like this, just tell him, 'Yes, I'm black, and I'm beautiful, and I don't care if you don't like me because of it.'"

Felicia's face brightened with the spirit of empowerment, although I think that "beautiful" may have held sway over "black." Still, racial pride assumed its place as a powerful tool, and I knew she'd wield it the best way she could.

Franklin is darker-complexioned than Felicia and I, but she'd taunt him with "Mommy and I are black, and you're brown," before collapsing into uncontrollable giggles.

CHAPTER 21

THE HYDE AMENDMENT:
POOR WOMEN, ALL WOMEN

The summer before I became the president of Planned Parenthood, the Hyde amendment was in effect provisionally, pending Federal District Judge John Dooling's decision on its constitutionality. In the year that followed, federal funds paid for 290,000 fewer abortions than the year before. However, the actual number of abortions performed on poor women dropped hardly at all. The effects of the Hyde amendment were mitigated by voluntary or court-ordered funding of abortions in some sixteen states and the District of Columbia. Most of these states, such as California, Connecticut, Pennsylvania, and New Jersey, were home to large numbers of poor women.

Elsewhere, most poor women who wanted abortions managed to pay for them, although at what price—not paying rent or utility bills? pawning household goods? diverting food and clothing money? traveling to another state to obtain lower-priced abortions?[1]

Some women were forced to end their pregnancies in much the way they had when abortion was still illegal. In 1979, Rosaura Jimenez, a twenty-seven-year-old Mexican American woman, died in the hospital from an infection following an illegal abortion done in Texas with an unsterilized catheter. One of twelve children of a family of migrant workers, she worked part-time in an electronics factory to support her five-year-old daughter, and was six months from receiving her bachelor's degree in education when she died.

Rosaura had two previous Medicaid-funded abortions, but because of the cutoff of funds, she'd been unable to get a third Medicaid abortion. Her scholarship check was in her pocket when she died, but instead of paying for a legal abortion with the money she needed for school, she'd sought a less expensive, illegal abortion. Her decision cost her her life.[2]

A Centers for Disease Control report in 1980 told of a thirty-seven-year-old woman in Georgia who died after trying to abort herself with a glass thermometer. She had already had twelve pregnancies, and after being denied a Medicaid-funded abortion, had consistently tried to self-abort. After being admitted to the hospital, she died of a pulmonary embolism after a hysterectomy.[3]

A woman in Louisiana died after a friend tried to give her an abortion by inserting numerous Q-Tips into her cervix. The woman was a single mother who had recently lost her job. She could not afford to pay for an abortion, and her state provided no assistance.

In South Carolina, a woman with a seven-year-old daughter sought to end her pregnancy at a private clinic. When the clinic told her that she would need a second-trimester abortion, and that it would cost between three hundred and five hundred dollars, she went to an illegal abortionist, who performed the procedure with unsterilized instruments and packed her vagina with gauze. Four days after her pregnancy was ended, the woman went to the hospital with a high fever caused by a severe infection. In order to save her life, the hospital had to perform a hysterectomy.[4]

Planned Parenthood affiliates tried to help the women who came to them with no means of ending an unwanted pregnancy, by providing abortions at low cost or by referring the women to clinics that would do so. Some affiliates had the funds to make loans to women, and arranged for repayment over an extended period.

On January 15, 1980, two and a half years after he'd lifted his injunction against the implementation of the Hyde amendment, Judge Dooling ruled that prohibiting the use of Medicaid funds for abortion was unconstitutional. Although Dooling restricted his decision to the question of whether the government should pay for "medically necessary" abortions, I doubt that so compassionate a decision as his would be handed down in today's courts. He wrote:

> A woman's conscientious decision, in consultation with her physician, to terminate her pregnancy because that is medically necessary to her health, is an exercise of the most fundamental of rights, nearly allied to her right to be, surely part of the liberty protected by the First Amendment. To deny necessary medical assistance for the lawful and medically necessary procedure of abortion is to violate the woman's First and Fifth Amendment rights. The irreconcilable conflict of deeply and widely held views on

this issue of individual conscience excludes any legislative intervention except that which protects each individual's freedom of conscientious decision and conscientious nonparticipation. Judgment must be for the plaintiffs. [5]

The secretary of the Department of Health and Human Services, Patricia Harris, immediately applied to the Supreme Court for a stay of the judgment, pending the department's appeal of the District Court's decision. The Supreme Court denied the request to block federal funding for "medically necessary" abortions, and the funding resumed, pending the Supreme Court's resolution of the case.

Rhonda Copelon, a young lawyer from the Center for Constitutional Rights, who had worked on the lawsuit from its inception (along with a number of other lawyers), would be arguing the case. It had been a hard-won opportunity for her. Because arguing and winning a landmark Supreme Court case is an achievement of distinction in the legal profession, the competition to do so is fierce and often unpleasant. Yes, my legal colleagues had muttered, Rhonda Copelon was brilliant, and yes, she knew all the ins and outs of the case—but was she the best choice to carry it to the High Court? A number of other names were put forward as alternatives, among them Janet Benshoof, of the American Civil Liberties Union, and Sylvia Law, a professor of law at New York University. Copelon's main competition, however, had been Harriet Pilpel, Planned Parenthood's general counsel, who'd had a long and distinguished legal career in reproductive and First Amendment law as well as appearances before some of the justices who would hear the arguments.

No one had doubted the abilities of any of the candidates. But concerns about physical appearance and temperament marked the turning point of this debate. Copelon, thin, dark-haired, and youthful, conveyed a feminist persona. Pilpel was a silver-haired woman in her late sixties. Pilpel's very presence, her supporters argued, would help to dispel the notion that the government was paying for the pleasures of "promiscuous welfare women."

But Copelon alone had researched not only the more probable lines of debate, but also the ways that the Hyde amendment introduced a religious tenet into government policy. If anyone could argue on this basis, Rhonda could, and her supporters carried the day.

On April 21, 1980, I climbed the marble steps of the Supreme Court for the first time to hear the oral arguments in the government's suit, *Harris v. McRae*. The white marble plaza that spanned the distance between the sweeping courthouse steps and the busy Washington avenue was bustling with activity, yet I was filled with a sense of awe and reverence. Here was the seat of the institution that had become the trusted guardian of justice and equality for my race. I knew, of course, that it had not always been so.

But in my memory, the Court had extended the protection of the Constitution to Americans who had so often been left out of its promise. It had made opportunities available to me that my grandparents could only strive for.

There is a tendency to speak softly upon entering the building, so as not to disturb the quiet majesty of its marble halls. This is true in the actual courtroom as well, with its vaulted ceilings, dark wood paneling, and floor-to-ceiling burgundy drapes. The seats reserved for the public are limited, and people often wait overnight outside the courthouse to be first in line to hear landmark cases. Once inside the courtroom, spectators are prohibited from taking notes, and one is left to meditate on the significance of the matters as they are discussed.

The marshal broke the hushed silence by crisply commanding everyone in the room to rise. As the judges stepped out together from behind the velvet drapes that were the backdrop of their seats on the elevated mahogany bench, I felt the authority of the law reaffirmed in pageantry. Although the composition and tenor of the Court have changed dramatically since I first witnessed this ritual, I am still moved by it—though never quite as much as that first time.

There before me stood Justice Thurgood Marshall, the man who had argued and won *Brown v. Board of Education of Topeka, Kansas* before the Court, and been the first black to be appointed to it. The wisdom that emanated from his aged, bronze face made it hard for me to look at anyone else.

But there was also Justice Harry Blackmun, the bespectacled former counsel to the Mayo Clinic who had written the *Roe v. Wade* decision. His dark, wavy hair framed his face, giving it a softness that made one think of a wise grandfather.

And then there was Justice William Brennan, diminutive in stature, with an ease and an impish bemusement that seemed to lurk just beneath the surface. His pleasant manner, however, belied the strength and convictions of his eloquent opinions.

These were men whose words I would read over and over as I became immersed in the battleground of the federal courts. And on this particular day, I found it hard to imagine that these same keepers of justice who had decided *Roe* might find that the government had a right to withhold resources with which a poor woman might exercise that right unless her life was in danger. But they had already ruled, in *Beal v. Maher*, to uphold the right to refuse funding for "nontherapeutic" abortions for poor women. How far would they go now?

The justices took their seats—and the formality of the Court soon disintegrated as the lawyers tried to make their opening statements and their

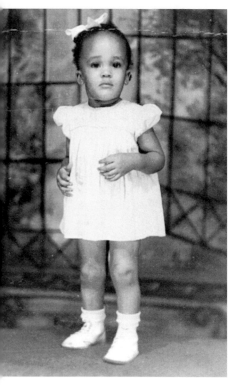

Standing up for myself as a toddler.

On the porch of my first home, 1241 Walton Avenue, with my best friend, Miss Sue—the same Miss Sue who watched as I tried to fly.

Posing for the camera outside 1241 Walton Avenue, around 1946.

Unless otherwise noted, photos are from author's personal collection.

Mama, Ozie Garrett Wattleton, wearing her pinstriped "preaching suit." This photo must have been taken around 1934, the time of Mama's first calling to the ministry.

My father, George Edward Wattleton, sitting proud atop one of his many cars. Note his signature fedora, perched on his bald head "that shone like new money."

Mama's family, the Garretts of Farmhaven, Mississippi, during the mid-1930s. My five uncles are standing in the back (from left to right): Robert, William Eugene (W.E.), Thomas, Coleman, and Ernest. In the front row are (from left to right): Aunt Alice, Aunt Evie, Mama Ola (my grandmother, who died one year before I was born), Aunt Ola, Grandpa Deanie, and Mama.

Aunt Ola and me, standing on the porch of 1241 Walton Avenue. After Mama Ola died in 1942, my aunts, Evie and Ola, came to live with us.

One of the only pictures I have of Jessie Wattleton, my grandmother on my father's side, taken when I was about five. Note the scar under my right eye—proof that I really did try to fly from a tree branch.

That's my beloved aunt Alice, for whom I'm named, sitting at the piano in our house in St. Louis, circa 1945–46. Her husband, David, is standing. By this time, they, too, had moved into our family home.

Nurse Wattleton, circa 1964. I guess it was fate; Mama tells me that back in kinder-garten, my teacher complained that I wouldn't stay in my seat—I followed her around all day, telling her, "I will help you with the babies."

Daddy, Mama, amd me, standing on the porch of Neil Hall at my graduation
from Ohio State's nursing school on June 14, 1964.

My husband at the time, Franklin
Gordon, treating our friends in
Dayton, Ohio, to some jazz piano
in the 1970s.

Learning the ropes of accounting with David Drewitt, at the Dayton Planned Parenthood affiliate.

Inside the workings of Planned Parenthood, 1978. This was my first executive committee meeting as president. David Andrews, my executive vice president, is seated in the chair on the right. Fred Smith, my mentor, who eventually became chairman of the national board, is seated second from left. Tenny Marshall, then chairwoman of the board, is seated next to me on the right (wearing glasses).

Sitting in my office in the summer of 1978, during my first year as president of Planned Parenthood. If I look tired, it's because I was fresh from my first battle, the *Abortion Eve* and the Planned Parenthood cartoon controversies.

Holding my daughter, Felicia, who was then two years old, in front of our old home in Dayton.

PHOTO © GORDON BAER—CINCINNATI

With Franklin and Felicia on vacation in Aruba, 1979.

Felicia and Mama, summer 1982.

This photo was taken in the slums of Old Dhaka, Bangladesh, during my first trip abroad as president of Planned Parenthood, in June 1979. The press of the curious crowds— who were awed by my height—got so tight that I had to have a path cleared so I could breathe.

With my friend and colleague Dan Weintraub, vice president of our international program, visiting one of our family-planning projects in Bangladesh on that first trip abroad in 1979.

Conferring with journalist Carl Rowan at Planned Parenthood's annual meeting, 1984.

One of my earliest national media appearances, on *Donahue*, debating Congressman Henry Hyde, whose Hyde amendment proposed cutting off funding for poor women's abortions. Note his hand-on-hip posture.

The look on my face says it all as I testified before the Senate in 1981 to defend Title X against the accusations of the Reagan administration. My colleague, Barbara Maves, is sitting on the left. Fred Smith is seated on the right of the photo.

With Gloria Steinem at the "March to Save Women's Lives," held on April 9, 1989, a few months before the *Webster* decision was to be announced.

Carrying the banner, on the frontlines of the march, with (from far left): Jesse Jackson, Veronica Hamill (in front of me), Felicia, Glenn Close (in sunglasses), Morgan Fairchild, Jane Fonda, Bella Abzug, Molly Yard, Marlo Thomas, Whoopi Goldberg, Cybill Shepherd. Penny Marshall and Pat Shroeder are standing just to the right of the banner.

Nothing could detract from my exhilaration during the 1989 march, not even the pro-criminalist hecklers standing on the sidelines attracting media attention with their signs.

Caught up in the whirlwind of the moment, rallying the crowds during my speech.

Marching along Constitution Avenue toward the Capitol, surrounded by thousands, including such stalwarts as (from left): Susan Sarandon, Betty Friedan, Kate Michelman of NARAL, Jesse Jackson, and Felicia. Gloria Steinem is on the right.

Not to be discouraged by the Court's decision in *Webster*, the pro-choice coalition organized "Mobilize for Women's Lives," a day of simultaneous rallies across America on November 12, 1989. In this photo, I am speaking in Austin, Texas, one of four stops along the way for me that day.

In New Orleans, another stop on my "Mobilize for Women's Lives" speaking trail, the gospel music rocked Pontchartrain Park.

Receiving an award from Ted Turner's Better World Society for Planned Parenthood's international work in the fall of 1989. Standing next to me are the other awardees.

With a family-planning client in Nepal during my last visit to Asia as president of Planned Parenthood in 1991.

Debating Randall Terry on *Donahue* on September 6, 1991, during the summer of Operation Rescue's Wichita siege.

Speaking out against the gag rule, George Bush's attempt to censor speech by stopping all mention of abortion in government-funded family-planning clinics. Actress Bonnie Franklin is third from the left. Patricia Ireland is second from the right.

PHOTO © ART STEIN

Celebrating Planned Parenthood's 75th Anniversary at the Washingto D.C., annual meeting, with Cicely Tyson, Helen Reddy, and Bella Abzug.

There is no greater joy than standing up for what I believe is right, alongside my daughter. At the April 5, 1992, March for Choice in Washington, D.C., just two days after my last day as president of Planned Parenthood.

Marching once again with Jesse Jackson, as well as the coalition from NOW (including Ellie Smeal, center, and Patricia Ireland) at the 1992 march.

Onstage in 1992, with Ellie Smeal, Patricia Ireland, and Gloria Steinem.

One of my favorite photos of Felicia and me, taken for a *New York Times* cover photo shoot in the summer of 1989.

arguments, despite numerous interruptions, diversions, challenges, and sarcastic asides from the justices.

The exchange between the government's attorney, Solicitor General Wade McCree, Jr., who was defending the Hyde amendment, and Justice William Rehnquist, following the Solicitor General's opening statement, was—for me—the beginning of my disillusionment about the ways of the Court:

Solicitor General McCree: . . . the district court seems to say that since some women as a matter of their religious convictions or conscience would seek an abortion that to refuse funding for them would somehow deny their First Amendment right to freedom of religion and free exercise of religion. We have a great deal of difficulty with that because it would seem that the free exercise clause prevents interference with [religious practice] but doesn't obligate the state to finance it. And we suggest in our brief that a person . . . has no right to expect the state to furnish him with religious objects, for example, a Bible or any religious artifacts to enable him freely to exercise his religion . . .

Justice Rehnquist: Do you think the Court would have ruled the same way had the government simply placed a very high tariff on Manischewitz, which is certainly part of a ritual of at least Orthodox and perhaps conservative Jewry? . . .

Solicitor General McCree: Oh, no, I think it would not be at all if the government had a sectarian purpose for doing that. Now, I—

Rehnquist: My question was did you think the Court would rule the same way? The only possible answer is that you don't know.

McCree: Of course, and I appreciate the Court's suggestion of that.

(Laughter).

Rehnquist: Don't you think the logic of the Court's ruling on the free exercise clause would have led to the same result in that hypothetical?

McCree: Not quite, because—

Justice Marshall: Mr. Solicitor General, why don't you recognize the difference between drinking wine and having a baby? [6]

As much as I loathed Judge Rehnquist's arcane argument drawing parallels between taxing wine and denying funding for poor women to exercise their most fundamental right to control their bodies, I was also offended by his trivialization of the free exercise of religion in all of its aspects, whether in the practice of conscience or the drinking of wines. This freedom is a core value of our constitutional principles.

When it was Copelon's turn, dressed in the dark suit and white blouse that seems to be the uniform of attorneys who appear before the Court, she began crisply and in modulated tones, as though to sound perfectly respectful:

> Mr. Chief Justice, and may it please the Court: This case is one of simple principle and singular magnitude. It involves the survival and health of potentially millions of poor women in the country, and it involves reaffirmation of the simple rule of the law of the written Constitution that this Court recognized in *Roe v. Wade* . . . If the district court found the Hyde amendment repugnant to the entire scheme of the Medicaid statute, [it is] also repugnant to the most minimal safeguards of the Constitution . . .[7]

Just as everyone had expected it would be, Copelon's presentation of the case was concise and eloquent. She remained strong under antagonistic probing from the justices, particularly Justice Rehnquist, who pressed to know why she believed the Court should disagree with the congressional decision that had instituted the amendment.

> **Rehnquist**: . . . You suggest we disagree with Congress in the [Hyde] judgment, whatever kind of a judgment it was?
>
> **Copelon**: . . . Your honor, yes, we suggest that the Court must disagree and—
>
> **Rehnquist**: And the Constitution disagrees?
>
> **Copelon**: That's right, and the reason that the Constitution disagrees, I think, is best illustrated if one looks at what the Court did in *Roe v. Wade.* . . . The conclusion that [there must be a] trade-off . . . between fetal life and maternal health and life is irrational.
>
> **Rehnquist**: When you say the word "irrational," I take it you mean literally those who voted to adopt the Hyde amendment belong in the loony bin?
>
> **Copelon**: No, Your Honor, I wouldn't say that at all.[8]

Even more unnerving than the verbal jabbing was the justices' seeming refusal to understand the impact that the amendment would have on real women. Indeed, the most persistent questioners all seemed to agree with the government that the evidence of the law's probable effects on poor women that was amassed by Judge Dooling had been irrelevant. If there was any compassion toward those women among these arbiters of the Constitution, it wasn't apparent in their probing.

I left the courtroom filled with foreboding. As Eve Paul and I walked down the hallway toward the massive front doors and sunlight, I asked her how she'd thought our side had done.

"I really think Rhonda did a fine job," she answered.

"But their questions seemed so hostile. Shouldn't we be worried?"

Eve warned me not to make a judgment about how the Court would rule based on the line of questioning of the justices: "You know, Faye, the briefs are what really count."

This was the first and last time I would leave an oral argument at the Supreme Court and not face a battery of journalists on the plaza. Since I didn't quite know what to make of the event, I was grateful for my anonymity in the bustling crowd.

Despite Eve's reassurances, I felt dubious that anything good could come of what I'd just seen.

On June 30, 1980, the Supreme Court ruled that the Hyde amendment was constitutional. Drawing upon the decision handed down in *Maher* in 1976, the judges found that:

> Although the government may not place obstacles in the path of a woman's exercise of her freedom of choice, it need not remove those not of its own creation. Indigency falls in the latter category. . . . The financial constraints that restrict an indigent woman's ability to enjoy the full range of constitutionally protected freedom of choice are not the product of governmental restrictions on access to abortions, but rather her indigency. . . .
>
> The remaining question . . . is whether the Hyde amendment is rationally related to a legitimate governmental objective. It is the government's position that the Hyde amendment bears a rational relationship to its legitimate interest in protecting the potential life of the fetus. We agree.[9]

The decision was close—five to four—but that was little solace, given its profound implications. Maybe because the decision would affect "only" poor women, much as *Bellotti* affected "only" minors, it didn't cause much of an uproar. After all, the "right" to abortion was still secure—it just wasn't accessible for some women—those toward whom society has always proved itself to be least sympathetic.

But the truth was that abortion was no longer secure and it was the beginning of the end for *all* women. The Court had declared that when it came to funding, the government did not have to remain neutral between childbirth and abortion—the opposite of its ruling in *Roe*. The government could push an interest in the fetus, using dollars to back its position. Congress could spend its money as it saw fit, even to discriminatory effect; and the women who could least afford to bear the brunt of these battles would pay the highest price. But if this discrimination roiled my sense of justice, I also knew that poor women were not the ultimate target.

It was around this time that, even as these losses played out on the national stage, affecting hundreds of thousands of women, my own personal struggles began to weigh heavily on me. All that Franklin and I had worked so hard for—our contentment as a family, our home, and the pleasure we shared in each other's career achievements—began to crumble.

The demands of running Planned Parenthood had increased tremendously because of the political opposition the organization was confronting. The situation was demanding more of my time and more of my emotions just at a time when Franklin found himself unsettled in his work. As my days became more hectic and his less satisfactory, the tensions between us grew. Franklin had never expected me to fulfill the traditional roles of wife and housekeeper—our marriage would have been hopeless from the start had that been the case—but the pace of my work was more than either of us had anticipated. The balance we'd established back in Dayton was now sorely strained.

I had held to my commitment not to let work interfere with our weekends. But the long daily commutes to the city and the frequent out-of-town travel often meant my arriving home exhausted late at night—too late for meaningful conversation at a time when the need for us to talk was growing more pressing. Now we found ourselves arguing when we were together, and the anger between us mounted.

My work became an instrument for survival. And when I wasn't at work, I found excuses, whenever possible, to take Felicia on any number of excursions in order to spare her the conflict that was beginning to fill our home. Before long, my concerns for Felicia took precedence.

One day, I walked into David Andrews's office in tears and said, "There's something I have to tell you."

Sympathetic, supportive, and wise without fail, he closed the door and sat down across from me. "My gosh, Faye, you look as if you've just seen a ghost. What is it?"

"I've decided that I'm going to get a divorce. Franklin and I can't live together in peace, and I can't bear the thought of Felicia's being caught in the middle of it all."

David was shocked by the announcement. He and his wife, Mimi, had visited Franklin and me in our home several times. I'm sure he thought we were happy. "Are you sure? Have you tried counseling?"

"Yes, I've tried counseling. But I really think things are past fixing."

"Do you have a lawyer?"

"No," I answered. "I was hoping that one of Planned Parenthood's attorneys could advise me on how to handle this quietly."

I couldn't let the impending separation and official end of my marriage affect Planned Parenthood in any way, certainly not at a time when the organization was coming under increasing scrutiny.

Within a matter of days, David had given me the name and telephone number of an attorney specializing in matrimonial law. When I first entered his office, the large and flamboyant lawyer seemed much more interested in recent coverage of me in a beauty magazine than in the troubles of my personal life, but soon we got down to business. A few minutes into our discussion, he said, "Let me give you some advice. The New York law is about to change—your feminist friends have really done it to you. If you don't get your divorce before the new no-fault equitable distribution law is passed, you're going to face the real possibility of having to pay your husband alimony if he makes a claim for it."

I was horrified. I was committed to ending my marriage, but I was hardly prepared to rush the proceedings along for economic reasons.

"Even if you decide to withdraw the action," the lawyer continued, "we need to get the papers filed immediately so you'll come under the old law if you decide to go ahead." Then he gloated one last time, "Boy, have your feminist friends done it to you." His belly shook from his whoop as he leaned back in his black leather swivel chair.

I left the office alone and upset. I wasn't ready for Franklin to be served with divorce papers. I suppose I hoped that I would somehow be able to get a divorce without going through all the turmoil of divorce. But since that was impossible, that night after Felicia was asleep, I told Franklin, "I'm tired of all this anger and fighting, and I'm worried about Felicia. I've decided to get a divorce."

Franklin responded, "Do what you have to do." His manner was impassive, as though he didn't take me seriously.

I didn't want Franklin to protest my decision, but I clung to the hope that we could remain civil to each other. He said nothing, so I continued, "I think it would really be better if you moved out so that we can keep conflict to a minimum until this is over."

To this he answered, "I have no intention of moving out. If you want to go through with the divorce, we'll simply put everything up for sale, split the proceeds, and leave it at that."

I couldn't imagine disrupting Felicia's home—certainly not at the same time that her family was in disorder—and I told Franklin so. The conversation ended there, and I suppose he assumed that it was all just talk and that I wouldn't go through with it until we had a few more verbal battles.

Nevertheless, I did proceed, and my determination to end our marriage never seemed so concrete as it did that Saturday morning when the court official arrived at our house with the action for divorce, which he served on Franklin. "How can you do this?" he asked as though he was hearing the news for the first time.

"I have to do it, Franklin. I don't want to stay married to you. I don't want Felicia to grow up like this."

"You're the only one who can stop this," he said, and demanded that I tear up the summons.

I wasn't willing to turn back.

A few weeks later, we met together with our respective lawyers to work out a property settlement. I wouldn't meet Franklin's demands, and he countersued for divorce. There were many days when the tension of living in the same house with Franklin while the divorce went along and the lawyers squabbled became more than I could bear. At work, I'd close the door to my office and drown my pain in tears of anger, regret, and sorrow.

Many years later, in a rural village in Nepal, an old man sitting in the sun on his porch would remind me of how I'd felt at this time of personal crisis. "You can hide happiness," he said. "But you can't hide trouble."

Still, I tried to maintain my privacy and hide my trouble. Only a few people at the office—David Andrews, my secretary, and Fred Smith— were aware of the turmoil in my life. Otherwise, I had no one to turn to— certainly not my mother, who had warned me that the marriage would not last. The demands of my position, which had often seemed so tyrannical, became my refuge.

The divorce was dragged out in a sixteen-month ordeal. I retained custody of Felicia, though Franklin was granted virtually unlimited visiting privileges. The financial issues were resolved. Fortunately, unlike most women who go through a divorce and are awarded child custody, as the chief executive officer of a large organization, I earned a comfortable enough income for my daughter and myself.

Felicia didn't seem outwardly disturbed by the breakup of our marriage. But there were times when when she revealed the anxieties borne of living in a tension-filled home. There was a phase when her drawings at school showed her father in the sky above our house while she and I walked along hand in hand below him. In her drawings, my head was on fire. I scheduled her for several sessions with a child psychiatrist, and it wasn't long before her disturbing drawings stopped.

CHAPTER 22

THE NEW RIGHT: DEFUNDING THE LEFT

The mood at the office on the morning of November 5, 1980, was somber. Over half of America's voters had just rejected the Democratic agenda and placed the leadership of their country in the hands of Ronald Reagan, a man who had run on a "traditional values," anti-choice platform; a man who had promised to work for "a constitutional amendment to restore protection of the right to life for unborn children" and to "support the congressional efforts to restrict the use of taxpayers' dollars for abortion."[1]

I'd stayed up late into the night watching the returns and thinking about the voters who had been willing to elect such a man. The pundits had been saying the voters were swayed by "pocketbook" and foreign policy issues, but how could they be deemed more important than our most basic rights? Had the opponents of abortion rights figured significantly in Reagan's victory? Had women streamed to the polls in great numbers, or had many of them stayed home?

"What can people be thinking?" I mumbled to myself throughout the night.

Would Ronald Reagan have been elected if his platform had included a promise to work for a constitutional amendment that applied government "protection" to the press or speech or religion? I thought yet again about David Garth and his advice, rejected by Planned Parenthood two years before, that we involve ourselves in politics and take part in the electoral process. We were now locked into a pro-criminalization administration for at least four years. For the moment the only tools we had to combat it would be the image-building and lobbying the board had allowed us.

Shortly before midnight, Tom Brokaw announced, on the NBC news, ". . . and for the first time in twenty-six years, the Senate will be in Republican hands . . ."

"What?!" I shouted into the solitude of my bedroom. It was late, but I had to call someone, to share my distress with another human being—to touch reality with someone who would understand immediately the implications of what was happening. I dialed David Andrews's number. "David, do you believe . . . ?"

"I know . . . I know. Mimi and I've been watching all evening. It's god-a-w-w-ful . . ."

The political activism of the New Right had staged an electoral upset. If the Republican platform had offered the vision, the Republican Senate could provide the machinery for achieving it. It now had the majority to lay the groundwork for effecting the Reagan agenda. Yes, the House would remain in Democratic hands for the next two years, probably more, but the Republican Senate had just won the power to rubber-stamp all federal judicial candidates that Reagan put forth. Unfolding before us was an era for women that would be every bit as bad as Garth had warned.

The senators had been elected on the same agenda Reagan had run on—one that vowed to "work for the appointment of judges at all levels of the judiciary who respect traditional family values and the sanctity of innocent human life."[2] Between the new president and new Senate, even if no vacancies arose on the Supreme Court, which was unlikely, they would certainly have the opportunity to transform the composition of the federal judiciary at the district and appellate levels.

After David and I finished imagining the worst, I flicked off the television. Sleep did not come easy. Running through my head was the sure sense that we were crossing the threshold of a new political era of attacks on women's reproductive rights. All the progress we'd made had been through the courts. We were not prepared to fight on the political terrain that was being laid for us. The New Right now had the strength to attack us at all levels and on all fronts. From education to contraception, to fetal research and abortion, the pro-criminalists would leave no aspect undisturbed. Those leading the Senate attacks would be people like Strom Thurmond (R-SC), who now headed the Judiciary Committee, and Orrin Hatch, a Mormon lay minister, who would now head the Committee on Labor and Human Resources. And newly elected were Jeremiah Denton from Alabama, Jake Garn from Utah, and Don Nickles from Oklahoma. These five men had proclaimed their intention to conduct a "moral crusade."

While the majority of public opinion may not have embraced Reagan's so-called social agenda, the country had been eager for his reassuring message after the turbulence of the early Seventies and the quiet demoralization of the Ford and Carter years. And most of those who shuddered at the prospect of change clung to the hope that the Supreme Court would continue to protect reproductive rights from the collusion of the White House and Senate. They seemed oblivious to or apathetic about the fact that the Court's very nature could be changed by nominations from the pro-criminalist White House and confirmations by the pro-criminalist Senate.

As if to underscore the fact that the political world as we knew it was no more, the first delegation that the new president received at the White House after his inauguration were representatives of "The March for Life."

Considering that so much of the campaign furor had been over abortion, the legislative assault on abortion began indirectly, when, one month after he took office, Reagan made his first budget proposal. Playing to the strong states' rights instincts of the New Right, and fulfilling his campaign promise to reduce the overall size of the federal bureaucracy, Reagan and his advisers proposed "returning" funding decisions for a wide range of health and social services to the state level. They suggested doing this by issuing so-called "block grants." Title X, which had enjoyed tremendous bipartisan support ever since 1969, when Nixon had signed it into law, was to be folded into one such package.

The Title X program of the Public Health Services Act provided federal support for family planning for the poor, so long as the funds weren't used for abortion-related services. Even with that restriction, it had played an essential role in the tremendous expansion of birth control services in many Planned Parenthood affiliates, my affiliate in Dayton being one example. Reagan's plan to fold the decade-old program into a block grant would obliterate it. Not only would Title X's share be indistinguishable from the blended proceeds of other programs in the package; the funds provided to Title X would be cut by twenty-five percent.

As though to add a note of disparagement, which showed where family planning figured in his priorities, Reagan proposed tying Title X into a bundle of unrelated programs, including immunization, hypertension prevention and treatment, rodent control, water fluoridation, and campaigns against lead-based paint poisoning and cigarette smoking. He did not propose to mandate that any money at all be allotted for family planning. If the states so chose, there was nothing to prevent them from spending the proceeds from the block grant on anything or everything *but* family planning within that bundle of programs.

The implications of returning funding decisions to the states were grave and far-reaching. For one thing, the legacy of unwanted childbearing is borne by the nation as a whole. To parcel the problem among many states is to shirk the responsibility for a problem with vast implications for our society. Another peril to family planning services was that as a federal categorical program, Title X had been insulated from the uncertainties of state politics. If Reagan succeeded, it would be subject to the decisions of state legislatures, which were much closer to the pressure points of the increasingly intense controversy over every aspect of family planning, even where abortion was not involved.

As an African American and as a woman, I have an especially deep fear of the states' rights approach to assuring minorities, the poor, and women access to the exercise of their constitutional rights, when those rights are in contention: Where would we have been then—and where today—if there had been no Federal Voting Rights Act—and funding to make voting accessible to *all* American citizens? And regarding healthcare, only through acts of Congress, through Medicaid and Medicare, have the poor and elderly been able to receive it. I'd grown up knowing that segregation and other discriminatory practices had the sanction of state legislations. And state laws banning information about contraceptive methods and abortion were the last to fall.

Quite apart from the threats and attacks by those opposed to family planning programs on moral or religious grounds, the states were facing severe cutbacks in federal aid in general. Between the fiscal crises that these reductions would stir, and the rising opposition, it seemed all but inevitable that programs addressing basic short-term survival needs for the poor—food, shelter, and care during illness—would take precedence over the prevention of pregnancy, especially any programs for poor women and teenagers, who were trapped in the reality of political voicelessness that has always been their lot.

To look at the block grants in this light was to see that they were hardly a simple matter of shifting governmental bookkeeping: They were a New Right–inspired attempt to take down many social and health programs that they opposed, including Title X, by stealth, without singling any out for public destruction. They called it "defunding the left."

When we first started to contact members of Congress to urge their rejection of Reagan's proposal, it quickly became evident that we would be fighting an uphill battle. Even in Planned Parenthood, the wisdom of the moment was that we should assume the loss of Title X. Ronald Reagan was simply too popular. "He will get his way," they sighed in resignation. "We should look for other means to support our programs."

Even within the Democratic House, which did have some leverage against him, we found few legislators willing to use it for fear of retaliation during the 1982 election campaigns. We might as well accept the reality, said dispirited colleagues, that the president had the mandate of the voters to reduce the size of government; we would simply have to accept the medicine, and fight in the states to get family planning funding from the reduced dollars the federal government sent back to them.

But as far as I was concerned, Title X was far more than an essential source of funding for our efforts to prevent unwanted pregnancy. It was a means for poor women and teenagers to control their reproductive lives, and the subtext of the assault was to toss every aspect of family planning into the same basket. It was my belief that any efforts to jeopardize Title X were part of the expanding spectrum of sabotage to frustrate women and deny them sexual liberty and reproductive control, and that abortion was the tip of the iceberg. Even if many of my colleagues at Planned Parenthood were willing to concede defeat, I was not. We had to fight for Title X. Our funding was our lifeblood and our enemies knew it. I felt within me that somehow we would win. Most affiliates agreed that we should put up a fight, but they weren't confident about the prospects of our prevailing.

Two months into the 1981 congressional session—one day after the assassination attempt on the president—the Senate Committee on Labor and Human Resources convened a hearing on Title X under the guise of examining whether the program had been a success. Days later, the House Subcommittee on Health and the Environment would do the same.

Orrin Hatch headed the Senate committee, which also included the freshmen Denton and Nickles and another Republican, Dan Quayle, of Indiana.

Senator Hatch had asked Jeremiah Denton, who had come to the Senate with the distinction of having been the nation's highest-ranking prisoner of the Vietnam War, to assist him in the presiding duties. Given the cast chosen to lead the interrogation, we saw clearly that the hearings would be an unmitigated assault on the program.

A week before the hearings were to begin, Bill Hamilton, the new director of our Washington lobbying office, called to say that we had received a request for me to appear before the committee. Fred Smith, the national board chairman, and Barbara Maves, the Muncie, Indiana, affiliate executive director and one of Dan Quayle's constituents, had also been invited. We assumed that the Senate committee would put together another panel of supporters as well.

We were to submit testimony in writing, so in addition to presenting the achievements of the program, every point of anticipated opposition would have to be scrupulously defended. Barbara and I would be allowed to make a brief opening statement and would then be questioned by the committee. Fred would answer questions only.

When I got to my Washington hotel, I received a message from Bill that our panel would be the only one to appear in support of Title X. It was a setup, blatantly unfair, and unlike any ploy we'd ever seen before. We had assumed that the hearing was going to be an assault on Title X, but only now was it clear that Planned Parenthood would bear the brunt of this challenge alone.

When I spoke to Bill from my hotel room that night, he confirmed, "As of tonight, ours is the only supportive group on the list."

"I can't believe they're really going to handle the hearing this way," I lamented.

In my first appearance before a congressional committee, I would face a new cast of characters, so there wasn't a lot that anyone could tell me, based on previous performances, about what to expect. I would have to rely on my intuition. This hearing would be as much about sizing up the newcomers as it was about Title X. As the hearing was shaping up, we would not be allowed to speak only for our twenty-five percent share of the program's funding. No, we were being called to defend Title X as though it were the exclusive purview of Planned Parenthood.

Shortly before the hearing was to begin, Barbara, Fred, and I arrived at the Dirksen Building. We walked down the long corridor leading toward the hearing room, past a line of those hoping to get seats. The line filled the hallway. Even I, who'd not been a hearing witness before, concluded, and Bill confirmed, that the turnout evidenced unusually strong interest in a forum that was not investigating criminal wrongdoing.

We gave our names as witnesses and the guard allowed us to enter the cavernous room. I shivered slightly, partly from nervousness and partly from the cool draftiness of the high-ceilinged chamber. We took our seats on the heavy, leather-upholstered wooden chairs in the front row, Fred and Barbara to my right. As always, I was anxious that I would forget an important point, make an error, or embarrass myself by appearing to be at a loss for words. To calm myself, I opened my folder to the statement that I would give, and to the list of points that I had to remember to try to make during the question-and-answer session that would follow our statements. I also hoped this would distract me from concerns roused by the display before us: Posters lined the walls of the hearing room, and sexuality education books and pamphlets were spread out on a large wooden table at the front of the room. Some of these materials were produced by us, some by others. Recognizing the covers of some of them from as far back as my Dayton days, I worried that I would be called to defend explicit points within them.

The room soon filled with the curious spectators. Then Senators Denton and Hatch, impeccably neat and conservatively dressed, entered, trailed by their young, freshly scrubbed aides. Nickles and Quayle would arrive even later, and Quayle would stay only long enough to acknowledge the presence of fellow Indianan Barbara Maves. After depositing their papers at their places at the elevated hearing bench, the senators stepped down to the hearing room floor and slowly walked around the pamphlet-laden table. We watched them as they stopped several minutes to peruse the covers, or flip through some of the booklets, shaking their heads as though in disbelief. In their solemnity, they reminded me of professional mourners viewing the open coffin of a stranger—respectfully somber and making the inspection for dramatic effect.

In later times, I would smile at such a carefully orchestrated spectacle, but this was my initiation and I was too nervous to see the humor in it. My teeth chattered slightly, and I clenched my jaw to stop them. I was too nervous to even muster any small talk with my seatmates.

Their silent drama completed, the senators seated themselves behind the authority of the heavy wooden pulpits that gave the room the air of a courtroom. Senator Denton instantly launched into a tirade about Planned Parenthood's counseling of minors based on a much-distorted view of our work.

> . . . Increasingly, it appears that family-planning clinics are serving teenagers in the absence of their parents' advice and counsel and often in contradiction of laws concerning sexual conduct in many of their own states.
>
> Moreover, in the role of sex educators, these clinics are promulgating their own version of morality in contradiction often to the values of the teenagers' parents and pastors. If we start with the assumption and establish it in the minds of our young that premarital sexual intercourse among children is acceptable and inevitable, then I believe we will see a continued growth of the problems attending teenage pregnancy and promiscuity which have marked so many young lives—indeed we will see a continued growth of other extremely dangerous and related sociological problems. . . .
>
> When grantees provide teens with values denying any need for self-restraint, with confidential birth control services, medical treatment and abortion counseling, it can hardly be said that we are encouraging youthful habits leading to their long-range happiness or promoting parental involvement. Parenthood is a lifetime vocation.[3]

On that last point, I strongly agreed. But Denton's construction of what clinics do had no basis in reality. We did not serve teens in contradiction to state law. As for the rest of what he had to say, clearly the senator had never sat in on a family planning counseling session when, typically, teenagers acknowledged that they were sexually active long before they'd arrived at the clinic. Many of them were already pregnant. Only a small proportion of those pregnancies were wanted.[4]

This opening put us on notice that the hearing would be as much a declaration of the New Right's moral manifesto as it would be a challenge to the value of Title X as a federal program in preventing unwanted pregnancy, or for that matter, to Planned Parenthood affiliates that received Title X funds. In the Senator's mind, sexuality among teenagers was evidence of the moral decline of America. And obviously Planned Parenthood, as the largest and oldest family-planning provider in the country, was thus the purveyor of values that were leading society to ruination.

That Denton would use teenagers to provide a framework for this inquisition was no surprise. Teenagers accounted for one-third of the Title X caseload. Teen sexuality has traditionally been a volatile political issue, exposing an especially sensitive area of ambivalence over the acceptance of sexuality as an aspect of our lives from infancy to death.

Denton accompanied his opening statement with a screening of *About Sex*. The film, which was *de rigueur* during the 1970s in urban teen clinics, depicts teenagers and a counselor engaged in a frank discussion of human sexuality and birth control. Candid though I knew this discussion to be, I was unprepared for the provocative introduction the senator from Alabama gave the film:

> Since a picture is worth a thousand words, as part of my opening statement, I invite my colleagues to view a film which is currently available and being used in a typical clinic. The film illustrates some of the fundamental issues we want to examine today. Because of the nature of the film, I have asked that children and adolescents be kept from the room for this segment of the hearing.[5]

Of course, at nine o'clock on a Tuesday morning there were no children or teenagers in the room. But Senator Denton had managed to imply that the audience was about to be subjected to an X-rated peep show. What the audience saw, after the presentation of credits accompanied by music of the Ghetto Brothers, was a racially and ethnically mixed group of teenagers and Angel Martinez, a well-regarded educator on sexuality, discussing the anatomy and physiology of reproduction and debunking a number of myths about how to prevent pregnancy.

Following the group discussion, Angel Martinez, now seen alone, addresses some of the subjects the group discussed—sexual thoughts and fantasies, masturbation, homosexuality, pregnancy, babies and birth control, and last, abortion. Much of his lecture is overlaid with visuals. Some of them are quite explicit, including a double exposure of a couple having sex. While discussing contraception, Angel displays various contraceptive devices. This discussion is interspersed with the image of the front of a Planned

Parenthood clinic (the only evidence in the film of Planned Parenthood as an entity) and with images of drugstore shelves holding contraceptives.

Angel's segment is followed by a discussion between a young woman and a physician about abortion.

> **Doctor**: Abortion is legal now. . . . This does not mean that abortion is a substitute for good contraception; that will never be the case. But abortion is a safe, easy procedure and, if it is done early, leads to very few complications and very few difficulties. . . . [6]

The film closes with teens displaying more maturity and insight about sexuality than our inquisitors would that day:

> **A Girl**: Two people involved in a relationship should consider each other as full human beings with a full spectrum of feelings. I think now more and more women are being more proud of their sexuality than of their sexiness.

> **A Boy**: A man and woman must share responsibilities in birth control as well as other things.[7]

The projector in the hearing room was barely off before Senator Hatch embarked on the offensive, with the same venomous flair that he would unleash on Anita Hill a decade later:

> Well, as I watched that I felt that is about as disgusting a film as I have seen, and it is incredible for me to imagine that something that gross would actually be shown to anyone, especially teenagers, in the name of sex education or for any other reason for that matter.
>
> As far as I am concerned, that film is pornographic. . . . I wonder how those infants will feel or these young people will feel when they grow up and realize that they were exploited like that, and in a way I feel we should apologize to those of you in the hearing room today who had to sit through that. . . .
>
> We have seen abortion touted as a painless, harmless, trouble-free procedure with few negative side effects. . . . In the name of open-mindedness, we have heard that masturbation is normal, acceptable, and even desirable. We have heard that homosexual relationships are as valid and natural as heterosexual relationships and that homosexual relationships should not be questioned or criticized but only accepted. By implication, we have heard that teenage sexual activity is inevitable. We have heard that the only problem with teenage sexual activity is that pregnancy may result.

We have seen teenagers encouraged to talk freely, openly and explicitly about the most intimate of personal matters with their peers, matters which they admittedly would be embarrassed to discuss with their own parents. . . . [8]

Perhaps what Senator Hatch found "gross," "pornographic," and "tasteless" was just one aspect of the American experience that he didn't want to publicly acknowledge existed. But whether the senator from Utah liked it or not, the film was in many ways no more than a snapshot of life as it is lived by many today. The teenagers in the film were not actors, but inner-city kids, uncoached, who were attending a family-planning clinic. Their realities are truths with which many other teenagers could identify.

Now came the substance of the hearing. Before Barbara, Fred, and I were called to the hearing table, Senator Howard Metzenbaum (D-OH) had registered his disapproval that no other organizations had been allowed to appear in defense of Title X. Senator Hatch had dismissed his complaint saying, "When you have two members of Planned Parenthood and you have these others [opposed to Title X funding], that is a balanced hearing. . . . We will proceed."[9]

And proceed we did. Barbara and I were interrogated, primarily by Senators Denton, Hatch, and Nickles, for over two hours—a long time for witnesses not accused of wrongdoing.

I was asked to speak first. When I placed my prepared remarks on the large oak table, I hoped no one would notice the slight trembling of my hands. I began my statement with a dry throat and a pounding heart, but conscious of the clicking cameras, I tried to muster a smile so I wouldn't look somber or frightened.

More for the *Congressional Record* than for the senators' ears, I proceeded to establish a few facts about Planned Parenthood, hoping to deflect the distortions certain to rain down on us. I told them that the primary mission of Planned Parenthood was to provide the means, through education and services, for women and men to responsibly manage their sexual and reproductive health and to exercise their reproductive decisions. And despite Senator Denton's opening remarks, we were not "promulgating [our] own version of morality." Rather, we aimed to provide tools that women and men could use in following the dictates of *their* personal moral beliefs on the basis of informed choice.

Having anticipated that teenagers, increasingly a public debate flashpoint, would be given a good deal of attention during the hearings, I hastened to describe the content of our education and counseling programs for minors. Explaining that we did much more than provide contraception, I cited our screening and treating of such other health problems as cancer, anemia, high blood pressure, diabetes, and sexually transmitted infections.

And because the senators had proved themselves bent upon characterizing Title X as encouraging promiscuity among poor women and teenagers, I reminded them that unwanted pregnancy was as much a fast road to poverty as it was a reflection of it.

As for the senators' attacks on our serving minors without parental consent, I again cited facts. More than half of the teenagers who came to our clinics did so with their parents' knowledge. But about a quarter of them had told us that if their parents *had* to be told, they would not come to us for contraceptive services—but neither would they stop having sex. I informed the senators that we did not blithely hand out contraceptives to teenagers, or adults, for that matter. Our clinics were run by professionals who cared about maturity, and about health, social, and family circumstances. In order to best serve the women who came to us, we had to consider each of them as an individual with her own rights, not simply an extension of her parents. If providing contraceptives to sexually active teenagers without parental consent made the difference between their being pregnant and their not being pregnant, we felt we had no choice.

Speaking to Denton's point that we were part of the exploding teenage pregnancy problem, I informed the senator that, in reality, the increase in the rate of teenage pregnancy was leveling off.

As would prove to be the rule in this hearing room where nothing Barbara and I said seemed to be heard, Senators Denton and Hatch did not respond to my statement at all. Instead, Denton continued his attempt to discredit Planned Parenthood by claiming that we pressured community groups to use our educational materials on sexuality, even when they were not reflective of community standards. As a case in point, he suggested that the film *About Sex* advocated that teenagers should not listen to their parents.

"Do you believe you can teach those kinds of facts without unjustified and harmful infringement on the moral and religious values of many of this country's families . . . ?" he asked.[10]

The idea that providing people with information about sexuality was the same as infringing upon "moral and religious values" made no sense to me, unless such "values" advocated ignorance. Knowledge is not infringement, *enforcement* is. And enforcement was just what the New Right agenda and Senator Denton were all about: compelling adherence to their standard of personal morality, by force of law. Senator Denton didn't seem to perceive the contradiction.

I answered:

> There are many young people who seek our services who cannot talk to their parents. . . . If my child could not come to me to discuss her concerns and her questions about her sexuality, I am comforted to know that

there is an agency in the community that can provide support to her during a difficult phase of her life.[11]

When the lights had first come up after the film, Senator Hatch charged that it had implied "teen sexual activity is inevitable." The reality is that sexual activity *is* inevitable—at any age. Surely not every teenager will have sexual intercourse, but most will. Maybe these senators never faced this fact in their youth, or maybe they did, and by carrying out their moral crusade they hoped for atonement. Maybe their children were unique among the teenage species and had never sneaked a drink, never tried marijuana, never experimented with sex and inadvertently caught a sexually transmitted infection or found themselves pregnant. Would they have felt they could come to their fathers if they had? And, if they had felt they could, and had come to them, how would the senators have treated their sons and, especially, their daughters?

I cannot speak for those senators or their children. But neither can they speak for me or mine, or for any parent or teenager. And the children of America—including the senators' and mine—are children not of their parents alone. They are, collectively and yet ever individually, our children; and I believe we owe all of them the best we can do to see that they live to grow up, and that they grow up to lead informed, productive, and compassionate lives. Any campaign to silence discussion of teenage sexuality when that discussion goes beyond the "Just Say No" approach is ultimately at odds with that end, inside or outside the U.S. Senate.

Senators Denton and Hatch saw the world as if through one set of lenses and we saw it through another. This became especially clear when they failed to respond to a particularly meaningful, and even brave, part of Barbara Maves's testimony.

Barbara had been asked to focus on her affiliate's services to teenagers, and in her prepared remarks, she recounted three stories that would not have been out of the ordinary at any Planned Parenthood clinic. The first concerned a mother distraught that her daughter had come to us for gonorrhea treatment and birth control but who came to realize that it was critical to safeguard her child's health and prevent an unwanted pregnancy. The second story was about a fourteen-year-old girl who'd run away from her mother to live with her father, who refused to assume responsibility for her. When she became pregnant, a neighbor brought her to the Muncie affiliate. In counseling, when the girl's father realized he would be legally responsible, he wanted her to have an abortion, although she wanted to keep the baby. It came out "that the young girl had always wanted a pet and fiercely resented never being allowed to have one. . . . Her father told his daughter that he would let her have a puppy if she would not have the baby, and she agreed."

Barbara continued:

> The third young woman . . . told me that she felt she needed birth control . . . that she . . . was not strong enough to continue saying no . . . I was hesitant . . . and I told the girl that we could not serve her, and that she should try to be strong and keep saying no. Sometime later the girl came [in pregnant], . . . went through our problem pregnancy counseling and chose to have her baby . . . I would see her from time to time. She had not married, and she said that she was not happy. She said that although she loved her baby, her baby had made her life very hard for her.
>
> I used to wonder whether the girl thought much about the fact that she had asked me for birth control before she had sexual intercourse and I had refused her.

Silence settled over the room. Even the television crews seemed captivated by the poignancy of the moment. Barbara concluded her testimony with a plea:

> The greatest wrong that you could do would be to oversimplify these grave and complicated matters. As you make decisions that may affect the future of the family-planning movement in this country, I trust that you will make them with the proper gravity and moral discrimination. Thank you.[12]

The only abortion-related issue that might have had any bearing on the hearings was whether Title X funds were being used to fund abortion services. But limiting the discussion to that did not serve the senators' purposes—not when the real point of the hearing was to demonize all of Planned Parenthood's work and thereby to malign all federally supported family-planning programs, thus rationalizing the destruction of Title X. Senator Nickles, the freshman senator from Oklahoma, still angling to confirm his credentials as a champion of the New Right, claimed to have received testimony, "from those qualified to give it," that Planned Parenthood's counselors did not act "in a neutral way." Instead, "if a girl is in school, young, unmarried, poor . . . abortion is often stressed either blatantly or subtly as the quickest, simplest, most practical solution." This, he asserted, was "poor counseling," regardless of how one felt about abortion.[13]

"What does this have to do with Title X?" I asked myself. But I maintained the professional passivity I'd learned long ago to mask my impatience, and explained in a flat voice that Planned Parenthood counselors discussed all alternatives with each client regardless of age. Only in accordance with the client's decision was a referral made to the appropriate service providers, whether to the local Birthright organization, which might support her through the pregnancy and help her in finding a job or other ways to support herself and her baby; to a Family Service Association agency, which could assist in arranging an adoption; or to a clinic in the local community that would enable her to end her pregnancy, if she chose to do so and the local Planned Parenthood did not provide the service.

I might have reminded the senator of how bleak a girl's future became if she was unmarried, poor, and pregnant; I thought about the girls at the Daytime Center. But such a reminder would surely have been brushed aside, for nothing the senators had said during these hearings demonstrated the least bit of compassion for the young or the poor.

Nickles challenged not only the moral legitimacy of our including abortion in any aspect of our counseling process, but the moral legitimacy of the act itself, which was prohibited by the Title X law:

Nickles: Ms. Wattleton . . . You are always talking about freedom and you are talking about choice. What about the choice of the unborn child to live? . . .

Me: I would point out to you that many people do not perceive a fetus as an unborn child, and reiterate that therefore their decision should be guided by their own ethical and moral and religious [beliefs].[14]

The explicit appearance of religious values in the proceedings of the highest legislative body of a secular nation, built on the principles of religious liberty, didn't seem to restrain the senator from Oklahoma.

Eventually, Nickles brought the discussion around to the subject of our five-year strategic plan, which the pro-criminalists had distorted, implying that it was part of a national plot to lure women into our clinics. Nickles wondered whether we set "targets" for increasing the number of abortions we did. I responded that our national plan was "not a goal, [but] an assessment of future need."

After some discussion of the number of teenagers who used Planned Parenthood abortion services each year (about one-third of the total of eighty thousand women of all ages who used our abortion services each year—a figure that was roughly in proportion with the national average), Nickles returned to our counseling procedures with special emphasis on when we discussed abortion with a client. As if to taunt me with a theme that would culminate fifteen years later in a national debate over the propriety of those who provided abortions in late months of pregnancy, he asked:

Nickles: What if they are four months pregnant?

Me: If they are four months pregnant, they are provided with care that is consistent with the medical standards of the community and the medical capabilities of Planned Parenthood. The affiliate may provide the service directly in the clinic or the woman may be referred to a health facility that provides the service.

Nickles: Six months?

Me: In most communities six months' gestation is as late as a woman can obtain an abortion. . . .

Nickles: Do you think that if the pregnant teenager knew what the body form of the fetus was at, say, four months or five months or six months, that would have a tendency to have them not want the abortion?

Me: My perception, as a nurse-midwife who worked in large urban hospitals before the Supreme Court decision, [is that] it would not deter them. They would again resort to illegal and unsafe means to end their pregnancies, out of desperation not to have an unwanted child. What it does do is to heap a great deal of guilt and shame on a woman who is often facing a difficult decision in her life. We believe that we should be supportive to her, not a source of repudiation.[15]

If services to teenagers and abortion had represented the first and second lines of attack on Planned Parenthood, then our escalated involvement in the political process represented the third. The senators found this activity "inappropriate for a government-funded organization."

It was over lobbying that Senator Hatch entered the questioning. "Some people," he said, "have made complaints that Planned Parenthood has been conducting lobbying efforts, or should I even say systematic lobbying efforts to promote Planned Parenthood's political, social, and financial interests."[16]

I replied with the same argument that I'd made to those within Planned Parenthood:

Senator Hatch, I would like to point out that Planned Parenthood did not initiate nor did we thrust this issue into the political arena. We believe that the decision should be left to the individual. When one does not have the means to carry [out] a decision as fundamental as childbearing, the government should be dispassionate in [providing services to support whatever choice is made].[17]

When Senator Hatch pressed further on this point and Barbara and I tried to point out that Planned Parenthood's political activities were financed by private donations, not federal funds, he seemed unwilling to hear or alter his attack. He cited a Planned Parenthood hot line located in Sacramento, California, that "urged people to vote, not necessarily because the presidential race was so important, but because"—and he quoted the hot line—" 'if you don't exercise that opportunity, you may be letting the opposition select the lawmakers who could limit your choices for years to come.' "

Had we used Title X money to make this statement, we would have violated the law. But as Barbara and I tried to make clear, Planned Parenthood had acted legally and ethically. But law and ethics weren't at issue; Planned Parenthood was.

So the senator continued—in Nickles's vein, promulgating the New Right's popular and cynical notion that we were part of a family-planning and abortion "industry." Hatch went so far as to say, "[I]t appears that family planners want to change the behavior, the attitudes, and the social values of our culture so that they conform with birth-prevention procedures and principles."

It was all but useless for me to say that "we are a voluntary organization . . . [of] concerned community residents with no personally vested interest in the family-planning services that we offer."[18]

At the end of Barbara's and my testimony, Senator Denton reflected upon the grave dangers that he believed we proponents of the "new morality" (or "old immorality") represented:

I don't think family is encouraged by what you all are doing in family planning. . . . Civilization has been here a short time, and it is fragile. It has failed before in nations, it has failed in societies. And usually the factor that causes it to fail is a breakdown in the institution of the family . . . I don't believe that the new morality you all are living with, in fact apart of really from the way you talk [*sic*], is new; I think it is the old immorality that delayed the dawn of civilization for millions of years and caused its fall every time it's been tried as something new. I don't think you can separate a choice as important, infinitely important as whether or not you go to bed with someone of the opposite sex, you can't separate that from some kind of effort to think about the consequences of that—in other words, morality.[19]

The tone of his statement was frighteningly familiar to me, echoing as it did, at the highest levels of government, the rhetoric of the tent revival crusades of my childhood: S-E-X was evil, a threat not only to the soul of the individual, but to the survival of civilization itself. To these senators, as to

Father Griese in Dayton, Planned Parenthood was like some perverse, sexual Pied Piper, leading the nation to damnation.

I stood up from the witness table limp and dazed. I had just been through initiation by fire. I was learning that a little adrenaline could go a long way toward loosening the tongue. In the midst of the inquisition, I hadn't stopped to reflect, hadn't had a moment to be uncertain, or the chance to make sure my statements were at least clear and complete, if not elegant. I'd just said what came to my mind and tried to keep the flashes of angry emotion out of the tone and out of the words. Had I done well enough? Racing through my head were points that I could have made more incisively.

As Barbara and I left the hearing room, we were deluged with congratulations and expressions of appreciation. Jeannie Rosoff came to me beaming, her concerns about me and what I might do to her organization now part of the past. Jeannie's smiling approval was a balm to the spirit. But the kudos that day did little to ease my tension. Given the "junkyard dog" aggression of the recently elected senators, I could see we were in for a long, hard season.

Two days later, the grilling about Title X started all over again in the House of Representatives. After the Senate hearings, I had developed a severe case of laryngitis, and testified before the House in a barely audible whisper.

Ultimately, the House reauthorized Title X for three more years as a separate program. But the subject of teen sexuality wasn't left undisturbed. The Senate Labor and Human Resources Committee agreed to authorize and fund, at the cost of thirty million dollars, a new program for "adolescent family life and pregnancy care"—the Adolescent Family Life Demonstration Projects Act. Sponsored by Senator Denton, and dubbed the "chastity bill" by the media, the bill was supposed to encourage the "study" of the effectiveness of promoting abstinence as a method of birth control. (Senator Ted Kennedy (D-MA) enlisted as a co-sponsor, reportedly at the behest of his sister Eunice Shriver.) Although we felt certain the program would not convince most teens to forgo sex, those who could be encouraged to do so would benefit from it. And by prevailing in the House, we'd made sure that if teaching chastity did not succeed, Title X would be there to offer alternatives to pregnancy—if the proposal was passed.

Now the Senate and House bills had to be reconciled in conference. Before negotiations on the overall budget began, the administration tried to persuade the Senate to accept the House health provisions—including Title X as a categorical grant—in order to avoid a protracted battle. President Reagan was perfectly happy to use the New Right's political machinery for his own purposes, but he had no intention of letting its pet programs interfere with more important matters—like getting a federal budget passed early in his presidency that would set the tone of his administration, and that would include major reductions in taxes and federal spending, at the same time that he proposed significant increases in defense appropriations.

It was reported that Title X and the chastity bill were the main bones of contention. Senators Hatch and Denton balked over preserving Title X as a categorical program. If they couldn't kill it outright, they wanted at least to give states control over how the funds would be used, and thus accomplish what a block grant would.

While the negotiations were taking place, we launched a massive education and lobbying campaign. In the midst of our agitation, Bill Hamilton suggested that we should try to meet with our most vocal congressional opponent, Senator Hatch.

When Bill and I entered Senator Hatch's office, he greeted us cordially, even graciously. As if seeking to establish rapport, he spoke of his wish to help people live better lives, and mentioned his work as a Mormon lay minister: how he had personally counseled people who were sexually promiscuous. Then he got to the point.

"Faye, I don't believe that the federal government should tell the people of Utah what to do. If we want to put restrictions on Title X we should be able to do it."

"But, Senator, Title X does not require the people of your state to accept the services. Its purpose is to simply make them available to low-income women and teens to use as they want."

"These programs just encourage teens to be promiscuous and to ignore their parents' teachings. The government shouldn't come between parents and their children."

We might as well have been living on different planets. It quickly became clear that we'd make no progress toward my hoped-for end.

Back in negotiation in the conference committee, Hatch offered to earmark funds to family planning within the block grant. However, when it became clear that Representatives Henry Waxman and John Dingell were not going to let go of Title X as a categorical program, Hatch finally agreed to keep it where it was, provided that the House agreed to the chastity bill, but not before the White House absolved him of responsibility for the defeat. On July 28, 1981, he received the following letter from Ronald Reagan:

Dear Orrin:

Thank you for your letter . . . regarding the conference on reconciliation between your Labor and Human Resources Committee and the House Energy and Commerce Committee. I regret that we do not have the votes to defeat the family-planning program and assuming this is the best you can do under the circumstances, I reluctantly conclude that the best course is to enter into the proposed conference agreement. Perhaps we can remedy some of the problems in the family-planning program administratively during the three years that it will remain as a categorical grant.

Thank you for your support and for the good job you are doing under difficult circumstances.

With kindest personal regards:
    (signed) Ron[20]

Title X survived as a categorical program authorized for three years. So this battle was won, but at a cost. Year after year for more than a decade, the program had been approved by Congress without opposition. But this was a new era. The lines of distinction between contraception and abortion would quickly dissolve under the hammering of the New Right's agenda. Title X, once hailed for being the one concrete program that reduced the need for abortion by preventing unintended pregnancy, was now being branded as "controversial." Members of Congress who had considered their support for Title X a political asset would soon come to dread the annual maneuvers of preventing the program from being killed while avoiding being labeled, themselves, as "pro-abortion." Eventually they would avoid association with Title X altogether, which would leave it tattered and struggling to survive.

I now felt even more strongly that the ties between our work and the political process were inextricable. If all women couldn't come before the lawmakers, at least we could. And I became more and more determined to keep repeating our message over and over again—no matter the heat I might be forced to take both from the opposition and from within my own organization.

During the following year, 1982, the United States General Accounting Office examined four Planned Parenthoods, and the Office of the Inspector General examined thirty-one for possible misappropriation of public funds. In September the GAO summed up its findings. "There was no evidence that Title X funds had been used to pay for abortions or to advise clients to have abortions," it said. And: "Lobbying by recipients was generally not paid for with Title X program funds and therefore not subject to federal lobbying restrictions."

While the report cleared Planned Parenthood of wrongdoing, it left an opening for future attack: "Some family-planning grant recipients' practices raised questions . . ." it said, and:

The Department of Health and Human Services (HHS) needs to set forth clear guidance on the scope of abortion restrictions in its title X program regulations and guidelines [and] . . . to make its guidance [on political activities] more specific and consistent.[21]

With the phrase "clear guidance," the groundwork was laid for what would become a decade-long regulatory tug-of-war—one that would result in the promulgation, and subsequent testing in court, of regulations that would deprive Planned Parenthood and other family-planning providers of the right to speak freely.

In the midst of the Title X battle, Franklin's and my divorce became final. It had been a long and bitter struggle to end our marriage, and when it was over, I felt a greater sense of failure and sadness than of relief and liberation. That slow, acrimonious, sad process was going on at the same time as I was trying to preserve the rights of women, and as I wrestled with the responsibilities of running Planned Parenthood. While I crisscrossed the country giving speeches, prepared for board meetings, managed a staff of over two hundred, plowed daily through the mountains of correspondence and reports on my desk, and dealt with affiliate concerns, I struggled to maintain emotional strength that was being sapped by the turmoil in my personal life.

And then I was a single mother. When Franklin and I were together, I'd found it hard to spread myself evenly between him and Felicia. After the divorce, she became my emotional center, the focus of my personal life. I have never believed that I could give her too much love, for she always returned it in abundance. Her happy giggles, her hugs, brought me joy at the end of a difficult day. And though Franklin was no longer a presence in her daily care, my attention to her needs—doctors' appointments, school meetings, shopping for that special dress and Hello Kitty knickknacks—was no trial; it was my emotional reward for loving her unconditionally.

During my fourteen years as president of Planned Parenthood, it was a rare night when I was on the road that I didn't talk with Felicia at length by telephone; sometimes we spoke several times a day. My schedule and hotel telephone numbers were typed up and left on her bulletin board. She knew that, unless I was on an airplane, I would take her calls and respond to her concerns. It was understood that when Felicia called, I was to be informed, no matter how important the task at hand.

Yet there were hardships for both of us. There was one experience, shortly after the divorce, when I was still very anxious about not having Franklin with her when I was away. I was in Syracuse to speak at that affiliate's annual benefit, and just before dinner, a man entered the small reception room and quickly came toward me. I saw anxiety in his taut features. "Ms. Wattleton, I'm the hotel manager. You have an urgent phone call."

My heart began to pound madly. Many thoughts passed through my mind in moments: Was there a fire? Is Felicia hurt, or worse? Has the baby-sitter taken off without warning? Is it Mama? If anything happened to Felicia in my absence, I'd feel that I had sacrificed her well-being for a cause—a sacrifice from which I could never recover, just as Margaret Sanger never recovered from the death of her young daughter.

"I think it's from your daughter," the hotel manager continued as I quickly excused myself and rushed toward the door, following after him. One part of me was profoundly relieved. He guided me to the nearest telephone. Even before I had the chance to say hello, I heard Felicia crying out, "I don't want that. I don't want to eat that!"

"Felicia. What's the matter?"

"Mommy," she cried, "Ruth won't give me anything to eat!"

"Why not?" I asked.

"She fixed me a hot dog. I told her that I didn't want it and she won't fix me anything else. I want pasta."

A wave of frustration swept over me. Not only did I have to contend with my own guilt at being away from her, but now, in the middle of an affiliate event as I was about to give a speech, I had to try to resolve my six-year-old daughter's tempest over not having what she thought was an acceptable supper.

I asked Felicia to pass the phone to the housekeeper. "Why is Felicia upset?" I demanded, setting aside my usual respectful demeanor spawned by the fear of losing a reliable baby-sitter. If Felicia had figured out how to get through to me at a cocktail party, she was upset. And if she was upset, I was upset. Whatever the housekeeper said, no explanation would be acceptable, but I had to go through the charade of gently asking.

"I fixed her a hot dog. The girl said she didn't want it," the young woman replied in a clipped Caribbean accent, furious with a crying—and, I was sure, by that time belligerent—Felicia. "I'm not going to be bothered with this little girl."

"Please give Felicia what she wants, and I'll see you when I get home tomorrow morning," I pleaded, trying to hold the anxiety and anger in my voice in check.

I hung up the telephone receiver, rearranged my mood, and went on to give my speech to the hundred or so gathered.

All the while, the rage that I'd heard in the baby-sitter's voice haunted me. Very little sleep came to me that night. As I waited for the half-light of dawn, I worried that the woman might somehow take her anger out on my child. The early flight could not get to La Guardia airport fast enough. The ride to New Rochelle was torture. When I arrived, Felicia had already gone off to school, and the baby-sitter was taking a late-morning nap. Without knocking, I flung open the door to her room, switched on the ceiling light, and demanded that the drowsy—and now, in my mind, lazy—woman leave immediately.

Without a word, she rose from the bed, packed her personal belongings into a small bag, and walked out of our house. I was expected in the office by late morning and I now had no child-care arrangements. Felicia was in school. At that moment, I didn't know what to do, but I didn't care; Felicia was safe. I'd manage. Somehow, things always worked out.

CHAPTER 23

TATTLE TALES: THE SQUEAL RULE

In 1985, I was invited by Planned Parenthood of Middlesex County, in New Jersey, to be its keynote speaker at a springtime social event for donors and supporters, held at an elegant faculty club at Rutgers University. The guests, like many Planned Parenthood supporters, represented the community establishment. Cocktails were served on a terrace overlooking the beautiful green lawns and gardens, lit by the gentle gold glow of the setting sun. Dinner followed in small clustered dining rooms, offering the opportunity for easy conversation.

At my table, I fielded the usual questions: "How long have you been president?" "How did you get involved in Planned Parenthood?" "I saw you on television last week. How do you stay so cool?" "How's your daughter?" "How old is she?" I reminded myself that although the questions were familiar to me, each person was asking for the first time, and usually out of genuine and sympathetic interest. There was pleasure even amid the routine, for such occasions were opportunities for relief from the daily burden of running a complex organization and the stress of increasing external dangers. And on virtually every occasion, some kind person would say, "I really appreciate what you're doing for women."

At about seven-thirty, the dinner came to a close and I was driven the short distance to the Presbyterian Church in New Brunswick, where I was to give a speech that was open to the public. About three hundred people had gathered in the large fellowship hall filled with metal chairs. Knowing that their interests probably lay more in social issues than in gritty realities, I spoke that night about individual responsibility for preserving reproductive rights. During the question-and-answer session that followed the speech, a man rose abruptly to his feet. I had noticed him earlier because, in jeans and a rumpled denim jacket, he'd stood out from the rest of the audience, who were, for the most part, well-dressed.

Waving his hands in the air, he shouted, "I will not rest until I have put a stop to you! You are a scourge!"

I'd heard this sort of railing before, but I was startled by this man's vehemence. He thrust his right hand into his pocket and continued to rant, "I will follow you wherever you go, to the streets of Washington, wherever it takes! I will put an end to you! You have turned my daughter into a prostitute! Because of you, she has turned her back on her family's teachings! She is out of control! Planned Parenthood is responsible and you must be stopped!"

The man then jerked his hand out of his pocket. I could see something in it. I couldn't see what it was, and had no other thought than that I might die. My heart began to pound.

The man then hurled the object toward me. It struck me in the chest as it fell to the floor at my feet with the clattering sound of plastic against a hard surface. A gasp went up from the assembly. Paralyzed by fear, I locked my eyes on my assailant as if my gaze would give me hypnotic protection.

Because the missile had not hurt when it hit me, I knew it was small, and probably harmless. Still, my knees weakened, my stomach churned, and I had to clutch the lectern for support. I couldn't stop looking at the man. Several people moved toward him; I signaled them to let him go on. He continued his harangue for a few more minutes that to me felt like an eternity. "I will follow you to Washington. I will follow you everywhere," he kept repeating.

When he finished, he stormed out of the large hall. I stooped down to pick up the small article lying at my feet. The label on the soft-pastel container identified our Trenton, New Jersey, affiliate as its source, but I was too nervous to make out the name of the person to whom the birth control pills had been dispensed. More than half of the pills were missing. In that man's eyes I was personally responsible for the weakening of his daughter's moral bearing—the symbol for something that had gone wrong in his family. To him, I was more than a symbol.

In my own life I could not, and have not, talked to my mother about sexuality. Doing so in my teens was unthinkable, though I had many questions. I feared Mama's stern religious rebuke. But there are myriad reasons why kids can't and don't approach their parents with their questions, and not the least of those reasons had cascaded forth upon the rage of my verbal assailant. Where are kids to turn if they won't go to their parents and can't seek help in a professional organization? To their own devices? I knew that

I would soon face these days from a parent's perspective. I remembered what it felt like to have questions and need answers. And I also knew what it was to need to protect one's child. Nevertheless, I believed that however protective we wished to be, those concerns should never be put before the needs of our children, whose entire futures were at risk. I believed this ever since my days in Dayton, when I'd argued for unrestricted services to teens and received phone calls from irate parents demanding to know whether their youngsters were coming to us, and what we were telling them and doing for them. I continued to believe it when this man hurled the birth control pill case at me. And I believe it now. Planned Parenthood's commitment to confidentiality, regardless of a woman's age, is both right in principle and right in practice.

Laws and regulations that claim to be designed to assure "parental involvement" in teenagers' sexual decisions have enormous appeal to parents and legislators alike.

When Title X of the Public Health Services Act was passed in 1970, it stated that "parental consent shall not be required" in order for unemancipated minors to receive contraceptives in federally funded clinics. But in 1981, when the program was reauthorized over the objections of Senators Denton, Hatch, and Nickles, Congress—in another effort to assuage the fears of those who charged that the program undermined the authority of parents—added language instructing "that grantees will *encourage participants in Title X programs* to include their families in counseling and involve them in decisions about services. The conferees believe that while *family involvement is not mandated*, it is important that families participate in the activities authorized by this Title as much as possible." (emphasis added) [1]

To carry out Reagan's promise to "remedy the problems of family planning administratively," the Reagan-appointed Secretary of the Department of Health and Human Services (DHHS), Richard Schweiker, proposed several regulations to implement the renewal of Title X. The first—which became known as the "squeal rule"—stated:

> When *prescription drugs* or *prescription devices* (emphasis added) are initially provided by the project to an unemancipated minor, [the project must] notify the minor's parents or guardian that they were provided within 10 working days following their provision. The project must tell the minor prior to the provision of services about this notification requirement.[2]

There were a number of disturbing aspects to this executive order. For one thing, we knew from studies conducted by the Alan Guttmacher Institute (AGI) that most teenagers would avoid going to clinics if they thought their parents might be told of their visits. For another, the squeal rule required that notice be sent only when "prescription drugs or devices" (pills, IUDs, diaphragms) were dispensed. There being no prescription contraceptives for boys, teenage girls were the obvious target of the new rule. If the clinics complied with it they would violate the young woman's privacy; if they didn't comply and the funding was withdrawn, hundreds of thousands of teenagers would be cut off from the means to prevent unwanted pregnancies.

The directive stated that the "notification requirement shall not apply in cases where a project is providing prescription drugs for the treatment of venereal disease," adding that "this is consistent with the overriding public health necessity of ensuring prevention of infection of others." In other words, sexually transmitted infections were a more serious problem than pregnancy. Given that the stated purpose of the rule was to encourage family participation in the services to minors, this exception was transparently hypocritical. After all, if one insists that parental involvement is *always* useful and productive, to exempt treatment for sexually transmitted infections from the requirements is disingenuous, at best.

Just as the Court had conceded, in constructing the judicial bypass system, that not all young women lived in homes with loving, caring parents, the DHHS rule makers allowed clinics to ignore the rule if "it would result in physical harm to the minor by a parent or guardian." But it had to be "illegal" harm. There had to be evidence of "child abuse, sexual abuse, or incest, or . . . other substantial grounds [for believing a minor might be harmed]."[3] Left to one's imagination was how, during the thirty to forty-five minutes spent with a teenager, a clinic worker was supposed to determine where the line between "substantial" or "unsubstantial" harm might be drawn.

Contradictions and hypocrisies aside, the motive for the squeal rule was obvious. It would not blatantly end Title X; but in fashioning an ethical and administrative nightmare, the Reagan administration had invented another means of blocking its availability to a large proportion of those being served.

The rule makers made certain that the rule would be enforced. Up until this time, the income of the person seeking services in a Title X–funded program was used to determine whether she was eligible to receive free services or must pay a nominal fee; her age didn't matter. Under the squeal rule, the income of the whole family would have to be calculated in order to establish her eligibility. Clinics that did not respect this particular aspect of the rule risked a cutoff of funding altogether, or worse, charges that they had misused government funds, which could result in criminal penalties. The only way teenagers could document their families' incomes was to tell their parents why they needed the information and hope that parents would be willing to divulge it.

The consequences of putting the squeal rule into effect were real.

A 1980 AGI study found that 59 percent of adolescents seventeen or younger attending family-planning clinics either were sure or thought their parents knew they were coming to the clinic. The remaining 41 percent said that their parents were not aware of their clinic attendance. Of that 41 percent, 23 percent said they would stop coming to the clinic if their parents had to be informed. However, only 2 percent said they would stop having sex. Basing its calculations on figures gathered two years earlier, the study projected that the squeal rule could result each year in 33,000 additional pregnancies among adolescents aged seventeen or younger. These pregnancies would lead to approximately 14,000 abortions, which, depending on state laws, might involve parental consent (or illegal abortions to avoid asking for consent); 9,000 out-of-wedlock births; 6,000 forced marriages and marital births; and 4,000 miscarriages.[4]

Because the Title X program was being held as proxy for attacks on Planned Parenthood, it became clear that we were being offered a Hobson's choice: If the DHHS rules were allowed to stand, we would either have to comply with them and notify the parents of every teenage girl who received prescription birth control from us—the overwhelming majority of our teenage clients—or we would be forced to provide sexually active teenagers with less effective nonprescription contraceptives—or even to cut off our contraceptive services to teenagers in the Title X–funded clinics. To escape the dilemma, we could have stopped serving teens altogether. If we honored the rules, our reputation as a provider of confidential services would be irrevocably compromised, and our own sense of integrity to our patients of every age would suffer devastating damage.

Worst of all, this could be the next step toward putting Title X out of business. Medicaid restrictions on abortions for poor women had disconnected them from federal support for abortion. Now, the squeal rule would cut off teenagers from confidential contraception. Planned Parenthood had, of course, existed long before Title X and would survive without it, but there was no mistaking the ultimate effect of the restrictions: to drive another wedge into the rights of all women to control their reproductive lives.

As I saw it, we had no choice but to fight the squeal rule. We could not become puppets of government repression, any more than Margaret Sanger had been. It would be two months from the time the regulations were first entered in the *Federal Register* to the time that the Reagan administration would have the legal authority to enforce its scheme. We had two months to mobilize our network of affiliates and supporters to protest the requirements. I realized this meant we had to be prepared for our first legal confrontation with the new and still-popular Reagan administration.

I convened my executive staff and an informal group of outside advisers whom I called my kitchen cabinet. As we gathered in the seventh-floor conference room, we vented our shared anger, frustrations, and fears about what this welter of assaults meant. No one argued for trying to accommodate the rules. Then we settled down to plan a course of action. Bearing in mind the recent distortions of Senators Hatch, Denton, and Nickles, Jeannie Rosoff of AGI cautioned, "We must be careful not to be seen as encouraging kids to have sex. The public won't like that. We need to show that we're serving kids who are already sexually active—that most kids go to Planned Parenthood with their parents' knowledge, but those who don't tell their parents usually have a good reason not to do so."

"We have to come at them from all sides," Herb Chao Gunther, of the Public Media Center, insisted. "A hard-hitting advertising campaign could really help people understand that this isn't just about teens, it's about all women."

We hoped that if we mounted a successful protest, the Department of Health and Human Services would decide to withdraw the regulations or modify them, although it was hard to imagine what could have been done to make them acceptable.

We all agreed that we had to present individual stories to convince the public that real kids would get hurt by this rule.

"We need to call a press conference to announce our plans. The best place to do it is on the enemy's territory," urged Timothea Pierce, our communications V.P. We knew that the squeal rule had already stirred up an editorial firestorm in major news organizations, and we hoped that our announcement would fan the flames and add pressure to DHHS to reconsider.

We held our press conference on April 14, 1982—in Washington—to announce our formal opposition to the squeal rule and our plans to bring a lawsuit if it wasn't withdrawn. The hotel conference room, about one-third the size of a ballroom, was filled to capacity when I stepped up to speak. The bank of microphones nearly covered the lectern's surface. As I began to read my statement, my throat threatened to tighten, but I proceeded.

We are vigorously opposed to these regulations to require parental notification. We find them inadequate and ill-advised at every turn. Under the guise of protecting minors' health, these regulations in reality thrust the government into the very fabric of the American family. While we totally support the concept of encouraging communications between parents and their teens, we categorically reject the notion that such involvement can be mandated by government fiat. . . . In the event [the regulations] are implemented, we will proceed immediately with a litigation strategy on behalf of the teens who will be denied the confidential services they so desperately want and need.[5]

In my written comments to DHHS, which we released that day, and which would later serve as the framework for our lawsuit, I pointed out that the Supreme Court had recognized the constitutional right not to have one's private affairs made public by the government. The lower courts had ruled that the privacy of medical records should be protected, especially when the records touched on sensitive material like pregnancy and contraception. "But the new regulation would," I charged, "require minors to give up established constitutional rights of confidentiality as a condition of receiving benefits to which they would otherwise be entitled." The last point was one of medical ethics: The squeal rule mandated the violation of physician-patient confidentiality.

I countered the government's claim that prescription contraceptives presented a major health hazard for teenagers by pointing out that teen pregnancy represented a much greater health risk.

I went on to discuss the impact the squeal rule would have on families. The forced revelations of a teenager's receiving birth control could cause family turmoil and chaos; even worse would be the revelations of a teenager's pregnancy—a pregnancy that might have been avoided had the teenager been able to receive contraception without notifying her parents.

I ended with: "In the event the department does promulgate this regulation, we will do everything in our power to prevent its implementation in order to shield young people from its hurtful impact."

Spotting a fight, the reporters pounced. The crucial question concerned what we would do if we lost the lawsuit.

"We will continue to do what we have always done, we will serve all our patients on a confidential basis. Whatever happens, we will not violate patient-physician confidentiality," I said without a second thought.

"But this is not about all your patients. This rule only affects minors."

"We will continue to serve them on a confidential basis."

"That could mean that you would lose your federal money. Will you give up your federal money?"

I should have anticipated this last question, but I hadn't. It was as if some part of me had thought we wouldn't actually need to seek settlement in the courts, even as we expressed our willingness to do so. The public outcry against the proposed rules had been so extraordinary: *The Wall Street Journal* reported that letters were pouring in to DHHS at a rate of seven thousand a week, and a review of a thousand of them showed that 80 percent were in opposition to the parental notification rule. Given the protest, it was easy to fall into the trap of assuming that the administration would withdraw the rule.

Even if we had to carry through on our lawsuit, I couldn't imagine that the courts would rule in the government's favor. But I still hadn't accurately calculated the relentless determination that fueled the campaign against us.

My response to the reporter's question was reflexive and unequivocal. After stressing that I didn't believe it would come to such a point, I said, "We will give up Title X funding if we are required to violate our long-standing policy of patient confidentiality."

I would never have misgivings about giving primacy to privacy. But even as I stood there, I wished I'd said, "We *won't* give up our funding—the Reagan administration will have to take it away, because we will not capitulate to a policy we know would hurt kids and their families and society as a whole."

The next day, the Associated Press story that ran in *The New York Times* reported my statement that Planned Parenthood would continue to provide confidential services to minors despite what the government had said about requiring parental notification, and that we could lose up to $30 million in federal funding if we did.

It continued: " 'Planned Parenthood has a long history of providing confidential services,' Miss Wattleton said. 'We will not abridge that policy, government regulations notwithstanding.' "[6]

The wire service story informed the affiliates of what I had said before I was able to report it to them myself. Although many of them expressed appreciation for my having taken such a strong stand, some were more wary, and didn't want me to foreclose their options to "find a way" to comply with the squeal rule without compromising their confidential services. Some said they couldn't justify losing funding that supported services for two-thirds of their caseload (low-income women) by defying a requirement that affected only one-third of it (teenagers). A vocal few were angry and took exception to my avowal. Their federal funds, they said, "[did] not belong to the national office. Therefore we had no right to make such a promise."

As David Andrews and I made the rounds of Planned Parenthood spring regional meetings, I began to see an erosion of the strong support that I had enjoyed from the executive directors. Their "you're one of us" was shifting toward "you're out of touch with us." Some suggested that I had abused my authority by taking such an uncompromising public stand without checking first with affiliate executive directors.

"I thought one of the reasons I was placed in this position was that the organization wanted leadership and visibility," I lamented to David when we had attended the last of the regional conferences. "Yes, and now they're saying, 'Where did *this* come from?'" he said, laughing.

Even in the face of affiliate wrath, I was unrepentant. At the press conference, I had stood up for our long-standing principles and would have expected to be condemned had I suggested we even consider compromising them by complying with the squeal rule. To this day, I find it hard to understand how there could be such disagreement over daring to defend our principles, even when it meant putting our funding at risk.

I appreciated the theories about "the ways organizations work." A consensus on exactly what I should say about the squeal rule would have been ideal; but the media wouldn't have waited around for a plebiscite.

Mainly, I believed that if our principles didn't anchor us, we would be weakened by internal strife and would drift into unending compromise and eventual irrelevance. My hope that we would not face an internal showdown over principle was bolstered by the court of public opinion. Thirty-nine state governments and the District of Columbia joined us in opposing the proposed rules, as did ninety major organizations—including the American Bar Association, the American Medical Association, the American Psychiatric Association, Catholics for a Free Choice, the Children's Defense Fund, the Salvation Army, the United Methodist Church, and the Young Women's Christian Association.

Perhaps it was because DHHS had been thrown into some confusion by such vocal opposition that Secretary Richard Schweiker didn't notify the press of his intention to issue the final regulations of the squeal rule until January 10, 1983—ten months after it could have been imposed. By this time, DHHS had received the reactions of over 120,000 individuals and organizations; by an overwhelming majority, they were opposed to the squeal rule.[7] In a press statement, Schweiker announced:

> This department has a deep responsibility to protect the health and safety of minor adolescents who are given prescription birth control drugs or devices paid for with taxpayer dollars. . . .
>
> As Congress recognized in its 1981 legislation, when Title X–funded clinics provide prescription contraceptives to minors, family involvement is an important protection for our children.
>
> While this rule does not mandate family participation, its great benefit is that it will provide an opportunity for family involvement where parents were previously kept in the dark. This will help remove a barrier between parents and adolescents [the secretary had called it a

"Berlin Wall" in testimony before the House Subcommittee on Health and the Environment], thereby encouraging more communication in many families. The new rule strikes a reasonable balance between the need to make federally funded family-planning services available to adolescents and the rights of parents in matters involving the health of their children.[8]

That very day—joined by the National Family Planning and Reproductive Health Association, a national nonprofit organization that represented about 75 percent of the direct recipients of Title X funds—we filed suit against President Reagan and DHHS. Our lawsuit codified the arguments we'd been voicing since the first press conference in April of the previous year. We asked for a permanent injunction against enforcement of the rule. As is often done in disputes with nationwide impact, actions were brought in a number of federal circuit courts.

On March 2, Judge Thomas A. Flannery of the United States District Court of the District of Columbia ruled on our suit, and permanently enjoined DHHS from enforcing the regulations.

Reading Judge Flannery's decision amid the turbulence of today's antichoice political climate takes me back, as did Judge Dooling's opinion in the Hyde amendment case, to what seems like a bygone era in jurisprudence:

> The regulations directly increase the risk of pregnancy for minors, and present the clinics with the choice of abridging physician-patient confidentiality, or sacrificing needed Title X funds. . . .
>
> Forty state governments, and dozens of health and welfare organizations have submitted statements to the secretary documenting their belief that teenagers will be deterred from attending family-planning clinics by a parental notification requirement. Despite the government's assertion to the contrary, this court is convinced that minors will avoid clinics if the regulations go into effect. The evidence also suggests that many minors will not quickly manifest the self-discipline counseled by the government, and will remain sexually active. It is quite clear that, as a result of these regulations, substantial numbers of adolescents will become pregnant and will either elect abortion, or suffer the consequences of unwanted pregnancies.[9]

The government appealed the ruling. However, on July 8, 1983 (my fortieth birthday), the U.S. Court of Appeals for the District of Columbia upheld the district court ruling in our case, saying that "in enacting the amendment to encourage family participation, Congress most definitely did not intend to mandate family involvement."[10]

The New York case followed a similar route. On March 14, 1983, federal judge Henry F. Werker in the Southern District of New York permanently enjoined the squeal rule from going into effect. He further prohibited the government from ever issuing regulations or guidelines intended to require parental notification. The Reagan administration appealed, but to no avail.

Having struck out at the appellate level, the government decided not to take the cases to the Supreme Court, and on November 30, 1983, the Reagan administration formally withdrew the squeal rule, though later it renewed its defense in a futile attempt to avoid paying our lawyers' fees.

While we knew that the battle was far from over, we had managed to hold the line for teenagers' lives. It also appeared that we had averted an internal confrontation, and had proved that we could still win—as we had before the recent setbacks in *McRae* and *Bellotti*—through the courts.

As the attacks from the White House and in Congress gained momentum, we had no choice but to expand our programs to challenge them. If we couldn't influence elections, we could at least fight the New Right's agenda in the courts with myriad lawsuits.

Believing that our work would rise or fall on these cases, I felt the only way to get through them was to build our own battery of lawyers to mount the legal challenges. Eve Paul agreed, and we decided to build a litigation program. Roger Evans, who had spent many years as a managing director of MFY Legal Services in Manhattan, was hired as the program's director.

Like our grassroots organizing and lobbying, and our advertising and media campaigns, we knew this legal battle was also going to be costly. Stewart Mott, who had led the formation of a political action committee, insisted that the one way to find the resources necessary to fund our expanding battles was through direct mail. He provided a loan to finance the development of a mailing list.

Craver, Matthews & Smith, the direct-mail consulting firm that had been so instrumental in building Common Cause and other progressive groups, developed our direct mail program. I quickly learned that letters to individuals were more than an opportunity to attract financial support; they were also vehicles for directly informing our supporters about the dangers pressing upon women's lives.

The direct-mail program showed promising results from the start. Not only did we get support from our existing donors; we also got high returns on letters sent to people for the first time. The size of their gifts was well above the average experience of other organizations.

But direct mail couldn't solve all our woes, and certainly not immediately. The program was still in the formative stage, and 1982 had been an especially difficult year. Besides the high costs of litigation and our media campaigns, we faced increasing demands from the affiliates for more services and more financial support. Looking out over the next two years, we concluded that our projected income would not be adequate to cover the cost of our services. We'd already cut as much as we thought we could without risking damage to our most critical programs, so it was with particular dread that I sat down at that year's budget meeting to discuss further cutbacks—cutbacks that would place our well-funded attackers at an advantage. I couldn't bring myself to do it, so I told the vice presidents, "Please go back to your divisions and think about how we can generate more revenue rather than cutting back our programs."

The following week, when we reassembled, David Andrews was the one out in front with a detailed plan: "If local grocery stores can market house-brand products, why couldn't Planned Parenthood with contraceptive products?" With his trademark optimism he proposed that the products could be marketed and distributed through the affiliates, producing revenue for them as well. "We could start on a limited basis— maybe with condoms—learn as much as we can about marketing a house brand, then move toward other products . . . foams, jellies, IUDs, even oral contraceptives."

For two years, we negotiated with American Home Products to license the Planned Parenthood name. The board was supportive and had given us the green light, and discussions with executive directors indicated that the majority approved. All seemed to be proceeding according to plan— until, several weeks before the 1984 annual meeting, when Sherri Tepper, the executive director of the Denver affiliate (the same director whose affiliate had produced the infamous cartoons), wrote to the executive directors and board presidents of all of the affiliates to blast the proposed agreement: Affiliates would find themselves flooded with questions about condoms, they wouldn't get the royalties that we promised them, and the good name of Planned Parenthood would forever be associated with condoms.

Enthusiastic support for the project was quickly transformed into alarm, and the project became the *cause célèbre* of that year's convention. No matter how we tried to counter Sherri's charges, the well had been poisoned, and other executive directors from large affiliates joined the opposing front. We'd been given a lesson on the power of a determined few to shift the inclination of the whole organization.

Then, American Home Products called David to say that they would consider finalizing the licensing agreement only if we would expand the product line to include contraceptive foams, jellies, and suppositories.

David phoned me with the news. "What should we do?" he asked anxiously.

It didn't take me more than a few seconds to weigh the sheer force of the opposition to the plan against its probable benefits. "Let's kill the program," I answered.

"What?" he asked in disbelief. And then, a few moments later, he said, "I guess you're right. We can't get our products sold even in our own clinics."

We'd invested so much time and energy. We'd had such high hopes for the project—hopes that transcended its original purpose of easing our financial woes. It could have broadened our name, given us the opportunity to educate greater numbers of people than we could ever possibly see in our clinics—and this was just the beginning of the awareness of the HIV/AIDS epidemic. But if we were receiving so much opposition to the prospect of distributing condoms, we didn't have a prayer with the other products. At the meeting that preceded the membership meeting, I recommended to the board that we not go forward. The members did not question my reasons. In fact, they seemed relieved.

Several years after the project ended, some affiliate directors urged us to renew the condom marketing project. By this time AIDS was taking a tremendous toll, and the affiliates were realizing that we'd lost an opportunity to play a vital role in the prevention of the disease. But the market was now flooded with other companies' products, and even if we could have secured a licensor, we could not possibly have redeveloped the concept without incurring tremendous losses.

After the divorce Felicia and I continued to live in our house in New Rochelle. The piano was gone. Franklin's jazz tape and record collections were gone. And most notably missing was Franklin's baritone voice, whose resonance had filled the rooms of the large house. I felt even more isolated than I had before. Our lovely home was now nothing more than a shelter.

The distance between our home and my office became increasingly harder to bridge. With no one to take me to the train station, I had to wake up and leave the house even earlier, so I could catch a taxi or the bus to the commuter train to the subway train, which took me to my office. If I was lucky, I'd get home by eight. Often, it was later, after Felicia was asleep. When I missed seeing her, I felt defeated and guilty that neither of her parents was with her.

But more significantly, I worried about what I would do if something happened to Felicia. There was an hour and a half between us. When I began to receive death threats, my worries grew a thousandfold. I knew it was time to leave New Rochelle. Although I now had little money to spare, I searched for a new home in Manhattan. There, I felt, Felicia would be safe. Eventually, we found a comfortable apartment in a building on Central Park West. It was far smaller and plainer than the home we were leaving, and it didn't have sweeping views of the park. But there were doormen and other security measures, and it was big enough for a babysitter to stay over so that there would always be someone in the apartment with Felicia. Again, Stewart Mott and Jean Mahoney, the chairperson of the PPFA board, came forward and kindly loaned me the additional money needed to make the down payment.

Felicia, then seven years old, was wary of moving. She had a happy life in New Rochelle—her friends; her large backyard, where they played on the swings and jungle gym; the wide shady streets where she rode her bike; the horseback riding lessons she'd started taking with her friend Inaka. I did my best to reassure her that there would be compensating privileges to living in the city, but she remained unconvinced. Nevertheless, the day the moving vans pulled up to our back door was one of the happiest days of my life. A chapter—the one in which I'd dreamed of building the life that I had not known as a child—had come to an end. A new chapter was about to begin for my daughter and me. I was excited about the possibilities that lay ahead.

I had enrolled Felicia at Brearley, a private girls' school on Manhattan's East Side. It was expensive, but it had been strongly recommended by the psychiatrist who had reviewed our family arrangements during the divorce. Soon, Felicia's misgivings gave way to a happy blur of second-grade academics and play dates with her new schoolmates.

I had always believed that it was equally important to nurture the spiritual aspect of Felicia's life. We attended church together every Sunday morning in New Rochelle. While we had never formally joined one there, I wanted us to join one in New York. Throughout my adulthood I had continued to attend church regularly, mostly within the Church of God, but sometimes not. I'd never become actively involved in church activities, because my childhood reticence about demonstrative religion remained with me. Then again, it may have been a matter of my being a preacher's kid who observed from the bench. I felt more comfortable there. I mentioned my search to Louise Tyrer, Planned Parenthood's vice president for medical affairs, whose parents had been Seventh-Day Adventist missionaries to China when she was born. She suggested that I try Marble Collegiate Church, where she was a member. Dr. Norman Vincent Peale, the author of *The Power of Positive Thinking*, was the senior minister there.

Marble Collegiate Church is the oldest continuing congregation in the United States. When I first entered the church on lower Fifth Avenue, I found its stained-glass windows and the carved and gilded chancel soaring toward the heavens at once imposing and warmly compelling. As Felicia had announced when she took her first step across the threshold of the

Brearley School, "Mommy, I want to go to school here," I now announced to myself, "I want to attend this church."

Dr. Peale was winding down his long career at Marble. His sermons focused on the teachings of the Bible as the framework for daily living; and, of course, there was always the intertwining theme of approaching life with a sense of empowerment. His messages engaged me. After he retired, his assistant, Arthur Caliandro, became the senior minister, and to my delight, I found the personal quality of his ministry even more accessible than the fiery preaching of his mentor, one of this country's greatest orators. I was hooked.

At Marble Collegiate Church I have yet to hear a sermon on hellfire and brimstone—the spiritual symbol of rejection of people for unacceptable behavior or moral turpitude—and the exemplification of the very intolerance I was fighting. However, I have heard many lessons on love, the virtue of encouragement and a positive outlook on life and toward others. These lessons were aligned with the way I was trying to live my life. The biblical basis for Arthur Caliandro's homilies had a familial authenticity that eased my abiding sense of disloyalty because this wasn't a Church of God.

The congregation was diverse in every respect. And the songs they sang, including "Jesus Loves Me This I Know" and "Amazing Grace," often touched a part of my emotions and my past that made it hard for me not to return every Sunday. As there had been in the churches of my childhood, here there were no grand public displays of emotion. The quiet formality reminded me of the years in Columbus, Nebraska. And unlike the churches of my childhood, these services were over in an hour.

I enrolled Felicia in Sunday school. Many were the Sunday mornings that Felicia groaned at having to rise early and dress for church. "It's so b-o-r-i-n-g," she would protest. I sympathized with her impatience and frustration, remembering my own childhood and the times when I'd sat through far longer sessions. But I also held the course, for I was now coming to understand at least part of my mother's commitment as I had never understood it before.

"Even if you don't want to listen," I reasoned with Felicia, "an hour a week of meditation is not too much to give. Just as I wouldn't think of letting you grow up without schooling, I can't let you grow up without being exposed to spiritual teachings."

I'm sure that my pontifications at those moments were of little interest to her. As she groaned and sullenly started to get dressed, I'd try to imagine the tongue-lashing I would have triggered if I'd protested going to church. Worse, I would have believed that I was on my way to hell.

Even though I attended Marble almost every Sunday, more as an example to Felicia than out of my own sense of urgency to do so, it would be twelve years before I would become a member. Breaking the ties that bind us to our spiritual roots is very hard to do.

When I told my mother that I was a member of a church that was not a Church of God, she had one thing to say: "I certainly would have been disappointed if you hadn't gone to church somewhere, with the raising you had."

CHAPTER 24

THE MEXICO CITY POLICY:
FIGHTING ON A NEW FRONTIER

In 1952 Margaret Sanger took her movement beyond the borders of the United States when she played a prominent role in establishing the International Planned Parenthood Federation, which is made up of national family-planning associations, including PPFA. This move coincided with the U.S. government's growing interest in international family planning. During the Eisenhower years, the federal government had begun to urge foreign governments to adopt population policies, and in 1961 this urging was codified in the Foreign Assistance Act. It authorized the Agency for International Development, the foreign aid branch of the U.S. State Department, to disburse funds to governments and organizations in developing countries in order to "increase the opportunities and motivation for family planning, and reduce the rate of population growth."[1] By 1985, the sums of money appropriated to AID by the U.S. Congress had reached a peak of $500 million.

By the late Sixties great attention was being given to the fragility of the earth's ecosystems and to the dangers posed to its diminishing resources by rapidly expanding populations, especially in the developing world. Satisfied with the progress it had made in reproductive rights and services in the United States, the Planned Parenthood leadership was open to the possibilities of extending its international work beyond its membership in IPPF. AID approached Planned Parenthood and suggested that it take over a contraceptive distribution operation to overseas mission hospitals through the Church World Service, but Planned Parenthood wasn't willing to just manage the shipment of contraceptives. It argued for funds for the provision of birth control information, the development of education programs, and the training and monitoring of clinic personnel.

This move by the national organization hadn't enjoyed the sweeping support of the affiliates. We were just then beginning to agitate for remaining focused on our domestic mission—many believed that an international program would dilute our resources. However, there were others who believed that the future of the world depended on controlling population growth. In 1971, when AID acceded to PPFA's conditions, the national board agreed—by a one-vote margin—to take on international work. Family Planning International Assistance was established as a special project of the national organization.

Shortly before my arrival at Planned Parenthood, Dan Weintraub had been named vice president for international programs. Dressed in his trademark safari shirts, khaki pants, and cowboy boots, you knew he was as much at home in the jungles of Costa Rica as he was sitting in his office, orchestrating the complicated business of acquiring and shipping reproductive healthcare supplies to hundreds of organizations in dozens of developing countries. He reveled in analyzing the political intrigues within the AID bureaucracy as well as within the foreign countries where we worked, and in finding ways to use those intrigues to enhance the programs we supported. He relished the middle-of-the-night calls from his regional directors in Asia, Africa, and Latin America. Yet Dan never lost touch with the heart of our complex international operation—giving women and men the means to manage their fertility.

In time, he and I would visit many parts of the developing world together—including Thailand, Bangladesh, the Philippines, India, Kenya, Burkina Faso, Ecuador, Bolivia, Sierra Leone, Liberia, Senegal, Zaire, and Brazil. We would visit an Indonesian outpost operated by Catholic nuns that was thirty kilometers beyond the point at which the Ministry of Health would consent to work. In Africa, we'd grab hard-boiled eggs, sardine sandwiches, and warm Fanta sodas to sustain us as we traveled in Land Rovers over bumpy trails through the bush, and across mountain passes to reach people living in isolated rural villages. We flew to remote villages, our small planes chasing chickens, cows, and goats from clearings so we could land. At the Calcutta airport, waiting for a plane that was twelve hours overdue, we would sleep in shifts, one of us standing watch to assure that the other wasn't bitten by rats. We would sleep in rooms in the mountains of Nepal with no electricity or heat, and we would be received in the royal and presidential palaces and government offices. But by far the most important times for me were those shared together with women in the communal yards of their villages, or in the dark and stuffy shacks of large urban slums—women who spoke to me of their lives in deeply emotional tones.

* * *

In the mid-Eighties, Dan and I went to Nepal to check on a number of our programs there. Dan, like David Andrews, had been a Peace Corps volunteer in Bolivia and an AID population officer in the Dominican Republic. He had studied dentistry but abandoned his training for the more exotic work of international development. We had left our car at the end of a road as the sun set behind the snow-covered mountains high in the Himalayas. Forty-five minutes later we were still climbing into the moonless night, on the way to a remote village, trekking cautiously but briskly, single file up the narrow mountain path. Our surefooted guides lit our way with flashlights. After an eternity of ascending steps, we came upon a wide clearing. Our leaders slowed and the small brightness in their hands faded. As my eyes adjusted to darkness, I made out the silhouette of a structure against the black but star-strewn sky. I gasped for breath in the thin, frosty night air and pulled my jacket tight about me. I heard the sound of voices emanating from the building: "Gah-ah-rah, gah-ah-rah, gah-ah-rah."

" 'Gah-ah-rah' means house in Nepali," our guide told us as we moved toward the low-slung, mud-sided, and tin-roofed building.

"Gah-ah-rah, gah-ah-rah, gah-ah-rah!" the women chanted in unison as we stepped onto the porch and through the door to stand at the back of the one-room school. Four kerosene lanterns lit the faces of thirty or so women and girls sitting on the dirt floor of the small room. The flickering light shone on their earrings and nose rings as they recited, following their teacher's lead.

This project, administered by the Nepal Jaycees, was funded by the Harry and Grace Steele Foundation, whose trustees Dick and Betty Steele had joined us for the trip. These girls and women were learning to read from books that contained health and family-planning information. They came to the school in the darkness after working in the rice and grain fields, fetching water, tending to their animals, and caring for their children, some of whom played quietly there in the lantern light. Tired though they must have been, they had walked barefoot over mountain trails, farther than we had, to attend class.

We were involved in this program for its family-planning aspect. But I felt that its more vital role was in teaching the women to read, for reading was a skill that would give them status in their families and villages. And status allowed them a greater measure of control over their lives. What's more, women's ability to practice family planning successfully is directly related to the level of education they have attained.

Only their teacher had formal schooling. An eighteen-year-old with a high-school education, she was considered highly educated and was paid three hundred Nepali rupees a month—about seven American dollars—to help them complete their six-night-a-week, six-month studies that would give them, at best, primitive reading skills.

"I am here so that I can learn to read the signs in town and in offices," one woman told me after class, in Nepali translated by our guides, as we talked with the students outside the school, in the shadows of the majestic mountains.

We wondered aloud to our hosts why the Nepal Jaycees devoted so much time and energy to help these women in scattered, isolated mountain villages. One of the project's leaders answered, "Am I not the son of a woman?"

The next day, as the sun warmed the snow-chilled air, we trekked the paths again with field-workers to the homes of women who were using family planning. They would determine if the women were experiencing any problems, and provide additional supplies and counsel them on other health matters. As usual, upon arriving in a village—all these villages were little more than a dozen houses and sometimes a store—we attracted a small crowd of curious followers. Dan asked the group what they had heard about America. One boy, who couldn't have been much older than twelve, proudly announced that he knew we had a king.

"What is our king's name?" Dan asked, laughing.

"Ronald Reagan," the boy answered, as though he was aiming to be at the head of the class of the puzzled onlookers.

"Where does King Ronald Reagan live?" Dan asked.

"In a white house." The boy's chest all but exploded with pride.

The authority of the "king" was soon to be felt all around the world.

Between 1961, when the Foreign Assistance Act was passed, and 1974, when the United Nations World Population Conference was held in Bucharest, Romania, the United States had been in the vanguard of family planning worldwide. At the conference, the American delegation called for increased funding to make family-planning programs more accessible to couples all over the world, and to integrate family-planning programs into development efforts. This vision was reflected in part of the plan of action released after the close of the conference:

> All couples and individuals have the basic right to decide freely and responsibly the number and spacing of their children and to have information, education and the means to do so; the responsibility of couples and individuals in the exercise of this right takes into account the needs of their living and future children, and their responsibilities towards the community.[2]

But we knew that federal support for our work abroad wouldn't last forever. The New Right, gaining a foothold in Congress, intended to see to that. In 1973, the same year that *Roe* was handed down and the year before the Bucharest conference, Senator Jesse Helms had succeeded in getting restrictions passed on funding for foreign family-planning programs. The Foreign Assistance Act was amended to state that none of the money could be "used to pay for the performance of abortions as a method of family planning to motivate or coerce any person to practice abortions."

Organized opposition to foreign aid for family-planning programs emerged around 1980, when Paul Marx, a Benedictine monk, founded Human Life International (HLI), the first international organization opposed to family planning. HLI's mission had been "to restore and promote Judeo-Christian values"[3] to the international work of the United States. The organization, based in Washington, D.C., sponsored programs and seminars in the United States that attacked every aspect of reproductive rights and family-planning programs other than those that promoted the so-called natural methods, and was a moving force in efforts to establish similar opposition in other countries.

Father Marx openly admitted that he focused his organization's attacks on family-planning efforts in developing countries because, in most of them, contraception was not widely available and abortion was still illegal. As far as he was concerned, those regions still offered hope of preventing the encroachment of family planning:

[We're] fighting the Planned Parenthood monster, the UN Fund for Population Activities, the U.S. Agency for International Development, the Rockefeller Foundation, and the Pathfinder Fund—all cramming baby-killing, sterilization and contraception down [Third World countries'] throats on a massive scale.[4]

Also in 1981, a year after the Security Council had ruled that the government could not use its funds to promote childbirth, two years after I had made my first trip abroad, and the year Reagan proposed dismantling Title X through block grants, the government made a move that would affect our foreign work directly and profoundly. First, Reagan's Office of Management and Budget proposed the elimination by 1983 of all international population assistance. Reagan turned down that proposal. But from that year on, he repeatedly asked Congress to severely cut appropriations to the Agency for International Development, for population assistance. Despite the president's wishes, for three years, Congress managed to maintain the funding at a steady level.

But a sympathetic Congress was not the sole decider of international family-planning assistance. Military and economic aid fell in part under the jurisdiction of Undersecretary of State for Security Assistance James Buckley, brother of journalist William F. Buckley, a devout Catholic and an outspoken proponent of antiabortion positions whom Reagan had appointed to the post. Almost simultaneously with the Office of Management and Budget's proposal, Buckley called for an assessment of AID's population program and an end to international family-planning assistance. Although AID did not respond to Buckley's demands, his attack had charged the international family-planning assistance with controversy and made even longtime supporters in Congress wary. He continued to harass the program until he left for a different post, in 1982. Two years later, Buckley reclaimed his Security Assistance position and took the lead in forcing a dramatic policy reversal on international family planning supported by the U.S. government.

The first sign of this reversal came in May 1984, while we were wrestling with domestic issues—most particularly with the attacks on Title X, with parental consent laws, and with the growing violence being leveled at our clinics. The draft of a new international population policy was issued not by Buckley, as we would have expected, but by the National Security Council.

We were bewildered by this new development. Some would argue that population growth can affect national security by destabilizing regions important to world peace—but the National Security Council was a most unlikely place for international population policy to originate. Years later the mystery was explained. In a February 24, 1992, cover story for *Time*, Carl Bernstein reported that the policy outlined in the draft was a concession to Pope John Paul II—one of the conditions for gaining his collaboration with the Reagan administration's efforts to reinforce the solidarity labor movement that was the linchpin needed to bring down communism in Poland.[5]

What this shift meant was that the NSC's draft policy could be made an Executive Order. It would not have to pass congressional muster in order to be imposed. That prospect became particularly disturbing when we read the contents of the draft.

The document presumed to speak for all Americans in stating that the United States

> does not consider abortion an acceptable element of family programs and will not contribute to those of which it is part. Nor will it any longer contribute directly or indirectly to famil-planning programs funded by governments or private organizations that advocate abortion as an instrument of population control.[6]

Although abortion was an accepted and constitutionally protected right in the United States, the White House was establishing different terms for the women of Bangladesh, Thailand, Egypt, or any developing countries where our government provided assistance for family-planning programs.

Once again, money would be the leverage for implementing an agenda that had the force of law: No federal funds could be provided to governments or organizations that provided or even advocated abortion, even if that money was kept separate from abortion-related services.

The furor that erupted in Congress and the media and the protests that sprang up all over the world in the wake of the announcement made it clear that this bit of American imperialism was unacceptable to most Americans. The Reagan administration, realizing that it was stirring up a hornet's nest, reconsidered the draft, and excluded the governments (but not the organizations) of countries such as Bangladesh and Nigeria, to which aid was given directly, in its final policy statement. That statement became the basis for the allocation of family-planning funds abroad.

Against this backdrop, the 1984 United Nations International Conference on World Population was held in Mexico City. To our dismay, James Buckley had been appointed chairman of the official U.S. delegation. In that role, he would have the opportunity to shape the evolving U.S. policy statement and to personally announce it to the world body of government representatives. This statement would influence the final positions of the conference.

On the morning of August 8, 1984, the main conference hall was hushed as Mr. Buckley walked to the imposing wooden pulpit. He began by acknowledging that ". . . a broad international consensus has emerged since Bucharest that economic development and population policies are mutually reinforcing . . ." He then drove a stake into the conscious choice and lives of the women of the developing world:

[W]here U.S. funds are contributed to nations which support abortion with other funds, the U.S. contribution will be placed into segregated accounts which cannot be used for abortion: second, the U.S. will no longer contribute to separate nongovernmental organizations which perform or actively promote abortion as a method of family planning in other nations: and third, before the U.S. will contribute funds to the United Nations Fund for Population Activities, it will first require concrete assurances that the UNFPA is not engaged in, and does not provide funding for, abortion or coercive family-planning programs.[7]

As I listened from my seat in the observers' section, I felt embarrassment and shame as an American. I was outraged at the sheer boldness of its political purpose, and hearing this dictate declaimed before a body consisting largely of people from poor countries who had few options to improve the quality of life for their people except through United States government aid, disgusted me.

Where was even a shred of consciousness for the lives of women for whom another birth could mean the difference between living and dying? What about the teenagers pressed into marriage and motherhood by their cultures, or of unwanted, exploited, and abandoned children on the streets in cities like Manila, Rio, and Mexico City? How could the government of a country that prided itself on its human rights policies have the audacity to espouse such regressive ideas? How hypocritical was our government in using its purse strings to impose on other countries restrictions that American women would not stand for?

The only rationale for this stand that had any logical basis was that the fall elections were approaching and the administration, which had not yet delivered on its commitments to the pro-criminalists on the domestic front, was making its best effort toward ideological purity—against women in foreign lands who could not vote in American elections. The stakes for this policy were unmercifully high, for the balance of survival in the lives of the women it affected was so delicate.

Throughout the remaining days of the conference, controversy raged over the pronouncement. The vice president of Kenya, Mr. Mwai Kibaki, reacted to its fundamental premise. Unlike the countries in the industrialized world, Africa and Asia, he said:

> . . . cannot wait for economic growth to put everything right. We cannot wait 150 years. . . . Our governments have to play a role in education, agriculture and other aspects of development. We must take a positive role in population too.[8]

While Mr. Kibaki's sentiments weren't unique, it was not governments (per Reagan's revised draft), but private organizations that would suffer from the restrictions—organizations with whom we worked; organizations like ourselves; organizations like the United Nations Fund for Population Activities, and like the International Planned Parenthood Federation of which PPFA was a member; and some special programs sponsored by U.S. universities.

Our own international program, Family Planning International Assistance, had grown to be the largest United States–based, AID-funded family planning program. In 1978, when I took over as president, our agreement with the State Department had been for $13,099,197; by 1988 it would grow to more than $22,000,000. We had international offices in Nairobi, Dhaka, Bangkok, Lagos, and Miami. Including those in our New York office, there were nearly one hundred staff members scattered around the world. Through Planned Parenthood flowed funds, primarily from AID, to

140 projects around the world, and these groups in turn served approximately 1.3 million women. All of this work was now in danger.

At the Mexico City Conference we issued a statement asserting that it was not the will of the American people for our government to take this position. A Gallup poll commissioned by the Rockefeller Foundation before the conference found that 78 percent of Americans with an opinion on this issue thought that the United States should provide family-planning support in countries where abortion was legal. And almost 40 percent of Americans agreed that United States funds should support both family planning and abortion in countries where abortion was legal.[9]

Of course our statement did nothing to influence the final conference declaration, which read:

> Governments are urged . . . [t]o take appropriate steps to help women avoid abortion, which in no case should be promoted as a method of family planning, and whenever possible, provide for the humane treatment and counseling of women who have had recourse to abortion.[10]

After we returned to the United States, the Population Crisis Committee, a Washington lobbying group, brought the U.S.-based international family-planning organizations together to discuss the implications of the new policy and what we should do. If there is a verbal equivalent to beating our chests, then that's what happened at this meeting. We assumed that we would achieve little success in fighting the proposal on purely constitutional grounds, as we were accustomed to fighting most of our battles—the rights protected by the Constitution do not extend to protect citizens of other countries from censorship by a U.S. president. And *McRae* had confirmed the government's power to control the purse strings to advance a particular dogma. But when we got down to discussing what we *could* do about it, I was dismayed to hear the rage diffuse into ambivalence, in what was becoming a familiar refrain: "How can we give up funds that serve so many for the sake of a point of principle that affects relatively few women?"

"But over five hundred thousand women *die* each year from childbirth-related causes—and another two hundred thousand from abortion—that isn't a few women. This isn't a philosophical point, we're talking about the lives of real women," I blurted out to my colleagues, frustrated with their buckling.

"How can we know what we know about women in developing countries and give in?" I challenged. "If we stick together, AID won't be able to defund us all."

The expressions on their faces ranged from impatience for a proposal that "might hurt our friends in AID" to disdain: "How dare you question my moral commitment." I knew some of them were thinking, "She's too strident," and "She's too aligned with the abortion issue, and has lost perspective."

I left the meeting frustrated and disgusted that my colleagues could not see that this policy was one more step toward disenfranchising all women from their reproductive rights. This time around, the stakes were international.

On the flight to New York, I remembered a trip that Dan and I had made to a small village outside the coastal city of Mombasa, in Kenya. There we joined some family-planning workers on their rounds. Our first stop came after a forty-five-minute ride over clay roads softened by spring rains and rutted by the heavy treads of four-wheel-drive vehicles. Having reached a cluster of mud and thatch houses, we walked on planks laid across the deep puddles, and negotiated our way to a courtyard swept clean as a kitchen floor. My eyes began to sting from the smoke of small fires. The women were gathered at the center, around black pots balanced on rocks over the open flames, cooking and tending their children; laughing and talking as they worked in a way that reminded me of Mama and Aunt Alice as they chatted with their customers while fitting their garments. The men who had not gone to seek work in Mombasa or Nairobi sat under trees nearby, drinking beer and chatting. Bare-bottomed children scampered around us as we perched on cane-bottomed stools alongside our escorts, who were following up on the women to find out if they were having problems with their birth control methods or other health needs.

I asked one thin, weary-looking woman who looked much older than her early thirties what method of birth control she used.

"The Pill," she answered.

"Why did you choose the Pill?"

"I don't want to have as many children as my mother."

Her mother had given birth to twelve children, she told me. How many pregnancies that woman had experienced, her daughter did not know.

Pressing on, I asked, "How many children do you want?"

"Seven or eight."

"Why?" I asked, not out of disapproval but out of sheer surprise. I adjusted my wonderment to the context, and hoped the woman hadn't seen my startled look. She wanted fewer children than her mother; seven was a lot less than twelve. More calmly, I asked, "Why do you want seven or eight, when your mother had many more?"

"It's too difficult to raise children these days. It takes a lot of money to feed them, it's very expensive to educate them, it takes more than we have to clothe them, and I want them to have it better than I did."

These were the very same words I had heard before—from the women I examined in the prenatal clinic back in Dayton and delivered at Harlem Hospital.

At another house, Dan asked, "What do women do here when they get pregnant and don't want to have the baby?"

One of the women in the group stood up and, without a word, walked inside the wooden shuttered house. When she returned, she carried a bottle filled with a bluish liquid. Dan unscrewed the cap and we sniffed the unmistakable smell of Clorox. It was explained that women in the village drank this liquid, hoping it would cause contractions. This was the same basic technique that the teenager back in Harlem had used. And just as this solution had done in Harlem, these substances could poison a woman's system, damage her organs, and kill her. The world over, regardless of race, custom, class, or religion, the story is still the same, and women's lives are put on the line for it.

As we debated how to address the Mexico City Policy, the bureaucrats at the Agency for International Development were dutifully planning its implementation. As I'd suspected, AID was worried that imposing the new regulation on all U.S.–based organizations at the same time would lead to wholesale rebellion. In an effort to avoid it, they announced that each organization would be asked to agree to the policy as its funding came up for renewal.

Despite their avowed belief in reproductive rights, all of the affected organizations that were up for renewal in 1984 and thereafter, with the exception of the International Planned Parenthood Federation, signed the new clause.

The United States government demanded that IPPF discontinue any monetary support to the 10 of its 119-member associations that engaged in abortion-related activities. IPPF was unwilling to bow to this demand, and on December 12, 1984, the United States Agency for International Development officially defunded the international federation. Ironically, its Western Hemisphere Region office signed the policy and continued to receive funding.

We wouldn't come up for renewal until 1988. In anticipation of AID's demand that we comply with the policy, I asked our lawyers to begin to prepare a lawsuit to challenge it. But first, I wanted to gain the consensus of my board. Milllions of dollars were at stake. I knew I had time to do so. I also had time to gather my recollections about the incalculable value of our work abroad.

During my last four years at the Dayton affiliate, groups of midlevel administrators from government and private family-planning organizations in developing countries had spent a week at a time with us, observing our operations and mobile services to poor urban and rural women and teenagers. In discussing with them how they could adapt our approach to fit the realities of their countries, I learned what it meant to have limited supplies, what it meant to come up against tribal and religious customs, what it meant when a woman's value was defined by the number of children she produced. I learned about the traditional methods used to space child-birth—for example, that in parts of Africa sexual intercourse was prohibited after the birth of a child until that child stopped nursing (between the ages of one and two), or until the child could carry a pipe or a small stool to his or her father, which usually happened around the same age.

Inevitably our conversations would reach beyond the subject of family planning to touch upon its larger cultural context—how the lack of educa-tion or marketable skills kept women locked into oppression. These were already familiar themes to me, anchored in my mother's dream that I become a missionary nurse to "Kenya Colony" and in my experiences at Harlem Hospital.

On becoming head of the Planned Parenthood Federation, I understood that if we were going to engage in international work, we must remain vigi-lant in service to our belief that voluntary family planning was a basic human right. We had to remain committed to making that right available to all women, and take particular care not to affiliate ourselves with govern-ments or organizations whose motives strayed from this vision.

I remembered a trip Dan Weintraub and I had made in 1979, when we traveled to a village clinic in a hilly northern province of Thailand. I spoke to a woman who helped me to see anew the tremendous lengths to which women will go, even when gravely ill, to control their fertility. Through a translator, the woman told us that she and her teenage daughter had walked a day and a half so that she could have her fallopian tubes tied at the clinic. When she smiled, she displayed teeth covered with the brown incrus-tation of years of chewing betel nuts. The woman was willing to remove her clothing for the examination and surgery, but not her elaborate headpiece, decorated with her wealth of beads and silver coins. She was the thirty-year-old mother of eleven, terminally ill with cancer.

In the Philippines, we visited an island where a tubal-ligation program was being run by the husband-and-wife team of Melanio and Carolina Gabriel, both of them doctors with the Iglesia ni Christo Church. The women who came to the clinic, some of them still in their early twenties and with several children, had chosen to end their childbearing years for good, rather than risk getting pregnant again in a country where abortion was illegal.

The Gabriels' clinic was set up in a large open space, a concrete-floored building in the center of the village. Except for the surgical lamp, which was moved from one stretcher to the next, the room was illuminated by sun-light. The structure was ventilated by the gentle breezes from the nearby waterways. Three or four women were lined up on parallel stretchers. A portable screen would maintain privacy during the surgery. The medical assistant cleaned the abdomen of one woman, while the surgeon closed with a silk suture the tiny incision through which she'd cut and tied another woman's fallopian tubes. The entire procedure lasted less than fifteen minutes. The women's slender bodies, having virtually no abdominal fat, made locating the soft tubes on either side of the uterus achievable. The setup the doctors had established allowed them to help many women in a short period of time. I was impressed by the quiet and, it seemed, unembarrassed acceptance with which the village women endured a relatively invasive procedure, despite a lack of privacy that an American woman would not have tolerated.

Dan and I also slogged through the garbage dumps of Cairo—massive areas of incineration where people are born, live, and die among rotting rubbish, their entire lives spent collecting the garbage of the city of Cairo, bringing the undifferentiated waste to dumps, sorting out anything of the slightest food value for their pigs, selling the rags and tradables, and burning the rest.

We were visiting a health clinic—an oasis in the midst of the garbage—run by the Coptic Christian Church. I felt a tremendous respect for the community workers who guided us, through the stench and the dense smoke that stung our noses and eyes, to the homes of women who alongside their husbands and children scraped together their living among the pigs that they raised. Unlike in Asia and sub-Saharan Africa in Egypt, the Muslim husbands monitored the conversations between their wives and the family-planning workers. As had the holy men we met who ran a program in Bangladesh, and as did the Pope Shenouda, the leader of the Coptic Orthodox Church, and Grand Mufti, the second-highest Islamic religious leader in Egypt, they supported family planning and claimed that their neighbors felt likewise. We were told that our support was wanted, needed, and appreciated.

Sometimes, as in Bangladesh, our work, which had begun with our commitment to the significant task of helping women to have fewer children, would expand to meet other needs—the provision of education, health services, and economic opportunities. The Bangladeshi family-planning workers lived in the slums they served.

With each trip that I would make over the years, I couldn't stop thinking of all I had seen. If I'd thought that my Dayton experience had informed me, I grew to understand that I'd only begun to conceive of the challenges that women faced in other parts of the world, a world I could never have imagined. I had seen girls as young as fourteen, married and pregnant, chattel of their husbands, with futures that promised more of the same, or worse. I always returned home determined to do everything within my power, everything within Planned Parenthood's power, to see that we continued to help them toward a better life.

The inextricable ties between a woman's reproductive capacity, inequality, poverty, and the struggle for survival were the same in Thailand and Bangladesh as they had been in rural Mississippi, Harlem, or Dayton. We could not help these women in every way, but we could help them to control their childbearing. Without the power to do so, they had no hope of breaking the pattern of their oppression.

In 1981, an Agency for International Development evaluation team had described Family Planning International Assistance as one of the best-managed and most capable operations involved in international family planning. Not only did we channel family-planning aid to organizations that needed it, AID said, but we accompanied our funding to family-planning clinics with a requirement that each program organize an income-producing feature; crafts, chicken and egg production, and organic and fish farming were among the most popular enterprises. These activities helped generate funds to support the organizations toward eventual self-sufficiency. They also elevated the women's self-esteem by helping them develop marketable skills and giving them some economic independence. By making a contribution to her family's welfare, a woman could enjoy the exercise of her own competence in other ways besides childbearing.

The Mexico City Policy—by jeopardizing the $20 million a year we received and distributed—put all of our international programs in jeopardy. I saw no possibility that we could agree to sign an oath that contradicted our principles and that used women of the developing world as political pawns by punishing them for doing something that was perfectly legal, although contested, in our country.

I longed for the day that we could return the full force of our focus to restoring Medicaid funding for poor women and to building public support against the proliferation of the dangerous laws restricting the rights of minors and to addressing the countless other, smaller infringements that were eroding reproductive freedom. Deep down I knew that it was easier to attack than to defend and that we didn't have the resources to defend equally effectively on all fronts that were under fire, even if the organization could muster the will to do so.

I had to admit that as dangerous as all the previous encroachments had been to a woman's fundamental rights, the Mexico City Policy had much broader and more treacherous implications. This time it was about free speech in other lands and the use of U.S. government funds to suppress it. If our opposition succeeded in censoring information about abortion abroad, American women could be next.

As each organization signed the policy, the reality of fighting AID by ourselves began to isolate us. Because Americans don't care so deeply about foreign aid, I knew that it would be hard to rally the grassroots and financial support necessary for the protracted and costly fight ahead. Yet we had no choice. Hundreds of thousands of women in the developing world were dying each year from illegal abortion, an international epidemic. Yes, they needed contraception, but they also needed to be protected from the lethal dangers of unsafe abortions. At the very least, if we took our fight against the policy to the courts, we might delay its imposition until the political landscape shifted and we found ourselves with a Congress more willing to nullify that fiat or even a president who would extinguish it altogether.

My executive staff and I prepared a thorough presentation for the January 1985 board meeting. At the meeting, after briefings and discussions about how we would effect the cutbacks necessary to balance our budget if we lost the funding, and debating all aspects of the policy and the ramifications of our challenging it, the board voted unanimously to reject any AID demand that we implement the Mexico City Policy. And they ratified my plan to bring a lawsuit, most likely to be filed in 1987, when our agreement with AID came up for renewal. It was one of the proudest moments of my presidency.

In the year that followed, Congress sent out a number of mixed signals. None were fatal to our cause, but none were helpful either. Congressmen kept telling us that we'd have to bow to the politics of compromise and that, precisely, was what disturbed me most deeply. Reproductive rights have no place in politics. Nevertheless, the court had allowed a woman's private decisions to be forced back into the legislative arena—including, now, the private decisions of women abroad.

While the Mexico City Policy was subject to its legislative roller-coaster ride, we embarked upon a full-scale media, advertising, and grassroots education campaign. If the American public was reticent about the subject of foreign aid in general, and even more mystified by what it all meant for reproductive health and women's rights, then our job would be just that much harder. We had to make sure the public understood that American aggression against women on the other side of the world was of profound relevance and danger to American women.

Doug Gould insisted that the campaign couldn't just be about the policy. He insisted we give it a human face. "Maybe if we give AID an identity that people can focus on, and not just a faceless bureaucracy, they will be more motivated to resist the policy."

Herb Chao Gunther of the Public Media Center prepared a hard-hitting and personal advertising campaign. We concentrated the ads at bus stops and locations near the State Department in Washington, where they could not be missed by the implementers.

As we revved up the public campaign, Dan and I traveled throughout the country and to Mexico City, where I held a press conference to apologize to the Mexicans for their inadvertent association with the Mexico City Policy and announced our decision to fight the policy; Dan and Doug led American reporters and television personalities on a trip to Bangladesh so they could capture in print and on film how the policy was affecting the lives of the women we were helping; and the affiliates worked hard to persuade their supporters to lobby their members of Congress to reverse the policy. It was the only time in my fourteen-year presidency that the board, the national organization, and the affiliates worked cooperatively without squabbling and without tension on a major public policy issue.

Our agreement with AID was scheduled to expire on December 31, 1987.

On Monday—January 13, 1987—our lawsuit challenging the legality and constitutionality of the Mexico City Policy was submitted to the U.S. District Court for the Southern District of New York. We charged that the policy was inconsistent with several provisions of the Foreign Assistance Act.

Our challenge presented a number of U.S. citizens (plaintiffs) who claimed violations of their First Amendment rights to speak with foreign nongovernmental organizations and individuals if that speech included information about the availability or benefits of safe, legal abortion. We charged that many of the groups with which the plaintiffs planned to work would not be able to associate with them because they would be forbidden to do so by the policy, and that AID would have compelled PPFA and other recipients of AID funds to extract agreements of silence from a large group of people.

We asked the court to find the "limits of the Clause . . . invalid and unenforceable" and asked that AID not be free to impose them. Further, we asked that AID be made to "inform organizations that [had] already agreed to the clause that it is of no force and effect." Finally, we asked the judge to "issue an injunction requiring that AID consider PPFA's application for a new Cooperative Agreement without regard to PPFA's position on reproductive freedom."[11]

We knew our lawsuit would be hard to win, not only because the courts are reluctant to interfere in foreign policy, but also because we weren't so sure that it would or could stretch the Constitution's protection to the individuals we were trying to serve by protecting the rights of the American citizens who were working with them. Fate did not smile on us when the case was assigned to Federal District Court Judge John Walker, cousin of then vice president George Herbert Walker Bush.

On September 30, 1987, when Walker handed down his decision, he agreed with AID's contention that the wisdom and constitutionality of the Mexico City Policy were not subject to court review because the policy had been handed down with presidential authority and was thus a "political" issue, not subject to judicial decision making.

My spirits sank when Eve Paul came into my office to tell me of the judge's decision. By the time Dan and David joined us, a collective gloom had gathered, as gray as the cloudy sky outside my window.

"Maybe you should consult your psychic," Dan joked. It broke the tension and we all laughed, as if at a joke at a wake.

"That's not a bad idea, Faye," David rejoined, in a tongue-in-cheek tone.

We had a brilliant litigation team and we all believed that we were on the side of the angels, but at this point we needed something more to pin our hopes on. So, the same day we lost in district court, we entered the United States Court of Appeals for the Second Circuit in New York to ask for a temporary restraining order requiring AID to continue funding us, and I called Desia, the psychic.

After a quick consultation, I told my colleagues that we would ultimately win.

Judge Walker's opinion was not the final word. As long as the appeals court decision was pending, there was a chance that we could prevail—or at least delay our doomsday. All the same, we would have felt much better had we been fighting the government's appeal rather than the other way around.

Four months after Judge Walker issued his decision, the Second Circuit Court of Appeals in New York unanimously overturned Judge Walker's ruling and sent our case back to the District Court. The appeals court suggested that the policy might violate the free speech rights of Americans working overseas in the hospitals or clinics that would have to choose between receiving U.S. family-planning aid and allowing their staff to talk to women about the availability of abortion.

It would be three years before we heard the final word from the Supreme Court.

While it was important to me to provide Felicia with comfort, security, and as many pleasures as I could afford for her, I also wanted her to understand that ours was a privileged life, and not something that she should take for granted, or feel entitled to. I suppose that like my mother before me, I wanted my daughter to have a sense of responsibility—a sense of a call to service. I couldn't think of a better way to convey these values to her than to bring her with me on some of my travels. She'd be witness to realities far harsher than anything she'd ever see in her relatively cloistered New York life, as well as acts of dignity and grace that she might never encounter in any other way.

So I'd try to arrange my international travel for the summer months, when the demands of my schedule lightened and she was on school holiday. By the time Felicia was ten, she was a regular and enthusiastic traveling companion. She'd sit patiently through endless meetings with government leaders, family-planning workers, and village women. The traveling conditions weren't always easy, and our schedule often saw us rising at four-thirty in the morning to catch a plane—but Felicia didn't complain once.

On our first trip together to Africa, we stopped in Senegal, in Burkina Faso, and then went to Kenya for the U.N. Women's Conference. When there was time, we'd take off on our own. The biggest treats for her were the few days we would take off to see the historic sites of the countries, ride elephants, or shop for unique souvenirs. In Senegal we took the ferry from the capital city of Dakar to the island of Gorée—now a national museum— where legend tells that over a million slaves passed through "the door of no return" into the seafaring ships that would carry them to the Americas and lives of bondage. If judged too weak or obstreperous, they were thrown into the shallow, shark-infested waters of the bay.

Standing with Felicia in the dark, dank passageway looking out toward the deep-sapphire waters, I remembered the times when my aunts had taken me down to the Mississippi River waterfront of St. Louis and shown me the concrete platform from which slaves had been sold.

It may have sounded preachy, but I reminded Felicia that because some of our descendants had suffered the shackles of slavery, and because some of them had sacrificed their lives, we had been born into freedom and privilege, and with these things came responsibility.

"I'm fighting against slavery too," I said softly to my not fully comprehending ten-year-old daughter, as I hugged her.

On another trip, in 1988, when Dan and I worried that the strain of the game being played out in Washington was undermining the morale of our international regional office staffs, we decided to visit all of the three regional offices—in Bangkok, Nairobi, and Miami—to reassure them that no matter what happened, Planned Parenthood would maintain a commitment to our international work.

Felicia was going to fly out alone to meet us in Bangkok. I still remember Mama's exclaiming, "You mean to tell me that you're going to let her fly all that way, all by herself?"

"Mama, what do you think that they'll do? Open the door and let her out of the airplane between New York and Bangkok?"

My mother did not appreciate the retort—after all, it was her granddaughter whom we were talking about. Although Felicia would soon be fourteen, in my mother's eyes she was still "the baby."

"Bangkok's halfway around the world," Mama informed me, unpersuaded.

Mama's objections notwithstanding, Felicia made it to Bangkok just fine.

However, one evening after a dinner that had been hosted for us by the Minister of Health of Thailand, Dan, Felicia, and I were riding back to our hotel in a tut-tut, one of those motorized rickshaws that bounce through that city's congested thoroughfares, when Dan pointed toward Patpong, the red-light district a few blocks from our hotel. It was a street lined on both sides with nightclubs and massage parlors.

"Do you want to take a walk through it?" he asked. "It's not that far out of the way."

I jumped at the offer. Dan asked the driver to stop, and we climbed out of the tiny vehicle onto the dusty paved street illuminated by the fluorescent lights of the dwellings that lined it. We wound our way through the glittering tawdriness made famous as a rest and relaxation stop during the Vietnam War.

As we moved more deeply into the cacophony, I ignored Felicia's tugs on my arm and her gentle pleas to head back to the hotel. I stood in open-mouthed fascination at the flagrant bawdiness of it all. The noise of the streets seemed to grow louder the farther we walked. The barkers stood in doorways, pulling at us and pleading with us to come into their dens. Intrigued by just what a massage parlor looked like, I suggested that we stop and take a look in one of them. Felicia grabbed my arm tight and urged, "No, Mommy, I don't want to go in."

"Felicia," I responded, squeezing her hand clutching the bend of my elbow, "it'll only be a few minutes. We won't stay. We'll just go in and look."

"You'll be safe—you're with us," Dan added.

Stepping just inside the door of one such establishment, Dan, Felicia, and I were stunned by what we saw when our eyes adjusted to the dimness: a one-way window that revealed a fluorescent-lit room of young women, with makeup so heavy that their young faces looked like those of painted dolls. Each of the girls—it was hard to imagine that some of them had even entered their teens, let alone moved out of them—was clothed in a modestly designed traditional Thai silk dress. They sat on risers with bold black numbers on placards across their chests. The cold glow of the lighting washed the life out of their skin.

Felicia continued to tug at my arm, and in an unusual show of emotion began to insist that we leave. Even now I remain amazed that I had failed to recognize the emotional significance that seeing the exploitation of other young women, some of them close to her own age, might have upon my daughter. In the engulfing shock at what I had sought to see, out of nothing more than curiosity, I had ignored her pain. For the rest of the night and the next day, Felicia refused to say a word to me.

In so many ways my lapse of judgment with regard to Felicia was not terribly different from the United States government's attitude toward women in the Third World. These girls were being exploited to serve economic ambition. They were being exploited as part of a game of power and political ambition. And because they had no power and no options, because they did not have the protection of the U.S. Constitution, they were subject to the degradation, by accident of their gender and by the powerlessness inherent in their age and economic status, that the enemies of reproductive rights would restore to the lives of American women.

My daughter had brought their pain home to me in a whole different way.

We couldn't give up. As long as women were oppressed, we couldn't give up. Each time I saw one more woman's suffering, I found myself less willing to countenance the views of others who counseled that "we have to find a compromise."

CHAPTER 25

BEARING THE CROSS
OF VIOLENCE

In the late Sixties, a gasoline-soaked cross was burned in the front yard of my parents' home in Washington Court House, Ohio.

My mother's small church sponsored a weekly radio religious program that aired her sermons. When in one of them she charged that the membership of the Ku Klux Klan was not deficient in doctors, lawyers, and other respected citizens of the community, as she had years earlier in Louisiana, her words angered some residents of that small southern Ohio farming community.

"One evening, I saw a brightness outside our bedroom window," my mother told me. "I wasn't used to seeing a light, so I went to see what it was. There was a cross of wood and rags about six feet tall burning away."

"Were you afraid?" I asked.

"No, I wasn't scared. I called the saints and they told me to stay inside. I said, 'I'm not scared. Y'all come. Let's gather around the cross and pray.'"

A few nearby members of my mother's congregation, taking courage from her courage, joined her in prayer around the burning symbol of racist terrorism.

When the congregation pressed the police to search for perpetrators, two young white men, members of the Klan, were eventually arrested. They confessed to their deeds and were charged, fined for vandalism, and released.

When I'd first entered the nursing profession, I hadn't known that I would someday confront the same sort of violence that my mother had faced in Washington Court House, the same sort of menacing attitude she'd experienced in that sleepy Louisiana town where she'd challenged the local establishment for refusing to worship God together in tolerance beneath the revival tent. But Planned Parenthood—serving as it did as a powerful agent in the defense of women's rights in the courts, Congress and state legislatures, and the media—also served as a lightning rod for those who wanted to restore the old order of women's subservience to their reproduction.

Because it is so much easier, so much more convenient, to attack the individual that personifies an organization's ideas, as head of Planned Parenthood, I became the focal point of a lot of the aggression against the organization. By the mid-Eighties, the sporadic picketing of the Seventies had become more organized and disruptive—a given aspect of my every public appearance. My hosts and supporters would often try to rationalize for me and themselves the unpleasantness of it by saying that their town was after all "the buckle of the Bible Belt." But after years of crisscrossing the country, I could discern no regional distinctions in people's attitudes for or against our cause.

And as the picketing was becoming more organized, disruptive, and routine, it was also becoming more aggressive, more personal. Placards no longer read "Planned Parenthood Kills Babies" or "Abortion Kills." Now they had my image pasted to them and they read, "Faye Kills Babies" and "Abortion Is Black Genocide." A woman at Yale University, seated somewhere in an audience of two thousand, yelled out "Murderer" at intervals throughout my delivery of a speech. I saw the picketers carrying poster-size color photographs of dead fetuses as they lined the road leading to an elegant country club in Waco, Texas, where I had been invited to speak at a Planned Parenthood dinner (and where, time having passed since that first frosty meeting with affiliate representatives, they were planning to start offering abortion services).

I saw hundreds of fundamentalist evangelicals from area churches bused to picket at the hotel where I was to appear in Pasco, Washington. And walking through Times Square in New York, I was singled out of hundreds of pedestrians by a microphone-toting street preacher: "Faye Wattleton, you should be ashamed of yourself, telling women to kill their babies, destroying our race." Her invectives continued until I was out of earshot.

And one evening, from the quiet sanctuary of a backstage dressing room, I listened to the angry chants of pro-choice and pro-criminalist demonstrators gathered outside an empty, darkened lecture hall at Pennsylvania State University before the doors had opened. I remember thinking at that moment about how much my privacy meant to me, and about all the angry voices, raised not just "outside," but in the corridors of power over the simple idea of a woman's privacy and the decisions that she should be trusted to make.

I stood for Planned Parenthood, and Planned Parenthood stood for the reproductive rights of all women. I intuitively understood that when the attacks were directed at me, they were directed at me as a symbol and not at me as a person. They did not know me. I couldn't take the ugly rhetoric and threats of violence against me to heart—neither could I let them silence me.

Nevertheless, I couldn't ignore the dangers, either. Soon after Franklin and I were divorced, I'd begun to receive death threats, and security guards had become necessities at all of my public appearances. Sometimes the threats received through the mail were serious enough to report to the U.S. Treasury's Bureau of Alcohol, Tobacco and Firearms. By the late Eighties, the FBI opened a file and routinely investigated the threats that seemed serious.

Uppermost in my concern was Felicia. She had been born into the circumstances of my work. I couldn't allow her life to be jeopardized. Our move to New York City had been my first effort to secure her safety. Once there, I often had to weigh the risks of her becoming fearful, even paranoid, against the need for prudence. We established a code system so that she wouldn't be lured to accompany someone on the pretext of being taken to me. Her school was alerted about the rare threats that seemed serious. The Brearley School's administration always expressed understanding and support. She was taught to run into the front door of the nearest apartment building, most of which had attendants, if someone accosted her. Felicia accepted the precautions as simply a part of our routine; she felt confident in having a rule to follow.

My experience with the growing threat of violence was hardly mine alone. My colleagues in the pro-choice movement all over the country were facing the same and worse.

In Granite City, Illinois, on August 12, 1982, an antiabortion group calling itself the Army of God (several groups went by that name) kidnapped Hector Zevallos, a doctor who performed abortions, and his wife. The couple was held at gunpoint for eight days. Of the three men who were convicted for the crime, one was found not guilty by reason of insanity. The other two, Don Benny Anderson and Matthew Moore, received prison sentences of thirty years each, to be added consecutively to another sentence of thirty years for their related crimes of firebombing and committing arson on two clinics in Florida.

The disturbances at abortion clinics would seem to accelerate after Congress or the Supreme Court dealt major setbacks to the pro-criminalist campaign. Senator Hatch's antiabortion constitutional amendment and Senator Jesse Helms's antiabortion statute in the Senate went down in defeat on

September 15, 1982. On October 26, arsonists attacked the Cherry Hill Women's Center, in Cherry Hill, New Jersey. On December 14, the Lovejoy Surgery Center, in Portland, Oregon, was bombed.

In 1983, the antiabortion camp suffered a rapid succession of defeats in midsummer. The Supreme Court affirmed and expanded *Roe v. Wade* in *Akron v. Akron Center for Reproductive Health* on June 15; on the same day the Senate again rejected Orrin Hatch's proposed constitutional amendment. Then the Washington, D.C., Court of Appeals declared the squeal rule invalid on July 13. On July 23 the New England Women's Services, in Boston, was bombed. The year ended with an arson attack at the Feminist Women's Health Clinic, in Everett, Washington.

Given the scattered nature of the attacks, we might have assumed them to be random—had we not known that leaders in the opposition had embarked upon a nationwide campaign of training in the tactics of terrorism and disruption. At the center of the more violent faction of the pro-criminalist movement was Joseph Scheidler, a devout Catholic who had taught theology at Mundelein College in Chicago in the mid-Sixties. After the *Roe v. Wade* decision, Scheidler became executive director of the Illinois Right to Life Committee. Asked to resign from the position in 1980 because of his strident tactics, Scheidler moved on to co-found Friends for Life, which aimed to become an umbrella group for antiabortion organizations around the country. Once again, he was forced to resign when the organization found his methods too offensive. He then founded his own group, the Pro-Life Action League.[1]

At an antiabortion conference in May 1984 in Fort Lauderdale, Scheidler challenged "every person who is not a cloistered nun or doing time in a federal penitentiary to come out in the streets at least two hours every month. Don't let a month pass when you haven't been there as a foot soldier. Almighty God wants to use you!"[2] In other speeches, Scheidler drew upon the Holocaust imagery that was now a standard part of the opposition rhetoric, labeling clinics "aboratoriums," and denouncing clinic employees for conducting "genocide."

Jean Emond, president of the antiabortion Debate Foundation, which had sponsored the conference and described itself as a nonprofit corporation "founded on the premise that all life is sacred," went even further. In the tones of the right-wing militias, he proclaimed to the activists in attendance, "We would rejoice . . . if tomorrow morning we picked up our newspapers and read that every butchery mill, every abortion clinic, in the United States were burnt to the bottom."[3]

The violence continued to escalate. On July 4, 1984, a bomb was planted next to the unoccupied offices of the National Abortion Federation, in Washington. Had it exploded, it would have been powerful enough to seriously damage the structure and injure or kill anyone unfortunate enough to have been inside. In September 1984, a Molotov cocktail burst through the window of the Cobb County clinic of the Planned Parenthood Association of the Atlanta Area. The bomb destroyed the waiting room, and caused extensive smoke damage. This incident was particularly unsettling because the Cobb County clinic provided no abortion services—only health and family planning programs. But then, of course, as the New Brunswick, N.J., incident had shown me, abortion was hardly the only aspect of our services that riled the passions and provoked the physical aggressions of those opposed to our work.

On Christmas, 1984, three clinics were bombed within three blocks of each other in Pensacola, Florida. One bomb completely gutted a doctor's office; the other two caused extensive damage at the Ladies Center and the West Florida Women's Clinic.[4] Two men were convicted for the bombings and each was sentenced to ten years in prison and fined $353,073. One of them—James Simmons—said he had been called upon by God to destroy the clinics. Two women were also convicted for conspiracy and sentenced to five years' probation. One of the women called the bombings "a gift to Jesus on his birthday."

A surly turn in the road was being made in the name of protecting "unborn lives." From my upbringing I understood, as naturally as I breathed, the sense of divine mission that our opponents spoke of and the companion single-minded dedication to its purpose. Nevertheless, I believed that perpetrating violence in the name of God was a perversion of that fervor. And if I respected the emotional force of devotion to a mission perceived as godly, I also knew that it would be difficult, through the rule of earthly laws, to quell those dangerous crusades born of the certainty of divine obligation.

Though the attacks would grow deadly by the early Nineties, 1984 would be the benchmark year for the sheer number of incidents of harassment and acts of violence—with 131 reported incidents, 30 of them bombings and arson.

On January 1, 1985, the Hillcrest Women's Surgery Center, in Washington D.C., was attacked with a bomb so powerful that it blew out 250 windows in an apartment building across the street. A man telephoned *The Washington Times* later in the day to claim credit for the bombing on behalf of the "Army of God, East Coast Division." He promised that the bombings would continue.[5] Three men were eventually convicted of seven additional bombings in the Washington area. One was sentenced to six years in prison (after an earlier sentence of ten years for the bombings was overturned on a technicality). Another was sent to jail for ten years, while the third was given a two-year sentence.

Although President Reagan continued to work toward making his campaign promises on reproductive rights a reality, 1985 opened with the president finally condemning the violence:

> During the past few months, there has been a series of bombings at abortion clinics throughout the country. I condemn, in the strongest terms, those individuals who perpetrate these and all such violent, anarchist activities. As president of the United States, I will do all in my power to assure that the guilty are brought to justice. Therefore, I will request the Attorney General to see that all federal agencies with jurisdiction pursue the investigation vigorously.[6]

But with the more mainstream antiabortion groups failing to condemn the violence (and with Scheidler going so far as to stoke the violent atmosphere by saying, "Personally, I don't have to take a tranquilizer to get to sleep every time an abortion clinic blows up"[7]) the president's words had little effect. In February, in Mesquite, Texas, a fire started with gasoline completely destroyed both a clinic and the shopping center complex in which it was located. Over $1.5 million in estimated damages resulted, and two firefighters were injured. The identity of the arsonist or arsonists remains unknown.

As the warlike destruction escalated, my predawn nightmares were riveted not on myself, but on the dangers to the affiliates and others. Perhaps I didn't dwell on my personal safety because I believed that worrying about it served no purpose and I knew that Mama was talking to God about it every day. But every time one of Planned Parenthood's clinics was attacked, David Andrews and others worked directly with the affiliate and the Bureau of Alcohol, Tobacco and Firearms to assist in the investigation, and to inform the media and the public of the continuing warfare being waged upon our clinics. BATF people carefully analyzed the bomb components and tracked their origins, and, collaborating with local law enforcement, managed to identify most of the builders of the bombs. Their percentage of arrests and convictions was high.

Meanwhile, our affiliates began to resemble fortresses as they found themselves forced to make major investments to secure their facilities. They installed sophisticated alarm systems, and doors void of keyhole locks, which could be filled with epoxy so that they could not be opened; they invested in bulletproof windows, and introduced elaborate check-in systems for patients. Doctors at clinics where the violence had been especially pronounced sometimes took to wearing bulletproof vests. But no measure of precaution could ease the stress of serving women under such dangerous conditions. The rate of staff turnover in the clinics was high. I couldn't fail to understand why fewer and fewer doctors were willing to put up with the dangers and aggravations of providing abortion services to women; but I feared that if we retreated in the face of such tactics, the opposition would only be empowered to step up their attacks.

Our best hope for prevailing lay in protecting reproductive healthcare providers, not just through improving defense measures at the affiliates, but by reaching the terrorists before they'd had the chance to wreak their havoc. In 1982, BATF, with the assistance of the FBI, had begun a national monitoring program in an attempt to determine whether the bombings were in any way connected. The Criminal Division of the Justice Department also began to investigate the bombings, and coordinated its inquiry with BATF's. Still, the frequency of the incidents mounted unchecked.

While we all knew of the danger that the lone terrorist could pose in the picket lines, Scheidler's activity—and the violent incidents that were becoming as predictable across the country as Fourth of July firecrackers— were convincing us that the bombings were part of a terrorist conspiracy being carried out by a loosely formed network of pro-criminalist groups. Within the pro-choice coalition, concern about the enormous security risks in clinics led to the urgent sentiment that preemptive action needed to be taken by the federal agency best equipped to do so. After all, President Reagan *had* requested that "all federal agencies with jurisdiction pursue the investigation vigorously."

Because the National Abortion Federation and Planned Parenthood were the only members of the pro-choice coalition that were actual abortion providers, the coalition concluded that our concerns about staff and patient security would carry the most weight with federal law-enforcement authorities. What's more, with 131 incidents of violence and disruption against clinics around the country,[8] we believed our episodes of violence couldn't be easily dismissed as isolated, regional incidents. Barbara Radford, the executive director of the National Abortion Federation, and I requested a meeting with William H. Webster, the former federal judge who was then the director of the Federal Bureau of Investigation.

On a cold, dreary day in January 1985, Barbara and I entered the stern and remote modern glass-and-concrete J. Edgar Hoover Building on Pennsylvania Avenue. Mr. Webster met us at his office door and invited us in with a pleasant smile and a firm handshake. In his dark pinstriped suit and horn-rimmed glasses, he seemed more like a corporate executive than the nation's top lawman. A few minutes later, we were joined by Assistant Director William Baker, who was in charge of congressional and public affairs.

Barbara and I told Mr. Webster and his colleague that we had come as representatives of the pro-choice coalition because of our alarm about the persisting violence against family-planning and abortion clinics across the country. "We don't want our concerns to be interpreted as dissatisfaction with BATF," I said, "but they investigate the violence *after* the fact. We believe there needs to be preemptive surveillance of the more radical elements to *prevent* the attacks."

Barbara went on to describe the conditions under which her clinics were operating. "We're having trouble recruiting and keeping doctors. They're being threatened in the parking lots of the clinics as well as at their private offices and even their homes."

She read a few passages from reports on Scheidler's activities within his Pro-Life Action League as evidence that he and his clan were conspiring with other organizations to commit violence. We pointed out the closely timed bombing of the Hillcrest Women's Surgery Center, in Washington, D.C., as a prime example for the suspicion of conspiracy.

Director Webster and Mr. Baker listened politely. When we were finished, Webster praised the BATF for doing a "superb job" in solving many of the crimes. "We are in close communication with BATF and are making our resources available to them," he assured us. "As far as we can see, there is no need to do anything further at this time."

"But we have verbatim reports on meetings to collaborate on ways to conduct violence against clinics," I said, amazed that anyone could interpret such reports as being anything but evidence of conspiracy. But Webster and Baker were unconvinced that Scheidler's war cries met the "guidelines" set for the Bureau's intervention, or that gatherings to discuss putting clinics out of business through violent tactics fell under "terrorist" or "national conspiracy" definitions, even if at those gatherings criminal measures were discussed. What's more, they didn't believe that the disparate locations of concurrent violence constituted sufficient evidence that a single group was coordinating the violence.

If their conclusions were correct and there was no pattern of disciplined coordination, the dangers were even more foreboding, because it meant that the atmosphere could be charged and could touch off the violent propensity of a lone terrorist not willing to persuade women that abortion was wrong, but determined to enforce his or her will to the fullest extent possible.

The FBI's 1983 and 1984 annual reports had defined terrorism as "the unlawful use of force or violence against persons or property to intimidate or coerce a government, the civilian population or any segment thereof, in furtherance of political or social objectives."[9] And yet Webster and Baker didn't believe we'd provided persuasive evidence of violence that fit their own definition of terrorism. "We will continue working with BATF and making our resources available to them," the director restated with finality.

That these men refused to acknowledge that pro-criminalist groups had conspired to commit violence; that they rebuffed our contention that the assaults we were being subjected to fit the definition of terrorism, frustrated us almost beyond words. They might at least have acknowledged that bombers were probably crossing state lines to commit their crimes and in doing so were subject to federal investigation. They chose, however, to downplay the strength of the evidence. It was becoming clear that loyalty to the reigning political orthodoxy—Reagan's promise on the violence notwithstanding—was taking precedence over common sense.

Now Barbara pressed our point: "These are loosely formed groups. We know that. And it's precisely because of their unorganized structure that they are so dangerous and they need to be put under surveillance. We need to identify those prone to violence if we are going to prevent someone in a clinic from being seriously injured or killed."

The director clarified the Bureau's "guidelines" that prevented them from engaging in any activities that might be construed as First Amendment violations. In an even, father-knows-best tone he said, "The Bureau came under attacks after civil rights groups discovered the FBI had spied on them."

I felt a flash of rage surge through me. It was true that in 1973, the Department of Justice had established some guidelines that had to be met before the Bureau could investigate groups that may have been engaged in violence and subversion. J. Edgar Hoover's excessive surveillance of civil rights groups engaged in lawful efforts to secure constitutional rights for all Americans had made those guidelines necessary. But I was outraged by the notion that the director of the FBI was using the guidelines established to protect civil rights groups to protect civil rights violators. More personally, Webster's excuse was an affront on two levels. Not only was he suggesting that the threats to women didn't warrant such a level of scrutiny; he had constructed an appalling parallel between violent protesters who were bombing clinics and the civil rights groups that had risked so much, through nonviolence, to secure African Americans—my people, me—claim to our constitutional rights.

The cordial atmosphere of the room became strained as Barbara and I struggled to remain respectful representatives of our cause and Webster endeavored to hold on to his patience. Barbara, the consensus-builder in the pro-choice coalition that she was, stiffened in her seat beside me as I responded, "There is a difference between civil rights organizations engaged in nonviolent protests against the injustices of racism, and groups engaged in kidnapping, shootings, arson, letter bombs, and other assaults against women carrying out their constitutional rights."

I could see that nothing we could say would convince them to be swayed from the position they had taken before our arrival.

Signaling that it was time to end the discussion, Webster suggested that if we had future concerns, we should get in touch with his deputy, Mr. Baker. I, determined to have the last word and hoping it might still have some impact, replied, "One of these days, Mr. Webster, someone is going to get killed. We've been lucky thus far, but it's only a matter of time. Maybe then, the FBI will consider the situation serious enough to get directly involved in surveillance of the criminal elements."

Although Mr. Webster had held his ground before us, in a later meeting between the pro-choice coalition and Dan Hartnett and Larry Eiken of the BATF, a representative was sent by the FBI to sit in on the meeting. He told us that since our meeting with the director, a Teletype had been sent to all Special Agents in Charge (SACs), asking them to take priority interest in the investigations of antiabortion activists and to provide whatever assistance was needed to the BATF. This was an obvious attempt to blunt the growing public criticism about the FBI's passivity without becoming explicitly involved and compromising the administration's standing with the pro-criminalist movement.

In March and April 1985, Representative Don Edwards (D-CA) held hearings in the House Judiciary Subcommittee On Civil and Constitutional Rights. Chairman Edwards emphasized that the purpose of the hearings was not to debate the abortion issue, but to "determine whether in specific instances unlawful activities directed against abortion clinics have infringed on constitutional rights of reproductive freedom." He went on to say, "To date, the role of the federal government in prosecuting clinic violence, apart from the bombings, has been limited or nonexistent. The Justice Department has available to it a statute making it a federal crime to interfere with the exercise of a constitutional right." Members of the committee opposed to legal abortion, namely William Dannemeyer (R-CA) and Michael DeWine (R-OH), wanted to use the hearings as a forum to condemn abortion. But Edwards stuck to his objective of investigating the violence.

Victoria Toensing, deputy assistant attorney general of the Department of Justice, which had supervisory authority over BATF, announced,

> Up to the present, the investigation of the many scattered abortion clinic attacks has failed to develop any evidence of a coordinated, organized campaign. Rather it appears that these crimes are independent actions by individuals or closely related groups of persons who share both a common philosophy or antipathy to abortion, plus a lawless love of violence.[10]

Toensing insisted that in order to show that the bombers were committing a federal crime, the accusers had to show that the bombers who crossed state lines *intended* to interfere with a protected right, and if that intent was not proved, potential victims of their bombings or other violent activities didn't merit federal involvement.

Edwards then questioned why investigations weren't taking place, based on the testimony heard at earlier hearings on clinic violence. Toensing replied that no other cases had been brought to the department's attention.

Edwards wasn't impressed with this argument, but Toensing insisted that incidents of violence ought to be handled by local law-enforcement authorities before the federal agencies were called upon. Webster, the former federal judge, backed Toensing when he told the subcommittee that "no right to abortion has been established against private interference," meaning that private individuals could interfere with abortion without violating one another's constitutional rights.

In disbelief, Congressman Edwards pressed Mr. Webster for clarification: "That no 'right to go to an abortion clinic' has what?"

Webster restated his point: "Has been established against private interference."

As in his meeting with Barbara and me, Webster fell back on civil rights movement precedent. But this time, he argued that decisions handed down in civil rights cases that established a federal mandate to protect the constitutional rights of African Americans did not necessarily apply to a woman's access to abortion.

Edwards pointed out that

[A] number of years ago, the local police in southern states didn't protect people who were trying to help others register to vote or petition the government to redress or hold a peaceful demonstration. . . . The federal government had to reach around and find a remedy. It took them a while. It took the bureau a while to involve itself. There is a parallel here, it seems to me, where there is severe harassment and violation of interference with the constitutional right going on. According to the testimony we have, the local police aren't fulfilling their obligations.[11]

Two weeks later, the National Association of Attorneys General unanimously urged the Justice Department to investigate violence against abortion clinics and harassment against clinic patients and staff.

The violence continued. In May 1985, in Sacramento, California, a man drove a World War II assault vehicle into the Pregnancy Consultation Center, ruining half the building. And in Oregon, three letter bombs were intercepted by the U.S. Postal Service before they reached the family-planning and abortion clinics to which they were addressed. Another letter bomb actually made it to the Portland Feminist Women's Health Center, but was intercepted there before it was opened.[12] These are but a small sampling of the 149 incidents of violence and disruption in 1985.

Later in the spring of 1985, Joe Scheidler again gathered antiabortion activists from all over the country to hold a "Pro-Life Activists Convention" in Appleton, Wisconsin, in a building upon which hung a banner reading: "Welcome Pro-Life Activists: Have a Blast!" At this meeting, he announced that he would be publishing a book titled *Closed: 99 Ways to Stop Abortion.* The delegates at the antiabortion convention vowed to inflict "A Year of Pain and Fear" on those providing or receiving abortions.

Scheidler elaborated, "We are going to go back to the doctors' homes, we're going to go to their offices, we are going to go into their clinics, we are going to talk with the young women. If somebody wants to call it harassment, so be it."[13] So it was that the Pro-Life Action Network, PLAN, was formed as a national network of organizations committed to using more violent methods of activism to limit abortion.

CHAPTER 26

THE SILENT SCREAM

"Sticks and stones may break my bones, but words can never hurt me."
In the playgrounds of my childhood, my playmates and I used that old familiar taunt to mock one another, sometimes in jest—and sometimes not. Of course, we all knew it wasn't true. Words did hurt. And they continue to hurt. Words can rally people to champion a cause. And then again, words can incite people to destroy one. Words can break our will, break our resolve to hold firm to our principles.

Early in the battle to preserve reproductive rights, the pro-criminalists harnessed the power of words to establish themselves as supramoralists. They defined themselves as "pro-life." Anyone who did not agree with them was "pro-abortion," a "babykiller," a "murderer," or an "accomplice to murder." They compared the battle for abortion rights with the Holocaust. And when words failed, they used images to shock and horrify—images of preserved fetuses immersed in jars, images of dead fetuses placed in garbage cans or wrapped in receiving blankets. They plastered those images on placards, in books, and in brochures. And the media broadcast them across the nation, often without analyzing and acknowledging the distortions implicit in them.

Leaders of the National Right to Life Committee were particularly adept at perpetuating such hateful rhetoric and such shocking and heartbreaking images. Even so, in the early years of my presidency of Planned Parenthood, I occasionally agreed to debate Jack Willke, who served from time to time as president of that committee.

I remember our last formal debate especially well. It was on a wet April in 1985 at the University of Puget Sound, in Tacoma, Washington.

A security guard escorted my assistant and me from the car to the back entrance of the meeting hall, where another guard led us through the door and into a room behind the auditorium. It reminded me of the small prayer rooms behind the pulpit in the churches of my childhood. The two comfortable sofas and the light of the table lamps offered a cozy contrast to the chilly night.

Willke sat confident in a gray metal folding chair as one of the leaders of the Washington State Right to Life Committee bathed him in idolatry.

"How are you, Faye?" he greeted me, without a smile. His glasses made his eyes seem unnaturally large, and the paleness of his skin and blond hair was a stark contrast to his navy blue suit. A gold pin in the shape of the soles of two tiny feet glistened in his lapel.

"I'm fine, Dr. Willke. How are you?" I responded formally, as one opponent acknowledges another before combat.

Willke nodded, then turned back to his colleague. I opened my briefing book and started to read over the points I needed to make in the few moments given to us at the beginning of the debate. As always, reading steadied my nerves.

Just before the debate was scheduled to begin, Willke pulled out a small tape recorder. "As part of my presentation, I would like to play a short passage from this tape," he announced. A surge of adrenaline sped through me. "Absolutely not!" I shot back.

Perhaps not wanting to appear too antagonistic, the dean overseeing the proceedings asked what was on the tape. (I already knew—Willke had tried the same maneuver when we had appeared together before the Washington Press Club.)

With all the authority of his profession, the doctor answered, "It's the heartbeat of a fourteen-week-old baby girl." (The opposition typically calculated the age of a fetus from the moment the sperm and egg had joined, although there is still no real way to establish that precise moment.)

"Dr. Willke, we can't permit you to play the tape," the dean ruled.

"But it's part of my presentation," Willke insisted.

"I won't remain on the stage if he is allowed to use it," I stated firmly, no more willing to agree to the amplification of a purported fetal heartbeat than Willke would have been to agree to my amplifying the sounds of women screaming in pain from the trauma of an abortion being performed without anesthesia on a dirty kitchen table, or my exhibiting human-size posters of bloodied, dead women.

"What are you afraid of, Faye?" the doctor taunted.

"Nothing. This debate will simply be over if you pull out that tape," I answered flatly.

"Dr. Willke," the dean's nervous voice broke in. "We can't allow you to use audio or visual materials."

Willke put the small black case back into his jacket pocket. I had prevailed in this skirmish, but I was furious. I granted the doctor no mercy when we stepped on stage and began our debate before the audience of students, faculty, and people of the community.

If Willke's aim was to persuade the audience that the fetus was an infant, entitled to the same rights that women were entitled to, mine was to reason that women, and their rights, must not be sacrificed in deference to his viewpoint.

"Who are you, Dr. Willke, to decide for any woman what her choices should be? Since you can never experience her condition, it would seem to me that you must defer to her wisdom. We can be trusted. After all, we are the mothers of children. You are not the arbiter of our morality. If you are so concerned about the fetus, why don't you champion the welfare of children already born?" I asked.

Willke answered, "The fetus is a pre-born child with all of its unique genetic makeup from the moment of conception. At six weeks the heart starts to beat. . . ."

Although his supporters formed a healthy-size part of the gathered crowd, by the time we got to the question-and-answer session that followed the debate, the hostile questions that were directed at Willke and the applause that accompanied my challenges showed me that my position was strongly supported that night, empowering my tongue to keep challenging.

When the encounter was over and the adrenaline rush diminished, I sat for a moment in the room where we had first confronted each other, collecting my thoughts. Once again I wondered what these gladiatorial theatrics—his and mine—had to do with the deeply private decision a woman had to make about a pregnancy she didn't want. I couldn't see how the barbs we'd traded served to advance a serious understanding of all that stood to be lost in the struggle to protect women's reproductive rights.

Certainly, in the heat of debate, my blood had run fast, and a sense of renewed commitment had galvanized my arguments; but I also knew that we were walking a dangerous line—that the intensity of debate rhetoric could fire the emotions of the unstable among our opposition. And as for those who were not quite opposed to choice, but not altogether for it, either, I was quite sure that the extreme words and images of debate would only deepen their moral conflicts about abortion and cause them to turn away.

None of Willke's efforts matched the level of mendacity that the film, evocatively titled *The Silent Scream*, achieved, or its harmful influence when it fell into the hands of the national media at the beginning of 1985. Produced by Dr. Bernard Nathanson and Don Smith, the chairman of a

California-based Crusade for Life (CFL), it purported to show that a twelve-week fetus had the ability to move away from danger and would scream in response to pain. Nathanson, a physician and a former abortion rights activist, was the narrator. He was a founder of the National Abortion Rights Action League (NARAL) and claimed to have performed thousands of abortions.

As the film opened, the swarthy doctor looked directly at the viewer, and in a slow, mournful voice said:

> Now we can discern the chilling silent scream on the face of this child who is now facing imminent extinction.[1]

Studying *The Silent Scream* at Planned Parenthood, what we saw was the fuzzy, barely visible outline of a fetus, magnified on a sonogram screen. The image would have been almost impossible to decipher had it not been for the incendiary narration that accompanied the doctor's pointer as it roved across the screen. Not willing to risk a viewer's failure to associate the image with an infant, Nathanson held up a doll next to the sonogram. The doll and the magnified image of the fetus were similar in size. It seemed to be the filmmakers' intent to imply that, like the doll, the fetus had a fully developed body—arms and legs that could shrink from pain, a mouth that could open to scream.

The facts of the matter were quite different. Were the fetus the age that Nathanson claimed—twelve weeks—it would have been less than two inches long, with small buds where limbs would eventually be and facial features that were the merest suggestion of what they would eventually become.

Nathanson went on to describe the assumed effects of the suction and curettage technique we would see being used to abort this fetus:

> Ultrasound imaging has allowed us to see this, and so for the first time we are going to watch a child being torn apart, dismembered, disarticulated, crushed and destroyed by the unfeeling steel instruments of the abortionist. . . .[2]

The metal probe (presumably the tip attached to the tube of a suction machine) that had been inserted into the uterus was discernible; but apart from that, the diffused images on the sonogram screen could have been almost anything. Nathanson suggested that we were watching a fetus's attempt to save itself:

> [T]he child's movements are violent at this point. It does sense aggression in its sanctuary. It is moving away, one can see it moving to the left side of

the uterus in an attempt, a pathetic attempt, to escape the inexorable instruments which the abortionist is using to extinguish its life.[3]

The film footage had been manipulated to emphasize Nathanson's point. Prior to the introduction of the probe, it runs in slow motion, and when the instrument is inserted, the film accelerates to regular speed. The change in the film speed makes it seem as though there is a dramatic change in fetal activity.

In this segment of the film, it's hard not to wonder how Nathanson reconciled his belief that abortion was murder with the making of the film. If abortion was murder, had he not been an accessory to this murder in order to get the film footage? Or was this, perhaps, the one kind of abortion that Nathanson and his colleagues condoned—one intended to preserve a woman's life?

Having "documented" the effects of abortion on a fetus, Nathanson moved on to discuss abortion as a procedure dangerous to a woman. Women, he suggested, were duped into having abortions by corrupt and sloppy abortion providers:

Women themselves are victims just as the unborn children are. Women have not been told of the true nature of the unborn child, they have not been shown the true facts of what an abortion really is. Women, in increasing numbers, hundreds, thousands, even tens of thousands, have had their wombs perforated, infected, destroyed. Women have been sterilized and castrated, all as a result of an operation of which they have had no true knowledge.[4]

Of course, the irony of those words lay in the fact that he was not describing current medical abortion practices, but rather the dangers women would be forced to face if his campaign was successful.

The images accompanying this part of the narrative consisted of docile-looking women—all of them white—with flowers in their hair, and wearing filmy gowns as they sat like wilting flowers in idyllic garden settings. The contempt for women that it showed was just as palpable as the conventional characterization of jaded or aggressive women having abortions "on demand." But here, women were being portrayed as hapless, forlorn victims of the venal "abortion industry."

We had seen this tactic before. Portrayals of women as creatures unable to make decisions for themselves were appearing more frequently in the rhetoric of the mid-Eighties, primarily through the efforts of Women Exploited by Abortion (WEBA), a group of women who professed that their deep remorse over their abortions stemmed from their not having been given the information they needed to make informed decisions. Some claimed that abortions had been "performed" on them against their will, and sometimes even without their knowledge. No such cases were ever verified. And disturbing as this portrayal of women as victims was, the concomitant notion was even more disturbing—that if women were not capable of making their own decisions, then the government ought to act *in loco parentis* to "protect" all women, just as it was acting to protect minors.

As adults, we all live with our decisions. Some women who have abortions deeply regret their choice and are guilt-ridden about it. But millions more have no regrets. And regrets or no regrets, the government is the agency least suited to interfering with that private decision that may or may not lead to regret. Outlawing the power to make decisions about our bodies, even if we later wish we hadn't made those decisions, is inconsistent with the concept of individual liberty.

At the close of the film, Nathanson hurled a few veiled threats at Planned Parenthood:

I accuse Planned Parenthood and all its co-conspirators in the abortion industry, of a consistent conspiracy of silence of keeping women in the dark with respect to the true nature of abortion. And I challenge all those purveyors of abortion to show this realtime video tape or one similar to it to all women before they consent to abortion.[5]

Of course, there was no conspiracy—the remotest suggestion of it was preposterous. But it was far from the most outrageous statement he had to make. Nathanson went on to state that abortion clinics were

increasingly . . . falling into the hands of the mob, of the crime syndicate here in the United States, and that this money, abortion money, is tainted, not only by the blood of the innocent victims of abortion, but by the dark hand of the crime syndicate in the United States.[6]

Given comments like those, one might think that objective viewers would dismiss the film outright. Such was not to be. When *The Silent Scream* was first released, it was shown in evangelical churches, on local TV stations, and extensively on the newly developed cable network systems of the religious right. However, it was not kept within those confines. On January 3, 1985, Senator Gordon J. Humphrey (R-NH) introduced the film into the *Congressional Record*, saying, "It is a film that I believe millions of Americans will see before long, and I believe it is a film that will change American history."[7] On January 22, 1985, the twelfth anniversary of the *Roe v. Wade* decision, President Reagan called *The Silent Scream* "chilling documentation of the horror of abortion. It's been said that if every member of Congress could see that film, they would move quickly to end the tragedy of abortion, and I pray that they will."[8] The film's producers quickly shipped off a copy to every member of Congress and to every member of the Supreme Court.

When *The Silent Scream* first appeared, we at the national office made no concerted effort to respond to affiliate reports that this "new film making the rounds in the fundamentalist churches" was "creating a real stir." Over the years, the steady barrage of incendiary propaganda had numbed our sensitivity. We failed to grasp the features of this film that would have a wholly different impact on the general viewing public, who could not be expected to be conversant with the medical and technical knowledge that we possessed or could easily obtain.

Sonogram images introduced a whole new visual element to the abortion debate, for they were windows into the womb, a place the public had previously been able to consider only in the abstract. Suddenly, the debate was no longer theoretical. It had a concrete meaning, a concrete site. Despite Nathanson's wild claims, the visual effects of the film so riveted the eye and the imagination that its fame—or notoriety—spread like wildfire.

On January 22, 1985, *The Silent Scream* reached a national audience when it was aired on *Nightline*. The title of the edition was "Abortion Debate: The Search for Middle Ground." In his opening commentary, Ted Koppel wasted no time in showing us what perspective the show would be taking on the abortion issue:

> Compromise. It is not a word that comes readily to mind on the subject of abortion. It is perhaps the hottest, the angriest, the most controversial issue in America today. But precisely because we hear so much from the extremes, tonight we're going to search for some middle ground. . . . Perhaps it is only a cherished illusion, but somehow we try to keep alive the notion that eventually, no matter how bitter a controversy, eventually the democratic system arrives at a workable compromise. It is also in the nature of our system, however, that neither side in a controversy will concede the possibility of compromise until all other options have been exhausted. On this twelfth anniversary of the Supreme Court decision which legalized abortion, there was no sign that either side is willing to make concessions.[9]

Koppel assumed that compromise was needed. But whose compromise, and on what? At the most conservative extreme there is no condition that justifies abortion. Most are willing to place the delimiting pole just short of the death of the woman. Others accept rape and incest as justification for ending an unwanted pregnancy. Essentially, the question ceases to be a debate about the morality of abortion and the right of the fetus to personhood, and becomes an issue of who gets to decide the rules for legal abortion—the woman or the state—and whose values of morality are to be imposed by the force of law. In its Solomonic wisdom, the Supreme Court answered that question when it concluded that the rightful arbiter is the woman whose body shelters and nourishes the fetus, in consultation with her physician. The Court decided that a woman should not be forced to sacrifice her body for potential life against her will, nor should she be prevented from doing so against her will. It found the compromise position. What other "compromise" can there be that does not deny the woman her right to decide what happens inside her own body?

But *Nightline* correspondent Jed Duvall showed coverage of the demonstrations and vigils held by both pro-choice and antiabortion activists to mark the anniversary of *Roe v. Wade*, and then read quotes from a number of leaders, including President Reagan, who had addressed the crowds gathered for the March for Life. Duvall then announced, "Antiabortionists today released for the first time a film that includes . . . scenes they claim will end the debate. They say it shows a twelve-week-old fetus struggling vainly to escape the abortionist's tool."[10]

This introduction certainly did not recognize the film as antiabortion propaganda. Quite the opposite. The fact that serious journalists were giving it such respectful coverage meant that it was worthy of serious consideration by the audience.

The show then cut to a clip from *The Silent Scream*, and Nathanson's saying, "And the body is now being torn systematically from the head. I am now outlining the child's head. The lower extremities have already been lost."[11]

Nightline then gave airtime to a number of legal abortion opponents and advocates, but no one offered a rebuttal to the film and no one countered Koppel's suggestion that the right to choice was one that could be settled by "compromise."

Two nights later, *20/20* followed with an even more provocative program on the subject. Hugh Downs opened the show with, "Tonight, three vital aspects of the most divisive issue of the Eighties—abortion. First, new tactics by pro-life groups. Some are resorting to violence; others are using a graphic film that leaves viewers gasping."

Geraldo Rivera, then a *20/20* correspondent, appeared on screen holding a jar in his hand that he claimed contained a fetus:

There has not been as large or as passionate an outpouring of public emotion since the movement to end the war in Vietnam. Within just the last few years, here in Washington and across the country, tens of thousands of people, many of whom had never been involved in anything more political than a PTA meeting, have gotten involved in the pro-life cause. Encouraged by priests and prelates, by television preachers and by the

President of the United States, a movement once considered way out on the fringe, a movement to change the law and ban virtually all abortions, now commands the support of perhaps half the American people.[12]

Rivera's last statement was shocking in its distortion of the facts.

Then *20/20* showed several minutes from *The Silent Scream,* along with segments from Ronald Reagan's recorded response to the film and voice-overs from Rivera that were the first evidence that journalists were beginning to question the veracity of the film's content.

President Reagan: For the first time through the new technique of real-time ultrasound imaging, we're able to see with our own eyes on film the abortion of a twelve-week-old unborn child.

Silent Scream **Narrator:** The abortionist has now dilated the cervix and is now inserting this suction tip, which you can see moving back and forth across the screen. This suction tip is the lethal instrument which will ultimately tear apart and destroy the child.

Rivera (as a voice-over): Narrated by a reformed abortionist, the film is being shown on some television stations and in churches across the land.

Silent Scream **Narrator:** Once again we see the child's mouth wide open in a silent scream. . . .

Rivera (as a voice-over): Intended to create revulsion and controversy, the film succeeds.

Silent Scream **Narrator:** And the body is being torn systematically from the head.

Rivera (as a voice-over): According to a survey of medical experts, there is absolutely no scientific proof that a fetus at this stage can experience pain. But the needs of true science were not why this film was made.

President Reagan: It's been said that if every member of the Congress could see this film of an early abortion, the Congress would move quickly to end the tragedy of abortion, and I pray they will.[13]

Some weeks earlier, Geraldo Rivera had interviewed me about a recent CBS/*Newsweek* poll for his segment on the program. In our conversation, he claimed the poll showed clear evidence that the pro-criminalists' campaign was gaining momentum, and now enjoyed the support of the majority of the American people.

I replied that, at best, the poll's findings were ambiguous. There was no evidence in tracking polls that there had been a shift in Americans' attitudes on the subject. In fact, the CBS/*Newsweek* poll had found that 83 percent of those interviewed believed that abortion should remain legal, "as it is now," in cases where a woman's life was at risk, and in instances of rape or incest. Furthermore, the polling companies that had tracked public opinion on abortion for years hadn't been able to corroborate his conclusion.

Rivera refused to give in to my point, and I certainly wasn't going to give in to his.

A few days later, the show called and asked if I would agree to being interviewed by Barbara Walters, who was replacing Rivera on the follow-up story. Although it meant taking time from a board meeting, I agreed. I felt certain that Barbara would allow me a fair airing of my conclusion.

Barbara began her interview where Rivera left off:

Barbara: There are many people who feel that the Right-to-Life movement is gaining momentum, and that there has been a change in the [public] viewpoint, especially in the past few years. Do you see this?

Me: We have seen no evidence of change in support of a woman's constitutional right to have an abortion. Certainly the intensity of the opposition to abortion by the Right-to-Life movement has clouded the understanding of the political reality. [But still] the political reality is that there is little support for the passage of a constitutional amendment or legislation restricting a woman's right to choose abortion. . . . In poll after poll, we have seen continuing and, in some cases, strengthening support for the right of women to make these decisions for themselves without government interference.

Barbara: Is it just perhaps that the pro-choice side is not as well organized, or doesn't picket themselves, or isn't as much out in the forefront? Is that it?

Me: I think we have been in the forefront; we are just not of the mind . . . to use the kind of tactics that the anti-abortion movement has used. I think we have sometimes mistaken the clamor of the anti-abortion movement for momentum. . . . Violence and harassment [are] sometimes misjudged as momentum in support of the antiabortion position. . . . [14]

We were taken off guard by the notion that the highly regarded television journalists of *Nightline* and *20/20* could take *The Silent Scream* as evidence of the growing force of the antiabortion movement. Women had needed them to challenge the film's many troubling premises, and they had failed. Lem Tucker of CBS would later admit, "We didn't balance it as we should have. . . . We let Nathanson have a free ride."[15]

We had to scramble to organize an effective counteroffensive to reclaim our losses in the wake of the opposition's public relations triumph. Immediately following the *Nightline* airing, we released a statement condemning the distortions and lies that were now being put forward by our opponents. The American College of Obstetricians and Gynecologists had had the foresight to do so the previous year, when it responded, not to *The Silent Scream*, but to a speech that President Reagan had given to the Annual Convention of the National Religious Broadcasters at the end of January 1984, in which he had declared, "There's another grim truth we should face up to: Medical science doctors confirm that when the lives of the unborn are snuffed out, they often feel pain, pain that is long and agonizing."[16] In its "Statement on Pain of the Fetus," the College said, "We know of no legitimate scientific information that supports the statement that a fetus experiences pain early in pregnancy."[17]

By the time Nathanson's claims in *The Silent Scream* were made public, the medical and scientific communities were ready to refute them. On *CBS Morning News*, just after the *Nightline* and *20/20* airings of *The Silent Scream*, Dr. John Hobbins of the Yale University School of Medicine, one of a panel of medical experts, said that no evidence existed that indicated that the fetus had the capacity to move purposefully, to percieve what Dr. Nathanson said it was percieving, or even to struggle, as Dr. Nathanson claimed it was struggling.[18] With specific reference to the film footage, Dr. Fay Redwine of the Medical College of Virginia stated firmly, "Any of us could show you the same image in a fetus who is not being aborted."[19]

Nevertheless, no matter how we scrambled to rebut the ideas put forward by *The Silent Scream*, no matter who joined us in our repudiation of the film, there was no denying our miscalculation—and no discounting the burdens that would likely weigh upon the affiliates' shoulders because of it. We were again on the defensive. Could a bill in Congress or a state legislature be far behind, restricting abortion on the basis of the "discoveries presented in the film"? The affiliates were furious with us and rightfully demanded immediate action.

I gathered together our team of outside advisers on media and political tactics—some of the best strategic minds in the country—to come up with a plan. Although I've never been privy to a war council, I suspect that our meeting on *The Silent Scream* resembled one. Bill Schneider, the political pollster (and now chief political correspondent for CNN), broke the bad news that we were fearing—that a significant proportion of those who had seen the coverage of *The Silent Scream* had believed its claims, and were more troubled by the idea of abortion than they had been before they saw it. Many of these people were young women, part of the generation who could take for granted the hard-earned right to control their fertility, without thinking about the conditions that had brought them this right. Their pro-choice inclinations were instinctive, not experiential. We had to reach them with the facts to counter the allegations of fetal pain and deliberate movement before the pro-criminalist propaganda took hold.

Herb Chao Gunther urged us to prepare another hard-hitting print advertising campaign—one that challenged the lies, but more crucially, reminded pro-choice Americans why it was so important for women to have the legal right to abortion. Our first two ads, "Nine Reasons Why Abortions Are Legal" and "Five Ways to Prevent Abortion," reframed the entire abortion discussion. The first was designed to reinforce a reader's pro-choice inclinations. The second made clear that, although we were advocates for the preservation of abortion rights, advocacy wasn't our sole focus. Through education, counseling, and contraceptive programs, we were actively involved in preventing the unwanted pregnancies that might end in abortions.

Herb worked with Doug Gould, who was now in charge of the communications division, to develop the advertising campaign. Doug never seemed to break his trot (physically or mentally) as we took our message to an ever-growing audience through reliable media contacts and attention-grabbing ads.

Roger Craver, our direct-mail consultant, delivered the draft of a direct-mail piece to our supporters within a few days of our meeting. With the guidance of a medical panel made up of professors of medicine and obstetrics and gynecology from prominent medical schools and leading hospitals, we created a factsheet and developed a brochure, "The Facts Speak Louder," for the affiliates to use to correct Nathanson's misrepresentations.

The medical panel viewed *The Silent Scream* and provided us with a report that concurred with those of the other medical experts:

> A scream cannot occur without air in the lungs. The fetus at 12 weeks is incapable of essential breathing. . . . Without a cerebral cortex (gray matter covering the surface of the mature brain), pain impulses cannot be received or perceived . . . [and] the mouth of the fetus cannot be identified in the ultrasound image with certainty. The statement that the viewer can see the open mouth of the fetus is a subjective and misleading interpretation by Dr. Nathanson. His conclusion is not supportable.[20]

Later, to emphasize the moral validity of abortion, we produced a short film titled *Personal Decisions,* a study of the lives of four ordinary women who had had abortions and were willing to discuss their reasons for their decisions.

By May, Dr. Nathanson admitted that the film was not entirely accurate. "It's metaphorical license. Everyone knows that," he said. "I don't think that really requires any comment. Of course it's metaphorical license. There is no such thing as a silent scream, is there?"[21]

But even with this imaginative confession, Dr. Nathanson had accomplished a great deal for his cause and inflicted damage to ours. The issue of personhood of the fetus had been so effectively raised by endowing it with infant characteristics (and with pain, a condition that engenders sympathy) that the Senate Subcommittee on the Constitution of the Judiciary Committee held a hearing on fetal pain in May 1985, with Dr. Nathanson as the star witness.

In welcoming Nathanson, Orrin Hatch, chairman of the subcommittee, called him "one of the leading authorities on the subject of abortion and fetal pain." Even Nathanson himself had never claimed such credentials.[22] Once again, Dr. Nathanson took his audience through a detailed narrative exposition of the film, expanding on various aspects in response to the senator's relentless questions.

Dr. Richard Berkowitz, a member of the American Board of Obstetrics and Gynecology whose work focused upon correcting congenital defects in utero, spoke in defense of a woman's right to abortion. He said, "While the images displayed in *The Silent Scream* are open to a variety of fanciful interpretations, they do not constitute visual proof that the fetus was fearfully reacting." He challenged Nathanson's "misuse of a technology" and concluded with, "I implore you . . . not to try to settle this issue with pseudoscientific claims that an early developing fetus is indistinguishable from a newborn baby."[23]

The hearings came to an inconclusive close.

Before long, it was rumored that *Silent Scream II* was in production. It would feature the same treatment as in the first installment, but would focus on second-trimester abortion. We continued our aggressive media and advertising campaign, as we were determined to change the context in which the new film would premiere. And we were successful. By the time *Silent Scream II* was released, its predecessor had been so soundly discredited that *Scream II* found little foothold in the American consciousness.

Still, we couldn't rest easy. By appealing to the persistent emotional ambivalence of Americans—even if it had to be achieved through fraud and deception—legal abortion opponents had found their best hope. The pro-criminalists knew that if the fetus could be humanized and women dehumanized by being either ignored or infantilized, the fetus could then compete with women for the protections of the law.

We were determined not to be caught off guard the next time around.

It's so easy but so dangerous to say, "No one pays attention to the words of the crazies, so just ignore them." While they may not manage to get their entire message accepted, they do score points, especially when their propaganda is cloaked in the respectability of a "doctor" or a "researcher." It becomes even more powerful when boosted by an "objective" media. Then the whole terrain of the debate and our language can shift—as it had shifted from women to fetal pain in *The Silent Scream*. Thankfully, Nathanson's statements had been so extreme that they became easy targets for our defense.

More important, *The Silent Scream* debacle, which started out so strong and ended in failure, showed us that a decade after *Roe v. Wade*, the pro-criminalist rebellion had stalled, fractured over goals, strategies, and semantics. While the "mainstream" organizations tried to use the political advantage of having a patron in the White House and control of the Senate to push through their agenda, things weren't going as they had hoped. Although the president was doing what he could through the power of executive orders, he still wasn't able to deliver a substantial blow to reproductive rights.

By 1986, the Senate was back in the hands of pro-choice Democrats, and Title X was still limping along despite cutbacks in funding. It became clear that a constitutional amendment overturning *Roe* was a remote hope, although the Senate Judiciary Committee was consistently confirming right-wing federal jurists. This forced the pro-criminalist movement to accept incremental gains instead of sweeping revisions. Still, incremental gains were like the rust under the fender that my father used to fret about. "By the time you know it's there," he would say, "it's too late."

Battling *The Silent Scream* didn't mean the luxury of a holiday from other fronts. Roger Craver had continued to remind us of his suggestion that a celebrity who enjoyed the admiration of the American public be asked to sign one of our fund-raising letters. We still confronted a daunting barrier to women's freedom in the proliferating parental notification laws—this was the most complex aspect of reproductive rights, and it had the weakest support. We could use the added prominence that would come from a celebrity's identifying with our uphill battles. There was no better image, insisted Roger and Win Forrest, our vice president for development, than Katharine Hepburn.

Ms. Hepburn's mother, Kate, had been a pioneer with Margaret Sanger in the birth control movement. Her father, a physician, had worked to establish the social health movement (a euphemism for venereal disease treatment). Because Ms. Hepburn had never been publicly associated with a cause, Roger and Win feared that persuading her not only to lend her name, but also to sign a letter, would be difficult. This was asking her to be a lot more than the honorary chair for a charity event, which she notoriously refused to do. She would be an advocate. "If you approach her personally," Win argued, "I'm sure you could convince her to do it."

"You have more confidence in my power of persuasion than I do," I remember moaning, intimidated at the prospect of approaching this woman whom the world and I admired so much.

Roger prepared a draft letter and Win suggested a way of approaching Ms. Hepburn through Mark Rydell, her director in *On Golden Pond* and a supporter of Planned Parenthood. I called Mark to see if he would help us. "I'll be happy to urge Kate to do it," he said. "I'm a big supporter of Planned Parenthood." His enthusiasm strengthened my courage.

A few days later, he phoned me. "Kate will speak with you," he said. I was on my own from there.

Not long after, I nervously opened the iron gate to Ms. Hepburn's East Side Manhattan town house. The door was flung open and there stood Katharine Hepburn, dramatically beautiful in her seventies, her presence filling the doorway. She was dressed in black baggy pants and a loose black shirt, which was brightened with a piece of vivid red cloth tucked casually in its pocket.

I'm sure that my startled expression was a familiar one. "Come in, come in," she said crisply.

I followed in her footsteps as she walked in her clogs up the stairway to a parlor that overlooked a beautiful shaded common.

Sitting nervously on her sofa, I did what every awestruck fan does in the presence of a celebrity. "Ms. Hepburn, I have admired your work for so many years," I stuttered.

"Yes" was her monosyllabic reply as her piercing eyes surveyed my face. Obviously she was not impressed by this flattery. At that moment, Nora, her sparrowlike assistant, entered silently with a tray of hot cranberry tea and finger sandwiches. I'd hardly taken a sip of tea when the movie legend got to the point. Tossing her head back, her aquiline nose angling upward, she asked, "What do you want from me?"

I prayed to God that I didn't drop my cup, as she rocked back and forth in her rocker.

Before I could explain, she began, "You know Mother and Dad worked with Margaret Sanger. Our family took a lot of heat for doing that."

She showed me pictures of her handsome parents and reminisced with warm admiration and pride about their pioneering work. "Mother and Dad were ahead of their time. He was a doctor, but our family was looked down on by our neighbors in Hartford because of their activities." And later she remembered the burdens, early in her life, of helping to care for her younger siblings. "I did the parent bit with my brothers and sisters," she said.

I saw my opening to connect her memories of her parents' pioneering struggle to our present battles in the birth control movement. "I hope you will agree to do something that we recognize you have never done before." She studied my face, unblinking. "We'd like you to sign a fund-raising letter that speaks about your parents' helping to start Planned Parenthood and the continuing importance of our work."

She wanted to know more about Planned Parenthood's current activities. I tried to summarize all that we were battling in a few minutes. "But," I ended, "we can't lose our focus on our primary mission that your parents were so dedicated to. Prevention is key. Our clinics continue to serve women in spite of the opposition."

"Yes, these antiabortion people are awful. Who's going to take care of all these unwanted babies?" Ms. Hepburn then said she would consider signing our letter.

"I would like to leave with you a draft of the letter that we're hoping you will sign. It primarily focuses on teens. You know the United States leads all developed countries in teenage pregnancy. . . . "

"Yes, and we have to do something about it." She hadn't needed to hear the rest of my spiel.

"You can adjust the letter according to your wishes," I emphasized several times, hoping that leaving it to her discretion would make her more willing to sign it. I left as nervously as I'd arrived, but feeling triumphant that I hadn't been turned down flat.

The next day, I received a call from Ms. Hepburn: "Faye Wattleton" (as she would always address me), "I have looked over this letter and it doesn't say exactly what I would like it to say." My heart sank. I figured she was about to reject our request.

"I think it needs to be much stronger," she said, her gravelly voice growing animated. "What I want it to say is that just because all these kids are screwing around doesn't mean that they have to have babies. So Planned Parenthood is stopping them from having babies. That's what I would like it to say."

At first speechless, I laughed and said, "Ms. Hepburn, we will try to change the letter to accommodate what you want to say."

With that the phone went dead.

That exchange began a long association between Planned Parenthood and Katharine Hepburn and a special friendship between the two of us. In time, letters that she approved and signed raised over four million dollars. Without her words, we surely wouldn't have been able fight as effectively to preserve what her parents had worked so hard to found when they put their social standing on the line seventy-five years earlier.

CHAPTER 27

LIFE-ALTERING DECISIONS

When Americans enter the voting booths to elect a president, the president's ability to appoint judges to the federal courts is not likely to play a prominent role in our decisions. Perhaps that's because the courthouse seems so remote, so distant from the turbulence of politics and the mundane concerns of our own daily lives. Or perhaps the processes by which judges get to the federal bench are so byzantine that it's easier for voters to just assume that everything will work out all right and trust that the president we select will handle jurist nominations responsibly.

The truth is, of course, that one of a president's most important powers is appointing judges to the federal judiciary, from which eminence their decisions shape the principles that govern our society. As a child, I had my backside dusted by the dry grasses of a southern roadside because the color of my skin had denied me the use of a toilet at a greasy Louisiana gas station. On railroad trains, I had eaten lunches from shoe boxes because I wasn't allowed to sit at a dining car table. Countless others of my race have endured far greater indignities. I have seen the tragedy of unequal treatment of women. I've seen some of them die because they had been denied access to safe and legal abortions. Federal judges had changed those things—federal judges who had been nominated by presidents and confirmed by senators.

It's hard for me to put into words how dangerous I think it is for voters to disclaim or just plain default on their responsibility for the federal judiciary. When they did this in 1980, a president was elected whose platform pledge was to place "judges at all levels . . . who respect traditional family values and the sanctity of innocent human life."

By the end of his first term, Reagan had made enormous strides toward making this promise a reality. Through retirements, resignations, and the establishment of new seats on the bench, he'd been able to make 360 life-time appointments, including three Supreme Court justices, and nearly half of all full-time appeals court judges. Planned Parenthood had never before become engaged in the confirmation proceedings of federal judges. We sat on the sidelines for most of Reagan's appointments, even though our very mission rested upon the decisions that those appointed would make; even though the tenor of the federal courts was being altered by the elevation of judges who questioned the foundation upon which reproductive rights rested.

We defaulted on our responsibility.

President Reagan's first two appointments to the Supreme Court— Sandra Day O'Connor, replacing Justice Potter Stewart in 1981, and Antonin Scalia, replacing William Rehnquist after Rehnquist became Chief Justice in 1986—passed with very little resistance. Ellie Smeal, at the National Organization for Women, had raised questions about the lack of clarity in O'Connor's judicial record on reproductive rights. But NOW, Planned Parenthood, and others who promoted women's interests were ambivalent about causing a stir, and thus diminishing the historic impact of Justice O'Connor's being the first woman to sit on the nation's highest court. Justice Scalia's nomination attracted even less attention than Justice O'Connor's had. His views seemed *so* extreme that it hardly seemed likely he would become a center of power on the Court. In both cases, we ratio-nalized that the strong liberal wing would counterbalance the inclinations of the recent appointees.

But their arrivals on the bench marked a decided rightward shift in the Court. We suddenly realized that our cause would be imperiled if that leaning went much further. A cottage industry of "Court watchers" sprang up, and their speculations were accompanied by a number of haunting "what ifs."

In 1986, when Reagan nominated William Rehnquist to succeed Chief Justice Warren Burger (who left the Court to head the commission to com-memorate the bicentennial of the Constitution), the atmosphere of con-cerned but distant observation began to change. Many questioned Rehnquist's ability, as Senator Paul Simon (D-IL) said, to present "a symbol of justice for all our people." The civil rights coalition opposed his promotion on the grounds of his past decisions in important civil rights cases. And given his opposition to both the *Griswold* and *Roe* decisions, his views on reproductive rights were completely unacceptable to us at Planned

Parenthood.¹ But our active resistance didn't go beyond a tepid press statement. We didn't intervene in the confirmation process.

However, on July 1, 1987, when President Reagan proposed federal judge Robert Bork to replace retiring Justice Louis Powell, we knew we had to take a stand on the issue. The Court now consisted of Justices Scalia, White, and Rehnquist on the right wing; Justices O'Connor and Stevens in the center; and Justices Blackmun, Brennan, and Marshall on the left flank. Not only did the ideological profile of the Court hang in the balance, but Judge Bork had regularly taken specific aim at the constitutional underpinnings of our principles. Both in his writings and in his public statements, he had been an outspoken opponent to the *Griswold* and *Roe* decisions. Bork's opposition was couched in great disdain for the Court's use of the constitutional right to privacy in its decision in favor of a woman's fundamental right to control her reproductive life. Of *Griswold v. Connecticut,* which allowed for the provision of birth control, he had written:

> The *Griswold* decision has been acclaimed by legal scholars as a major advance in constitutional law, a salutary demonstration of the Court's ability to protect fundamental human values. I regret to have to disagree . . . The Griswold opinion fails every test of neutrality. The derivation of the principle was utterly specious, and so was its definition. In fact, we are left with no idea of what the principle really forbids.²

And as far as *Roe* was concerned, at his confirmation hearings to sit on the U.S. Court of Appeals for the District of Columbia, six years before, Bork had said:

> I am convinced, as I think most legal scholars are, that *Roe v. Wade* is itself an unconstitutional decision, a serious and wholly unjustifiable judicial usurpation of state legislative authority.³

If Judge Bork were to be confirmed, the liberal edge would become razor thin, with only the aging Blackmun, Brennan, and Marshall certain to represent the philosophy of the Court that had handed down the *Roe* decision. If Bork stayed on the Court long enough to out-sit the liberal wing, he, along with Scalia, White, and Rehnquist, could tip the scales hard to the right. And if recent cases brought before the Court were any indication of a trend, there was every possibility that he would be involved in the reconsideration of landmark decisions—perhaps even the reconsideration of *Roe.* Our course of action was clear. We had no choice but to actively oppose his confirmation.

Judge Bork was Reagan's most striking move to fulfill his campaign promise, and would suffer the full force of those opposed to it. We soon found ourselves part of a massive anti-Bork movement. The Court-watchers on our side of the battle had thoroughly researched the backgrounds, speeches, and writings of all likely Supreme Court nominees. Bork had been at the top of most of their lists. Given his prominence during the Watergate crisis and his reputation as a "brilliant jurist" within his ideologically right-wing positions, he would have been exactly the nominee that Reagan was looking for. Therefore, by the time Judge Bork's name was sent to the Senate Judiciary Committee, his work had been thoroughly scrutinized. All negative research about him became ammunition at that moment when the name of this U.S. Court of Appeals judge was sent to the Senate Judiciary Committee to be promoted to the Supreme Court.

In an effort to escape this well-informed opposing campaign, the Senate Judiciary Committee punted with the confirmation hearings: While we could submit written statements, only private individuals could testify for and against the nominee—no organizational representatives would be allowed time to express their views on the hearing floor.

We were at once offended and distraught by this manipulation of a process that would offer the public its only chance to hear open debate over a judge's philosophical worthiness to preside over the rules that underlie our society before he was elevated to the bench upon which he could sit for life. This is when we decided that if we couldn't speak directly to the Senate, we would speak directly to the American people to alert them to the dangers and persuade them to oppose Bork's confirmation. Once again, my kitchen cabinet convened to plot our strategy.

The hearings were scheduled to begin on September 15. We had only two and a half months in which to take our campaign to the public. We began immediately by publishing and broadcasting newspaper and radio advertisements to enlist the public's attention and support. One of our headlines read: "Robert Bork's Position on Reproductive Rights — You Don't Have Any."

The media instantly responded to the campaign. We were being called by the television networks, CNN, radio stations, and print outlets all over the world. It had become standard practice for me to go to work dressed camera-ready, since I never knew when a television crew might show up for an interview, so this latest onslaught of media interest was not difficult to accommodate. The affiliates joined vigorously in the campaign, and their efforts resulted in thousands of messages to the Senate. Our allies' efforts were meeting with similar response. Altogether, we represented a diverse and formidable front. The coalition against Bork was the strongest and most united effort I saw during my years as president of Planned Parenthood.

* * *

If we weren't going to be allowed to express our views in the Senate hearing, we made our feelings especially clear in the statement we delivered to the Senate Judiciary Committee. We wrote that this was the first time we had taken a position on the appointment of a Supreme Court justice, but that the dangers represented by Bork's nomination warranted a vigorous response.

> Based on what we know about Judge Bork's judicial outlook and temperament, his philosophical rigidity, his preoccupation with judicial theory even at the expense of human justice, his trivialization of the fundamental right to privacy, and his obeisance to legislative enactments, we believe millions of "real people" stand to lose a great deal if Judge Bork's nomination to the Supreme Court is not stopped. . . . His detachment from the human consequences of his doctrinaire views may make him a curiosity in the classroom, but could create a monster in the highest court . . . The judge doesn't recognize the role of the court which most Americans consider to be its central purpose: that of correcting the transgressions of the legislative branch as they intrude upon the liberties and freedoms of the individual.

Our recommendation was strong, simple, and unequivocal:

> Judge Bork's judicial radicalism and ideology are out of the mainstream. They pose a threat to the stability and continuity that the American people reasonably expect from the Supreme Court of the United States. Judge Bork should not be confirmed.[4]

But nothing we could have said or written for the hearing could compare with the effect that Bork himself had on the public during the televised hearings. His opening statement served as an alarm. He informed the committee that his views were

> neither liberal nor conservative . . . simply a philosophy of judging which gives the Constitution a full and fair interpretation but, where the Constitution is silent, leaves the policy struggles to the Congress, the president, the legislatures and executives of the fifty states, and to the American people.[5]

In other words, he believed that when the Constitution did not *specifically* permit or prohibit a form of action, the legislative and executive branches could make decisions as they chose. In Robert Bork's world, then, the courts were to uphold only those freedoms that were clearly enunciated in the Constitution; the rest was to be left to the states. If he'd been on the bench when *Griswold* had been decided, he would not have found a state law banning contraception as unconstitutional, since the Constitution did not mention contraception. If he'd been on the bench when *Roe* was considered, his statements made it clear that he would not have found abortion constitutional, because the Constitution did not specify the right of privacy as giving rise to reproductive rights. Neither did it specify women's rights. After all, when the Constititution was first written, slavery was legal and women did not have the right to vote.

Later, Senator Orrin Hatch, who supported Bork's nomination, asked him specifically, "I presume your concerns about the reasoning of the *Roe v. Wade* case do not necessarily mean that you would automatically reverse that case as a Justice of the Supreme Court?"

Judge Bork avoided answering the question directly; he responded that he would demand confirmation of the constitutional foundations of the particular rights to privacy upon which the case was based. Given Judge Bork's earlier condemnation of *Griswold* and *Roe,* there was little doubt that he would find them "erroneous" and "not compatible with original intent" of the framers of the Constitution.

After days of televised testimony and relentless probing by the Democratic members of the Committee, Bork seemed to have to work harder to argue his views, and his arguments began to appear less and less coherent. Each argument raised new questions about his previous positions, and his new verbal contortions raised suspicions that they were being made solely for the confirmation hearings. The more Americans saw and heard of him, the less they liked him. And by the time his record on the subject of privacy—a word that, in these hearings, served as a proxy for abortion rights—was laid out for public scrutiny and interpreted by those of us who were talking directly to the people, most Americans were opposed to him.

On October 23, 1987, fifty-eight senators enacted the mandate of their constituents and rejected Bork's nomination. It was the largest vote—ever—against a Supreme Court nominee. Of course, Bork didn't see his rejection as reflecting the will of the American people. After his defeat, he attacked Planned Parenthood and People for the American Way as being primarily responsible for his defeat.

Whether or not our campaign was the determining factor in Bork's rejection, after the fact, there was a great controversy within Planned Parenthood over whether we should have gotten so visibly involved. Although no one argued with the position we'd taken, some thought we shouldn't have screamed it from the pages of *The New York Times* and *The Washington Post.* We had played a more high-profile role in the defense of women's rights than we had in any other federal judicial confirmation, and many within the organization would have preferred that we remain discreetly within the ranks of the loyal backup.

At our fall gathering, where complaints were aired and debated, some affiliates denounced our involvement. One former chairman of the executive committee approached me and, after praising our success, added, "I hope that you're not planning to oppose any more Supreme Court nominees. You've opposed once, and that's enough."

Since the president can put up as many candidates as he wishes, I found that unacceptable. Freedom is not about how many times you defend it, but how faithful you are to its defense. Standing by while *any* unacceptable candidate ascended to the Court didn't make sense to me. There were those who saw my purpose as "just being a crusader." When all is said and done, maybe that is what I am, but I have never viewed myself as such. As far as I was concerned, I was merely living up to the principles on which I was reared: "Stand up for what you believe in," Mama had always preached. As I came to know more about the roots of the movement I led, I began to understand that I was also fighting to fulfill the high-minded ideals of Margaret Sanger. I was doing so not because anyone gave me permission, not because it was politically correct, but because my choices had been restricted and I had touched and absorbed the pain of those who did not have a choice at all. I always felt in my soul, "But for the Grace of God, so go I."

However much I believed in the relentless defense of fundamental rights, I knew we couldn't trust the Senate Judiciary Committee to feel the same way. Unfortunately, in subsequent confirmation proceedings, this uncertainty proved founded when the Democratic-controlled committee began to shrink from bruising battles with Republicans on the committee, who were determined to exact retribution for the crushing defeat of their judicial standard-bearer. A "don't ask, don't tell" approach to the president's nominees began to emerge. The president began to nominate judges whose philosophies were harder to pin down in writing or speech trails. Without that evidence, it was nearly impossible for us to consolidate sufficient opposition to prevent their confirmation.

By the time Anthony Kennedy, a U.S. circuit judge from California, was proposed, there was little energy available to challenge his confirmation. The National Abortion Rights Action League vocally challenged his nomination, and cautioned the Senate Judiciary Committee: "Perception of Kennedy as a moderate, compromise candidate must not be allowed to overshadow his actual record . . . The White House packaged Robert Bork as a moderate; a full 70 days of careful review proved that label wrong."[6]

The precariousness of the Court was the harvest that we would continue to reap for our years of caution and restraint in defense of women's lives.

CHAPTER 28

FREEDOM OF SPEECH
ON THE LINE

Looking back on one issue at a time, it would be easy to isolate each battle that we were fighting—in the courts and in Congress—as if each were a discrete entity unto itself. The truth is, all of the battles were connected, intertwined even, both as I experienced them in the course of a day and as they related to one another over the years.

By the mid-Eighties, we were drawing on all our resources to preserve choice. Even the staunchest defenders of women's rights were growing weary. Calls for "compromise" became more frequent. Those of us wary of such notions as "searching for common ground" were looked upon as "strident" instigators instead of defenders of freedom.

By 1987, the forces that had been building against reproductive rights in battle after battle reached critical mass when President Reagan introduced the "gag rule." From the beginning, Title X funds could not be used for abortion services. Now, with the gag rule regulations, the Reagan administration was decreeing that all *mention* of abortion cease in Title X–funded clinics, presenting us with the most dangerous challenge to carrying out our clinical services since Title X was enacted in 1981.

The broad purpose of the gag rule was the same as the Mexico City Policy—to censor speech about abortion. However, unlike the more aggressive Mexico City Policy, which prohibited U.S. government funds from even going to an organization that provided any abortion services, the domestic gag rule suggested that if organizations chose to offer such services, they could do so with their own monies as long as such activities did not touch Title X services.

The gag rule found its roots in the 1981 Title X hearings and in President Reagan's promise to Orrin Hatch to "remedy . . . some of the problems in the family-planning program administratively," and was nurtured by the New Right's incremental gains. When the Supreme Court ruled in *McRae v. Califano* that Congress could use its control of the government purse strings to foster one policy over another, it provided the opening for the president to do likewise, through administrative orders. In the case of the gag rule, the president used executive orders that had the force of law to mandate censorship of speech about abortion.

After the Title X hearings in Congress in 1981, the General Accounting Office and the Inspector General had embarked upon audits of Planned Parenthood and similar organizations to confirm that we weren't violating the law by using Title X monies to fund abortion-related or political activities.

After almost a year of probing, the audits produced no evidence of rampant transgressions. The GAO did, however, find some problems and suggested that Congress might want to issue some guidelines concerning how federal family-planning funds may be used.

It wasn't Congress but the administration that provided "guidance," back in 1982, when it developed regulations for the disbursement of Title X funds. The draft proposed forcing agencies receiving Title X funds to separate family-planning facilities and abortion facilities, even to the extent of having separate entrances and exits, examining tables, even separate blood pressure cuffs. Because of widespread protest, this draft never made it into the Federal Registry.

Five years later, in July of 1987, in a speech before antiabortion leaders, President Reagan announced that, within thirty days, the Department of Health and Human Services would publish the proposed regulations that became known as the "gag rule," prohibiting abortion counseling in Title X clinics, in the Federal Register. His chief domestic policy adviser, Gary Bauer, a New Right activist, was the architect of these DHHS regulations:

(a) A project supported under this subpart may take no action which encourages, or advocates abortion as a method of family planning, or which assists a woman in obtaining an abortion as a method of family planning . . . Prohibited actions include the following:

   (1) Lobbying for the passage of proabortion legislation, providing speakers to argue for abortion as a method of family planning, or paying dues to organizations that advocate abortion as a method of family planning;

(2) Using legal action to make available in any way abortion as a method of family planning;

(3) Developing, assisting in the development of, posting or disseminating in any way materials (including printed matter and audiovisual materials) that advocate abortion as a method of family planning.[1]

The Alan Guttmacher Institute laid out the potentially devastating consequences:

Title X projects would not be able to counsel a woman about abortion or give her information about where to obtain an abortion, even if she has a medical condition where abortion should be considered to protect her life or health. This will affect, for example, women with cancer, cardiac disease, circulatory disorders or diabetes and women pregnant with an IUD in place and women who test positive for HIV infection. Moreover, Title X projects would not be able to provide even the most neutral information about abortion to women at risk for bearing a fetus with serious disease, congenital or genetic problems, such as women who are infected with the AIDS virus and women who carry genetic anomalies.[2]

The gag rule was a wake-up call to those who had tried to ignore the Mexico City Policy: This wasn't about funding organizations in faraway lands. These were our clinics, in American cities. Even if we seriously considered accommodating the regulations, it would be as it would have been with the squeal rule, a logistical and financial nightmare, if not an outright impossibility. And then there were the philosophical implications of the rule. If we acceded to it, we would be compromising one of our fundamental principles, that a woman should be empowered to make an informed decision about her fertility based on a thorough understanding of *all* her options. And yet if we did not accept the rule, the affiliates risked losing over $37 million a year in Title X money. Not only would this loss have a serious impact on our services, it could mean the end of existence for some of the smaller affiliates, and for non–Planned Parenthood organizations who relied almost exclusively on Title X monies.

Had this threat occurred anytime in the past, we could have turned to the congressional champions of Title X to defeat it. But by the mid-Eighties, there weren't many left to turn to. After years of battering, even those members of Congress who had trumpeted their support for the program were now avoiding the "controversy." They feared that a vote for Title X without restrictions would be used against them as a vote for abortion—it didn't seem to matter to them that the Title X program was actually a way to *prevent* that most "controversial" procedure, abortion.

After 1985, Title X was never again given the multiyear authorization it had once enjoyed. In fact, from that year onward Title X funds were appropriated without official reauthorization for the program to even exist. If we were without strong advocates in Congress, even to get the program renewed, fighting the administration's gag rule through congressional action would be hard to do.

I felt we had to make the fight regardless of our prospects of succeeding. The affiliates were not so sure. Vigorous debate broke out. Some affiliates would not consider compromise, but were reluctant to take a strong stand against those affiliates who declared that they would abide by the regulations if they were enacted rather than lose their funding. Still other affiliates didn't know what they would do if they actually faced the rule.

I could not conceive of acquiescing. Freedom of speech is fundamental to American democracy; it is the First Amendment to the Constitution. And the gag rule stood to affect far more than just Title X organizations. If doctors, nurses, and women could be censored, who would be next?

The gag rule debate only threw more fuel on another fire that had been smoldering within Planned Parenthood for a number of years. When in the early Eighties we became convinced that we couldn't take Title X for granted, the affiliates began to look for ways to secure themselves in the event that the program was shut down.

The long-simmering possibility of affiliates' expanding their services was raised in the context of concerns about funding and about the developing competition from health maintenance organizations that offered a broader range of health services, including reproductive healthcare. The board had initially agreed that we should resist efforts to dilute our mission, and we resisted the affiliates' suggestions for expanding their services to nonreproductive health services.

By the late Eighties, almost a decade had passed since I had been the director of Planned Parenthood of Miami Valley. I may not have been entirely sensitive to the realities as they were currently lived by the affiliates, but in the most practical terms, I believed that the particular services that we provided were needed more than ever. There was no evidence that reproductive health services, including contraception, abortion, and treatment of sexually transmitted infections (especially to teenagers and poor women), were becoming less controversial. And I believed it likely that the new corporate health providers would want to avoid these issues.

More important, I also believed that a mission that loses its focus is doomed to fail. Movements evolve to meet a need, and that need was far from being fully met. If we lost sight of the need, we lost sight of our reason for being. The liberation of women, through the power to control their bodies, was more essential than ever.

And it was a question of credibility as much as guiding principle. Large numbers of Americans had come to support us because of our uncompromising family-planning services and our consistently strong voice in the defense of women's reproductive rights. We had to stay true to that image if we were to keep the support and mobilize it in our battles.

In 1987, almost ten years after the initial conflict over extending our services, a task force of affiliate and national representatives had recommended that our focus remain on reproductive health—but broadly defined from contraception to childbirth; from screening for sexually transmitted infections to minor gynecological services. Nevertheless, the concept of comprehensive healthcare continued to gain currency among affiliates. At the national office, we began to consult with outside healthcare experts about adapting our services to the changing marketplace. But that wasn't enough for the affiliates: They lobbied the board to be allowed to make their own arrangements.

Planned Parenthood of Niagara Falls asked to be given approval to offer the same range of services that a family-care physician would provide. They argued that not only were such services needed, they were also a way of attracting family-planning clients. Over my objections that we had no means of monitoring a program projected to offer everything from contraceptives to cardiac care, the board okayed the request, on an experimental basis.

At that moment, I began to understand how Margaret Sanger must have felt when the organization to which she'd devoted her life changed its name from the American Birth Control League to Planned Parenthood, and with it shifted the organization's focus from women to families. Although the Niagara program never fulfilled its promise, that did not diminish the calls for "transforming" our clinics into comprehensive health services.

Nevertheless, like our fight against Bork's nomination, our fight against the gag rule was a unified effort. Most of the affiliates agreed that we had to mobilize our supporters as never before. Maybe we were fighting it to forestall our day of reckoning—that moment when the affiliates had to decide whether they would withhold information from women in order to conform to governmental censorship, continue to receive Title X funds and risk losing their right to use the Planned Parenthood name, or whether they would stand firm on our principles of informed consent, and, if we lost our fight, lose the government support.

Because the gag rule was handed down by the Department of Health and Human Services, it, like the squeal rule, was subject to a comment period before going into effect. While we assumed that we would ultimately turn to the courts, we began our "Ninety Day Campaign to End the Gag Rule."

This time, instead of having one or two executive directors joining us in our strategy meetings, an advisory committee of affiliate representatives was formed to oversee the structuring and progress of the entire campaign.

Because the outcome of this particular battle affected them so directly, it was essential that they be involved in every aspect of its execution. We needed their input to be certain that we understood the dangerous nuances of the gag rule for the clinics. The value of coming together at all levels of the organization to fight the censorship, even if it simply offered a sense of organizational momentum, was important at this point in our history.

On February 2, 1988, six months after the first appearance of the gag rule, the Reagan administration published the final regulations, giving notice that they were scheduled to go into effect in Title X clinics on March 3, 1988.

On that same day in February, in separate lawsuits, the Planned Parenthood Federation of America, the National Family Planning and Reproductive Health Association (along with the state of Massachusetts), and the American Civil Liberties Union (along with the city and state of New York) sought to overturn the regulations in three different jurisdictions.

On February 15 our lawsuit before District Court Judge Zina L. Weinshienk in Colorado temporarily blocked enforcement of the gag rule, pending a hearing. She described the regulations as being "an unduly burdensome interference with a woman's freedom to decide whether to terminate her pregnancy," and added that, based on the First Amendment, they would impose "an uncomfortable straitjacket" on the woman's physician in providing information.[3]

A few days later, a similar ruling was handed down by District Court Judge Louis Stanton, in New York.

Meanwhile, we were making some progress in our campaign in Congress. The Senate Labor and Human Resources Committee released a report on a bill to reauthorize Title X through fiscal year 1991. While fully recognizing the long-standing prohibition in the Title X statute on the use of family-planning funds for abortion, the report made clear the committee's intent that the prohibition "not be extended to include information about abortion."[4]

On March 3, the day the rule was to go into effect, Judge Walter J. Skinner nullified the regulations, permanently and nationwide. He found no compelling reason why it could be in the government's interest to place such stringent restrictions upon free speech; to the contrary, he found the providers' First Amendment rights to offer full information to their patients critical to those patients' health.

On June 15, 1988, Judge Weinshienk issued a permanent injunction against the gag rule. She wrote that DHHS "lacked statutory authority to enact the regulations," and went on to say that implementation of the regulations would result in "irreparable injury" to both Title X–funded clinics and their clients "because the regulations in question are unconstitutional." Judge Weinshienk also stated that the regulations impermissibly "represent[ed] content-based censorship" that "significantly impair[ed]" the First Amendment rights of clinics and patients and that they "intrude[d] upon a woman's fundamental right to decide to have an abortion."[5]

But on June 30 came the first decision in favor of the gag rule—by Judge Louis Stanton, who had initially blocked the gag rule in the New York case.

In an echo of the Supreme Court decision allowing the Hyde amendment to cut off funding for poor women's abortions, Judge Stanton concluded that the regulations "reflect[ed] DHHS's decision to favor childbirth over abortion" and that, since not all healthcare providers were bound by limitations on abortion-related speech, the regulations did not constitute "invidious discrimination of ideas."[6]

All three appellate opinions were appealed. In the meantime, Judge Weinshienk's injunction against the gag rule stood. We would wait four years before the ultimate outcome was known.

By this time, our battles were beginning to seem like efforts to buy time. Perhaps if we fought long enough, the New Right agenda would wear out its welcome and we'd find ourselves with a political climate and a court system more favorable to our cause. But even forestalling our opposition meant enduring a battering storm. When I was most caught up in the turmoil, I'd sometimes recall an experience I'd had that seemed like a guiding metaphor.

On a cold and blustery February morning not long after I became president of Planned Parenthood, I boarded an eight-seater commuter airplane in Columbia, Missouri. I had given a speech the night before and was scheduled to give two speeches later that day in Kansas City, two hundred miles away. When I reached the gate, I was informed that due to overbooking, I would have to occupy the copilot's seat if I wanted to get to Kansas City on time. Having traveled many miles in small aircraft to isolated parts of the world, I had come to expect the unexpected, so it was with utter calm that I strapped myself into my seat in the tiny cockpit to travel beside the pilot.

We were nearing our destination when, in the distance, the clear blue sky gave way to a curtain of dense and forbidding darkness. I asked the pilot if this was an unusual cloud formation; he told me that it was the usual pattern for a cold front, and that we'd probably encounter sleet and snow when we hit it. Sure enough, just as he lowered the wing flaps to slow us down for our descent, icy rain and sleet began to pummel the little plane. All the incidental sounds of the pilot's work were soon muffled by the persistent, deafening roar of the plane's engines and the pounding of sleet on metal. Several moments later, the pilot's frantic turning of the knobs of his radio drew my attention away from the clouds and back into the cabin. He kept saying something I couldn't hear into a microphone he held to his lips.

At last I heard the voice of the air traffic controller: "Come in, Royal 101. Come in, Royal 101."

A spasm of terror sped through my body and my heart began to pound—the controller in Kansas City couldn't hear us.

The increasingly agitated pilot futilely changed the dial of the radio from one channel to another, and kept repeating, "This is Royal 101. Come in, Kansas City." Finally, he blurted out that the electrical system of the plane was "gone." Only then did I notice that with the exception of the compass and the gauge that read our altitude, which said we were 5,000 feet above the ground, all the gauges on the cockpit panel were holding steady at zero. My heart pounded faster and faster.

"Are we in danger?" I asked, hoping that the answer wasn't as obvious as it seemed.

My question was answered by the beads of sweat covering the pilot's forehead.

"Are we going to crash?"

"I don't know."

I began to plot my strategy for survival. Maybe if I sat on my hands, it would cushion the impact. I carefully examined the windows. I wondered if it would be possible to jump out just before the plane hit the ground—and had to stifle a nervous impulse to laugh at my own absurdity. I was terrified.

"What do we do now?" I asked.

"I don't know," he said again.

The pilot told me he was on furlough from a major airline and he wasn't familiar with the landing pattern in Kansas City. Given the low cloud cover, he was afraid that once we dropped out of the clouds, we'd find ourselves headed straight for a building.

"So what do we *do*?" I persisted.

"We can try to go back up above the clouds."

"Well, why don't we?"

"The wing flaps are down, and without the electrical system I can't raise them. And the de-icer is gone."

My throat was very dry. In a quiet, high-pitched voice, I pressed, "Do you think we're going to die?"

"I don't know," he blurted out, "but I'm trying to think, so I need some quiet."

Feeling like a chastened schoolgirl, I quickly—and briefly—apologized.

Moments later, in a more comforting tone, he said that it would be difficult to ascend with the flaps down, but he was going to try to get us above the storm to sunny skies and attempt a visual landing. "It might take a while, but we have plenty of fuel. . . . I'll probably get an FAA complaint lodged against me, but that's better than plowing into a building."

Turning the plane westward, he asked me to search for an opening in the clouds, then revved the engines. After what seemed like a millennium, the bouncing aircraft began a slow but steady climb.

I searched for any hint of separation in the clouds. After a further millennium, I spotted a small break. We flew through it—and into brilliant sunshine above a carpet of clouds that looked like billowing white cotton.

The relieved pilot announced to the other passengers that we were unable to put down in Kansas City because of "trouble in the electrical system," and that he was attempting to find a suitable place to land.

He then gave me a second assignment: search for another break in the clouds—this time beneath us—so he could descend through it and get beneath the storm. Then he might be able to identify an airstrip or another suitable spot for an emergency landing. He assured me that we could land on a highway or in a field if necessary. As the tension in my body drained, I took up the quest. I cannot recall a happier moment than when I spotted a break in the white foam. We descended through the cloud opening and circled a water tower to identify the name of the town over which we were flying. It turned out that we were back near Columbia. The other passengers told the pilot that if we followed the highway, we'd end up at the airport where we'd started.

Escaping the terror of death, all I could think about was how I was going to miss the first of my two speeches in Kansas City. But the pilot quickly brought my thoughts back to the issue at hand. We still faced one final challenge: With no electrical system, the landing gear would have to be operated manually. He took an instruction book from a compartment, flipped to the page titled "Manual Landing," and handed the booklet to me.

"Turn the crank nineteen rotations . . . ," I read.

When we finally touched down, sighs of profound relief could be heard throughout the tiny aircraft.

I didn't have much time to reflect upon what I had just experienced—I had to find a way to get to Kansas City. I rented a car and again headed north. When I arrived, the organizers of the affiliate events weren't happy that I was late, even though they knew that the Kansas City airport had been closed because our plane had "disappeared."

As my battles over a woman's most fundamental rights wore on, I sometimes felt a strange affinity with the pilot of that tiny aircraft. Like the passengers on that commuter plane, secure in their seats and taking for granted the pilot's ability to land the plane safely, so much of the general public had taken for granted that reproductive rights would not be destroyed.

But even when he'd lost contact with the flight controller and lost the use of his instruments, the pilot still had his compass to steer by. At Planned Parenthood, our compass was our principles. And as long as we clung to our compass to guide us in our battles, we would not crash. We just had to keep flying.

CHAPTER 29

MARCHING TO SAVE
WOMEN'S LIVES

J ust before the 1988 primaries, three members of my executive staff asked to meet with me. They didn't tell me what about, but when they sat down across from me at the desk, their solemn expressions and edgy postures commanded my attention. They kept glancing out the window and at each other. One of them finally spoke up. "We've been given information about an anti-choice candidate. He was present when the woman he was involved with had an abortion. The procedure was performed in a hospital. There are doctors who were present who are prepared to verify this."

If this information was passed to the press it would be a big story, a bombshell that could expose the hypocrisies of our opposition, and we all knew it.

My jaw went slack as a flash of total disbelief took hold of me. Don't lose it, I told myself as they went on to rationalize their proposal. I had to struggle to remind myself that these weren't malicious people, but rather individuals committed to choice and very weary from witnessing hypocrisy in the pursuit of political ambition.

I appreciated that they, like all of us, had been fighting on all fronts, in what seemed to be a war without end. I appreciated how physical and emotional fatigue, especially after years of the pressures of constant siege, from one corner or another, could misshape one's perspective.

After eight years of wreaking havoc on women's rights, Reagan was leaving office. All indicators were pointing to George Bush as his pro-criminalist successor. This meant that we were about to be locked into four more years with an administration that would be at least as hostile, if not more so, to reproductive rights as Reagan's. Having once been pro-choice, Bush would need to prove his anti-choice stance to his right-wing supporters.

But quite apart from the trials of facing another four years of an anti-choice White House and the probability of increased opposition in Congress, what the three in my office were suggesting was probably illegal—as a 501(c)(3) nonprofit organization, we couldn't attempt to influence the outcome of any elections. And most important, I couldn't imagine any action more antithetical to everything we stood for. After a few moments of tempering my reaction, my response was immediate and unequivocal. "I am horrified at the prospect of your even considering such an act. If we believe in the privacy of individuals, we cannot pick and choose whose privacy we will honor. You will have nothing to do with such a caper, and you'd better hope that this doesn't find its way into the press," I threatened. "If it does, I'll assume that you defied my order and played a role in getting it there. You will be history as far as Planned Parenthood is concerned."

They stared at me, stunned. After a few moments, one said, "Well, I have my constitutional rights."

"You certainly do," I answered. "But you have no constitutional right to employment at Planned Parenthood. You had better pray that this doesn't go any further," I repeated, adding, "I don't want to know the name of the alleged politician. I don't want the burden of knowing."

After further heated exchanges, my colleagues, in whom, for years, I had placed great trust, left my office grim-faced and angry. I sat incredulous for a moment, frustrated, irritated, and sad over this rare instance of a standoff. I took pride in having a generally collegial relationship with my executive staff, and I found the give-and-take of our meetings stimulating and rewarding. They were never reluctant to give me their opinions. A strong camaraderie had developed out of our ability to approach an issue with differences of opinion, yet manage to mold those differences into a common vision stronger than any single point of view.

But in this instance, there wasn't any give-and-take. I had instantly slammed the door on their proposal, allowing no time for listening to their reasoning, much less for convincing them to see things my way. And I'd surely left them feeling vulnerable about losing their jobs if someone else leaked the information.

I didn't enjoy feeling like a tyrant, but I couldn't countenance what they were up to. I regretted having alienated my staff, and at that moment, I felt isolated. I relied on them, and the other vice presidents who reported directly to me, for their wisdom in particular areas and their invaluable contributions toward the operation of the national organization. But I also relied on them for the emotional support they provided when the storms within and around Planned Parenthood were especially turbulent. They were my trusted colleagues, and yet I'd had no choice but to stop them in their tracks. At that moment, the larger purpose of the organization and its mission had to be served.

Either Planned Parenthood believed in privacy or it didn't. Despite our anxieties about our opposition, we couldn't ignore our principles— principles that demanded our offering others compassion and confidentiality without drawing moral distinctions. If estrangement from my colleagues was the price I had to pay, so be it. I cannot fight without them, I told myself. But we can't become hypocrites, another voice weighed in.

In the summer of 1988, I received a call from the U.S. surgeon general's office asking if I would participate in a delegation of pro-choice representatives to discuss our views on the mental and physical effects of abortion for a report President Reagan had commissioned Dr. C. Everett Koop to prepare.

When Dr. Koop had been appointed surgeon general in 1981, the pro-choice coalition feared that he would use the prominence of his position to attack reproductive rights. Our worries were founded largely on Dr. Koop's association with an antiabortion film, *Whatever Happened to the Human Race*, that he had narrated. In one particularly provocative segment of the film, the camera panned across a field of salt chunks and water in which hundreds of dolls, resembling dead babies, were scattered, and then fixed on Koop, standing amid the sea of dolls. In his deep voice he echoed the warnings of Senator Jeremiah Denton (R-AL) during the Title X hearing, and Dr. Bernard Nathanson of *Silent Scream* fame:

Since [1973], at least six million unborn babies have been aborted. To give you some idea of how many that is—you are looking at one thousand dolls, multiply that by six thousand and add a million a year and you see the slaughter of innocence.[1]

However, once he'd taken office, Dr. Koop had not used his position as an anti-choice pulpit, as we'd feared. Instead, surely disappointing his sponsors and supporters, he'd directed his energies toward the threats of cigarette smoking and the emerging AIDS epidemic. In refusing to back down on his position that condoms should be widely distributed, he'd incurred the wrath of those who believed that AIDS was God's curse for sinful acts— and attracted the guarded support of those of us who'd been wary that real health issues would be forsaken for ideological views.

As we waited in his outer office, the bearded, bespectacled surgeon general, in his white military uniform complete with epaulets and ribbons, a cup of coffee in one hand and a doughnut in the other, passed by us on the way to his sanctum. We surveyed one another warily. A few minutes later, Dr. Koop's secretary ushered us into his wood-paneled, flag-bedecked office.

Explaining his assignment, Dr. Koop informed us that we were the first delegation with whom he would consult in carrying out the presidentially ordered investigation on abortion. "I plan to meet with hundreds of people," he told us. Although I had some suspicion about just how he would use our presentation, I told myself that perhaps our being at the head of the line of pro-choice delegations was evidence of his respect for us.

Getting down to the substance of our meetings, David Grimes, then a professor in obstetrics and gynecology at the University of Southern California and a former head of the surveillance branch of the Centers for Disease Control, reeled off the statistical data he had marshaled about the abortion-connected mental and physical disturbances that President Reagan had presupposed. While David admitted there had not been a great deal of reliable research on the subject, he said he had found no information that lent support to a definitive conclusion that most women who terminated unwanted pregnancies were psychologically impaired by the experience. On the other hand, he pointed out, there was substantial evidence that women who carried unwanted pregnancies to full term were more likely to experience depression and other emotional problems than women who'd had abortions. David offered the statistics to support that summary. More important, he understood the statistics in their most human terms. As an obstetrician-gynecologist and a professor at a large, urban medical center, he had firsthand knowledge of the realities of women's reproductive lives.

Jackie Forrest, a researcher at the Alan Guttmacher Institute, cited additional research that affirmed David's conclusions. And then Dr. Jaroslav Hulka, from the University of North Carolina, Chapel Hill, and I drew upon our personal experiences to convey the many reasons why women decide to end unwanted pregnancies.

Dr. Koop listened respectfully to our presentations. We had no sense of whether anything we'd said may have influenced him toward modifying the content of his report. He told us only that he had not asked for this political hot potato but, as a servant of the president of the United States, he was obliged to fulfill the assignment. After again reminding us that he would be meeting with a wide range of groups, and that he intended to wrap up his inquiry quickly, he thanked us crisply but genially. As we rose to leave, David said respectfully, but assertively, one doctor to another, "We hope that you will draw upon the objectivity of your medical background in listening to the different points of view." Dr. Koop made no promises. We left his office as we'd been received, with courtesy and respect.

My preconceptions about Dr. Koop as a zealous pro-criminalist had not been confirmed. I suspected that neither had his suppositions about us been confirmed. And indeed, that first meeting formed the foundations of a respectful working association.

Later that year, Dr. Koop requested our input on the development of an AIDS brochure, *Understanding AIDS: America Responds to AIDS*, that would eventually be mailed to every household in the United States. Although the pamphlet had been watered down to an all but ineffectual degree to satisfy the conservative agenda of the Reagan administration, the very fact that Dr. Koop had reached out to an organization whose purposes he had condemned was a measure of fairness, courage, and determination to maintain a degree of professional integrity regardless of ideological distortions.

The surgeon general's final report on the effects of abortion on a woman's mental health was never officially released. But in January 1989, Dr. Koop wrote a letter to the newly elected George Bush, discussing the report and its findings:

> The health effects of abortion on women are not easily separated from the hotly debated social issues that surround the practice of abortion.[2]

Although we'd been hopeful that he would confine his report to the objective data, both pro and con, Dr. Koop would not confirm an association between abortion and mental health.

> I regret, Mr. President, that in spite of a diligent review on my part of many in the public health service and in the private sector, the scientific studies do not provide conclusive data about the health effects of abortion on women. I recommend that consideration be given to going forward with an appropriate prospective study.[3]

Although we were not surprised—we knew the political vise in which the surgeon general was locked—we were grateful to know that at least one person in the administration, and one crucial to our work, wouldn't claim that legal abortion drove women into mental illness.

After the 1988 election, with George Bush in the White House, there was no reason to believe that he wouldn't be moving the federal judiciary even further to the right, no reason to believe that the power of executive orders wouldn't be wielded with new vigor in an effort to roll back women's reproductive rights, or that the bitter congressional battles wouldn't proceed apace. In fact, frustrations and fears had reached a boiling point.

Shortly after Bush was elected, the National Organization for Women

(NOW), with Molly Yard as its president, announced—once again without consulting the other members of the pro-choice coalition—that it was calling for pro-choice supporters nationwide to march on Washington in the spring "to save women's lives." Ellie Smeal would coordinate it, and once again, the pro-choice coalition was trapped between the need to fulfill the overcommitments of our individual organizations and the need to present a unified front with our colleagues in the battle to preserve reproductive freedom. None of us, including NOW, had the money in our budgets for such a mammoth task. But without the full participation of the pro-choice coalition it would be all but impossible to pull off the march, all but impossible to make the strong statement that only a march could make. What we couldn't afford was to invite unfavorable comparisons to the March for Life, which drew fifty to a hundred thousand marchers every January 22 to mourn *Roe v. Wade*.

Despite the resentful grumbling, Ellie, always passionate, put us in our places. "Look, women's lives are on the line," she exhorted us. "We didn't need your permission to announce this march. We have got to take direct action—to make sure that this new administration knows just how strong the opposition is to any further weakening of women's reproductive rights—or we're going to lose everything. And with the Supreme Court considering *Webster v. Reproductive Health Services* [which would shape the future of the abortion debate], the justices need to see our opposition, and Congress does, too." Ellie had made her point in no uncertain terms. We knew there was no more time for squabbling.

In order to cover the expenses of the march—buses, permits, sound system, Porta Potties—we'd have to approach our donors for extra support. Someone in the coalition suggested that we combine our donor lists, take out any duplications, and make a single appeal for the march. It seemed like a good idea to me and an efficient way to raise funds. What's more, many of us used the same firm, Craver, Matthews and Smith, for our direct-mail solicitations.

Nevertheless, combining our lists for a single mailing proved very tricky to negotiate. Although none of us would have access to the final lists, the bigger organizations were afraid that donor names would be pilfered; the smaller organizations, already vulnerable to being overshadowed, worried that their supporters would contribute to the collective appeal for the march rather than to their organizations.

Impatient with the bickering, I finally announced, "I don't care what any of you do. As for Planned Parenthood's part, I will be asking Craver, Matthews and Smith to draw up a letter to our four hundred thousand national donors, asking them to send us a gift to support our participation in the march."

Fearing that our donors might also be their donors, the other organizations didn't want us to have the advantage. Finally setting aside partisan concerns, we all agreed to ask Craver, Matthews and Smith to combine our lists and send out an appeal letter that we'd all sign. We were all surprised by Craver's news that our donor lists overlapped only about 20 percent. The mailing enabled us to raise the necessary funds to pull off the massive demonstration.

Once this was settled, I was scheduled to leave for a four-month sabbatical. I would return just in time for the march. There were several reasons for my taking a leave. I'd been working full throttle for almost eleven years, and in that time had weathered the storms of a divorce and relocation, and fought the countless battles inside and outside Planned Parenthood. The growing number of speech engagements and media requests meant a heavy travel schedule, often speaking under contentious conditions. I was extremely exhausted in ways that ten-day leaves of absence couldn't begin to remedy. I was convinced that the new Bush administration would escalate the attacks, and if I didn't restore my inner resources, I feared I would not be at my best.

David Andrews would serve as acting president in my absence, and I didn't feel a moment's anxiety in handing over the responsibilities of running the organization to him. He knew my values and my administrative methods better than anyone I'd ever worked with, and he knew the inner workings of the organization as well as I did.

In those first few weeks away from my office, I felt as though I'd been dropped into a foreign land—one where there were no airplanes to catch, no affiliate complaints, no budget problems to solve, no personnel problems to take care of, no television, radio, newspaper, or magazine interviews to do, no crises to address. I could go to bed early and sleep past six the next morning.

Before the start of my leave, I'd agreed to write this book. I figured that in my time away, I would get a good start on it. I went to the Caribbean for two weeks—the first time I had gone anywhere for so long with no work-related activities and without Felicia. I thought I'd find the peace I needed to reflect on what I wanted the book to say. It turned out, though, that the sun, the sea air, and the gentle rhythms of life on the island conspired together, and my body gave way to the cumulative fatigue. I managed to get a broad outline structured, but I spent a good part of my time sleeping as though I'd never slept before.

Before I knew it, the sabbatical was over, and I was back at my post at Planned Parenthood the week before the march on Washington was scheduled to take place. I couldn't have hoped for a more exhilarating way to return.

The timing of the march—Sunday, April 9, 1989—was deliberate. Two weeks later, on April 26, the Supreme Court was to hear the arguments in

Webster. Hundreds of thousands of women, men, and children were expected to show Congress and the Court where most Americans stood on the issue.

Earlier, we'd learned that an antiabortion group had applied for a permit to erect four thousand white crosses on the Washington Mall, to create a "Cemetery of the Innocents," and we'd sought a court order against the permit. We feared that the visual image of our marching past the white crosses would create the negatively charged atmosphere we were hoping to avoid. We also worried that the crosses, with their spiked bases, might be pulled from the ground and used as weapons in the event of verbal provocation escalating into physical conflict. NOW, believing that it could handle all security issues, had not wanted us to interfere, but as co-sponsors, we now had a vested interest in the safety and success of the march. We'd gone forward anyway with the court-order request, which was eventually denied on First Amendment grounds.

April 9 dawned gray and drizzly, but daffodils and forsythia promised the profusion of cherry blossoms that would soon brighten the city. Felicia and I had flown down to Washington the night before the march in order to attend the pre-rally gathering in a Senate Office Building hearing room the following morning. When we walked into the room, the enthusiastic energy of those already gathered gave me the confidence that this was the start of an historic day for women. We had received reports of hundreds of buses that were coming from all parts of the country; of chartered airplanes and trains. On the basis of reports it was getting from organizers around the country, NOW predicted that a million people would be marching this day.

As the hearing room filled, I thought about my first appearance in one of these rooms, so many years earlier, when I'd tried to defend Title X from the wrath of Senators Denton, Nickles, and Hatch. On this day, the room was crowded with advocates for reproductive freedom. They ranged from ordinary people committed to preserving women's rights and willing to put their bodies on the line to defend them, to famous Hollywood stars like Glenn Close, Jane Fonda, Bonnie Franklin, Whoopi Goldberg, Penny Marshall, Susan Sarandon, and Cybill Shepherd. There were senators and grandmothers, men and small children. There were old veterans of protest marches, and people who had never done anything political before, let alone march in the street.

After a formal welcome, celebrity after celebrity spoke of their commitment to choice and their determination to do everything they could to see to it that no more ground was lost. With each speech, the exuberance in the room rose. By midmorning, the gathering had taken on the aura of a pregame pep rally. Around eleven, this excitement spilled out of the hearing room and into the Washington streets, as we all made our way to the Mall at the foot of the Washington Monument.

As a car moved Jean Mahoney, PPFA's national chairperson, Felicia, and me toward the staging area of that large expanse, the air began to pulsate with the beats of rock and folk music. Felicia and I threaded our way through the masses of people toward a path that would lead us to an area that had been fenced off for "VIPs."

Reporters had gathered alongside the temporary barrier and shouted out questions as we passed by. One called me by name and asked a question that caught me off guard: "Why do you think so few black women have appeared for the march?"

I thought it was a little early in the day for such a rush to judgment, but with only seconds to organize my thoughts, I answered, "Social movements are not the luxury of people who are engaged in the daily struggle for survival. If it seems that the presence of blacks is disproportionately small, it reflects more on economic disparity than a lack of interest in being able to have children when we want them."

It wasn't the most eloquent statement I'd ever made, but I believed what I said. I also believed that as much as I was there to speak for Planned Parenthood, I was also there as a woman and as an African American. I hadn't forgotten who would disproportionately bear the devastating consequences of the regulations our government was so eager to put forward if the Supreme Court allowed it. If they couldn't be there to represent themselves, I was there to do my best to speak on their behalf.

After this brief exchange, Felicia and I walked on toward the tent filled with reporters awaiting abbreviated interviews. The question asked most often that morning was, "Why are you here?" I answered: "This is a day when George Bush and all those who attack reproductive rights will see that the silent majority will be silent no more. We know that the battles will go on, but today we're here to show the strength of support for choice."

Shortly before noon, when the march was scheduled to begin, we began to line up for the parade down Constitution Avenue and toward the Capitol. The center of the banner that proclaimed "March for Women's Lives/March for Women's Equality" would be carried by Molly Yard, Gloria Steinem, Bella Abzug, and Ellie Smeal. Felicia and I would walk near the right-hand edge of the column, with Jesse Jackson to our left side, and Betty Friedan and her daughter just to our right. Representatives of organizations in the pro-choice coalition were dressed in white and wore purple sashes, in symbolic alliance with the suffragettes. A truck filled with photographers drove a half block ahead of us, recording our paces and our chants, "Not the church, not the state, women must decide their fate!" and "We're gonna kick back/Bush's attack!"

Behind us marched hundreds of thousands—mothers and daughters, husbands, sons, and brothers; physicians, lawyers, and activists; and nine hundred Columbia University students who had arrived on eighteen buses and carried placards that read "9 Votes Can't Force 9 Months." Many of our fellow participants also carried tricolored banners of purple, white, and gold. Others hung coat hangers from their clothes and held high signs that read "Never Again."

As we marched, we resisted the jeering encroachments of a small but vocal contingent of pro-criminalist demonstrators who trailed alongside us, mocking us. Several carried large placards of pictures of dead fetuses. One carried a large crucifix. Some, dressed as babies in bloomers and crying "What about the babies?", carried small white crosses, which, they said, signified abortions performed each day.

When we arrived at the long flight of steps leading up to the Capitol Building and the stage that overlooked the Washington Monument, our formation collapsed into disarray, and for a moment panic swept over me as we were squeezed toward steps that were too narrow to accommodate the sudden crush of bodies. I held on to Felicia as we tried to press through the narrow passage. Jesse, the veteran marcher, understood the situation, warning, "Hold tight, this is where it gets rough." I grabbed his hand too, and the three of us inched our way forward, toward the rear of the platform to await our turns to speak.

There were over thirty speakers that day—politicians, and movie stars, Gloria, Ellie, Molly, Bella, and Kate Michelman (from NARAL) among them. There were people representing a wide range of organizations, from the labor movement to the gay rights movement to the Hispanic rights movement. There were senators and congressmen. People were jockeying to be moved up on the schedule. Though no one said as much, I suspected that the real concern was the desire to speak before the crowd dwindled. As it turned out, there was no danger of that happening. By four o'clock the end of the parade was just leaving the Mall.

Of the march in Washington on that cloudy April day, we would say that over half a million people joined in demanding that women's reproductive rights be secured. The U.S. Park Service said the figure was closer to three hundred thousand.

"We've been robbed," we said to each other.

"The Park Service does it all the time," veterans of earlier demonstrations told us. But we all knew that our point had been made.

Felicia and I actually did need to get back to New York that night to attend the funeral, in Queens, of Franklin's ninety-six-year-old mother, who had died earlier that week. She was a kind lady who, in her lucid years, had written me long, loving letters. Though she was deaf, we would spend hours chatting, through written notes, when she came to visit Franklin and me in Dayton. We'd had little contact since the divorce, but I felt very sad when her daughter, Claudinne, called to say that she had passed away. I was scheduled to speak three-quarters of the way into the program, so Felicia and I would have to race to the airport to catch our flight.

The rally started with Molly Yard's voice bellowing from the loudspeaker system, "Our voices will be heard! Our protests will be heard! We are still unloading buses at the parking lot!"[4]

I waited my turn, hour after hour, listening to speaker after speaker, chatting with Felicia and others, taking pictures, being interviewed by the press, and drinking hot tea to ward off the damp chill. The buoyancy of the crowd and the rhetoric of the speakers inspired me.

When my name was introduced, the roar from the sea of people made my knees go weak. "Good luck, Mommy," whispered Felicia encouragingly to me as I moved toward the podium, hardly feeling my legs and feet move beneath me. Over the years I had given hundreds of speeches, but never before had I felt the electricity that I experienced as I stepped to the microphone that day. When I looked out at the crowd nothing else mattered more than what I was about to say. Barbara Snow, my speechwriter, and I had worked diligently for three days on what I would say. I had read my speech over and over again on the flight down.

Mama used to call the power of that moment when all anxieties disappeared and she was carried forward by her message "the power of the Holy Spirit." I felt it as a joining together of my most essential sense of purpose and the powerful convictions of the marchers. We were all participants in seeking an ideal. And because we were there together to stand for something, the speeches became a collective experience that was larger than the speaker, larger than the crowd, larger than the occasion itself. I began:

This is an historic day in the reproductive rights movement. For many of us, marching on Washington for a noble cause brings back memories— painful, yet exhilarating memories. Being here today also reminds us that freedom can never be taken for granted. There are always those who would take it from us. They are the apostles of fear and ignorance. They are the instruments of hatred and control. They ask women to submit themselves to the tyranny of repression.

As a black American, I say it is an insult and a shame to compare anti-abortion terrorism and harassment with the civil rights movement of the 1960s. Just as the nonviolent civil rights movement faced violence, we do as well.

As a moral person, I know that morality must be taught in the home, preached from the pulpit and practiced in our personal lives. In America, morality cannot be dictated by Jesse Helms or George Bush.

The roar from the crowd drowned out my last words, and I had to wait a bit for it to die down.

And as a woman, I know that the power of the government to control women's reproduction is more frightening than any other tyranny, and more binding than any other prison.

There can be no *equal* rights without *abortion* rights!

If we cannot decide when we will bear children, what good is access to the boardrooms of corporate America?

If we cannot protect our health and our lives, what good is equal pay, equal opportunity, or equity in any other aspect of American life?

And if it is assumed that women are too limited to be trusted to make moral decisions without the direction of Mr. Bush, how can we be trusted to raise the children of America—and thereby shape the future of America?

Again the last phrase went unheard. With each question the volume of cheers carried me and my challenge to a higher emotional pitch.

We are here today to say to the Congress and the Supreme Court that American women will *not* die again as a result of illegal abortion. If there is any retrenchment on women's reproductive rights, there will be a groundswell of rebellion in this country. Americans want abortion to remain safe and legal. Americans refuse to brand women criminals because they choose to take charge of their health and their destinies. And Americans will not tolerate women dying at the whim and the will of complete strangers.

As I said these words, all of the years of outrage over the continuing attacks on women poured out of me in a sweeping purge. I felt more confident about our mission that day than ever before. As much as I knew the dangers that lay ahead, I also knew that we had reached a milestone. For most women in America there would be no returning to the dangers. We had to make sure this was true for all women, everywhere.

Eight years ago, George Bush and Ronald Reagan came to Washington, pledging to get the government off our backs. That's where we want them. *Off* our backs. Out of our bedrooms. *Away* from our doctors' offices.

In a pluralistic nation, private morality must be just that—private! . . .

Their time would be better spent dealing with the major issues facing our country and our globe. They should feed hungry children, house homeless children, and educate ignorant children.

As we join together today in support of women's equality and women's lives, let us remember: We have inherited the legacy of the civil rights movement of the Sixties. It is *we* who represent the *majority* of Americans who cherish their hard-won personal freedoms. And to the world, it is we who say "Read our lips!" "No more back alleys!" "Never again!"[5]

I turned to head for the back of the platform, the cheering of the crowd enveloping me. Bella Abzug, who had given her speech hours earlier, but who had stayed to hear me, was sitting off to the side, grinning. "That was great!" she said. Few words at that moment could have meant more than hers. I felt as though I would collapse with the release of tension within me.

A step or two later, I spotted Felicia, smiling and rushing toward me. "Mommy, you were so-o-o-o-o good. Oh, my God, you were so-o-o-o-o good." I hugged her, and in that hug experienced once again the depth of the bond between us. There is no greater joy for me than knowing I have made my daughter proud. I knew that she knew I was doing this for her.

CHAPTER 30

WEBSTER: WRECKING ROE

The case of *Webster v. Reproductive Health Services*—the case whose out-come we'd hoped to influence by marching in Washington—had begun three years earlier in Missouri. In 1986, the Missouri state legislature passed a law drafted at the behest of the Missouri Catholic Conference. The law, which was overwhelmingly approved, declared that:

- No public funds could be used for "encouraging or counseling a woman to have an abortion not necessary to save her life";[1]
- "Before a physician performs an abortion on a woman he has reason to believe is carrying an unborn child of twenty or more weeks gestational age, the physician shall first decide if the unborn child is viable";[2]
- It would be "unlawful for any public employee within the scope of his employment to perform or assist an abortion not necessary to save the life of the mother";
- No "public facility" could be used "for the purpose of performing or assisting an abortion not necessary to save the life of the mother."[3]

Nearly a decade after *McRae v. Califano*, the 1976 case that challenged the Hyde amendment's cutoff of Medicaid funds to poor women seeking abortions, Missouri was attempting to apply the same principles at the state level: The government could use its resources in a non-neutral manner to impose its philosophy of favoring childbirth over abortion. This time, how-ever, the state decided to test the boundaries even further than prohibiting the use of public (government) funds to "encour[age] or counsel" a woman to have an abortion unless it was "necessary to save her life." In its next restriction, which required a physician to perform tests to determine if a twenty-week-old fetus would be able to sustain life outside the womb, the Missouri state legislature was interfering in the practice of medicine. This aspect of the law was nothing short of high cynicism, given that there was—and is—no medical evidence that fetuses are viable at twenty weeks. Their lungs are not sufficiently developed to permit survival, even with the most advanced intervention. Furthermore, amniocentesis, the only test at that time by which a doctor could determine viability, is painful to the woman and risky to the fetus. It can even induce labor, ending the life that the Missouri law ostensibly sought to preserve.

The last two provisions of the law—that no public employees could perform or assist in performing abortions, and that no public facilities could be used for performing or assisting in the performance of abortions—extended the principles opposed in *McRae* a giant step further. For the first time since *Roe v. Wade*, the restrictions had reached beyond poor women and teenagers, to include *all* women who might seek to exercise their constitutional right to end an unwanted pregnancy in public facilities, regardless of whether they could afford to pay for the procedure. The law did not apply to private hospitals operated by religious denominations.

The lawsuit seeking to block this egregious policy was filed in July 1986, and in March of the following year, Federal District Judge Scott Wright ruled the law unconstitutional and blocked its enforcement, citing *Roe* and stating it "inappropriate for this Court to conduct an inquiry into such a difficult and philosophical question" as when life begins.[4]

As expected, William Webster, the Missouri attorney general, appealed Judge Wright's decision. On March 26, 1987, the Eighth Circuit Court of Appeals barred the law in even stronger tones than had the low court and continued to prevent its implementation.

Missouri, however, continued to press its case. The Supreme Court agreed to hear both sides of the argument on April 26, 1989, three years after it had been passed.

On the morning the *Webster* arguments were to be presented, the courthouse plaza was filled with contentious protesters for and against the Missouri law. I had flown down to Washington early to hear the oral arguments, which were scheduled for 10 A.M.

As I took my seat in the courtroom that April morning, I looked about me. This was a case upon which the whole of the reproductive rights movement was riveted. It held the potential to reverse the reality of sixteen years of legal abortion, and those gathered to hear it represented the stalwarts in the defense of a woman's right to choose. On the wooden cushion-seated bench in front of me sat Sarah Weddington, her blond hair in a pouffe framing her translucent skin. The youthful idealism of this Texas lawyer had eventually prevailed in *Roe v. Wade*. Her presence on the lecture circuit kept alive our consciousness of how short the time had been that women had gained complete control over their reproduction.

Next to Sarah sat Molly Yard, from NOW, her gray hair twisted in a bun at the nape of her neck. I had grown to admire and respect her. When I'd learned that she had been fighting for women's equality since her college days, I thought of my mother, and of her perseverance in her mission from girlhood to maturity.

When the judges entered, to take their seats in their high-back burgundy leather chairs, I was struck by the shift in the visual makeup of the Court since my last visit over a decade earlier to hear the arguments in *McRae*. Gone were Justices Stewart, Burger, and Powell. Now seated were Justices O'Connor, Scalia, and Kennedy, along with Chief Justice Rehnquist and Justice White, who disputed the constitutional bedding of *Griswold* and *Roe*. Still sitting were Justices Blackmun, Brennan, Marshall, and Stevens.

Since Missouri was appealing to the Court to reverse the earlier decision, William Webster, tall, dark, and squarely built, opened the session. After a few preliminary procedural questions, Justice John Paul Stevens, who seemed to be the most aggressive toward the state official, exposed Webster's lack of forethought on how the law was to be enforced.

Justice Stevens: General Webster, can I ask you one clarifying question? What is the consequence of a violation of that section? If the doctor should go ahead and do it, is he committing any kind of misdemeanor or crime?

Mr. Webster: . . . Any post-viability abortion would be prohibited under Missouri statute.

Justice Stevens: I am just asking if one violates Section 205 or 210 or 215, is there any sanction for violation?

Mr. Webster: To my knowledge there is no sanction for violation.

Justice Stevens: It is not a misdemeanor? What is the state's method of enforcement, then? . . .

Mr. Webster: I would presume [it] would be . . . to prevent either the [public] facilities from performing those services or to prohibit the expenditure of the funds themselves.

Justice Stevens: What if a doctor who had a patient in a public hospital went ahead and performed [an abortion] in the first trimester. . . . Is there any sanction against the doctor if he did that?

Mr. Webster: This particular chapter . . . carries a . . . misdemeanor penalty for violations of the initial sections, but there is no operative language in the 1986 statute.

Justice Stevens: So it would be a misdemeanor then?

Mr. Webster: Arguably, it would be a misdemeanor.

Justice Stevens: What is your opinion? Don't you know?

Mr. Webster: My opinion is that there is no language in that section which was adopted here which would suggest that it would make it a criminal offense, only that it is directed to those bodies expending the public funds themselves.

Justice Stevens: Is it your opinion as the chief law-enforcement officer of the state that it would be a misdemeanor?

Mr. Webster: We wouldn't view that violation as a misdemeanor, no.

Justice Stevens: Is there any enforcement provision other than injunctive relief?

Mr. Webster: That is the only enforcement power that we would presume contained in the language which was enacted in the 1986 statute.[5]

Charles Fried, special assistant to the United States attorney general in the Bush administration, struck straight at the heart of reproductive rights in his opening statement:

Today, the United States asks this Court to reconsider and overrule its decision in *Roe v. Wade* . . . we are not asking the Court to unravel the fabric of enumerated and privacy rights [which] the Court has woven in [other] cases. . . . Rather, we are asking the Court to pull out one thread. And the reason is well stated in *Harris v. McRae*: abortion is different. It involves the purposeful termination, as the Court said, of potential life. And I would only add that in the minds of many legislators who pass abortion regulation, it is not merely potential life but human life.[6]

This frontal assault of *Roe* by the president's emissary in such powerfully concise terms shocks me even now.

Frank Susman, who had argued before the Supreme Court against Missouri's restrictive abortion law—particularly its insistence upon parental consent—back in *Danforth*, was once again representing the opposition to the Missouri law. He began his argument by responding to Charles Fried's statement:

> I think the solicitor general's submission is somewhat disingenuous when he suggests to this Court that he does not seek to unravel the whole cloth of procreational rights, but merely to pull a thread. It has always been my personal experience that when I pull a thread, my sleeve falls off. There is no stopping. It is not a thread he is after. It is the full range of procreational rights and choices that constitute the fundamental right that has been recognized by the Court. For better or for worse, there no longer exists any bright line between the fundamental right that was established in *Griswold* and the fundamental right that was established in *Roe*.[7]

As might have been expected, when the attorney finished his presentation, Justice Antonin Scalia went on the assault.

Justice Scalia: Excuse me, you find it hard to draw a line between these two but easy to draw a line between the first, second, and third trimester?

Mr. Susman: I do not find it difficult—

Justice Scalia: I don't see why a court that can draw that line can't separate abortion from birth control quite readily.

Mr. Susman: If I may suggest the reasons in response to your question, Justice Scalia, the most common of what we generally in common parlance call contraception today . . . act as abortifacients . . . Things have changed. The bright line, if there ever was one, has now been extinguished. That's why I suggest to this Court that we need to deal with one right, the right to procreate. We are no longer talking about two rights.[8]

Given the combative tone on both sides of the questioning, it was hard to surmise how the Court would decide. I remembered Eve's caution, ten years before, that courtroom performances were not reliable indicators of how the Court would rule.

The lawyers on Planned Parenthood's staff, and legal scholars generally, agreed that although it wasn't likely that the Court would bow to Fried's request and overturn *Roe*, it very well might allow Missouri to implement its restrictions, and in so doing allow other states to do the same. But still, we were hopeful that the Court would not ignore public sentiment.

All that confidence generated by the April rally was shattered on July 3, 1989, when the Court announced its five-to-four decision upholding the Missouri law, whose preamble stated:

> The laws of the state of Missouri should be interpreted and construed to acknowledge on behalf of the unborn child at every stage of development, all the rights, privileges, and immunities available to other persons, citizens, and residents of [the] state, subject only to the Constitution of the United States. . . . The life of each human being begins at conception.[9]

The Court concluded that "the state intended its abortion regulations to be understood against the backdrop of its theory of life."[10]

By allowing the preamble to stand, it had confirmed the state's powers to advance religious dogma in its public policies. Even if preambles aren't laws, and are therefore unenforceable, they form the philosophical framework of laws. Even if the Missouri preamble does not "by its terms regulate abortion," the Supreme Court had allowed the official position of the State of Missouri to stand, declaring the fetus to be a person, "with all the rights, privileges, and immunities" of a person, "subject only to the Constitution of the United States," something that the Court itself had refused to do in *Roe v. Wade*.

The overarching reality was that, because the Court was allowing states to claim that the rights of the fetus were superior to a woman's and thus to deny women access to abortion in all publicly funded facilities, *Roe* as we knew it ceased to exist. *Webster* had endorsed a religious point of view about the initiation of life, and granted states the power to enforce a growing number of restrictions on abortion. And if abortion was inaccessible, what was the practical difference in its being found illegal?

And the *Webster* decision had left the door open, foreboding even more control by the state. In her concurring opinion, Justice Sandra Day O'Connor promised, "When the constitutional invalidity of a state's abortion statute actually turns on the constitutional validity of *Roe v. Wade*, there will be time enough to reexamine *Roe*. And to do so carefully."[11]

It was Justice Harry Blackmun who spoke for most Americans, including the hundreds of thousands of pro-choice demonstrators on the Washington Monument Mall three months earlier, when he wrote in an angry dissent:

> Never in my memory has a plurality announced a judgment of this Court that so foments disregard for the law and for standing decisions . . . I fear for the future . . . I fear for the liberty and equality of the millions of women who have lived and come of age in the 16 years since *Roe* was

decided . . . For today at least the law of abortion stands undisturbed. For today the women of this nation still retain the liberty to control their destinies. But the signs are evident and very ominous and a chill wind blows.[12]

Indeed, a chill wind did blow. Although no law has been passed to enforce this official point of view, it did have some bizarre and ironic consequences. Perhaps the most extreme of these incidents came when an imprisoned pregnant woman in Missouri sued for her release, claiming that her "unborn child," of necessity "imprisoned" with her, had been incarcerated in violation of rights guaranteed to persons in the Thirteenth and Fourteenth Amendments of the Constitution. The suit was dismissed on the grounds, in spite of the Missouri law's preamble, that in *Roe v. Wade* the Supreme Court held that a fetus is not a "person" entitled to the protection of the Fourteenth Amendment.[13]

Words like "protectable interests in the life, health and well-being" of "unborn children" are all quite open to interpretation by those enforcing the laws. The lengthy process of complaining to the court and waiting for a decision does not halt the progression of the woman's predicament, for pregnancy is not a lifelong condition. Any public official who wants to do so, in Missouri or any other state that sees fit to follow its lead, can earn political spurs by prosecuting women for a whole range of alleged activities that might "harm" a fetus, or by defending individuals who assert that they are fighting on its behalf. By the end of 1989, two Missouri state judges had already acquitted pro-criminalist protesters of trespassing on the property of abortion clinics, accepting their claims that they were protecting fetal interests.[14]

The preamble also refers to the "protectable interests" of the fetus's "natural" parents. I don't argue that men's interests in their unborn progeny are nonexistent, but as long as women alone bear the burden of pregnancy and childbearing, their to determine the course of their pregnancies residing within and drawing upon the sustenance of their bodies must be the preeminent right, and it must be theirs alone. The design of nature (Mama would say, "God") makes it impossible to accord the status of personhood to the fetus without compromising the personhood of the woman carrying it.

And of course the "protectable interests" of a parent don't touch upon the tragedy of fetuses conceived in rape and incest. But the Missouri law, and the justices on the Supreme Court who ruled in its favor, had allowed for the possibility that those who want to make the rules for a woman may attempt to force her to carry such a fetus to term because its "father" had a "protectable interest."

The distance had just been cut shorter between the plight of women living under the yoke of the Missouri law as we neared the end of the twentieth century, and the plight of the women that Margaret Sanger had tried to save in New York City tenements in the early years of this century.

Flying back to New York after finishing the press interviews on the day the decision was announced, I felt depressed, but not defeated. *Roe* was still technically in place, and Congress might be persuaded to pass federal protections to stanch the flow of restrictions from state legislatures. Riding across the Triborough Bridge from La Guardia Airport as I had done hundreds of times before, I found myself enveloped in a sense of aloneness. Felicia was away at riding camp, and for once I found myself grateful for the prospect of quiet—even if a lonely quiet.

Later that night, I called David Andrews, with whom I had spoken at various times over the course of the day: "David, it seems to me that the Court has shown us that it can change its mind, just as politicians do. Now it has given the opposition new weapons with which to fight us. This battle will never stop," I moaned.

David, who was almost always upbeat, seemed subdued. "Yeah, you're right. This is pretty bad."

"It seems to me that the only way to fix this is to fix the Constitution."

David didn't ask me what I meant by that, and I was too exhausted to offer any further insights about what seemed to be springing out of my intuition.

The next week, expecting to find a kindred spirit, I called Bella Abzug, with whom I often commiserated when the struggle became especially difficult. "I think we need to go for a reproductive rights amendment to the Constitution," I announced.

With volume that could not be mistaken for anything but emphasis, my good friend challenged me in no uncertain terms: "Are you crazy? Don't say that to *anyone*! If you do, even people who have long supported your leadership will assume that you've really lost it."

It hadn't occurred to me that I was being anything more than practical, searching for a long-term solution rather than, like a leaky faucet, letting the constant drip of restrictions corrupt women's rights. Facing the countless skirmishes at the state level and again failing to take the offense seemed to me the insane thing to do. The only way I could imagine stopping the gradual erosion of reproductive rights was by explicitly securing them in the Constitution.

Bella—lawyer, seasoned feminist, and veteran politician—would hear none of my argument. "Let me tell you something. You don't know what it means to pass a constitutional amendment. You just don't know. Are you nuts? Are you crazy?" she demanded in utter exasperation.

"No, you're right. I don't know. But I'm not crazy, either." I stood my ground. "How much clearer does it have to be before we get it? We won't be winning this war anytime soon, unless we take control."

"Look, I know what it means to try to get a constitutional amendment passed, okay?" she repeated. "We weren't able to do it with the ERA. Hatch and Helms haven't done it with their 'fetus is a person' amendments. Who's to say we could even come up with language that would satisfy everyone? And who's to say how it will be interpreted if you do get that far? What amendments will get attached to the amendment? You'll bring out every crazy in the world to fight us," she predicted. And then, lecturing me now more softly, and in her best Bronx enunciation, she said, "Honey, let me tell you something, okay? Change is not made by constitutional amendments. It's made by elections. It's made by building strong political movements nationally, and often on a state-by-state basis. I know what it takes and I'm telling you that you're wrong."

"I may be wrong, but I really think this is what it's going to take, Bella. Women may not lose *all* of their reproductive rights this year or next year; maybe not even in our lifetimes. But that doesn't mean that more and more women aren't going to be cut off from exercising them."

"Listen, I'm a friend of yours," she finally said. "I support your work. I support everything that you've done. You're the best that we have in the women's movement, but I'm telling you, don't talk about this kind of thing. People will think that you're off your rocker, honey."

"It won't be the first time I've been called crazy and I doubt that it will be the last, but I know the stakes are higher now than ever before. We can't just ignore that fact and go on as if the Earth hasn't shuddered." I was frustrated that I hadn't been able to at least get my friend to consider my thinking, and I was sure that she was maternally chagrined by my willfulness. After our conversation ended, I experienced one of those moments of isolation, when I believed within my heart that I was right, and realized that very few, if any, of my usual allies would ever agree. At such times, it was as though I could see far down the line to that place where, ultimately, others would arrive and understand.

My executive staff was as wary as Bella had been, although a little more restrained in saying so. "It will take a lot of money." "It will take a long time," they said.

And just as I'd responded to Bella, I responded to them, "Don't you see? It's going to take a lot of money and time either way. The opponents of reproductive rights will not give in. They'll use their new weapon to hammer away at them, and there may be more weapons to come. Women's lives are too high a price to pay." They looked at me in silence, as though thinking, "Maybe she has a point, but this will pass."

* * *

Two weeks after the *Webster* decision was handed down, our outside advisers, who now included Jim Hart, a Democratic fund-raiser, as well as John Deardourff, a well-known Republican political consultant, flew to New York to help us plan our response to the new realities.

I had spoken with Roger Craver earlier. Not knowing that I'd been thinking the same thing, he'd urged, "Planned Parenthood has got to take the lead to initiate a reproductive rights amendment. You're the only one who can do it. And you have to move fast to capture the momentum of the negative reaction."

I told him I shared his views and had gone so far as to suggest it to my staff—to a very much less than enthusiastic response.

"Sure, they'll be against you," he'd answered with his typical pragmatism. "But if you can get it started, get out in front, they'll have to follow. It's what Ellie does so well."

But my proposing to amend the Constitution was a bit different from NOW's proposing an abortion summit or a Washington march. "Maybe so," I'd replied. "But I'll never convince Planned Parenthood to go along with it." I was certain of that.

In our strategy session, Roger took up this conversation where it left off. "If you get it started," he said, pressing his original argument, "they'll have to join in."

"I'm not so sure," I countered.

Not dissuaded, Roger proceeded as though there wasn't a single worry in my head: "You'll have to move quickly, mobilize voters who are angry and afraid that legal abortion will not survive. If we don't bring them in now, we may never have a chance to build a broader base of support to protect reproductive rights."

Several of those gathered around the conference tables hadn't heard any mention of amending the Constitution before this meeting, and they looked at Roger as though he had two heads. Others listened to him with polite tolerance. Our allies were clearly in the minority.

But Roger's assessment of the mood of the country after *Webster* was on target. A Louis Harris poll conducted on July 14, a few days before our meeting, had reported that the public opposed the decision by a margin of 58 percent to 39 percent and affirmed its support for *Roe v. Wade* by 61 percent to 37 percent. Six in ten of those polled were opposed to the Supreme Court's reversing *Roe v. Wade*; 72 percent said that every woman should have the right to decide for herself in the matter of abortion. So unpopular was the *Webster* decision that the pollsters found a precipitous 34 percent drop in the public's approval rating of the Supreme Court. We'd reached the high watermark of public fear.

Roger tried to persuade us that the conditions were ideal for a massive counterattack. This was the moment at which the adrenaline born of fear could be channeled toward our cause, and our defensive posture, forced upon us by an increasingly unpopular Court, could be transformed into an offensive one.

Herb Gunther suggested that a national media campaign could be built to give a constitutional amendment movement a voice and a face. "It could contribute to an atmosphere of urgency and outrage, and force politicians to give pause before using their newly issued powers to weaken the power of women to make and exercise their reproductive choices."

Into the high-energy atmosphere of the room, John Deardourff introduced a note of caution, urging us not to get our hopes too high—we should not underestimate the tremendous investment, both financial and otherwise, that a constitutional amendment endeavor would require. He reminded us of the fate of the Equal Rights amendment, and that we should not underestimate the depth of the resources that would be put up to defeat us.

I was not undaunted by the complexity of getting the public to see a clear picture of what was happening. *The New York Times* reported that its poll showed that over half of those surveyed had no idea what the decision had said and meant. While the shock of the Court's ruling might energize women, there was also a definite risk that women might assume that *Roe v. Wade* had been overturned or greatly diminished and again resort to unsafe measures rather than fighting back. Reassuring women that abortion was still legal could result in a sense of complacency in the face of the emerging dangers.

The question was, How far could I expect Planned Parenthood to move? First, there was the question of the board. Over the years of my tenure, it had evolved into a powerful voice for affiliate interests, and would certainly oppose an amendment campaign if the affiliates were against it, even if the board believed it was the right thing to do.

While I knew that affiliates were all deeply concerned about *Webster*, I doubted that this genuine concern would transform itself into a commitment to an amendment campaign. And without their support, we would have no mechanism at the local level to mobilize voters.

Nevertheless, we decided to test the waters. Knowing the August 1989 board meeting was coming up, we sent a paper out to the members, outlining the ramifications of the *Webster* decision, and broaching the possibility of building the political machinery that could eventually allow us to embark upon a successful amendment campaign.

However, instead of asking the board to consider approving a constitutional amendment campaign outright, I suggested that they might want to authorize a program that would strengthen Planned Parenthood as the kind of political force that David Garth had described. Maybe we needed to go beyond the limitations of our lobbying efforts; the time had come to become directly involved in electoral politics. In my heart, I doubted I could build a strong consensus for even this proposal. But without trying, I would never know, although I would be subject to the criticism that I was on yet another power trip for personal aggrandizement.

Even if, perchance, the ideas met with the board's approval, I knew from past experience that the strategy of the campaign itself was likely to become a bone of contention, and with enough affiliate pressure, the board would reverse itself. And there was also the danger that any proposal would get so tangled with limitations so "things don't get out of control," that it would never get off the ground. The power increasingly flowed from the affiliates and not the national board. Then I remembered Mama's refrain, "Nothing ventured, nothing gained." I had to keep trying to make progress, wherever I could.

A little more than a month after the Court had jolted women's rights, the thirty-five members of Planned Parenthood's national board assembled in New York City. Our board represented a range of philosophical viewpoints—its members were neither strictly conservative nor strictly liberal. I had no idea what their response would be to our discussion paper.

The windowless hotel ballroom we were meeting in felt like a bunker as we got right down to the issue on everyone's mind—the *Webster* decision and what our response should be.

Eve Paul explained the details of the Supreme Court's decision. We discussed the possible motivations for each of the justices' opinions, the possible outcomes of the cases challenging every aspect of *Roe* that were still in the judicial pipeline, and the health of the jurists remaining on the progressive flank of the Court. Then the board turned to the subject of how we should address *Webster*.

Lydia Neumann, the vice president for public affairs, outlined a strategy that could ultimately get a constitutional amendment passed, though, she said, we were not recommending that Planned Parenthood commit to such a goal. Building state-by-state organizations through non-tax-deductible organizations would give us the ability to conduct significantly more lobbying and to get involved in endorsing and opposing candidates.

The board discussion of the constitutional issues that we presented spanned beyond our organizational issues. The members reported significant interest in their communities in stopping the momentum of legislatures and the Court. To my surprise, they were actually interested in discussing the idea of a constitutional amendment. There were, however, strong reservations about it. They worried about the danger that we'd end up dividing our ranks over partisan issues. And some were concerned about the tremendous challenges of reaching the two-thirds mandated level of consensus required for the would-be amendment to pass Congress. Others worried that if we did not produce a credible offensive, Planned Parenthood's image would be damaged.

Still others felt that the ambiguities in the Constitution should be preserved, as they played to our favor in that the Constitution could be interpreted broadly. "I think that the United States has the most remarkable constitution in the world—it doesn't have a lot of amendments to it," a college professor from California asserted. "I see the proposal as a fix, but I'm not sure. I like some ambiguity in the Constitution. I think it gives me more rights than a constitution that spells out every right I have."

I pointed out that the pro-criminalists in Congress and the strongly right-leaning Court were now using ambiguities to give states the power to decide in favor of increasing restrictions.

Then there were the usual internal concerns. Some worried that such an undertaking could divert Planned Parenthood from our service delivery mission; others that it might in some way affect our financial support among people not happy about our getting involved in partisan politics or attempting to tamper with the Constitution. If our activities were not carefully separated, such an operation might cost us our 501(c)(3) status. Would we be able to go it alone—would we be able to get other pro-choice organizations to collaborate with us? We would have to dedicate substantial resources over a lengthy period of victories and defeats to create a prospect of success. Did we have the staying power to make a credible campaign while fighting battles on so many other fronts?

A lawyer from Montana cautioned that we shouldn't rush to judgment about what was impossible. "After all," he said, "the conventional wisdom that a Supreme Court nominee couldn't be blocked on philosophical grounds was disproved by the Bork defeat. Perhaps a constitutional amendment *could* get passed."

As I listened to the discussion, I reflected on the march that had been called earlier in the spring, when NOW had not asked for a consensus before staking a public position. We had no choice but to join in, albeit reluctantly, if we didn't want the pro-choice side to be tagged as divided and weak. But that gathering couldn't begin to compare in scale with a constitutional amendment campaign. However, it did demonstrate how individuals and organizations, initially reluctant to an idea, could be brought together if shown a vision of how it could succeed, and that others were determined to make the effort.

After well over an hour's debate, the still-dubious board authorized the board chairperson, Anne Saunier, and me to consider their concerns and to make a recommendation about a constitutional amendment campaign. Our proposal was to be mailed to them before the board meeting that immediately preceded the annual convention. Then they would decide their position on the matter.

In the months between the August board meeting and the annual convention, Eve and her staff convened a council of law scholars, including Walter Dellinger, Laurence Tribe, and Harriet Pilpel, to analyze the requirements for framing a constitutional response to the *Webster* decision. They were less than enthusiastic about the idea. And they were more than a little skeptical about coming up with language for an amendment that might have a prayer of being passed by Congress without amendments that could make the situation even worse, and that would also gain sufficiently strong approval of the whole pro-choice movement. My worst fears already seemed to be materializing: Even our allies were acquiescing to the loss, reserved in their commitment to fight back.

A month before the annual meeting, the board reconvened. By then the members' inclination on the constitutional amendment issue was even less enthusiastic than that of the lawyers. As a result, the proposal we sent to the affiliates was a carefully worded document that deliberately avoided that now frightening word *amendment*, and resolved to direct our efforts toward securing the "constitutional protections" of reproductive rights. We could do this through lawsuits, legislative battles, and eventually by entering the electoral process on a limited basis. My passion to act decisively was frustrated. But I was neither surprised nor greatly troubled by the board's ultimate indecision. We weren't disagreeing over our principles; rather, we had different perspectives on the urgency of the dangers to women and what to do about it.

Soon enough, the affiliates would give us face-to-face their views on our position.

What always restored my energy and perspective were family occasions and the holidays. Just as Felicia's birth had occurred during a Planned Parenthood annual meeting, which always took place in the autumn, so her birthday often fell that same week. I always felt guilty about being away from home then. But, trying to reassure my daughter how much her birthday meant to me, I invested special effort in the celebrations, which I usually arranged to unfold the week before Felicia's birthday.

Amid the preparations for the most important event of the year in the life of Planned Parenthood and the stress that it brought, I also sorted out the details for her most important event of the year and the joy that it brought. I made reservations at the place of her choice—whether a party room where a clown would twist balloons into animal shapes and paint the faces of Felicia and her friends, or, when she was ten, the Hard Rock Cafe. I'd send out invitations, get the cake, and assemble what often seemed to be the most important item of the event—festive-looking bags of party favors. Sometimes I'd find myself feeling like a rubber band come the middle of October, but there was nothing like the pleasure of seeing Felicia blow out

378 / Life on the Line

the candles as her friends all sang "Happy Birthday." Or, in the case of the Hard Rock Cafe, hearing the entire room join in.

And as soon as I returned from the meeting, Halloween was upon us. We usually found the makings for Felicia's costumes in my closet or at the five-and-dime store. Inspiration came from the cultural icons of the moment: Her Tina Turner year—with a big blond wig, heavy makeup, short black leather skirt, black fishnet stockings, and black high heels—was my favorite. Then there were themes inspired by life in New York City. One year she went as a bag lady, using Tina's blond wig, transformed from glamour to scraggliness by large hair rollers tangled through its masses. She'd found an old bathrobe of mine, and finagled her father's favorite pair of worn Stan Smith sneakers. Baggy stockings and an oversized old overcoat completed her costume. Dragging a shopping cart behind her, she took off for her trick-or-treat rounds in our apartment building.

After Halloween comes Thanksgiving, our favorite holiday. Even as a small child, Felicia relished joining me in shopping for the groceries and accessories that would transform our living room into a dining room of two or three rented round tables that we decorated with linen cloths, flowers, and the china that I seemed to use only once a year. Our home, opened to at least a dozen friends, sometimes to as many as twenty-five, became an echo of my childhood when friends and relatives from down south had converged on 1241 Walton. Mama would sometimes come up from Atlanta, and my friend Sarah often flew in from Ohio.

The night before, and well into the early-morning hours of the big day itself, the preparations went on: chopping vegetables for the cornbread-and-oyster dressing; washing green beans, spinach, and chard; boiling sweet potatoes for Felicia's favorite marshmallow-and-potato balls; and grinding fresh cranberries, oranges, and walnuts into relish. It had all seemed so simple to do at the outset of the evening, but as the hours wore on, a sense that all this fun *could* become drudgery would set in.

Felicia and I would wake early on Thanksgiving morning. After putting the fresh turkey into the oven and preparing the yeast dough for my once-a-year, never-fail homemade rolls, we'd head to the Planned Parenthood offices, which offered an unobstructed view of the Macy's Thanksgiving Day Parade. We loved watching the giant balloons as they floated down from the height of the windows on Broadway. Afterward, we'd make one quick stop at the Little Pie Company to pick up Felicia's favorite sour cream apple-walnut pies for dessert, and then it was back home to the mad flurry of last-minute table setting, candle lighting, and figuring out the logistics of getting every dish out of the oven and onto the table perfectly done and piping hot—although I have yet to succeed in doing this. By the middle of the afternoon the friends would begin to arrive, and our home would fill with the laughter and good cheer that always more than validated our labors of love.

As the intensities of the Planned Parenthood battles grew, my workdays routinely stretched to fill twelve and thirteen hours—each day a dizzying whirl of meetings, memos and letters, budget balancing, and interviews. Those moments when I completely put aside the stress of it all and savored a family life became my lifeline and recharged me emotionally. Aside from my work, my life was dedicated to Felicia. After the most wretched days, hearing her "Hi, Mommy!" as I walked in the door washed away my troubles in purest joy.

By the late 1980s, I had come to dread the fall of every year and the Planned Parenthood convention that it always brought with it. I gladly carried out my usual responsibilities—managing the day-to-day operations of the organization, making three to four speeches each month and regular media appearances on the latest controversy in Congress or the Supreme Court, and overseeing the preparations for the meeting of over a thousand participants. These tasks in themselves, and their incumbent anxieties, I willingly accepted as part of my job as president. But with each passing year, I was finding it harder and harder to accept the knot of unease that grew steadily in the pit of my stomach from Labor Day until the convention in late October or early November.

The primary purpose of the annual meeting has always been to provide the opportunity for the discussion of common interests and to honor those whose contributions were in keeping with our mission. However, by the late Eighties, it had come to serve more and more as a forum for the airing of the affiliates' grievances against the national organization. I suspected that the 1989 meeting would be as contentious as any I'd ever attended.

As the delegates gathered at the sprawling Town & Country Hotel in San Diego, the lush tropical vegetation and swaying palms could hardly soothe the emotionally charged atmosphere. Anne Saunier, who had been a strong, uncompromising voice for reform, was handing over the gavel to Ken Edelin. In the midst of all that was shifting, I yearned for continuity wherever it could be found, including the chair. *The Boston Globe* had this to offer upon Ken's election: "Board members and others who know both Edelin and Wattleton . . . wonder how two people with such robust egos will get along over the long term."[15]

I had high regard for Ken. He had become a powerhouse in the prochoice movement following the tragic persecution he'd suffered in 1973 when, as a young resident in obstetrics and gynecology at Boston City Hospital, Ken had performed a second-trimester abortion on a seventeen-year-old girl. Although *Roe v. Wade* had been decided, his actions placed him in the path of a vindictive city attorney and the budding backlash to *Roe*.

During an investigation, it was discovered that in attempting to perform an abortion, Ken had opened the uterus to remove the fetus after saline injections failed to cause contractions. Ken's accusers asserted that the fetus had been legally "born," and that he should have saved it. He was charged with manslaughter.

Ken was put on trial in January 1975. Assistant District Attorney Newman Flanagan argued that the "baby boy" was born when Dr. Edelin detached the placenta from the uterine wall. Ken's defense argued that the young physician had performed a legal abortion protected by the 1973 Supreme Court decision. Although he was found guilty as charged, the Supreme Judicial Court of Massachusetts eventually overturned the conviction.

My heart had gone out to the handsome, somber-faced physician as, night after night in Dayton, I'd followed the national news coverage of the trial. Long before I met him, I had admired Ken and his courage and personal sacrifice for women. As a board member, he'd always been a strong supporter of my endeavors. I looked forward to working with him—although, truthfully, at this moment I would have appreciated not having a changing of the guard, no matter who it was.

On the floor of plenary sessions, affiliates voiced their fears that our proposal, especially electoral involvement, would threaten their community support, and that any grand scheme was impossible to tackle successfully. They saw it as a Trojan horse from which a constitutional amendment would surely pour out. I made no attempt to conceal my ultimate vision. Neither was I unclear about my authority in the organization. If they didn't want the organization to go forward, I could not defy such restraint. And yet, they did not trust my words and my motives. Perhaps the power of my burgeoning visibility after *Webster* was handed down increased their anxieties. Whatever the cause, a lack of faith in a leader's integrity seriously undermines the ability to lead effectively.

Some of the sentiment was driven by the fear the dramatically altered ground rules had provoked, and I was urging that we couldn't just let it be, that we had to act, and act boldly. I had become a lightning rod, attracting the anger over the endless battles, the fears of what the future held, and the frustrations at my refusal to accommodate the situation in a gentle manner.

The hallways buzzed as delegates debated my motives as they imagined them to be. The most frequently raised of these was that my need for personal glory took precedence over the interests of the organization. Such an indictment would have been wrenching had I not known in my heart how totally wrong they were. I'm human, and I might have a vain nerve in my body. In fact, I have a lot of them. But the thousands of miles I had traveled each year, the media exposure, the honorary degrees, and myriad other awards had more than fulfilled any vainglorious needs I might have harbored. For me, this was purely and simply about women and making certain that their rights were safeguarded. Why else would I risk their thinking I'd "lost it"? Why else would I be willing to put myself at great risk of failure, at greater risk of physical harm, and at even greater risk of weakening my role within Planned Parenthood? Why else would I have made such enormous personal sacrifices? Truly, it would not have mattered to me who led the campaign, so long as the protections that needed to be built were built.

In the end, despite the resistance, we made some progress. The membership voted to appoint a task force to study the options for "securing constitutional protections" of reproductive rights. They were even willing to investigate entering electoral politics by setting up a 501(c)(4), which would also allow us to expand our lobbying activities—the very idea that had caused a small riot when David Garth had proposed it ten years earlier.

There would be a special membership meeting in the spring to decide on our next moves.

As at every annual meeting, everyone who cared to had their say. They'd made their arguments and placed their votes, and could return home content that the necessary controls on the national organization had been put back in place and reinforced. I found myself more than a little worn down by the sheer weight of process and dissension. Yes, we'd made progress, but as a colleague would later say to me, "I know how you feel. Although you win the battles, you simply get tired of having them."

CHAPTER 31

REBUILDING THE
RIGHT TO CHOOSE

By the late summer of 1989, with the new Bush administration now hitting its stride and with every evidence that things were only going to get worse for reproductive rights believers, NOW called for another march in Washington. Buoyed by the success of the April demonstration and deeply disturbed, as we all were, about the *Webster* decision, this time they targeted Sunday, November 12, as the day of action. Again, they'd made the announcement without consultation—but this time, most of us in the pro-choice coalition wouldn't go along. We wouldn't agree to march down Constitution Avenue, when the Court had turned so much power back to the states. Besides, we couldn't hope for the turnout we'd achieved at the April march a few months earlier; and a significantly smaller crowd would be interpreted as evidence of a sense of discouragement within the movement.

We were in one of our coalition meetings. Kate Michelman, from NARAL, was presiding. The atmosphere in the room was enormously strained. Some agreed with NOW, but an inclination to capitulate to their latest announcement was not in evidence among the majority. *Webster* had changed our world. We couldn't simply continue as before—not even in the way we protested.

"Remember Vietnam?" Ellie Smeal appealed, more toward those who were engaged in the peace movement, twenty years earlier, than to the rest of us. "We marched and marched until the war was ended."

Bella Abzug turned to her longtime colleague, Molly Yard, and pointed out: "You know, we had to get out into the states to get anywhere with ERA."

We didn't want to undermine NOW, and didn't want to end the day in utter disunity. So we hammered out another compromise. We would spread out all over the country to support smaller simultaneous rallies in major cities. If we pulled this off, it would display a nationwide opposition to the Supreme Court's ruling, while demonstrating support for the preservation of reproductive rights. NOW could organize the Washington march; the rest of us would work within our organizations and together to plan demonstrations in different cities—all on the same Sunday. Calling it "Mobilize for Women's Lives," we appealed to our donors for extra money to help support the local organizers' efforts and to defray our costs.

Doug Gould plotted an itinerary that called for me to cover four rallies coast to coast—on the same day. When I first took a look at it, I thought that he had lost his mind.

"The only way we can get this done," he admitted, "is to rent a private jet, saving the waiting time at airports and not being locked into airline schedules."

"What about my ability to hold on to my coherence?" I challenged him, half seriously.

Given my previous experiences in small planes, I was less than thrilled at the prospect. Nevertheless, I didn't have much of a choice if I wanted to get from Kennebunk, Maine, to New Orleans, to Austin, Texas, to Los Angeles, all in one day.

On November 11, the night before the scheduled events, Felicia, Doug, several members of his staff, media representatives, actress Polly Bergen, and I boarded a privately chartered jet and flew up the coastline to Portland, Maine, arriving around midnight. An ABC News crew, reporters from *Glamour* magazine, and the Pacifica Radio network would be with us for the entire day.

In Portland, a caravan of cars was waiting to take us to Kennebunk—the location of a key rally of the day, only a couple of miles from George Bush's summer home. The location, well covered by the media and visibly associated with the president, would convey a strong message of who was responsible for a federal court system that was dismantling *Roe v. Wade*.

A candlelight vigil was scheduled for six o'clock the next morning. "We have to be out by five-thirty," I reminded Felicia as I switched off the light in our motel room.

Rousing her did not prove difficult. Knowing that the television crew would come to our room to start filming at that early hour was a powerful internal wake-up alarm for both of us. Trailed by the crew and their apparatus in the chilly darkness, we headed for the First Parish Unitarian Church in Kennebunk for the candlelight vigil. Giant maples lined the streets, and the ground was carpeted with a profusion of bronze, gold, and vivid yellow leaves. With the white frame homes and steepled churches, it was as though we were entering a New England scene from a Norman Rockwell painting.

As we approached, I could see that the churchyard was already filled with hundreds of people. A long line of cars waited to enter the parking lot, and people afoot streamed toward the stately white frame building. By the time Sherri Huber, of the Maine legislature, Polly Bergen, Kate Michelman, and I stepped out onto the back porch of the church social hall, where we would be giving our speeches, nearly 2,500 people had gathered, each holding a small, white, lighted candle. The dramatic impact of all those small flames illuminating our faces against the first hints of dawn sent goose bumps up my arms.

"We hold our candles to banish the darkness, and what better place to begin than on our president's back porch," I reminded the crowd. Polly, Kate, and Sherri spoke of our determination to bring a thousand points of light to end the darkness of ignorance, intolerance, and oppression. As the sun began to rise, we entered the sanctuary of the church, where the press lined the back wall. Sound systems amplified our speeches into outer rooms filled with people who could not get into the packed sanctuary.

Polly stepped up to the microphone. To a hushed audience, she spoke of walking down a dark street forty years before, up some stairs, down a dark hallway, through a door, and into a dark room where she risked her life to end an unwanted pregnancy. She told of the wrenching pain as the contents of her uterus were removed. She told of the infection and of her subsequent sterility—she would never be able to bear a child. There were more than a few wet eyes when Polly finished telling why she felt she had to do everything in her power to save other women from such fear and such a fate. After Polly, Kate began to turn the hushed atmosphere of the room into applause and cheers.

When it was my turn, I said:

The Webster decision invited states to invade our most personal and private decisions, to ignore our needs, to put fetuses first. This is no fresh breeze of freedom! This is a piercing gust of oppression.

Compulsory pregnancy, forced cesarean sections, surveillance and detention of pregnant women—these are not fiction! These are chilling, logical outcomes that protect fetuses at the expense of women—laws that reduce women to instruments of the state. . . .

Let us remember the words of one of our most inspired and noble leaders, Elie Wiesel . . . "What hurts the victim most is not the cruelty of the oppressor, but the silence of the bystander."

Let us shape our lives by that credo, and let us never abandon our commitment to the vulnerable and voiceless.[1]

When the speeches ended, I was scheduled for an on-camera interview with Maria Shriver for *NBC Sunday Morning*. The hundreds of attendees inside the church had to remain silent as the large open space became a sound studio.

Peering into the lens of the camera, I felt disconnected from the anchorwoman, who was speaking to me from New York through the small earphone in my right ear. I saw only my own reflection in the dark glass circle.

After the interview ended, we headed to the airport and immediately took off for New Orleans. The fifteen thousand marchers who had gathered in the brilliant, hot southern sun under the giant oaks of Pontchartrain Park were ringed by a noisy group of counterdemonstrators carrying placards condemning us for murder, their chants amplified by a small megaphone carried by a man who seemed to be their leader. But the melodic voices of the gospel singers for whom New Orleans is so justly famous rose in spiritual counterpoint and lent the pro-choice rally the hallowedness of a church camp meeting.

As I headed to the stage, Terri Bartlett, executive director of Planned Parenthood of Louisiana, greeted me with the warmth of her honey-sweet southern accent; the sound of it pulled me back to the days of my childhood in Franklin, Louisiana, ninety miles south of New Orleans. Then, it was the white women on the street and in the stores who greeted each other with "How y'all doing?" On this day, black and white together demonstrated in common purpose against oppression of (in some theories) another kind. My speech built upon the one I had given in Kennebunk:

> It's about time politicians stopped pandering to an extremist fringe. To "save lives," zealots burn clinics. To "defend womanhood," they threaten and taunt pregnant women who enter clinics. To "help" teenagers, they trick them with phony promises and indoctrination centers that masquerade as health clinics.
>
> Operation Rescue is the guerrilla faction of the antiabortion movement. Despite their claims to the contrary, their only resemblance to the civil rights struggle is their resemblance to the Ku Klux Klan—a similar blot on our nation's history . . .[2]

Amid applause and cheers, and signs lofting messages like "Keep Abortion Legal," "Mobilize for Women's Lives," "Motherhood by Choice, Not by Chance," and "Pro Choice is Pro Child," we were once again headed for the airport and were soon in flight to Austin, Texas.

I tried taking short naps during each lap of the trip. The grinding pace was starting to wear me down, and I had to make it through Los Angeles. When we landed in Austin, I headed for the ladies' room at the private airport to steam my crumpled purple suit and freshen my makeup. When I walked into the vaulted halls of the capitol building the crowd outside had begun to dwindle from its peak of 15,000 people. As I approached the speakers' platform on the terrace overlooking the capitol grounds, Ann Richards, who would be the next governor of the state, ran toward me with arms extended and embraced me as she said, "We're *so* glad you're in Texas."

I'd arrived just as Jim Hightower, then Texas's cowboy-booted secretary of state, was finishing his speech to applause and cheers from the crowd.

I walked out to the stage just as it was my turn to speak:

> How much longer must the pro-choice majority endure the tyranny of an extremist minority? . . .
>
> For too long, pro-choice voters have given politicians a free ride, because we didn't want to be labeled "single-issue voters."
>
> But we are proud to be "single-issue" if our single issue is saving the lives of women—if our single issue is guaranteeing that every child is a wanted child—if our single issue is rejecting the cynical manipulation of politicians who ignore our needs and then count our votes! We will be single-issue voters from now on.[3]

The crowd cheered robustly at the last line.

By the time I climbed the narrow sling steps into the silver aircraft, I was beginning to feel as though I couldn't think. Fatigue washed over me, but it didn't squelch my excitement over encountering so many thousands of people across the country that day who were determined not to let women lose their right to reproductive choice. I hoped that my colleagues were encountering similar enthusiasm—in New York; Washington, D.C.; Chicago; Milwaukee; Jefferson City, Missouri; Lincoln, Nebraska; Laramie, Wyoming; Miami; Portland, Oregon; and San Francisco, among other cities. The thought of it filled me with pride. The press would later report that a thousand "Mobilize for Women's Lives" events were held in more than 150 cities.

Thrilling though the April rally in Washington had been, there was something even more exhilarating about meeting people where they lived. Surely it touched upon my long-submerged memories of the revival and camp meeting circuits. It was as if my life had come full circle. "This is what it's all about," I kept saying to Felicia. "Ordinary people all over the country."

The day ended with a reception for Hollywood supporters in the cavernous lobby of the Creative Artists Agency. We had been unable to get there in time for the rally; but Bella Abzug had made it, flying down from Seattle. Before the reception, Felicia and I checked into our hotel room, and I collapsed onto the bed the moment we walked in. It seemed that I'd been asleep five minutes when Felicia roused me an hour later, telling me: "Mommy, wake up. It's time to get ready."

Within minutes we were whisked off to a gathering in a community where image and industry are one and the same, and in a state whose governor had provoked outrage when he'd made large cuts in the state's family-planning program.

For me, the evening's reception passed as in a hazy dream. Fifty thousand people had turned out for the Los Angeles event. It was the largest pro-choice rally in the history of the city, and was said to have caused "worse-than-usual" traffic tie-ups.

The memory of the lusty cheers of 2,500 hearty Maine pro-choice supporters that had opened our day linked itself in my mind to the mellow company of the California pro-choice supporters, Jeff Bridges, Polly Bergen, and Michael Milken among them. It was my last speech of the day. I could barely think, let alone speak. *How do political candidates do this day in and day out?* I asked myself. I condemned the acts of the anti-choice governor for cutting funding for family planning, and urged all present to use their power and influence on behalf of women, to stop his regressive politics.

By the time we returned to the hotel, Doug had spoken with various contacts around the country. I may have been tired to the bone, but the reports that in every city the crowds had exceeded expectations made me excited all over again. The crowd in Washington had stretched from the Lincoln Memorial to the Washington Monument and was estimated at over two hundred thousand supporters. NOW had been right—people every-where wanted to march! They were stirred by the threats to reproductive rights. Maybe, I thought, finding the energy and commitment for a national political movement to ensure reproductive rights in the Constitution wasn't impossible.

The highs of our day of triumph contrasted sharply with increasing evi-dence that our fears about the Bush administration were materializing. Before I'd left for that big day of flying and rallies, Marcy, my secretary, informed me that Dr. Koop was on the line. I greeted him as an old colleague.

"Faye," he said in his to-the-point, no-nonsense, country doctor tone, "I'm coming up to New York and I'd like to meet with you."

He gave no clue to what was on his mind, but it wasn't hard to imagine that, having failed to endorse the Reagan/Bush political agenda on both abortion and AIDS, he had fallen out of favor. "I have a meeting scheduled at my lawyer's office to work on the contract for my book," he said. "I think it would be best for you to meet me there." Unspoken was the message that even though he was reaching out to me as a professional colleague, he didn't want to be seen coming out of Planned Parenthood's offices.

In the quiet privacy of the law firm's empty conference room, I sat across the table from the man who had given greater prominence to his office than any other since the Surgeon General's Report on Smoking in 1964, and who had earned the respect of most Americans, even those who didn't share his point of view.

"You know, Faye, I have grown to respect you as someone who believes deeply in your cause, and carries out your work with dignity and reason. But you must understand: The reason that I do not feel the same way you do about abortion is that I've spent my professional life treating and saving the lives of babies. I cannot believe that abortion is an acceptable practice."

For the first time ever, I was able to say to an abortion opponent, one of the most visible abortion opponents in America, that I respected his work as a pediatric surgeon and as surgeon general, as well. And I added, "My views are also based on my life's work. I've spent my career serving women, and I can't forget those who have been injured and killed as the result of illegal abortion."

Our views, forged in our dedication to health, were irreconcilable, but we could meet on the common ground of understanding.

"The reason I wanted to meet with you," Dr. Koop continued, "is to tell you that I'm going to be leaving the Bush administration before my term as surgeon general is over. I wanted you to know about it before it was announced in the press."

There had been rumors, so I was not surprised by his announcement, but still, his words jolted me.

"The simple indignities that I am going through are intolerable," he said, and went on to describe the cancellation of his reserved parking place and dining room privileges. "These are small things, but I know it's time to go." Dignified, but with the quiet sadness of humiliation, he told me, "We're negotiating acceptable terms for my pension. As soon as that's done, I'll go."

I found myself wondering whether the day would come when I would reach the same conclusion about life within Planned Parenthood. With each battle, I had become more convinced than ever that we were fighting for something larger than reproductive rights—that the larger struggle was over women's power. The leverage being used to oppress us today was reproduction, just as it had been in Margaret Sanger's time. As the assaults on women grew more cynical, more inhumane, we could little afford the costs of internal organizational strife, and yet it seemed to be growing. And my endurance, like Dr. Koop's, was waning.

From the days just after the announcement of my appointment as president of Planned Parenthood to the day I resigned, I was increasingly frustrated by the carping of those who would have done things differently. As the organization's visibility and credibility grew more prominent, the attempts to stifle my leadership seemed to escalate.

My staff and supporters would say, "Just ignore them," but I felt pained and exasperated. The hostility took a quantum leap in 1989, a watershed year for reproductive rights—the year of the march; of *Webster*; of the cross-country barnstorming, the year the media began what seemed like relentless coverage. My increased prominence as a spokesperson exacerbated the fears within Planned Parenthood that I would say or do something that would spur further opposition toward our work or "paint us in a corner."

My frustration was hardly eased by my certainty that had I been white and male, I would have been lauded by my own or at the very least been charged far less often with being "out of control" or "too strong" or "unable to understand affiliates' needs." Certainly I would never have been undermined by false comments like "The board set aside a slush fund for her clothes."

I didn't concern myself too much with the questions about my competence. While I had harbored self-doubts about ascending to positions of greater responsibility, once in them, I never doubted my ability to rise to the challenges of the work to be done. My itinerant childhood had educated me in meeting new and unpredictable circumstances and finding the fortitude to survive them, one after another, with a lesson learned.

Furthermore, according to the benchmarks of success, we were thriving—despite *Webster* and because of it. Public support for our philosophy and our work had never been stronger: The numbers of our national donor list grew from 85,000 individuals in 1978 to 365,000 in 1989. (The one-million mark would be achieved in 1991.) The aggregate budget for the headquarters and affiliates grew from $116.7 million in 1978 to $331.5 million in 1989; and $50.9 million of that amount was the headquarters budget, which in turn included all expenses of the international program. The national staff now included over 200 people who worked in New York, Washington, D.C., and in three domestic and three international offices. Affiliates were providing education and medical services to nearly four million people. Despite the cutoff of funding from the Agency for International Development, our international programs were reaching 625,000 more women in the developing world than in 1978.

In the beginning, I had vigorously debated with those who challenged me on how I ran the organization or what I said publicly in articulating our mission. But now, I would listen quietly, even impassively, to the complaints and the resistance to my proposals for moving the organization forward. I would try to answer the challenges as they came—but I felt less bothered by them. A part of me had simply accepted that no matter what I did, I would never be allowed the pleasure of the organization's unified backing.

Over the years, I wondered whether the objections had to do with my being an African American woman, but I never could convince myself that this was the case, so much as it was my refusal to compromise on the principles of the organization. When those principles collided with funding—as our enemies made sure that they did over and over—the tensions grew between us. As my board became more sensitive to affiliate pressures, even those who strongly supported me muted their praise. But even in the increasingly heated cauldron of resistance, I believed that we had to remain true to our beliefs and if we did so, the support would flow to us.

The basis for my longevity was first and foremost my talented, stable, hardworking, and loyal staff. My executive staff, some of them already in position when I arrived, became a surrogate family. We rarely socialized outside the office, but during the workweek, the synergy of our teamwork was remarkable. Had that not been the case, I would not have had the longest tenure of all of Planned Parenthood's presidents.

I had also enjoyed positive relationships with all the chairs of the board, from Tenny Marshall to Ken Edelin. Jean Mahoney, Allan Rosenfield, and Anne Saunier filled in an unbroken band of supporters. None, however, had guided me quite so much as Fred Smith. I longingly recalled one of Fred's stated beliefs: "One of the key roles of the board is to protect the CEO, so that she can do her job."

Nevertheless, the vocal opponents within the organization were no less effective than the zealots battering us from the outside.

Around 1987, I'd been asked not to attend nominating committee meetings of the national board. "You have too much influence on board decisions," I was told. So at the beginning of that committee's meetings, I would make a brief presentation on the skills that I felt the board needed, and was then excused from the deliberations. It was inevitable that the distance between me and the board would grow, since each new member was usually a stranger to me when they joined.

As for the affiliates, while most were supportive, more than a few among them charged that I was unresponsive to their concerns. Having come to the presidency after being an affiliate executive director, I'd had a pretty clear sense of what their needs were, and I'd made every effort to meet them. Soon after my appointment, I created a new division whose sole purpose was to address affiliate concerns and to develop programs to help them.

And much in the fashion of my mother, who believed it her duty to accept every invitation to speak that came her way, I felt obliged to honor the invitations of the affiliates, no matter how small the installation or how difficult it was to reach. I didn't want to lose touch with "real life" as the affiliates were experiencing it, and I incorporated their requests into my schedule, even when those occasions so often took me away from my most important responsibility—my daughter. Only when invitations interfered with weekends or Felicia's school holidays did I decline them. Twenty to thirty times a year I'd rise at dawn to throw a few things into a suitcase, creep into my slumbering daughter's room, kiss her good-bye, and be out the door to catch a seven o'clock flight. That way I could keep commitments for luncheon speeches or be interviewed by the media (or sometimes do both), be it in Odessa, Texas; Chicago, Illinois; or San Francisco, California.

The irony of the tensions between the national office and the local organization was that the national fights were almost always made on behalf of the affiliates' needs. Whether fighting for Title X, or against the squeal rule, the gag rule, and clinic violence, we were involved mostly to ensure that the affiliates could continue to serve women. But at the heart of all the affiliate resistance toward me was my role as the head of a large, decentralized organization and my views on our role as a liberation movement.

The philosophical differences between those who believed, as I did, that Planned Parenthood was above all else a movement for the sexual and reproductive liberation of women and men, and those who believed that Planned Parenthood was foremost a business, came into sharper focus under the threat of our losing federal funding.

I understood that our public battles had often left us vulnerable in any number of ways, from government funding to destruction of our facilities. But I also believed that the most dangerous thing we could do was to shrink from our commitment.

Planned Parenthood was probably no worse than any other dysfunctional family; none of us forthrightly acknowledged that differences in philosophy existed among us. Thus, instead of being aimed at my philosophy, the criticism focused on me personally. I was said to be aloof because I didn't "hang out" with executive directors and board members at meetings. It was just that after long hours of negotiating myself and the organization through external challenges and internal conflicts, after consulting with my staff to manage the controversies of the moment, after sitting in meetings all day, absorbing all that I was hearing, and thinking about how my leadership could be more effective, after shaking hands, hugging friends and enemies alike, and "just trying to be gracious" (Mama's words)—I would head straight off to bed at the end of the day to get some rest so that I could do my best to meet everyone's needs and wishes for more personal contact over our early-morning breakfasts.

Around this time, one executive said to me, quite matter-of-factly and without rancor, "You know, you're really bigger than the organization now." Although I believed that she intended no offense, I was taken aback by her assessment. I felt that I was the person I'd always been, working twelve- to fourteen-hour days with one agenda—to see that the organization succeeded. In my heart, I felt as much devoted to Planned Parenthood as ever; yet something was pulling me toward a broader meaning for the federation.

Our public affirmation in 1989, through the two marching campaigns, played a large part in my will to continue in the face of such resistance and isolation. And so, I think, did my sheer determination and stubbornness. I came to understand as never before the words of David Garth's colleague Judy Brenner, who advised me that "a high public profile will protect you from your enemies within the organization."

The anxiety I felt about my sense of growing estrangement from Planned Parenthood was tempered by the enduring love and joy of Felicia. She was growing up and blossoming into an independent person in her own right. The occasions where we could spend long periods alone together were becoming fewer and farther between; but those times that we could arrange became my islands of respite and renewal. Whether we were suspended on the seat of a chairlift together or rocking in the small cabin of a sailboat in the waters around the Galapagos Islands, I found deep satisfaction in her unconditional love. Watching her grow up to be a person that I would like to have as a close friend was sheer joy. The consistency of her presence in my life centered me emotionally and gave all that I was doing a special purpose.

CHAPTER 32

RESISTING THE GAG

While the rights of women had been seriously compromised by the Court's decision in *Webster* in 1989, as the Eighties gave way to the Nineties, the erosion of women's reproductive rights picked up momentum in the United States and throughout the world. While we fought President Reagan's executive order to restrict speech in Title X clinics at home, we continued to fight the battle against the restriction of speech in AID-funded clinics abroad.

In March 1990, just over two years after he'd been ordered to reconsider Planned Parenthood's challenge to the constitutionality of the Mexico City Policy, Judge John Walker, of the Federal District Court in New York City, again dismissed our lawsuit, this time finding the policy "within the statutory and constitutional power of the government."[1] The U.S. government could disassociate its funding from any foreign group of its choosing that was involved with abortion.

We had not expected the federal judge to rule otherwise. But neither time nor other battles had diminished our commitment to defending women in developing nations from the policy. And we were determined never to conspire with the government to increase the number of women dying each year in less developed countries by forcing the organizations with whom we worked to deny them information and help. How could we oppress women by enforcing abroad restrictions that we believed were wrong and unconstitutional in our own country? How could we claim adherence to the principles of informed choice if we denied women the information to make their own decisions? How could we implement a policy that we knew would cost women their lives?

The Second Circuit Court of Appeals granted our request to hear our case quickly. On August 30, 1990, we received a letter from the Agency for International Development telling us that it had concluded we would not prevail in our legal battle and thus it was ending our agreement of almost twenty years, effective October 31, 1990.

Two weeks later AID's assumption proved to be on target. The three-judge panel rejected our appeal, deciding that the policy did not violate our First Amendment rights, because it stated that Planned Parenthood could use its own funds to establish "an abortion-related facility next door."[2]

But the judges had failed to understand that the Mexico City Policy had explicitly prohibited referrals. Not only could a foreign clinic not give a woman any information about abortion, but it couldn't even tell her where she *could* go to get information. This censorship became an obstacle that kept women from getting to that facility "next door."

Our only hope lay in an appeal to the Supreme Court. We also asked the appeals court to order AID to continue funding us, according to our old agreement, until it had reviewed our lawsuit. On October 29, 1990, our request was denied, and two days later our funds were officially stopped. Despite our publicity and lobbying efforts, Congress had not come through and nullified the policy, and we'd run out of judicial options. Still, the lives of women in the developing world compelled us to keep trying. On January 17, 1991, we filed a petition with the High Court, asking it to review the Second Circuit Court's denial of our request for a review of our appeal.

I still remember June 3, 1991, the day Eve and Dan came to my office to tell me that our request had been denied. We all sat silent, numb with disbelief. Until that moment, there had been a sliver of hope, but now, the Supreme Court had allowed the government to censor the words and actions that could save women's lives.

The end of AID funding did not mean the end of our international work, but we knew that it would take years to build the private philanthropy to match the heft of government largess. With private donations, we were able to continue serving over thirty projects, even though these were only a third of the 94 projects, serving over 1.2 million people, that we'd funded before the cutoff. By 1991 the program would rebound to fund 46 projects in 26 countries, with $5 million in private support.

The international family-planning organizations that agreed to the censorship had drawn upon that now-too-familiar rationalization that it would be better to serve many women with contraceptive services than to lose funding, and they negotiated with AID to receive the funds that had once come to us. When I encountered them in a group or individually, I found it hard to remain civil toward them. I felt they'd accepted blood money. And I was still convinced that had all our organizations stood united against the Mexico City Policy, we would have had the leverage necessary to persuade Congress that the policy was unacceptably dangerous and that legislation reversing the policy was urgently needed.

"Congress is our last chance," Dan concluded. A change in Congress or the White House could turn things around. If we kept the issue alive, didn't let Congress conclude that it was all working out, we could keep the door from being locked.

In autumn 1991, anxious to learn firsthand the impact of Mexico City on our international work, I made my last journey to Asia as president of Planned Parenthood.

Arriving in Dhaka, Bangladesh, late at night, a little more than ten years after my first visit, I felt as though I was being introduced to the city for the first time. The cars and rickshaws still jockeyed with one another for a place on the crowded roadways, but this time the automobiles outnumbered the thin, muscular Bangladeshis who negotiated their three-wheeled cycles and vibrantly costumed human cargo through the thick traffic. And the thoroughfares themselves were now broad and continuous stretches of pavement rather than bumpy lanes broken by patches of gravel that had been left after disastrous typhoon flooding. Despite the restrictions on electrical power, the inky sky sparkled with the incandescent lights of newly constructed tall buildings. As for our accommodations, this time we stepped not into the dingy Sheraton, where we had stayed on our last visit, but into the glittering glass and marble pavilion of the Sonargaon Hotel, resplendent in plush hand-loomed carpets and bustling with Japanese and European businessmen. Tropical fruit and flowers drenched me with fragrance when I entered my frigidly air-conditioned room to rest from the day-long journey.

The morning after our arrival, we climbed into our eight-seater van and set off for Old Dhaka to visit Concerned Women for Family Planning, a program started by Mustafi Khan, whom I had met when she came to visit the affiliate in Dayton as part of our international management-training program. Because women were not allowed to leave their neighborhoods without their husbands, Concerned Women paid its family-planning workers a small income to distribute birth control information and supplies to women in their homes. In a decade, Concerned Women for Family Planning had grown from a few women, whose workers lived and distributed contraceptive information in the slums of Dhaka, into a thriving multi-centered social-service and economic-development organization. They had made a commercial enterprise of the training center by adding a store, a restaurant that employed women, and social-welfare and health programs.

Although we were no longer funding them, we'd kept them as our first stop. Their headquarters were now located near downtown Dhaka, and we found ourselves entering a compound of buildings rather than the old cramped and cluttered office. There we were greeted by the ever-gracious warmth of Mustafi Khan's smile.

"We had to promise AID that we wouldn't have anything to do with abortion or they would force us to give up our money," she told us as we sat down for tea and several of her colleagues joined us. "Since AID funds over 90 percent of our work, we had no choice. If we hadn't agreed we would have lost everything. We told AID that we would abide by the policy—but we still send women to safe services. What can we do?" Her manner showed less resignation than pragmatism. Though it was not said and we did not press the point, they had their ways of serving women. In Bangladesh, abortion performed in the first ten weeks of pregnancy was not prosecuted by the government.

The livelihood of Concerned Women depended on its yearly $510,000 from the U.S. government—a tremendous boon to a country where the average person's annual income was less than $200. We listened as the women told of their struggles, their dark almond-shaped eyes flashing in anger and disgust at the limitations that endangered them. An organization that had been in the forefront of legal reform in Bangladesh had been reduced to subterfuge.

The next day we met with the minister of health and family welfare, Chowdhury Kamal Ibne Yusuf. A large, dark-haired man snappily dressed in a light, cream-colored suit, the minister had been vocal among the several countries dependent on AID funding who had objected to the Mexico City regulations.

"Six thousand women die each year in Bangladesh, that we know about, as a result of illegal abortions. These are only the ones who come to the hospitals and clinics," he said sadly. "We don't know how many die in the fields and the rural areas."

Mr. Yusuf's statement chilled me, eliciting the horrible thought of a woman's suffering and dying for one reason—she was a woman in a poor country. But now our government had added another reason—the help that could have saved this woman was sacrificed on the altar of political ambition. I was angered and saddened by the thought that our government had succeeded in inflicting its pro-criminalist views upon women in any land, but especially in a country where so many women had so few options to avoid its mean-spirited purposes.

After our meeting with the minister, we set out on the part of these journeys I always liked best: making the rounds with the family-planning community workers in the crowded slums. These experiences of seeing, smelling, hearing, and touching deepened my knowledge of the conditions in which women lived their lives. If I ever felt any temptation to compromise, these visits strengthened my resolve.

As our van wound its way through the narrow roads lacing the sprawling ancient city, hardly a woman was to be seen. The few women we did see were mostly in purdah, wearing ankle-length black robes, their faces covered in black veils, as dictated by orthodox Islamic practice.

Our first stop was one of the Concerned Women's centers, where a group of about fifteen women who lived and worked in the area came to meet us. We asked them, "What do you tell women now when they want to end an unwanted pregnancy?"

The women looked embarrassed and uncomfortable. I explained to them that Planned Parenthood had not agreed to the policy, but knew that since they worked for Concerned Women of Bangladesh, which received funding from our government, they had pledged not to discuss abortion with their clients.

After more furtive glances and short nervous laughter, two or three of the women spoke up. "Well, we send them to the BAPSA. They take care of everything."

Supported by Planned Parenthood with funding from the Steele Foundation, the Bangladesh Association for the Prevention of Septic Abortion was a nongovernmental organization that provided menstrual extractions, a procedure that uses a syringe to suction out the contents of the uterus before pregnancy is diagnosed. The practice was gaining acceptance in many of the developing countries where abortion was officially illegal but commonly practiced, and where surgical facilities were inadequate.

By referring women to BAPSA, the field-workers were not abiding by their pledge, but the reality of their work forced them to surreptitiously violate the agreement that jeopardized women's lives. The Mexico City Policy forced them to ignore the suffering that they witnessed every day and lie about their actions or go out of business because they refused to concede to the censorship requirements.

Two of the community workers were to guide us through the quarter. It was a muggy morning and the sun beat down on our heads with fierce brutality. My thin cotton blouse and skirt clung to my skin as we followed the workers through the maze of precariously constructed shelters of the slum—tiny, one-room shanties. Home to up to twelve people, the shanties' small sizes often made it necessary for their occupants to sleep in shifts.

The first family we stopped to visit lived in a makeshift shelter. We were told that the young woman who greeted us was in her early twenties, but she looked at least ten years older. She carried a child in her arms, while another clung to the soiled skirt of her sari. While the community workers asked her about her birth control and proudly showed us the records of her reproductive history and birth control usage that they kept so carefully, the child in the young mother's arms drew my attention.

According to the records, she was almost two years old. Judging by her tiny size, she looked no more than eight or nine months old, but her wrinkled, dry face made her features look much older. Her legs were scrawny, her belly distended, and in a land of raven-haired people, her hair was the color of reddish mud. The white lace-trimmed cotton dress hung limply from her dusty lifeless skin. Her large eyes stared without expression.

I asked the mother if she would allow me to hold her child while she spoke with the workers. When I took the little girl in my arms, I found her even lighter than I had expected. She didn't squirm or look anxiously toward her mother, although she did manage to let out one barely audible cry. Her brother, who peered up from his mother's side, was round-faced and appeared healthy. When I asked the mother how often she was able to give her family meat, she replied, "About once a week." When I asked if there was enough for everyone, she answered, "No, not always."

Judging from the appearance of the little girl in my arms, it seemed she was suffering from kwashiorkor, an often fatal condition of severe protein deficiency. We rarely see the ailment in the United States, even in the most deprived areas. In Bangladesh, boys represent more security for their parents and are therefore more valued than girls. The little girl was probably getting what was left after the food was apportioned to her older brother and parents. Before returning the child to her mother's arms, I hugged her unresisting body, as I had often done at Kiddies.

At the beginning of our opposition to Mexico City, it seemed that our hopes in Congress were well placed.

In the fall of 1989, the spring of 1990, and again in 1991, the House Foreign Affairs Subcommittee had held hearings on the policy. After the last review, on May 14, 1991, the full House Foreign Affairs Committee incorporated language reversing the policy into the 1992 Foreign Assistance Act Reauthorization bill. An attempt to strike the new language was defeated by a full House vote in June 1991, the first time since the inception of the Mexico City Policy in 1984 that the House had voted in favor of reversal.

Following the House action, the Senate began consideration of the foreign aid bill. Despite President Bush's veto threat, the Senate Foreign Relations Committee also approved language, offered by Senator Nancy Kassebaum (R-KS), that would reverse the policy.

On July 29, the full Senate began consideration of the 1992–93 foreign aid bill. Senator Jesse Helms threatened a filibuster of Senator Paul Simon's floor amendment to authorize $20 million for the United Nations Fund for Population Activities (UNFPA), which had been defunded in 1986 for supporting programs in China that were allegedly coercive. But Senator Simon's amendment stipulated that none of the U.S. aid could be used in UNFPA's China program. In order to forestall a filibuster, a cloture vote, requiring sixty votes for approval, was taken, with the understanding that if cloture was invoked, the UNFPA provision would be approved and there would be no further challenge to the Mexico City provision. The vote was 63–33, and both provisions were passed by voice vote.

However, in September 1991, the House and Senate conference committee decided to back away from overturning the Mexico City Policy despite the fact that, for the first time, both houses of Congress had voted to overturn the policy. In exchange, the conferees agreed to retain Senator Simon's provision restoring a U.S. contribution to UNFPA. The issue became moot, however, when Congress killed the entire foreign aid reauthorization bill at the end of the year.

It wouldn't be until April 1992, a month after my resignation from the presidency of Planned Parenthood and halfway through the fiscal year, that Congress and the president reached agreement on legislation providing appropriations for foreign aid for the remainder of the fiscal year 1992. The trade-off for ensuring safe passage of the full bill had been to preserve it as an essentially status quo measure: Neither the amendment that Paul Simon advanced to resume funding to UNFPA nor another that would reverse the Mexico City Policy were to be included. We had lost, and our only hope would be the 1992 presidential elections.

Our hopes were finally realized when, on January 22, 1993— two days after his inauguration—with the stroke of his executive pen, President Bill Clinton ended the enforcement of the gag rule and the Mexico City Policy of 1984.

As had been clear since before the Eighties ended, we were no longer fighting a series of sequential battles. Instead, we were caught up in a host of simultaneous battles—about sexuality education, about Title X, about abortion—that were played out on four stages: in Congress, in the courts, in the state legislatures, and in public opinion.

As we fought the Mexico City Policy abroad, we continued to fight the imposition of the gag rule at home. The three cases protesting the gag rule had entered the appeals courts by 1988, two appeals contesting district court decisions to block its implementation and one contesting a decision to uphold it.

On May 8, 1989, a three-judge panel of the U.S. Court of Appeals for the First Circuit upheld Judge Walter Skinner's decision in *Commonwealth of Massachusetts, et. al. v. Secretary of Health and Human Services* to strike down the domestic gag rule. The judges concluded that President Reagan had planned an unconstitutional governmental intrusion on the relationship between the woman and her physician and that the rule represented

400 / Life on the Line

the censorship of advocacy based on content (the content, or subject, being abortion). It was therefore a violation of the First Amendment protecting freedom of speech.

On November 1, 1989, the Second Circuit Court of Appeals in New York upheld Judge Stanton's 1988 decision upholding the gag rule. Echoing Stanton's decision, it ruled that the Department of Health and Human Services could ban the provision of any information about abortion in clinics receiving Title X funding while mandating compulsory referrals of all pregnant women for maternity care—unless Congress explicitly stated otherwise. The appeals court favored the government's right to spend its money as it pleased, even if that meant putting conditions on it that two other circuits ruled unconstitutional.

On September 6, 1990, Judge James Logan of the U.S. Court of Appeals for the Tenth Circuit in Denver, like Massachusetts, struck down the regulations on constitutional grounds and continued Judge Weinshienk's permanent order against their enforcement. He reasoned that the failure to provide information about abortion might lead some to conclude that it was no longer a legal option and thus that failure was an obstacle to a Title X client's freedom to choose abortion. Furthermore, Logan wrote that medical ethics required a physician to include all legal alternatives in their medical advice, and that included abortion as long as it remained a legal alternative.

The First and Tenth Circuit Appeals Court decisions to strike down the gag rule and the Second Circuit decision to uphold it were disputes among the appellate-level courts that only the Supreme Court could settle. On May 29, 1990, the Court agreed to review one of the cases—the Second Circuit decision, which upheld the gag rule. And on October 30, 1990, the Supreme Court heard the oral arguments for this decision. This case was known as *Rust v. Sullivan.*

Appearing for the Bush administration, U.S. Solicitor General Kenneth Starr justified the regulations as being consistent with the law that created the Title X program, which, he asserted, was designed to provide only "preventive . . . preconception services"—not counseling and treatment for pregnant women. Under this interpretation, when pregnancy was diagnosed, the government-funded clinic became "the transition out to another healthcare provider." General Starr did not see the gag rule as a violation of doctors' rights to free speech, because doctors were free to provide abortion counseling in other settings besides Title X–funded family-planning clinics.[3]

Arguing on behalf of the City and State of New York and Planned Parenthood of New York City, Harvard Law School Professor Laurence Tribe vigorously disagreed with Starr's theoretical creation. "We depend on doctors to tell us the whole truth whoever is paying the medical bill, the patient or the government, whether in a Title X clinic or in the Bethesda

Naval Hospital," he said. But under the gag rule, Tribe told the court, "Truthful information that may be relevant is being deliberately withheld from people who have every reason to expect it."[4]

There was no question about who our Constitution protected in the domestic gag rule challenge. Or so we thought. I would not let myself believe that the Supreme Court of the United States would allow the censorship of speech. Admittedly, it had upheld the government's right to fund some programs and not others, according to the government's own interests. But speech was different. Speech was protected in the First Amendment of the Constitution. It is the fundamental principle of liberty.

We would not learn the fate of the domestic gag rule until months later, in May 1991. Meanwhile, the Supreme Court was to undergo yet another dramatic shift.

On July 20, 1990, Justice William Brennan announced his decision to leave the Supreme Court at the end of the session. Given the importance of the cases in the federal circuits that would redefine the future of reproductive rights—and given that the gag rule was to be heard in the Supreme Court's next session—the announcement, although not surprising because of the justice's age, reverberated throughout the pro-choice community. Not only was one more departure from the progressive flank of the Court alarming; it also provided President Bush with his first opportunity to make an appointment.

The president's position on abortion and his relentless assault on Title X left us with little doubt that he would not put forth an acceptable nominee. And we figured he'd heed the lessons his predecessor had learned about recommending a candidate for the court whose judicial opinions, writings, and speeches created a body of work that could be analyzed and attacked. We expected him to nominate a jurist who had spent relatively little time on the federal bench, and therefore contributed little to the written or spoken record for public scrutiny. David Souter, a judge from the First Circuit Federal Court of Appeals in Boston, proved to be just the man.

As was often the case when announcements of significance to our work were made, there was little time to call for a Planned Parenthood referendum. Instantaneous media coverage demanded instantaneous response. As Planned Parenthood's spokesperson, I was once again responsible for deciding what position we would take on the nominee. Our official policy was to oppose any public official who did not support reproductive rights. But even after close analysis of Souter's record, our legal advisers could find no evidence of his inclination one way or the other.

After Bork, the Republicans were taking no chances. We couldn't take a chance either—not with the Supreme Court now so closely divided on reproductive rights. After consulting with the board officers and my

402 / Life on the Line

management team, I concluded that if in the course of the nomination proceedings Souter did not acknowledge his support for the *Griswold* and *Roe* decisions—the two pillars of reproductive rights—we would oppose his confirmation.

On the night of Souter's nomination, I was invited to appear on ABC's *Nightline* with Elliott Mincberg of People for the American Way, Attorney General Richard Thornburgh, and Senator Warren Rudman, a New Hampshire Republican who was Souter's chief sponsor. When Chris Wallace, who moderated the program, asked me where Planned Parenthood stood on the issue of the clarity of judicial philosophy, I responded, "When those issues reflect our . . . fundamental constitutional rights, it's altogether appropriate that these questions be asked."[5]

Senator Rudman, revealing the sensitivity now attached to Supreme Court nominations, asserted that, although the American public "has every right to extract [Souter's] judicial philosophy . . . If anybody really believes that a nominee to the United States Supreme Court should sit before the United States Senate and prejudge a series of cases on civil rights, on abortion, on a whole range of criminal issues, then they are perverting the process."[6]

I reminded the senator that, since Planned Parenthood considered the right of privacy and the right to reproductive determination fundamental human rights, we felt that any nominee who didn't make known his or her views on these rights did not deserve to sit on the Supreme Court.

Senator Rudman again distorted the point, commenting, "What Ms. Wattleton would really like to know is how he will vote on *Roe v. Wade.* The president doesn't know that. I don't know that, and she is not entitled to know that."[7]

I could not resist a barb: "Well, I think that the American people are certainly entitled to know . . . Perhaps Senator Rudman does not understand that the right established . . . in *Roe v. Wade* was established on the basis of the Constitution's protection of privacy, which is what we're concerned about."[8]

Not long after this airing of *Nightline*, a delegation of affiliate representatives (board members and executive directors) asked to meet with me just before the start of the August board meeting.

"We hope the federation will stay on the sidelines on the Souter nomination. I feel certain that he is not anti-choice," said one board member from Seattle, who had been a clerk for a Supreme Court justice.

"We don't believe he's a Robert Bork," said another.

Then the delegation informed me that it planned to press for the national board to create a committee composed of national board members and affiliate representatives who would decide what position Planned Parenthood should take whenever future Supreme Court nominations were posited by the president.

"Well," I said, betraying no emotion, "I think such a process would make it very difficult to speak quickly when the impact can be the greatest."

I couldn't begin to fathom the nightmare of delegating our response to fast-breaking news events to a committee. We would be haggling on the sidelines while our colleagues in other organizations and our opponents defined the issue that had come under the spotlight. By 1990, the national media usually turned to us first, giving us the opportunity to frame the pro-choice position. They wouldn't wait around if we weren't ready to respond immediately. We could lose not only our place as a reliable voice for women, but the public visibility upon which so much of our support, including financial support, depended. I believed that our mission and our policies were clear enough to guide whatever I needed to say, and found myself resisting what seemed to be one more attempt to bridle my leadership.

After my visitors had departed and the door was closed, I erupted to David, my ever-supportive colleague, subjecting him to one more soliloquy. I could understand this visit if I had overstepped the boundaries of our principles every other time I opened my mouth. But I hadn't and wouldn't. We had more support than ever before. In spite of our internal strife, the world saw us as a united movement, because we gave a consistent message. Now they wanted me to go to a committee to be told what to say.

"This is ridiculous," I raged.

"They say they want leadership, and when they get it, they say, 'What is this?'" David said, then laughed heartily. I found myself laughing, despite my fury.

The delegation, as promised, raised with the board the issue of a committee to deliberate on Planned Parenthood's position on Supreme Court nominees. I described how we decided on our response to such events and others—and assured the board that I took great care to analyze the situation and its meaning for Planned Parenthood and that I sought the advice of my staff, AGI, and, almost always, a set of outside experts. The board deliberated the matter before deciding to leave the authority in my hands. I had prevailed, but the message of containment was not lost on me.

Despite the antagonism within Planned Parenthood over the matter, Souter's confirmation proceedings were tranquil in comparison with the Bork hearings. We lobbied members of the Judiciary Committee individually. Senator Paul Simon agreed to probe Mr. Souter's ideas on the constitutional underpinnings of reproductive rights, and we asked others to reject his confirmation if he avoided answering. The Democrats on the committee promised to do so.

Souter managed to evade a gentle inquiry about his opinions on the constitutional foundation for reproductive rights, and even the most liberal members of the panel were disinclined to pursue the subject beyond a few perfunctory questions. His nomination was approved by the Judiciary

Committee with a vote of 13 to 1, and by the full Senate on October 2, 1990, with a vote of 90 to 9.

The Senate had been in pro-choice Democratic hands when all of the justices (except Sandra Day O'Connor) nominated by the Reagan and Bush administrations were confirmed. With the exception of Robert Bork, the nominees were all allowed to ascend to the Court without revealing their views on Planned Parenthood's—and women's—threshold issues.

The next day I responded to the Senate's approval:

> Yesterday, the Senate overwhelmingly confirmed David H. Souter to the United States Supreme Court. In doing so, our elected officials once again demonstrated a decided lack of regard for the real-life problems of American women and their families.
>
> Americans once counted on the Supreme Court to preserve and protect our fundamental rights of privacy and self-determination. We can no longer. Judge Souter has made it clear he believes that legal abortion remains an open question. In other words, our rights continue to be up for grabs.[9]

We would have to wait to see how the new justice would rule, on a case-by-case basis, before learning his opinions on a matter central to the lives of over half of our country's citizens and on a struggle that jeopardized the right of every American to speak freely without government censorship.

On May 23, 1991, the decision in *Rust v. Sullivan* was handed down. By a split of five to four, with David Souter in the majority, the Supreme Court upheld the gag rule. Chief Justice Rehnquist delivered the opinion of the majority:

> We agree with every court to have addressed the issue that the language of the Title X Act is ambiguous . . . [and] does not speak directly to the issues of counseling, referral, advocacy, or program integrity. If a statute is "silent" or ambiguous with respect to the specific issue, the question for the court is whether the agency's answer is based on a permissible construction of the statute. . . .
>
> Based on the broad directives provided by Congress in Title X in general and 1008 in particular, we are unable to say that . . . a ban on counseling, referral, and advocacy within the Title X project, is impermissible.[10]

The legacy of the 1981 Title X hearings conducted by Senators Hatch, Denton, and Nickles now haunted us with finality. The hearings had led to General Accounting Office and Inspector General audits. The audits had in turn led to a report stating that "clear guidance on the scope of abortion restrictions needed to be provided" to Title X recipients. And that recommendation had led first to the squeal rule and now, more ominously, to the gag rule.

Though this case was as much about freedom of speech as it was about informed consent, the essence of the Court's decision was brutally frank:

> In *Maher v. Roe*, we . . . held that the government may "make a value judgment favoring childbirth over abortion, and . . . implement that judgment by the allocation of public funds." Here the government is exercising the authority it possesses under *Maher* and *McRae* to subsidize family-planning services which will lead to conception and child birth, and declining to "promote or encourage abortion." . . . [T]he government has not discriminated on the basis of viewpoint; it has merely chosen to fund one activity to the exclusion of the other.[11]

The Court stated that the language of the Title X act was "ambiguous" and thus did not "speak directly to the issues of counseling, referral, advocacy, or program integrity,"[12] and that "Title X program regulations do not significantly impinge upon the doctor-patient relationship."[13] In so stating, the Court failed to address—just as the appeals courts had in allowing restrictions on the distribution of AID funds to foreign organizations—the practical question: How do you get the woman from the Title X clinic to the "separate and independent" program, if you can't refer her to it or even, as the government admitted, allow the Yellow Pages listing abortion providers to be placed on the premises of a Title X clinic?

I wondered if the justices could even imagine what it was like to be young, poor, or both, in a government-funded birth control clinic. I wondered if they tried to understand how the flow of information there is seamless with the care provided. It is virtually impossible to separate the provision of physical care from the words of guidance that are spoken upon the discovery of a pregnancy. Now, a woman who discovered she was pregnant during a Title X–clinic visit for contraception couldn't discuss or have information given to her about all of the legal options available to her. She couldn't even be given a piece of paper with a list of telephone numbers of sources of information. To any question on abortion that clinic personnel might receive, the government would require the doctor or nurse to say, "The project does not consider abortion an appropriate method of family planning and therefore does not counsel or refer for abortion." More than halfway through a generation of legality, the Court was allowing the government to return abortion for the poor to the realm of ignorance and rejection.

Ironically, the justices cited a venue where they would not allow the government to use taxpayers' money to censor speech: the university. They wrote: ". . . [T]he university is a traditional sphere of free expression so fundamental to the functioning of our society that the government's ability to control speech within that sphere . . . is restricted by the . . . doctrines of the First Amendment."[14] In other words, if Title X–funded clinics had been located at universities, the gag rule would have been struck down.

The Court seemed to ignore the fact that Title X clinics are often the only source of medical care for low-income women and teenagers. Adapting a refrain from *McRae*, the majority in the Court allowed themselves a callousness to the struggles of the poor.

> Petitioners contend, however, that most Title X clients are precluded by indigence and poverty from seeing a healthcare provider who will provide abortion-related services. But once again, even these Title X clients are in no worse position than if Congress had never enacted Title X. "The financial constraints that restrict an indigent woman's ability to enjoy the full range of constitutionally protected freedom of choice are the product not of governmental restrictions on access to abortion, but rather of her indigence."[15]

Justice Blackmun did not miss the deeper significance for all Americans when he offered a scathing dissent for the minority of the Court:

> Until today, the Court never has upheld viewpoint-based suppression of speech simply because that suppression was a condition upon the acceptance of public funds. Whatever may be the government's power to condition the receipt of its largess upon the relinquishment of constitutional rights, it surely does not extend to a condition that suppresses the recipient's cherished freedom of speech based solely upon the content or viewpoint of that speech. . . .
>
> It cannot seriously be disputed that the counseling and referral provisions at issue in the present cases constitute content-based regulation of speech. Title X grantees may provide counseling and referral regarding any of a wide range of family planning and other topics, save abortion. . . .
>
> Until today, the Court has allowed to stand only those restrictions upon reproductive freedom that, while limiting the availability of abortion, have left intact a woman's ability to decide without coercion whether she will continue her pregnancy to term . . . Today's decision abandons that principle, and with disastrous results. . . .
>
> In its haste further to restrict the right of every woman to control her reproductive freedom and bodily integrity, the majority disregards established principles of law and contorts this Court's decided cases to arrive at its preordained result . . . [O]ne must wonder what force the First Amendment retains if it is read to countenance the deliberate manipulation by the government of the dialogue between a woman and her physician. This is a

course nearly as noxious as overruling *Roe* directly, for if a right is found to be unenforceable, even against flagrant attempts by government to circumvent it, then it ceases to be a right at all.[16]

With *Rust v. Sullivan* decided, the focus of our fight would shift again to Congress. Meanwhile, the debates accelerated within Planned Parenthood over whether we should hold true to our commitment to providing women with full and nonjudgmental information and services or whether the affiliates would be allowed to "work out arrangements" with the government to hold on to their Title X funding:

"Our lawyer has figured out a way for us to live within the rule and give women the information they need. If our doctors diagnose a pregnancy in a woman in a Title X clinic, he won't say anything to her about her options."

"But what does the doctor tell her if she asks, 'What can I do?'" I would inquire.

"He would say, 'I can't talk to you about that. I'll send you next door to another service. They will help you with your options.'"

That scenario would have been illegal under the regulations, because the gag rule prohibited the clinic from referring a woman to a provider that did offer abortion-related counseling and/or services; but the very notion that a Planned Parenthood clinic would withhold information from a woman who requested it was anathema to me.

The rift within the organization was widening. Something had to be done before we broke apart over *Rust*. After discussing the growing tensions at its winter meeting, the board had approved my recommendation that we organize a federation-wide retreat so we could have the chance to work through some of the animosity building up between the national organization and the affiliates, and among the affiliates themselves. We scheduled a three-day assembly of affiliate executive directors, board presidents, and national board and staff for June, in San Antonio, Texas. There, secluded within Trinity University's campus, we would discuss our vision of what Planned Parenthood should be, and what we should do in the likely event that Congress didn't act and the Bush administration went ahead and imposed the gag rule.

Although I doubted that any minds would be changed about how to address the gag rule, I saw the San Antonio conclave as a way to help us to bridge the divide. I hoped that talking in small, informal groups and eating meals and spending leisure time together would allow us to see each other in ways that might help us to overcome our antagonisms, even if we couldn't rally around the same course of action. I believed that we all had the interests of women at heart, and that we had to try to find a way of coming together over one of the fundamental principles of informed consent.

Because the House and Senate votes on the gag rule weren't expected until July, the media remained interested in the issue. ABC's *Prime Time Live* asked if they could send a crew to San Antonio to film a segment on Planned Parenthood, me, and our fight against censorship in government family-planning clinics. I saw their request as a timely and phenomenal opportunity to keep the dangers of the gag rule in the forefront of public attention and thus bring increased pressure to bear upon congressmen and senators. After consulting with other members of my executive staff and with Ken Edelin, and after gaining ABC's commitment that they would be as unobtrusive as possible during the one or two hours that they planned to film, I agreed to let them cover our gathering.

When we arrived in Texas, my assistant, Tim Lannan, told the outside consultants we'd engaged to facilitate the retreat about the news program's interest so that they might make arrangements to accommodate the filming if we decided to go ahead with the coverage. I was surprised when he came to me later that day to tell me the consultants were strongly opposed to the idea. I was further taken aback when he informed me that he agreed with their position.

"They believe that this retreat is supposed to be a safe place for the affiliates. Letting the outside media come in will do violence to what we're trying to do."

"A safe place? What does that mean? What about missing the opportunity of getting the dangers of the gag rule before millions of people for fifteen minutes of prime time network television?" I asked. Not only would we not be able to fight the oncoming battles if we were divided, but we also couldn't fight alone.

Then, in a flourish that really stung, Tim added, "Faye, this is exactly why the affiliates are so upset. They see you as trying to promote yourself." In his words I heard the all-too-familiar message that all that I was doing to raise the visibility of Planned Parenthood and its mission was for my own self-aggrandizement.

Far more frustrating than this accusation regarding my personal motives was the affiliates' steadfast refusal to see that challenging the gag rule in every appropriate venue *was* defending them and their work. Aside from a small program to fund nurse-practitioner training in Pennsylvania, not a penny of Title X funding flowed into the national organization. I believed that everything we were doing to capitalize on our opportunities, including my media appearances, offered evidence that the national office was an advocate for affiliates' needs.

However, just as Tim and the consultants had predicted, ABC's presence became the focus of resentment. Some vocal affiliate representatives saw this as an invasion—and my allowing it as proof of my lack of concern for their troubles. No one challenged me directly, and the filming went off with little disruption. But I felt a chill wherever I walked.

Had she been by my side, Mama might have quoted, "I have prophetic powers and understand all mysteries and all knowledge and if I have all faith, so as to remove mountains but do not have love, I am nothing."[17] *Love* would not be the word to describe the emotions of that moment, but more than anything else, I wanted to "remove mountains" for my organization. I had to keep pressing forward.

By the end of the retreat, the tensions had receded, and many people expressed appreciation for the opportunity to come together to find out how to communicate better with one another. But I couldn't forget the strains. Above all, I found myself very tired—not of the fight for women, but of the fight for and within Planned Parenthood.

CHAPTER 33

AN ABORTION PILL:
TOO GOOD TO BE TRUE

By the early 1990s, it was estimated that more than half of all the pregnancies in the United States were unintended. Eighty-four percent of all counties throughout the country had no abortion services at all. Because of the disruptions and violence carried out by pro-criminalists, fewer doctors were willing to be trained to perform abortions, and as those who did would eventually be retiring from the practice of medicine, their numbers were dwindling. A medical alternative to the 1.53 million surgical abortions performed each year in the United States would hold the potential to drastically alter the nature of the reproductive rights debate. It could make the option of early pregnancy termination realistically available to greater numbers of women and would require less public intervention by others. And in the poorest parts of the world, where deaths due to childbirth and related causes were continuing at epidemic rates, an alternative to surgical abortion held the promise of rescuing hundreds of thousands of women each year from injury and death.[1]

By the end of the Eighties, RU-486, sometimes called "the abortion pill," developed in France in 1980 by the pharmaceutical giant Roussel-Uclaf, seemed to offer just such an alternative. In early surgical abortion, the tissue is removed by suction. However, with RU-486, the contents of the uterus pass without the use of a surgical instrument. According to published reports, it is almost a hundred percent effective in ending a pregnancy when used with a companion hormone up to six weeks from the first day of the last menstrual period.

RU-486 is given to a pregnant woman by a physician after her pregnancy is diagnosed. Two days later, she returns to get a second drug, known as a prostaglandin, and returns home to await the contractions of her womb and the passage of its contents, whose development has been blocked by the first drug. Side effects—nausea, cramping, and heavy and prolonged bleeding—are rarely reported. In a tiny percentage of cases, the uterus does not empty completely, necessitating a surgical abortion.

But since its development, RU-486 was available primarily to women in France. On a spring morning in 1991, Sheldon (Shelley) Segal, then director of Population Sciences for the Rockefeller Foundation, Louise Tyrer, Planned Parenthood's vice president of medical affairs, and I were about to make one more try at getting RU-486 released from its French custodians for U.S. distribution.

As we rode through the glistening wake of early-April morning showers, the sublime beauty of Paris shone in stark contrast to the obstinance of the Roussel-Uclaf pharmaceutical company executives with whom we were going to meet for the third time. Neither the freshly washed breeze and the fragrance of blossoms, nor my colleagues' good-natured reassurances could lighten my spirits. For two years we'd been having discussions with the holders of the most important breakthrough in birth control for women since the development of oral contraception, and they had proved to be a stubborn lot.

There had been reports of conflict within Roussel-Uclaf over the prospect of releasing RU-486 outside France. We knew that the company's largest shareholder, the German chemical manufacturer Hoechst A.G., had been opposed to that prospect because they feared political controversy. Hoechst was said to be reacting to pro-criminalist insinuations that purveyors and sponsors of the drug were doing to fetuses what the Nazis had done to Jews. Hoechst was particularly sensitive to such claims because its ancestor company had manufactured cyanide gas for the death camps.[2] We knew it would be very difficult to overcome Hoechst's opposition.

I wondered out loud whether a similar compound, maybe even a better one, couldn't be developed and moved through the FDA approval process by the time the people at Hoechst and Roussel-Uclaf got around to making up their minds. "At the rate we're going," I said to my companions, "it will be the next century before women catch so much as a glimpse of the drug in the United States." I was arguing rhetorically, without opposition from Shelley and Louise. Each of us knew that our previous meetings had ended in heady anticipation and invariably dissolved into frustrated disappointment as the company offered one reason after another not to release the drug.

When we learned that Etienne Emile Baulieu, a French physician and researcher who had encouraged Roussel-Uclaf to pursue the development of RU-486 as an abortifacient, would again be bringing his witty presence to our discussions, as an adviser to Roussel-Uclaf, we hoped that the company was serious this time about releasing RU-486. The distinguished scientist had been involved in fertility control research for over twenty years and was considered an expert on hormones. Baulieu had first become interested in fertility control in 1961, as a postgraduate researcher at Columbia University. Though few realized it at the time, the quest for an abortion pill started in 1970, when receptor cells were discovered in the uterus that receive the effects of progesterone, the hormone vital to the maintenance of early pregnancy. Anything that blocks the hormone's effect will imperil the pregnancy. Later, Baulieu and his team theorized that if a substance could be found that deceived the receptor cells by mimicking the progesterone without doing the work of the hormone of pregnancy, it could block its vital role.

Baulieu challenged the researchers at Roussel-Uclaf to look for or create chemicals—known as antihormones—that would serve as progesterone impostors. Baulieu suggested to Roussel's chemists that the antihormones might be synthesized by grafting a complex atom cluster onto a progesterone-like molecule. This would make it chemically different from progesterone even though the attachment mechanism remained so similar that the uterus would receive it as a progesterone. In 1980 Roussel's chief chemist, George Teutsch, succeeded in this search. Thus was born a molecule registered as Roussel-Uclaf 38486, shortened to RU-486.[3]

While these developments were taking place in France, the U.S. pharmaceutical industry's contraceptive-technology research and development had come to a virtual standstill. In the face of all the controversy surrounding abortion, and the wariness spawned by the Dalkon shield liability lawsuits, there were few economic incentives for U.S. companies to pursue further innovation in reproductive technologies. Nor were the National Institutes of Health being funded at the level that would give reasonable expectation for breakthroughs in contraception. On top of all this, the Reagan and Bush administrations chilled the research climate by imposing executive prohibitions on any fetal tissue research when that tissue was obtained through surgical abortion. Such tissue had been the medium through which research scientists had made so many discoveries—including the polio vaccine. Suspicion that women would seek surgical abortions to profit from the harvest of fetal tissue for research purposes was fed by the turbulence of the abortion conflict.

Even in France, all did not go smoothly for RU-486. On October 26, 1988, Roussel-Uclaf announced that it was pulling the drug off the market, because of the "polemic" surrounding the company's new pill.[4] After years of clinical trials, the drug had been on the French market for only one month. Wolfgang Hilger, chief executive officer of Hoechst, proclaimed that the drug violated the company's credo to support life. He also expressed fear that boycott threats by U.S. antiabortion activists could cripple Hoechst Celanese, his company's $6-billion-a-year U.S. subsidiary.

The day of the announced withdrawal, 9,500 doctors and researchers were gathered in Rio de Janeiro for the World Congress of Gynecology and Obstetrics. Roussel-Uclaf's decision drew outrage and protest there, turning a group of professionals not generally known for political militancy into an instant collective of impassioned activists.

Shelley, who was at the Rio conference, attacked Roussel-Uclaf for "betraying its partnership with the medical profession."[5] Etienne Baulieu, also in Rio, condemned his colleagues back in France, and asserted that the decision was bad for women's health and bad for medical research. The French government, which owned a 36.25 percent stake in the company, now faced tremendous pressure to intervene.

Two days later, the French health minister, Claude Evin, put Roussel-Uclaf on notice that if it didn't reverse the decision, the patent for RU-486 would be transferred to another company. "I could not permit the abortion debate to deprive women of a product that represents medical progress," said Evin. "From the moment government approval for the drug was granted, RU-486 became the moral property of women, not just the property of the drug company."[6]

Roussel-Uclaf relented, and made the drug available in clinics run by the French government, but only after placing stringent controls on its distribution. As in the case of legal narcotics, each dosage was to be numbered and had to be accounted for. In order to ensure that women didn't travel to France to obtain RU-486, women weren't eligible to receive the abortifacient unless they could show proof that they had lived in the country for at least three months.

As I read about the RU-486 saga and watched television news coverage of the protest, I expected a push to make the drug available to women in our country. Given the passion of its support, maybe it had a real chance.

"I think it's quite possible," said Shelley when he'd returned to New York. "Edouard Sakiz [chairman of Roussel-Uclaf] and I have been friends and colleagues since early in our careers. I think he'd really consider the possibility."

"Do you think he would consider Planned Parenthood clinics as a site for clinical trials?" I pressed expectantly.

"Given the credibility of Planned Parenthood clinics as well as their experience in conducting clinical studies on new contraceptives, I can't see why not." Shelley duly arranged the meeting.

A small study of RU-486 was being conducted at the University of Southern California by the same David Grimes who had been a part of our delegation to Everett Koop. But I knew that if the drug was to be approved by the Food and Drug Administration, it would have to be administered under FDA supervision to thousands of women in order to gather sufficient data on its effectiveness, side effects, and complications, to protect it against attacks that it was harmful and had not been adequately studied.

Assuming that Roussel-Uclaf had an interest in making the drug available in the United States, we wanted to explore the possibility of the company's granting Planned Parenthood permission to apply to the FDA for the right to conduct the clinical trials. Prior to our meeting, Roussel-Uclaf had demanded that we sign a confidentiality agreement: We could not reveal that the company was talking to anyone about the possible distribution of RU-486 in the United States.

Shelley, Louise Tyrer, and I had made our first trip to Paris in January of 1989—six months before the *Webster* decision was handed down. Dr. Sakiz sent his car and driver to our hotel that morning to take us to the company's headquarters on Boulevard des Invalides. I had imagined an imposing facility of grand French architecture. Instead, we pulled up before a modest modern glass building and stepped into a spacious but unadorned entrance hall. Dr. Sakiz, reed thin and impeccably groomed, greeted us graciously. He had arranged for Etienne Baulieu and the executives managing the RU-486 program to meet with us. After the cordial introductions and pleasantries over tea, Dr. Sakiz made a polite but swift exit. The remaining executives and scientists were to handle our day-long meeting. We felt encouraged when we heard that the company had been thinking of distributing RU-486 outside France. That they were considering Britain as a location for their first trial made us more hopeful that they'd be willing to place the drug in a country where abortion was controversial. Britain's pro-criminalist movement was one of the most vigorous in Europe.

But midway through our meeting, Dr. Sakiz rushed back into the room, waving a sheaf of papers and saying, in a "see what I mean" tone, "This is what it's all about. This is the opposition that RU-486 will face if we allow it to go to the United States! Can you guarantee us that we will not have to put up with this?" Before we could reply, he demanded, "What do you know about these people?"

Lost for a response that would not upset him further, I thumbed quickly through the pages, and saw that the Christian Action Council was threatening to boycott the company's products if RU-486 was released in the United States.

Bluffing confidence, I said, "I have never heard of them, and if I haven't heard about them, they're probably one of hundreds of groups who make threats of all sorts. I wouldn't get too excited. There has never been a successful boycott of a corporation by antiabortion activists."

"Can you promise that we won't face boycotts?" Dr. Sakiz insisted again.

"No, we can't promise," I answered for the group.

At that, he picked up the thick sheaf of pages and stalked out of the room.

We returned to our discussions, which had progressed to the value of RU-486 in developing countries. Certain that everyone seated around the table would agree, I said, "This drug has the potential to do more good in developing countries than in our own." Appealing to their sense of social responsibility, I continued, "The governments of poor countries lack facilities to test new technology. They often follow the lead of the United States in accepting new drugs."

"RU-486 will never go to developing countries," said one of the executives in a tone flat with finality.

He couldn't be serious, I thought; but this was no time to argue.

Over the course of the day we were queried closely about Planned Parenthood's clinics and how they operated, and whether we'd be able to meet our interrogators' standards. I was getting the picture that they wanted us to be able to account for the whereabouts of every pill by serial number, and I was starting to feel strong suspicions that getting the drug would not be so easy to accomplish. That didn't daunt me. I knew that our international program shipped and kept track of millions of cycles of birth control pills all over the world. We should be able to keep track of them in our clinics, I figured. Roussel-Uclaf's concerns that the drug not fall into the hands of teenagers further illuminated their fears over the moral complexities of abortion, but it was their fear of being boycotted that colored every aspect of our discussion. They seemed to worry about everything except the women who needed what the company had serendipitously discovered. Not once did it enter their concerns. RU-486 was just a product to them, and a troublesome one at that.

By late afternoon, the executives had expressed a willingness to work with us to explore the best way to establish a testing program.

As soon as I returned to New York, I asked David Andrews to write Dr. Sakiz expressing our hope that we could proceed quickly toward an agreement so we could file for the FDA's permission to begin testing RU-486 in Planned Parenthood clinics.

Roussel-Uclaf's response to David's letter brought our hopes tumbling down.

We have accepted to explore with Planned Parenthood the situation and the possible solutions for the USA. But there is no will on our side at this time to make the full dossier available for submission to the FDA, as we have made no decision to register and sell outside of France.[7]

This letter came during my four-month sabbatical when David was serving as acting president. Though hesitant to break our agreement that I would be contacted only in an extreme emergency, he phoned me with the news.

"It's just going to take longer than we thought," I answered, as much to soothe my own disappointment as to encourage him.

In the time between our meeting and the receipt of Roussel-Uclaf's letter, Louise Tyrer had reported to the board about our meeting and they had responded with unqualified enthusiasm. This new initiative was in keeping with tradition. Margaret Sanger herself and Planned Parenthood supporters had played pivotal roles in envisioning and supporting the early research on the birth control pill. For years, affiliates had participated in clinical studies on various birth control methods. And, given our experience in such research, and our capability in managing the abortion controversy, we believed that our clinics were the perfect theater for testing RU-486.

The board authorized a large reserve of funds for that purpose and urged us to plan a research-protocol business and marketing strategy. The Abraham Foundation gave us a large grant in support of these activities. But the fate of RU-486 distribution outside France once again became the source of much speculation. Rumors circulated wildly that Etienne Baulieu was courting socialites and potential investors for an independent company to be established to distribute the drug. Various venture capitalists announced they had reached an understanding with Roussel-Uclaf. But we would later learn that most of the delegations who made anticipatory pilgrimages to Paris had been given the same "not so fast" message. The company's executives were alleged to have announced that they wouldn't allow the drug into the United States until the president of the United States supported its entry. Some said that the Catholic-dominated German holding company was hindering discussions.

Whatever the cause, two years had passed between our first talks and that lovely spring morning in 1991 in Paris when Shelley, Louise, and I were heading in for another round of talks with Roussel-Uclaf. That we were there at all was due in large part to Shelley's unfailing optimism, his insistence that we keep the lines of communication active. The cynicism I felt as we once again entered the double glass doors of the pharmaceutical behemoth was tempered by the addition of George Zeidenstein, president of the Population Council, to our delegation. The Population Council is an international organization that conducts biomedical, social-science, and public-health research. If anyone could convince Roussel-Uclaf to spring the drug at last, I believed he could, for he and Shelley were free of the political baggage of the reproductive rights battles that the rest of us carried.

This time, Edouard Sakiz led the meeting. "Unless Hoechst tells me not to do so, I intend to allow doses of the drug to come into the United States for testing by June of 1991," he said. Under a 1983 agreement between Roussel-Uclaf and the Population Council, he believed he had the authority to begin clinical testing of the drug in the United States.

He turned to George: "You already have what is needed to bring the drug into the United States. Why don't you exercise your rights? With some modifications of the agreement, you can start."

But George wanted assurances that the company would continue to supply the drug after the testing period was completed. No doubt he was thinking of the small studies in which Roussel-Uclaf had provided just enough RU-486 for a specific protocol, and then frustrated the researchers by refusing to continue supplying the drug for additional studies on the most effective dosages.

"We'll have to get back to you on that," Edouard replied.

"Well," said George, "I have an ethical problem with investing time, energy, and money into testing, only to find that you won't continue to supply the drug when the testing is done. What would be the point?"

Although much was left unresolved, and although the company had disappointed us in the past, that evening we toasted our new agreement as Dr. Sakiz's guests at one of Paris's finest restaurants, Taillevent. It was one of those sparkling evenings in Paris about which one only reads in gourmet magazines. It was a very long way from 1241 Walton Avenue.

Flying back to New York, I was still plagued with doubt about the reliability of the French commitment. And sure enough, several weeks after our meeting, Dr. Sakiz called George to tell him that he had been advised by a Hoechst board member not to release the drug without affirmative approval from that company. Not until 1994 did Roussel-Uclaf agree to release RU-486 to the Population Council for testing and marketing.

By the time the studies were completed in a variety of Planned Parenthood and non–Planned Parenthood settings, and before the application was submitted to the FDA to approve RU-486 for manufacturing and marketing, another drug was offering the promise of achieving the same objective through different means. Methotrexate, which had already been approved by the FDA to treat cancer, was being studied in different parts of the country as an abortifacient. Since it had already been approved for one purpose, it could not be withdrawn from the market, because it was found to be effective for another purpose. But the FDA had urged additional studies to establish the appropriate dosage for pregnancy terminations and to identify side effects. As I had hoped years earlier, another avenue had been opened to avert the continuing, predicted hurdles of RU-486. Although methotrexate may not be the perfect drug, neither is RU-486. Nevertheless, I feel confident that, one way or another, before the millennium, women will have a medical alternative to surgical abortion.

Louise Tyrer had been on the executive staff of Planned Parenthood when I was appointed president, but I came to know her in a whole new way in working so closely with her on the RU-486 project. Her story reminded me of the reasons, both unique and universal, that led each of us to join the struggle for women's reproductive freedom. The passion of her voice and the vividness of her experience bear witnessing:

> I can't forget what we're fighting for. I grew up in China, where my father was a doctor and ran a mission hospital. It was still common then to see Chinese women with bound feet. I'd see these women trying to manage harvesting wheat crops, pregnant, and with small children at their side. My father would come home and tell us about women who had been brought to the hospital almost dead from impacted labor. I dreamed then of becoming a missionary doctor like my father.
>
> I was a resident at Los Angeles County General Hospital between 1945 and 1948. My first assignment in Ob/Gyn was in two wards of sixty women each. All of them were illegal-abortion cases and they would come in with severe infections or hemorrhages. We had two private rooms, always full, where we put the women who were dying. We had women in the wards with curtains drawn around them waiting to go into those rooms.
>
> Then the police would show up. They always got there remarkably fast. I don't know how they knew to come. I guess the ambulance drivers brought them there. We'd just say that the patient was too critically ill to talk with them and that they would have to come with some sort of affidavit and/or warrant. If they were particularly insistent we would talk to the women and say that obviously the person they'd gone to hadn't done a good job, and had caused all this problem. 'Do you want to talk to the police and tell them who it was?' we'd ask. Invariably they would not. They were so grateful to be free of their pregnancies that even if their abortions had nearly cost them their lives, they didn't want to squeal on the person who had done it for them.
>
> During the war, almost all the antibiotics went to the men in the service. We were only allowed to administer antibiotics to patients with subacute bacterial endocarditis. So when these women came in, we couldn't give them anything to fight their infections. As a result they developed sepsis and septicemia and they died.
>
> Any patient that was critical on admission to the hospital got a red blanket. Some had gas gangrene. Their skin would turn black and it would crackle anywhere that you touched the skin because of the gas released by the bacteria that had been introduced in their systems by unsterile instruments. They would go into coma and septic shock and die.
>
> Seeing someone dying from tetanus was terrible—those convulsions— and their teeth clenched and froth would come from their mouths. I had never seen anything like this. The ones who got well would go home in about three days. The ones that didn't—some of them died within twenty-four hours, some of them suffered for five days or more.

The women usually came by themselves, and we'd call a relative if things seemed especially bad. We would say, "You may not live, and we have to be able to notify somebody." Then they would give us a relative to put in the chart.

Occasionally we'd hear about what had actually been done to them. The worst case that I handled was when I was in practice in Reno, sometime between 1960 and 1970. An Indian girl was brought into the emergency room. She was about seventeen years old and had gotten pregnant. Some Indian boys decided they would help her have an abortion. They all got drunk and they used a can opener—you know, the short triangular-pointed one and went up in her vagina to try and extract the products of conception and do an abortion on her. They went up into her vagina, I suppose by feel. They ripped a hole in her bladder and they ripped a hole through her vagina into her rectum.

She was in deep shock by the time they brought her in. They hadn't gotten anywhere near the cervix, so she was still about four months pregnant. We had to give her about five pints of blood before we could even take her to surgery. We did a colostomy and had to put a catheter in her bladder. We closed the bladder rip through the vagina. About three days later the girl had a spontaneous abortion. Why she didn't die, I'll never know.[8]

The Christian Action Council was not only creating problems for us in France, it was about to cause serious trouble on the home front. For some years we'd had the support of America's leading corporations, which had managed to sidestep the contention of the reproductive rights movement. Those who did support us usually earmarked their contributions for research, education, or buildings. Corporate support was only about 5 percent of our budget, but it meant a great deal to us. The credibility that such endorsements bestowed was at least as valuable as the actual dollars given. It was important that we receive support from every sector of our society—from the kid who sent us a portion of an allowance, to major conglomerates.

The AT&T Foundation had supported our education programs for twenty-four years. By 1990 we were receiving $50,000 a year for teen pregnancy prevention. Our relationship with the foundation had always been cordial; and as it repeatedly expressed approval of our work, I felt confident that we could rely on its support for the foreseeable future.

In 1988, the Christian Action Council had begun a campaign to boycott corporate supporters of Planned Parenthood. The Christian Action Council had been founded in 1975 in Minneapolis, Minnesota, by C. Everett Koop (yet to become surgeon general), the Reverend Harold O. J. Brown, a longtime antiabortion activist, and others. Established as a Protestant counterpart to the National Right to Life Committee and the American Life League, which were both originally predominantly Catholic, the Christian Action Council courted that segment of its constituency that supported a strict fundamentalist interpretation of the Bible. AT&T was on the list of corporations targeted for boycotts and other pressures to persuade them to discontinue their support of PPFA.

In late 1989, we knew that the CAC had made threats to the sportswear company Patagonia, and BPC, the British oil company, both of whom had rebuffed them. However, as rumors persisted, and realizing that our corporate support could be vulnerable, I called Reynold Levy, president of the AT&T Foundation, to arrange a meeting to discuss how Planned Parenthood could mobilize grassroots support to counter the Christian Action Council. The foundation was considering a renewal of our funding.

"The pressure on AT and T could become intense," I warned.

Reynold assured me that we needn't concern ourselves on this matter. AT&T preferred to handle the challenge in its own way, and he didn't anticipate any problems in continuing our funding.

"But you don't know what these people are like," I pressed him. "Not countering their threats will only give the impression that you think they represent a significant opposition to the foundation's support of Planned Parenthood."

"We don't want to get a lot of conflict started," he insisted.

I'd heard this reasoning before. It usually signaled a naive belief that an accommodation could be made with the pro-criminalist demands. I could not persuade Reynold that those who favored his foundation's support of us had no way of neutralizing those opposed to it if they didn't know what was happening.

Some weeks after our conversation, he called to inform me that the decision would probably be made to discontinue our funding. Given his earlier assurances, I was taken aback, but not surprised. He told me that they were getting a lot of opposition from within the company because of their grant to us. When I asked him to tell me about the nature and amount of the opposition, he declined. I pleaded again that the AT&T Foundation not give in. Sensing that my entreaties were in vain, I shifted my argument.

"If you are determined to give in to these people, please don't make it public," I implored him. "It will only give aid and comfort to the people who are opposed to women's reproductive rights. And it will cut us off at the knees." I also feared that it would have a dampening effect on our support from other corporations. I offered a strategy in which we would be spared a modicum of dignity: "Phase out the funding over a period of a year or two, so that it looks as though you've just changed your priorities."

I had little hope that he would reconsider and repel the threats of the pro-criminalists, who by targeting AT&T's funding of our education program were once again demonstrating that their focus was not just on abortion but on all our work.

On March 12, I received a formal letter from Reynold Levy, which stated that the AT&T Foundation was withdrawing its support because of concern from employees, customers, suppliers, and shareowners that their support was being used to fund abortion. AT&T did not want to give this impression, as its grants were intended, not to fund abortion, he reminded me in his letter, but to "strengthen families and help teenage parents to raise their children to become independent adults and to avoid unwanted pregnancies."[9]

A day after Reynold's letter to me, Jane Redfern, senior vice president of the foundation, wrote to Douglas Scott, director of public policy for the Christian Action Council:

> Noting Planned Parenthood's increasing role in abortion rights advocacy, the trustees of AT&T Foundation recently concluded that we are unable to clarify to our constituents' satisfaction the distinction between funding of Planned Parenthood's educational programs and taking a position in support of abortion . . . Therefore, the trustees have decided that the AT&T Foundation will no longer provide philanthropic support to Planned Parenthood. . . .[10]

Reynold Levy also wrote to AT&T employees, completing the circle of public humiliation for us:

> Our funding of Planned Parenthood, part of an effort to reduce the number of unwanted teenage pregnancies, has supported educational projects, not clinical or abortion-related activities. While the foundation trustees have not viewed this as taking a position on abortion, increasingly many employees, customers and share owners . . . have viewed it as such. AT&T does not take a position on the highly personal issue of abortion; to do so would be presumptuous, because it is a matter of personal conscience.[11]

I called him in a rage. "I can't believe that you have not only discontinued the funding of the very programs that prevent the need for abortion, you have done so precipitously, and you have done so in a public way that only encourages attacks on other companies that support us."

He remained coolly detached. Now believing that there was no point in reasoning with him, I promised, "Planned Parenthood will not sit by and allow a public company to be used as a tool of right-wing zealots. We will do everything possible to make sure that the public understands AT and T has capitulated to right-wing pressures."

The Christian Action Coalition wasted no time chronicling its victory to its supporters:

AT&T is off the hook! . . . Even the corporate giants are sensitive to public opinion. You, the powerful buying public that chooses to use or not to use specific products or services, have made a difference and won a victory for life! . . .[12]

The only course left to us was to reveal the offense to the public through paid advertisements in major newspapers. We asked Herb Chao Gunther to prepare the campaign. Even if we could not save our funding, perhaps we could prevent other corporations from following in AT&T's footsteps if we made them understand that the silent majority supportive of Planned Parenthood could be mobilized. I made one final, futile attempt to get the company to change the way it was implementing its decision. I attempted, unsuccessfully, to meet with AT&T's chairman, Robert Allen.

Within days, we placed full-page ads in the *The New York Times* and in Newark's *Star Ledger*. *The Wall Street Journal* and the *Los Angeles Times* refused to accept them. The headline read: "AT&T Hangs Up on Planned Parenthood."

We drafted a letter to AT&T that was signed by prominent business leaders, academicians, celebrities, and shareholders, urging reinstatement of our funding. We also released a press statement, and wrote to our 600,000 supporters, urging them to contact AT&T to express their opinion. And we encouraged AT&T stockholders, users of AT&T services, employees of AT&T, and PPFA friends to express their views about the decision directly to the chairman, Robert Allen, whose address we provided. AT&T employees were also urged to contact Reynold Levy demanding that their contributions to PPFA via United Way campaigns be matched by the company.

As was now standard within Planned Parenthood, there was criticism of our publicly criticizing major institutions. But to have remained silent would have been tantamount to capitulating to the Christian Action Council, as the AT&T Foundation had done. We had to make it clear that similar actions would lead to even greater controversy than our opponents could muster. I understood the risk, but the greater risk of the tyranny of a fringe element imposing its will, unchallenged, on a public company was, to me, unthinkable.

The response to our fervent campaign far exceeded our expectations. AT&T employees organized a fund-raising campaign to restore the funding. An invitation to participate in this campaign was received by about

305,000 employees via the company's E-mail system. AT&T had to install extra lines to handle the volume of protest from outside. One of our donors offered to contribute $10,000 if we were able to get four other donors to do the same—to replace the $50,000 grant.

But addressing the offense with a short-term media blitz and fund-raising campaign could not repair the damage done not just to Planned Parenthood but, more important, to women. We decided to try to get a resolution on the 1991 AT&T shareholders ballot that would instruct the foundation to restore funding to Planned Parenthood. Ann Lewis, of the American Jewish Congress and an AT&T shareholder, agreed to put forth a resolution to be voted on at the April 1991 shareholders' meeting.

AT&T tried to block the move by asking the Securities and Exchange Commission to investigate our actions, claiming that we were interfering in a matter related to the company's ordinary business, that the company had redirected funding to other organizations engaged in teen pregnancy prevention and parenting programs, and that our campaign had been false and misleading.

After an investigation of our activities, the SEC ruled against AT&T, and the shareholder proposal was allowed to go on the ballot of its April 17, 1991, shareholders' meeting. Liz Holtzman, then comptroller of the City of New York, organized an effort among comptrollers in major cities to vote the AT&T shares in their retirement funds in favor of the resolution.

It is generally all but impossible to get a ballot measure passed when that measure is opposed by management, as this one was. A 3 percent vote will guarantee a place on the ballot for the following year; a 5 percent vote will ensure a place on the ballot for the next three years; a 10 percent vote is considered a victory that will undoubtedly result in a change of policy. We came painfully close. By not remaining silent when women's lives were on the line, we were able to generate 9.5 percent support for our proposal.

CHAPTER 34

THE WICHITA SHOWDOWN: PRIVATE
DECISIONS, PUBLIC DEBATE

It was 1991, and Felicia and I had just returned from the two weeks we always took together at the end of summer, before she returned to school. That year we'd traveled to the Galapagos Islands, so it wasn't until we returned from the long flight from South America that I began to learn about all that happened while we were away.

There was a message on my answering machine from David Andrews, who told me, "Phil Donahue would like you to be in Wichita in two days to appear on his show about the Wichita siege. And guess who you'll be up against?"

I didn't want to think about it.

"Randall Terry. Phil says you're the only one who can handle Terry, and he won't do the show without you."

After the serene doldrums of the equator, I was hardly ready to face the full force of the abortion debate. But I didn't have a choice. The man was too dangerous to go unchallenged.

Randall Terry and Operation Rescue, an aggressive faction of the pro-criminalist movement, had first emerged in the news in November 1986. A former used-car salesman from Rochester, New York, Terry had dropped out of high school and become a born-again Christian. He would eventually proclaim his purpose: "to reform this culture . . . the arts, the media, the entertainment industries, medicine, the sciences, education—to return to right and wrong, a Judeo-Christian base."[1] One of his aunts had worked for Planned Parenthood of Rochester.

Terry assumed a place on the national stage at the 1988 Democratic National Convention in Atlanta, Georgia. To grab the media spotlight, hundreds of Terry's supporters had descended upon the city to picket the convention. Their plan was to create a spectacle by blockading abortion clinics throughout Atlanta and to be arrested en masse for trespassing. They taunted and jeered at the women who attempted to enter the Atlanta Northside Family Planning Services, the Atlanta Surgical Center, and the Midtown Hospital, calling them whores, lesbians, and murderers.

Before the convention was over, 134 of these protesters had been arrested. Many remained in jail because they refused to give their real names. "Jane Doe" and "John Doe," they called themselves, so that formal charges could not be pressed. Terry was arrested twice, but released both times on bail raised by his supporters.

By the end of 1989, Operation Rescue had become a national phenomenon. By its own estimate, 37,000 of its ranks had been arrested for participating in clinic protests around the country.[2] The organization's tactics were attracting so much attention that it even garnered the support of John Cardinal O'Connor, of the Archdiocese of New York, and The Moral Majority's Jerry Falwell, who contributed $10,000 toward Terry's release in a subsequent arrest.[3]

In 1991, Operation Rescue decided to make Wichita, Kansas, the site of a major antiabortion campaign. Encouraged by Governor Joan Finney and welcomed by Wichita mayor Bob Knight, Terry and his cohorts targeted Women's Health Care Services. This clinic, owned by Dr. George Tiller, was one of the few facilities in the country that provided second-trimester abortions, and Operation Rescue intended to capitalize on the widespread ambivalence toward late-term abortions. Its organizers also figured that a sustained campaign in one location, especially in Middle America, would best serve to draw national media attention.

About eighty Operation Rescue members—a mere trickle, given the numbers soon to arrive—entered Wichita the week of Sunday, July 14. Unfortunately, in an effort to avoid confrontation with Terry and his followers, Wichita's three abortion clinics had arranged to close for that week. I say "unfortunately" because I believe that closing clinics actually encourages terrorists, and is a response that should never be considered. It is the responsibility of law-enforcement agencies to protect the clinics and those engaged in lawful activities. No one was surprised when Terry pronounced this triple capitulation a victory for his forces. Since they were picketing closed clinics, the protests for that week were peaceful and no arrests were made.

Then Terry revealed that Operation Rescue planned to stay in Wichita for the summer. Now the real struggle began. For six weeks, the life of this small midwestern city was daily subjected to willful damage and disruption.

426 / Life on the Line

Law-enforcement authorities were overwhelmed by the challenges posed by the hundreds of agitators who had installed themselves there.

Dr. Tiller went to court and filed a lawsuit against Operation Rescue, requesting that the court immediately restrain and prohibit members of the group from trespassing and from blocking entry to his clinic or exit from it; from harassing and abusing patients and workers; from obstructing the work of his clinic with noise; and from "harassing and intimidating or physically abusing Dr. George R. Tiller and his family." The complaint requested that each defendant be levied a contempt penalty of $25,000 a day for the first violation of the order, and double that amount for each successive violation.[4]

On Tuesday, July 23, Federal District Judge Patrick F. Kelly, reported to be a devout Catholic, granted all of Dr. Tiller's requests, including the penalties for contempt of the judge's order, which was later extended to include the other abortion clinics in Wichita.

When he was served with Judge Kelly's order, Terry brazenly threw it to the street. "What injunction? . . . Our injunction comes from God,"[5] he reportedly said. At that point, the police began making arrests—over 200 on that Tuesday alone. The next day, ignoring the injunction, 550 Operation Rescue followers blocked the entrance to the Women's Health Care Services clinic. They, along with Terry and his colleagues Pat Mahoney and Jim Evans, were arrested. Evans was released under an order not to return to the scene.[6]

It was reported that Mayor Bob Knight and City Manager Chris Cherches had told Police Chief Rick Stone that his officers were to first let protesters block the gate to the clinic, and only then start arresting them, using minimum force. But the following Monday, Judge Kelly ordered federal marshals to keep open the entrance to Tiller's clinic. Up to this point, arrests among the interlopers and the local residents who supported them had been for violations of city ordinances, such as loitering and trespassing. Violating Judge Kelly's order now meant committing a federal offense. The protesters' response was to move across the street, which allowed employees and patients to enter the clinic without direct interdiction. Operation Rescue official Joe Slovenic, a Cleveland minister, told the hundred or so protesters, "We've done everything we can physically do today."[7]

On July 31, Terry and Mahoney, who'd been arrested on the first day of the injunction, were released from jail after assuring Judge Kelly that they would stop blocking access to abortion clinics. However, once out, Terry said he could not force his followers to abide by his pledge. By early August, nearly 2,000 protesters, including almost a hundred members of the clergy, had been arrested.

In the midst of the siege, I called Dr. Tiller in Wichita to thank him for his courage in the face of the egregious assaults at his clinics. A rumor was circulating among colleagues in the pro-choice community that Tiller was beginning to question whether he should continue to oppose the law to limit second-trimester abortions—still pending in the Kansas state legislature. If he ceased to oppose the restrictions, Operation Rescue would count his submission as a major moral victory, and one that validated the effectiveness of the group's tactics.

I didn't presume to understand the pressure Dr. Tiller was under. But I knew one thing for certain: If he yielded to people who would never give up until all of women's reproductive rights were lost, the few doctors in the country who did still perform late abortions would most likely be subjected to even more intense harassment, if not violence. Ultimately, I knew, a vital source of service, often in the most tragic circumstances, could be lost. Late-term abortions are often needed when, for example, pregnancy would make a chronic condition worse, as in the case of a low-income woman whose pregnancy would not kill her but impair her for life; or when a couple who discovers that the fetus in a wanted pregnancy has been blighted by a congenital defect that would mean certain death after delivery; or when a twelve-year-old has been impregnated through incest but the pregnancy has not been discovered until the advanced stages.

Dr. Tiller thanked me for calling and expressed his sense of isolation under the daily barrage. Though it may have been small comfort, I ended the conversation with the heartfelt assurance that his courage was an inspiration to us all.

On Monday, August 5, Judge Kelly, who had by this time himself been confronted by protests on the lawn of his home and had received several death threats, held a two-hour court hearing on whether to extend his temporary restraining order into a more permanent preliminary injunction. He decided in favor of the injunction and promised to jail anyone who defied it—including Kansas governor Joan Finney and the Roman Catholic bishop of the Wichita diocese, Eugene Gerber. Governor Finney had addressed an Operation Rescue rally a few days prior to the injunction, and Bishop Gerber had participated in a blockade of a clinic.

At a news conference immediately following the hearing, Kelly declared that the court had taken charge. He had given up hope of city officials handling the situation appropriately since they seemed to be showing support for Operation Rescue's actions: Not only the City Council members, but the governor, too, had attended the Operation Rescue demonstrations.

Following Judge Kelly's order, Mayor Knight said that city officials would continue following the advice of City Attorney Joe Allen Lang and the city's law department to arrest all lawbreakers and bring them to trial, because:

A stance which preempts the legal rights of the demonstrators, or a less vigorous arrest policy which ignores the legal rights of the parties against whom the demonstrations are directed, may subject this city to legal actions.[8]

On August 7, two days after filing the preliminary injunction, Kelly handed down his opinion. In it, he accepted the plaintiff's argument, which referred to a Reconstruction-era law known as the Ku Klux Klan Act (1985(3)), originally passed by Congress in 1871 to protect the civil rights of African Americans. In basic terms, the act forbids conspiracies designed to deprive a person or class of persons of the equal protection of the laws or of equal privileges and immunities under the laws and Constitution of the United States. Numerous federal courts had subsequently expanded its protection to include gender-based aggression. Kelly concluded that "a conspiracy motivated by gender-based animus is actionable under [the law] 1985(3)."[9]

Operation Rescue was no stranger to the evolution of 1985(3). Two years earlier, in the fall of 1989, when Operation Rescue announced plans to try to close down clinics in the Washington, D.C., area, a coalition led by NOW, Planned Parenthood, and local clinics, and represented by the NOW Legal Defense and Education Fund, struck back by going to federal court in Virginia prior to the demonstration. In that case, the district court put a ban on the blockades, saying that they constituted a conspiracy to deprive women seeking abortions of their civil rights and therefore violated the Ku Klux Klan Act, ruling that the blockades interfered with the women's right to travel.[10] The federal appeals court in Richmond upheld the lower court ruling. It was being appealed to the Supreme Court as *Bray v. Alexandria Health Services.*

Back in Wichita, George Bush's Justice Department entered the case for Operation Rescue by arguing in a lengthy brief that the federal courts had no jurisdiction in these cases because the Ku Klux Klan Act did not apply to women seeking abortions.

Since many women had come from other states to Dr. George Tiller's clinic to obtain late-term abortions, this emphasis on travel was significant. In the past, the courts had decided that the right to an abortion could be protected only from government interference. In the 1871 statute, the Ku Klux Klan Act, the right to travel was protected not only from government action but from private interference as well. Judge Kelly had accepted this argument: there was certainly sufficient evidence of private interference by Operation Rescue.

Operation Rescue appealed Kelly's ruling and requested a stay of the federal jurist's lock on their activities during the appeal. Bush administration Justice Department lawyers, under Attorney General Richard Thornburgh's direction, flew out to the Kansas court to Operation Rescue's aid, just as it had intervened in Virginia six months earlier to disrupt NOW's case. If let stand, the ruling of the district court could undercut the Justice Department's argument before the High Court that the Ku Klux Klan Act did not apply to women seeking abortion. The Bush administration had to protect its position, fearing that if the courts agreed with the clinics, laws that it favored would be struck down—laws that already discriminated against women seeking abortions, such as the Hyde amendment and parental-consent requirements that were, arguably, gender-based animus.

Judge Kelly granted the government's request for a stay, but not without first saying, "I am disgusted by this move by the United States."

On August 8, three days after Kelly issued the preliminary injunction and called on U.S. marshals to back it up, demonstrators again tried to block the entrance to Tiller's clinic. About twelve marshals and thirty-five police officers in riot gear were at the scene. Two people were arrested—an unidentified man and a Catholic priest, who were charged with battery for allegedly running into a police officer.[11]

The law-enforcement agencies were gaining control of the situation. While demonstrators continued to pile up behind police barricades, they made few attempts to cross the barricades or to lie down in front of cars trying to enter the parking lots.[12] On Sunday, August 11, at a rally of about three thousand people, Operation Rescue leaders announced that they would be leaving Wichita in two weeks.

However, on August 20, about 150 demonstrators stormed Tiller's clinic, knocking down two sawhorse barricades, scaling a wrought-iron fence, and blocking the driveway while several others knelt in front of a car carrying a patient. About 130 adults and 10 children were arrested. Police Captain George Scantlin commented, "It was the most aggressive they've been so far. No question."[13]

Over 2,600 arrests and $650,000 in police and court costs later, the siege ended with separate rallies in Wichita—one by the pro-criminalists (25,000 people attended), and one by pro-choice supporters (about 5,000 attended).[14]

Three years later, on August 19, 1994, Dr. Tiller was shot and seriously wounded outside his clinic by a known pro-criminalist activist.

After David Andrews had informed me of the proposed showdown with Randall Terry on Phil Donahue's show, I shifted my attention from the virtually unthinkable to the comfort of the immediately manageable. I called Bruce Clark, my close friend and hairstylist, to see if he could squeeze me in the next day. "I have to do *Donahue*," I pleaded. For twelve years of television news shows and magazine photo shoots, Bruce had never failed me, whether it was for 6:30 A.M. or 11:30 P.M. studio calls. He was always there to listen to my latest travail or triumph and lift my spirits with words of encouragement or a wonderful haircut. I loved him as the brother I never had. "Okay, come in tomorrow at eleven," he sighed.

I might have worried about what I was going to say on *Donahue*, but I never worried about how I would look after Bruce's work was done. Like me, and like my mother before me, Bruce believed that being well-groomed was an essential part of being an effective communicator. Though he has never said so, I felt that he saw his work as his vicarious contribution to the cause.

The next morning, September 6, I headed for Wichita. When we landed, two members of the uniformed police force boarded the plane and walked up to my seat. I felt immediate panic that something had happened to Felicia or a member of my family.

"Ms. Wattleton, we're here to take you to the fairgrounds coliseum," they informed me. When I realized their purpose, my fear subsided. Given the uproar of the summer, having my security so tightly guarded was a comfort. Before the other passengers could disembark, they escorted me to a waiting police cruiser on the airport tarmac. Clearly, this was not going to be a routine television appearance.

My parents and I had traveled through Wichita when I was a child. Now, as lush cornfields rolled past the windows, I found myself recalling our journeys to the Kansas State camp meeting in Topeka—Mama, Daddy, and me. I remembered sitting in the backseat in one of my nylon dresses, and visualized the silhouettes of Mama and Daddy in front of me. I opened the window of the air-conditioned squad car to feel the Kansas breeze blow hot in my face once again. At that moment, I missed Daddy more than I ever had.

Finally, I turned my attention back to the task at hand. As I reviewed the briefing papers prepared for me by my staff, I casually asked Sam Rodriguez, one of our staff members who was responsible for handling my advance arrangements, how many people were expected at the coliseum. "A full house," he answered.

"What do you mean a full house?"

"Oh, five thousand."

I thought I'd misheard him. "Five thousand what?!"

"People," he said, laughing. "That's how many the coliseum will seat. The tickets were snapped up within hours of their availability."

"You're joking."

Sam shook his head, and went on to explain that the *Donahue* show had evenly distributed the tickets to pro-choice and pro-criminalist advocates. We could expect twenty-five hundred passionately vocal partisans on either side of the divide.

The contrast between my memories of the tent revivals, which gathered in scores of the shouting and singing faithful, and my nervous anticipation over participating on national television in one of the most contentious debates of our time, before thousands of potential combatants, was more than I could conceive. For once, I was terrified.

When we arrived at the large auditorium, Phil, caught up in the whirl-wind of activity that always preceded his shows, was pacing back and forth with the energy of a veteran ringmaster.

"Don't you think you've gone a little crazy here?" I asked him.

He laughed. "Maybe you're right. But, kid, we're here, so we've got to make this work."

Out on stage, Phil animatedly warned all present that if they became unmanageable he would simply have their microphones turned off and deny them the opportunity of getting their views out on national TV.

As Randall Terry walked onto the stage, I felt the charged energy in the air. My pulse pounded faster than usual. I tried to coax my jaw muscles into permitting a smile. Be pleasant and relaxed, I lectured myself. No matter how obnoxious he gets, don't let him get to you.

As soon as we had settled into our straight-backed upholstered armchairs, Randall Terry began to expound upon my sins and the willingness of God to forgive me if I "turned to Him." I thought, This is going to be the longest hour of my life.

When we were before the camera, Phil began:

Ladies and gentleman across America, I am pleased to welcome you to your heartland. This is the city that has found itself on the front page of every newspaper in the world in recent weeks. This is also a city of very civic, compassionate, generous, proud Americans. This is Wichita, Kansas![15]

Taking Phil's compliment to heart and heeding his rallying cry that, although "not everyone in this hall will agree with any single observation throughout this hour . . . [we] are going to see if we can accept the challenge of discussing one of the most emotionally charged issues in our land today,"[16] the audience was very well behaved.

After deferring to "the lady" to begin, after my opening remarks, Randall Terry began, "Abortion is the brutal murder of an innocent child . . . God almighty judges this country for this holocaust."[17]

When, during the first commercial break, Terry resumed insulting and proselytizing me, I resolved that during the next break I would not cope with his agitation in the few minutes allowed to wipe my brow, get a dusting of face powder, and collect my thoughts. So when he started in, "Faye, you're selling your people down the river, you should be ashamed,"

I turned and fairly snarled, "If you don't leave me alone I will ask the show's producer to make you leave the stage during the breaks." I was furious.

He left me alone after that—he wasn't willing to forfeit the rock star–level adulation of his admirers if he had to be ushered out. Immediately following Phil's "We'll be right back," Terry's fans would cluster at the foot of the stage, calling out, "We're praying for you!" or "Thank you for saving my baby. I was going to have an abortion!" Then they would turn, glower at me, and whirl back to their seats.

Later, on the air, he would attack me on one of his favorite themes: my race and Planned Parenthood's supposed racist origins.

Terry: Phil, there are three black people right here who all just clapped their hands in agreement with me. Why? Faye—listen to me. Let me finish! Margaret Sanger, the founder of Planned Parenthood, was an avowed racist. She wanted to eliminate the black community. She said so again and again and she, Faye Wattleton, knows this and has never disavowed the racist statements of Margaret Sanger. She even said so in a 1984 interview in the *Washington Times.* You have—and to say that abortion for black women is somehow a favor to them, to kill their offspring— you have been bought, Faye. You have been bought!

Donahue: Let me just—give me a chance here! Give me a chance.

Me: Mr. Terry, I think it is outrageous that you have chosen to use my race to exploit your point of view.

Terry: No! They're using your race to exploit you, Faye! . . . You're a black woman. That's why they hired you.

Me: I do not need you to tell me what my choices are about my life and my body because I am a black person.

Terry: No, that's not my point.

Me: I can make that choice for myself, just as every black woman can make that choice for herself. And we are not inherently incapable of deciding without you.[18]

One of the last exchanges of the show followed a question about how Planned Parenthood counseled women who were facing an unwanted pregnancy—particularly, about why we didn't encourage them to put their children up for adoption.

Me: I think that women do make the choice to continue their pregnancies, to have the babies and to give them up for adoption. But that choice should not be made by people in the street. It should be made by the woman involved and it must be her choice.

Terry: At least she's admitting it's a baby. At least she's admitting it's a baby that is being killed and that it should be placed for adoption.

Me: What I said was, "continue a pregnancy and have the baby."

Terry: You don't have a frog today. It's not a frog or a ferret that's being killed. It's a baby.[19]

Now turning my head directly toward him, and with all the rage that I felt for the pain he had caused women, I let go of my last restraint and attacked him personally: "I'm fully aware of that. I am fully aware of that . . . Mr. Terry, since I have had a baby and I don't believe you have."[20]

The coliseum erupted in cheers of support, laughter, and whistles.

Having trained my gaze on Terry along with my anger, I saw that, briefly, some stark emotion froze his features. The color drained from his face. Instead of his usual glib aplomb, for a moment he seemed stunned, speechless, even hurt. I had struck a sensitive nerve. What really motivates this man? I wondered. Had I pierced a veil covering buried hurt and anger that were being channeled into his assaults on women?

Farther along the way, we got another dose of incendiary words from Mr. Terry: "Dr. George Tiller's going to do hard time when this is all over. He is a mass murderer. He is an enemy of humanity."[21]

At last, the hour that seemed like a year was over. As usual, I left the set with weak knees, and started to think of all the things that I should have said—all the points that I should have made. But then I asked myself, what had brought us to Wichita? What had provoked 5,000 people in a town of 300,000 to show up for a television show? Yes, it was Donahue—but it was so much more. After all these years of legal contraception and abortion, how could these debates still spark such intense emotion? How could a matter so *personal* as a woman's decision whether or when to have a child evoke such *public* emotion? Why should a woman's body be the target of social chaos? What phenomena had created the Randall Terrys of this world—and those whose deeds ran darker even than his words?

I had been posing these questions to myself over and over from my very first years with Planned Parenthood. And I always came to the same conclusion. The root conflict was not about abortion. It was about the liberation of women and the power and responsibility that such liberation vested in us.

The fear of such power is not restricted to men, for there are also women who fear claiming it for themselves and allowing it for other women. It is deeply threatening to change the balance of power in human relationships. It is more reassuring to have clearly defined boundaries of power than to hand over authority to those who have not traditionally been entrusted with such authority. A new order, one in which women are vested with the enormous power of choosing for themselves whether they will bring new life into this world, is more than some can tolerate or accept.

CHAPTER 35

THE END OF THE LINE

September 24, 1991, dawned brilliantly sunny and warm. The passage of summer and the promise of fall were carried on the gentle breeze that met me as I rushed out of the front door of my apartment building and into the car that would take me to the airport. I was headed for Utica, New York, to make a speech at a Planned Parenthood event that night.

Felicia had left for school a few minutes earlier. Next month she'll be sixteen, I thought as we hugged each other good-bye.

I promised as I had hundreds of times before, as much to reassure myself as to comfort her, "I'll call you tonight and give you my hotel room number."

The last-minute bustle of packing and instructions had left me strangely short of breath. Since I routinely worked out at a gym two or three times a week, and was rarely out of breath, except after a demanding hour on the tennis court, I took notice. As I settled into the comfortable seat of the car for the twenty-minute ride from our apartment to La Guardia Airport, I felt oppressively tired, as if I'd just finished a hard day's work.

Although the day had just begun, I kept thinking of the two hours later that day that I always reserved for a break on such trips. I used that time—after the media interviews and before the pre-dinner cocktail party and speech—to work on my speech and to call my office for messages or to manage any crisis that may have erupted. Sometimes I did media interviews by telephone on controversies breaking in other parts of the country. Occasionally an interview would be taped at a local television station for play on the network evening news or for CNN or *Nightline*. But as tired as I felt on this particular morning, I was certain that all I would do this time was sleep.

At the airport I scrambled out of the car, checked my bag, and rushed down the long corridor toward the gate, where a small commuter airplane waited. I glanced down at my watch and saw that, as usual, I had only a few minutes to spare. I quickened my pace. But then, suddenly, I began to feel slightly dizzy. There was a tightness in my chest, as though a heavy hand were pressing against it. Then a sharp pain began to travel up my arm and my neck, straight to my left temple. I had never felt—nor have I since felt—such a frightening sensation. I remembered that my aunt Alice had been felled by a stroke several years earlier. And, although my blood pressure has always been on the lower end of normal, my nursing instincts vaulted me into the fear that I might be disabled by a brain hemorrhage. I stopped for a few moments until the pain subsided and I felt in control of my body again.

Moving more slowly now, but decisively, I continued toward the gate.

Buckled into my seat on the plane, I thought about the sensation I'd just experienced and the sense of panic it had engendered. I couldn't tell myself, "Oh, it's nothing." Despite the fact that my doctor had assured me I was fine after my annual physical examination a few months earlier, I could not dismiss my body's warning to slow down.

I don't think anyone around me knew just how deeply I was feeling the strain. I was good at bottling it all in, just as I would that day. If the pains recurred, I would take care of them at that point. For the moment, I had an audience to satisfy and an affiliate not to disappoint.

The whole of 1991 had been a year of escalating tensions. In the beginning of the year, there was a general consensus between the pro-choice coalition and our supporters in Congress that something needed to be done to protect the rights secured by *Roe*. Not only had the *Webster* decision put it in jeopardy, it seemed likely that Bush would be able to capitalize on his Gulf War popularity to get reelected in 1992. A second term would give him the opportunity to appoint two to three more right-wing Supreme Court justices. If the Senate confirmed them, there was a high probability that *Roe* would be overturned, or so deeply injured that its protections would become academic.

It was Don Edwards (D-CA), chair of the House Judiciary Subcommittee on Civil and Constitutional Rights, who took the initiative by creating the Freedom of Choice Act, which would have supposedly codified *Roe v. Wade* within a federal statute. In general, a state:

(1) may not restrict the freedom of a woman to choose whether to terminate a pregnancy before fetal viability;

(2) may restrict the freedom of a woman to choose to terminate a pregnancy after fetal viability unless such a termination is necessary to preserve the life or health of the woman; and

(3) may impose requirements on the performance of abortion procedures if such requirements are medically necessary to protect the health of women undergoing such procedures.[1]

But even before the statute began its legislative journey, it came under fire from those who opposed the very idea of it, and who proceeded to bind it in restrictive language. Undermining the foundation of the bill, the additional wording now stated:

Nothing in this Act shall be construed to:

(1) prevent a state from protecting unwilling individuals or private health-care institutions from having to participate in the performance of abortions to which they are conscientiously opposed;

(2) prevent a state from declining to pay for the performance of abortions; or

(3) prevent a state from requiring a minor to involve a parent, or guardian, or other responsible adult before terminating pregnancy.[2]

"Everyone here in Washington believes this is the only way we can get freedom of choice passed," said Bill Hamilton, my Washington-based colleague, trying to explain the rationale behind these precedent-setting limitations on a federal proposal ostensibly designed to guarantee the rights enunciated in *Roe*. But there was no excusing these three points that so flagrantly undermined the rights of poor women and teenagers who were already paying a high price for this conflict over reproductive rights for all women.

Having spent decades opposing parental-consent restrictions for teenagers and funding discrimination against poor women in the courts, Congress, and state legislatures, it would have been utterly hypocritical for Planned Parenthood to support a federal statute that would reverse everything we had so vigorously opposed. I immediately made our opposition public, announcing that we would not support such a travesty, even if it meant not getting a freedom of choice act passed.

Hoping to persuade the pro-choice coalition to unify behind the bill, Senator Alan Cranston (D-CA) called a meeting with all of us, along with Senate and House supporters, to discuss our objections.

The heads of the pro-choice organizations were arranged in a semicircle of chairs facing the members of Congress, who sat on the comfortable sofa and chairs in the soon-to-be-retiring California senator's office. Our staff members sat in a second circle behind us. Kind-faced and studious, Don Edwards started the conversation by reiterating his desire to see *Roe* protected. "But I don't want to move the legislation if you people in the pro-choice coalition aren't going to get behind it."

While we were unanimous in expressing our appreciation of his leadership, it quickly became clear that we were divided into two philosophical camps—those who would simply not support the bill with the restrictive amendments, and those who believed that, for pragmatic reasons, the modifiers were the only way that anything was going to make it through Congress. The ACLU, NOW, and Planned Parenthood were in the minority as we stood our ground in refusing to agree to the restrictions. Even Bill Hamilton and I disagreed on the issue, but he knew that, based on our policies, we had no choice but to take this position. He also knew that I wouldn't tolerate being undercut in this meeting.

I tried to explain to the gathered senators and congressmen the impact the bill would have on our clients. Ira Glasser, executive director of the ACLU, and Mort Halperin, also of the ACLU, tried to get them to understand the moral impossibility of the ACLU's challenging each of the restrictions in lawsuits against the states, only to agree to them in Congress.

And then I heard words from Senator Packwood that I thought I'd never hear. "I can't support your position," he said. "We have to do something about parental-consent requirements or we'll never get anything passed. With one or two changes on the Court, *Roe* could be history."

I was flabbergasted. Here was a senator who had been an early leader in state abortion reform and with whom we had collaborated on so many occasions to defeat anti-choice legislation, a senator from a state where parental-consent requirements had been solidly defeated by citizens on a statewide ballot referendum that year, a senator who had threatened to read the telephone book aloud on the floor of the Senate to filibuster the defeat of such anti-abortion legislation. "Bob, I cannot believe that you would be willing to support the first federal legislation that reverses the gains that you have spent years helping to achieve."

The senator's face flashed impatience with my impertinence.

But it seemed that even our staunchest supporters were weakening under the steady onslaught of the forces they had so long defied, running for cover under the banner of "pragmatism." We're really in for some tough times, I thought, my heart sinking with the recognition that an era of battling was ending and one of accommodation was taking hold. That meant a new kind of battle, a broadening struggle within our ranks that could do more damage to our cause than even our enemies had been able to do. I felt myself go limp with frustration, fury, and profound disappointment as it sank in that some of us gathered in that room had begun to *accept* the perceived political realities rather than continue to resist them. Yet a part of me also empathized with the simple human quality of battle fatigue. It's settling in everywhere, I thought.

Sensing the tension building in the room, Mort Halperin jumped in. "Well, as long as the legislation has been introduced, let's see how far we can move it without restrictions. Don, you could hold hearings on the parental-consent restrictions. We could bring kids to testify about their horrible experiences. We may be able to get the amendments killed if we can make people understand what happens in real life."

But the senators and congressmen were not persuaded by Mort's idea. They told us that they just wanted to get something passed—"while we still can."

Growing exasperated at the fruitless back-and-forth, I challenged, "Now, let me get this straight," my eyes flashing at no one in particular but at the sheer lunacy of our discussion. "You're saying that we should work for a federal bill that says that states can impose parental-consent language and gives in to states' denial of payment for abortions for poor women?"

No one could bring themselves to say "yes," but no one offered a denial, either.

As the discussion turned to bickering over the interpretation of the specific language of the restrictions, Barbara Boxer (D-CA) started to lecture us on the art of politics. "Look, you people need to understand something. You need to be realistic here. Politics is about compromise. You want it all. If you can't get it all, you have to decide what you can live with."

Because Ira Glasser, Molly Yard, and I were the only organization leaders who would not agree to even consider the proposed federal restrictions, it was clear that she was scolding us in particular. The fact that we headed the largest organizations in the pro-choice movement made us obstacles they couldn't ignore.

Ira turned to Barbara, his Brooklyn accent growing thicker with his anger:

I don't need you to tell me what politics is all about. I've been doing this legislative work for twenty-five years. I know how to compromise and what compromise means, but this isn't it. This is selling out that part of our constituency that needs us most. We're shooting ourselves in the foot before we even get started. Why should we do that? This is supposed to be the Freedom of Choice Act. You're asking us to agree to a bill in advance of a fight that says the most vulnerable women will have no freedom of choice at all. We just aren't going to do it.

On the shuttle back to New York, Ira and I commiserated with one another. "You know," he observed sadly, "I've always felt a little queasy as a man in these situations, especially when the sentiment is so lopsided. But today I didn't care. We can't let this happen to women."

No further action on the Freedom of Choice Act was taken in 1991.

After the Supreme Court had ruled back in May that the government had the green light to implement the gag rule, we reconvened the advisory group that had planned the Ninety-Day Campaign to End the Gag Rule when Reagan had first announced it. When the Court upheld the government's right to censor free speech, our only remaining hope was to convince Congress to block implementation. Since there were still affiliates who believed "something could be worked out," we hoped this politically charged endeavor would forestall a confrontation between them and the national organization.

I dreaded the idea of standing before Congress, the press, or the American people and trying to justify compromising our principles for the sake of government funding. I refused to believe we had to make such concessions. Although, by our own choice, our political hands were tied because of our reluctance to get involved in elections, I believed that if we worked hard enough, we could still mobilize enough opposition to persuade Congress to stand up to the president.

"Let's not spend all our energy painting useless and damaging scenarios," I argued over and over again. "We should put all of our energy into convincing Congress to nullify the rule. After all, both houses are in Democratic, and presumably pro-choice, hands." But I knew that, although Congress had been working against the rule since it had been handed down, when push came to shove, it always gave up the fight whenever President Bush made threatening statements.

But then, on November 8, President Bush reiterated his vow to veto the fiscal 1992 Department of Labor–Health and Human Services (HHS)–Education appropriations bill over the freedom of speech language it contained. On November 19, Bush made good on his earlier threat and vetoed the bill.

Meanwhile, in the most vigorous lobbying effort that we had ever mounted, the entire Planned Parenthood Federation joined other reproductive health and rights organizations to prevail upon every member of Congress to overturn the veto. We used every technique at our disposal—from paid print, radio, and television advertisements to direct-mail alerts, to telegrams to persuading major political contributors to call key members of Congress, to arranging visits to their offices by their constituents.

In a clever maneuver designed to preempt the strong opposition to the gag rule, the Bush administration issued a memo promising, "Nothing in these regulations is to prevent a woman from receiving complete medical information about her condition from a physician."[3]

Within hours of the president's veto, the House voted on a motion to override it. As we watched the tally, the tensions of the past months reached an unbearable height in the eternity of those minutes. The final tally fell twelve votes shy of the two-thirds majority needed to nullify the president's rejection. It was the closest we had ever come to overriding a presidential veto since Reagan had been elected in 1980. But close wasn't good enough for the women whose lives were on the line. After so much effort, it was the most bitter defeat we had ever experienced. If censorship was going to be allowed, what other sacred right would be next?

It was a sad day indeed when Thurgood Marshall announced his retirement from the Supreme Court a year after William Brennan had announced his. It was an affront to Justice Marshall's legacy that, on July 1, 1991, President Bush nominated Judge Clarence Thomas as the "best-qualified" successor to fill his position on the bench. Fifteen months earlier, Bush had appointed Mr. Thomas to the District of Columbia Court of Appeals. Before that, from 1982 to 1990, he had served as Reagan's chairman of the Equal Employment Opportunity Commission. When reporters suggested that the president's selection was the kind of quota-based decision that Bush had so publicly abhorred, he responded that he had kept his promise to the "American people and to the Senate by picking the best man for the job on the merits. And the fact he's minority, so much the better. . . . I would strongly resent any charge that might be forthcoming on quotas when it relates to appointing the best man to the Court."[4]

Nevertheless, the fact that an African American was being put up to succeed an African American made it hard not to believe that there wasn't a racial component to Mr. Thomas's nomination. Furthermore, to hold him up as best qualified to replace Thurgood Marshall was preposterous. Nothing in his legal career, nor in the promise of it, could begin to match such African American scholars and jurists as Derrick Bell, Leon Higginbotham, or Constance Motley.

More threatening to our particular cause was the fact that Thomas had demonstrated his clear objections to *Roe v. Wade* and the constitutional principles underpinning it. Although like Souter, Thomas had produced little oral or written evidence of his views on reproductive rights, we did know that he had praised an anti-abortion essay that made caustic references to "the conjured right to abortion," and had signed a report made for President Reagan on the family, authored by Gary Bauer, the architect of the gag rule, attacking not only *Roe*, but also *Planned Parenthood of Central Missouri v. Danforth*, and *Eisenstadt v. Baird*, which upheld the right of unmarried people to use contraceptives. (During the confirmation hearings, Judge Thomas said that he signed the report without reading it.)

After Souter's confirmation, we worried that the Supreme Court was now more heavily weighted toward right-wing extremism than ever before. A reconsideration of *Roe v. Wade* in some form was virtually inevitable. It was now frighteningly possible that Judge Thomas's views could seal the fate of women's reproductive rights.

On the basis of his record, NOW and NARAL opposed the judge's nomination even before he appeared before the Senate Judiciary Committee. However, Planned Parenthood was still fraught from within with conflict over taking public stands against Supreme Court nominees. The board's executive committee decided that, initially, we should take a more cautious stance. We should wait to hear the nominee's views. In my mind there was little likelihood that he would warrant such forbearance, but I remained publicly silent. However, we did urge the judiciary committee to ask the right questions.

Meanwhile, sensitive to Judge Bork's claims that he had been given insufficient support, the White House deployed Senator John Danforth (R-MO) to guide Judge Thomas's candidacy through the Senate process.

When the hearings before the Senate Judiciary Committee commenced on September 10, I listened to Judge Thomas testify that he'd never read or thought about the historic *Roe* decision. Not only was there evidence that he had both spoken and written about it, he had been studying at Yale University Law School when *Roe* was decided. It seemed hard to imagine that such a distinguished law school wouldn't have fostered some discussion among its students about a major constitutional landmark.

As the hearings proceeded, it also became clear that although the Senate was making some effort to downplay the *Rust v. Sullivan* decision in which Justice Souter had provided the deciding vote, the committee was still not in the frame of mind to press vigorously on Judge Thomas's views about reproductive rights. On the other hand, the committee didn't hesitate to question the judge closely on other "unsettled" doctrinal questions—discrimination law and laws governing social welfare, for example—nor did he refuse to express his philosophy on these matters. Reproductive rights had become the hot button, and the senators touched it ever so gingerly. Thomas didn't refuse to answer all questions on privacy, but he did refuse to acknowledge that privacy was a right that belonged to a woman considering the termination of her pregnancy.

After a week of questions and testimony, PPFA board chairperson Ken Edelin, who had joined me in Washington for the hearings, and I decided that we'd heard enough to announce Planned Parenthood's opposition to the nominee. We planned to make our statement during one of the committee's intermissions, but we quickly discovered that speaking to the media was going to be difficult. In a well-orchestrated White House strategy that we hadn't encountered before, Senator Danforth would position his six-foot-plus frame at the microphones just before the committee would break and would talk into the cameras until the hearings resumed. After waiting futilely through several recesses, we realized we were going to have to be more assertive. Catching a brief pause in his monologue, I moved aggressively into the sliver of silence to announce that we had a statement to make. Danforth relinquished the microphone without protest:

> In nominating Judge Souter last year for the Supreme Court, the Bush administration sought to tip the scales against *Roe v. Wade* and other court decisions that safeguard reproductive rights. Now, by putting forward Judge Thomas, the White House seeks to decisively weight the Court in favor of the anti-choice agenda.
>
> If confirmed, we believe that Judge Thomas would be a powerful voice for restricting reproductive rights well into the twenty-first century. Planned Parenthood calls on all Americans who believe that the Constitution protects the right to privacy to vigorously oppose his confirmation.[5]

When the committee decided to allow organizational representatives to appear before it, on September 19, to speak for and against Mr. Thomas, I joined a panel, along with Kate Michelman, Sarah Weddington, and former Vermont governor Madeline Kunin, to oppose Clarence Thomas's confirmation to replace Thurgood Marshall.

I spoke of the threat Judge Thomas's confirmation presented, and the importance of seeing reproductive rights in the context of other fundamental rights:

> I have no doubt that if this committee suspected that a nominee were prepared to overrule *Brown v. Board of Education* . . . it would insist upon answers to clarify the nominee's beliefs and intentions. As an African American, I fully appreciate the significance of *Brown* . . . And as a woman, I recognize that . . . *Roe* [is also] fundamentally important to the well-being of American women and families. . . . All Americans, regardless of gender or race, are beneficiaries of these landmark decisions that have recognized inalienable human rights. It is unfortunate that Judge Thomas is unwilling to acknowledge their universality, their constitutional soundness, and the rights and freedoms that emanate from them. . . . We urge you to refuse to confirm Clarence Thomas.[6]

The hearings acquired a whole new layer of meaning when Anita Hill was called to appear. On October 11, my staff and I sat riveted before our office television set as the law professor made her appearance before the Senate Judiciary Committee. In contrast to the dignified responses of Anita Hill, the sexually prurient behavior of the Senate Judiciary Committee members was a disturbing metaphor for the plight of women in the hands of powerful men even in this day and age. Still, after this performance, we were certain that Clarence Thomas wouldn't stand a chance of assuming a seat on the Court.

Even in the face of so many disappointments, I had clung to my deep respect for the Court. But now, no matter what the outcome of the hearings, there was no question that the dignity and authority of the Court had been tarnished, certainly for as long as this candidate, whose conduct had been linked with the discussion of pubic hairs and sexual slurs, sat on the bench. We couldn't help but think of sexual harassment in the workplace every time we heard Clarence Thomas's name or read a Supreme Court opinion on which it appeared. Why did no one—not George Bush, not Clarence Thomas, and not the Senate Judiciary Committee—put a stop to this travesty?

I know that in the eyes of many African Americans my position would be seen as disloyal. But as unfair as some might judge it, I believe that as African Americans, we are always subject to greater scrutiny and held to higher standards than white Americans. This is even more true when we reach rarefied positions of power and influence, such as the Supreme Court.

In spite of this unseemly circus, and the lack of courage to call it off, the Judiciary Committee voted 7 to 7, automatically sending his nomination to the full Senate without recommending his confirmation. On October 15, in a deeply divided vote of 52 to 48, the Senate confirmed Clarence Thomas to sit for the rest of his life on the U.S. Supreme Court.

Time has only confirmed our worst fears about Justice Thomas. He is philosophically isolated in the far right wing of the Court with Justice Scalia. He has forgone any claim to a compassionate understanding of the impact of the Constitution and its laws upon the lives of real people, especially oppressed people. And his opinions on reproductive rights cases have been abhorrent. But our worst fears notwithstanding, he has yet to become more than a marginal figure on the Court. And so far, David Souter has emerged as a solid centrist on the Court.

The hearings created such anger and outrage among women that a backlash was inevitable. I firmly believe that had there been no Clarence Thomas nomination, George Bush would have been reelected in 1992, and the twelve-year Republican dynasty would have continued.

* * *

By the end of 1991, our allies were in retreat—both individuals in Congress like Bob Packwood and institutions like the Court, with such newly installed judges as David Souter and Clarence Thomas. Nevertheless, we had won some modest victories. Aside from both the House and Senate approving legislation affirming international family-planning policies, without restrictions, in July of 1991, Title X, though much diminished from its glory days, had managed to hobble along while other programs were being destroyed. On July 17, the Senate voted to permanently over-turn the gag rule by passing Senator John Chafee's (R-RI) Title X Pregnancy Counseling Act of 1991. Without contradicting the leader of his party directly, the Chafee bill required the secretary of Health and Human Services to ensure that women who received Title X services were provided with information and counseling regarding *all* of their legal options. On July 30, surprising all skeptics, the House Energy and Commerce Committee also voted to overturn the gag rule and reauthorize the Title X family-planning program for five years.

But we all understood how fragile our success was. A lawsuit was moving toward the Supreme Court challenging a multifaceted restrictive Pennsylvania law that would require a woman to notify her husband of her intention to have an abortion; require physicians to describe the fetus's development and then make a woman wait twenty-four hours after her request to have the procedure; require a second physician to be present during an emergency abortion performed after twenty-four weeks; and require the surgeon to perform the emergency abortion in a way that would maximize the chances for fetal survival. It could be the vehicle for an outright reversal of *Roe v. Wade.*

The violence in Wichita had raged throughout the summer of 1991, and the Supreme Court would soon decide *Bray v. Alexandria Reproductive Health Services,* which challenged Operation Rescue's, and their collaborators', violent tactics.

Despite the growing support for Title X in Congress, the awareness that the Bush administration could implement the gag rule at any time assured that the tensions over the gag rule and possible loss of federal funding would headline our annual convention scheduled for Washington, D.C., that fall.

The funding anxieties revealed themselves in a contentious issue that always lay beneath the surface: the formula by which affiliates paid dues to support the national organization. Many believed that it was unfair to some of the affiliates and that, in general, too much money was flowing out of their coffers to support our work at the national level. At that time, about 10 percent of our $40 million budget came from affiliates. Half of this sum was rebated to them. The membership had set up a task force to study the complaints, and after a year of work, the report was scheduled for a vote.

Given the tremendous need for support to fight the national battles, I believed this move was just one more attempt to restrain my leadership. With fewer dollars, there would be less visibility and, perhaps, less controversy. While the move distressed me because I knew that support would result in throttling our programs, I didn't feel the same intensity of emotions as in the early years. My attitude was, "We'll take it as it comes."

In the report sent out to the affiliates prior to the meetings, the task force had recommended that affiliate support to the national office remain flat for several years. This recommendation had been met with broad opposition, and a counterproposal had been circulated calling for a reduction in affiliate support.

I had been scheduled to do a *Good Morning America* interview the day before the official opening of the convention. I had risen at 5:30 A.M to be ready for the television studio transportation that would pick me up in front of the hotel at 6:30 A.M.

This also happened to be the same morning we'd planned to have hundreds of Planned Parenthood representatives lobby members of Congress. There was going to be a breakfast briefing on the Hill before the delegates set off to visit congressional offices, and many of them were emerging from the hotel just as I was leaving for the ABC studios.

The day had dawned dark and soggy, and by the time we'd gathered out under the portico of the hotel, the rain was coming down in sheets. Few cabs were in sight to carry the long line of drowsy activists to the Hill. Just then, a black ABC stretch limousine pulled up to the door and the driver popped out, bearing a sign with my name. Embarrassed by the seeming luxury of my circumstances, and knowing the commotion it was bound to generate, I urged a group of damp conventioneers into the vehicle. "It's on the way," I promised without consulting the driver and without concern for getting to the studio quickly.

Unfortunately, my effort did not avert censure. At noon, I was approached by one of the board officers, who said, "People are outraged that you're being driven around in a limousine."

I didn't have the energy to say anything more than "I didn't ask ABC to send a limousine."

This incident fed into the tenor of the convention. It didn't take much time to guess that when the last session was called to order, it would be four hours of torture.

Jeff Brand, the executive director from Greater Northern New Jersey, was among the first to speak:

I am particularly sympathetic to the concerns that have been expressed about the financial condition of the national office . . . because when I first became an executive director in 1982, my affiliate was still reeling from the big Title X cut and for the last ten years my affiliate has been forced to live with basically a flat funding from its primary funding source. But I am confident that the national office, like its affiliates, will find creative, effective, and interesting ways to not only continue to provide services but to increase the provision of services like its affiliates have over the last decade. [7]

A round of applause followed Jeff's speech.

I was numbed by the arrogance of this sermonette, and the debate that had led up to it. Over the years, there had always been squabbles over how much support the national organization should receive from the affiliates, and a regular demand to know what the affiliates got for their money. When I was an affiliate executive director, I had even vigorously joined in such squabbles. This is why, as president, I had been especially conscientious about serving affiliate needs. And in spite of everything we'd faced, we and the affiliates were thriving as never before. They had ever-increasing caseloads, ever-larger budgets and buildings, and a nationwide visibility unmatched in our history. And I believed that it was my leadership and the efforts of the national organization that had made a substantial contribution to this success. But there was no countering the fear of Title X cutbacks, or the sense that the national organization had prospered at the affiliates' expense.

When it was announced that the membership had voted 268 to 117 to reject the task force's moderate recommendation in favor of cutting support to the national organization by several million dollars over the next three years, cheers and applause filled the room. I found myself thinking that I'd reached a point of no return, as though the cumulative effect of all of the criticism, attacks on my leadership, and the interminable attempts to undermine everything I tried to do, were finally too much to bear.

As Ken Edelin announced the result of the vote and made a small joke, my eyes scanned the audience. I saw many who had, over the years, encouraged and supported my leadership. They remained silent during the long session of speeches. I spotted the director from San Diego who had crafted this plan for denying us adequate funding and who led the drive to get it passed, and I thought once again how it was the determined focus of a few that kept turning the tide against us, whether inside or outside the organization. And I thought of the satisfaction that the executive directors from Chicago, Minneapolis, Los Angeles, Maryland, and Washington,

D.C., must have felt. Whatever the repudiation enshrined in the actions of the membership, I knew that I had done my best.

I was tired in every way. I'd been tired before, but now I didn't think I had the energy or the inclination to fight on as part of the Planned Parenthood movement.

CHAPTER 36

LIFE GOES ON

"I'm Murray Schwartz," said the friendly voice from across the continent. "I produced the Merv Griffin show for over twenty years. Since the show ended I've been looking for someone to launch a new talk show with. I think the American audience is more intelligent than what they see on television these days. Frankly, I'm pretty disgusted with what has happened in my industry. I believe that people are tired of it and it's time for a new kind of show that will cover sensible issues important to everyone's life. Until now, I haven't been able to find someone with whom I wanted to develop a television project, but last night I think I found that person."

Murray's call had come the year before, following my July 1990 appearance on *Nightline* in connection with the Souter nomination. I'd never taken the proposal for television opportunities seriously before. Nothing had seemed nearly as interesting or as compelling as what I'd been doing. As Mama would have described her own diligence, I too was "working for my soul's salvation." There had always been another battle to fight.

But lately, things had been changing—in me and around me. The mounting difficulties of life at Planned Parenthood and my evolving acceptance that the battles outside the organization would go on for many years—in large part because of our reluctance to engage in them as directly as our opposition—began to shift my sense of dedication. The years of hope and determination with which I had countered PPFA irresolution and calls for restraint had taken their toll. I didn't feel defeated, but I was overwhelmingly weary.

Murray's ideas kept swirling in my mind. After our conversation, I began to think that perhaps a talk show would offer me the opportunity to have a broader influence on the range of issues I cared about, which concerned many more aspects of women's and men's lives than reproductive rights. Murray and I agreed to meet several weeks later, when he'd be on the East Coast.

I liked him the moment I met him, and was impressed with his idea of doing a show that covered lively issues—things other than emotional and sexual dysfunction or marital infidelities; a show structured to create enough tension and drama to make people think and care about what was going on in the world.

"I believe that a show that combined celebrity interviews with information and provocative debate could really work," Murray suggested. He favored the idea of a program that traveled to different parts of the country as Merv Griffin's had, to keep it rich and interesting to the American public. I agreed to continue our discussions. I also agreed to let him begin to pitch the idea to some of his colleagues in the television industry. ABC and Buena Vista (Disney) made verbal commitments to develop a show—but for different reasons, each of them backed out before the contract stage. Eventually, Tribune Entertainment made an offer to launch a program to be taped in Chicago from station WGN. The talks had continued through the summer of 1991. But they were still just that: talk, nothing firm.

Flying home after the Planned Parenthood annual convention in Washington that October, I replayed the events over and over again in my head—the controversy over the limousine, the punitive business meeting in which our funds had been slashed, the concern over my clothes and my public speaking appearances. I kept trying to make sense of everything, to find a reason to go on. But this time, those mental exercises I'd practiced since childhood to carry myself through the hard times didn't work anymore.

I opened the door to our apartment and Felicia, hearing the latch, called out, "Hey, Mommy!" and came running from her room. I hugged her more tightly than I ever had. Though she was nearly as tall as me now, I pulled her into my lap as I slumped onto a stool at our kitchen counter. "I'm thinking about leaving Planned Parenthood," I blurted out.

Perhaps I ought to have kept this to myself longer, but I had to say it to someone I could trust. If I made the decision to go forward, until the terms for the show could be worked out, I couldn't risk further unsettling the situation at Planned Parenthood by telling anyone there—not even David.

The expression in Felicia's lacy-lashed, large brown eyes shifted from joy at my arrival to terror at my surprise announcement. "But what are you going to do?" she asked nervously.

When I saw her fears, a lump rose in my throat. "Well, I think I'm going to do that talk show we've been discussing," I told her.

"But what if it doesn't work out?" Felicia persisted.

I blustered faint confidence. "If it doesn't work out, we'll just have to figure out something else, but the contract will guarantee my present salary for a year. That will give me time to make other plans if the pilot show doesn't sell."

This didn't seem to reassure my daughter very much. Dampening her sunny spirits made me feel guilty about dropping this emotional bomb on her without warning. It also made me confront the reality that any major decision I made would have a powerful impact on my child's emotional equilibrium. In an effort to ease her anxiety, I told her, "I haven't made a final decision. I'll make up my mind when I get back from Nepal."

Felicia was now a junior in high school. College was right around the corner. Since she didn't know what she wanted to be, I'd been encouraging her to view her college years as an opportunity to explore, rather than a mandate to train for a profession as I had done. Given the satisfaction that she took from her studies, and the excellence of her straight-A work, it was simply understood that her private-school education would lead to an expensive private-university education. The burden of paying for it would be mine. I had some savings, but it would take more than I had. I couldn't afford to be unemployed.

Felicia had blossomed into an all-around typical teenager. She was tall, but not quite as long-legged as me, with a blend of her father's full mouth and my high cheekbones; and a temperament that shifted from sultry sweetness to adolescent rebellion and back again. She loved tennis and volleyball, and she loved art. She frequently complained about our church-going, and never understood why I didn't think that disco-hopping every Friday and Saturday night was the greatest idea. But she'd grown into an honest and honorable person of strong will and values. If I had placed an order for a child of certain characteristics before she was born, I would have shortchanged myself, because I could never have imagined how many qualities and capacities she possessed.

By late summer, Murray and I had been unable to work out an agreement, but Tribune Entertainment continued to pursue the idea independently. During discussions in my agent's office, Robert Lance, George Paris, the company's vice president for programming, Darryl Porter, vice president for business and development, and I agreed to develop a program that would offer "intelligent debates about controversial subjects."

By November, Tribune was anxious to solidify an agreement. I found myself thinking about the challenge of getting viewers to understand why they should care about one topic or another. I thought that the process might not be that different from helping to clarify reproductive issues in dialogue with audiences on the college circuit, where I was being invited to speak more and more regularly. I enjoyed the students' vitality, and their responsiveness made me feel more and more confident about holding the attention of hundreds in a nationwide television audience.

My trip to Southeast Asia dashed any hopes I might have had that it would renew my spirits or point to the path I should take toward pressing on in my struggles within Planned Parenthood. If I needed a signal, I got it at the December board meeting. It came in discussions with the board officers on the impact of the membership vote on the national office program and how I would manage the loss of millions of dollars from the affiliates to support our programs over the next few years.

"I don't see how we can do it," I said, and pointed out that the costly legal and political battles were escalating, not diminishing, and that the affiliates wanted more services in return for less support. "Our budget is already stretched thin. It's as though we're being punished for our success," I remarked.

One of the vice chairpersons of the board turned to me and said, in a voice sharp with impatience, "You know, people really aren't interested in hearing about your problems anymore."

After the board meeting, the treasurer of the board took me aside and said, "The board would like you to provide us with a list of your outside speaking engagements." The public utilities executive from Fort Worth drawled, "At this point we don't want to know what honorariums you receive. We just want a list."

This pair of incidents seemed more personal than ever before. I had positive and supportive relations with the officers of the board, even if they didn't buffer the attacks on me as had the officers of the early years. Yet I was feeling more isolated than ever. My loyal staff and my growing external visibility had kept me going, but even they were no longer enough to sustain me. First thing Monday morning, I called my agent and asked him to tell the Tribune Entertainment people that I'd sign the option to develop the show.

I called my mother to tell her that I'd decided to leave Planned Parenthood. "Well," she said after a long pause, "my prayers have been answered."

Several mornings later, I asked David to come into my office. He would be the first to know. For sixteen years—since our days together at the National Executive Directors Council—we'd worked side by side, rallying one another toward success and supporting one another through the difficult times. As he bounced jauntily into my office and sat down across from me at my desk as he'd done hundreds of times before, I felt an overwhelming sense of sadness for the first time since I'd made my decision. For a fleeting moment, "Maybe I shouldn't do this" passed through my mind.

But there was no turning back. "I've decided to resign. I've agreed to develop a talk show that will be nationally syndicated."

David sunk into his chair. His jaw went slack, and the color drained from his face. All of the exuberance and humor with which he had entered the room, and which never failed him, had vanished.

"Is it final?" he asked, almost inaudibly.

"Yes. I've already signed the agreement."

"When will you be leaving?"

"Around the first part of April, although I'll be available for consultation into early summer, if I'm needed."

As though musing to himself, David commented, "The federation has no idea of the loss that it is about to suffer. You've had a lot of offers over the years, but I never thought there would be anything that would cause you to give up this work."

I couldn't say anything more—there was nothing left to say. For a minute or two my office fell uncharacteristically silent.

Then, ever generous, David rallied. "Well, this is terrific for you. A wonderful opportunity. I know you'll be wonderful at it. This is really great," he added, willing enthusiasm back into his voice. A smile spread stiffly across his face.

It didn't feel great. Something in me had wanted him to say, "You can't do this. You're too valuable for us to lose. What can we do to keep you?" Not that I would have changed my mind, and not that David would ever do anything but support me in my decisions.

"You'll find this ironic," he said. "Jill Cobrin just informed me late yesterday that the million dollar key person life insurance policy that the board requested be taken out on your life has been approved. I guess we won't be needing it now," he said, laughing sardonically.

The paradox of their recent decision was that even as the aggression against my leadership intensified, the board concluded that if I died suddenly, Planned Parenthood would suffer considerable damage. The fundraising successes directly related to my efforts would be lost, and the organization's public visibility would be diminished. The management of our worldwide program would be disrupted. The policy would ease the organization's transition to new leadership. I didn't consider the idea macabre. It was strictly a business decision that companies and organizations made. I supported the need to do it. I did not, however, miss the irony of the manner of this acknowledgment of my value.

A few moments later, the vice presidents gathered in my office. Three were in Washington and connected by speakerphone. After everyone was settled into the chairs around my desk, I said simply, "I've decided to leave the federation."

There was silence and blank stares on their faces, as they seemed to try to make sense of what I was saying.

Dan Weintraub broke the silence. "The federation is losing its most valuable asset," he said matter-of-factly.

At that moment, all of the places that Dan and I had traveled together— Egypt, Nepal, Thailand, Kenya, Bolivia, Brazil, and Ecuador—flashed through my mind.

Next to him sat Eve Paul. I remembered the many discussions and debates we'd had over a host of legal issues and lawsuit strategies—from handling affiliate legal problems to determining how far we could get involved in politics, from protecting the Planned Parenthood name from unauthorized use to dealing with landmark Supreme Court decisions. Eve's work was superb, and she had never wavered in her commitment to the welfare of the organization or her loyalty to me.

Larry Broadwell, the vice president for finance and administration, had first come to the federation to stay "two years to get things straightened out," and was now in his tenth year. Larry, proud to be a St. Louis native, sat quietly staring at me as though he could not believe what he had just heard. I couldn't remember when we last had a blemish on our annual audits. He had helped to manage our Bermuda insurance company into a reliable source of medical malpractice coverage for the affiliates. I felt proud that during the time we'd worked together, the financial reserves necessary to see the organization through difficult times had grown from $1.5 million when I arrived, to over $11 million.

I felt especially guilty when I looked over at Michael Policar, our vice president for medical affairs, and Lynne Abraham, vice president for communications. Michael had joined the staff only a few months earlier, having left a teaching position at the University of California San Francisco Medical School and a position as medical director at Planned Parenthood of Alameda, San Francisco. He looked both stricken and astonished. Lynne, who had also been hired recently, didn't react much. She was a New Yorker, and hadn't uprooted her family and personal life to make a move across the continent.

Jane Johnson, in charge of affiliate development, and Steve Dennin, in charge of the fund-raising programs, remained silent over the open line from Washington. Our affiliate-accreditation process was used as a model for other organizations, and the affiliates considered our regional offices one of the most important aspects of our operations. The direct-mail program was projected to raise $18 million.

When Jane, Steve, and Sally Patterson, who was in charge of public affairs, returned to New York the next day, they came to my office with somber faces and warm hugs. Now did not seem to be the time for extended reminiscences, though the weight of our shared past was such a presence in that room.

Each of them made a few inquiries: "When do you plan to leave?" "Does the board know?" "What will your show be about?"

After a few more minutes, I said, "I never promised you I'd turn out the lights at Planned Parenthood." I laughed awkwardly and stood to signal that the meeting was ending. Each of the six vice presidents embraced me. The power of their silence struck me more profoundly than their words ever could have. These were the people who had made it possible for me to carry on, sometimes in the face of very difficult odds. David, Dan, and Eve had been with me from the beginning (Louise Tyrer had retired a year earlier). In many ways they were my family. If I was leaving the struggles and tensions of my work behind, I was also leaving them, and I didn't like that idea one bit. A part of me felt guilty that I was letting them down; I worried about their future under a new president.

After they left my office, David and I talked about my plans a little bit more and then discussed the transition. I was certain he would be asked once again to step in as acting president. Needing something concrete to do, David said, "We need to make a list of our major donors and other supporters to notify them before the press release goes out."

At precisely ten o'clock, my secretary buzzed me to announce that the board officers were on the conference line. David stayed in my office, sitting silently across from me at my desk.

Although Ken Edelin knew the nature of the announcement, the others did not, so Ken opened the conversation with, "Thank you all for making yourselves available on such short notice. Faye has an announcement that she would like to make."

Again, after I announced my decision there was silence on the line.

"Well," Ken entered the vacuum, "you've given us a helluva ride."

Mailgrams announcing my resignation went out to the rest of the board and to all of the affiliates, and a press release was issued:

Faye Wattleton, president of Planned Parenthood Federation of America, announced today that she will leave her position in late March to host a new television program focusing on issues facing American women and men in the 1990s. . . .

Ms. Wattleton quickly set the tone for her tenure at Planned Parenthood. At the news conference announcing her appointment, she made it known that Planned Parenthood, previously a low-profile organization, would become highly visible and aggressive in the battle to defend abortion rights. She moved quickly to establish a strong lobbying presence in Washington, to mobilize grassroots support, to launch a far-reaching program of litigation, and to implement hard-hitting advertising programs. Within a few years, Planned Parenthood was repositioned as a forceful advocacy group and a leader in the fight for reproductive freedom. . . .

Reacting to Ms. Wattleton's resignation, PPFA Chairperson Kenneth C. Edelin, M.D., voiced a view that is undoubtedly shared by Planned Parenthood's 22,000 staff and volunteers nationwide: "Planned Parenthood could not have had a better leader, at a better time, than Faye Wattleton. Under her direction, Planned Parenthood grew to become one of the most respected and most effective health and advocacy movements in the world. Faye Wattleton piloted us through difficult times with the grace, wisdom, and dedication born of her rich and challenging experience. She is a true visionary, and we will miss her. But she leaves behind a legacy of inspiration and commitment that is sure to serve the federation well in all the years to come."

Indeed, Planned Parenthood is poised for action in the important election year ahead. Undaunted by a narrow defeat in the fight to overturn the gag rule on federally funded family-planning clinics, PPFA is lobbying for a new legislative effort to reverse this dangerous and unethical regulation. Planned Parenthood also led a coalition of pro-choice organizations to hear a Pennsylvania case that will provide an opportunity to reaffirm—or overturn—the landmark *Roe v. Wade* decision. And, as November 1992 draws near, Planned Parenthood is determined to channel the outrage and dismay of millions of pro-choice voters into electoral clout.

In all the success that lies ahead for Planned Parenthood Federation of America, the legacy of Faye Wattleton will play a lasting and invaluable role.[1]

My last Planned Parenthood board meeting was on February 22, 1991. Business was taken up in a routine manner. At the end of the meeting, Ken announced that, although the meeting had extended more than an hour beyond schedule, a brief presentation had been planned, as this would be my last board meeting.

My staff had organized a series of slides covering the fourteen years of my presidency; as they flashed on the screen, Ken read from a script prepared by the staff of the communications division. In the darkness of the room, I felt completely disconnected from the colored images that flashed before us, and from everything that Ken said. I felt emotionally wrung out, dry. We all knew that we were participating in a formality—it was the correct thing to do.

Afterward, champagne poured into plastic stemmed glasses was passed to each board member. Ken offered a toast, and Sharon Allison, one of the delegation of three who had rebuked me fourteen years earlier in El Paso, Texas, for the damage that they believed I had done to the organization, presented me with an engraved Steuben bowl. I felt a strange blend of regret and relief that the pressure would soon be released, and pride that I had done my best, that the Planned Parenthood movement was stronger than I had found it. For as much as it had taken out of me and as much as it had given to me, I knew that if I'd had it to do again, I would do so without hesitation.

Before the meeting convened, I had been asked to make a final report to the board. Because a search committee was about to be formed to recruit my replacement, the board members had wanted me to describe my responsibilities. I had asked the human resources department to compile my average weekly hours and classify how I spent them, as summarized from my time sheets for the past year. The report showed that the average was in excess of sixty hours per week, divided between management, fund-raising, acting as spokesperson, and international work.

Forty-five minutes into the descriptions and the questions that it stimulated, Ken asked me to conclude. "People need to catch their planes," he said. Andy Greensfelder must have felt the same way when he had prepared a presentation on why my candidacy for the presidency should be approved and the discussion was cut short in the interest of those who had to catch flights to the Super Bowl. Midway through my description, my career at Planned Parenthood had officially ended, as the group thinned out and people rushed off to the airports.

It would be two more months before I would clear out my files and desk. My last day would be April 3, 1992. David, as I had expected, was asked once again to carry the responsibility of acting president. He and I worked every day on plans for a smooth transition, meeting with each vice president to review each division's status and goals. I still had speaking commitments at, among others, Planned Parenthood of Northern New England, Planned Parenthood of North Central Indiana, and Pennsylvania State University.

As the time for my departure neared, my staff arranged a reception for me in our large conference room. Their many warm expressions of appreciation and affection were a dramatic contrast to the ceremonious farewell given by the board of directors. Perhaps this was as it should have been— for my staff were the ones who had made it possible for me to make it through all the ups and downs. The eleventh-floor lobby had been decorated with bright-colored paper garlands and large bouquets of fresh flowers. After a catered lunch, each division had made a presentation of poems, songs, comedy, wicked skits and other skewers, as well as emotionally delivered thank-yous. Felicia made a surprise appearance. After I'd said my thanks with a sense of gratitude as deep as any I've ever felt, they presented me with a certificate of commission for a wall hanging by noted artist Lew Knauss. At the end, many sets of eyes, including mine, were brimming with tears.

*   *   *

Back in January, the announcement of my forthcoming show had appeared in the same edition of the *Chicago Tribune* that covered the decision of the Tribune-owned WGN-TV superstation, reaching 40 percent of the country, to drop all religious programming after more than thirty years. The anti-abortion activists in the Chicago area were outraged not only by the pros-pect that the Catholic archdiocese would lose a forum, but that I would gain one.

Joe Scheidler of the Pro-Life Action Network, whose home base is Chicago, quickly went into action. He called Tribune's corporate offices and threatened boycotts, picketing, and other disruptions. When we'd all discussed the possibility of such objections during the negotiations, the Tribune Entertainment executives seemed to relish the idea of controversy. "It will be good for the show," they chuckled.

But a few weeks after Scheidler had begun to wage his campaign, Darryl Porter called me in New York. "We want you to take a low profile from now on," he ordered.

I was stunned. "But I'm still Planned Parenthood's president and until I leave, I intend to live up to my obligations."

He was not to be dissuaded, so I agreed not to take on any additional speaking engagements, although I was troubled by this shift in attitude so early on. My resignation from Planned Parenthood had already been tendered. Whatever happened, I had to keep moving ahead, just as I had done all of my life.

Within a couple of months, I began to wonder if the show would ever come to be.

I had been asked by Velma Cato, who had been hired by *Tribune* as the executive producer, and George Paris to participate in a conference call with *Tribune*'s seven television-station managers. Mystified by this request, I asked for an explanation. "Oh, they have some questions," Velma responded breezily. "I'm sure that you'll be able to handle them," she laughed.

I joined them on the line. The managers, all of them men, were connected from Los Angeles, Houston, Chicago, Philadelphia, New York, Boston, and Washington. If the strong enthusiasm that had been reported by the executives of Tribune had ever existed among its station managers, it had evaporated by this first week of July. I learned that none of them were under any obligation to air programs produced by Tribune Entertainment. "We don't think you can produce a commercially viable show," one said bluntly. "We think you'd be better suited to anchor a late-afternooon news-magazine show."

I was stunned by their announcement. Velma and George had given me no preparation on how to handle the television station-mangers, so I put up the best defense I could. "We're planning to do the kind of show that we've been negotiating for months. But regardless of the subject matter," I said, trying to be persuasive, "doesn't it really depend on whether the audience wants to spend an hour with me?"

To this, one of the executives answered, "I asked my secretary before coming to this call whether she'd ever heard of you and she hadn't. We'll lose a lot of money getting the audience acquainted with you."

"Women who watch daytime talk shows aren't smart enough or interested in current events," said another.

I couldn't believe what I was hearing. My breath stuck in my throat. Finally, one of the station managers asked me point-blank, "Let's put it this way, are you willing to do a show on women with big breasts during ratings week?"

In a flash, the tentativeness that had been caused by the ground shifting beneath me turned to indignation. "No, absolutely not! I won't do a show on women with big breasts during any week—I haven't spent my career working for the elevation of women only to come to this."

I felt angry, betrayed, and terrified. The future that had looked so filled with possibility was now beginning to look like a blank slate. I concluded that the station managers were envisioning a show built not around my talents, but around how I would fit into the talk-show mold as they knew it. They were, after all, looking for me to do trash television and were now doubting whether I could pull it off. Their instincts were right.

As I was making my way through negotiations and disappointments, life's harsher realities were brought home to me. Felicia and I were scheduled to spend a week together in Barcelona, Spain, at the Olympic games, so I tried to focus on the preparations for our trip. A few days before we were to leave, I checked my voice mail for messages. "Faye, call me as soon as you get in." It was Nell Braxton's voice.

When my best friend from childhood read about my appointment as president of Planned Parenthood in *The New York Times*, we had taken up our friendship as though there had never been a twenty-year gap. Our families were soon spending Thanksgiving together as an annual ritual, and I cherished the long dinners that Nell and I had committed ourselves to. We'd talk of everything going on in our lives: her work as assistant to Paul Moore, the Episcopal bishop of the archdiocese of New York; her husband Bertram and their two teenagers, Bert III and Erica; my work; Felicia's finding the right college; my current romantic interest.

This time, I felt instinctively from the urgency of my friend's voice that this was not a call to arrange a time for our next dinner. I hope something hasn't happened to Bert, I thought as I dialed her number.

"Nell, what is it?"

"Third died this afternoon."

I could not believe what I was hearing. Their handsome twenty-three-year-old son, a joy to everyone who had met him, and standing at the portal of his career as a writer, had died earlier in the day in a freak accident. Sitting on a second-story window ledge, he had lost his balance, fallen backward, and was killed instantly when his neck absorbed the impact of his body hitting the ground.

All I could say was, "Oh, no! Oh, no!" over and over again.

Felicia heard my words and saw my face. "What is it? What is it?"

When I hung up the telephone, I broke the news to her—news that still did not seem real.

"Mommy, I had such a crush on Third all my life," Felicia wept. "He was so gorgeous and always so nice to me."

The truth was that Third had been as much a big brother to Felicia as he was the focus of her adolescent attraction—and he'd been a very special brother at that.

After comforting my sobbing daughter, as I walked the few short blocks to Nell and Bert's apartment alone, I thought about how my life would be if I lost Felicia. She was the center of my life, and I could not imagine finding a purpose that could begin to replace all that she meant to me.

By the time I reached Nell's door, I could only hug her and hug her as she sobbed. Words cannot reach such emotion.

When Felicia and I returned from Barcelona, the taping of the test shows proceeded as planned, except that, after the religious-programming uproar, the Tribune-owned WGN had decided not to allow us to use their studios. The twelve test shows were taped at WBBM, the CBS network affiliate in Chicago. The best takes were to be used in a single presentation tape for marketing the show to network affiliates in major media markets. The subjects ranged from "Women in the Church" to "Sexuality in the '90s." I was astonished and touched by the caliber of the guests who agreed to travel to Chicago to participate on the shows' panels, among them Joseph Califano, former secretary of the Department of Health and Human Services, and Wendy Kaminer, the author of *I'm Dysfunctional, You're Dysfunctional.* Both said they'd agreed to come because they admired my work and wanted to support me.

I quickly discovered that doing the shows wasn't the same as handling a large auditorium of people in a freewheeling question-and-answer session. It was makeup artists, hairdressers, wardrobe designers, TelePrompTers, camera angles, floor directors, commercial breaks, midshow conferences with the executive producer, panels of guests, and studio audiences that ranged in age from teenagers to the elderly. There seemed to be an endless number of elements to cope with in preparing for each forty-eight-minute show and getting it "in the can." We taped two shows a day, and by the time we'd finished the second taping, I'd remove the thick layers of makeup, return to my hotel room, and collapse into exhausted slumber.

Word was traveling around Chicago that I was doing a show, and at the last taping, the studio was crammed with extra chairs to accommodate the people who had lined up outside the studio in hopes of being members of the audience. Tribune flew Felicia out from New York to join the wrap party. And yet, although there were smiles and compliments, something didn't seem quite right. There wasn't enough enthusiasm. No one said, "This show's going to be a big hit."

November is the time when production companies promote their products to stations around the country for the second half of the season. Tribune showed little activity during this critical sales month. We waited anxiously to hear of stations' agreeing to air the show—but there was only silence.

It came as no surprise to me when, a week before Christmas 1992, my agent, Robbie Lantz, called me to say that after three months, the two principals, George Paris and Don Hacker, wanted to meet with us.

"They're coming to tell us they're not going to do the show," I told Robbie worriedly.

"No, no," said the longtime agent of such celebrities as Elizabeth Taylor and William Rehnquist. "No, they wouldn't do that to you," he assured me. "I think they want to meet to discuss the production schedule."

Arriving an hour late for the meeting, Don Hacker hustled into the Tribune sales office, where Robbie and I sat nervously talking to George Paris.

"We think Faye's better suited for an afternoon show," Hacker commented, before telling us that they'd decided not to go ahead with the project. None of its stations would agree to carry my show. No one gave any explicit reasons when Robbie asked why, and after a few more moments of discussion, we left Tribune's offices.

For the first time since nursing school—if not the first time in my life—I had no idea what I was going to do next. I was forty-eight years old. So much of my life still lay ahead, and up to now, each step of my career had always been marked for me. Now I could not see the marker.

Felicia was midway through her senior year of high school and in the midst of finalizing her applications to six colleges: Harvard, Brown, Yale, Wesleyan, the University of Pennsylvania, and Stanford. Oddly, this Christmas season was not one of remorse for me. Perhaps my optimism was sustained by Mama's quoting Romans 8:28 during moments of travail: "We know that all good things work together for good to them that love God . . ."

I began to reach out to friends who might recommend my candidacy for corporate boards. Years ago Fred Smith had suggested that my administrative talents would be extremely useful in such a role. "Sure," they said when

I offered myself up for inspection. "You'd be ideal, a great asset." Weeks later they would call, much less enthused, to report regretfully that the chief executive officer was very concerned that the pro-criminalists would cause trouble. Ironically, it wasn't while I was at the barricades but after I'd walked away that I experienced the most daunting threat to my child's and my own well-being. The phenomenon was frightening and frustrating. But just as I had no power to change or deepen others' perceptions of me, neither did I have any regrets. "I'll just keep putting one foot in front of the other," I told my friends. And that's exactly what I did. Each day I made a list of colleagues and friends to call. I was still receiving many invitations to speak on college campuses and before various women's professional groups—not that I harbored any illusion that I could sustain our lifestyle for long on the speaker's circuit.

Although I was usually called upon to speak about reproductive rights, invariably the subject was broadened during the question-and-answer sessions.

"Do you think a woman can cope with having it all—a career and a family?"

"How do I confront sexual harassment on my job? I need my job."

"I'm just a college student. How do I get involved?"

"What are the differences between women's and men's healthcare?"

"I'm not a feminist, that label has a bad connotation now. But what do you think women need to do to break down discrimination?"

These were not routine questions for me. Within them, I heard a searching, a longing for different ideas, an acknowledgment that the battles of the past were important. But I also heard a message that the rubble of the struggle for women's equality contained little that related to their experiences.

I would challenge their rejection of the feminist label. "Are you saying that you're not committed to working for the interests of women?" No one replied, "Yes, that's what I mean." But what I was beginning to understand is that they were searching for a different way to frame their aspirations and their needs.

This is when I began to dream of the possibility of establishing a think tank that would research and study the issues that women will face in the twenty-first century, and that would formulate public and debate strategies to address the persisting inequities women face in our society. I recognized that there were many university-based policy centers and several located in Washington, D.C., that primarily addressed government policies. Nevertheless, I concluded that there was a need for something broader with a core institutional mission of educating and influencing public thinking and debate on a wide range of issues that are crucial to women.

* * *

In the fall of 1993, Felicia was heading for college. She'd been accepted at all six of the universities to which she'd applied, and together we'd visited each of the campuses, and a few others that hadn't made her final list. It didn't take her long to decide. "If a black person has a chance to go to Harvard, they should go," she'd said. So we packed up and headed for Cambridge, Massachusetts.

I was so proud of my daughter. She had graduated from Brearley with honors and had spent the summer as an editorial assistant at *Vogue* magazine. As we drove north along I-95, I remembered her as a small child, and how I'd reveled in her affection, her brightness of spirit, and the joy she gave. I'd once wondered to a friend if I could ever bear to see her grow into independence. The friend had reassured me by saying, "When it's time for her to go, you'll be ready for her to leave."

It was time for her to go. But I wasn't ready. I felt guilty about my sadness, because I felt it was born of selfishness. I had not lost a child. She was moving on to her next station of independence. I was in a stew of conflicting emotions. I believed that not only must she go, but I insisted that she go to another city. My words—"I have only one requirement; you must apply to a college outside the New York metropolitan area"—were as much a mantra for my own fortitude to encourage her growth as for her reluctance to exuberantly embrace the venture that would bring her closer to adulthood.

When we drove onto the Harvard campus, our van loaded to the brim, the reality that our lives would never be the same again struck with full force. Yes, she would come home for holidays and the summers, but never again would the rhythms of our lives be the same. I had no doubt that in the future things would be wonderful. But they would be different. I didn't want them to be different.

My profound sadness was intensified when we opened the door to Felicia's assigned room and saw that it was dingy and dirty. Felicia turned to me and said, "Mommy, I want to go home." But then we quickly discovered that, actually, good fortune had smiled on her. She'd been assigned to a single room with a private bath. Our shock turned to gratitude, and just as Jan, my onetime roommate, and I had done back at Ohio State, we set about brightening her room with pretty cotton curtains and spreads and a colorful rag rug.

When Felicia was mostly settled and it came time for me to return to New York, the tears began to well up inside me. But I didn't want her to see me this way—it was her moment of excitement, her moment of anticipation and of adventure. I was determined not to spoil it. But every day for the next six weeks the tears came as I mourned the life that had gone with my child.

I clung fiercely to my faith that in time my life's path would be revealed to me again. I thought of my mother's favorite scripture in the Twenty-third Psalm, ". . . Surely goodness and mercy shall follow me all the days of my life. . . ." Within it I found solace that I was not alone in my personal isolation. Our lives were evolving and something was upholding us. Even at this dark moment in my soul, I could still feel gratitude.

Eventually my emotional strength and confidence returned, and I began to reconstruct my life. Staying in touch with old friends, newer friends, and colleagues had resulted in more support and more new opportunities than I could ever have imagined. Eventually the invitations to join corporate and foundation boards began to arrive.

In a moment of encouragement, Arthur Caliandro, senior minister at Marble Collegiate Church, had offered, "Remember, on Palm Sunday Jesus was lauded with hosannas and praise. By Friday, he was betrayed, condemned, and crucified. On Easter Sunday he was resurrected to a higher spiritual plane. This is an affirmation that we can pass through the darkest hours of the soul and survive to greater achievements."

It was a moment of hope, as though a door had opened through which I could glimpse a future of possibilities, a future in which I have always believed.

Through the efforts of Herb Chao Gunther, David Andrews, and Eve Paul, the seed of an idea for a national policy center on women's issues began to germinate. On August 25, 1995, the Center for Gender Equality was incorporated in New York City with an endowment of one million dollars.

AN OPEN LETTER TO MY DAUGHTER

I have thought a great deal about what to say to you at the close of this chronicle of my life. Because our lives are so intertwined, this is as much your story as mine. Yet, when I think of you alone, I envision your future and my hopes for you and all the women of your generation.

When I look at your life, I see a world of choices that I could not have imagined when I was your age. I think of the rights that you take for granted—rights that would not exist if not for the grit and determination of all those women who resisted oppression. And at the close of the twentieth century, I think about how your rights are being seriously threatened. I wonder whether you fully appreciate how important it is to accept the responsibility of protecting your freedom. I pray that you will never forget that you are the beneficiary of the struggles and sacrifices of others, and that your children in turn will reap the investment you make in their future.

You have studied the life of Sojourner Truth, and though you have cautioned me not to allow her to become "a cliché" in my speeches, I hope you will indulge me once again, for I find the lessons of inspiration in her life as relevant today as they were 150 years ago.

As you know, when the first national women's rights convention was held in Worcester, Massachusetts, in October 1850, Sojourner Truth was the only black female delegate in attendance. Born in 1797, Sojourner had spent the first forty years of her life in slavery and servitude. When her owner promised her freedom, then rescinded his promise, she left his farm in Ulster County, New York, and, after a brief contract with another farmer, headed for New York City. She changed her name from Isabela to Sojourner Truth—a name she believed would be taken as a sign that her calling to the ministry came from God. Like your grandmother, Sojourner traveled the highways and byways, calling sinners to repentance. And like your grandmother, she quickly found herself esteemed both for her speaking powers and the lather of her humor as she gained a large following among white audiences as well as black ones.

Sojourner Truth eventually joined the abolitionist movement, where her activism, and the zeal of her women colleagues, engendered society's criticism. This censure, combined with the unequal treatment of women by their male colleagues within the movement itself, prompted her to embrace women's rights as part of her crusade, and she joined forces with Elizabeth Cady Stanton, Lucretia Mott, and Susan B. Anthony in the fledgling suffragette and women's rights movements.

At the women's rights convention, Sojourner found herself in the midst of a forum of educated white women whose issues she did not fully understand, such as the right to own land and the right to wear pants. (Your grandmother would not have approved of the latter demand.) As a former slave, Sojourner found these issues of little relevance to her. Hers was the same sentiment often expressed by African American women today toward the women's liberation movement. So when she was asked her opinion on one such issue, she replied, "Sisters, I'm not clear what you be after. If women want any rights more than they've got, why don't they just take them and not be talking about it."[1]

I've often thought of the power embodied in her simple admonition to the women of that forum, and how relevant her instructions remain for women in their struggles today and for you and your generation in particular.

Women's rights are incontrovertible, Sojourner Truth was telling us. They are our birthright. All we have to do is claim them. It seems that women have not fully absorbed the wisdom of this former slave, who understood women's potential more clearly than we do today. Women have made phenomenal progress since she spoke in Worcester, but until the day arrives when all women decide that our rights are not negotiable, our future choices will not be secure.

Sojourner's life was transformed from slavery to a ministry of liberation. Similarly, your grandmother left the cotton fields of Mississippi to fulfill a mission of religious salvation. Neither allowed themselves to be shackled by convention. Instead, they ignored the rules of what they were supposed to do for the sake of what they believed they were called to do. I've never heard your grandmother question her calling or her right to fulfill it—not when she encountered opposition because of her gender, not when she faced danger because of her race, and not when it meant long separations from her family and friends. I doubt that Sojourner did either. But most importantly, they both believed in themselves—they believed that they had the power within themselves to shape their own destinies. Neither would be denied her future, whether here on earth or in the great beyond. Their effectiveness lay in their strength of persuasion, in their appeal to the sentiments of decency, civility, and godliness, and above all in their refusal to cede their personal power to the will of others.

It's more than blood that binds your grandmother, you, and me. On the surface, your grandmother's and my missions in life could hardly have been more different. Beneath it, they are driven by the same guiding principles. My mother believes in the ultimate power of God in every earthly purpose. Yes, I believe in God, but I also believe in the power of human beings, if given the means, to manage their lives and to work for a better existence for others. Your grandmother crisscrossed the country with a message of salvation from eternal damnation. I have traveled many of the same roads, and more, with a message of respect, tolerance, and compassion—salvation from the injustices of this world.

Over the years, I have come to understand and even revere those qualities about your grandmother, for I now recognize that these are the roots of who I am. I've come to appreciate how essential Mama's beliefs and values were in shaping my own values. Through her teachings and through her example, she gave me the code of ethics—your grandmother calls them "principles"—by which I live: honesty, loyalty, integrity, respect and compassion for others, diligence, perseverance, and faith in God. She taught me right from wrong. For her, the lines were never fuzzy.

I have tried to convey the same principles to you, although with less absolutism. Your dresses may have been short enough to give your grandmother and me heart attacks, and school dances were not forbidden, but you were taught not to compromise your fundamental values for the sake of acceptance. You were also taught to keep your heart open to an empathic understanding of how you would feel "if that were me."

Through the example of my life, I've tried to demonstrate that it's our continuing responsibility to challenge inequality, intolerance, and oppression—the darkness that snuffs out the flames of hope.

Often we've talked about the differences between your grandmother's standards and those by which you were reared. You've wondered how your own evolving values fit into the picture. As I did and your grandmother before me, you must find your own way. You've been taught to believe in yourself and to live by your principles. It won't be any easier for you than it was for your grandmother or for me. It will require courage. Your life's possibilities will expand or shrink in direct proportion to the strength of your courage.

You are a member of a privileged class. I don't just mean the conventional privilege of affluence. More importantly, your privilege is of a heritage rich in values, academic achievement, and exposure to a world far beyond that of most people your age. This privilege carries a high price tag—the obligation of service and especially the duty of leadership. Leadership may not come easy to you, for it is a cloak that women do not wear comfortably, regardless of our ethnic, political, or social backgrounds. We're conditioned to avoid appearing to be leaders, for this means wielding power, and powerful women are viewed as threatening. We are taught in many different ways that it's not feminine to use power in a forthright manner. Yet the judicious use of power is the cornerstone of leadership. When we shrink from power, the result is that women are forced into circuitous machinations that sap our ability to protect our choices and to contribute the fullest measure of our potential to our world.

The women of your generation must wear the raiments of power and leadership with as much self-possession as the women in your grandmother's and Aunt Alice's sewing room wore their beautiful new clothes. Leadership is not the exclusive purview of those appointed to national platforms. Each of us can practice it every day of our lives. And leadership isn't solely about individual achievement. For when we act together, we have the power to shape the future in ways that we never can individually. You certainly understood the power of collective leadership when you and your classmates united to persuade the administrators in your high school to create a more culturally diverse curriculum.

As we enter the twenty-first century, the stakes have never been higher for women to assert the power of our leadership. Now is the time for women of your generation to become invested in the political process, for your lives are on the line. In this last national political cycle of the twentieth century, the next president of the United States will probably have the opportunity to shape the Supreme Court that will arbitrate the rules of law for your children. Because of the Court's retrenchment, women's rights— especially women's reproductive rights—are held together by a very fragile political thread. What will the next president do? If the Congress remains anti-choice, women could lose a great deal that has been gained in our ability to make our own decisions about our own lives. Americans' fundamental rights, women's rights, your rights, your children's rights, must not be allowed to hang in the balance.

Religious tenets will continue to be used as a vehicle to undermine the power of your womanhood. Freedom of religion and freedom of speech are America's most cherished liberties. They are the rights that protected the traditions of your ancestors. But no matter how strong a force religion has been in shaping your grandmother's life, my life, and yours, we are still free to choose or reject it—and we have been taught never to impose it on others. I implore you to recognize the sacredness of this freedom, the inestimable value of not being forced to bow down to the gods of others, and the uncompromising determination that is needed to protect this right. Do not allow the denial of your first liberty to be a weapon of your oppression.

As an African American, I'm secure in the belief that our Constitution protects you from discrimination because of your skin color and that the state cannot officially control your destiny because of your race. But you were female long before you understood what it meant to be African American. And it pains me to say that, as a woman, you are not equally secure from government oppression because of the unique reproductive characteristics of your gender. My training and experience as a nurse and nurse-midwife were invaluable in teaching me, as Margaret Sanger's profession taught her, that a woman's health and her right to control her reproduction are inextricably linked to her ability to achieve equality.

My determination has been driven by the repugnant idea of the government in a free society intruding into the most private aspects of a woman's life and body. I find the powers that the courts have granted the states so profoundly objectionable that I once suggested that reproductive rights should be explicitly secured in the Constitution. I was roundly criticized as being unrealistic and extreme. Perhaps I *was* unrealistic, but I was not extreme—and bearing the criticism was vastly less important to me than saving women's lives. Nothing is more essential to your personal liberty than protecting your body from the intrusions of governmental edicts. Private does not mean a little government regulation. What's private is private.

During the past four years the restoration of the reproductive rights that were lost during the Reagan and Bush era was not due to the united efforts of women, but by the political sweep of the presidential pen. The domestic and international gag rules, which would have prohibited women from receiving information about abortion, failed not because the Supreme Court ruled that the president couldn't censor speech, but because time expired before the Bush administration could figure out how to impose them. What frightens me most is that women—especially the young women of your generation— seem unaware of this. They simply do not recognize the seriousness of the dangers that loom over a right so fundamental as their "right to be." Those who are committed to reversing women's progress are expert in using the powers of the law, especially in the states, and executive orders to narrow the choices of your future and to deny you the potential of the power that is within you.

Be especially mindful that women's reproductive rights will continue to be at the heart of the struggle for women's equality. Within your rights to control your fertility is vested enormous power, the power to control the entry of life into the world. Some believe such power should not be entrusted to you, for they fear the destruction of the old order of women living in subservience to sexual and reproductive control. They fear all that it means for women to be equal in every respect. Who will have the power to make the decisions about the most intimate aspects of your body and your life force? By whose moral and religious values will you live? Who will make the decisions about your daughter's body and the choices in her life? Will she, or will the government?

You must not languish in the complacency of "it's all so boring" or "I don't have time to get involved." It is never too early to get involved. Remember, your grandmother began her ministry at seventeen. She also taught me from the Bible that it is "the little foxes that spoil the vines." If you do not keep yourself informed, some will exploit your detachment and will whittle and whittle at the vines of your rights. Without your resistance, their resolutions will eventually weaken the sustaining promise of your liberty, embodied in the promise of our Constitution.

You've been encouraged to be an independent thinker. In your brief life, encounters with injustice have energized your spirit of resistance. I've seen your reaction when you believed I was dealing with you unfairly; I've seen the sadness and indignation in your eyes when we sat together in the villages of the poorest women of the world. You've grown up in the thick of one of the most important social movements of the twentieth century. You've been taught the value of hard work and diligence. The doors of opportunity have been opened wide for you. But it's not the privilege to which we are born, but what we make of our lives that counts. You must now continue the fight.

How will you put your talents to work for women? How will you use them to shape your future? Will you take risks? Will you use the system to work in the interests of all women, especially the most vulnerable women? Will you do this without apology?

The irony of this struggle is that if the women of our country, of our world, united to end inequality, it would be eradicated. The potential is within us, within you. In solidarity, women need not fear the price of claiming what is ours—our right to full equality and opportunity. I believe there are some steps we can take that will help us to overcome our reticence to use our powers, to, as Sojourner Truth said, "take them and not be talking about it." I offer these to you in the hope that they will guide you as you seek to fulfill your own mission in life:

- Be informed. Be vigilant! You can't defend your rights if you don't understand them, if you don't know how you got them, and if you don't know who wants to destroy them. Take nothing for granted, for if you do so, you will not take pains to protect your rights.
- Do not shrink from power. Feel a sense of who you really are deep within, and do not rely on the approval of others as your primary source of affir-

mation. You have the power within yourself to create beneficial change for yourself and for others.

- Don't ever compromise your fundamental rights. Would you sit still if the government attempted to control *The New York Times*? Wouldn't it be unthinkable if each edition were reviewed by government censors? Felicia, the sanctity of your body is even more precious.
- Don't ever let anyone convince you that a cause cannot be won. It may take time and it may be painful, but nothing of value has been attained without struggle. And so much is lost when we cannot summon the courage of our convictions.
- Don't be afraid to fail. Try to see your setbacks as learning opportunities. I certainly did, when I discovered that I could not fly and then mounted my tricycle the next day to move on to my next adventure. Learn to ignore those who undermine your resolve and your vision. Some of history's greatest advances have been born of frustration and setbacks yielding to perseverance.
- Support other women. Remember—we live in a society that does not value women enough. We must support each other when we speak out and when we challenge barriers. I deeply hope that the women of your generation will be more mutually supportive of each other than the women of my time have learned to be.
- Embrace every level of the political process. It is a ubiquitous force in our lives, and women must be reasonably represented and involved at every level if public policies are to reflect our aspirations and protect our rights.
- Do not allow yourself to grow weary of the struggle for equality. This struggle has endured for hundreds of years, and sadly, I don't foresee it being achieved in our lifetimes, perhaps not even in your children's lifetime. If you accept inequities, what hope will your children have of enjoying the rights that you now possess? If we don't give in, if we don't despair when we experience setbacks, we can protect our gains and make progress toward the day that our rights and aspirations will no longer be contested because we are women.
- Change is rarely immediate. This has been one of the most difficult lessons I have had to learn. Change usually comes in increments, and over time, as though to entice us to persist.
- Maintain your grace and dignity, even when you are subjected to the most distasteful lack of civility. Whether you like it or not, you are a role model, and your conduct and your life influence others. What do you want to exemplify?

Remember: the recorded history of the world is essentially a story of liberation, of the triumph of freedom over oppression. But the victories were usually hard-won. We—your grandmother, you, I, and all those who join the struggle for equality—are in good company with those who made the sacrifices and "fought the good fight" before us.

Not too long ago, I asked your grandmother if she believed that the price she paid to pursue her mission was too high. "No, Lordy. I have no regrets," she said. "I'd do it all over again."

I, too, have no regrets, for in you, I see the future.

Killed in Albany by Vote of 15 to 3," *New York Times*, March 8, 1967, 1.

3. Christopher Tietze, *Induced Abortion: Population Council Fact Book* (New York: Population Council, 1979).
4. Linda Charlton, "Abortion Brokers Are Under Study," *New York Times*, February 10, 1971, L45, L47.
5. Jane Brody, "Abortion Agencies Assailed on Foes," *New York Times*, February 12, 1971, L38.
6. From a hearing held by Manhattan Borough President Percy Sutton, New York, October 16, 1970.
7. *State of New York v. Abortion Information Agency, Inc.*, Supreme Court, Special Term, New York County, 69 Misc. 2d 825; 323 N.Y.S. 2d 597, May 13, 1971.
8. "New Abortion Rules Take Effect, Complicating Confused Picture," *New York Times*, October 20, 1970, L29.
9. Richard Nixon to Cardinal Terence Cooke, May 6, 1972, in *ASA Newletter* (New York: Association for the Study of Abortion, Fall 1972), 5.
10. Ibid.

Chapter 14: *Roe v. Wade*: Completing the Revolution

1. *Roe v. Wade* and *Doe v. Bolton*, Supreme Court Reporter, 410 U.S. 116, (1978), 179.
2. Interview with Sarah Weddington by Faye Wattleton.
3. *Roe v. Wade* and *Doe v. Bolton*, Supreme Court Reporter, 153.
4. Ibid., 163.
5. James C. Mohr, *Abortion in America: The Origins and Evolutions of National Policy, 1800–1900* (New York: Oxford University Press, 1978), 126.
6. W.L. Atlee and D.A. O'Donnell, *Report of the Committee on Criminal Abortion*, 22 Transactions of the AMA 241 (Philadelphia: Collins Printer, 1871), as quoted in *Webster's Historians Brief*, 246–247.
7. Letter by Pat Robertson for the Christian Coalition of Chesapeake, Va., cited in "Equal Rights Initiative in Iowa Attacked," *The Washington Post*, August 23, 1992, A15.
8. "Pastoral Plan for Pro-Life Activities," National Conference of Catholic Bishops, November, 1975.

Chapter 16: Family Values: Holding It All Together

1. Faye Wattleton, speech to Planned Parenthood Federation of America, Kansas City, Mo., January 29, 1977.

Chapter 17: Reproductive Rights Under Siege

1. Christine Brim, "Abortion Clinics Under Siege," *Seven Days*, May 5, 1978, 2:23–24; NARAL Report, "Violence Against the Right to Choose," 1978; "Highland Clinic Hit by Fire," *St. Paul Pioneer Press*, February 24, 1977; "Abortion: Arson at Clinic," *St. Paul Dispatch*, February 24, 1977.
2. "Letters May Provide Clues in Fire-Bombing of Clinic," *Omaha World Herald*, August 19, 1977.
3. NARAL Report, "Violence Against the Right to Choose."
4. *Holy Bible, The New Revised Standard Version*, (Nashville, Tenn.: Division of Christian Education of the National Council of the Churches of Christ in the United States, 1989), Romans 12:19–21.
5. NARAL Report, "Violence Against the Right to Choose"; "Trespassers or Saviors?" *Cincinnati Post*, April 22, 1978.
6. "Clinic Dealing in Abortions Is Set Afire," *Cleveland Pain Dealer*, February 19, 1978, 1-A; also, "Antiabortion Violence: Incidents of Arsons, Bombings, and Attempts, 1977–1989," National Abortion Federation, 1990.
7. News release, Public Interest Relations, February 2, 1978.
8. "Planned Parenthood's New Head Takes a Fighting Stand," *New York Times*, February 3, 1978.
9. "Faye Wattleton Working for the Family," *Essence*, March 1980, 64.
10. Jacqueline Warsaw, "To Have or Have Not . . . Children," *Working Woman*, June 1978, 47.
11. "Faye Wattleton Working for the Family," *Essence*, March 1980, 64.
12. Planned Parenthood–World Population, "Statement on Abortion Eve," May 1, 1978.

Chapter 18: Refusing to Surrender the Poor

1. Planned Parenthood–World Population, *Washington Memo*, Washington, D.C., June 24, 1977, 4.
2. *Congressional Record*, July 28, 1976, 20885.
3. *Congressional Record*, August 10, 1976, 8633.
4. Ibid., 26792.
5. Ibid., 26787.
6. *McRae v. Califano*, amended complaint, District Court for the Eastern District of New York, September 30, 1976, 3–4.
7. *Maher v. Roe*, Supreme Court Reporter, 432 U.S. 464, (1977), 2378.
8. Ibid., 2390.
9. "A Proposal for Planned Parenthood Federation of America," by Garth Associates, Inc., New York, January, 31, 1979, 2.
10. Ibid., 8–9.

NOTES

Foreword

1. Faye Wattleton, President, Planned Parenthood Federation of America, press statement, July 3, 1989.

Chapter 1: Indomitable Spirit

1. *Holy Bible, The New Revised Standard Version* (Nashville, Tenn.: Division of Christian Education of the National Council of the Churches of Christ in the United States, 1989), Proverbs 3:6.

Chapter 2: The Roots of Conviction

1. *Holy Bible, The New Revised Standard Version*, (Nashville, Tenn.: Division of Christian Education of the National Council of the Churches of Christ in the United States, 1989), Mark 16:15.
2. Ibid., Ephesians 5:22–24.

Chapter 5: Preacher's Daughter

1. *Gospel Trumpet*, 1909, in Merle D. Strege, *Tell Me the Tale: Historical Reflections on the Church of God* (Anderson, Ind.: Warner Press, 1991), 7.

Chapter 6: Budded, Blossomed, and Bloomed

1. *Holy Bible, The New Revised Standard Version*, (Nashville, Tenn.: Divi-

sion of Christian Education of the National Council of the Churches of Christ in the United States, 1989), Romans 7:19–21.

Chapter 10: Harlem: An Awakening

1. D.P. Swartz, M.D., and M.K. Pananjpe, M.D., "Abortion: Medical Aspects in a Municipal Hospital," *Bulletin of the New York Academy of Medicine*, vol. 47, no. 8, August, 1971, 846.
2. Jane Brody, "Abortion: Once a Whispered Problem, Now a Public Debate," *New York Times*, January 8, 1968, L28.

Chapter 11: Prenatal Care and Parental Consent

1. *Holy Bible, The New Revised Standard Version*, (Nashville, Tenn.: Division of Christian Education of the National Council of the Churches of Christ in the United States, 1989).

Chapter 12: Mama's Loss, Planned Parenthood's Gain

1. Linda Gordon, *Woman's Body, Woman's Right: A Social History of Birth Control in America* (New York: Penguin Books, 1976, 1990), 95–116.
2. From Federal Criminal Code, Section 211, cited in Ellen Chesler, *Woman of Valor: Margaret Sanger and the Birth Control Movement in America* (New York: Simon & Schuster, 1992), 68.
3. David Kennedy, *Birth Control in America: The Career of Margaret Sanger* (New Haven and London: Yale University Press, 1970), 94–96.
4. Chesler, *Woman of Valor*, 373.

Chapter 13: The New York Reform: A New Day for Women

1. Planned Parenthood Policy Statement, from Margaret Sanger, *My Fight for Birth Control* (Elmsford, N.Y.: Maxwell Reprint Company, 1931, 1959), 56.
2. Sydney Schanberg, "Abortion Change Killed in Albany by Vote of 15 to 3," *New York Times*, March 8, 1967, 1.
3. Christopher Tietze, *Induced Abortion: Population Council Fact Book* (New York: Population Council, 1979).
4. Linda Charlton, "Abortion Brokers Are Under Study," *New York Times*, February 10, 1971, L45, L47.
5. Jane Brody, "Abortion Agencies Assailed on Foes," *New York Times*, February 12, 1971, L38.
6. From a hearing held by Manhattan Borough President Percy Sutton, New York, October 16, 1970.
7. *State of New York v. Abortion Information Agency, Inc.*, Supreme

Court, Special Term, New York County, 69 Misc. 2d 825; 323 N.Y.S. 2d 597, May 13, 1971.
8. "New Abortion Rules Take Effect, Complicating Confused Picture," *New York Times*, October 20, 1970, L29.
9. Richard Nixon to Cardinal Terence Cooke, May 6, 1972, in *ASA Newletter* (New York: Association for the Study of Abortion, Fall 1972), 5.
10. Ibid.

Chapter 14: *Roe v. Wade*: Completing the Revolution

1. *Roe v. Wade* and *Doe v. Bolton*, Supreme Court Reporter, 410 U.S. 116, (1978), 179.
2. Interview with Sarah Weddington by Faye Wattleton.
3. *Roe v. Wade* and *Doe v. Bolton*, Supreme Court Reporter, 153.
4. Ibid., 163.
5. James C. Mohr, *Abortion in America: The Origins and Evolutions of National Policy, 1800–1900* (New York: Oxford University Press, 1978), 126.
6. W.L. Atlee and D.A. O'Donnell, *Report of the Committee on Criminal Abortion*, 22 Transactions of the AMA 241 (Philadelphia: Collins Printer, 1871), as quoted in *Webster's Historians Brief*, 246–247.
7. Letter by Pat Robertson for the Christian Coalition of Chesapeake, Va., cited in "Equal Rights Initiative in Iowa Attacked," *The Washington Post*, August 23, 1992, A15.
8. "Pastoral Plan for Pro-Life Activities," National Conference of Catholic Bishops, November, 1975.

Chapter 16: Family Values: Holding It All Together

1. Faye Wattleton, speech to Planned Parenthood Federation of America, Kansas City, Mo., January 29, 1977.

Chapter 17: Reproductive Rights Under Siege

1. Christine Brim, "Abortion Clinics Under Siege," *Seven Days*, May 5, 1978, 2:23–24; NARAL Report, "Violence Against the Right to Choose," 1978; "Highland Clinic Hit by Fire," *St. Paul Pioneer Press*, February 24, 1977; "Abortion: Arson at Clinic," *St. Paul Dispatch*, February 24, 1977.
2. "Letters May Provide Clues in Fire-Bombing of Clinic," *Omaha World Herald*, August 19, 1977.
3. NARAL Report, "Violence Against the Right to Choose."
4. *Holy Bible, The New Revised Standard Version*, (Nashville, Tenn.: Divi-

sion of Christian Education of the National Council of the Churches of Christ in the United States, 1989), Romans 12:19–21.

5. NARAL Report, "Violence Against the Right to Choose"; "Trespassers or Saviors?" *Cincinnati Post*, April 22, 1978.
6. "Clinic Dealing in Abortions Is Set Afire," *Cleveland Pain Dealer*, February 19, 1978, 1-A; also, "Antiabortion Violence: Incidents of Arsons, Bombings, and Attempts, 1977–1989," National Abortion Federation, 1990.
7. News release, Public Interest Relations, February 2, 1978.
8. "Planned Parenthood's New Head Takes a Fighting Stand," *New York Times*, February 3, 1978.
9. "Faye Wattleton Working for the Family," *Essence*, March 1980, 64.
10. Jacqueline Warsaw, "To Have or Have Not . . . Children," *Working Woman*, June 1978, 47.
11. "Faye Wattleton Working for the Family," *Essence*, March 1980, 64.
12. Planned Parenthood–World Population, "Statement on Abortion Eve," May 1, 1978.

Chapter 18: Refusing to Surrender the Poor

1. Planned Parenthood–World Population, *Washington Memo*, Washington, D.C., June 24, 1977, 4.
2. *Congressional Record*, July 28, 1976, 20885.
3. *Congressional Record*, August 10, 1976, 8633.
4. Ibid., 26792.
5. Ibid., 26787.
6. *McRae v. Califano*, amended complaint, District Court for the Eastern District of New York, September 30, 1976, 3–4.
7. *Maher v. Roe*, Supreme Court Reporter, 432 U.S. 464, (1977), 2378.
8. Ibid., 2390.
9. "A Proposal for Planned Parenthood Federation of America," by Garth Associates, Inc., New York, January, 31, 1979, 2.
10. Ibid., 8–9.
11. Ibid., 5.

Chapter 19: How Many Daughters Must Die?

1. From a speech by Karen Bell, Portland, Oregon, October 1991.
2. *Planned Parenthood of Central Missouri v. Danforth*, Supreme Court Reporter, 428 U.S. 52 (1976), 2832.
3. *Planned Parenthood of Central Missouri v. Danforth*, 392 F Supp. 1362 (1975).
4. *Planned Parenthood of Central Missouri v. Danforth*, Oral Arguments, Supreme Court of the United States, March 23, 1976, 18–21.

5. Ibid.
6. From an interview with Frank Susman by Alwynne Wilbur.
7. *Planned Parenthood of Central Missouri v. Danforth*, Supreme Court Reporter, 428 U.S. 75 (1976), 2843.
8. *Planned Parenthood of Central Missouri v. Danforth*, Supreme Court Reporter, 428 U.S. 92 (1976), 2851.
9. Ibid., 2832.
10. *Planned Parenthood of Central Missouri v. Danforth*, Supreme Court Reporter, 428 U.S. 101 (1976), 2856.
11. *Baird v. Bellotti*, 393 F Supp. 847 (1975).
12. *Baird v. Bellotti*, Supreme Court Reporter, 428 U.S. 132 (1976), 2858.
13. *Baird v. Bellotti*, Supreme Court Reporter, 433 U.S. 132 (1979), 647–648.
14. Interview with Jamie Sabino by Alwynne Wilbur, April 23, 1993.
15. *Abortion and Women's Health* (New York: Alan Guttmacher Institute, 1990), 29.
16. Susanne Yates, Ph.D., and Nita J. Pliner, J.D., M.A., "Judging Maturity in the Courts: the Massachusetts Consent Statute," *American Journal of Public Health*, June 1988, 647.
17. Jones, Forrest, Goldman, Henshaw, Lincoln, Rosoff, Westhoff, and Wulf, "Teenage Pregnancy in Industrialized Countries," 1986.
18. *Sex and America's Teenagers* (New York: Alan Guttmacher Institute, 1994).

Chapter 20: Standing Firmly on Middle Ground

1. Alan Guttmacher Institute, *Washington Memo*, May 18, 1979, 3.
2. Razelle Frankl, *Televangelism: The Marketing of Popular Religion* (Carbondale: Southern Illinois University Press, 1987), 3.
3. David Anderson, UPI, November 5, 1980, General News.
4. Sue Warner, "The Other Conventions," *Washington Post*, August 4, 1980, B3.
5. Connie Paige, *The Right to Lifers: How They Operate; Where They Get Their Money* (New York: Summit Books, 1983), 166–167. Also Alan J. Mayer et al., "A Tide of Born Again Politics," *Newsweek*, September 15, 1980.
6. "Penthouse Interview: Jerry Falwell," *Penthouse*, March 1981.
7. Alison O'Neill, "Politics in the Pulpit," *Washington Post*, November 3, 1980, D1.
8. John Banker, "Anti-Abortion Rally Turns into Anti-O'Connor Rally," UPI, September 4, 1981, Domestic News.

9. Richard Viguerie, *The New Right: We're Ready to Lead* (Falls Church, Va.: Viguerie Company, 1980), 159.

Chapter 21: The Hyde Amendment: Poor Women, All Women

1. District Court Judge M. Joseph Blumenfeld in *Women's Health Services Inc. v. Maher*, in "The Impact of Restricting Medicaid Financing for Abortion," by James Trussell, Jane Menken, Barbara L. Lindheim, and Barbara Vaughan, *Family Planning Perspectives*, May/June 1980.
2. Ellen Frankfort and Frances Kissling, "Investigation of a Wrongful Death," *Ms.*, January 1979, 66–68.
3. "The Impact of Restricting Medicaid Financing for Abortion," 129.
4. Frankfort and Kissling, "Investigation of a Wrongful Death," 82.
5. *McRae v. Califano*, 491 F Supp. 630 (1979), 742.
6. *Harris v. McRae*, Supreme Court of the United States, Oral Arguments, April 21, 1980, 17–18.
7. Ibid., 24.
8. Ibid., 29.
9. *Harris v. McRae*, Supreme Court Reporter, 65 L Ed 2d (1980), 804, 809.

Chapter 22: The New Right: Defunding the Left

1. *Official Proceedings of the Thirty-Eighth Republican National Convention, Republican Platform*, Washington, D.C., Republican National Committee, 1980, 183.
2. Ibid.
3. U.S. Senate Committee on Labor and Human Resources: Hearing Before the Committee, 97th Congress, March 31, 1981, 3.
4. Ibid., 15–16.
5. Ibid., 3–4.
6. Ibid., 7.
7. Ibid., 7.
8. Ibid., 8–9.
9. Ibid., 11–12.
10. Ibid., 44–45.
11. Ibid., 45.
12. Ibid., 33–34.
13. Ibid., 10.
14. Ibid., 74–75.
15. Ibid., 78–79.
16. Ibid., 47.
17. Ibid., 47.
18. Ibid., 49.

19. Ibid., 84–85.
20. Letter from President Ronald Reagan to Senator Orrin G. Hatch, July 28, 1981.
21. Report by the Comptroller General of the United States, "Restrictions on Abortion and Lobbying Activities in Family Planning Programs Need Clarification," September 24, 1982.

Chapter 23: Tattle Tales: The Squeal Rule

1. Public Law 97–35.
2. Squeal Law, *Federal Register*, vol. 47, no. 35, February 22, 1982.
3. Ibid.
4. Aida Torres, Jacqueline Darroch Forrest, and Susan Eisman, "Telling Parents: Clinic Policies and Adolescents' Use of Family Planning and Abortion Services," *Family Planning Perspectives*, vol. 12, no. 6, December 1980, 290.
5. Faye Wattleton, President, Planned Parenthood Federation of America, press statement, April 14, 1982.
6. "Contraceptive Clinics Pledge Confidentiality," *New York Times*, April 15, 1982, A28.
7. Alan Guttmacher Institute, *Washington Memo*, December 27, 1983.
8. Department of Health and Human Services, Washington, D.C., press statement, January 10, 1983.
9. *Planned Parenthood v. Schweiker*, United States District Court of the District of Columbia, March 2, 1983, 667.
10. *Planned Parenthood v. Schweiker*, 559 F Supp. 658 (1983).

Chapter 24: The Mexico City Policy: Fighting on a New Frontier

1. The Foreign Assistance Act of 1961, (a) and (b) of 22 U.S.C. 2151.
2. "World Population Plan of Action," United Nationals World Population Conference, Bucharest, 1974.
3. From the Mission Statement, Human Life International, Front Royal, Va.
4. *3rd Human Life International*, interview with Father Paul Marx, Human Life International, Front Royal, Va.
5. Carl Bernstein, "The U.S. and the Vatican on Birth Control," *Time*, February 24, 1992, 35.
6. "White House Draft Statement," printed in *Congressional Record*, Senate, June 18, 1984.
7. James L. Buckley, "Family Planning Programs," delivered at the United Nations International Conference on Population, Mexico City, August 8, 1984.
8. "Mexico '84: Conference Report," *People*, vol. 11, no. 4 (1984), 6.

9. Planned Parenthood Federation of America, *International News*, New York, September 14, 1984.
10. *The Report of the International Conference on Population in Mexico City*, Recommendation 18(e), 1984, 21.
11. *Planned Parenthood Federation of America v. Agency for International Development*, Complaint, U.S. District Court for the Southern District of New York, January 13, 1987, 32–33.

Chapter 25: Bearing the Cross of Violence

1. Patricia Donovan, "The Holy War," *Family Planning Perspectives*, January/February 1985, 9.
2. Ibid., 8.
3. Ibid., 8.
4. Ibid., 6.
5. Ibid., 5.
6. Statement by President Ronald Reagan, The White House, Office of the Press Secretary, January 3, 1985.
7. *Newsweek*, January 14, 1985, 25.
8. "Incidents of Violence and Disruption Against Abortion Providers," National Abortion Federation, Washington, D.C., 1990.
9. Donovan, "The Holy War," 6.
10. Abortion Clinic Violence Hearing, House of Representatives, Subcommittee on Civil and Constitutional Rights, Committee on the Judiciary, Washington, D.C., April 3, 1985, 141.
11. Ibid., 116–117.
12. "Violent Attacks Against Planned Parenthood and Other Reproductive Health Clinics," *PPFA Fact Sheet* (New York: Planned Parenthood Federation of America, 1985).
13. Gary Potter, "Joe Scheidler: New Era of Pro-Life Activism Begins," *The Wanderer*, April 26, 1985.

Chapter 26: *The Silent Scream*

1. *The Silent Scream* as submitted to the *Congressional Record*, Senate, January 3, 1985, S16.
2. Ibid., S16.
3. Ibid., S16.
4. Ibid., S17.
5. Ibid., S17.
6. Ibid., S17.
7. Ibid., S15.
8. Fetal Pain Hearing, Senate, Subcommittee on the Constitution, Committee on the Judiciary, Washington, D.C., May 21, 1985, 1.

9. "Abortion Debate: The Search for Middle Ground," ABC *Nightline*, Show #957, January 22, 1985.
10. Ibid.
11. Ibid.
12. ABC *20/20*, New York, January 24, 1985.
13. Ibid.
14. Ibid.
15. "Abortion Bias: How Network Coverage Has Tilted to the Pro-Lifers," *TV Guide*, vol. 33(45), November 9, 1985, 14.
16. "Remarks at the Annual Convention of the National Religious Broad-casters, January 30, 1984," *Public Papers of the Presidents of the United States, Ronald Reagan, 1984*, Book 1: January 1–June 29, 1984 (Washington, D.C.: U.S. Government Printing Office, 1986), 119.
17. "A False Scream," *New York Times*, March 11, 1985, A18.
18. Ibid.
19. Ibid.
20. *The Facts Speak Louder* (New York: Planned Parenthood Federation of America, April 1985).
21. Mary Schmich, "Birth of a Radical," *Chicago Tribune*, May 5, 1985, Tempo, 1.
22. Fetal Pain Hearing, Senate, Subcommittee on the Constitution, Com-mittee on the Judiciary, Washington, D.C., May 21, 1985, 3.
23. Ibid., 26–28.

Chapter 27: Life-Altering Decisions

1. "Analysis of Justice Rehnquist's Lone Dissents," National Organiza-tion for Women Legal Defense and Education Fund, Washington, D.C., 1986.
2. Robert H. Bork, "Neutral Principles and Some First Amendment Problems," *Indiana Law Journal*, vol. 47, no. 1, fall 1971, 1.
3. Hearings before the Subcommittee on Separation of Powers of the Senate Judiciary Committee, 97th Congress, 1st session, June 1, 1981, 310.
4. Statement by Faye Wattleton of Planned Parenthood Federation of America, submitted to the Judiciary Committee, U.S. Senate, on the Nomination of Robert H. Bork to be Associate Justice of the Supreme Court of the United States, Hearings before the Committee on the Judiciary, October 5, 1987, 5893–5897.
5. Opening Statement of Robert H. Bork to be Associate Justice of the U.S. Supreme Court, Hearings before the Committee on the Judiciary, U.S. Senate, September 15, 1987, 103.
6. Testimony by Kate Michelman, Executive Director of the National

Abortion Rights Action League, on the Nomination of Anthony
Kennedy to the Supreme Court of the United States, presented to the
Senate Judiciary Committee, December 17, 1987.

Chapter 28: Freedom of Speech on the Line

1. Department of Health and Human Services, 42 CFR Part 59, *Federal
   Register*, September 1, 1987.
2. Alan Guttmacher Institute, *Washington Memo*, Washington, D.C.,
   December 14, 1987.
3. Alan Guttmacher Institute, *Washington Memo*, Washington, D.C.,
   March 1, 1988, 1.
4. Ibid.
5. Alan Guttmacher Institute, *Washington Memo*, Washington, D.C.,
   July 6, 1988, 3.
6. Ibid., 4

Chapter 29: Marching to Save Women's Lives

1. "Whatever Happened to the Human Race," video narrated by C. Everett
   Koop, 1978.
2. Quote from letter in "A Measured Response: Koop on Abortion," *Family
   Planning Perspectives*, vol. 21, no. 1, January/February 1989, 31.
3. Quote from letter in "A Measured Response," 32.
4. Speech by Molly Yard, President, National Organization for Women,
   Washington, D.C., April 9, 1989.
5. Speech by Faye Wattleton, President, Planned Parenthood Federation
   of America, Washington, D.C., April 9, 1989.

Chapter 30: *Webster:* Wrecking *Roe*

1. Mo. Rev. Stat. 188.205, 1986.
2. Mo. Rev. Stat. 188.029, 1986.
3. Mo. Rev. Stat. 188.210 & 188.215, 1986.
4. Alan Guttmacher Institute, *Washington Memo*, Washington, D.C.,
   March 26, 1987.
5. *Webster v. Reproductive Health Services*, U.S. Supreme Court, Oral
   Arguments, recorded by Alderson Reporting Co. as printed in *The
   New York Times*, April 27, 1989.
6. Ibid.
7. *Webster v. Reproductive Health Services*, U.S. Supreme Court, Oral
   Arguments, recorded by Alderson Reporting Co. as printed in *The
   New York Times*, April 27, 1989.
8. Ibid.

9. Mo. Rev. Stat 1.205-1(1)(2), 1986.
10. *Webster v. Reproductive Health Services*, 851 F Supp. 1076, 1988.
11. *Webster v. Reproductive Health Services*, U.S. Supreme Court, No. 88–605, Concur, July 3, 1989, 5.
12. *Webster v. Reproductive Health Services*, U.S. Supreme Court, No. 88–605, Dissent, July 3, 1989, 2.
13. *Unnamed Fetus v. Ashcroft, et al.*, Order to Dismiss, Document 25, #89-CV-4328, U.S. District Court for the Western District of Missouri, 1990.
14. UPI, August 17, 1989, interview with St. Louis County Counselor Bob Fox. Also Barbara Brotman, "Abortion Decision Fallout Gathers," *Chicago Tribune*, August 20, 1989.
15. Ethan Bronner, "Planned Parenthood Gives New Role in an Old Cause," *Boston Globe*, October 22, 1989, 4.

Chapter 31: Rebuilding the Right to Choose

1. Speech by Faye Wattleton, President, Planned Parenthood Federation of America, Kennebunk, Maine, November 12, 1989.
2. Speech by Faye Wattleton, President, Planned Parenthood Federation of America, New Orleans, Louisiana, November 12, 1989.
3. Speech by Faye Wattleton, President, Planned Parenthood Federation of America, Austin, Texas, November 12, 1989.

Chapter 32: Resisting the Gag

1. *Planned Parenthood Federation of America v. Agency for International Development*, U.S. District Court for the Southern District of New York, March 7, 1990, 18–19.
2. *Planned Parenthood Federation of America v. Agency for International Development*, U.S. Court of Appeals for the Second Circuit, Opinion, September 19, 1990, 11.
3. *Rust v. Sullivan*, U.S. Supreme Court, Oral Arguments, October 30, 1990.
4. Ibid.
5. "Bush Names Supreme Court Nominee," ABC *Nightline*, Show #2391, July 23, 1990.
6. Ibid.
7. Ibid.
8. Ibid.
9. Faye Wattleton, President, Planned Parenthood Federation of America, press statement, October 3, 1990.
10. *Rust v. Sullivan*, U.S. Supreme Court, No. 89–1981, Opinion, May 23, 1991, 8.

11. Ibid., 15–16.
12. Ibid., 8.
13. Ibid., 8.
14. Ibid., 24.
15. Ibid., 27.
16. Ibid., 5–13.
17. *Holy Bible, The New Revised Standard Version* (Nashville, Tenn.: Division of Christian Education of the National Council of the Churches of Christ in the United States, 1989), I Corinthians 13:1–2.

Chapter 33: An Abortion Pill: Too Good to Be True

1. Stanley Henshaw, "Abortion Services in the U.S.: 1991 and 1992," *Family Planning Perspectives*, vol. 26, no. 3, May/June 1994, 105.
2. Steven Greenhouse, "A Fierce Battle," *New York Times Magazine*, February 12, 1989, 24.
3. Ibid., 24.
4. Ibid., 25.
5. Ibid., 25.
6. Ibid., 24–25.
7. Letter from J. Orsini, Executive Vice President, Roussel Uclaf, to David Andrews, Acting President, Planned Parenthood Federation of America, February 2, 1989.
8. Interview with Louise Tyrer by Faye Wattleton, May 15, 1996.
9. Letter from Reynold Levy, President, AT&T Foundation, to Planned Parenthood Federation of America, March 12, 1990.
10. Letter from Jane Redfern, Senior Vice President, AT&T Foundation, to Douglas Scott, Christian Action Coalition, March 13, 1990.
11. Letter from Reynold Levy, President, AT&T Foundation, to AT&T employees, March, 1990.
12. Letter to supporters, Christian Action Council, Falls Church, Va., April 16, 1990.

Chapter 34: The Wichita Showdown: Private Decisions, Public Debate

1. Susan Faludi, "Where Did Randy Go Wrong?" *Mother Jones*, November, 1989, 26.
2. Planned Parenthood Federation of America, *Insider*, New York, February 15, 1990.
3. Henry King, "Cardinal O'Connor Indicates Interest in Rescue," *The Wanderer*, October 12, 1989; and Susan Faludi, "Where Did Randy Go Wrong?" *Mother Jones*, November 1989, 27.
4. *Women's Health Care Services v. Operation Rescue*, U.S. District Court for the District of Kansas, Complaint, 9–11.

5. "Abortion Protesters Arrested," AP, July 24, 1991.
6. Matt Schofield, "Anti Abortion Leaders Arrested," *Kansas City Star*, July 25, 1991.
7. Judy Lundstrom Thomas and Jim Lyn, "Federal Judge Orders U.S. Marshals to Keep Abortion Clinic Entrance Open," UPI, July 29, 1991.
8. Judy Lundstrom Thomas, "Federal Judge Orders Operation Rescue to Stop Blocking Wichita Clinics," *Knight-Ridder Newspapers*, August 5, 1991.
9. *Women's Health Care Services v. Operation Rescue*, 773 F Supp. 258, 1991.
10. *Women's Health Care Services v. Operation Rescue*, 123 F Supp. 183, 1989.
11. "Anti-Abortion Protest Arrests Resume," UPI, August 9, 1991.
12. Michael Abramowitz, "The War in Wichita," *Washington Post*, August 9, 1991.
13. John Hanna, "Protesters Storm Wichita Clinic," AP, August 20, 1991.
14. Peter Irons, "Little Rock, 1957; Wichita, 1991," *New York Times*, August 10, 1993. Also "Injustice in Wichita," editorial, *New York Times*, August 9, 1991; Don Terry, "Tough Choices in Tense Times for Wichita Judge," *New York Times*, August 9, 1993; Michael Abramowitz, "The War in Wichita," *Washington Post*, August 9, 1991; Thomas and Lyn, "Federal Judge Orders U.S. Marshals to Keep Abortion Clinic Entrance Open."
15. "War in Wichita: Pro-Life Versus Pro-Choice," *Donahue*, Transcript #3288, September 6, 1991, Multimedia Entertainment Inc.
16. Ibid.
17. Ibid.
18. Ibid.
19. Ibid.
20. Ibid.
21. Ibid.

Chapter 35. The End of the Line

1. Freedom of Choice Act, H.R. 25, House of Representatives, 102nd Congress, January 3, 1991, 4–5.
2. Ibid., 5.
3. Health and Human Services, 1991–1992 Chronology, *Congressional Quarterly Almanac*, 598.
4. "Excerpts from News Conference Announcing Court Nominee," *New York Times*, July 2, 1991.
5. Statement by Faye Wattleton, President, Planned Parenthood Federation of America, September 12, 1991.

6. Testimony by Faye Wattleton, President, Planned Parenthood Federation of America, before the Judiciary Committee, U.S. Senate, on the Nomination of Clarence Thomas to the United States Supreme Court, September 19, 1991.
7. Planned Parenthood Federation of America, Annual Meeting, Washington, D.C., October 1991.

Chapter 36: Life Goes On

1. "Faye Wattleton Resigns as President of Planned Parenthood," news release, Planned Parenthood Federation of America, January 9, 1992.

Afterword: An Open Letter to My Daughter

1. Jacqueline Bernard, *Journey Toward Freedom: The Story of Sojourner Truth* (New York: Feminist Press at the City University of New York, 1967, 1990).

ACKNOWLEDGMENTS

It is impossible to adequately express my gratitude to the people whose love, lives, and support are so deeply invested in this memoir—as it was lived and as it was written. In every challenge of my life, I have received help and encouragement that have made it possible for me to succeed. The creation of this book was no exception, for it is richly endowed with the goodwill and support of family, friends and colleagues.

I am especially indebted to Nancy Friday and Norman Pearlstine for upholding before me the importance of the message and not allowing me to lose perspective when the road got rocky. I thank them also for guiding me to Robert Levine, who became my agent and my friend. Bob's vision, when others saw little, and his indomitable enthusiasm at every phase of the book's development, was a blessing of fortune that only the gods could bestow. Thank you, David Andrews, for your unfailing loyalty and enthusiasm. Your role in the success of my life's work deserves far more credit then there was space to describe on these pages. Bob Woodward and Henry Kissinger's patience and wise counsel in the early structure of this book was an invaluable template from which I worked for two years.

I have learned in this, my first publishing venture, that there are many hands that are put to the tasks of transforming the author's voice into a cogent record of thoughts and experiences. They are an intimate part of the process of transforming the raw material into the book you now hold in your hands. None were more vital than Jenna Laslocky's editorial assistance and Erin Rossitto's and Alwynne Wilbur's research acumen. Jenna's collaboration in shaping the mountain of material on reproductive rights and my life into an intertwined journal of an era of women's history, bespeaks a rare combination of temperament and talent that I took as a sign that this book was meant to be. Erin's unerring diligence and hard work, so kindly given on every aspect of the book, strengthens my optimism that the young women of my daughter's generation have the dedication to continue the struggle for women's rights and will do what it takes to preserve them.

I thank also Linda Grey and Cheryl Woodruff of Ballantine Books, and their staff for their support and commitment to entering this book into the public dialogue at a moment in history when women's lives are on the line. Gary Brozek's and Leah Odze Epstein's day-to-day management of the final editorial logistics was a study in grace and perseverance, and I thank Barbara Shor and Julie Garriott for their work. I look forward to the long months ahead as the public gets acquainted with *Life on the Line* through the competent efforts of Kim Hovey and John Conti at Ballantine, Cathy Saypol at CSPR, and Grada Fischer at the Fischer-Ross Group.

And then there is another circle of friends whose support and counsel made it possible for me to shoulder the burden of this journey:

Thank you Aunt Alice and Uncle Robert, Sarah and Lowell Black, Herb Chao Gunther, Louis Harris, Tom Layton, Anna Morris, Jim and Bose Obi, Eve Paul, George Parrott, Ken Pelletier, Charlie Rice, Louise Tyrer, Dan Weintraub, Bobbie Wunsch, Gary Yates, and Denise Young. You formed a ring of encouragement and support in ways that were individually unique and collectively powerful.

The loyalty of my former staff and colleagues in the reproductive rights movement was shared in many forms including research assistance, personal recollections and generously offered suggestions and resources. Among them I thank Lisa Abelman, Trish Adams, Julian Allen, Sharon Allison, Valerie Beckles, Karen and William Bell, Janet Benshoof, Polly Bergen, Joy Callender, Sherri Chessen, Ade Coker, Constance Cook, Gail Esterman, Roger Evans, Will Fitzpatrick, Nicki Gamble, Nell Gibson, Ira Glasser, Doug Gould, Ross Graham, Andrew Greensfelder, Sandra Grymes, Michele Haberland, Lee Hall-Smith, Bill Hamilton, Linda Hamlin, Peggy Jarman, Jane Johnson, Yohannes Kassa, Amy Knight, Jon Knowles, Tim Lannan, Tenny Marshall, Claire McCurdy, Howard Moody, Fannie Porter, Cory Richards, Gloria Roberts, Jeannie Rosoff, Jamie Sabino, Andrea Salwen, Harriet Schick, Carol Selton, Sheldon Segal, Margery Sly, Barbara Snow, Roberta Spivak, Robyn Stein, Frank Susman, Roberta Synal, Susan Tew, Sarah Weddington.

Finally, but most importantly, I could not have sustained the strength necessary to write this book without the love, encouragement, suggestions and critiques of Mama and Felicia. The long hours that my mother allowed me to probe the deep reservoirs of our lives and her Bible added a richness to this book and our love that will remain with me for the rest of my life. And Felicia's uninterrupted love and patience with the disruptions in the routine of our lives been a remarkable performance at any age. The fact that she was still a teenager marks another reason why I am such a proud mother.

Many who have touched and influenced my life are mentioned in this book and there are many more that could be included here. If I attempted to do so, the pages would be endless. To each of you I offer my deepest and most humble gratitude.

ABOUT THE AUTHOR

Faye Wattleton consults with American business and political leaders and with heads of state, ambassadors, and cabinet ministers around the world on family-planning issues. She holds fifteen honorary degrees, is a member of the National Women's Hall of Fame (1993), and has won numerous awards, including the Jefferson Award for the Greatest Public Service Performed by a Private Citizen (1992) and the Margaret Sanger Woman of Valor Award (1996). Ms. Wattleton makes her home in Manhattan.